William Carew Hazlitt, Richard Price, Thomas Warton

History of English Poetry from the 12th to the Close of the 16th Century

William Carew Hazlitt, Richard Price, Thomas Warton

History of English Poetry from the 12th to the Close of the 16th Century

ISBN/EAN: 9783744666367

Printed in Europe, USA, Canada, Australia, Japan

Cover: Foto ©ninafisch / pixelio.de

More available books at **www.hansebooks.com**

THE HISTORY OF ENGLISH POETRY.

LONDON:

TURNER

CHISWICK PRESS:—PRINTED BY WHITTINGHAM AND WILKINS,
TOOKS COURT, CHANCERY LANE.

SKETCH OF THE HISTORY OF ANGLO-SAXON POETRY.

[The history of English poetry begins in lands where the name of England was not known. Not in our "island home" was our mother tongue in its earliest stage first spoken, but in parts of the Danish land, the Anglish and Saxish provinces, in Friesland, Jutland, and the neighbouring isles, whence the first Teutonic settlers and invaders came, to people our England. They brought with them the legends of their continental homes; and the one weird poem which has come to us from them whole, though much meddled with by later hands, is our national epic. But before we give an account of it, and the rest of our forefathers' poetry, we must say somewhat of the forms of Anglo-Saxon verse, and must note that, for convenience of classification, the continuous changes in our language have been separated into the following stages:

I. Anglo-Saxon or Old English, with regular inflexions, up to 1100 A.D.
II. Semi-Saxon or Transition English, in two stages, (1) when the inflexion signs were struggling for superiority, from 1100 to 1500 A.D.;¹ (2) when the final *e* had gained the victory, but the vocabulary was almost wholly Anglo-Saxon, as in Laȝamon, 1150-1250 A.D.
III. Early English, 1250-1500 A.D. when the vocabulary received large French importations, and the final *e* gradually became grammatically valueless.
IV. Middle English, 1500-1620 A.D.—*F.*]

---

¹ [See the preface to Dr. Richard Morris's *Old English Homilies*, I. Early English Text Society, 1868; and his sketch of the characteristics of the Transition Period of our language in Section 1 below.]

[Sketch of the History of Anglo-Saxon Poetry.

BY HENRY SWEET, OF BALIOL COLLEGE, OXFORD.

THE forms and traditions of Anglo-Saxon poetry[1] are those which are common to all the old Germanic nations. The essential elements of Anglo-Saxon versification are accent and alliteration. Each long verse has *four* accented syllables, while the number of unaccented syllables is indifferent, and is divided by the cæsura into two short verses, bound together by alliteration: *two* accented syllables in the first short line, and *one* in the second, beginning with any vowel or the same consonant. Instead of two there is often only *one* alliterative letter in the first short verse. The alliterative letter of the second short verse must belong to the first of the two accented syllables. Of this metre in its strictest and simplest form the following line of Beowulf is an example :—

> Á ríce to rúne | rǽdes eáhtedon.

---

[1] The standard work for the study of Anglo-Saxon poetry is the collection of Grein, published under the title of *Bibliothek der Angelsächsischen Poesie*, in four vols., the first two containing critical texts of all known poems, the third and fourth a complete poetical dictionary. In his *Dichtungen der Angelsachsen* Grein has given a literal translation of nearly all the poems. In the *Bibliothek* will be found a complete list of all previous editions and translations, nearly all of which, it may be added, are entirely superseded by Grein's work. It will therefore be necessary only to mention those works which have appeared since the publication of Grein's *Bibliothek*. These are the edition of the fragments of Waldhere by Professor Stephens and by Grein, as an appendix to his edition of Beowulf and Finnesburg, and Heyne's edition and translation of Beowulf, the former of which has appeared in two editions. A volume of *Metrical Homilies, or Lives of Saints* is preparing for the Early English Text Society, under Mr. Skeat's editorship.

Here are two accents in each short verse, both accented syllables in the first short verse, and the first in the second beginning with the letter *r*. In the line

eórmenláfe | æðelan cynnes

there are only two alliterative letters, *eo* and *æ*, which, being vowels, are allowed to be different.

As remarked above, the number of unaccented syllables is indifferent; the same remark applies, within certain limits, to an excess of *accented* syllables also. The most important of these limitations is that all additional accents in the second short verse must come *before* the alliterative syllable. Generally speaking, the number of accents in an ordinary long line does not exceed *five*:

micel mórgenswég | mǽre þeóden.
fæder on láste | siððan forð gewát.

Such is the general structure of the great majority of Anglo-Saxon verses. More elaborate modifications are, however, occasionally introduced, generally in solemn, lyrical passages. The most important characteristic of these metres is the regular introduction of unaccented syllables, each accented syllable being followed by one or more unaccented, the last foot but one of the line (containing the alliterative letter) especially being often a dactyl. This kind of verse often resembles the ancient hexameter, when read accentually. The comparison of the two following lines will at once show how much of the character of Anglo-Saxon verse depends on the use of unaccented syllables:

mícel mórgenswég | mǽre þeóden.
rínca to rúne gegángan | hí ða on réste gebróhton.

This kind of verse is also generally characterised by an increased number of accented syllables, generally not less than six, often more:

ðónne hi mǽst mid him | mǽrða gefrémedon.
geófian mid góda gehwílcum | ðeáh he his gíngran ne sénde.
geheáwann ðísne mórðres brýttan | geúnne me mínra gesýnta.
fíra beárn on ðíssum fǽstum clómmum | ongínnað nu ýmb ða fýrde þéncean.

More rarely we meet with an increased number of accented, without unaccented syllables; the effect is peculiar, and quite different from that of the hexameter-like lines quoted above; two lines of the *Wanderer* afford a good example:

hwǽr cwóm meárg? hwǽr cwóm mágo? | hwǽr cwóm máððumgifa?
hwǽr cwóm símbla gesétu? | hwǽr síndon séledreámas?

Different as these metres are, they all belong to the same type, which is represented in the simplest form in the verse of Beowulf first quoted. All the variations reduce themselves to:—

(1.) Insertion of additional feet before the alliterative syllable of the second short line.

(2.) Regular use of unaccented syllables.

(3.) Increase in the number of accents in the first short verse.

So that the only really arbitrary feature is the varying number of accents in the first short verse; although this license, like all others in Anglo-Saxon poetry, is always regulated by the metrical feeling of the poet, and often depends on the more or less regular use of unaccented syllables. The strictest part of the line is the second short verse: only one alliterative letter is allowed, and its position and that of the inserted syllables are fixed (compare also the remark about the dactylic feet). This tendency to metrical concentration and strictness at the end of the line is common to all metres; it is alike evident in the structure of the classical hexameter and of the modern rhyming metres. The alliteration, though not the essence of the Anglo-Saxon versification, is a necessary element of it, being indissolubly connected with the accentuation. It cannot therefore, like modern rhyme, be omitted or modified at pleasure. There are also traces of rhyme, and one poem, commonly called the *Rhyming Poem*, is composed throughout of very elaborate rhymes.

An essential feature of Anglo-Saxon poetry is the use of poetic words and phrases: words being employed in poetry which do not occur in prose, or prose words and phrases being used in a peculiar sense. There is also a strong tendency to apposition, which in some cases almost amounts to parallelism, as in Hebrew poetry: " dæt ic *sænessas* geseon mihte, *windige weallas*," so that I could see the sea-headlands, the windy walls; " dæt ðu us gebrohte *brante ceole*, hea hornscipe, ofer hwæles eðel," that thou mightest bring us in a steep vessel, a high-prowed ship, over the whale's country (the sea). In this last example the two adjectives are exactly parallel, and have practically the same meaning. This tendency is strikingly shown in the frequent use of an adjective in apposition to a substantive, instead of attributively: "hæfdon swurd nacod, heard on handa," we held in our hands keen swords unsheathed.

This simplicity and freedom of form, which is characteristic of the earliest poetry of all the Teutonic nations, has led narrow-minded and superficial writers to describe Anglo-Saxon poetry as lines of bad prose, joined together by alliteration; forgetting that the highest artistic excellence is attainable in many ways, and that the metrical laws which suit one language, are totally out of place in another of different structure. A strict and unvarying system of versification, like the Homeric hexameter, in which a battle and a cooking operation are described in the same metre, would have seemed intolerable to a Northern poet: he required one which would adapt itself to every phase of emotion and change of action, which in describing prosaic incidents, such as will occur in every narrative poem of any length, could be let down nearly to the level of ordinary prose, with an effective transition to the more concentrated passages. The leading principle in Anglo-Saxon poetry is to subordinate form to matter. No brilliancy of language or metre is accepted as a substitute for poverty of thought or feeling; purely technical poetry, with a few trifling exceptions, is not known. This tendency is clearly brought out by a comparison of the closely allied poetry of the Scandinavians, as carried to its highest point of development in Norway and Iceland. Here the original metrical system, essentially the same as the Anglo-Saxon, was at an early period brought to a high degree of perfection. The number of syllables was made invariable, the alliteration was refined and regulated, and rhymes, both initial and final, were introduced, the original alliteration being still preserved. But these technical advantages were counterbalanced by an almost total stagnation of any higher artistic development. Lyric and dramatic poetry, traces of which are found in the earliest poems of Edda, remain undeveloped, and at last poetry degenerates into a purely mechanical art, valued only in proportion to the difficulty of its execution. The Anglo-Saxons, on the other hand, whilst preserving the utmost technical simplicity, developed not only an elaborate epic style, but what is more remarkable, produced lyric and didactic poetry of high merit, and this at a very early period, certainly at least as early as the beginning of the eighth century.

Important characteristics of Anglo-Saxon poetry are concifeness and directness. Everything that retards the action or obscures the main sentiment of the poem is avoided, hence all similes are extremely rare. In the whole poem of Beowulf there are scarcely half a dozen of them, and these of the simplest character, such as comparing a ship to a bird. Indeed, such a simple comparison as this is almost equivalent to the more usual "kenning" (as it is called in Icelandic), such as "brimfugol," where, instead of comparing the ship to a bird, the poet simply calls it a sea-bird, preferring the direct assertion to the indirect comparison. Such elaborate comparisons as are found in Homer and his Roman imitator are quite foreign to the spirit of Northern poetry.

A marked feature of Anglo-Saxon poetry is a tendency to melancholy and pathos, which tinges the whole literature : even the song of victory shows it, and joined to the heathen fatalism of the oldest poems, it produces a deep gloom, which would be painful were it not relieved by that high moral idealism which is never wanting in Anglo-Saxon poetry. This tendency was, no doubt, strengthened by the great political calamities of the Anglo-Saxons, their precarious hold upon Britain, their civil and foreign wars, which ultimately brought about their national extinction. Descriptions of nature are not unfrequent in Anglo-Saxon poetry, and form one of its most characteristic features; for descriptions of natural scenery are generally unknown in early literature, and are often rare in many, which are otherwise highly developed. Elaborate descriptions of gardens may be found in Homer and the Italian poets, but hardly any of wild nature. In the lyrical German poetry of the thirteenth century, there is evidence enough of a strong feeling for nature, but there is no distinctness or individuality—nothing but general allusions to the brightness of the flowers and the song of the birds, which soon petrify to mere formulæ. In Anglo-Saxon poetry, on the other hand, such passages as the descriptions of Grendel's abode in Beowulf (p. 11 below), have a vividness and individuality which make them not inferior to the most perfect examples of descriptive poetry in modern English literature,—perhaps the highest praise that can be given. This characteristic forms a strong bond of union between the two literatures, so different in many other respects, and it is not impossible that some of the higher qualities of modern English poetry are to be assigned to traditions of the old Anglo-Saxon literature, obscured for a time by those didactic, political, and allegorical tendencies which almost extinguished genuine poetry in the Early English period. The bulk of the poetical literature that has come down to us is considerable, but the pieces are of various degrees of value, and some of them are totally destitute of poetical merit. There can be no doubt that the works we possess do not fairly represent the actual literature. They have not been handed down to us from generation to generation, and preserved in many MSS., as is the case with the literatures of ancient Greece and Rome; where, if a work is lost, we are to a great extent justified in assuming it to have been of inferior merit. We know that for many centuries after the Conquest books written in the old language were considered as waste parchment, and utilized accordingly; and that great havoc was made among the monastic libraries at the Reformation. The consequence is that many of the finest poems are mere fragments, and those that are preserved have escaped total destruction by a series of lucky chances, and, with a few trifling exceptions, are preserved only in single manuscripts.

The chronology and authorship of the poems are in most cases very uncertain. Several of them were certainly composed before the German colonization of Britain, however much they may have been altered and interpolated in later times. It is equally certain that by far the greater number of the other poems were composed in Northumbria. Cædmon we know to have been a Northumbrian, both from the express testimony of Bede, and from the fact of a few lines of his being preserved in the original northern dialect. The name of Cynewulf is introduced into several poems contained in the Exeter and Vercelli MSS., three times in a kind of acrostic in Runic letters, once in a riddle or rather charade on his own name. As all these poems are written in the ordinary West-Saxon dialect, it was at first supposed that Cynewulf was a native of the south of England; but when the Runic inscription of the Ruthwell cross in Dumfriesshire was deciphered, and shown to be a fragment of a poem of Cynewulf's, which is preserved entire in the Vercelli MS., it became at once evident that the poems of Cædmon and Cynewulf in their present shape are copies of Northumbrian originals, altered to suit the southern dialect. How far the analogy holds good for the remaining poems of unascertained authorship is uncertain. As we know that literature was first cultivated in the north, there is an *à priori* probability in the case of all the older poems that they were either composed by Northumbrians, or at least were first written down in Northumbria. Indeed, there are only two poems of any merit to which we can assign with any certainty a southern origin. These are the ode on the battle of Brunanburg, and the narrative of the battle of Maldon, which were, no doubt, composed immediately after the events they record. King Alfred's translation of the metres of Boethius is almost entirely destitute of poetical merit.

It is probable that the earliest poetry of the Anglo-Saxons consisted of single strophes, each narrating, or rather alluding to, some exploit of a hero or god, or expressing some single sentiment, generally of a proverbial or gnomic character. Such is the poetry of savage nations. The next stage is to combine these strophes into connected groups. The third is to abandon the strophic arrangement altogether. With regard to the poetical form, it is tolerably certain that in the earliest stage there was no difference between poetry and prose; in fact, poetry was entirely unformal—simply a concentrated prose. Of all civilized poetical literatures, the most primitive is that of the ancient Hebrew, which is only distinguished from prose by the symmetry and mutual correspondence of its sentences. This parallelism we have recognized as a frequent, though not essential, ingredient of Anglo-Saxon verse; it is also strongly developed in the earliest Scandinavian poetry. It seems, therefore, not improbable that the Anglo-Saxon poetry in its earliest stage consisted of lines of prose connected only by parallelism. When alliteration had developed itself and become a constant element of the poetic form, the parallelism would gradually fall into disuse, as in Latin literature the regular alliteration of Nævius becomes sporadic in Virgil.

Almost the only example of strophic poetry in Anglo-Saxon is the poem known as *Deor's Complaint*. The poem is obscure, and has been handed down to us in a corrupt and mutilated state, but its strophic character is unmistakeable. The first and last two strophes consist of six lines each, and all six strophes end with the same refrain. All the old Scandinavian epic and mythological songs are strophic; and the connection between the strophes is often so little evident that it is a work of difficulty to arrange them in proper order; in short, the regular epos is hardly developed at all. It is not impossible that *Deor's Complaint* is a solitary remnant of the same stage of Anglo-Saxon poetry; the poem deals exclusively with the historical and mythological traditions common to all the Teutonic nations, and may easily have been composed before the migration to England. It must, however, be borne in mind that the use of a primitive form is quite compatible with a comparatively recent origin of a poem, especially one of a half lyric character, like *Deor's Complaint*. The other epic pieces seem to be quite destitute of strophic arrangement, most of them exhibit the epos in its most advanced and artistic form, although the greater bulk of the epic poetry being preserved only in fragments, it is difficult to determine whether these fragments form part of a regular epos, or are merely epic songs like those of the *Edda*. It is probable that some of them may belong to this latter class, of which we have an undoubted specimen, composed in historical times, the *Battle of Maldon*. Every genuine national epos presupposes a stage of literature, in which these short historical songs were the only narrative poems existing; for the genuine epic, which is regarded by those for whom it is composed as history, and nothing else, is never invented, but has to draw on the common national stock of historical and mythological tradition. How far the original substructure of separate songs is still visible in the finished epos, depends entirely on the genius of the manipulator, and his command of his materials. If he is destitute of invention and combination, he will leave the separate poems unaltered, except, perhaps, in cases of repetition and very obvious contradiction, and merely cement them together by a few lines of his own. Many of the Eddaic poems are in this stage: they are patchwork, evidently executed long after the true epic spirit had died. Very often the connecting and complementary passages are written in prose, so that the genius of a Lachmann is hardly needed to cut out the interpolation. But if the traditions contained in these songs are handled by a poet, that is to say, a man of invention, combination, and judgment, they are liable to undergo considerable modifications. There will be room for original work in connecting the various incidents and introducing episodes, in removing incongruities and repetitions, and in fusing together two or more different renderings of the same tradition. In short, the use of traditional material does not in the slightest degree preclude originality. This has often been overlooked by critics who have endeavoured to analyse such poems as the *Iliad* or *Nibelungenlied* into their original songs; the result in the case of the *Nibelungenlied* is that the dissector, after employing an elaborate apparatus of brackets, parentheses, and italics, is obliged to confess that the excised passages not only mar by their absence the symmetry of the whole, but are often superior to those which are allowed to remain. We know that Shakespeare founded his *Julius Cæsar* on Plutarch, but we do not wish to see his play cut up according to the chapters of North's Plutarch.

The only national epic which has been preserved entire is Beowulf. Its argument is briefly as follows:

The poem opens with a few verses in praise of the Danish kings, especially Scild, the son of Sceaf. His death is related, and his descendants briefly traced down to Hroðgar. Hroðgar, elated with his prosperity and success in war, builds a magnificent hall, which he calls Heorot. In this hall Hroðgar and his retainers live in joy and festivity, until a malignant fiend, called Grendel, jealous of their happiness, carries off by night thirty of Hroðgar's men, and devours them in his moorland retreat. These ravages go on for twelve years. Beowulf, a thane of Hygelac, king of the Goths, hearing of Hroðgar's calamities, sails from Sweden with fourteen warriors to help him. They reach the Danish coast in safety, and, after an animated parley with Hroðgar's coast-guard, who at first takes them for pirates, they are allowed to proceed to the royal hall, where they are well received by Hroðgar. A banquet ensues, during which Beowulf is taunted by the envious Hunferhð about his swimming-match with Breca, king of the Brondings. Beowulf gives the true account of the contest, and silences Hunferhð. At nightfall the king departs, leaving Beowulf in charge of the hall. Grendel soon breaks in, seizes and devours one of Beowulf's companions, is attacked by Beowulf, and after losing an arm, which is torn off by Beowulf, escapes to the fens. The joy of Hroðgar and the Danes, and their festivities, are described, various episodes are introduced, and Beowulf and his companions receive splendid gifts. The next night Grendel's mother revenges her son by carrying off Æschere, the friend and councillor of Hroðgar, during the absence of Beowulf. Hroðgar appeals to Beowulf for vengeance, and describes the haunts of Grendel and his mother. They all proceed thither; the scenery of the lake, and the monsters that dwell in it are described. Beowulf plunges into the water, and attacks Grendel's mother in her dwelling at the bottom of the lake. He at length overcomes her, and cuts off her head, together with that of Grendel, and brings the heads to Hroðgar. He then takes leave of Hroðgar, sails back to Sweden, and relates his adventures to Hygelac. Here the first half of the poem ends. The second begins with the accession of Beowulf to the throne after the fall of Hygelac and his son Heardred. He rules prosperously for fifty years, till a dragon, brooding over a hidden treasure, begins to ravage the country, and destroys Beowulf's palace with fire. Beowulf sets out in quest of its hiding place with twelve men. Having a presentiment of his approaching end, he pauses and recalls to mind his past life and exploits. He then takes leave of his followers one by one, and advances alone to attack the dragon. Unable from the heat to enter the cavern, he shouts aloud, and the dragon comes forth. The dragon's scaly hide is proof against Beowulf's sword, and he is reduced to great straits, when Wiglaf, one of his followers, advances to help him. Wiglaf's shield is consumed by the dragon's fiery breath, and he is compelled to seek shelter under Beowulf's shield of iron. Beowulf's sword snaps asunder, and he is seized by the dragon. Wiglaf stabs the dragon from underneath, and Beowulf cuts it in two with his dagger. Feeling that his end is near, he bids Wiglaf bring out the treasures from the cavern, that he may see them before he dies. Wiglaf enters the dragon's den, which is described, returns to Beowulf, and receives his last commands. Beowulf dies, and Wiglaf bitterly reproaches his companions for their cowardice. The disastrous consequences of Beowulf's death are then foretold, and the poem ends with his funeral.

It is evident that the poem as we have it, has undergone considerable alterations. In the first place there is a distinctly Christian element, contrasting strongly with the general heathen colouring of the whole. Many of these passages are so incorporated into the poem, that it is impossible to remove them without violent alterations of the text; others again are palpable interpolations. Such are the passages where Grendel is described as a descendant of Cain. Perhaps the strongest instance is one where we have a christian commentary on a heathen superstition. We are told that the Danes, in order to avert the miseries brought on them by Grendel, began to offer sacrifices to their idols. Then follow some verses beginning: "Such was their custom, the hope of heathens; they thought of hell, but knew not the Lord, the Judge of deeds, &c."

Without these additions and alterations, it is certain that we have in Beowulf a poem composed before the Teutonic conquest of Britain. The localities are purely continental: the scenery is laid among the Goths of Sweden and the Danes; in the episodes, the Swedes, Frisians, and other continental tribes appear, while there is no mention of England, or the adjoining countries and nations. It is evident that the poem, as a whole, cannot have been composed directly from the current traditions of the period: the variety of incidents, their artistic treatment, and the episodes introduced, show that the poet had some foundation to work upon, that there must have been short epic songs about the exploits of Beowulf current among the people, which he combined into a whole. In the poem as it stands, we can easily distinguish four elements: the prologue, the two chief exploits of Beowulf against Grendel, the dragon, and the episodes.

The attempt to eliminate these elements in their original form would be lost labour, as we have no means of determining the degree of alteration they have undergone; an alteration which, however, to judge from the remarkable unity and homogeneousness of the whole work, must have been considerable; otherwise we should hardly fail to perceive some traces of the incongruity and abrupt transition which betray a clumsy piece of compilation. The episodes would be less liable to alteration than those passages which form part of the main narrative, and it is highly probable that among them the oldest parts of the poem are to be found. Many of these episodes are extremely obscure, partly from the corrupt and defective state of the text, partly from the elliptical way in which they are told, evidently leaving a good deal to be filled up by the hearer, to whom the traditions on which they are founded were naturally familiar.

The following literal translations will give some idea of the style of Beowulf. The first is the description of Grendel's abode; the second is part of Hrodgar's farewell address to Beowulf; the third is part of the description of Beowulf's funeral, with which the poem ends:

"They hold a hidden land: where wolves lurk, windy nesses, perilous fen-tracts, where the mountain-stream shrouded in mist pours down the cliffs, deep in earth. Not far from here stands the lake overshadowed with groves of ancient trees, fast by their roots. There a dread fire may be seen every night shining wondrously in the water. The wisest of the sons of men knows not the bottom. When the heath-stalker, the strong-horned stag, hard-pressed by the hounds, coursed from afar, seeks shelter in the wood, he will yield up his life on the shore sooner than plunge in and hide his head. That is an accursed place: the strife of waves rises black to the clouds, when the wind stirs hostile storms, until the air darkens, the heavens shed tears."

1358-1377.

"Strange it is to say how mighty God generously dispenses wisdom, riches, and virtue among men: he has power over all! Sometimes he at will allows to wander the thoughts of the mighty race of man: grants him in his country worldly joys, a man-sheltering city to hold, lands and wide empire, so that for his folly he thinks not of his end. He lives in revelry; neither sickness nor age afflict him, gloomy care besets not his heart, nor does strife assail him from any side with hostile sword, but the whole world follows his will. He knows not misfortune, until pride begins to grow and blossom within him, when the guardian of the soul sleeps. The sleep is too heavy, bound with sorrows, the murderer near at hand, who shoots with cruel bow. Then he is wounded in the heart through the sheltering breast by the bitter shaft. He cannot ward off the strange influence of the accursed spirit. The riches he held so long seem to him now too little, greed hardens his heart, he seeks not fame with gifts of rings (of gold), but forgets and neglects the future, because of the honour which the Lord of glory formerly granted him. Then comes the end: the worn-out body falls, doomed to death. Another succeeds, who distributes the hoarded gold without stint, heeds not the former owner. Shun this baleful vice, dear Beowulf, best of men! Choose what is better, eternal wisdom! Cherish not pride, illustrious champion! Now is the flower of thy might for a time: soon will sickness or sword part thee from thy strength, or fire's embrace, or the sea's flood, or sword's gripe, or flight of spear, or sad old age assail thee, and veil in darkness the glance of thine eyes. Soon, prince, will death overpower thee!"

"Then the men of the Goths wrought a mound on the hill, high and broad, easily seen from afar by all wave-farers, and built in ten days the warrior's beacon: they raised a wall round his ashes, as honourably as the wisest men could devise it. They placed in the mound rings and gems, all the treasures, of which hostile men had spoiled the hoard. They let the earth hold the treasure, the heritage of earls, where it still remains, as useless to men as it was before. Then round the mound rode a troop of nobles, twelve in all; they wished to mourn the king with fitting words: they praised his courage and deeds of valour, as is right for a man to praise his dear lord with words, and love him in his heart, when his soul has departed from his body. So the Goths mourned their lord's fall, his hearth-companions said that he was the mildest and most humane of world-kings, the gentlest to his people, and most eager for glory."

Most of the other national epic pieces are mere fragments. Two of them, Widsid and Finnesburg, are of special importance, on account of their intimate connection with Beowulf. The greater part of the first of these poems is taken up by a long list of kings and nations, which Widsid, a minstrel of noble Myrging family, professes to have visited. The only passages of the poem which have any poetical worth are those in which the wandering life of the minstrel is described with considerable picturesqueness and power; the main interest of the poem is historical and geographical. An allusion of the poet in the introductory verses to a visit he had made to Eormenric, king of the Goths, who died A. D. 375, has been assumed as a criterion for determining the age of the poem, but there seems reason to doubt whether Widsid himself ever existed at all. The name Widsid, literally the "wide wanderer," is suspicious, and a comparison with many names of Odin of like significance in the Scandinavian mythology, makes it probable that Widsid is a purely mythological person, probably Odin himself. This does not diminish the value of the lists of kings and nations put into his mouth, many of which are found also in Beowulf. There can be no doubt, from the want of any mention of England and the intimate knowledge displayed of the continental tribes, that this poem was composed before the conquest of Britain. The subject of the other poem is the attack on Fin's palace in Friesland, which is also alluded to in Beowulf. The poem is a mere fragment. Two inconsiderable fragments of the epic of Waldhere have also been preserved.

Lastly, there remains one poem, which although not strictly epic in form, yet has a certain connection with the poems treated of above, being founded on the common traditions of the north. This is the piece called *Deor's Complaint*, mentioned above as remarkable for its strophic form. It is indeed almost lyric in its character. Deor, the court-poet of the Heodenings, complains that he is supplanted by his rival Heorrenda, but consoles himself by the reflection that as Weland and other heroes survived their misfortunes, so may he also regain his former prosperity.

Next in importance to these legendary poems are the two historical pieces Byrhtnod and Brunanburg, the former purely narrative, the latter showing a decided lyrical tinge. Byrhtnod (otherwise known as the "Battle of Maldon"), is meagre in form, being in fact little better than alliterative prose, yet shows considerable dramatic power, and is animated throughout by a strong patriotic feeling. The language and general tone of the poem show that it must have been composed immediately after the battle it celebrates (A. D. 993); it is even possible that the poet himself took an active part in it. This historical character gives the poem its special interest; in it we recognise the epic song in its most primitive stage, unaltered and unadorned by tradition. The beginning and end of the poem are lost, but the context shows that there cannot be many lines missing. The argument of the poem is as follows:—The "ealdorman" Byrhtnod assembles a body of men to oppose the landing of a body of Danish pirates at Maldon in Essex. They offer to return to their ships in peace, if Byrhtnod will agree to pay them any sum of money they may fix. Byrhtnod rejects all terms, and prepares to oppose their landing. The bridge over the Pant is successfully defended, but as the tide ebbs, the Danes ford the stream higher up, and attack the English on their own ground. Byrhtnod falls, and a general flight ensues. Many of the best men however rally and the fight is renewed.

The Brunanburg battle song commemorates the great victory of

Æðelſtan over the Danes and Scotch at Brunanburg. This piece is inſerted in the Saxon Chronicle under the year 938 inſtead of the uſual proſe entry. This deliberate ſubſtitution, together with the general ſtyle of the poem, ſhows that it is not a popular ſong, but was compoſed expreſſly for the Chronicle. This piece is inferior in intereſt to Byrhtnod. The language and metre are dignified and harmonious, but there is a perceptible tendency to bombaſt and overcharging with epithets, while the fineſt paſſages have rather the character of reminiſcences from the common poetical traditions than of original invention. Nevertheleſs as a whole it is a noble poem, and ſtands alone in our literature. Its ſubſtance is as follows:—King Æðelſtan and his brother gained life-long glory at Brunanburg. From early dawn till ſunſet the Northmen and Scotch fell. Two kings, eight earls were ſlain, and a countleſs hoſt beſides. Anlaf, the Northern king, fled over the dark ſea with a ſad remnant, and Conſtantine, the King of Scotland, left his ſon on the battle-field; nor had they cauſe to boaſt of their meeting with the ſons of Edward. Then the brothers returned to the land of the Weſt-Saxons, leaving behind them the wolf and raven to tear the ſlain. Never was a greater ſlaughter in this iſland, ſince firſt thoſe proud warriors the Engliſh and Saxons croſſed the broad ſea, overcame the Welſh, and won their lands!

There are ſeveral other poems of inferior merit incorporated into the *Chronicle*. The beſt perhaps is the ſhort piece commemorating the releaſe of five cities from the Daniſh yoke by Edmund (A. D. 942): it ſhows ſomething of that ſkilful command of proper names, which forms ſo eſſential an element of Roman poetry.

Beſides the national epics there are a large number of narrative poems founded on religious ſubjects. Theſe poems are entirely national in treatment: the language, coſtume and habits are purely Engliſh; there is no attempt at local or antiquarian colouring. The moſt important of theſe poems are thoſe of Cædmon, of whoſe life and compoſitions an intereſting account is given by Bede in his eccleſiaſtical hiſtory. The ſubſtance of his account is this:—Attached to the monaſtery of the Abbeſs Hild at Whitby was a certain man named Cædmon. Cædmon, never having learned any poems, often uſed to ſteal out of the houſe, when the harp was paſſed round at feſtive meetings. On one of theſe occaſions he retired to the cattle-ſtall, and there fell aſleep. A man appeared to him in a dream, and commanded him to ſing ſomething. He excuſed himſelf at firſt, but finally when aſked to ſing of the beginning of things, he began a poem, which he had never heard before. When he awoke, he remembered the words, and added many more in the ſame metre. The abbeſs then perſuaded him to forſake worldly life, and become a monk. He learnt the whole of the Bible hiſtory, and all that he remembered he ruminated, like a pure animal, and turned it into the ſweeteſt poetry, and his teachers wrote it down from his mouth. He ſang of the creation of the world, and the origin of the human race, the whole hiſtory contained in Geneſis, the departure of the

Israelites from Egypt and their entering into the promised land, and many other scripture narratives,—of the incarnation, passion, resurrection and ascension of Christ, of the coming of the Holy Ghost and the apostolic doctrine, also of the terror of the day of judgment, the torments of hell and delights of heaven, and he composed many other poems about the beneficence and justice of God, and never would make any poems on secular or frivolous subjects. Hild was abbess from 657 to 680. The first lines of Cædmon are preserved at the end of a MS. of Bede's *Ecclesiastical History* of the early part of the eighth century. They agree very closely with Bede's translation of them in the history, and as they are in the old Northumbrian dialect we may conclude that in them we have the exact words of the poet. The great bulk of his poetry is contained in a much later MS. written in the usual southern dialect. The beginning of this MS. corresponds in matter to the first lines of Cædmon in their oldest form, but there is such discrepancy in the actual words and expressions, that the authenticy of the later MS. has been denied. However, the comparison of the analogous discrepancies between the two versions of Cynewulf's poem of the *Cross*, also preserved both in the original northern form and in a southern MS., shows that either the original poems were liable to considerable variations or that the southern transcribers took great liberties with their originals; probably both causes worked together. In the case of these lines of Cædmon such variations are quite conceivable. Their poetical merit is not high; they form merely an introduction to a longer poem, and as such might easily have been altered afterwards by the poet himself. We may have in the earlier lines the rough draft, which appears in the later MS. in a revised and expanded form. The contents of the later MS. agree also with Bede's enumeration, although it contains only a part of his poems. Cædmon's poetry naturally falls into four divisions. The first consists of the poems founded on the book of Genesis, which seem to be preserved entire, with the exception of a few leaves cut out in the MS., down to the intended sacrifice of Isaac. Then follows the departure of the Israelites from Egypt. All the other Old Testament narratives are lost except that founded on the adventures of Daniel. The New Testament pieces are chiefly represented by Christ's descent into hell. This poem is not mentioned by Bede, probably because it is not strictly a scripture narrative. There are besides several smaller pieces founded on New Testament narratives, some of doubtful authenticity.

It has exercised an unfortunate influence on the due appreciation of Anglo-Saxon poetry that Cædmon has always been held up as its most important representative. Although his poetry contains many fine passages and always shows considerable metrical power, it is as a whole inferior to that of the other religious poets. The most serious fault of his poetry is the almost total want of constructive power and command of his material, which often reduced his poems to mere paraphrases. Thus, to the narrative of the creation and fall is appended a circumstantial and tedious list of the descendants of Adam, and the length of their lives, followed by the remaining history contained in the Book of *Genesis*. This feature of Cædmon's poetry is the more striking as it contrasts remarkably with the perfect structure of *Judith* and the religious epics of Cynewulf. The best portions of his poetry are those which narrate the creation and fall of the rebellious angels. These passages have all the grandeur of Milton, without his bombastic pedantry.

Of the poem of *Judith* only the last three cantos are preserved; the first nine, with the exception of a few lines of the last, are entirely lost. The fragment opens with the description of a banquet, to which Holofernes invites his chiefs. Then follows the death of Holofernes at the hands of Judith, the attack on the Assyrian camp at daybreak, and slaughter of the Assyrians. Mutilated as it is, this poem is one of the finest in the whole range of Anglo-Saxon literature. The language is of the most polished and brilliant character; the metre harmonious, and varied with admirable skill. The action is dramatic and energetic, culminating impressively in the catastrophe of Holofernes' death; but there is none of that pathos which gives Beowulf so much of its power: the whole poem breathes only of triumph and warlike enthusiasm. In constructive skill and perfect command of his foreign subject, the unknown author of *Judith* surpasses both Cædmon and Cynewulf, while he is certainly not inferior to either of them in command of language and metre.

The name of Cynewulf has already been mentioned as contained in several poems. These are the cycle of hymns on the threefold coming of Christ, commonly known as Cynewulf's Crist, the Passion of St. Juliana, both in the Exeter MS., and the Elene or Finding of the Cross in the Vercelli MS. His name is also contained in a charade prefixed to the collection of riddles in the Exeter MS. The poem of Elene is immediately preceded in the MS. by a work of a similar character, relating the adventures of St. Andrew among the cannibal Marmedonians, ending, like the Elene and Juliana, with an epilogue, wherein the poet, after briefly alluding to the fates of the other apostles, expresses penitence for his sins. There is every reason for believing that the conclusion of this piece, which is unfortunately cut out, contained an acrostic similar to that in the Elene, and from their marked resemblance of language and style, that the two poems are by the same author. The poem of Elene is preceded by a short piece called the Dream of the Cross, evidently composed by Cynewulf as an introduction to the longer poem, and expressly alluded to in the epilogue of the Elene. There are several other pieces contained in the Exeter book, which from evidence of style seem also to be Cynewulf's. These are the Life of St. Gudlac, and the descriptive poem of the Phœnix, and several smaller lyric pieces, the most important of which are the Wanderer and the Seafarer.

These passages in which the poet introduces his name, are also of value, as affording some biographical data. They tend to show that in his youth Cynewulf held the post of minstrel at the court of one of the Northumbrian kings, and that in one of those civil wars which desolated Northumbria in the 8th century, he was driven into exile. In his old age a total change came over Cynewulf, which he himself attributes to the miraculous vision of the cross. Up to this time he confesses that he was a frivolous and sinful man, given over to worldly pursuits; but after being commanded by the cross to reveal his vision to men, he devoted himself entirely to religious poetry. To this period of his life belong, therefore, the longer narrative poems, all of which are founded on religious subjects. The internal evidence, on which these results depend, may not be altogether trustworthy; but the main result, viz. that Cynewulf was a minstrel by profession, and not, as formerly supposed, a churchman, seems incontrovertible. The most valuable and characteristic of Cynewulf's poems are the early lyric pieces; the longer poems, although always distinguished by grace of diction and metre, pathos, and delicacy of feeling, are inferior to *Beowulf* and *Judith* in the specially epic qualities.

The shorter poems of Cynewulf show lyric poetry in its earliest stage, in which the narrative and descriptive element is still to a great degree predominant: the lyric idea is enclosed, as it were, in an epic frame. The *Wanderer* and the *Wife's Complaint* both turn on the miseries of exile and solitude. In the former of these poems, which is the more important, the Wanderer bewails the slaughter of his lord and kinsmen, the destruction of their burg, and the hardships of his wanderings. Into this half-epic matter are woven reflections on the excellence of constancy and silent endurance, and on the transitory nature of earthly things: the ruins which cover the face of the earth are but presages of that general destruction to which all things are tending; the world grows old and decrepit day by day. The *Seafarer* is fragmentary, and therefore somewhat obscure. Its general subject is the dangers and hardships of the sea, and the fascinations of a sailor's roving life, with a purely lyrical undercurrent of ideas similar to those of the *Wanderer*. These poems have a wonderful harmony of language and metre, which is of course quite lost in a translation. The following piece is a literal rendering of a few lines of the *Seafarer*:—

"He cares not for harp, or gifts of gold; his joy is not in woman, nor are his thoughts of the world, or of aught else except the rolling waves; but he yearns ever to venture on the sea. The groves resume their flowers, the hills grow fair, the heath brightens, the world shakes off sloth. All this only reminds him to start on his journey, eager to depart on the distant tracts of ocean. The cuckoo also reminds him with his sad voice, when the guardian of summer sings, and bodes bitter heart-sorrow. (The cuckoo's song is here taken in the double sense of a bad omen and harbinger of summer—*Rieger*.) The man who lives in luxury knows not what they endure who wander far in exile! Therefore now my mind wanders out of my breast over the sea-floods, where the whale dwells, returns again to me, fierce and eager, screams in its solitary flight, impels me irresistibly on the path of death over the ocean waters."

The *Ruin* is, unhappily, a very mutilated fragment. It describes a ruined castle, whose builders have long since passed away. This poem, together with the *Wanderer* and *Seafarer*, are the finest lyric pieces we possess. The *Complaint of the Soul to the Body*, and *The Blessed Soul's address to the Body*, treat of a favourite subject of the middle ages. Other short poems of a lyrical and didactic character have for their subjects the various fortunes of men, the various arts of men, the falsehood of men, the pride of men. These pieces are of no great literary merit, but their antiquarian value, as illustrations of life and manners, is considerable. The *Father's Advice to his Son*, is, as the title shows, purely didactic. The Gnomic poems consist of a string of aphorisms and proverbs strung together, often in a somewhat disconnected manner. Many of the passages are extremely poetical, and the poems generally bear a striking resemblance to the Norse Hávamál, and like them, belong no doubt to the earliest stage of poetry, however much they may have been altered in later times. The curious poem, *Salomon and Saturn*, consists also of a variety of gnomic sentences, mixed, however, with a variety of other matter, in the form of a dialogue. Much of the poem is of foreign origin, and often wildly extravagant, but many passages have a strongly heathen character, and are probably fragments of some older piece resembling the Eddaic Vafþrúdnismál. *Solomon and Saturn* treats of the divine virtue, personified under the mystic name of " Paternoster," of " vasa mortis," the bird of death, of the fall of the angels, of the good and evil spirits that watch over men to encourage them to virtue or tempt to evil, of fate, old age, and various moral and religious subjects. Many passages of the poem are of high poetic beauty. The *Riddles* of Cynewulf are very pleasing. Many of them are true poems, containing beautiful descriptions of nature; and all of them have the charm of harmonious language and metre.

The religious lyric poetry is chiefly represented by the metrical psalms. The translation is a very fine one, far superior to any modern version. The language and style show that it was originally composed in the Northern dialect. The imperfect scholarship of the translator makes it doubtful whether the work is to be ascribed to Aldhelm, as suggested by Dietrich. Several metrical hymns and prayers, of little value, have also been preserved. The most valuable of the religious lyrics is the " Dream of the Cross," composed by Cynewulf, as an introduction to the *Elene*. The following is an abridged translation of the poem:—

" Lo! I will tell of the best of visions, which I dreamed at midnight. I thought I saw a noble tree raised aloft, encircled with light, bright with gems and molten gold. On it gazed all the angels of God, men, and all this fair creation; for it was no felon's gallows, but a noble victorious tree, and I was stained with sins. My mind was sad, awestruck at the fair sight, as I watched its changing hues:

now it was wet with blood, now bright with gold. I lay there a long while, gazing sorrowfully on the Saviour's tree, till I heard a voice: the best of woods began then to speak: 'It was long ago (I remember it still), when I was hewn on the borders of a forest, torn from my roots. Strong foes seized me, bore me on their shoulders, and fixed me on a hill. There they bade me raise aloft their felons. Then I saw the Lord of mankind hasten courageously, ready to ascend me. The young hero girded himself, he was God Almighty, resolute and stern of mood; he ascended the lofty gallows, proudly in the sight of many, eager to redeem mankind. I trembled, when the King embraced me, yet I durst not bow to earth; I could easily have felled all my foes, yet I stood firm. They pierced me with dark nails, the wounds are still visible on me, open gashes of malice. I durst not harm any of them, and they reviled us both together. I was all stained with blood; it poured from the hero's side, when he had yielded up his spirit. Many cruel fates have I endured on that hill! The Lord's body was shrouded in black clouds; deep shade oppressed the sun's rays. All creation wept, mourned the king's fall: Christ was on the rood. Nobles came, hastening from afar; I beheld it all. I was sorely oppressed with sorrow, yet I bowed humbly before those men, yielded myself readily into their hands. They took Almighty God, and raised him from the cruel torment. They laid him down weary in his limbs, stood around at the head of the corpse, gazing on the Lord of heaven, and he rested there a while, weary after the great toil. They began then to work an earth-house, cutting it in white stone, and placed in it the victorious king. They sang then a lay of sorrow, disconsolate at eventide, when they departed weary from the noble prince. He rested there with a scanty retinue. The corpse grew cold, the fair life-dwelling. They began then to fell us all to the ground: that was a terrible fate! They buried us in a deep pit, but the Lord's disciples found me, and adorned me with gold and silver. Now thou hast heard, dear friend, what sorrows I have endured. On me the Son of God suffered, therefore I now tower gloriously under the heavens, and I can heal all who revere me. Once I was the hardest of tortures, the most hateful to men, until I cleared for them the way of life.'"]

The History of English Poetry.

SECTION I.

N the foregoing account of Anglo-Saxon poetry, Mr. Sweet has intentionally passed over several Saints' Lives and other like productions which are hardly to be distinguished from alliterative prose in short lines, and are not really metrical. The Percy Society's Anglo-Saxon *Passion of St. George* (1850), Mr. Earle's *Saint Swithun*, &c., are of this class; and the third series of Ælfric's *Homilies* (mainly lives of saints), on which Mr. Skeat is now engaged for the Early English Text Society,[1] will probably prove to be so.

We now pass on to the Second or Transition stage of English, which is generally called Semi-Saxon. Its first stage,—1100-1150, A.D.—contains no very striking specimens in any species of composition Its substance was Anglo-Saxon, with degrading forms, and slightly mixed with Norman-French. The Saxon, a language subsisting on uniform principles, and polished by poets and theologists, however corrupted by the Danes, had much perspicuity, strength, and harmony: while the Norman-French imported by the Conqueror and his people—though of mixed origin (principally Latin, with a slight admixture of Teutonic and Celtic),—was a tongue of great beauty and power.

[Norman and Saxon struggled for the mastery, and] in this fluctuating state of our national speech, the French predominated [for a time]. Even before the Conquest the Saxon language began to fall into contempt, and the French, or Frankish, to be substituted in its stead: a circumstance which at once facilitated and foretold the Norman accession. In the year 652, [if we may trust the spurious History of Ingulphus] it was the common practice of the Anglo-Saxons to send their youth to the monasteries of France for educa-

---

[1] [This society has undertaken to print all our unedited Anglo-Saxon MSS. Those of the time of Alfred are under Mr. Sweet's charge; the later ones will be edited by Dr. R. Morris, Mr. Skeat, and Mr. Lumby.]

tion:[1] and not only the language but the manners of the [Franks] were esteemed the most polite accomplishments.[2] In the reign of Edward the Confessor, the resort of Normans to the English court was so frequent, that the affectation of imitating the Frankish customs became almost universal; and the nobility were ambitious of catching the Frankish idiom. It was no difficult task for the Norman lords to banish that language, of which the natives began to be absurdly ashamed. The new invaders [are said, but probably in error, to have] commanded the laws to be administered in French.[3] Many charters of monasteries were forged in Latin by the Saxon monks for the present security of their possessions, in consequence of that aversion which the Normans professed to the Saxon tongue.[4] Even children at school were forbidden [says the spurious Ingulphus] to read in their native language, and instructed in a knowledge of the Norman only.[5] In the meantime we should have some regard to the general and political state of the nation. The natives were so universally reduced to the lowest condition of neglect and indigence, that the English name became a term of reproach: and several generations elapsed before one family of Saxon pedigree was raised to any distinguished honours or could so much as attain the rank of baronage.[6] Among other instances of that absolute and voluntary submission with which our Saxon ancestors received a foreign yoke, it is said [in the spurious Ingulphus] that they suffered their hand-writing to fall into discredit and disuse;[7] which by degrees became so difficult and obsolete, that few beside the oldest men could understand the characters.[8] In the year 1095, Wolstan bishop of Worcester was deposed by the arbitrary Normans: it was objected against him, that he was "a superannuated English idiot, who could not speak French."[9] It is true that in some of the monasteries, particularly at Croyland and Tavistock, founded by Saxon princes, there were regular preceptors in the Saxon language: but this institution was suffered to remain after the Conquest as a matter only of interest and necessity. The religious could not otherwise have understood their original charters. William's successor, Henry I., gave an instrument of con-

---

[1] Dugd. *Mon.* i. 89.
[2] Ingulph. *Hist.* p. 62, *sub ann.* 1043.
[3] But there is a precept in Saxon from William I. to the sheriff of Somersetshire. Hickes, *Thes.* i. Par. i. p. 106. See also Præfat. *ibid.* p. xv.
[4] 'The Normans, who practised every specious expedient to plunder the monks, demanded a sight of the written evidences of their lands. The monks well knew that it would have been useless or impolitic to have produced these evidences, or charters, in the original Saxon; as the Normans not only did not understand, but would have received with contempt, instruments written in that language. Therefore the monks were compelled to the pious fraud of forging them in Latin; and great numbers of these forged Latin charters, till lately supposed original, are still extant. See Spelman, in *Not. ad Concil. Anglic.* p. 125; Stillingfl. *Orig. Eccles. Britann.* p. 14; Marsham, Præfat. ad Dugd. *Monast.*; and Wharton, *Angl. Sacr.* vol. ii. Præfat. pp. ii. iii. iv. See also Ingulph. p. 512. Launoy and Mabillon have treated this subject with great learning and penetration.'
[5] Ingulph. p. 71, *sub ann.* 1066.
[6] See Brompt. *Chron.* p. 1026; Abb. Rieval, p. 339.
[7] Ingulph. p. 85. [8] *Ibid.* p. 98, *sub ann.* 1091. [9] Matt. Paris. *sub ann.*

firmation to William archbishop of Canterbury, which was written in the Saxon language and letters.¹ That monarch's motive was perhaps political: and he seems to have practised this expedient with a view of obliging his queen who was of Saxon lineage, or with a design of flattering his English subjects, and of securing his title already strengthened by a Saxon match, in consequence of so specious and popular an artifice. It was a common and indeed a very natural practice, for the transcribers of Saxon books to change the Saxon orthography for the Norman, and to substitute in the place of the original Saxon Norman words and phrases. A remarkable instance of this liberty, which sometimes perplexes and misleads the critics in Anglo-Saxon literature, appears in a voluminous collection of Saxon homilies preserved in the Bodleian library, and written about the time of Henry II.² It was with the Saxon characters, as with the signature of the cross in public deeds, which were changed into the Norman mode of seals and subscriptions.³ The Saxon was [of course] spoken in the country, yet not without various adulterations from the French: the courtly language was [Norman-] French, yet perhaps with some vestiges of the vernacular Saxon. But the nobles in the reign of Henry II. constantly sent their children into France, lest they should contract habits of barbarism in their speech, which could not have been avoided in an English education.⁴ Robert Holcot, a learned Dominican friar, confesses that in the beginning of the reign of Edward III. there was no institution of children in the old English: he complains that they first learned the French, and from the French the Latin language. This he observes to have been a practice introduced by the Conqueror, and to have remained ever since."⁵ There is a curious passage relating to this subject in Trevisa's translation of Hygden's *Polychronicon*.⁶ "Chyldern in scoles, aȝenes þe usage and manere of al oþere nacions, buþ compelled for to leve here oune longage, and for to construe here lessons and here þingis a Freynsch; and habbeþ suþe þe Normans come furst into Engelond. Also gentilmen children buþ ytauȝt for to speke Freynsch fram tyme that a buþ yrokked in here cradel, and conneþ speke and pleye wiþ a child his brouch: and uplondysch⁷ men wol lykne hamsylf to gentile men, and fondeþ⁸ with gret bysynes for to speke

---

¹ Wharton, *Auctor. Histor. Dogmat.* p. 388. The learned Mabillon is mistaken in asserting, that the Saxon way of writing was entirely abolished in England at the time of the Norman Conquest. See Mabillon, *De Re Diplomat.* p. 52. The French antiquaries are fond of this notion. There are Saxon characters in Herbert Losinga's charter for founding the church of Norwich, temp. Will. Ruf. A.D. 1110. See Lambarde's *Diction.* v. NORWICH. See also Hickes, *Thesaur.* i. Par. i. p. 149. And Præfat. p. xvi. An intermixture of the Saxon *w* is common in English MSS. [up to 1200, A.D.; the ð was used still later, and the þ after 1500; indeed, the latter is still seen in our *ye* for *the*.]
² MSS. Bodl. NE. F. 4. 12.   ³ Yet some Norman charters have the cross.
⁴ Gervas. Tilbur. *de Otiis Imperial.* MSS. Bibl. Bodl. lib. iii. See Du Chesne, iii. p. 363.
⁵ *Lect. in Libr. Sapient.* Lect. ii. 1518.
⁶ Lib. i. cap. 59, MSS. Coll. S. Johan. Cantabr. Robert of Gloucester, who wrote about 1280, says much the same: edit. Hearne, p. 364.
⁷ upland, country.   ⁸ try.

Freynſch for to be more ytold of. Thys manere was moche yuſed tofore þet furſte moreyn; and ys ſeþe ſomdel ychaunged. For John Cornwall, a mayſtere of gramere chaungede þe lore in gramere ſcole, and conſtruccion of Freynſch into Englyſch: and Richard Pencryche lernede þat manere techynge of hym, and oþere men of Pencryche. So þat þe ȝer of oure Lord *a thouſand thre hon ;red foure ſcore and fyve*, [and] of þe ſecunde Kyng Richard after þe conqueſt nyne, in al þe grammere ſcoles of Engelond childern leueth Freynſch and conſtrueþ and lurneþ an Englyſch,"[1] &c. About the ſame time, or rather before, the ſtudents of our univerſities were ordered to converſe in French or Latin.[2] The latter was much affected by the Normans. All the Norman accounts were in Latin. The plan of the great royal revenue-rolls, now called the pipe-rolls, was of their conſtruction and in that language. Among the Records of the Tower, a great revenue-roll on many ſheets of vellum, or *Magnus Rotulus*, of the Duchy of Normandy for the year 1083, is ſtill preſerved indorſed in a coæval hand ANNO AB ICARNATIONE DNI M⁰ LXXX⁰ III⁰ APUD CADOMUM [Caen] WILLIELMO FILIO RADULFI SENESCALLO NORMANNIE.[3] This moſt exactly and minutely reſembles the pipe-rolls of our exchequer belonging to the ſame age in form, method, and character.[4] But from the declenſion of the barons and prevalence of the commons, moſt of whom were of Engliſh anceſtry, the native language of England gradually gained ground; till at length the intereſt of the commons ſo far ſucceeded with Edward III., that an act of parliament was paſſed [in 1362], appointing all pleas and proceedings of law to be carried on in Engliſh;[5] although the ſame ſtatute decrees, in the true Norman ſpirit, that all ſuch pleas and proceedings ſhould be enrolled in Latin.[6] Yet this change did not reſtore either the Saxon alphabet or language. It aboliſhed a

---

[1] From the contemporary MS. Cotton. Tiberius, D. vii., collated with Harl. MS. 1900, in Dr. R. Morris's handy book for ſtudents, *Specimens of Early Engliſh*, 1250-1400, A.D. p. 338-9.—F.]

[2] In the ſtatutes of Oriel College in Oxford, it is ordered that the ſcholars or fellows, "ſiqua inter ſe proferant, colloquio Latino, vel ſaltem Gallico, perfruantur." See Hearne's *Trokelowe*, p. 298. Theſe ſtatutes were given 23 Maii, A.D. 1328. I find much the ſame injunction in the ſtatutes of Exeter College, Oxford, given about 1330; where they are ordered to uſe "Romano aut Gallico ſaltem ſermone." Hearne's MSS. Collect. No. 132, p. 73, Bibl. Bodl. But in Merton College ſtatutes mention is made of the Latin only (cap. x.). They were given 1271. This was alſo common in the greater monaſteries. In the regiſter of Wykeham biſhop of Wincheſter, the domicellus of the prior of St. Swythin's at Wincheſter is ordered to addreſs the biſhop on a certain occaſion in French. A.D. 1398. Regiſtr. Par. iii. fol. 177.

[3] Privately printed by Petrie, 1830, 4°. Two other rolls of the Norman era have been publiſhed by Stapleton, 1848, 2 vols. 8°.]

[4] Ayloffe's *Calendar of Ant. Chart.* Pref. p. xxiv. edit. 1774.

[5] But the French formularies and terms of law, and particularly the French feudal phraſeology, had taken too deep root to be thus haſtily aboliſhed. Hence, long after the reign of Edward III., many of our lawyers compoſed their tracts in French. And reports and ſome ſtatutes were made in that language. See Forteſcut. *De Laud. Leg. Angl.* c. xlviii.

[6] Pulton's Statut. 36 Edw. III. This was A.D. 1363. The firſt Engliſh inſtrument in Rymer is dated 1368. *Fœd.* vii. p. 526.

token of subjection and disgrace, and in some degree contributed to prevent further French innovations in the language then u'ed, which yet remained in a compound state, and retained a considerable mixture of foreign phraseology. In the meantime, it must be remembered that this corruption of the Saxon was not only owing to the admission of new words, occasioned by the new alliance, but to changes of its own forms and terminations, arising from reasons which we cannot investigate or explain.[1]

[The Transition Period of the English language, between 1100 and 1250 A.D., may be divided into two stages, 1100-1150, 1150-1250. The characteristics of the language of each of these stages are its successive changes from Anglo-Saxon, principally in inflexions; and of these changes, between 1100 and 1300 A.D., we are enabled to present[2] the following sketch:—

Changes from 1100 to 1150.

(This period includes part of the *A.-Sax. Chronicle*, and some prose pieces as yet inedited. No poetical compositions of this period have, as yet, been found.)

The changes are mostly *orthographical* ones.

1. The older vowel endings, *a*, *o*, *u*, were reduced to *e*. This change affected the oblique cases of nouns and adjectives, as well as the nominative, causing great confusion in the grammatical inflexions, so that the termination

an	became	en.
um	,,	en.
ena	,,	en.
on	,,	en.
as	,,	es.
ath	,,	eth.
ra, ru	,,	re.
od, ode	,,	ed, ede.

The older endings were not wholly lost, but co-exist along with the modified forms.

2. C is sometimes softened to *ch*, and *g* to *y* or *i*, but *sc* remains intact.

3. An *n* is often added to a final *e*, and *n* often falls off, especially in the endings of nouns of the *n* declension and in the definite declension of adjectives.

Changes from 1150 to 1250,

(Including pieces in Dr. R. Morris's *Old English Homilies*, Laȝamon, &c.)

Great grammatical changes take place, and orthographical ones become fully established.

[1 This subject will be further illustrated in the next Section.]
[2 By the kindness of Dr. Richard Morris, who drew up the present insertion.]

1. The indefinite article *an (a)*, is developed out of the numeral *an* (one). It retains moſt of the older inflexions.

2. The definite article becomes *the, theo, thet (that)*, inſtead of *ſe, ſeo, thæt*.

There is a tendency to drop ſuffixes, and to uſe an uninflected *the*. *The* occurs as a plural inſtead of *tha* or *tho*.

3. Plurals of nouns end in —*en* or —*e* inſtead of the older *a* or *u*, thus conforming to the *n* declenſion.

4. The plural ending —*es* is often ſubſtituted for —*en*.

5. Genitive plural —*es*, is occaſionally found for —*e* or —*ene*.

6. Confuſion in the genders of nouns, ſhowing a tendency to aboliſh the older diſtinction of maſculine, feminine and neuter nouns.

7. Adjectives ſhow a tendency to drop certain caſe endings:
  (1.) The gen. ſing. maſc. indef. declenſion.
  (2.) The gen. and dat. fem. of indef. declenſion.

8. Dual forms are ſtill in uſe, but are leſs frequently employed.

9. New pronominal forms come into uſe:

 ha, a = he, ſhe, they; *is (hiſe)* = *hire* = her;
 his, is = *hi, heo* = them; *me* = *men* = *man* = Fr. *on*.

That is uſed as an indeclinable relative (1) for the indeclinable *the*: (2) for *ſe* and *ſeo*. *Which, whoſe, whom, what*, come in as relatives.

10. The *n* of *min, thin*, drops off before conſonants, but is retained in the oblique caſes.

11. The genitive caſes of the pronouns are becoming mere poſſeſ-ſives.

Mi-ſelf, thi-ſelf, for *me ſelf, the ſelf*.

12. The infinitive frequently omits the final *n*, as *ſmelle* = *ſmellen*. The infinitive often takes *to*, as in the earlier text of Laȝamon.

13. The gerundial or dative infinitive ends in —*en* or —*e*, inſtead of —*ene* (= *enne, anne*).

14. The *n* of the paſſive participle is often dropped, as *icume* = *icumen* = come.

15. The preſent participle ends in —*inde* (for *ende*).

The participle in *inde* often does duty for the dative infinitive in —*ene*, as *to ſwimende* = *to ſwimene* = to ſwim.

This corruption is found before 1066.

Shall and *will*, are uſed as auxiliaries of the future tenſe.

16. The above remarks are baſed on the Southern dialect, but the Ormulum has a general diſregard for nearly all inflexions.

(1.) The article is uninflected in the ſingular, and for the pl. we only find the nom. *tha*.

That is a demonſtrative, and not the neuter of the article.

(2.) The gender of nouns is much the ſame as in modern Engliſh.

(3.) The genitive *s* is uſed for maſc. and fem. nouns.

(4.) *Theȝȝ, theȝȝre, theȝȝm*, are uſed for *hi, heore, heom*. Ȝho = ſhe, for *heo*.

(5.) Verbal plurals end in *en* inſtead of *eth* (except imper. pl.)

(6.) The particle *i* (or *ge*) is dropt before the paſſive participle.

(7.) Inflexion is often loft in the 2nd perf. pret. of ftrong verbs.

(8.) The *Ancren Riwle, St. Marharete, &c.* have *fch* for *fc*, which change feems to have taken place after 1200.

There is a mixture of dialect in thefe latter works, and there is more fimplicity of grammatical ftructure than in *Laʒamon*, &c.

(9.) *Arn* occurs, as in the Ormulum, for *beoth* or *find*.

Changes from 1250 to 1300.

(1.) The def. article has not wholly loft in the Southern dialect the gen. fing. fem. and acc. mafc. inflexions: *tho* is the plural in all cafes.

(2.) The gender of nouns is much fimplified, owing to lofs of adjective inflexions.

(3.) Plurals of nouns in *en* and *es* are ufed indifcriminately.

(4.) The genitive *es* becomes more general, and often takes the place

>(1.) Of the older —*en* or —*e*. (n. decl.)
>(2.) Of *e* (fem. nouns).
>(3.) Of the plural —*ene* or —*e*.

(5.) Dative *e* (fing. and pl.) is often dropt.

(6.) Dual forms rare; and loft before 1300.

(7.) Adjective inflexions are reduced to *e*.

The gen. pl. —*re* is retained in a few cafes, as *al-re*, as well as the gen. fing. —*es* in a few pronominal forms, as *eaches, otheres*.

(8.) The gerundial infinitive in *e* or *en* is more common than in —*ene*.

(9.) Some ftrong verbs become weak.

(10.) Prefent participles in —*inge* make their appearance in the fecond text of Laʒamon, fay 1270 A. D.

All thefe points are fubject to occafional exceptions caufed by dialectal differences. Thus, the Kentifh of the thirteenth century, as far as we know it, has older forms than the weftern, as exhibited in *Laʒamon*, as *fe* = the (m.) *si*, f. &c., while the *Ayenbite* of the fourteenth century is more inflectional in many refpects than the *Ancren Riwle* and *St. Marharete*.

Having thus ftated the characteriftics of the two ftages of the Tranfition Period, in the firft of which we have, as above noted, no poetry, we proceed to give a lift of the principal poetical works known to us in manufcript in the fecond ftage of the Tranfition Period, and the Early Englifh Period—with fome extenfion,—only warning our readers that our dates are in many cafes hypothetical ones, as it is very difficult to fettle the date of an old romance or poem known to us only through a late and often altered copy. Of the MS. of the latter we know the date, but it would be abfurd to give that date to the early original.

As it would be impoffible, under exifting circumftances, to notice in detail all the Early Englifh Poems that have been printed, or made known in modern times, we truft that the reader will be content with our lift of the principal ones, and the volumes containing moft of the minor ones, so that he may examine for himself those that he does not find described in the course of the *History:*

Before 1200 A.D.
    Poetical pieces from the Lambeth MS. 487.

From 1200 to 1250, A.D.
    Dr. R. Morris's Old English Homilies (Early English Text Society), pp. 1–182.
    ? The Grave, in Thorpe's Analecta.
    Ormulum (ed. White).
    Laȝamon, the 1st text (ed. Madden).
    St. Marharete, the 1st text (ed. Cockayne).
    St. Katherine (ed. Morton, Abbotsford Club).
    St. Juliana (ed. Cockayne).
    The Poetical Pieces in Dr. R. Morris's Eng. Homilies (pp. 182—287).
    Later versions of the Moral Ode.

From 1250 to 1300 A.D.
    Genesis and Exodus (ed. Dr. R. Morris).
    Bestiary (ed. by T. Wright in Reliq. Antiq., and by Dr. R. Morris in Old English Bestiary, &c., Early English Text Society, 1871).
    Laȝamon, 2nd text (ed. Madden).
    Cuckoo Song and Prisoners' Prayer (ed. A. J. Ellis, Philolog. Soc., 1868).
    The Owl and Nightingale (eds. Stevenson and T. Wright; Stratmann, best edition).
    ✓ The Religious Pieces from the Jesus MS., in Old English Bestiary, 1871.
    Havelok the Dane (eds. Madden and Skeat).
    O. E. Northern Psalter (ed. Stevenson, for Surtees Society).
    Athanasian Creed (Hickes's Thesaurus).

1264-1327. Political Songs (ed. T. Wright, Camden Society).
1280-1300. Hendyng's Proverbs (ed. T. Wright and R. Morris).
    Lyric Poetry, Harl. 2253 (ed. T. Wright, Percy Society).
    Harrowing of Hell, Maximon &c., Harl. 2253 (ed. Halliwell, &c.).
    ✓ Horn (ed. Michel, Roxburghe Club; ed. Lumby, Early English Text Society; ed. Mätzner and Goldbeck in their Sprachproben, best edition).

Close upon 1300 A.D., but probably after, to judge by *ou* for *u*.
    Romance of Alexander (in Weber's Metrical Romances, vol. i.).
    Robert of Gloucester (Cotton MS.—*not* the version printed by Hearne).
    Lives of Saints (ed. Furnivall[1]); SS. Brandan and Beket (Percy Society); Popular Science (ed. T. Wright); and the rest in the Harleian MS. 2277.

1303.   Robert Manning of Brunne's Handlyng Synne, MS. about 1370 (ed. Furnivall, Roxburghe Club).
    ——— (?) Meditations on the Lord's Supper.
    Cursor Mundi, or Cursur o Worlde[2] (in hand for the Early English Text Society, 2 parallel texts).

1310-20? Metrical Homilies (ed. Small).
1310-20? Pieces in Digby MS. 86. Maximian, Dame Siriz, Vox and Wolf, &c. (*Rel. Ant.*, Mätzner, Hazlitt, &c.) Harrowing of Hell, &c.
1320?   Poem on the times of Edward II. (ed. Hardwicke, Percy Society).
1320-30? All the Romances and pieces in the Auchinleck MS. in the Advocates' Library, Edinburgh, of which a list is given in Sir Walter Scott's edition of Sir Tristram, and Mr. D. Laing's Penniworthe of Wit, &c. (Abbotsford Club, 1857). The principal are:—Bevis of Hampton (Maitland Club); Guy of Warwick (Abbotsford Club); Sir Tristram (ed. Scott);

[1 The contraction i^c was by mistake printed *ic* instead of *ich*, in this edition.—F.]
[2 There are a great many *u*'s for *ou*'s in *Cursor Mundi* (Cotton MS.), and Dr. R. Morris is inclined to think that the *oldest* text, from which many dialectal copies have been made, was written before 1300; but this original has not yet been found.]

Otuel (Abbotsford Club); Roland and Vernagu (Abbotsford Club); Orfeo and Heurodis (ed. Laing); Arthour & Merlin (Abbotsford Club); Seven Sages (Weber); Syr Degore (Abbotsford Club); Guy and Alquine; Lai le Freine, King of Tars, and Horn Child (Ritson); Liber Regum Anglie; Assumption of the Virgin; Joachim, our Lady's Mother; Amis and Amiloun (Weber); Owayn Miles; Harrowing of Hell; Body and Soul; Pope Gregory; Adam; St. Margaret; St. Katherine.

1325 ? Shoreham's Poems (ed. T. Wright, Percy Society).
1338. Robert Manning of Brunne's Chronicle (Part I. ed. Furnivall; Part II. ed. Hearne).
1340 ? The Psalms wrongly called Shoreham's (Brit. Mus. Addit. MS. 17,376).
1340 ? Alisaunder, a fragment, with William of Palerne (Skeat's ed.).
1340-8. Hampole's Pricke of Conscience (ed. R. Morris, Philological Society) and Minor Poems.
1350. William of Palerne, or William and the Werwolf (ed. Madden, Roxburghe Club; Skeat, Early English Text Society).
1352. Minot's Poems (ed. Ritson).
1360 ? Early English Alliterative Poems (ed. R. Morris, Early English Text Society), and
Gawayne & the Green Knight, Cotton MS. Nero, A. x. (ed. Madden, Roxburghe Club; R. Morris, Early English Text Society; See too Percy Folio, ii. 56). The coarse paintings in the cotton MS. are later than the text.
Respecting the age of the Cotton MS., however, Sir F. Madden observes (*Sir Gawayne*, 1839, 301): "It will not be difficult, from a careful inspection of the manuscript itself, in regard to the writing and illuminations, to assign it to the reign of Richard the Second; and the internal evidence, arising from the peculiarities of costume, armour, and architecture, would lead us to assign the romance to the same period, or a little earlier."
1360 ? Morte Arthure (eds. Halliwell, Perry, and Brock, the two latter for the Early English Text Society, from the Thornton MS. about 1440 A.D.).
? The Gest Hystoriale of the Destruction of Troy (ed. Donaldson and Panton, Early English Text Society).
1362. Piers Plowman, Text A (ed. Skeat, Early English Text Society).
1366 ? Chaucer's Romaunt of the Rose.[1]
1369. Chaucer's Boke of the Duchesse.
Rewle of St. Benet (Northern).
1373 ? Chaucer's Life of St. Cecile.
Chaucer's Assemble of Foules, and Palamon and Arcite.
1375. Barbour's Brus (ed. Hart, Anderson, &c.; Pinkerton, Jamieson, James; best ed. Skeat, 1870).
About 1375. All the pieces in the (Southern) Vernon MS.,[2] of which Mr. Halliwell printed an incomplete and incorrect list.[3] The chief are:
*Old and New Testament, abridged.
Saints' Lives, &c. (Other Brit. Mus. MSS. are Harl. 2277, 4196

[1 Mr. Henry Bradshaw disputes the Glasgow MS., the only one known of any English translation of the Rose, being Chaucer's version.]

[2 A very imperfect duplicate of this MS., the Simeon or Additional MS. 22,283, is in the British Museum.]

[3 The Vernon MS. has these Lives, &c, which are not in the earlier Harl. MS. 2277. (The numbers are those of Mr. Halliwell's list). How the Martyrs be God's Knights, "Now bloweth this newe fruyt that late bigon to springe," (1st line of Lives.) 2 New Year's Day, 3 Twelfth Day (Epiphany), 4 St. Hillare, 5 St. Wolston, St. Edward, and William of Normandy, 6 St. Fabian, 7 St. Agnes, 8 St. Vincent, 9 St. Juliane, 10 St. Blase, 11 St. Agace, 12 St. Scolace, 13 St. Valentin, 14 St. Juliane, 15 St. Mathi[as], 16 St. Gregori, 17 St. Longius, 18 St. Edward the King, 19 St. Cuthberd, (20 St. Benet), 21 St. Julian, 22 St. Bride, 23 St. Oswald, 24, St. Chadde, 40 St. Pernele, 42 St. Adboruh, 44 St. Aylbriht, 45

30 *List of Early English Poems.* S. 1.

        (Northern), Egerton, 1993 ; Additional, 10301, 10626). Mr. Earle has printed the St. Swithin and St. Mary of Egypt.
   *Barlaam and Josafaph.
   *La Estorie del Evangelie translated (to the Nativity).
   *Gospels illustrated by Stories.
   Wm. of Nassington's Mirror of Life, from Jn. of Waldby's Speculum Vitæ.
   †Hampole's Prick of Conscience.
   The Prikke of Love.
   Bodie and Soule (ed. T. Wright, in Mapes's Poems, pp. 340-6).
   Christes Passion ; Christ and the Devil, &c.
   Castell off Loue (ed. Weymouth, Philological Society, 1864).
  *†Kyng Robert of Cicyle, &c.
   Kyng of Tars and Soudan of Dammas (ed. Ritson, Metr. Rom.).
  *Proverbs and Cato.
   Stacions of Rome (ed. Furnivall, Early English Text Society, 1867).
   Virgin and Christ's Cross (ed. Morris, Early English Text Society, 1871).
  *†Pistyl of Sweet Susan.   Stimulus Amoris.
   Hampole's Perfect Living.   Contemplative Life.
   Mirour of St. Edmund.   Abbey of the Holy Gost, or Conscience.
   Spiritum Guidonis.   *Life of Adam and Eve.
   Piers Plowman, Text A. (ed. Skeat, Early English Text Society).
  *Joseph of Arimathæa, or the Holy Graal (ed. Skeat, Early English Text Society, 1871).
   Lives of Pilate and Judas (ed. Furnivall, Philological Society).
   Minor Poems (some printed).
1370-80. Sir Amadas, Avowyng of Arthur, &c. (eds. Stephens and Robson).
1377   Piers Plowman, Text B. (ed. Crowley, T. Wright ; Skeat, best edition, Early English Text Society).
1377 ? *Sir Ferumbras (Ashmole MS. 33).
   Chaucer's Troylus and Cresseyde.[1]
1380 ?* Piers Plowman, text C. (ed. Whitaker).
1384 ? Chaucer's House of Fame.
   Chaucer's Anelida and Arcite, Complaynt of Mars and Venus, and minor pieces.
   Chaucer's Legend of Good Women.
1387 ? Chaucer's Canterbury Tales.[2]
   Sowdane of Babyloyne and Sir Ferumbras (Roxburghe Club).
   Barbour's Troy Book, MSS. fragments.
   Audelay's Poems (Percy Society).

    * Copied, and in hand for the Early English Text Society.
    † Of this, another MS. has been printed.

St. Aeldrede, 46 St. Botulf, 47 St. Patrik, 50 St. Athelwold, 55 St. Mildride, 58 St. Allix (different metre), 59 St. Gregory, 60 The 7 Sleepers, 61 St. Dominick, 62 King St. Oswold, 65 St. Perpolyt, 69 St. Egwyne, 73 St. Justine, 74 St. Leger, 75 St. Francis. Also in different metre :—87 Sancta Paula, 89 Virgin in Antioch, 90 ditto, Miracle of a Virgin, 91 Sithia and Climonen, 92 St. Theodora, 93 St. Bernard, 94 St. Austin, 95 St. Savyn. The Beket is different too.

    The earlier Harl. MS. 2277 has these Lives, &c. not in the Vernon :— 4 Leynte, 6 Pascha, 7 Ascencio, 8 Pentecost, 13 Letanie, 14 Rouisons, 18 Quiriac, 19 Brendan, 24 Teofle, 46 Denis, 47 Luc, 48. 11,000 Virgins, 49 Symon and Jude, 50 Quintin, 51 All Saints, 52 All Souls, 53 St. Leonard, 54 St. Martin, 55 Edmund Confessor, 56 Edmund King, 63 St. Anastace, 65 Invencio Stephani.

    The following are lost from the beginning of Harl. MS. 2277 :—Hillarij, Wolstani, Fabiani, Sebastiani, Agnetis, Vincencij, Juliani conf[essoris], Juliani hosp[itis], Brigide, Blasij, Agathe, Scolastice, Valentini, Juliane virginis, Mathie apostoli, Oswaldi, Cedde conf[essoris], Gregorij, Longij, Patricij, Edwardi Juuenis, Cutberti, and (part) Benedicti.

[¹ The prose *Boece* was probably written before *Troylus*.]
[² The prose *Astrolabe* contains the date 1391.]

	The altered verſion of Wm. of Naſſington's Mirrour of Life, (from Jn. of Waldhy's Speculum Vitæ).
1390?	Barbour's Lives of Saints (MS. in Camb. Univ. Library, about 40,000 lines).
	Troy Book, Bodleian MS.
1392-3.	Gower's Confeſſio Amantis (ed. Pauli, a poor text).
1394?	Pierce the Ploughman's Crede (ed. Wolfe, Rogers, Whitaker, T. Wright; Skeat, Early Engliſh Text Society, beſt ed.).
1395?	Plowman's Tale (ed. 1687, Wright's Polit. Poems, ii.)
1395?	Richard Maydenſtoon's Pſalms (Rawlinſon MS. A. 389).
	The Lay Folks' Maſs Book (ed. Simmons, Early Engliſh Text Society, in the preſs).
1399.	Depoſition of Richard II. (ed. T. Wright for the Camden Society, and in Political Poems, vol. ii.).

After 1400 A.D. *e* final rapidly loſt ſuch grammatical value as it had at the cloſe of the 14th century. Many copies of earlier romances, &c., are preſerved for us only in 15th century MSS.

?	Morte Arthure, from MS. Harl. 2252, ab. 1440-50, A.D. (ed. Panton, Roxburghe Club; ed. Furnivall).
1410.	Lydgate's Tranſlation of Boethius.
1414.	Brampton's Penitential Pſalms (Percy Society).
1414-25.	Poems of James I. of Scotland.
1420?	Mirk's Duties of a Pariſh Prieſt (ed. Peacock, Early Engliſh Text Society).
1420?	Occleve's De Regimine Principum (ed. T. Wright, Roxburghe Club): Minor Poems (ed. Maſon, 1796, and thoſe in MS.)
1420.	Siege of Rouen (Archæologia, xxi, xxii.).
1425?	Palladius on Huſbandry, tranſlated (ed. Lodge, Early Engliſh Text Society; in the preſs).
1426.	Lydgate's Pilgrim (from De Guileville).
1430?	Partonope of Blois (ed. Buckley, Roxburghe Club).
1430?	Minor Poems of Lydgate (ed. Halliwell, Percy Soc. Others are in MS. at Trinity College, Cambridge, &c. &c.)
1430?	Merlin, Douce MS. 236, 1296 lines (differs from Affleck copy).
	Athelſton (and other pieces in Reliquiæ Antiquæ, ii.).
1430?	Poem on Freemaſonry (ed. Halliwell).
1430?	Chevelere Aſſigne (ed. Utterſon, Roxburghe Club; H. H. Gibbs, Early Engliſh Text Society).
1430-40.	Lincoln's Inn MS. 150; Ly beaus Diſconus; Merlin, &c.
1430?	Ancient Myſteries from the Digby MS. (Abbotsford Club).
1430.	Political, Religious, and Love Poems (ed. Furnivall, Early Engliſh Text Society).
1430?	Engliſh verſe tranſlation of *Speculum Humanæ Salvationis*. Mr. Hy. Huth's MS.
1430?	Sir Generides (ed. Furnivall, Roxburghe Club; Lydgate's verſion is in a MS. at Trinity College, Cambridge).
	Robert of Cycille (ed. Halliwell, in Nugæ Poeticæ).
	The Siege of Jeruſalem (2 verſions).
	Jon the Gardener, and Poems on Herbs (MS. Trinity College, Cambridge, in hand for Early Engliſh Text Society).
1430?	Hymns to the Virgin and Chriſt, the Parliament of Devils, &c. (ed. Furnivall, Early Engliſh Text Society).
1430-40?	The poems in the Cambr. Univerſity MS. F f 2, 38. Many of the minor poems have been printed. The principal pieces are:—
	Commandments, 7 Works, 5 Wits, 7 Sins and Virtues.
	The Good Man and his Son, Merchant and Wife, Merchant and Son (all printed).
	Erle of Tolous (ed. Ritſon, Metr. Rom., iii. 93-114).
	Syr Eglamoure (ed. Halliwell, Thornton Rom. 121-176. See too Percy Folio, ii. 338.)

Syr Tryamoure (ed. Halliwell, Percy Society. See, too, Percy Folio, ii. 78.)
Octavian (ed. Halliwell, Percy Society, 1844).
Seven Ages (imperfect, differs from Affleck copy).
Guy of Warwick (12156 lines, perfect). Another copy at Caius College, Cambridge. Copies of Lydgate's translation are in the Bodleian, and in Harleian MS. 5243.
Le Bone Florence of Rome (ed. Ritson, Metr. Rom. iii. 1-92).
Robert of Sicily (ed. Halliwell, 1844).
Sir Degare (imperfect. See too Percy Folio, i. 344).
†Bevise of Hampton.

1430? Lydgate's Siege of Thebes, and other Poems.
1430, 1460, &c. The Babees Book, Russell's Book of Courtesy, &c. (ed. Furnivall, Early English Text Society).
1430. Two Alexander Fragments (ed. Stevenson, Roxburghe Club).
1440? Lyfe of Ipomydon (Harl. MS. 2252, later ed. Weber.)
1440? Arthur (ed. Furnivall, Early English Text Society).
1440? Torrent of Portugal (ed. Halliwell).
1440? Sir Gowther (ed. Utterson).
1440? Poems of Charles Duke of Orleans (Roxburghe Club).
1440? Those pieces in the Thornton MS. which do not belong to a much earlier date. See a list of the contents of the MS. in Mr. Halliwell's "Thornton Romances" for the Camden Society. The principal poems are:
Morte Arthure (ed. Halliwell, ed. Perry, and best ed. Brock).
†Octavyane, †Syr Isumbrace, †Erle of Tholouse, †Syr Degravante, †Syr Eglamoure.
Tomas off Erssfeldoune (ed. Laing, in Select Remains).
Syr Perecyvelle of Gales (ed. Halliwell, Thornton Rom. 1-70.)
Awnetyrs of Arthur at the Tarne Wathelan (ed. Laing, in Select Remains, and Madden in Syr Gawayne, 15-128).
Wm. of Nassington on the Trinity (ed. Perry, Early English Text Society).
Sayne Johan, &c. (ed. Perry, Early English Text Society).
1443. Bokenam's Lives of Saints (Roxburghe Club).
1440-50? Henry Lonelich's Saynt Graal (ed. Furnivall, Roxburghe Club) and Merlin; both imperfect.
Songs and Carols (ed. Wright, Percy Society and Warton Club).
1450? Sir Degrevvaunt (ed. Halliwell, Thornton Romances, 177-276), and many poems in Cambridge University, MS. F f 1, 6.
1450? Chester Plays (ed. T. Wright, Shakespeare Society).
1455? The Buke of the Howlat, by Sir R. de Holande (ed. Pinkerton, 1792; Bannatyne Club, 1823).
1460. Wyntown's Chronicle (ed. Macpherson, 1795).
1462? The Wright's Chaste Wife (ed. Furnivall, Early English Text Society).
Wey's Pilgrimage to Jerusalem (Roxburghe Club, and Mr. H. Huth's MS.).
1460? Towneley (or Widkirk) Mysteries (ed. Surtees Society).
1460? Play of the Sacrament (ed. Stokes, Philological Society).
1460? York Mysteries (Lord Ashburnham's MS.)
1460? Miscellanies from the Porkington MS.
1460? Liber Cure Cocorum (ed. R. Morris, Philological Society).
1460? Tundale's Visions, &c. (ed. Turnbull).
1460? Blind Harry's Wallace (ed. Jamieson, &c.)
1460? Knight and his Wife, and Life of St. Katherine (ed. Halliwell).
1460? The pieces in the Cotton MS. Caligula A ii. from older originals.
†Eglamor of Artus.
†Octavian Imperator.
Launfal Miles (ed. Ritson, Metr. Rom.).
Ly beaus Disconus, or The Fayre Unknown (ed. Ritson, Metric. Rom. ii.; ed. Hippeau; see also another copy in the Percy Folio, ii. 415).

---

† Of these, other MSS. have been printed.

The Nightingale, from John of Hoveden's Latin. He wrote the *Practica Chilindri* in the Chaucer Society's Essay, Part 2.
Emare (ed. Ritson, Metr. Rom.).
Ypotis (Vernon MS.; in hand for Early English Text Society).
Stacions of Rome, St. Gregory's Trental, (ed. Furnivall, 1866, Early English Text Society).
Urbanitas (ed. Furnivall, Babees Book, Early English Text Society, 1868).
†Owayne Miles (another MS. pr. at Edinburgh). †Tundale.
Sege of Jerusalem (see Vesp. E. xvi. leaf 78).
†Isumbras.
St. Jerome. St. Eustache. Minor Poems.

1460? The Rule of the Moon, &c. (in hand for Early English Text Society, ed. Furnivall).
1468? Coventry Mysteries (ed. Halliwell, Shakespeare Society).
1470. Harding's Chronicle (printed). See MS. Selden B. 26: Harl. 661.
1460-88. Henryson's Poems (ed. Laing).
1500? Lancelot of the Laik (ed. Skeat, Early English Text Society).
1500? Partenay or Lusignan (ed. Skeat, Early English Text Society).
? Robert the Devyll (ed. Herbert, 1798).
1500? Doctrynall of Good Servauntes, &c. (circa 1550, repr. Percy Society).
1450-1500. Caxton's Book of Curtesy, 3 versions (ed. Furnivall, Early English Text Society.)
1480-1515. Dunbar's Poems (ed. D. Laing).
1506-30. Hawes's Poetical Works (W. de Worde, &c., Percy Society, &c.).
Death and Life (Percy Folio Ballads and Romances, iii. 56).
1508. Golagrus and Gawayne, &c. (ed. Madden ; ed. Laing).
1513? Scotish Field (Percy Folio Ball. and Rom. i. 199).
1520? John the Reeve (Percy Folio Ball. and Rom. ii. 550).
Sir Lambewell, „   „   i. 142.
Eger and Grime „   „   i. 341.
Merlin,   „   „   i. 417.
1520? Gawin Douglas's Works.

[The reader is also referred to the section of English Poetry in the Class Catalogue of MSS. in the British Museum, now being made under Mr. E. A. Bond's direction; to Mr. Coxe's Catalogue of the Oxford College MSS.; Mr. Kitchin's, of the Christchurch MSS.; the Index and Catalogue of the Cambridge University Library, of Corpus Christi Coll. Cambridge: of the Ashmole, and other collections in the Bodleian Library; in Trinity College, Dublin ; in Sir Thomas Philipps's and Lord Ashburnham's collections ; and to the Reports of the Historical Manuscripts Commission under the Master of the Rolls, &c. &c. Mr. W. Aldis Wright is cataloguing the MSS. in Trinity Coll. Cambridge.]

Among the Digby MSS. in the Bodleian library, we find a religious or moral Ode, consisting of one hundred and ninety-one stanzas, [the original of which[1], if it should be discovered, may be as old as] the Conquest[2]; but [it is certain that the earliest MS. we have of this poem, Lambeth 487, is not earlier than the latter half of the 12th century, if it is not after 1200 A.D.[3]] It exhibits a

---

† Of these, other MSS. have been printed.
[1] *Ling. Vett. Thes.* Part i. p. 222. There is another copy not mentioned by Hickes, in Jesus College library at Oxford, MSS. 85, *infra citat*. This is entitled *Tractatus quidam in Anglico*. The Digby manuscript has no title.
[2] [Morris's *Old English Homilies*, Early English Text Society, 1868, p. vi. note.]
[3] Sir F. Madden attributes the Digby MS. to the reign of Henry III. He enumerates five other MSS. of the Ode: Jesus Coll. 29 ; Trin. Coll. Camb. B. 14, 52; Lambeth, 487, f. 39 b. ; and two others in the Egerton MS. 613, in the Br. Mus.; and printed in Dr. Morris's *Old English Homilies*, p. 159. The copy

regular lyric strophe of four lines, the second and fourth of which rhyme together: although these four lines may be perhaps resolved into two Alexandrines; a measure concerning which more will be said hereafter, and of which it will be sufficient to remark at present that it appears to have been used very early. For I cannot recollect any strophes of this sort in the elder Runic or Saxon poetry; nor of any of the old Frankish poems, particularly of Otfrid, a monk in Weissenburgh, who turned the evangelical history into Frankish verse about the ninth century, and has left several hymns in that language;[1] of [the Strickers,] who celebrated the achievements of Charlemagne;[2] and of the anonymous author of the metrical life of Anno, archbishop of Cologne. The following stanza is a specimen [of the Lambeth MS., but with the lines arranged as in the Digby MS.]:[3]

> Sendeth sum god biforen eow[4]
> The hwile thet ȝe muȝen to hovene,
> For betere is an elmesse biforen
> Thenne both efter souene.[5]

That is, "Send some good thing before you to heaven while you

---

in the Egerton MS. 613, was printed by Mr. Furnivall for the Philological Society (*Transactions*, 1858, pt. II. p. 22), and partly in Morris's *Old English Homilies*, p. 288.]

[1] See Petr. Lambec. *Commentar. de Bibl. Cæsar. Vindebon.* pp. 418, 457. [A modern German translation, by Kelle, of Otfrid's poems has just been published.]

[2] See Petr. Lambec. *ubi supr.* lib. ii. cap. 5. There is a circumstance belonging to the ancient Frankish versification which, as it greatly illustrates the subject of alliteration, deserves notice here. Otfrid's dedication of his evangelical history of Lewis I., king of East France, consists of four-lined stanzas in rhyming couplets: but the first and last line of every stanza begin and end with the same letter: and the letters of the title of the dedication respectively, and the word of the last line of every tetrastic. Flacius Illyricus published this work of Otfrid at Basil, 1571. But I think it has been since more correctly printed by Johannes Schilterus. It was written about the year 880. Otfrid was the disciple of Rhabanus Maurus. [Schilter's book was published under this title: *Schilteri Thesaurus antiquitatum Teutonicarum, exhibens monumenta veterum Francorum, Alamannorum vernacula et Latina, cum additamentis et notis Joan. Georg. Schertzii.* Ulmæ, 1727-8. 3 vols. in fol. The *Thesaurus* of Schilter is a real mine of Francic literature. The text is founded on a careful collation of all the MSS. to which he could obtain access; and these, with one exception, perhaps—the *Life of St. Anno*—are highly valuable for their antiquity and correctness. In the subsequent editions of this happiest effort of the Francic Muse, by Hegewisch, Goldman, and Besseldt, Schilter's oversight has been abundantly remedied. The *Strickers* (a name which some have interpreted *the writer*), is written in the Swabian dialect; and was composed towards the close of the thirteenth century. It is a feeble amplification of an earlier romance, which Warton probably intended to cite, when he used the Strickers' name. Both poems will be found in Schilter; but the latter, though usually styled a Francic production, exhibits a language rapidly merging into the Swabian, if it be not in fact an early specimen of that dialect in a rude uncultivated state.—*Price*.]

[3] St. xiv.

[4] "Sende god biforen him man,
þe hpile he mai to heuene;
For betere is on elmesse biforen
Danne ben after reuene."

This is from the Trinity MS. at Cambridge, written about the [middle of the 13th century, in Mr. Wright's opinion.] Cod. membran. 8vo. Tractat. I. See Abr. Wheloc, *Eccles. Hist. Bed.* p. 25, 114.

[5] MSS. Digb. A 4, membran.

can: for one alms-giving before death is of more value than feven afterwards." The verſes might have been thus written, as two Alexandrines:

> Sendeth ſum god biforen eow the hwile thet ʒe moʒen to hovene,
> For betere is an elmeſſe biforen, thenne both after ſouene.[1]

Yet alternate rhyming, applied without regularity, and as rhymes accidentally preſented themſelves, was not uncommon in our early poetry, as will appear from other examples.

In the archiepiſcopal library at Lambeth, among other [Tranſition Engliſh] homilies in proſe, there is a homily or exhortation on the Lord's prayer in verſe,[2] which we may place with ſome degree of certainty [about the year 1200]:

> Vre feder thet in heovene is
> Thet is al ſothful i wis.
> Weo moten to theos weordes iſeon
> Thet to live and to ſaule gode beon.
> Thet weo beon ſwa his ſunes iborene
> Thet he beo feder and we him icorene
> Thet we don alle his ibeden
> And his wille for to reden, &c.—(lines 1-8.)
> Lauerd God we biddeth thus
> Mid edmode heorte ʒif hit us.
> Thet ure ſoule beo to the icore
> Noht for the fleſce forlore.
> Thole us to biwepen ure ſunne
> Thet we ne ſteruen noht therinne
> And ʒif us, lauerd, thet ilke ʒifte
> Thet we hes ibeten thurh holie ſcriſte.—AMEN.[3]
> —(Lines 298-305.)

In the valuable library of Corpus Chriſti College in Cambridge, is a ſort of poetical biblical hiſtory, extracted from the books of Geneſis and Exodus.[4] It was probably compoſed about [1250]. But I am chiefly induced to cite this piece, as it proves the exceſſive attachment of our earlieſt poets to rhyme: they were fond of multiplying the ſame final ſound to the moſt tedious monotony, and without producing any effect of elegance, ſtrength, or harmony. It begins thus:

> Man og to luuen that rimes ren.
> The wiſſed wel the logede men.
> Hu man may him wel loken
> Thog he ne be lered on no boken.
> Luuen God and ſerven him ay
> For he it hem wel gelden may.
> And to alle Criſtenei men
> Beren pais and luue by-twen

---

[1] As I recollect, the whole poem is thus exhibited in the Trinity MS. [and in all the others except the Digby.—Sir F. Madden's information.]

[2] [The whole of this Lambeth MS. 487, written before 1200, has been edited for the Early Engliſh Text Society, by Dr. R. Morris, in his *Old Engliſh Homilies*, 1867-8. The verſe Lord's Prayer is on pages 55-71 of Part I.—F.]

[3] [The Story of Geneſis and Exodus. An early Engliſh ſong, about A.D. 1250. Now firſt edited from a unique MS. in the library of Corpus Chriſti College, Cambridge. With Introduction, Notes, and Gloſſary. By Richard Morris. Early Engliſh Text Society, 1865.]

[4] Quart. minor. 185. Cod. membran. [487,] f. 21, b.

> Than fal him almighti[n] luuven.
> Here by-nethen and thund abuuen,
> And given him bliffe and foules refte[n],
> That him fal earvermor leften.
>
> Ut of Latin this fong is dragen
> On Engleis fpeche on fothe fagen,
> Criftene men ogen ben fo fagen,
> So fueles arn quan he it fen dagen.
> Than man hem telled fothe tale
> Wid londes fpeche and wordes fmale
> Of blifies dune, of forwes dale,
> Quhu Lucifer that devel dwale
> And held hem fperd in helles male,
> Til God frid him in manliched,
> Dede mankinde bote and red.
> And unfpered al the fendes fped
> And halp thor he fag mikel ned.
> Biddi hie fingen non other led.
> Thog mad hic folgen idel-hed.
>
> Fader god of alle thinge,
> Almigtin louerd, hegeft kinge,
> Thu give me feli timinge
> To thaunen this werdes beginninge.
> The, leuerd God, to wurthinge
> Quether fo hic rede or finge.[1]

We find this accumulation of identical rhymes in the Runic odes, particularly in the ode of Egill cited above, entitled *Egill's Ranfom.* [At the end of the Cotton MS. of the *Owl and Nightingale*, are feven religious metrical pieces which are printed in one of the modern editions[2] of that poem, and alfo in Dr. Richard Morris's *Old Englifh Beftiary*, &c., (E. E. T. Soc. 1871,) together with other verfions from the Jefus Coll. MS., which give hints towards fettling the date, &c. of the poems. Among thefe is] a poem on the fubjects of death, judgment, and hell torments, where the rhymes are fingular, and deferve our attention:

> Non mai longe lives thene,
> Ac ofte him lieth the wrench:
> Feir weder turneth ofte into reine,
> An wunderliche hit maketh his blench,
> Tharvore, mon, thu the bithench,
> Al fchal falewi thi grene.
> Weilawei! nis kin ne quene
> That ne fchal drincke of deathes drench.
> Mon, er thu falle of thi bench,
> Thine funne thu aquench.[3]

To the fame period of our poetry I refer a verfion of Saint Jerom's French pfalter, which occurs in the library of Corpus Chrifti College at Cambridge [and in Cotton MS. Vefp. D. vii.[4]]. The [ninety-ninth] pfalm is thus tranflated:

---

[1] [Nafmith's Cat. No. 444. It is defcribed by Dr. Morris as in the Eaft Midland dialect.]

[2] [Edited by T. Wright for the Percy Society, 1843.]

[3] Bibl. Cotton. MSS. Calig. A ix.—vi. f. 243. [Sir F. Madden pointed out that there is another copy in Jefus Coll. Oxf. 29, f. 252, b.]

[4] [Printed from this MS. by Mr. Stevenfon for the Surtees Society, 1843-7, 2 vols. 8vo.—F.]

> Mirthhes to lauerd al erthe that es
> Serues to lauerd in fainenes.
> Ingas of him in the fight,
> In gladefchip bi dai and night.
> Wite ye that lauerd he God is thus
> And he vs made and oure felf noght vs,
> His folk and fchepe of his fode :
> Ingas his yhates that ere gode :
> In fchrift his porches that be,
> In ympnes to him fchriue yhe.
> Heryes of him name fwa fre,
> For that lauerd foft es he ;
> In euermore his merci effe,
> And in ftrende and ftrende his fothneffe.[1]

In the Bodleian library there is [another MS. of this] tranflation of the Pfalms, (No. 921, *olim* Arch. B. 38,) a folio on vellum, written in the fifteenth century.[2] A fourth copy written in the reign of Edward II. has been purchafed for the Britifh Mufeum. This verfion may be afcribed to the period of his predeceffor. The Bodleian MS. alfo contains the Nicene creed[3] and fome church hymns verfified; but it is mutilated and imperfect. The nineteenth pfalm runs thus:

> Heuenes tellen Godes blis
> And wolken fhewes loūd werk his,
> Dai to dai worde rife right,
> And wifdome fhewes niht to niht,
> And pai nare fpeches ne faihes euen.
> Of whilk wat noht es herde war fteuen.
> In al the werld out yhode war rorde
> And in ende of erþ of pame þe worde.
> In funne he fette his telde to ftande
> And bridegome he als of his boure comād.
> He gladen als eten to renne þe wai
> Fro heghift heuen his outcoming ai,
> And his gainrenning til heht fete
> Ne is gwilk mai hide him fro his hete
> Lagh of louerd vnwemned iffe
> Turnand faules in to bliffe
> Witnes of louerd es euer trewe,
> Wifdom leuand to litel newe
> Louerdes rightwifnes riht hertes fainand
> Bode of louerd light eghen lighand
> Drede of louerd hit heli iffe
> In werlde of werld ai ful of bliffe,
> Domes of louerd ful fō þe are ai
> Righted in pame felue are pai
> More to be yorned ouer golde
> Or fton derwurpi þat is holde,
> Wel fwetter to mannes wombe,
> Ouer honi ande te kombe.

This is the beginning of the eighteenth pfalm :

---

[1] [Cott. MS. Vefp. D, vii. fol. 70.]   [2] [Sir F. Madden's information.]
[3] Hickes has printed a metrical verfion of the creed of St. Athanafius: to whom, to avoid prolix and obfolete fpecimens already printed, I refer the reader, *Thefaur. Par.* i. p. 233. I believe it to be of the age of Henry II. [In 1835, Mr. Thorpe publifhed his edition of the Pfalter in Anglo-Saxon from a MS. in the Bibl. Imper. at Paris.]

> I fal loue the louerd of bliffe
> Strengh mine louerd feftnes min effe
> And in fleing min als fo
> And mi lefer out of wo.

I will add another religious fragment on the crucifixion, in the shorter measure [of the middle of the thirteenth century]:

> Vyen i o the rode fe,
> Faft nailed to the tre,
> Jefu mi lefman,
> Ibunden, bloc ant blodi,
> An hys moder ftant him bi,
> Wepande, and Johan :
> Hys bac wid fcuurge ifwungen,
> Hys fide depe iftungen,
> For finne and lowe [love] of man ;
> Weil aut [well ought] i finne lete
> An neb wit teres wete,
> Thif i of loue can.[1]

In the library of Jesus College at Oxford [MS. Arch. I. 29], I have seen [an early English] poem of another cast, yet without much invention or poetry. [This Jefus MS. is of the latter half of the thirteenth century. Another MS. of the first half of the same century is in the British Museum, Cotton, Caligula, A. ix.[2]] The poem[3] is a contest between an owl and a nightingale about superiority in

---

[1] MSS. Bibl. Bodl. 57, f. 102, b. [In MS. Bodl. 42, are two ftanzas of a metrical verfion of a paffage in the Meditations of St. Auftin, very fimilar to Warton's fragment, and the fame lines occur on a piece of vellum inferted in a MS. in the Cath. Lib. Durh. written in the middle of the thirteenth century. Both texts are printed in Mr. Furnivall's *Political, Religious, and Love Poems*, for the Early Englifh Text Society, p. 214.]

[2] The latter has been edited by Mr. T. Wright for the Percy Society, and very carefully by Dr. Stratmann (Krefeld, 1868), with a full collation of the Jefus MS. The Jefus MS. was printed by Mr. Stevenfon for the Roxburghe Club, and his Gloffary contains fome aftonifhing miftakes.]

[3] [Nicholas de] Guldevorde is the author of the poem which immediately precedes in the manufcript, as appears by the following entry at the end of it, in the handwriting of [Thomas Wilkins, LL.B., rector of St. Mary, Glamorganfhire. Sir F. Madden's Corr.] : " On part of a broken [fly?] leaf of this MS. I find thefe verfes written, whearby the author may be gueft at :

> " 'Mayfter Johan eu greteth of Guldworde tho,
> And fendeth eu to feggen that fynge he nul he wo,
> On thiffe wife he will endy his fonge,
> God louerde of hevene, beo us alle amonge."

The piece [which is printed in Dr. Morris's *Old Englifh Beftiary*, &c., Early Englifh Text Society, 1871] is entitled and begins thus:

> *Ici commence la Puffyun Ihu Chrift en engleys.*
> " Ihereth eu one lutele tale that ich eu wille telle
> As we vyndeth hit iwrite in the godfpelle :
> Nis hit nouht of Karlemeyne ne of the Duzpere,
> Ac of Criftes thruwynge," &c.

It feems to be of equal antiquity with that mentioned in the text. The whole manufcript, confifting of many detached pieces both in verfe and profe, was perhaps written in the [thirteenth century. It is attributed to Nicholas de Guilford, who was poffibly related to John de Guilford].

voice and singing. It is not later than [Edward] I.[1] The rhymes are multiplied, and remarkably interchanged:

> Ich was in one sumere dale:
> In one swithe diȝele hale,
> Iherde ich holde grete tale,
> An ule[2] and one nihtegale.
> That plaid was stif & starc and strong,
> Sum hwile softe and lud among.
> And either aȝen other swal
> And let that uvele mod ut al.
> And either seide of othres custe,
> That alre worste that hi wuste;
> And hure and hure of othres songe
> Hi heolde plaiding swithe stronge.[3]
>
> [—*Stratmann*, p. 1.]

The earliest love-song which I can discover in our language, is [in Harl. MS. 2253]. I would place it before or about the year 1200. It is full of alliteration, and has a burthen or chorus:[4]

> Blow northerne wynd,
> Sent thou me my suetyng;
> Blow northerne wynd,
>   Blou, blou, blou.
> Ichot a burde in boure bryht
> That fully semly is on syht,
> Menskful maiden of myht,
>   Feir ant fre to fonde.
> In al this wurhliche won,
> A burde of blod & of bon,
> Never ȝete y nuste[5] non
>   Lussomore in londe. *Blou, &c.*

From the same collection I have extracted a part of another amatorial ditty, of equal antiquity, which exhibits a stanza of no inelegant or unpleasing structure, and approaching to the octave rhyme. It is, like the last, formed on alliteration:

> In a fryht as y con fare fremede
> Y founde a wel feyr fenge to fere,
> Heo glystnede ase gold when hit glemede,
> Nes ner gome so gladly on gere,
> Y wolde wyte in world who hire kenede,
> This burde bryht, ȝef hire wil were;
> Heo me bed go my gates, lest hire gremede,
> Ne kepte heo non hevyng here.[6]

In the following lines a lover compliments his mistress named Alysoun:

---

[1] [Sir F. Madden seems inclined to identify Nicholas de Guilford with the vicar of Porteshom, near Abbotsbury.]
[2] owl. [3] MSS. Coll. Jes. Oxon. 86, membr.
[4] [Printed in Ritson's *Ancient Songs*, 1792, p. 26; 2nd ed. i. 58; and in T. Wright's *Specimens of Lyric Poetry* (Percy Soc. 1842), which contains all the songs quoted from the MS. (about 1307 A.D.) by Warton. It was not thought desirable, therefore, to retain Warton's very lengthy extract, and only the commencement has been given.]
[5] knew not.
[6] MSS. *ibid.* f. 66. [*Hevyng* is hoving, stopping. Sir F. Madden, judging from internal evidence, supposes that this piece was written shortly after 1307, to which date he assigns the execution of the MS.]

Bytuene Merſhe ant Aueril
When ſpray biginneth to ſpringe,
The lutel foul hath hire wyl
On hyre lud to ſynge,
Ich libbe in louelonginge
For ſemlokeſt of alle thynge.
He may me blyſſe bringe;
Icham in hire baundoun;
An hendy hap ichabbe yhent
Ichot from heuene it is me ſent.
From alle wymmen mi love is lent
And lyht on Aliſoun.

On heu hire her is fayre ynoȝ,
Hire browe broune, hire eye blake,
With loſſum chere he on me loh :
With middel ſmal and wel ymake,
Bote he me wolle to hire take, &c.¹

The following ſong, containing a deſcription of the ſpring, diſplays glimmerings of imagination, and exhibits ſome faint ideas of poetical expreſſion. It is extracted from the ſame inexhauſtible repoſitory. I have tranſcribed the whole:²

Lenten ys come with love to toune,
With bloſmen ant with briddes roune,
   That al this bliſſe bryngeth;
Dayes eȝes in this dales,
Notes ſuete of nyȝtegales,
   Uch foul ſong ſingeth.

The threſtelcoc³ him threteth oo,
Away is huere wynter wo,
   When woderoue ſpringeth;
This foules ſingeth ferly fele,
Ant wlyteth on huere wynter wele,
   That al the wode ryngeth.

The roſe rayleth hir rode,
The leves on the lyȝte wode
   Waxen al with wille :
The mone mandeth hire bleo
The lilie is loſſum to ſeo;
   The fenyl and the fille.

Wowes this wilde drakes,
Miles murgeth huere makes.
   As ſtreme that ſtriketh ſtille
Mody meneth, ſo doh mo.
Ichot ycham on of tho,
   For love that likes ille.

---

¹ Harl. MSS. fol. 2253 63, b.
² [The following ſtanza formed the opening of this ſong as printed by Warton. It appears to have been inadvertently copied from a poem in the parallel column of the manuſcript, Harl. 2253. (See Wright's *Lyric Poetry*, p. 45.)

"In May hit muryeth when hit dawes,¹
In dounes with this dueres plawes,²
   Ant lef is lyȝt on lynde;
Bloſmes bredeth on the bowes,
Al this wylde wyȝtes wowes,
   So wel ych under-fynde."—*Price.*]

³ throſtle, thruſh.

---

¹ "it is mery at dawn."   ² plays.

The mone mandeth hire lyȝt,
[So doth the femly fonne bryȝt,]
   When briddes fyngeth breme,
Deawes donketh the dounes
Deores with huere derne rounes,
   Domes forte deme.

Wormes woweth under cloude,
Wymmen waxith wounder proude,
   So wel hyt wol hem feme :
Ȝef me fhal wonte wille of on
This wunne weole ẏ wol forgon
   Ant wyht in wode be fleme.¹

This fpecimen will not be improperly fucceeded by the following elegant lines, which a contemporary poet appears to have made in a morning walk from Peterborough, on the bleffed Virgin ; but whofe genius feems better adapted to defcriptive than religious fubjects :

Now fkruketh rofe ant lylie flour,
   That whilen ber that fuete favour
      In fomer, that fuete tyde ;
Ne is no quene fo ftark ne ftour,
Ne no leuedy fo bryht in bour
      That ded ne fhal by-glyde :
Whofo wol fleyfh-luft for-gon
And hevene-bliffe abyde,

---

¹ MSS. *ibid.* ut fupr. f. 71, b. In the fame ftyle, as it is manifeftly of the fame antiquity, the following little defcriptive fong, on the Approach of Summer, deferves notice.—*MSS. Harl.* 978, f. 5 :

"Sumer is i-comen in,
   Lhude fing cuccu :
Groweth fed, and bloweth med,
   And fpringeth the wde nu.
      Sing cuccu.

Awe bleteth after lomb,
   Lhouth after calve cu ;
Bulluc fterteth, bucke verteth :
   Murie fing, cuccu,
      Cuccu, cuccu :
   Wel finges thu cuccu ;
Ne fwik thou nauer nu.
   Sing cuccu nu,
   Sing cuccu.

That is, "Summer is coming : Loudly fing, Cuckow! Groweth feed, and bloweth mead, and fpringeth the wood now. Ewe bleateth after lamb, loweth cow after calf ; bullock ftarteth, buck *verteth* :¹ merrily fing, Cuckow! Well fingeft thou, Cuckow, Nor ceafe to fing now." This is the moft ancient Englifh fong that appears in our manufcripts, with the mufical notes annexed. The mufic is of that fpecies of compofition which is called *Canon in the Unifon*, and is fuppofed to be of the fifteenth century. [See Chappell's *Popular Mufic of the Olden Time*, 23-5, and references there given to other fongs of the fame character ; alfo Mr. Alexander J. Ellis's careful edition of this fong and the Prifoner's Prayer in the *Philological Society's Tranfactions*, 1868. Mr. Richard Taylor has drawn attention to the fimilarity of this fong to fome of the lays of the *Minnefingers*, collected by Mr. Edgar Taylor, 1825.]

---

¹ goes to harbour among the fern.

> On Jhefu be is thoht anon,
> That therled was ys fide.¹

To which we may add a fong, probably written by the fame author, on the five joys of the bleffed Virgin, [a common topic, treated by Shoreham and other poets:]

> Afe y me rod this ender day,
> By grene wode, to feche play;
> Mid herte y thohte al on a May.
> Sueteft of alle thinge;
> Lythe, and ich ou telle may
> Al of that fuete thinge.²

In the fame paftoral vein, a lover, perhaps of the reign of King John, thus addreffes his miftrefs, whom he fuppofes to be the moft beautiful girl, "bituene Lyncolne and Lyndefeye, Northampton and Lounde":³

> When the ny3tegale finges, the wodes waxen grene;
> Lef and gras and blofme fpringes in Averyl, y wene.
> Ant love is to myn herte gon with one fpere fo kene
> Ny3t and day my blod hit drynkes, myn herte deth me tene.⁴
>
> Ich have loved al this 3er that y may love na more,
> Ich have fiked moni fyk, lemmon, for thin ore,
> Me nis love never the ner, ant that me reweth fore;
> Suete lemmon, thench on me, ich have loved the 3ore.
>
> Suete lemmon, y preye the of love one fpeche,
> While y lyve in worlde fo wyde other nulle y feche.⁵
> [With thy love, my fuete leof, mi blis thou mi3tes eche,
> A fuete cos of thy mouth mi3te be my leche.]

Nor are thefe verfes, in fomewhat the fame meafure, unpleafing:

> My deth y love, my lyf ich hate, for a levedy fhene,
> Heo is brith fo daies li3t, that is on me wel fene.
> Al y falewe, fo doth the lef in fomer when hit is grene;
> 3ef mi thoht helpeth me no3t, to wham fhal I me mene?

Another, in the following little poem, enigmatically compares his miftrefs, whofe name feems to be Joan, to various gems and flowers. The writer is happy in his alliteration, and his verfes are tolerably harmonious:

> Ichot a burde in a bour, afe beryl fo bry3t,
> Afe faphyr in felver femly on fy3t,
> Afe jafpe⁶ the gentil that lemeth⁷ with ly3t,
> Afe gernet⁸ in golde and ruby wel ry3t,
> Afe onycle⁹ he ys on yholden on hy3t;
> Afe diamaund the dere in day when he is dy3t:
> He is coral y-cud with Cayfer ant kny3t,
> Afe emeraude a morewen this may haveth my3t.
> The my3t of the margarite haveth this mai mere,
> For charbocle iche hire chafe bi chyn ant bi chere.
> Hire rode ys as rofe that red ys on rys,¹⁰

---

¹ Harl. MSS. 2253, f. 80; [*Lyric Poetry*, p. 87.]
² MS. *ibid.* f. 81, b; *Lyric Poetry*, p. 94.   ³ London.
⁴ MSS. *ibid.* f. 80, b. [The confufion, adverted to above, prevailed in the difpofition of this fong. The prefent copy follows the MS.—*Price.*] Ritfon's *Anc. Songs*, p. 30.   ⁵ MSS. *ibid.* f. 80, b.
⁶ jafper.   ⁷ ftreams, fhines.   ⁸ garnet.   ⁹ onyx.   ¹⁰ branch.

With lilye white leves loſſum he ys,
The primroſe he paſſeth, the parvenke of prys,
With aliſaundre thareto, ache ant anys:
Coynte¹ as columbine ſuch hire cande² ys,
Glad under gore in gro ant in grys
He is bloſme opon bleo bri3teſt under bis
With celydone ant ſauge aſe thou thi ſelf ſys, &c.
From Weye he is wiſiſt into Wyrhale,
Hire nome is in a note of the ny3tegale;
In an note is hire nome, nempneth hit non,
Who ſo ryzt redeth, ronne to Johon.³

The curious Harleian volume, to which we are ſo largely indebted, has preſerved a moral tale, a compariſon between age and youth, where the ſtanza is remarkably conſtructed. The various ſorts of verſification which we have already ſeen, evidently prove that much poetry had been written, and that the art had been greatly cultivated before this period.

Herkne to my ron, } *Of elde al hou yt ges.*
As ich ou tell con,
Of a mody mon, } *Soth withoute les.*
Hihte Maximion,
Clerc he was ful god, } *Nou herkne hou it wes*⁴.
So moni mon undirſtod.

For the ſame reaſon, a ſort of elegy on our Saviour's crucifixion ſhould not be omitted. It begins thus (*Lyric Poetry*, p. 85):

I ſyke when y ſinge,
For ſorewe that y ſe,
When y with wypinge
Bihold upon the tre,
Ant ſe Jheſu the ſuete
Is hert blod for-lete,
For the love of me;
Ys woundes waxen wete,
Thei wepen ſtill and mete,
Marie, reweth the.⁵

Nor an alliterative ode on heaven, death, judgment, &c. (*Lyric Poetry*, p. 22.):

Middel-erd for mon wes mad,
Un-mihti aren is meſte mede,
This hedy hath on honde yhad,
That hevene hem is heſt to hede.
Icherde a bliſſe budel us bade,
The dreri domeſdai to drede,
Of ſunful ſauhting ſone be ſad,
That derne doth this derne dede,
Thah he ben derne done.
This wrakefall werkes under wede,
In ſoule ſoteleth ſone.⁶

Many of theſe meaſures were adopted from the French chanſons.⁷ I will add one or two more ſpecimens.

---

¹ quaint. ² [kind, nature. Sir F. Madden's corr.] ³ MSS. *ibid.* f. 63.
⁴ MSS. *ibid.* f. 82, [printed in *Reliquiæ Antiquæ*, i. 119-125. There is another copy in the Digby MS. 86, leaf 134 back, ab. 1320 A.D.]
⁵ *Ibid.* f. 80.
⁶ MS. Harl. 2253, f. 62, b. ⁷ See MSS. Harl. *ut ſupr.* f. 49, 76.

On our Saviour's paſſion and death:

> Jeſu for thi muchele mi3t
> Thou 3ef us of thi grace,
> That we mowe dai ant nyht
> Thenken o thi face.
> In myn herte hit doth me god,
> When y thenke on Jeſu blod,
> That ran doun bi ys ſyde;
> From is herte doune to his fot,
> For ous he ſpradde is herte blod
> His wondes were ſo wyde.¹

On the ſame ſubject:

> Lutel wot hit any mon
> How love hym haveth y-bounde,
> That for us o the rode ron,
> Ant bohte us with is wounde;
> The love of him us haveth ymaked ſounde,
> And y-caſt the grimly goſt to grounde:
> Ever ant oo, ny3t ant day, he haveth us in is tho3te,
> He nul nout leoſe that he ſo deore bo3te.²

The following are on love and gallantry. The poet, named Richard, profeſſes himſelf to have been a great writer of love-ſongs:

> Weping haveth myn wonges³ wet,
> For wikked werk ant wone of wyt,
> Unblithe y be til y ha bet,
> Bruches broken, aſe bok byt:
> Of levedis love that y ha let,
> That lemeth al with luefly lyt,
> Ofte in ſonge y have hem ſet,
> That is unſemly ther hit ſyt.
> Hit ſyt and ſemeth noht,
> Ther hit ys ſeid in ſong
> That y have of them wroht,
> Ywis hit is al wrong.⁴

It was cuſtomary with the early ſcribes, when ſtanzas conſiſted of ſhort lines, to throw them together like proſe. As thus:

"A wayle whyt as whalles bon | a grein in golde that godly ſhon | a tortle that min herte is on | in tounes trewe | Hire gladſhip nes never gon | whil y may glewe."⁵

Sometimes they wrote three or four verſes together as one line:

With longyng y am lad | on molde y waxe mad | a maide marreth me,
Y grede, y grone un-glad | for ſelden y am ſad | that ſemly for te ſe.
Levedi, thou rewe me | to routhe thou haveſt me rad | be bote out of that y bad | my lyf is long on the.⁶

Again,

---

¹ MS. Harl. 2253, f. 79. Probably this ſong has been ſomewhat moderniſed by tranſcribers.

² Ibid. f. 128. Theſe lines afterwards occur, burleſqued and parodied, by a writer of the ſame age.

³ [cheeks, A. S. pang, Ital. guancia.]

⁴ MSS. Ibid. f. 66; [Lyric Poetry, p. 30-33.]

⁵ Ibid. f. 67. [Mr. R. Taylor refers us to Hoffmann's Fundgruben 1830; Danſke Kiæmpe Viſer, 1787; and Raynouard, Poeſies des Troubadours, ii. Poeme ſur Boece, p. 6.]

⁶ Ibid. f. 63, b.

Mofti ryden by Rybbes-dale | wilde wymmen for te wale | ant welde wuch ich wolde:
Founde were the feyreft on | that ever wes mad of blod ant bon | in boure beft with bolde.[1]

This mode of writing is not uncommon in ancient manufcripts of French poetry. And fome critics may be inclined to fufpect, that the verfes which we call Alexandrine, accidentally affumed their form merely from the practice of abfurd tranfcribers, who frugally chofe to fill their pages to the extremity, and violated the metrical ftructure for the fake of faving their vellum. It is certain, that the common ftanza of four fhort lines may be reduced into two Alexandrines, and on the contrary. I have before obferved that the [old Englifh] poem cited by Hickes, confifting of one hundred and ninety-one ftanzas, is written in ftanzas in the Bodleian, and in Alexandrines in the Trinity manufcript at Cambridge. How it came originally from the poet I will not pretend to determine.

Our early poetry often appears in fatirical pieces on the eftablifhed and eminent profeffions; and the writers, as we have already feen, fucceeded not amifs, when they cloathed their fatire in allegory. But nothing can be conceived more fcurrilous and illiberal[2] than their fatires when they defcend to mere invective. In the Britifh Mufeum, among other examples which I could mention, we have a fatirical ballad on the [Confiftory Courts, and the vexation which they caufed to the peafantry. The whole ballad is printed in Mr. T. Wright's *Political Songs*, for the Camden Society, 1839, pp. 155-9, and we quote a few lines againft the Summoners, whom we know from Chaucer's fketch, eight years later:—]

> Hyrd-men hem hatieth, ant vch mones hyne,
> For everuch a parrofshe heo polketh in pyne,
> Ant claftreth with heore colle:
> Nou wol vch fol clerc that is fayly
> Wende to the byfshop ant bugge bayly,
> Nys no wyt in is nolle.[3]

The elder French poetry abounds in allegorical fatire; and I doubt not that the author of the fatire on the [legal] profeffion, cited above, copied fome French fatire on the fubject. Satire was one fpecies of the poetry of the Provençal troubadours. Gaucelm Faidit, a troubadour of the eleventh century, who will again be mentioned, wrote a fort of fatirical drama called the Herefy of the Fathers, *Heregia del Preyres*, a ridicule on the council which condemned the Albigenfes. The papal legates often fell under the lafh of thefe poets: whofe favour they were obliged to court, but in vain by the promife of ample gratuities.[4] [There is a very lively and fevere fatire (erroneoufly attributed to Hugues de Bercy,) belonging to the 12th or 13th century, which is called by the writer *Bible Guiot de Provins*,] as containing nothing but truth.[5]

---

[1] Harl. MSS. 2253, f. 66.
[2] [I doubt whether they faid one word more than the oppreffions they fuffered juftified.—*F.*]
[3] Harl. MS. 2253, f. 71.
[4] Fontenelle, *Hift. Theatr. Fr.* p. 18, edit. 1742.   [5] See Fauchet, *Rec.* p. 151.

In Harl. MS. 2253, I find an ancient French poem, yet respecting England, which is a humorous panegyric on a new religious order called *Le Ordre de bel Eyse*. This is the exordium :—

> Qui vodra a moi entendre
> Oyr purra e aprendre
> L'estoyre de un Ordre Novel
> Qe mout est delitous e bel.[1]

The poet ingeniously feigns that his new monastic order consists of the most eminent nobility and gentry of both sexes, who inhabit the monasteries assigned to it promiscuously; and that no person is excluded from this establishment who can support the rank of a gentleman. They are bound by their statutes to live in perpetual idleness and luxury: and the satirist refers them for a pattern or rule of practice in these important articles, to the monasteries of Sempringham in Lincolnshire [where Robert Manning of Brunne dwelt for a time[2]], Beverley in Yorkshire, the Knights Hospitallers, and many other religious orders then flourishing in England.[3]

When we consider the feudal manners and the magnificence of our Norman ancestors, their love of military glory, the enthusiasm with which they engaged in the Crusades, and the wonders to which they must have been familiarized from those eastern enterprises, we naturally suppose, what will hereafter be more particularly proved, that their retinues abounded with minstrels and harpers, and that their chief entertainment was to listen to the recital of romantic and martial adventures. But I have been much disappointed in my searches after the metrical tales which must have prevailed in their times. Most of those old heroic songs have perished, together with the stately castles in whose halls they were sung. Yet they were not so totally lost as we may be apt to imagine. Many of them still partly exist in the old English metrical romances, which will be mentioned in their proper places; yet divested of their original form, polished in their style, adorned with new incidents, successively modernised by repeated transcription and recitation, and retaining little more than the outlines of the original composition. This has not been the case with the legendary and other religious poems written soon after the Conquest, manuscripts of which abound in our libraries. From the nature of their subject they were less popular and common, and being less frequently recited, became less liable to perpetual innovation or alteration.

In the reign of [Edward II.], a poem occurs, the date of which may be determined with some degree of certainty. It is a satirical song or ballad, written by one of the adherents of Simon de Mont-

---

[1] [It will be found in the second volume of Barbazan's *Fabliaux*, p. 307. "La Bible au Seignor de Berze" is a more courtly composition, and forms a part of the same collection, p. 194. The earlier French antiquaries have frequently confounded these two productions.—*Price*. *L'Ordre de Bel Eyse* is printed also by Wright, *Political Songs of England*, 1839, p. 137. Mr. Wright assigns it to the reign of Edward II.]

[2] [*Handlyng Synne*, Prologue, edit. Furnivall.]

[3] MSS. ibid. f. 121.

fort earl of Leicester, a powerful baron, soon after the battle of Lewes, which was fought in the year 1264, and proved very fatal to the interests of the king. In this decisive action, Richard king of the Romans, his brother Henry the Third, and Prince Edward, with many others of the royal party, were taken prisoners:[1]—

> Sitteth alle stille, ant herkneth to me:
> The kyn of Alemaigne, bi mi leaute,
> Thritti thousent pound askede he[2]
> For te make the pees in the countre,
>   And so he dude more.
>   Richard, thah thou be ever trichard,
>   trichen shall thou never more.
>
> Richard of Alemaigne, whil that he was kyng,
> He spende al is tresour opon swyvyng:
> Haveth he nout of Walingford o ferlyng;
> Let him habbe, ase he brew, bale to dryng,
>   Maugre Wyndesore.
>   Richard, thah thou, &c.

These popular rhymes had probably no small influence in encouraging Leicester's partisans, and diffusing his faction. There is some humour in imagining that Richard supposed the windmill to which he retreated, to be a fortification; and that he believed the sails of it to be military engines. In the manuscript, from which this specimen is transcribed, immediately follows a song in French, seemingly written by the same poet, on the battle of Evesham fought the following year; in which Leicester was killed, and his rebellious barons defeated.[3] Our poet looks upon his hero as a martyr, and particularly laments the loss of Henry his son, and Hugh le Despenser justiciary of England. He concludes with an English stanza, much in the style and spirit of those just quoted.

[Daines Barrington, in his *Observations on the Statutes*, 1766,] has observed, that this ballad on Richard of Alemaigne probably occasioned a statute against libels in the year 1275, under the title, "Against slanderous reports, or tales to cause discord betwixt king and people."[4] That this spirit was growing to an extravagance

---

[1] [Printed entire in *Political Songs*, ed. Wright, 1839, p. 69. The first and second stanzas have therefore been thought a sufficient specimen of the production.]

[2] The barons made this offer of thirty thousand pounds to Richard.

[3] f. 59. It begins,

"Chaunter mestoit | mon ever le voit | en un duré langage,
Tut en pluraunt | fust fet le chaunt | de noitre duz Baronage," &c.

[4] [Privately printed by Palgrave, 1818, with three other pieces from the same source. Sir F. Madden's information. It has also been included in Ritson's *Ancient Songs*, ed. 1829. A version of it was made by Sir Walter Scott, at the request of Ritson, and has been reprinted in the [second edition] of his *English Songs*, vol. ii. Mr. Geo. Ellis made another metrical translation, which perished with many of Ritson's MS. treasures.—*Park*.

This Norman ballad has since been printed in the new edition of Ritson's *Ancient Songs*. Political songs seem to have been common about this period: both English, Norman, and Latin, the three languages then used in England, seem to have been enlisted into the cause of Simon de Montfort. I have somewhere seen a Latin poem in his praise; and, in the following passage from a MS. containing his miracles (for Simon, like Harold, and Waltheof, and most of the popular heroes of those days, was looked upon as a saint), and written apparently no very long time

which deserved to be checked, we shall have occasion to bring further proofs.

I must not pass over the reign of Henry III. who died in the year 1272, without observing that this monarch entertained in his court a poet with a certain salary, whose name was Henri d'Avranches.[1] And although this poet was a Frenchman, and most probably wrote in French, yet this first instance of an officer who was afterwards, yet with sufficient impropriety, denominated a *poet laureate* in the English court, deservedly claims particular notice in the course of these annals. He is called *Master Henry the Versifier*:[2] which appellation perhaps implies a different character from the royal *Minstrel* or *Joculator*. The king's treasurers are ordered to pay this *Master Henry* one hundred shillings, which I suppose to have been a year's stipend, in the year 1251.[3] And again the same precept occurs under the year 1249.[4] Our Master Henry, it seems, had in some of his verses reflected on the rusticity of the Cornish men. This insult was resented in a Latin satire now remaining, written by Michael Blaunpayne, a native of Cornwall, and recited by the author in the presence of Hugh, abbot of Westminster, Hugh de Mortimer, official of the archbishop of Canterbury, the bishop elect of Winchester, and the bishop of Rochester.[5] While we are speaking

---

after his death, we have apparently the fragment of a hymn addressed to him when canonized by the popular voice. MS. Cotton. Vesp. A. VI. fol. 189. "Anno Domini m° cc^{mo} lx° v^{to} octavo Symonis Montis Fortis sociorumque ejus pridie nonas Augusti.

"Salve Symon Montis Fortis,
    tocius flos milicie,
Duras penas passus mortis,
    protector (?) gentis Anglie.
Sunt de sanctis inaudita,
Cunctis passis in hac vita
    quemquam passum talia : (*sic.*)
Manus, pedes amputari ;
Caput, corpus vulnerari ;
    abscidi virilia.
Sis pro nobis intercessor
Apud Deum, qui defensor
    in terris exterritas. (*sic.*)

Ora pro nobis, beate Symon, ut digni efficiamur promissionibus Christi." There are found many political songs in Latin, which shows that the monks took much interest in politics.—W.]

[1] See Carew's *Surv. Cornw.* p. 58, edit. 1602.
[2] Henry of Huntingdon says, that Walo *Versificator* wrote a panegyric on Henry the First : and that the same Walo *Versificator* wrote a poem on the park which that king made at Woodstock. Leland's *Collectan.* vol. ii. 303, i. 197, edit. 1770. Perhaps he was in the department of Henry mentioned in the text. One Gualo, a Latin poet, who flourished about this time, is mentioned by Bale, iii. 5, and Pits, p. 233. He is recommended in the *Policraticon*. A copy of his Latin hexametrical satire on the monks is printed by Mathias Flacius, among miscellaneous Latin poems *De corrupto Ecclesiæ statu*, 1557, p. 489.
[3] "Magistro Henrico Versificatori." See Madox, *Hist. Excheq.* p. 268.
[4] *Ibid.* p. 674. In MSS. Digb. Bibl. Bodl. I find, in John of Hoveden's *Salutationes quinquaginta Mariæ*, "Mag. Henricus, versificator magnus, de B. Virgine," &c.
[5] MSS. Bibl. Bodl. Arch. Bodl. 29, viz : "Versus magistri Michaelis Cornu-

of the *Versifier* of Henry III., it will not be foreign to add, that in the thirty-sixth year of the same king, forty shillings and one pipe of wine were given to Richard the king's harper, and one pipe of wine to Beatrice his wife.[1] But why this gratuity of a pipe of wine should also be made to the wife, as well as to the husband who from his profession was a genial character, appears problematical according to our present ideas.[2]

The most ancient English metrical romance which I can discover, is entitled the *Geste of King Horn*.[3] It was evidently written after the Crusades had begun, is mentioned by Chaucer,[4] and probably still remains in [something near] its original state. I will first give the substance of the story, and afterwards add some specimens of the composition. But I must premise, that this story occurs in very old French metre in the manuscripts of the British museum;[5] [but

---

bienfis contra Mag. Henricum Abricensem coram dom. Hugone abbate Westmon. et aliis." fol. 81, b. *Princ.* "Archipoeta vide quod non sit cura tibi de." See also fol. 83, b. Again, fol. 85:

"Pendo poeta prius te diximus Archipoetam,
Quam pro postico nunc dicimus esse poetam,
Imo poeticulum," &c.

Archipoeta means here the *king's chief poet*.
In another place our Cornish satirist thus attacks master Henry's person:

"Est tibi gamba capri, crus passeris, et latus apri;
Os leporis, catuli nasus, dens et gena muli:
Frons vetulæ, tauri caput, et color undique mauri."

In a blank page of the Bodleian MS., from which these extracts are made, is written, "Iste liber constat Fratri Johanni de Wallis monacho Ramefeye." The name is elegantly enriched with a device. This MS. contains, amongst other things, *Planctus de Excidio Trojæ*, by Hugo Prior de Montacino, in rhyming hexameters and pentameters, viz. fol. 89. Camden cites other Latin verses of Michael Blaunpain, whom he calls "Merry Michael the Cornish poet." *Rem.* p. 10. See also p. 489, edit. 1674. He wrote many other Latin pieces, both in prose and verse.
Compare Tanner in *Joannes Cornubiensis*, for his other pieces. *Bibl.* p. 432, notes, f, g. [The poems of Michael Cornubiensis (in Latin) are preserved, as Mr. Wright informs us, in MS. Cotton. Vesp. D. 5, 49. The same gentleman states that in the British Museum there is more than one copy of the verses quoted by Warton. In one (MS. Reg. 14 C. xiii. 269), they are said to have been recited at Cambridge before the university and masters.]

[1] *Rot. Pip. an.* 36 *Henr. iii.* "Et in uno dolio vini empto et dato magistro Ricardo Citharistæ regis, xl. sol. per Br. Reg. Et in uno dolio empto et dato Beatrici uxori ejusdem Ricardi."

[2] [Beatrice may possibly have been a *jugleress*, whose pantomimic exhibitions were accompanied by her husband's harp, or who filled up the intervals between his performances. This union of professional talents in husband and wife was not uncommon. In a copy of the ordonnances for regulating the minstrels, &c. residing at Paris, a document drawn up by themselves in the year 1321, and signed by thirty-seven persons on behalf of all the *menestreux jougleurs et jougleresses* of that city, we find among others the names of Iehanot Langlois et Adeline, fame de Langlois Jaucons, fils le moine et Marguerite, la fame au moine. See Raynouard, *De la Poesie Françoise dans les xii. et xiii. Siècles*, p. 288.—*Price.*]

[3] See Mätzner and Goldbeck's text in their *Sprachproben.*—F.]

[4] Rim. Thop. 3402, Urr.

[5] MSS. Harl. 527, b. f. 59, Cod. membr. [*King Horn* has been edited for the Early English Text Society; it was included (from Harl. 2253) in Ritson's col-

it is probably not] a translation: a circumstance which will [affect] an argument pursued hereafter, proving that most of our metrical romances are translated from the French.

[The] king of the Saracens lands in the kingdom of Suddene, where he kills the king named Allof [or Mury]. The queen, Godylt, escapes; but [the king] seizes on her son Horne, a beautiful youth aged fifteen years, and puts him into a galley, with two of his play-fellows, Athulph and Fykenyld: the vessel being driven on the coast of the kingdom of Westnesse, the young prince is found by Aylmer king of that country, brought to court, and delivered to Athelbrus his steward, to be educated in hawking, harping, tilting, and other courtly accomplishments. Here the princess Rymenild falls in love with him, declares her passion, and is betrothed. Horn, in consequence of this engagement, leaves the princess for seven years; to demonstrate, according to the ritual of chivalry, that by seeking and accomplishing dangerous enterprises he deserved her affection. He proves a most valorous and invincible knight: and at the end of seven years having killed King Mury, recovered his father's kingdom, and achieved many signal exploits, recovers the Princess Rymenild from the hands of his treacherous knight and companion Fykenyld, carries her in triumph to his own country, and there reigns with her in great splendour and prosperity. The poem itself begins and proceeds thus:[1]—

> Alle beon he blithe
> That to my song lythe:
> A sang ich schal ʒou singe
> Of Murry the kinge.
> King he was biweste
> So long so hit laste.
> Godhild het his quen,
> Faire ne miʒte nou ben.
> He hadde a sone that het horn.
> Ne no rein upon birine,
> Ne sun[n]e upon bischine.
> Faiser nis no[n] thane he was,
> He was briʒt so the glas,
> He was whit so the flur:
> Rose red was his colur.
> In none kinge-riche
> Nas no[n] his iliche.
> Twelf feren he had
> That alle with him ladde.
> Alle riche manes son[n]es,
> Alle hi were faire gomes,
> With him for to pleie,

---

lection. It is substantially the same story as *Ponthus of Galicia*, printed in 1511, 4to. In 1845, M. Francisque Michel completed for the Bannatyne club his long-promised volume on this subject. It is entitled, " Horn et Rimenhild. Recueil de tout ce qui reste des poemes, relatifs a leurs Aventures, composés en François, en Anglais, et en Ecossais, dans le xiii. xiv. xv. et xvi. Siècle."]

[[1] The following extracts have now been collated with the Early English Text Society's edit. of *Horn*, 1866, from the Cambridge University MS.]

Meſt he lu[u]ede tweie ;
That on him het hathulf child,
That oth[er] Fikenild.
Athulf was the beſte,
Fikenylde the werſte.
Hit was upon a ſomeres day,
Alſo ich ȝou telle may,
Murri the gode king
Rod on his pleing
Bi the ſe ſide,
Aſe he was woned ride,
He fonde by the ſtronde,
Ariued on his londe,
Schipes fiftene
With ſarazins kene :
He axede what iſoȝte
Other to londe broȝte.

But I haſten to that part of the ſtory where Prince Horne appears at the court of the king of Weſtneſſe :

The kyng com in to halle,
Among his kniȝtes alle ;
Forth he clupede Athelbrus,
That was ſtiward of his hus,
Stiwarde, tak nu here
My fundlyng for to lere,
Of thine meſtere
Of wude [and] of riuere,[1]
Ant tech him to harpe
With his nayles ſcharpe,[2]
Thou tech him of alle the liſte
That thee eure of wiſte,
Biuore me to kerue,

---

[1] So Robert de Brunne, of King Marian. Hearne's *Rob. Glouc*. p. 622.
   "Marian faire in chere
   He couthe of wod and ryvere
   In alle maner of venrie," &c.
[Sir F. Madden points out that the phraſe is from the French, and inſtances the following :
   "Tant ſeit apris qu'il liſe un bref
   Car ces ne li eſt pas trop gref,
   D'eſchas, *de rivere*, et de *chace*,
   Voil que del tot apreuze e face."
   —*Roman du Rou* (MS. Harl. 1717, fol. 79).]

[2] In another part of the poem he is introduced playing on his harp :
   "Horn ſette him abenche,
   Is harpe he gan clenche,
   He made Rymenild a lay,
   Ant hue ſeide weylaway," &c.

In the chamber of a biſhop of Wincheſter at Merdon caſtle, now ruined, we find mention made of benches only. *Comp. MS. J. Gerveys, Epiſcop. Winton*, 1266. "Iidem red. comp. de ii. menſis in aula ad magnum deſcum. Et de iii. menſis, et una parte, et ii. menſis ex altera parte cum treſſellis in aula. Et de i. menſa cum treſſellis in camera dom. epiſcopi. Et v. *formis* in eadem camera." *Deſcus*, in old Engliſh *dees*, is properly a canopy over the high table. See a curious account of the goods in the palace of the biſhop of Nivernois in France, in the year 1287, in Montf. *Cat. MSS.* ii. p. 984, col. 2.

And of the cupe ferue,[1]
In his feiren thou wife
Into other feruife;
Horn thu underuonge,
Tech him of harpe and fonge
Ailbrus gan lere
Horn [and] his yfere:
Horn in herte laʒte
Al that he him taʒte,
In the curt and ute,
And elles al abute,
Luuede men horn child,
And meft him louede Rymenhild
The kynges oʒene dofter,
He was meft in thoʒte,
Heo louede fo horn child,
That neʒ heo gan wexe wild:
For heo ne miʒte at borde
With him fpeke no worde,
Ne noʒt in the halle
Among the kniʒtes alle,
Ne nowhar in non othere ftede:
Of folk heo hadde drede:
Bi daie ne bi niʒte
With him fpeke ne miʒte,
Hire foreʒe ne hire pine,
Ne miʒte neure fine.
In heorte heo hadde wo,
And thus hire bithoʒte tho:
Heo fende hire fonde
Athelbrus to honde,
That he come hire to,
And alfo fcholde horn do,
Al in to bure,
For heo gan to lure,
And the fonde feide,
That fik lai that maide,
And bad him come fwythe
For heo nas nothing blithe.
The ftuard was in herte wo,
For he nufte what to do,
Wat Rymenhyld byfuʒte
Gret wunder him thuʒte;
Abute horn the ʒonge
To bure for to bringe,
He thoʒte upon his mode
Hit nas for none gode;
He tok him another,
Athulf, hornes brother.
Athulf, he fede, riʒt anon
Thu fchalt with me to bure gon,
To fpeke with Rymenhild ftille,
To wyte hure wille,

---

[1] According to the rules of chivalry, every knight before his creation paffed through two offices. He was firft a page: and at fourteen years of age he was formally admitted an efquire. The efquires were divided into feveral departments; that of the body, of the chamber, of the ftable, and the carving efquire. The latter ftood in the hall at dinner, where he carved the different difhes with proper fkill and addrefs, and directed the diftribution of them among the guefts. The inferior offices had alfo their refpective efquires. *Mem. Anc. Cheval.* i. 16, *feq.*

> In hornes ilike,
> Thu schalt hure biswike:
> Sore ihc me ofdrede
> He wolde horn mis-rede
> Athelbrus gan Athulf lede
> And into bure with him ȝede:
> Anon upon Athulf child
> Rymenhild gan wexe wild:
> He[o] wende that Horn hit were,
> That heo hauede there.

At length the princess finds she has been deceived; the steward is severely reprimanded, and Prince Horn is brought to her chamber; when, says the poet:

> Of his feire siȝte
> Al the bur gan liȝte.[1]

It is the force of the story in these pieces that chiefly engages our attention. The minstrels had no idea of conducting and describing a delicate situation. The general manners were gross, and the arts of writing unknown. Yet this simplicity sometimes pleases more than the most artificial touches. In the mean time, the pictures of ancient manners presented by these early writers strongly interest

---

[1] There is a copy, much altered and modernized, in the Advocates' library at Edinburgh, W. 4, i. Numb. xxxiv. [and another in MS. Harl. 2253, temp. Edw. II. printed in Ritson's *Romances*, vol. 3.] The title *Horn-childe and Maiden Rimnild*. The beginning:

> "Mi leve frende dere,
> Herken and ye shall here."

[The bishop of Dromore considered this production "of genuine English growth;" and though his lordship may have been mistaken in ascribing it, in its present form, to so early an æra as "within a century after the Conquest;" yet the editor has no hesitation in expressing his belief, that it owes its origin to a period long anterior to that event. The reasons for such an opinion cannot be entered upon here. They are too detailed to fall within the compass of a note, and though some of them will be introduced elsewhere, yet many perhaps are the result of convictions more easily felt than expressed, and whose shades of evidence are too slight to be generally received, except in the rear of more obvious authority. However, to those who with Mr. Ritson persist in believing the French fragment of this romance to be an earlier composition than *The Geste of Kyng Horn*, the following passage is submitted, for the purpose of contrasting its highly wrought imagery with the simple narrative, and natural allusion, observed throughout the English poem:

> "Lors print la harpe a sei si commence a temprer
> Deu ki dunc lesgardast, cum il la sot manier!
> Cum les cordes tuchot, cum les feseit trembler,
> A quantes faire les chanz, a cuantes organer,
> *Del armonie del ciel lie pureit remembrer*
> Sur tuz ceus ke i sunt fait cist à merveiller
> Kuant celes notes ot fait prent sen amunter
> E par tut autre tuns fait les cordes soner."—*Price*.

Both Mr. Wright and Sir F. Madden believe the French romance of *Horn* to be a translation from the English *Gest*, and the former points out, as one ground for his opinion, that the French MSS. (of which there are three, all imperfect) exhibit traces of additions and embellishments, and that many new names are interpolated. Sir F. Madden adds that the French romance of *Atla* declares that *Horn* (there called *Aelof*) was translated from English into French.]

the imagination; especially as having the same uncommon merit with the pictures of manners in Homer, that of being founded in truth and reality, and actually painted from the life. To talk of the grossness and absurdity of such manners is little to the purpose; the poet is only concerned in the justness and faithfulness of the representation.

Hickes has printed a satire on the monastic profession; the MS. of which was written [a little before the year 1300, according to Sir F. Madden, but early in the following century, Mr. Wright inclines to believe. It is printed (the spelling modernised) by Ellis,[1] and from the Harl. MS. 913, leaf 3, &c., by Mr. Furnivall.[2]] The poet begins with describing the land of indolence or luxury:

> Fur in see, bi west Spaynge,
> Is a lond ihote Cokaygne;
> Ther nis lond under hevenriche,[3]
> Of wel of godnis hit iliche.
> Tho3 paradis be miri[4] and bri3t
> Cockaygn is of fairir si3t.
> What is ther in paradis
> Bot grasse, and flure, and grene ris?
> Tho3 ther be joy,[5] and grete dute,[6]
> Ther nis mete bote frute.
> Ther nis halle, bure,[7] no benche,
> Bot watir, manis thurs[t] to quenche, &c.

In the following lines there is a vein of satirical imagination and some talent at description. The luxury of the monks is represented under the idea of a monastery constructed of various kinds of delicious and costly viands:

> Ther is a wel fair abbei,
> Of white monkes and of grei,
> Ther beth bowris and halles:
> All of pasteiis beth the walles,
> Of fleis, of fisse, and rich[e] met,
> The likfullist that man mai et.
> Fluren cakes beth the scingles[8] alle,
> Of cherche, cloister, boure, and halle.
> The pinnes[9] beth fat podinges
> Rich met to princez and [to] kinges ....
> Ther is a cloister fair and li3t,
> Brod and lang, of sembli si3t.
> The pilers of that cloistre alle
> Beth iturned of cristale,
> With harlas and capitale·

---

[1] *Specimens*, vol. i.
[2] [In *Poems and Lives of Saints*. Phil. Soc. Trans. 1858, part II. p. 156. The MS. was lent to Hickes by Tanner, but in 1698 it was the property of Bishop More. How it came into the Harleian Collection, Sir F. Madden professes himself unable even to guess.]
[3] Heaven. Sax.
[4] Merry, cheerful. "Although Paradise is chearful and bright, *Cokayne* is a much more beautiful place."
[5] ioi, Orig.   [6] Pleasure.   [7] [A chamber.]
[8] *Shingles.* "The tiles, or covering of the house, are of rich cakes."
[9] The pinnacles.

A Satire on the Monastic Profession.

Of grene jaspe and rede corale
In the praer is a tre
Swithe likful for to se,
The rote is gingeuir and galingale,
The siouns beth al sedwale.
Trie maces beth the flure,
The rind, canel of swet odur :
The frute gilofre of gode smakke,
Of cucubes ther nis no lakke. . . . .
There beth iiii. willis[1] in the abbei
Of triacle and halwei,
Of baum and ek piement,[2]
Ever ernend[3] to ri3t rent;[4]
Of thai stremis al the molde,
Stonis preciuse[5] and golde,
Ther is saphir, and uniune,
Carbuncle and astiune,
Smaragde, lugre, and prassiun:,
Beril, onix, toposiune,
Ametist and crisolite,
Calcedun and epetite.[6]
Ther beth birddes mani and fale
Throstil, thruisse, and ni3tingale,
Chalandre, and wood[e]wale,
And other briddes without tale,
That stinteth never bi her mi3t
Miri to sing[e] dai and ni3t. . . .
Yi[t]e I do 3ow mo to witte,
The gees irostid on the spitte,
Flee3 to that abbai, God hit wot,
And gredith,[7] " gees al hote, al hote," &c.

Our author then makes a pertinent transition to a convent of nuns, which he supposes to be very commodiously situated at no great distance, and in the same fortunate region of indolence, ease, and affluence:

An other abbai is therbi
For soth a gret fair nunnerie;[8]
Up a river of swet milke
Whar is plente grete of silk.
When the someris dai is hote,
The 3ung[e] nunnes takith a bote
And doth ham forth in that river
Both with oris and with stere :
Whan hi beth fur from the abbei,
Hi makith ham nakid for to plei,

---

[1] Fountains.
[2] This word will be explained at large hereafter.   [3] Running, Sax.
[4] Course, Sax.
[5] The Arabian philosophy imported into Europe was full of the doctrine of precious stones.
[6] Our old poets are never so happy as when they can get into a catalogue of things or names. See *Observat. on the Fairy Queen*, i. p. 140.
[7] Cryeth. [Anglo-Sax.] [See Conybeare's *Illustr. of A.-S. Poetry*, 1826, 3-8, and Thorpe's *Cædmon*, 1832, Pref.—*Madden*.]
[8] [*La grange est pres des bateurs* ; ("Said of a Nunnerie thats neere vnto a Fryerie:) the Barne stands neere the Thresher's."—Cotgrave, under *Bateur*.—*F*.]

And lepith dune in to the brimme
And doth ham fleilich for to fwimme :
The zung[e] monkes that hi feeth,
Hi doth ham up, and forth hi fleeth,
And comith to the nunnes anon,
And euch monke him takith on,
And fnellich[1] berith forth har prei
To the mochil grei abbei,[2]
And techith the nunnes an oreifun
With jambleue[3] up and dun.[4]

---

[1] Quickly, quickly. [Anglo-Saxon.]
[2] "To the great abbey of Grey Monks."
[3] Lafcivious motions, gambols. Fr. *gambiller*.
[4] Hickes, *Thes*. i. Par. i. p. 231 *feq*. [A French fabliau, bearing a near refemblance to this poem, and poffibly the production upon which the Englifh minftrel founded his fong, has been publifhed in Barbazan, *Fabliaux et Contes*, 1808, iv. 175.—*Price*. But Mr. Wright has pointed out that Price errs in defcribing the fabliau as fimilar to the Englifh poem, and fpecifies, on the other hand, an old Dutch poem which, from the fpecimen he affords, certainly exhibits a ftriking refemblance.]

The fecular indulgences, particularly the luxury, of a female convent, are intended to be reprefented in the following paffage of an ancient poem, called *A Difputation bytwene a Cryftene mon and a Jew*, [from a MS.] written [near the end of the 14th century.] MS. Vernon, fol. 301 :

"Till a Nonneri thei came,
But I knowe not the name ;
Ther was mony a derworthe[1] dame
    In dyapre dere :[2]
Squiȝeres[3] in vche fyde,
In the wones[4] fo wyde :
Hur fchul we lenge[5] and abyde,
    Auntres[6] to heare.
Thene fwithe[7] fpekethe he,
Til a ladi fo fre,
And biddeth that he welcum be,
    'Sire Water my feere.'[8]
Ther was bords[9] i-clothed clene
With fchire[10] clothes and fchene,
Seþþe[11] a waffchen,[12] i wene,
    And wente to the fete ;
Riche metes was forth brouht,
To all men that gode thouht :
The criften mon wolde nouht
    Drynke nor ete.
Ther was a wyn ful clere
In mony a feir mafere,[13]
And other drynkes that weore dere,
    In coupes[14] ful gret :

---

[1] Dear-worthy. [2] Diaper fine. [3] Squires, attendants.
[4] Rooms, apartments. [5] Shall we tarry. [6] Adventures.
[7] Swiftly, immediately.
[8] My companion, my love. He is called afterwards, "[Sir] Walter of Berwick."
[9] Tables. [10] Sheer, clean.
[11] Or *fithe*, i. e. [afterwards : but perhaps we fhould read *feththe thei*, "afterwards they."—*Price*.]
[12] Wafhed. [13] Mazer, great cup. [14] Cups.

This poem was designed to be sung at public festivals:[1] a practice, of which many instances occur in this work; and concerning which it may be sufficient to remark at present, that a Joculator or bard was an officer belonging to the court of William the Conqueror.[2]

Another [Early English] poem cited by the same industrious antiquary [and since printed by Mr. Cockayne], is entitled *The Life of Saint Margaret*. The structure of its versification considerably differs from that in the last-mentioned piece, and is like the French Alexandrines. But I am of opinion that a pause, or division, was intended in the middle of every verse: and in this respect its versification resembles also that of [Warner's] *Albion's England*, or Drayton's *Polyolbion*, which was a species very common about the reign of Queen Elizabeth.[3] The rhymes are also continued to every fourth line. It appears to have been written about the time of [Henry III.]. It begins thus:[4]

> Seinte Margarete was: holi maide 't god
> Ibore heo was in Antioche: icome of cunde blod
> Terdose hire fader het: while bi olde dawe
> Patriarch he was wel he3: 't maister of the lawe
> He ne bileouede on ihesu crist no3t: for he hethene was
> Margarete his 3unge dou3ter: ipaid therwith no3t has
> For hire hurte bar anon: cristene to beo
> The false godes heo het deuelen: that heo mi3te aldai iseo—.

In the sequel, Olibrius, lord of Antioch, who is called a Saracen, falls in love with Margaret: but she being a Christian and a candidate for canonization, rejects his solicitations, and is thrown into prison.[5]

> Meidan Maregrete one nitt in prisun lai
> Ho com biforn Olibrius on that other dai.

> Sihthe was schewed him bi
> Murththe and munstralsy,[1]
> And preyed hem do gladly,
> With ryal rechet.[2]
> Bi the bordes up thei stode," &c.

[1] As appears from this line:
  "Lordinges gode and hende," &c.

[2] His lands are cited in Doomsday Book (*Gloucestershire*.) "Berdic, Joculator Regis, habet iii. villas et ibi v. car. nil redd. See Anstis, *Ord. Gart.* ii. 304.

[3] It is worthy of remark, that we find in the collection of ancient Northern monuments published by M. Biorner, a poem of some length, said by that author to have been composed in the twelfth or thirteenth century. This poem is professedly in rhyme, and the measure like that of the heroic Alexandrine of the French poetry. See Mallet's *Introd. Dannem*, &c., ch. xiii.

[4] I direct, Fr. "I advise you, your," &c. [The writer of this Life in the Bodleian MS., who is quite as likely to have understood the author's meaning, reads, "I preye you:" words bearing no doubt the same signification then as they do at present."—*Price*. This extract has now been taken from edit. Cockayne, 1st text, 1866.]

[5] [Edit. Cockayne (2nd text), p. 37].

---

[1] Afterwards there was sport and minstrelsy.
[2] *i. e.* recept, reception. But see Chaucer's *Rom. R.* v. 6509:
  "Him woulde I comfort and *rechete*."
[Cheer, from Fr. *rehaitier*.—Sir F. Madden's inform.] And *Tr. Cresf*. iii. 350.

Meidan Maregrete, lef up on my lay,
And Ihefu that thou leveſt on, thou do him al awey.
Lef on me, ant be my wife, ful wel the mai fpede.
Auntioge and Afie fcaltou han to mede :
Ciclatoun¹ ant purpel pal fcaltou haue to wede :
Wid all the metes of my lond ful wel I feal the fede.²

This piece was printed by Hickes from a MS. in Trinity College library at Cambridge, [and has been lately re-edited]. It feems to belong to the manufcript metrical *Lives of the Saints*,³ which form a very confiderable volume, and were probably tranflated or paraphrafed from Latin or French profe into Englifh rhyme before the year 1[3]00.⁴ We are fure that they were written after the year

---

¹ Checklaton. See *Obs. Fair.* Q. i. 194.
² The legend of *Saint Julian* in the Bodleian, is [in profe, with verfes at the end, which Sir F. Madden notes, are not in MS. Reg. 17 A. xxvii. Both texts are now in type for the Early Englifh Text Society, ed. Cockayne.] MSS. Bibl. Bodl. NE. 3 xi. membran. 8vo. iii. fol. 86. This MS. I believe to be of the age of Henry III. or King John : the compofition much earlier. It was tranflated from the Latin. Thefe are the laft five lines :

" Hpen brihtın o vomer vei pinopeð hiſ hpeate,
And penpeð þæt burti cheſ to hellene heate,
He more beon a conn ı ʒobeſ ʒulbene ebene,
De tunbe ðiſ oſ Latın to Enʒliſche lebenne
And he þæt her leart onprat ſpa aſ he cuþe. AMEN."

That is, "When the judge at doomſday winnows his wheat, and drives the dufty chaff into the heat of hell; may he be a corn in God's golden Eden, who turned this book [from] Latin," &c. [Sir F. Madden points out that thefe lines are taken from an inedited profe life of St. Hugh (MS. Digby, 165, fol. 114.) See Hume's monograph on St. Hugh, 1849, for fome curious particulars refpecting that fingular tradition.]
³ The fame that are mentioned by Hearne, from a MS. of Ralph Sheldon. See Hearne's *Petr. Langt.* pp. 542, 607, 608, 609, 611, 628, 670. Saint Winifred's Life is printed from the fame collection by Bifhop Fleetwood, in his *Life and Miracles of S. Winifred*, p. 125, ed. 1713.
⁴ It is in fact a metrical hiſtory of the feſtivals of the whole year. The life of the refpective faint is defcribed under every faint's day, and the inſtitutions of fome Sundays, and feaſts not taking their rife from faints, are explained on the plan of the *Legenda Aurea* written by Jacobus de Voragine, Archbifhop of Genoa, about the year 1290, from which Caxton, through the medium of a French verſion entitled *Legend Dorée*, tranflated his *Golden Legend*. The *Feſtival* or *Feſtiall* by Myrk (fee preface to Myrk's *Duties of P. Prieſts*, Early Eng. Text Society), is a book of the fame fort, yet with homilies intermixed. See MSS. Harl. 2247 and 2371, and 2391, and 2402 and 2800 *feq*. Manufcript lives of faints, detached and not belonging to this collection, are frequent in libraries. The *Vitæ Patrum* were originally drawn from S. Jerome and Johannes Caffianus. In Grefham College library are metrical lives of ten faints, chiefly from the *Golden Legend*, by Ofberne Bokenham, an Auguſtine canon in the abbey of Stoke-clare in Suffolk, tranfcribed by Thomas Burgh, at Cambridge, 1477. *The Life of St. Katharine* appears to have been compofed in 1445. MSS. Coll. Grefh. 315, [but now MS. Arundel Br. Muſ. 327: Printed for the Roxb. Club, 1835, 4to. Some other *Lives of Saints* have been printed by the Philological Society, ed. Furnivall (*Tranfactions*, 1858, Pt. ii.); the *Life of St. Quiriacus*, with the *Legends on the Croſs*, from a Saint's Lives' MS., is in the preſs for the Early Englifh Text Society, under the editorfhip of Dr. Morris. The *Life of St. Katharine* is alfo in MS. Publ. Lib. Camb. Ff. ii. 38, and has been printed by Halliwell (*Contrib. to Early Engl. Lit.*, 1849).] The French tranflation of the *Legenda Aurea* was made by Jehan de Vignay, a monk, foon after 1300.

1169, as they contain the *Life of Saint Thomas Becket*.[1] In the Bodleian library are three manuscript copies of these *Lives of the Saints*,[2] in which the *Life of Saint Margaret* constantly occurs;

---

[1] Ashmole cites this Life, *Instit. Ord. Gart.*, p. 21. And he cites S. Brandon's *Life*, p. 507. Ashmole's MS. was in the hands of Silas Taylor. It is now in [the Bodleian]. MSS. Ashm. 50. [7001.]

[2] MSS. Bodl. 779, Laud, L 70. And they make a considerable part of a prodigious folio volume, beautifully written on vellum [about 1400], and elegantly illuminated [of which the first foliated text has the title] : " *Here begynnen the tytles of the book that is cald in Latyn tongue Salus Anime, and in Englysh tonge Sowlehele.*" It was given to the Bodleian library by Edward Vernon, Esq., soon after the civil war. I shall cite it under the title of MS. Vernon. Although pieces not absolutely religious are sometimes introduced, the scheme of the compiler or transcriber seems to have been, to form a complete body of legendary and scriptural history in verse, or rather to collect into one view all the religious poetry he could find. Accordingly the *Lives of the Saints* a distinct and large work of itself properly constituted a part of his plan. There is another copy of the *Lives of the Saints* in the British Museum, MSS. Harl. 2277; and in [the Bodleian] MSS. Ashm. *ut supr.* This MS. is also in Bennet College library [and elsewhere : MS. Laud. 108 ; MS. Ashmole, No. 43 [6924] ; Cotton MS. Julius, D ix. and Add. MS. 10, 301, &c.] The Lives seem to be placed according to their respective festivals in the course of the year. The Bodleian copy (marked 779) is a thick folio, containing 310 leaves. The variations in these manuscripts seem chiefly owing to the transcribers. The *Life of Saint Margaret* in MS. Bodl. 779, begins much like that of Trinity Library at Cambridge.

"Old and yonge I preye you your folyis for to lete," &c.

I must add here, that in the Harleian library, a few Lives, from the same collection of *Lives of the Saints*, occur, MSS. 2250, 23 f. 72, b. *seq.* chart. fol. See also *Ib.* 19, f. 48.

The *Lives of the Saints* in verse, in Bennet library, contain the martyrdom and translation of Becket, Num. clxv. This MS. is supposed to be of the fourteenth century. Archbishop Parker, in a remark prefixed, has assigned the composition to the reign of Henry II. But in that case, Becket's translation, which did not happen till the reign of King John, must have been added. See a specimen in Nasmith's *Catalogue of the Bennet MSS*. 1777, p. 217. There is a MS. of these Lives in Trinity College library at Oxford, but it has not the Life of Becket, MSS. Num. lvii. In pergamine, fol. The writing is about the fourteenth century. I will transcribe a few lines from the *Life of St. Cuthbert*, f. 2, b :

" Seint Cuthberd was ybore here in Engelonde,
God dude for him meraccle, as ʒe scholleth vnderstonde.
And wel ʒong child he was, in his eigtethe ʒere,
Wit children he pleyde atte balle, that his felawes were :
That com go a lite childe, it thoʒt thre ʒer old,
A swete creature and a fayr, yt was myld and bold :
To the ʒong Cuthberd he ʒede ' sene brother,' he sede,
' Ne ʒench than noʒt such ydell game for it ne oʒte noʒt be thy dede :'
Seint Cuthberd ne tok no ʒeme to the childis rede
And pleyde forth with his felawes, al so they him bede.
Tho this ʒonge child y seʒ that he is red forsok,
A doun he fel to grounde, and gret del to him tok,
It by gan to wepe sore, and his honden wrynge,
This children hadde alle del of him, and bylevede hare pleyinge.
As that they couthe hy gladede him, sore he gan to siche,
At even this ʒonge child made del y liche,
' A welaway,' qd seint Cuthberd, ' why wepes thou so sore
' Sif we the haveth oʒt mysdo, we ne scholleth na more.'
Thanne spake this ʒonge child, sore hy wothe beye,
' Cuthberd, it falleth noʒt to the with ʒonge children to pleye,

but it is not always exactly the same with this printed by Hickes; and, on the whole, the Bodleian Lives seem inferior in point of antiquity. I will here give some extracts:

From the *Life of Saint Swithin*:[1]

> Seint Swithin the confessour : was her of Engelande,
> Biside wyncheftre he was ibore : as ic vndirftonde :
> By the kinges day Egberd : this gode man was ibore,
> That tho was king of Engelond : and fomwhat ek bifore ;
> The ei3teothe king he was that com : after Kenewold the kynge,
> That feint Berin dude to Criftendom : in Engelond furft bringe :
> Ac feynt Auftin hadde bifore : to criftendom ibro3t
> Athelbri3t the gode king : ac al the londe no3t.
> Ac fitthe hit was that feint berin : her bi wefte wende,
> And turnde the king Kenewold : as our louerd him grace fende :
> So that feint Egberd was kyng : tho feint fwithin was ibore
> The ei3teteothe he was : after kenewold that fo longe was bifore, &c.
> Seint Swithin his bifchopriche : to alle gode drou3 (line 51)
> The toun alfo of Wyncheftre he amended enou3,
> For he let the ftronge brugge : withoute the eft 3ate arere
> And fond therto lym and fton : to worcmen that ther were.

From the *Life of Saint Wolftan* :

> Seynt Wolfton byffcop of Wirceter was then in Ingelonde,
> Swithe holyman was all his lyf, as ich onderftonde :
> The while he was a yonge childe, good lyf hi ladde ynow,
> Whenne other children orne play, toward cherche hi drow.

> 'For no fuche idell games it ne cometh the to worche,
> 'Whanne god hath y-proveyd the an heved of holy cherche.'
> With this word, me nyfte whidder, this 3ong child wente,
> An angel it was of heven that our lord thuder fent."

I will exhibit the next twelve lines as they appear in that mode of writing: together with the punctuation.

> "Þo by-gan feint Cuthberd. for to wepe fore
> [And by-leuede al þis ydel game, nolde he pleye no more.[1]]
> He made his fader and frendis. fette him to lore
> So þat he fervede boþe ny3t and day. to plefe god þe more
> And in his 3oughede ny3t and day. of fervede godis ore
> Þo he in grettere elde was, as þe bok us hap yfed
> It byfel þat feint Aÿdan. þe biffchop was ded
> Cuthberd was a felde with fchep. angeles of heven he fe3
> Þe biffchopis foule feint Aÿdan. to heven bere on he3
> Allas fede feint Cuthberd. fole ech am to longe
> I nell þis fchep no longer kepe. afonge hem who fo afonge[2]
> He wente to þe abbeye of Germans. a grey monk he þer bycom
> Gret joye made alle þe covent. þo he that abbyt nom," &c.

The reader will obferve the conftant return of the hemiftichal point, which I have been careful to preferve, and to reprefent with exactnefs ; as I fufpect that it fhows how thefe poems were fung to the harp by the minftrels. Every line was perhaps, uniformly recited to the fame monotonous modulation, with a paufe in the midft ; juft as we chant the pfalms in our choral fervice. In the pfalms of our liturgy, this paufe is expreffed by a colon: and often, in thofe of the Roman miffal, by an afterifk. The fame mark occurs in every line of this manufcript, which is a folio volume of confiderable fize, with upwards of fifty verfes in every page.

[[1] *Early Englifh Poems and Lives of Saints*, edit. Furnivall, pp. 43-7 ; *St. Swithun*, ed. Earle, 1861, pp. 78-81.]

[[1] Inferted from Add. MS. 10,301. Sir F. Madden's inform.]
[[2] "Take them who will."—*Price*.]

Seint Edward was tho vr kyng, that now in hevene is,
And the biſſcoppe of Wirceſter Brytthege is hette I wis, &c.
Biſſcop hym made the holi man ſeynt Edward vre kynge
And undirſonge his dignite, and tok hym cros and ringe.
His buſhopreke he wuſt wel, and eke his priorie,
And forcede him to ſerve wel God and Seinte Marie.
Four ȝer he hedde biſſcop ibeo and not folliche fyve
Tho ſeynt Edward the holi kyng went out of this lyve.
To gret reuge to al Engelonde, ſo welaway the ſtounde,
For ſtrong men that come ſithen and broughte Engelonde to grounde.
Harald was ſithen kynge with treſun, allas!
The crowne he bare of England which while hit was.
As William Baſtard that was tho duyk of Normaundye [1]
Thouhte to winne Englonde thoruȝ ſtrength and felonye:
He lette hym greith foulke inouȝ and gret power with him nom,
With gret ſtrengthe in the ſee he him dude and to Engelonde com:
He lette ordayne his oſt wel and his baner up arerede,
And deſtruyed all that he fond and that londe ſore aferde.
Harald hereof tell kynge of Engelonde
He let garke faſt his oſte agen hym for to ſtonde:
His baronage of Engelonde redi was ful ſone
The kyng to helpe and eke himſelf as riȝt was to done.
The warre was then in Engelonde dolefull and ſtronge inouȝ
And heore either of othures men al to grounde flouȝ:
The Normans and this Engliſch men day of batayle nom
There as the abbeye is of the batayle a day togedre com,
To grounde thei ſmiit and flowe alſo; as God yaf the cas,
William Baſtard was above, and Harald bi-neothe was. [2]

From the *Life of Saint Chriſtopher:*

[3] Seint Criſtofre was ſaraȝin: in the lond of Canaan,
In no ſtede bi him daye: ne fond me ſo ſtrong a man:
Four & tuentie fet he was long: & thicke & brod inouȝ,
Such mon bote he were ſtrong me thinȝth hit were wouȝ:
Al a contrai where he were: for him wolde fleo,
Therfore him thouȝte that no man: aȝen him ſcholde beo.
With no man he ſeide he nolde beo: bote with on that were
Hexiſt louerd of alle men: & vnder non, other uere.

Afterwards he is taken into the ſervice of a king:

Criſtofre him ſeruede longe; (l. 17)
The kyng louede melodie: of harpe & of ſonge;
So that his iugelour adai: to-fore him pleide faſte,
& anemnede in his rym: the deuel atte laſte:
Tho the kyng ihurde that: he bleſcede him anon, &c. [4]

From the *Life of Saint Patrick:*

Seyn Pateryk com thoru Godes grace to preche in Irelonde
To teche men ther ryt believe Jheſu Cryſte to underſtonde:
So ful of wormes that londe he founde that no man ni myghte gon,
In ſom ſtede for worms that he nas wenemyd anon;
Seynt Pateryk bade our lorde Cryſt that the londe delyvered were,
Of thilke foul wormis that none ne com there.

---

[1] [See Small's *Metrical Homilies*, p. xvi.]   [2] MS. Vernon. fol. 76, b.
[3] MSS. Harl. *ut ſupr.* fol. 101, b.

"Seint Criſtofre was Sarazin in ðe lond of Canaan
In no ſtede bi his daye ne fond me ſo ſtrong a man
Four and tuenti fet he was long and þiche and brod y-nouȝ, &c."

[4] [*Early Engliſh Poems and Lives of Saints*, edit. Furnivall, 1862, pp. 59-60.]

From the *Life of Saint Thomas Becket:*[1]

> Gilbert was Thomas fader name : that the true was and gode
> And lovede God and holi churche ; fiththe he wit underſtod.
> The croice to the holie lond ; in his ȝunghede he nom,
> And mid on Richard that was his man : to Jeruſalem com,
> There hi dude here pelrynage : in holi ſtedes faſte
> So that among the Sarazyns : ynome hi were atte laſte, &c.

[One authority[2] attributes theſe *Lives* to the cloſe, and another[3] to the middle, of the thirteenth century.[4] The former remarks: "The ſtyle and language of theſe Lives of Saints would lead us at once, from their ſimilarity to the Chronicle aſcribed to Robert of Glouceſter, to attribute them to the cloſe of the thirteenth century, and perhaps to the ſame writer. Had Warton[5] looked into theſe *Lives* a little more attentively, he would have found the *Legend of St. Dominic*, who died in 1221, and that of *St. Edmund of Pountney*, who was canonized in 1248. But in the latter legend we have deciſive proof that theſe lives were written in the reign of Edward I."]

Theſe metrical narratives of Chriſtian faith and perſeverance ſeem to have been chiefly compoſed for the pious amuſement, and perhaps edification, of the monks in their cloiſters. The ſumptuous volume of religious poems which I have mentioned above[6] was undoubtedly chained in the cloiſter or church of ſome capital monaſtery. It is not improbable that the novices were exerciſed in reciting portions from theſe pieces. In the Britiſh Muſeum[7] there is a ſet of legendary tales in rhyme, which appear to have been ſolemnly pronounced by the prieſt to the people on Sundays and holidays. This ſort of poetry[8]

---

[1] [*Life and Martyrdom of Thomas Becket*, edit. Black (Percy Soc.), p. 1.]

[2] [Madden's note in *H. E. P.* ed. 1840, i. 17. Guernes, an eccleſiaſtic of Pont St. Maxence in Picardy, wrote a metrical life of Thomas à Becket, and from his anxiety to procure the moſt authentic information on the ſubject, came over to Canterbury in 1172, and finally projected his work in 1177. It is written in ſtanzas of five Alexandrines, all ending with the ſame rhymes, a mode of compoſition ſuppoſed to have been adopted for the purpoſe of being eaſily chanted. A copy is preſerved in MS. Harl. 270, and another in MS. Cotton, *Domit.* A. xi. See *Archæol.* vol. xiii. and Ellis's *Hiſt. Sketch*, &c. p. 57."—*Park.*]

[3] [*Life and Martyrdom of St. Thomas A Becket*, ed. Black, Introd.]

[4] [Warton ſuppoſed them written in the reign of Richard I.]

[5] In the Cotton library I find the lives of Saint Joſaphas and the Seven Sleepers: [compoſed in the French of the thirteenth century, and in a hand of the time. Sir F. M.'s corr.] Brit. Mus. MSS. Cott. *Calig.* A ix. Cod. membran. 4to. ii. fol. 192:

> Ici commence la vie ꝺe ſeinꞇ Ioꞃaphaȝ.
> Ki vouꞇꞇ a nul bien æntendre
> Per eſſample poeꞇ mulꞇ apreꞃꝺre,

iii. fol. 213, b. *Ici commence la vie de* Seꞇ Dormanȝ.

> La verꞇu ðeu ke tut ıur ꝺure
> E ꞇuꞇ ıurȝ eꞃꞇ cerene e pure.

Many legends and religious pieces in Norman rhyme were written about [the time of Edward I.] See MSS. Harl. 2253, f. 1, membr. fol. *ſupra citat.* p. 15.

[6] Viz. MS. Vernon.

[7] MSS. Harl. 2391. 70. The dialect is perfectly Northern.

[8] That legends of Saints were ſung to the harp at feaſts, appears from *The Life of Saint Marine*, MSS. Harl. 2253, fol. memb. f. 64, b.

was also sung to the harp by the minstrels on Sundays, instead of the romantic subjects usual at public entertainments.[1]

> " Herketh hideward and beoth stille,
> Y praie ou ʒif hit be or wille,
> And ʒe shule here of one virgin
> That was ycleped saint Maryne."

And from various other instances. [But Sir F. Madden very properly doubts whether this expression means, in many cases, any thing further than an invitation to the listeners to attend to the recital.]

Some of these religious poems contain the usual address of the minstrel to the company. As in a poem of our Saviour's descent into hell, and his discourse there with Sathanas the porter, Adam, Eve, Abraham, &c. MSS. *ibid.* f. 57.

> " Alle herkeneth to me now,
> A strif wolle y tellen ou:
> Of Jhesu and of Sathan,
> Tho Jhesu wes to hell y-gan."

Other proofs will occur occasionally. [The lives of St. Josaphat and of the Seven Sleepers are attributed by the Abbé de la Rue to Chardry, an Anglo-Norman poet, who also wrote *le petit plebs*, a dispute between an old and a young man on human life. Stephen Langton, archbishop of Canterbury in 1207, wrote a canticle on the passion of Jesus Christ in 123 stanzas, with a theological drama, in the Duke of Norfolk's library, and Denis Pyrannus, who lived in the reign of Henry III., wrote in verse the life and martyrdom of King St. Edmund in 3286 lines, with the miracles of the same saint in 600 lines: a manuscript in the Cott. Library, Dom. A. xi. See *Archæologia*, vol. xiii.—*Park.*]

[1] As I collect from the following poem, MS. Vernon, fol. 229:—

" *The Visions of Seynt Poul won he was rapt into Paradys.*

> " Lusteneth lordynges leof and dere,
> ʒe that wolen of the Sonday here;
> The Sonday a day hit is
> That angels and archangels joyn iwis,
> More in that ilke day
> Then any odur," &c.

[It was enjoined by the ritual of the Gallican church, that the Lives of the Saints should be read during mass, on the days consecrated to their memory. On the introduction of the Roman liturgy, which forbad the admixture of any extraneous matter with the service of the mass, this practice appears to have been suspended, and the Lives of the Saints were read only at evening prayer. But even in this the inveteracy of custom seems speedily to have re-established its rights; and there is reason to believe that the lives of such as are mentioned in the New Testament were regularly delivered from the chancel. Of this a curious example, the "Planch de Sant Esteve," has been published by M. Raynouard in his "Choix des Poesies originales des Troubadours [Paris, 1817];" where the passages from the Acts of the Apostles referring to St. Stephen are introduced between the metrical translations of them. From France it is probable this rite found its way into England; and the following extract from the piece alluded to above will show the uniformity of style adopted in the exordiums to such productions on both sides of the Channel:

> " Sezets, senhors, e aiats pas;
> Se que direm ben escoutas;
> Car la lisson es de vertat,
> Non hy a mot de falsetat."

" Be seated, lordings, and hold your peace (*et ayez paix*); listen attentively to what we shall say; for it is a lesson of truth without a word of falsehood." It has been recently maintained, that the term "lording," of such frequent occurrence in the preludes to our old romances and legends, is a manifest proof of their being

Extract from "Soulehele."

In that part of Vernon's manuscript entitled "Soulehele,"[1] we have a translation of the Old and New Testament into verse, which I believe to have been made before the year 1300 [though the MS. is some seventy-five years later]. The reader will observe the fondness of our ancestors for the Alexandrine: at least, I find the lines arranged in that measure:—

>   Oure ladi and hire suftur stoden vndur the Roode,
>   And seint jon and marie magdaleyn with wel sori moode :
>   Vr ladi biheold hire swete sone ; heo gon to wepe sore,
>   That thre teres heo let of red blod, tho heo nedde watur no more.
>   Vr lord seide : " Wommon, to her thi sone ibrouħt in gret pyne
>   For monnes gultes nouthē her, and nothing for myne."
>   Marie weop wel sore, and bitter teres leet ;
>   The teres fullen uppon the ston doun at hire feet.
>   " Allas, my sone, for serwe wel ofte " seide heo,
>   " Nabbe ich bote the one, that honguft on the treo ;
>   So ful icham of serwe, as any wommon may beo,
>   That i schal my deore child in al this pyne iseo :
>   How schal I, sone deore, hou haft i thouȝt liuen with outen the,
>   Nufti neuere of serwe nouȝt, sone, what seyft thou me ?"
>   Thenne spak Ihesus wordus goode tho to his modur dere,
>   Ther he heng vppon the roode : " here I the take a fere,
>   That treweliche schal serue the, thin owne cosin Jon,
>   The while that thou alyue beo among alle thi son :"
>   " Ich the hote, jon," he seide, " thou wite hire bothe day and niht,
>   That the Gẏwes, hire fon, ne don hire non vnriht."
>   Seint Jon in the ftude vr ladi in to the temple nom ;
>   God to seruen he hire dude, sone so he thider com ;
>   Hole and seeke heo duden good that heo founden thore,
>   Heo hire serueden to hond and foot, the laffe and eke the more.
>   The Pore folk feire heo fedde there, heo seȝe that hit was neode,
>   And the seke heo brouȝte to bedde, and mete and drinke gon heom beode.
>   With al heore mihte ȝong and olde hire loueden, bothe syke and fer,
>   As hit was riȝt, for alle and sūme to hire seruise hedden mefter.
>   Jon hire was a trewe feere, and nolde nouȝt fro hire go,
>   He loked hire as his ladi deore ; and what heo wolde, hit was ido.[2]

"composed for the gratification of knights and nobles." There are many valid objections to such a conclusion ; but one perhaps more cogent than the rest. The term is a diminutive, and could never have been applied to the nobility as an order, however general its use as an expression of courtesy. By way of illustration, let it also be remembered, that the "Disours" of the present day, who ply upon the Mole at Naples, address every ragged auditor by the title of "Eccellenza."—*Price.*]

[1] [The first foliated part of the MS. A prose translation of Ailred's *Regula Inclusarum*, or *Rule of Nuns*, is on the preceding unfoliated leaves. Both treatises are in the hands of editors for the Early English Text Society.—F.]

[2] MS. Vernon, fol. 8.

SECTION II.

HITHERTO we have been engaged in examining the state of our poetry from the Conquest to the year 1[3]00, or rather afterwards. It will appear to have made no very rapid improvement from that period. Yet, as we proceed, we shall find the language losing much of its ancient obscurity, and approaching more nearly to the dialect of modern times.

The first poet whose name occurs in the reign of Edward I., and indeed in these annals, is Robert of Gloucester, a monk of the abbey of Gloucester. He has left a poem of considerable length, which is a history of England in verse, from Brutus to the reign of Edward I. It was evidently written after the year 1278, as the poet mentions King Arthur's sumptuous tomb, erected in that year before the high altar of Glastonbury church[1]: and he declares himself a living witness of the remarkably dismal weather which distinguished the day on which the battle of Evesham above mentioned was fought, in the year 1265.[2] From these and other circumstances this piece appears to have been composed [after] the year [1297].[3] It is exhibited in the manuscripts, is cited by many antiquaries, and printed by Hearne, in the Alexandrine measure; but with equal probability might have been written in four-lined stanzas. This rhyming chronicle is totally destitute of art or imagination. The author has clothed in rhyme the fables of Geoffry of Monmouth, which have often a more poetical air in Geoffry's prose. The language is not much more easy or intelligible than that of many of the [Early English] poems quoted in the preceding section: it is full of Saxonisms, which indeed abound, more or less, in every writer before Gower and Chaucer. But this obscurity is perhaps owing to the western dialect, in which our monk of Gloucester was educated. Provincial barbarisms are naturally the growth of extreme counties, and of such as are situated at a distance from the metropolis; and it is probable that the Saxon heptarchy, which consisted of a cluster of seven independent states, contributed to produce as many different provincial dialects. In the mean time it is to be considered, that writers of all ages and languages have their affectations and singularities, which occasion in each a peculiar phraseology.

---

[1] Pag. 224, edit. Hearne.   [2] Pag. 560.
[3] [Sir F. Madden's corr., founded on the mention in the piece of the canonization of St. Louis in 1297. Sir F. M. refers to the Cotton MS. Calig. A. xi. (from which Dr. R. Morris has printed an extract in his *Specimens*) as nearly coeval with the author, and as the proper basis of a new edition. He tells us that Waterland's annotated copy of ed. Hearne (erroneously taken from Harl. MS. 201 in chief measure), is in the Bodleian. Mr. Furnivall notes that there is a MS., one of a class, with great differences, in the library of Trinity College, Cambridge. Mr. W. Aldis Wright is preparing a new edition of Robert of Gloucester for the Rolls Series.]

[The MSS. of Robert of Gloucester divide themselves naturally into two classes. Taking the Cotton MS. as the type of what we may call the earlier recension, and the MS. in Trinity College Library, Cambridge, as the type of the later, the two classes may be readily distinguished by a reference to the beginning of the reign of King Stephen. Up to this point the MSS. of the two recensions agree roughly in their contents, those of the later having insertions in various places and of various lengths, amounting altogether to between eight and nine hundred lines. From this point they differ entirely; the reigns from Stephen to Edward I. occupying in the earlier recension about three thousand lines, while in the later they are compressed into about six hundred of an entirely different character. In the Cotton MS. King Stephen's reign begins thus:

> Steuene þe bleis þat god kniʒt . & stalwarde was also
> þo þe king was ded is vncle . an oþer he þoʒte do.

In the Trinity MS. it begins:

> þo com stephene þe bleys⸴ mid strēgþe & quaintise
> & seide he wolde be king⸴ in alle kūnes wyse.

This distinction furnishes a ready test of the class to which any MS. belongs. Tried by it, we find that the known MSS. of the earlier recension are Cotton Calig. A. xi., Harl. 201, Add. MSS. 18631 and 19677 in the British Museum, and MS. S. 3. 41 in the Hunterian Museum, Glasgow. The MSS. of the later recension are Sloane 2027 in the British Museum; Ee. 4. 31 in the University Library, Cambridge; R. 4. 26 in the Library of Trinity College, Cambridge; Bodleian, Digby 205; Lord Mostyn's MS.; and MS. 2014 in the Pepysian Library. The MS. in the Herald's College, of which the readings are quoted in the notes to Hearne's edition, contains a mixture of prose and verse, and cannot be assigned to either recension. Besides these there formerly existed two others, of which one belonged to the famous Thomas Allen of Gloucester Hall; the other, quoted by Camden in his *Remaines*, was in the possession of John Stow the antiquary; but of these no trace has yet been found. The passages from the former, given in Hearne's *Appendix*, shew that it probably belonged to the later recension.][1]

Robert of Gloucester thus describes the sports and solemnities which followed King Arthur's coronation:

> The kyng was to ys paleys, tho the servyse was ydo,[2]
> Ylad wyth his menye, and the quene to hire al so.
> Vor hii hulde the olde vsages, that men wyth men were
> By them sulue, and wymmen by hem sulue al so there.[3]
> Tho hii were echone yset, as yt to her stat bycom,
> Kay, king of Aungeo, a thousend kynʒtes nome

---

[1] [Mr. W. Aldis Wright's addition.]
[2] "when the service in the church was finished."
[3] "They kept the antient custom at festivals, of placing the men and women separate. Kay, king of Anjou, brought a thousand noble knights clothed in ermine of one suit, or *secta*."

> Of noble men, yclothed in ermyne echone
> Of on fywete, and feruede at thys noble feft a non.
> Bedwer the botyler, kyng of Normandye,
> Nom al fo in ys half a uayr companye
> Of on fywyte¹ vorto feruy of the boterlye.
> By uore the quene yt was alfo of al fuche corteyfye,
> Vorto telle al the noblye thet ther was ydo,
> They my tonge were of ftel, me ffolde noʒt dure therto.
> Wymmen ne kepte of no kynʒt as in druery,²
> Bote he were in armys wel yprowed, & atte lefte thrye.³
> That made, lo, the wymmen the chaftore lyf lede,
> And the kynʒtes the ftalwordore,⁴ & the betere in her dede.
> Sone after thys noble mete,⁵ as ryʒt was of fuch tyde,
> The kynʒts atyled hem aboute in eche fyde,
> In feldes and in medys to preue her bachelerye.⁶
> Somme wyth lance, fome wyth fuerd, wyth oute vylenye,
> Wyth pleyynge at tables, other atte chekere,
> Wyth caftynge,⁷ other wyth ffettinge,⁸ other in fom oʒyrt manere.
> And wuch fo of eny game adde the mayftrye,
> The kyng hem of ys ʒyfteth dude large corteyfye.
> Vpe the alurs of the caftles the laydes thanne ftode,
> And byhulde thys noble game, & wyche kynʒts were god.
> All the thre hexte dawes⁹ ylafte thys nobleye
> In halles and in veldes, of mete and eke of pleye.
> Thys men come the verthe¹⁰ day byuore the kynge there,
> And he ʒef hem large ʒyftys, euere as hii wurthe were.
> Byffopryches and cherches, clerkes he ʒef fomme,
> And caftles and tounes, kynʒtes that were ycome.¹¹

Many of thefe lines are literally translated from Geoffry of Monmouth, [and more from Wace.] In King Arthur's battle with the giant at Barbesfleet, there are no marks of Gothic painting. But there is an effort at poetry in the defcription of the giant's fall:

> Tho gryflych ʒal the ffrewe tho, that griflych was ys bere:
> He vel dounʒ as a gret ok, that bynethe ycorue were,
> That yt thoʒte that al hul myd the vallynge ffok.¹²

That is, "Then horribly yelled the fhrew, that fearful was his braying: he fell down like an oak cut through at the bottom, and [it feemed that]¹³ all the hill fhook with his fall." But this ftroke is copied from Geoffry of Monmouth, who tells the fame miraculous ftory, and in all the pomp with which it was perhaps dreffed up by his favourite fablers. "Exclamavit vero invifus ille; et velut quercus ventorum viribus eradicata, cum maximo fonitu corruit." It is difficult to determine which is moft blameable, the poetical hiftorian or the profaic poet.

It was a tradition invented by the old fablers, that giants brought

---

¹ "brought alfo, on his part, a fair company cloathed uniformly."
² [gallantry.]   ³ thrice.   ⁴ [fuite.]
⁵ "Soon after this noble feaft, which was proper at fuch an occafion, the knights accoutred themfelves."
⁶ [The ftate preparatory to knighthood.]   ⁷ [Cafting the ftone.—M.]
⁸ [Aiming with fpears or javelins.]
⁹ "All the three higheft or chief days. In halls and fields, of feafting, and turneying, &c."   ¹⁰ fourth.   ¹¹ Pag. 191, 192 [edit. 1810.]   ¹² Pag. 208 [ibid.]
¹³ [Mr. Garnett's correction.]

the stones of Stonehenge from the most sequestered deserts of Africa, and placed them in Ireland; that every stone was washed with juices of herbs, and contained a medical power; and that Merlin the magician, at the request of King Arthur, transported them from Ireland, and erected them in circles, on the plain of Amesbury, as a sepulchral monument for the Britons treacherously slain by Hengist. This fable is thus delivered, without decoration, by Robert of Gloucester:

> "Sire kyng," quoth Merlin tho, "suche thinges y wis
> Ne beth for to schewe noȝt, but wen gret nede ys,
> For ȝef ich seide in bismare, other bute yt ned were,
> Sone from me he wold wende the Gost, that doth me lere:"[1]
> The kyng, tho non other nas, bod hym som quoyntyse
> Bi thenke aboute thilke cors, that so noble were and wyse,[2]
> "Sire kyng," quoth Merlyn tho, "ȝef thou wolt here caste
> In the honour of hem, a werk that euer schal y laste,[3]
> To the hul of Kylar[4] send in to Yrlond
> Aftur the noble stones that ther habbet[5] lenge y stonde;
> That was the treche of geandes,[6] for a quoynte werk ther ys
> Of stones al wyth art y mad, in the world such non ys.
> Ne ther nys nothing that me scholde myd strengthe a doun caste.
> Stode heo here, as heo doth there, euer a wolde laste."[7]
> The kyng somdel to lyȝhe,[8] tho he herde this tale,
> "How myȝte," he seyde, "suche stones so grete & so fale[9]
> Be y brort of so fer lond? & ȝet mest of were,
> Me wolde wene, that in this lond no ston to worche nere."
> "Syre kyng," quoth Merlyn, "ne make noȝt an ydel such lyȝhyng.
> For yt nys an ydel noȝt that ich telle this tythyng.[10]
> For in the farreste stude of Affric geandes while sette[11]
> Thike stones for medycine & in Yrlond hem sette,
> While heo woneden in Yrlond, to make here bathes there,
> Ther vnder for to bathi, wen thei syk were.
> For heo wuld the stones wasch, and ther inne bathe y wis.
> For ys no ston ther among, that of gret vertu nys."[12]
> The kyng and ys conseil radde[13] tho stones forto fette,
> And with gret power of batail, ȝef any mon hem lette.
> Uter the kynges brother, that Ambrose hette al so
> In another maner name, y chose was ther to,

---

[1] If I should say any thing out of wantonness or vanity, the spirit, or demon, which teaches me, would immediately leave me. "Nam si ea in derisionem, sive vanitatem, proferrem, taceret Spiritus qui me docet, et, cum opus superveniret, recederet." Galfrid. Mon. viii. 10.

[2] "bade him use his cunning, for the sake of the bodies of those noble and wise Britons."

[3] "if you would build, to their honour, a lasting monument."

[4] "To the hill of Kildare."   [5] have.

[6] "the dance of giants." The name of this wonderful assembly of immense stones.

[7] "Grandes sunt lapides, nec est aliquis cujus virtuti cedant. Quod si eo modo, quo ibi positi sunt, circa plateam locabuntur, stabunt in æternum." Galfrid. Mon. viii. x. 11.

[8] somewhat laughed.   [9] so great and so many.   [10] tyding.

[11] "Giants once brought them from the farthest part of Africa," &c.

[12] "Lavabant namque lapides et infra balnea diffundebant, unde ægroti curabantur. Miscebant etiam cum herbarum confectionibus, unde vulnerati sanabantur. Non est ibi lapis qui medicamento careat." Galfrid. Mon. *ibid*.

[13] [advised or counselled].

>   And fiftene thousant men this dede for to do
>   And Merlyn for his quoyntise thider wente al so.[1]

If anything engages our attention in this passage, it is the wildness of the fiction; in which, however, the poet had no share. I will here add Uther's intrigue with Ygerne:

>   At the fest of Estre tho kyng sende ys sonde,
>   That heo comen alle to London the hey men of this londe,
>   And the leuedys al so god, to his noble fest wyde,
>   For he schulde crowne here, for the hye tyde.
>   Alle the noble men of this lond to the noble fest come,
>   And heore wyues & heore do3tren with hem mony nome,
>   This fest was noble ynow, and nobliche y do;
>   For mony was the faire ledy, that y come was therto.
>   Ygerne, Gorloys wyf, was fairest of echon,
>   That was contasse of Cornewail, for so fair nas ther non.
>   The kyng by huld hire faste y now, & ys herte on hire caste,
>   And tho3te, thay heo were wyf, to do folye atte laste.
>   He made hire semblant fair y now, to non other so gret.
>   The erl nas not ther with y payed, tho he yt vnder 3et.
>   Aftur mete he nom ys wyfe myd stordy med y now,
>   And, with oute leue of the kyng, to ys contrei drow.
>   The kyng sende to hym tho, to by leue al ny3t,
>   For he moste of gret consel habbe som insy3t.
>   That was for no3t. Nolde he no3t the kyng sende 3et ys sonde.
>   That he by leuede at ys parlemente, for nede of the londe.
>   Tho kyng was, tho he nolde no3t, anguyssous & wroth.
>   For despyte he wolde a wreke be, he swor ys oth,
>   Bute he come to amendement. Ys power atte laste
>   He 3arkede, and wende forth to Cornewail faste.
>   Gorloys ys casteles a store al a boute.
>   In a strong castel he dude ys wyf, for of hire was al ys doute.

---

[1] Pag. 145, 146, 147. That Stonehenge is a British monument, erected in memory of Hengist's massacre, rests, I believe, on the sole evidence of Geoffry of Monmouth, who had it from the British bards. But why should not the testimony of the British bards be allowed on this occasion? For they did not invent facts, so much as fables. In the present case, Hengist's massacre is an allowed event. Remove all the apparent fiction, and the bards only say, that an immense pile of stones was raised on the plain of Ambresbury in memory of that event. They lived too near the time to forge this origin of Stonehenge. The whole story was recent, and, from the immensity of the work itself, must have been still more notorious. Therefore their forgery would have been too glaring. It may be objected, that they were fond of referring every thing stupendous to their favourite hero Arthur. This I grant: but not when known authenticated facts stood in their way, and while the real cause was remembered. Even to this day, the massacre of Hengist, as I have partly hinted, is an undisputed piece of history. Why should not the other part of the story be equally true? Besides the silence of Nennius, I am aware that this hypothesis is still attended with many difficulties and improbabilities. And so are all the systems and conjectures ever yet framed about this amazing monument. It appears to me to be the work of a rude people who had some ideas of art: such as we may suppose the Romans left behind them among the Britons. In the mean time I do not remember, that in the very controverted etymology of the word *Stonehenge*, the name of Hengist has been properly or sufficiently considered. [The etymology referred to by Mr. Ritson is evidently the most plausible that has been suggested: Stan-henge—hanging stone: *Observations*, &c. In addition to this it is supported by an authority of high antiquity:

> "*Stanheng* ont non en Anglois,
> *Pierres pendues* en François."—Wace's *Brut*.—Price.]

In another hym felf he was, for he nolde noȝt,
Ȝef cas come, that heo were bothe to dethe y broȝt.
The caftel, that the erl inne was, the kyng by fegede fafte,
For he myȝte hys gynnes for fchame to the other cafte.
The he was ther fene nyȝt, and he fpedde noȝt,
Igerne the conteffe fo muche was in ys thoȝt,
That he nufte non other wyt, ne he ne myȝte for fchame
Telle yt bute a pryve knyȝt, Ulfyn was ys name,
That he trufte meft to. And tho the knyȝt herde this,
"Syre," he feide, " y ne can wyte, wat red here of ys,
For the caftel ys fo ftrong, that the lady ys inne,
For ich wene al the lond ne fchulde yt myd ftrengthe wynne.
For the fe geth al aboute, bute entre on ther nys,
And that ys vp on harde roches, & fo narw wei it ys,
That ther may go bote on & on, that thre men with inne
Myȝte fle al the lond, er heo come ther inne.
And noȝt for than, ȝef Merlyn at thi confeil were,
Ȝef any mygte, he couthe the beft red the lere."
Merlyn was fone of fend, y-feid yt was hym fone,
That he fchulde the befte red fegge, wat were to done.
Merlyn was fory ynow for the kynges folye,
And natheles, " Sire kyng," he feide, " here mot to maiftrie,
The erl hath twey men hym next, Bryȝthoel & Jordan.
Ich wol make thi felf, ȝef thou wolt, thoru art that y can,
Habbe al tho fourme of the erl, as thou were ryȝt he,
And Olfyn as Jordan, and as Brithoel me."
This art was al clene y do, that al changet he were,
Heo thre in the otheres forme, the felve at yt were.
Aȝeyn euen he wende forth, nufte no mon that cas,
To the caftel heo come ryȝt as yt euene was.
The porter y fe ys lord come, & ys mefte priuey twei,
With god herte he lette ys lord yn, & ys men beye.
The contas was glad y now, tho hire lord to hire com
And eyther other in here armes myd gret joye nom.
Tho heo to bedde com, that fo longe a two were,
With hem was fo gret delyt, that bitwene hem there
Bi gete was the befte body, that euer was in this londe,
Kyng Arthure the noble mon, that euer worthe vnderftonde.
Tho the kynges men nufte amorwe, wer he was bi come,
Heo ferde as wodemen, and wende he were ynome.
Heo a faileden the caftel, as yt fchulde adoun a non,
Heo that with inne were, ȝarkede hem echon,
And fmyte out in a fole wille, and foȝte myd here fon :
So that the erl was y flawe, and of ys men mony on,
And the caftel was y nome, and the folk to fprad there,
Ȝet, tho thei hadde al ydo, heo ne fonde not the kyng there.
The tything to the contas fone was ycome,
That hire lord was y flawe, and the caftel ynome.
Ac tho the meffinger hym fey the erl, as hym thoȝte,
That he hadde fo foule y-low, ful fore hym of thoȝte,
The contaffe made fom del deol, for no fothneffe heo nufte.
The kyng, for to glade here, bi clupte hire and cufte.
"Dame," he feide, " no fixt thou wel, that les yt ys al this ?
Ne woft thou wel ich am olyue ? Ich wole the fegge how it ys.
Out of the caftel ftilleliche ych wende al in priuete,
That none of myne men yt nufte, for to fpeke with the.
And tho heo mifte me to day, and nufte wer ich was,
Heo ferden riȝt as gydie men, myd wam no red nas,
And foȝte with the folk with oute, & habbeth in this manere.
Y lore the caftel and hem felue, ac wel thou woft y am here.

> Ac for my caſtel, that is ylore, ſory ich am y now,
> And for myn men, that the kyng and ys power ſloȝ.
> Ac my power is now to lute, ther fore y drede ſore,
> Leſte the kyng vs nyme here, & ſorwe that we were more.
> Ther fore ich wole, how ſo yt be, wende aȝen the kynge,
> And make my pays with hym, ar he to ſchame vs brynge."
> Forth he wende, & het ys men that ȝef the kyng come,
> That hei ſchulde hym the caſtel ȝelde, ar he with ſtrengthe it nome.
> Tho he come toward ys men, ys own forme he nom,
> And leuede the erles fourme, & the kyng Uter by com.
> Sore hym of thoȝte the erles deth, ac in other half he fonde
> Joye in hys herte, for the contaſſe of ſpouſhed was vnbonde,
> Tho he hadde that he wolde, and payſed with ys ſon,
> To the contaſſe he wende aȝen, me let hym in a non.
> Wat halt it to telle longe? bute heo were ſethth at on,
> In gret loue longe y now, wan yt nolde other gon;
> And hadde to gedere this noble ſone, that in tho world ys pere nas,
> The kyng Arture, and a doȝter, Anne hire name was.[1]

In the latter end of the reign of Edward I. many officers of the French king, having extorted large ſums of money from the citizens of Bruges in Flanders, were murdered: and an engagement ſucceeding, the French army, commanded by the Count of Saint Pol, was defeated; upon which the King of France, who was Philip the Fair, ſent a ſtrong body of troops, under the conduct of the Count of Artois, againſt the Flemings; he was killed, and the French were almoſt all cut to pieces. On this occaſion the following ballad was made in the year 1301.[2]

> Luſtneth, lordinges, bothe ȝonge ant olde,
> Of the Freynſhe-men that were ſo proude ant bolde,
> Hou the Flemmyſshe-men bohten hem ant ſolde,
>   Upon a Wedneſday,
> Betere hem were at home in huere londe,
> Then for te ſeche Flemmyſshe by the ſee ſtronde
> Wharethourh moni Frenſhe wyf wryngeth hire honde,
>   Ant ſyngeth, weylaway.
> The Kyng of Fraunce made ſtatuȝ newe,
> In the lond of Flaundres among falſe ant trewe,
> That the commun of Bruges ful ſore can a-rewe,
>   And ſeiden amonges hem,
> Gedere we us togedere hardilyche at ene,
> Take we the bailifs by tuenty ant by tene,
> Clappe we of the hevedes an oven o the grene,
>   Ant caſt we ẏ the fen.
> The webbes ant the fullaris aſſembleden hem alle,
> And makeden huere conſail in huere commune halle,
> Token Peter Conyng huere kyng to calle
>   Ant beo huere cheventeyn, &c.

Theſe verſes ſhow the familiarity with which the affairs of France were known in England, and diſplay the diſpoſition of the Engliſh towards the French at this period. It appears from this and previous inſtances, that political ballads, I mean ſuch as were the

---

[1] *Chron.* p. 156[-60, *ut ſupr.*]
[2] The laſt battle was fought that year, July 7. [The ballad is in Harl. MS. 2253, fol. 73, and is printed entire in Wright's *Political Songs*, 1839, p. 187. A ſpecimen only has therefore been retained, from the text of 1839.]

vehicles of political satire, prevailed much among our early ancestors. About the present era we meet with a ballad complaining of the exorbitant fees extorted, and the numerous taxes levied, by the king's officers.[1] There is a libel remaining, written indeed in French Alexandrines, on the commission of trayl-baston,[2] or the justices so denominated by Edward I. during his absence in the French and Scotish wars about the year 1306. The author names some of the justices or commissioners, now not easily discoverable: and says, that he served the king both in peace and war in Flanders, Gascony, and Scotland.[3] There is likewise a ballad [written in the reign of Edward II.] against the Scots, traitors to Edward I., and taken prisoners at the battles of Dunbar and Kykenclef, in 1305 and 1306.[4] The licentiousness of their rude manners was perpetually breaking out in these popular pasquins, although this species of petulance usually belongs to more polished times.

Nor were they less dexterous than daring in publishing their satires to advantage, although they did not enjoy the many conveniencies which modern improvements have afforded for the circulation of public abuse. In the reign of Henry VI., to pursue the topic a little lower, we find a [satire] stuck on the gates of the royal palace, severely reflecting on the king and his counsellors then sitting in parliament.[5] But the ancient ballad was often applied to better purposes: and it appears from a valuable collection of these little pieces, lately published by my ingenuous friend and fellow-labourer Dr. Percy, in how much more ingenuous a strain they have transmitted to posterity the praises of knightly heroism, the marvels of romantic fiction, and the complaints of love.

[In] the reign[s] of [the three Edwards],[6] a poet occurs named

---

[1] MSS. Harl. 2258, f. 64. There is a song half Latin and half French, much on the same subject. *Ibid.* f. 137, b.

[2] See Spelman and Dufresne *in v.* and Rob. Brunne's Chron., ed. Hearne, p. 328.

[3] MSS. Harl. *ibid.* f. 113, b.

[4] *Ibid.* f. 59. [This will be found in Wright's *Political Songs*, 1839. The ballad against the French is in Ritson's *Anc. Songs*, 1792.—Price.]

[5] This piece is preserved in the Ashmolean Museum, with the following Latin title prefixed: "*Copia scedulæ valvis domini regis existentis in parliamento suo tento apud Westmonasterium mense marcii anno regni Henrici sexti vicesimo octavo.*" [See Hearne's *Hemingi Chartularium.*—Ritson.

[6] "In the third Edwards time was I,
   When I wrote all this story;
   In the house of Sixille I was a throwe;
   Dan Robert of Malton that ye know,
   Did it write for felaws sake."

" By this passage he seems to mean that he was born at a place called Malton; that he had resided some time in a house in the neighbourhood called Sixhill; and that *there* he, Robert de Brunne, had composed at least a part of his poem during the *reign of Edward III.*—Ellis.] MSS. Bibl. Bodl. 415. Cont. 80, pag. Pr. "Fadyr and sone and holy goste." And MSS. Harl. 1701. [The Harleian MS., like the Bodleian, if Warton followed the Bodleian manuscript, professes to be a translation from the French of Grosseteste. But this may be a mere dictum of the

s. 2. Robert Mannyng of Brunne's "Handlyng Synne." 73

Robert Mannyng, but more commonly called Robert de Brunne. He was [born at Brunne in Lincolnshire, and became] a Gilbertine canon in the [priory of Sempringham, where he remained fifteen years. He afterwards removed to] Sixhille, a house of the same order, and in the same county. He was [not] merely a translator. He [turned] into English metre, or rather paraphrased [with large omissions and additions] a French book, written by [William of Wadington, and falsely attributed to Bishop Grosseteste], entitled *Manuel Peche*, or *Manuel de Peche*, that is, the Manual of Sins. This translation was [not printed till of late years].[1] It is a long work, and treats of the decalogue and the Seven Deadly Sins, which are illustrated by many legendary stories. This is the title of the [copies of the MS.]: *Here bygynneth the boke that men clepyn in Frenshe Manuel Peche, the which boke made yn Frenshe Robert Groosteste byshop of Lyncoln.* From the Prologue, among other circumstances, it appears that Robert de Brunne designed this performance

---

transcriber. All we gather from the work itself is an acknowledgment of a French original called *Manuel Peche*, whose author was clearly unknown to De Brunne. Had it been written by a man of Grosseteste's eminence, it would hardly have been published anonymously; nor can we suppose this circumstance, if really true, would have been passed over in silence by his translator. Be this as it may, the French production upon which De Brunne unquestionably founded his poem, is claimed by a writer calling himself William of Wadington, and that in language too peculiar and self-condemning to leave a doubt as to the justice of his title:

> " De le françeis vile ne del rimer,
> Ne me deit nuls hom blamer,
> Kar en Engletere fu ne,
> E norri, e ordiné, e alevé.
> De une vile sui nomé,
> Ou ne est burg ne cité, &c.
> De Deu seit beneit chescun hom,
> Ke prie por Wilhelm de Wadigton."
> *Manuel Peche*, Harl. MSS. 4657.

De Brunne, however, is not a mere translator. He generally amplifies the moral precepts of his original; introduces occasional illustrations of his own (as in the case of Grosseteste cited in the text), p. 74, and sometimes avails himself of Wadington's Latin authorities, where these are more copious or circumstantial than their French copyist. Wadington's work, according to M. de la Rue (*Archæologia*, vol. xiv.), is a free translation of a Latin poem called *Floretus;* by some ascribed to St. Bernard, and by others to Pope Clement. But *Floretus* is so short that it cannot fairly be taken as Wadington's original, any more than the Bible and Church Services can. The following lines in one of Manning's stories—

> " Equitabat Bevo per silvam frondosam,
> Ducebat secum Merswyndam formosam,
> Quid stamus? cur non imus?
>
> By the leved wode rode Bevolyne,
> Wyth hym he ledde feyre Merswyne,
> Why stond we? why go we noght?—

have been identified by Sir F. Madden as part of the unique Latin legend of St. Edith, by Goscelin (MS. Rawl. Bodl. 1027). They are not in Wadington's French, and are only part of De Brunne's many additions to the latter.]

[1] [Edit. Furnivall, 1862 (Roxb. Club), with William of Wadington's French original, in parallel columns.]

to be fung to the harp at public entertainments, and that it was written or begun in the year 1303:[1]

> For lewdè[2] men y undyrtoke,
> On Englyfsh tunge to make thys boke:
> For many ben of fwyche manere
> That talys and rymys wyl blethly[3] here,
> Yn gamys and feftys, and at the ale[4]
> Love men to leftene trotevale[5]: (l. 43-8) &c.
> To alle Cryftyn men undir funne,
> And to godè men of Brunne;
> And fpeciali, alle be name
> The felaufhepe of Sympryngháme,[6]
> Roberd of Brunnè greteth yow,
> In al godeneffe that may to prow.[7]
> Of Brymwake yn Keftevene[8]
> Syxe myle befyde Sympringham evene,
> Y dwelled yn the pryorye
> Fyftenè yere yn conpanye,
> In the tyme of gode Dane Jone
> Of Camelton, that now ys gone;
> In hys tyme was Y there ten yeres,
> And knewe and herde of hys maneres;
> Sythyn wyth Dane Jone of Clyntone
> Fyve wyntyr wyth hym gan Y wone.
> Dane Felyp was mayfter that tyme
> That y began thys Englyfsh ryme,
> The yeres of grace fyl[9] than to be
> A thoufand and thre hundred and thre.
> In that tyme turned y thys
> On Englyfshe tunge out of Frankys (l. 57-78).

From the work itfelf I am chiefly induced to give the following fpecimen; as it contains an anecdote relating to bifhop Groffetefte, who will again be mentioned:

> Y fhall yow telle as y have herd
> Of the bysfhope Seynt Roberd,
> Hys toname[10] ys Groftest
> Of Lynkolne, fo feyth the geft.

---

[1] fol. 1, a.   [2] laymen, illiterate.   [3] gladly.
[4] So in *Pierce Ploughman*, fol. xxvi. b. edit. 1550.—
"I am occupied every day, holy day and other,
With idle tales *at the Ale*, &c."

Again, fol. 1, b—
"Foughten *at the Ale*
In glotony, godwote, &c."

And in the *Plowman's Tale*, p. 185, v. 2110—
"And the chief chantours at the *nale*."

[5] truth and all.
[6] The name of his order.   [7] Profit.
[8] A part of Lincolnfhire. *Chron. Br.* p. 311.
"At Lincoln the parlement was in
Lyndefay and Keftevene."
See a ftory of three monks of Lyndefay, *ibid.* p. 80. [The county of Lincoln is divided into the hundreds of Lindfay and Kifteven.—*Park.*]   [9] Fell.
[10] Surname. See Rob. Br. *Chron.* p. 168. "Thei cald hi this toname," &c. Fr. "Eft furnomez," &c. On St. Robert of Lincoln, fee p. 82 *note*.

> He lovede moche to here the harpe,
> For mannys wytte hyt makyth ſharpe.
> Next hys chaumbre, beſyde hys ſtody,
> Hys harpers chaumbre was faſt therby.
> Many tymes, be nyghtys and dayys,
> He had ſolace of notes and layys,
> One aſked hym onys, reſun why
> He hadde delyte in mynſtralſy?
> He anſwered hym on thys manere,
> Why he helde the harper ſo dere:
> "The vertu of the harpe, thurghe ſkylle and ryght,
> Wyl deſtroye the fendes[1] myght;
> And to the croys, by godè ſkylle,
> Ys the harpè lykened weyle. (p. 150, l. 4742-59).
> Tharefor, gode men, ye ſhul lere,
> Whan ye any glemen[2] here,
> To wurſchep God at youre powere,
> As Davyd ſeyth yn the ſautere:[3]
> Yn harpe, yn thabour, and ſymphan gle[4]
> Wurſchepe God; yn trounpes and ſautre;
> In cordys, an organes, and bellys ryngyng;
> Yn all theſe, wurſhepe ye hevene kyng," &c.[5] (l. 4768-75).

But Robert de Brunne's largeſt work is a metrical chronicle of England.[6] The former part, from Æneas to the death of Cadwallader, is tranſlated from an old French poet called Maſter Wace or Gaſſe, who manifeſtly copied Geoffry of Monmouth,[7] in a poem

---

[1] the *Devil's*.   [2] harpers; minſtrels.   [3] pſalter.
[4] Chaucer, R. *Sir Thop.* v. 3321:—
> Here wonnith the queene of Fairie,
> With harpe, and pipe, and *Simphonie*.

[5] Fol. 30, b. There is an old Latin ſong in Burton which I find in this MS. poem. Burton's *Mel.*, part iii. § 2. Memb. iii. p. 423.

[6] The ſecond part [tranſlated from the French of Peter Langtoft,] was printed by Hearne in 1725. Of the firſt part Hearne has given us the Prologue, Pref. p. 96; an extract, *ibid.* p. 188; and a few other paſſages in his Gloſſary to Robert of Glouceſter. [The whole of it will be iſſued in the Rolls Series in 1871.] It appears from *Chron.* p. 337, that our author was educated and graduated at Cambridge.

[How long Mannyng was employed upon his tranſlation of Langtoft does not appear; but that he had not finiſhed it in 1337 is clear from a paſſage on p. 243 of the printed copy (of 1725) of the Second Part; and indeed he, elſewhere, expreſsly tells us:

> "Idus that is of May left I to wryte this ryme,
> B letter & Friday bi ix. that ʒere ʒede prime."

The dominical letter, as Hearne obſerves, ſhould be D: ſo that the poet finiſhed his work, upon which he had probably been engaged for ſome years, upon Friday, the 15th May, 1339."—*Ritſon*. The only perfect MS. of the Chronicle known is a vellum one in the Inner Temple library; a more modern and abridged copy of Part II. is in Lambeth, MS. 131. (Sir F. Madden's inform.) But the Lambeth copy of Part I., on the old cloſe-ribbed paper of the 14th century, was judged by the experts of the Britiſh Muſeum to be at leaſt as early as the Temple vellum copy, while Dr. Richard Morris, our chief authority on Early Engliſh dialects, judges the dialect of the Lambeth MS. to be much nearer the Eaſt-Midland of Manning than the decidedly northernized Temple MS. From the Lambeth MS., therefore, Mr. Furnivall has printed his edition of Part I. for the National Series of the Maſter of the Rolls, 1871.—F.]

[7 Whether written 'Euſtace, Euſtache, Wiſtace, Huiſtace, Vace, Gaſſe, or Gace, the name through all its diſguiſes is intended for one and the ſame perſon, Wace of Jerſey. Mr. Tyrwhitt was the firſt to reſcue this ingenious writer from the

commonly entitled *Roman des Rois d'Angleterre*. It is esteemed one of the oldest of the French romances; and was commenced under the title of *Brut d'Angleterre*, in the year 1155. Hence Robert de Brunne calls it simply the *Brut*.[1] This romance was soon afterwards

---

errors which had gathered round his name; and M. de la Rue has fully established his rights, by supplying us with an authentic catalogue of his works, and exhibiting their importance both to the historian and antiquary. [Wace's *Brut* was printed by Le Roux de Linçy at Rouen in 1836.] De Brunne was induced to follow the *Brut d'Angleterre* in the first part of his Chronicle, from the copiousness of its details upon British history. But the continuation noticed in the text was the production of Geoffri Gaimar, a poet rather anterior to Wace; and is supposed to have formed a part of a larger work on English and Norman history. *Le Roman du Rou*, or the History of Rollo, first duke of Normandy, is another of Wace's works; and *Les Vies des Ducs de Normandie*, which is brought down to the sixth year of Henry I., a third. But the reader who is desirous of further information on this subject, is referred to the 12th, 13th, and 14th volumes of the *Archæologia*, where he will find a brief but able outline of the history of Anglo-Norman poetry, by M. de la Rue.—PRICE. See also M. Joly's comparison of Wace with his rival chronicler of Normandy, in his *Benoit de St. More et le Roman de Troie*, Caen, 1870, and M. Edelestand du Meril's treatise on *Wace et ses Ouvrages*.—F.]

In the British Museum there is a fragment of a poem in very old French verse, a romantic history of England, drawn from Geoffry of Monmouth, perhaps before the year 1200. MSS. Harl. 1605, 1, f. 1. In the library of Dr. Johnston of Pontefract, there was a MS. on vellum, containing a history in old English verse from Brute to the eighteenth year of Edward II.; and in that of Lord Denbigh, a metrical history in English from the same period to Henry III. Wanley supposed it to have been of the handwriting of the time of Edward IV.

[1] The *Brut of England*, a prose chronicle of England, sometimes continued as low as Henry VI., is a common MS. It was at first translated from a French chronicle [MSS. Harl. 200], written in the beginning of the reign of Edward III. The French have a famous ancient prose romance called *Brut*, which includes the history of the Sangreal. I know not whether it is exactly the same. In an old metrical romance, the story of *Rollo*, there is this passage (MS. Vernon, f. 123):—

"Lordus ȝif ye wil lesten to me,
Of Croteye the nobile citee
As wrytten i fynde in his story
Of *Bruit* the chronicle," &c.

In the British Museum we have *Le petit Bruit*, compiled by Meistre Raufe de Boun, and ending with the death of Edward I. MSS. Harl. 902, f. 1. It is [a separate compilation, made in 1310, as shown by Sir F. Madden, in his Preface to *Havelock the Dane*]. In the same library I find *Liber de Bruto et de gestis Anglorum metrificatus;* (that is, turned into rude Latin hexameters). It is continued to the death of Richard II. Many prose annotations are intermixed. MSS. *ibid.* 1808, 24, f. 31. In another copy of this piece, [there is at the end *qd Peckward*, which may merely mean that Peckward was the copyist]. MSS. *ib.* 2386, 23, f. 35. In another MS. the grand *Brut* [that is, as Sir F. Madden notes, *Caxton's Chronicle*] is said to be translated from the French by "John Maundeuile parson of Brunham Thorpe." MSS. *ibid.* 2279, 3.

[It was first printed by Caxton, in 1480, under the title of *The Chronycles of England*, and under the same title was twice republished. In 1483 it appeared, with a few alterations and considerable additions, under the title of *Fructus Temporum*, and these are later impressions.]

[In the *Chroniques Anglo-Normandes*, 1836, will be found part of Geoffrey Gaimar, of the continuation of the *Brut*, of the Chronicle of Benoit de Sainte More, &c. The *Roman du Rou* was printed in 1827, and a translation of part of it, by Mr. E. Taylor, with notes, in 1837. Laȝamon's *Brut* was published from the Cotton MS., as elsewhere mentioned, in 1847.]

continued to William Rufus, by Geoffri Gaimar, in the year 1146.[1] Thus both parts were blended, and became one work. Among the royal MSS. in the British Museum it is thus entitled: *Le Brut, ke maistre Wace translata de Latin en Franceis de tutt les Reis de Brittaigne.*[2] That is, from the Latin prose history of Geoffry of Monmouth. And that Master Wace aimed only at the merit of a translator, appears from his exordial verses:—

> Maistre Gasse l'a translatè
> Que en conte le veritè.

Otherwise we might have suspected that the authors drew their materials from the old fabulous Armoric MS., which is said to have been Geoffry's original.

An ingenious French antiquary supposes, that Wace took many of his descriptions from that invaluable and singular monument, the *Tapestry of the Norman Conquest*, preserved in the treasury of the cathedral of Bayeux,[3] and engraved and explained in Ducarel's *Anglo-Norman Antiquities*. Lord Lyttelton has quoted this romance, and shewn that important facts and curious illustrations of history may be drawn from such obsolete but authentic resources.[4]

The measure used by Robert de Brunne, in his translation[5] of the former part of our French chronicle or romance, is exactly like

---

[1] [*Anglo-Norman Metrical Chronicle with Notes and Appendix, &c.*, edited by T. Wright, 1850, 8vo.] See Lenglet, *Biblioth. des Romans*, ii. pp. 226-7, and Lacombe, *Diction. de la veille Lang. Fr.* pref. p. xviii. And compare Montfauc. *Catal. Manuscr.* ii. p. 1669. See also M. Galland, *Mem. Lit.* iii. p. 426, 8vo.

[2] 3 A xxi. 3. [Sir F. Madden observes, that this is only in part the *Brut* of Wace.] It occurs again, 4 C xi. *Histoire d'Angleterre en vers, par Maistre Wace*. In the Cotton library [an early English MS.] occurs twice, which seems to be a translation of Geoffry's History, or very like it. Calig. A ix. and Otho. C 13. [Since printed under the care of Sir F. Madden, 1847, 3 vols. 8vo.] The translator is one Laʒamon, a priest, born at Ernly on Severn. He says, that he had his original from the book of a French clergyman, named *Wate* [Walter Calenius, archdeacon of Oxford,] which book Wate the author had presented to Eleanor, queen of Henry II. So Laʒamon in the preface, "Bot he nom the thridde, leide ther amidden: tha makede a frenchis clerc : Wate (Waʒe) wes ihoten," &c.

[3] *Rec.* p. 82, edit. 1581. Mons. Lancelot, *Mem. Lit.* viii. 602. And see *Hist. Acad. Inscript.* xiii. 41, 4to. [M. de la Rue has advanced some very satisfactory reasons for supposing this tapestry to have been made by, or wrought under the direction of, the Empress Matilda, who died in the year 1167. (See *Archæologia*, vol. xviii.) It was evidently sent to Bayeux at a period subsequent to the death of its projector, at whose demise it was left in an unfinished state. Wace probably never saw it. At all events, could it be proved that he did, he disdained to use it in his *History of the Irruption of the Normans into England*, his only work where it could have assisted him; since his narrative is at variance with the representations this monument contains.—*Price.* But Mr. Bolton Corney has sought to controvert the opinion that the tapestry was presented by the Empress Matilda, and maintains that it was executed for the chapter of Bayeux at their own cost.]

[4] *Hist. Hen. II.* vol. iii. p. 180.

[5] [The work here cited is in course of editing for the Master of the Rolls' Series by Mr. Furnivall. See notes, p. 75.]

that of his original. Thus the Prologue, [from the northernized Temple MS.]:

>Lordynges that be now here!
>If ye wille, liftene and lere
>All the ftory of Inglande,
>Als Robert Mannyng wryten it fand,
>And on Inglyfch has it fchewed,
>Not for the lerid, bot for the lewed;
>For tho that in this land[e] wone
>That the Latyn no Frankys cone,
>For to half folace and gamen
>In felawfchip when thai fitt famen.
>And it is wifdom forto wytten
>The ftate of the land, and haf it wryten,
>What manere of folk firft it wan,
>And of what kynde it firft began.
>And gude it is for many thynges,
>For to here the dedis of kynges,
>Whilk were foles, and whilk were wyfe,
>And whilk of tham couthe moft quantyfe;
>And whylk did wrong, and whilk [did] ryght,
>And whilk maynten[e]d pes and fyght.
>Of thare dedes fall be mi fawe,
>And what tyme, and of what law,
>I fall you fchewe fro gre to gre,
>Sen the tyme of Sir Noe:
>Fro Noe unto Eneas,
>And what [thynges] betwixt tham was,
>And fro Eneas till Brutus tyme,
>[That kynd he telles in this ryme.]
>Fro Brutus till Cadwaladres,
>The laft Bryton that this lande lees.
>Alle that kynd, and alle the frute
>That come of Brutus that is the Brute;
>And the ryght Brute is told no more
>Than the Brytons tymè wore.
>After the Bretons the Inglis camen,
>The lordfchip of this lande thai namen;
>South, and north, weft, and eaft,
>That calle men now the Inglis geft.
>When thai firft [came] amang the Bretons,
>That now ere Inglis than were Saxons:
>'Saxons' Inglis hight all oliche.
>Thai aryved up at Sandwyche,
>In the kynges tyme Vortogerne
>That the lande walde tham not werne, &c. (l. 1-44).
>One, mayfter Wace, the Frankes telles;
>The Brute, all that the Latyn fpelles,
>Fro Eneas till Cadwaladre, &c.
>And ryght as mayfter Wacè says,
>I telle myn Inglis the fame ways, (l. 57-62) &c.[1]

The fecond part of Robert de Brunne's *Chronicle*, beginning from Cadwallader, and ending with Edward I., is tranflated in great meafure from the fecond part of a French metrical chronicle, written in five books by Peter Langtoft, an Auguftine canon of the monaftery of

---

[1] [Furnivall's edit. pp. 1-2.]

Bridlington in Yorkshire, who wrote not many years before his translator. This is mentioned in the prologue preceding the second part:

> Frankysche speche ys cald Romaunce,[1]
> So sey this clerkes and men of Fraunce.
> Peres of Langtoft, a chanoun
> Schaven y[n] the hous of Brydlyngtoun,
> On Romaunce al thys story he wrot
> Of Englishe kynges, &c.[2]

As Langtoft had written his French poem in Alexandrines,[3] the translator, Robert de Brunne, has followed him, the prologue excepted, in using the double distich for one line, after the manner of Robert of Gloucester, as in the first part he copied the metre of his author Wace. But I will exhibit a specimen from both parts. In the first, he gives us this dialogue between Merlin's mother and King Vortigern, from Master Wace:

> "Dame," seyde the kyng, "welcom be thou :
> Nedlike at the y mot wyte how [4]
> Who than gat [5] thy sone Merlyne,
> And on what manere was he thyne."
> His moder stod a throwe [6] and thought
> Er sche to the kyng onswered ought :
> When scheo had stande a litel wyght,[7]
> Sche seyde "by Marye bright,
> That I ne sey ne nevere knew
> Hym that this child on me sew.[8]
> Ne wiste neuere, ne y ne herd,
> What maner wyght wyth me so ferde ;[9]
> Bot this thyng am y wel of graunt,[10]
> That I was of elde avenaunt ;[11]
> On com to my bed, y wyst,
> And with force me clipte and kyst :
> Als [12] a man y hym felt,
> And als a man he me welt ; [13]

---

[1] The Latin tongue ceased to be spoken in France about the ninth century, and was succeeded by what was called the Romance tongue, a mixture of Frankish and bad Latin. Hence the first poems in that language are called Romans or Romants. *Essay on Pope*, p. 281. In the following passage of this chronicle, where Robert de Brunne mentions Romance, he sometimes means Langtoft's French book, from which he translated : viz. *Chron.* p. 205 :

> "This that I have said it is Pers sawe ;
> Als he in Romance laid, thereafter gan I drawe."

See Chauc. *Rom. R.* v. 2170. Also *Balades*, p. 554, v. 508. And Crescembin, *Istor. della Volg. Poes.* vol. i. L. v. p. 316, *seq.*
[2] [Furnivall's edit., 579, l. 16709-14.]
[3] Some are printed by Hollinsh. *Hist.* iii. 469. Others by Hearne, *Chron. Langt. Pref.* p. 58, and in the margin of the pages of the Chronicle. [A portion appears in the *Chroniques Anglo-Normandes*, already referred to : it extends from William the Conqueror to Henry I.]
[4] "I must by all means know of you."   [5] begot.
[6] awhile.   [7] *white*, while.   [8] begot.   [9] [fared.—*Ritson*.]
[10] assured.   [11] [of a fit age.—*Ritson*.]   [12] as.   [13] *wielded*, moved.

And als a man he spak to me.
Bot what he was, myght y nought se.¹

The following, extracted from the same part, is the speech of the Romans to the Britons, after the former had built a wall against the Picts, and were leaving Britain:

We haue yow closed ther most nede was;
And ȝyf ye defende wel that pas
Wyth archers² and wyth mangeneles,³
And wel kepe the carneles;
Theron ye may bothe scheote and kaste:
Wexeth bold, and sendeþ yow faste!
Thenk, your fadres wonne fraunchise,
Be ye na more in otheres servise,
Bot frely lyves to your lyves ende:
We taken now leve fro you to wende (p. 239, l. 6797-6800).

---

¹ [Ed. Furnivall, pp. 282-3, l. 8039-58.]
² Not *bowmen*, but apertures in the wall for shooting arrows, viz., in the repairs of Taunton Castle, 1266, *Comp. J. Gerneys, Episc. Wint.* "Tantonia. Expense domorum. In mercede Cementarii pro muro erigendo juxta turrim ex parte orientali cum Kernellis et Archeriis faciendis, xvi. s. vi. d." *Archiv. Wolves. apud Wint.* *Kernells* mentioned here and in the next verse were much the same thing: or perhaps Battlements. In repairs of the great hall at Wolvesey Palace, I find, " In kyrnillis emptis ad idem, xii. d." *Ibid.* There is a patent granted to the monks of Abingdon, in Berkshire, in the reign of Edward III. " Pro kernellatione monasterii." Pat. an. 4, par. 1.
³ Cotgrave has interpreted this word, an old-fashioned sling. V. *Mangoneau*. See *Rot. Pip.* An. 4 Hen. iii. (A.D. 1219). "Nordhant. Et in expensis regis in obsidione castri de Rockingham, 100*l.* per Br. Reg. Et custodibus ingeniorum (engines) regis ad ea carianda usque Bisham, ad castrum illud obsidendum, 13*s.* 10*d.* per id. Br. Reg. Et pro duobus coriis, emptis apud Northampton ad fundas petrariarum et mangonellorum regis faciendas, 5*s.* 6*d.* per id. Br. Reg."—*Rot. Pip.* 9 *Hen. III.* (A.D. 1225). "Surr. Comp. de Cnareburc. Et pro vii. cablis emptis ad petrarias et mangonellos in eodem castro, 7*s.* 11*d.*" *Rot. Pip.* 5 *Hen. III.* (A.D. 1220). " Devons. Et in custo posito in 1. petraria et 11, mangonellis cariatis a Nottingham usque Bisham, et it eisdem reductis a Bisham usque Notingham, 7*l.* 4*s.*" See *infr.* Mangonel also signified what was thrown from the machine so called. Thus Froissart: " Et avoient les Brabançons de tres grans engins devant la ville, qui *gettoient* pierres de faix et *mangoneaux* jusques en la ville."—Liv. iii. c. 118. And in the old French *Ovide* cited by Borel, *Tresor.* in v.:

" Onques pour une tor abatre,
Ne oit on Mangoniaux descendre
Plus briement ne du ciel destendre
Foudre pour abatre un clocher."

Chaucer mentions both *Mangonels* and *Kyrnils,* in a castle in the *Romaunt of the Rose,* v. 4195, 6279. Also *archers, i. e. archeriæ,* v. 4191. So in the *Roman de la Rose,* v. 3945:

" Vous puissiez bien les Mangonneaulx,
Veoir la par-dessus les Creneaulx.
Et aux archieres de la Tour
Sont arbalestres tout entour."

Archieres occur often in this poem. Chaucer, in translating the above passage [if we have his translation,] has introduced guns, which were not known when the original was written, v. 4191. The use of artillery, however, is proved by a curious passage in Petrarch to be older than the period to which it has been commonly referred. The passage is in Petrarch's book *de Remediis utriusque fortunæ,* undoubtedly written before the year 1334. " G. Habeo machinas et balistas. R. Mirum,

Vortigern, King of the Britons, is thus described meeting the beautiful Princess Rouwen, daughter of Hengist, the Rosamond of the Saxon ages, at a feast of wassail. It is a curious picture of the gallantry of the times, [or, at least, Wace's conception of that gallantry.]

> Hengist that day dide his myght,
> That all was glad, kyng and knyght,
> And als thei were best in gladyng,
> And wel cuppe-schoten[1] knyght and kyng,
> Fro chaumbre cam Ronewenne so gent,
> Byfore the kyng in halle scheo went.
> A coupe wyth wyn sche hadde in hande
> And hure atyr[2] was wel farande.[3]
> Byfore the kyng o knes sche hir sette
> In hure langage ful faire him grette.
> "Wassayl, my lord! Wassail!" seyd sche.
> Then, asked the kyng, what that myght be.
> On that langage the kyng ne couthe.[4]
> Bot a knyght that speche had lered[5] in youthe.
> Breyth highte[6] that knyght, y-born Bretoun,
> That wel spak langage of Saxoun.
> Thys Breth was the kynges latynier.[7]
> And what scheo seyde teldyt Fortyger.

---

nisi et glandes æneas, quæ flammis injectis horrisono sonitu jaciuntur.—Erat hæc pestis nuper rara, ut cum ingenti miraculo cerneretur: nunc, ut rerum pessimarum dociles sunt animi, ita communis est, ut quodlibet genus armorum." Lib. i. Dial. 99. See Muratori, *Antiquitat. Med. Æv.* tom. ii. col. 514. Cannons are supposed to have been first used by the English at the battle of Cressy, in the year 1346. It is extraordinary that Froissart, who minutely describes that battle, and is fond of decorating his narrative with wonders, should have wholly omitted this circumstance. Musquets are recited as a weapon of the infantry so early as the year 1475. "Quilibet peditum habeat balistam vel hombardam." Lit. Casimiri III. an. 1475. *Leg. Polon.* tom. i. p. 228. These are generally assigned to the year 1520. I am of opinion that some of the great military battering engines, so frequently mentioned in the histories and other writings of the dark ages, were fetched from the Crusades. See a species of the catapult, used by the Syrian army in the siege of Mecca, about the year 680. *Mod. Univ. Hist.* b. i. c. 2, tom. ii. p. 117. These expeditions into the East undoubtedly much improved the European art of war. Tasso's warlike machines, which seem to be the poet's invention, are formed on descriptions of such wonderful machines as he had read of in the Crusade historians, particularly William of Tyre.

[1] [Drunk: *enivré.—Wace.* See Cotgrave under *yvre*.] [2] attire.
[3] [well facing, fitting, very becoming.—*Ellis*.]
[4] was not skilled. [5] learned. [6] was called.
[7] Interpreter. [Formerly printed *Latimer*. Mr. Wright is quite correct in his surmise, that Latimer is a mere ignorant misreading of the MSS. for Latiner.] Thus, in the romance of *King Richard*, Saladin's *Latiner* at the siege of Babylon proclaims a truce to the Christian army from the walls of the city. Signat. M. i.

> "The Latemere tho tourned his eye
> To that other syde of the toune,
> And cryed trues with gret soune."

In which sense the French word occurs in the *Roman de Garin*, MSS. Bibl. Reg. Paris, Num. 7542. [Printed in 1833-5, 2 vols. by M. Paulin Paris, and again by Du Meril, in 1845:]

> "Latimer fu si sot parler Roman,
> Englois, Gallois, et Breton, et Norman."

[See Selden's *Table-Talk*, edit. 1860, p. 179.]

"Sire," Breth feyde, " Ronewenne yow gretes,
And kyng calles, and lord yow letes.¹
Thys ys ther cuftume and ther geft,
Whan they arn at ther [ale or] feft.
Ilk man that loues, ther hym beft thynk,
Schal fey ' Waffail,' and to him drynk.
He that haldes fchal fey, ' Waffayl,'
That other fchal feye ageyn, ' Drynk hayl.'
That feys [Waffeyl] drynkes of the coppe,
Kiffing his felawe he gyveth hit uppe.
' Drynk hail,' he feyth, and drinketh ther-of,
Kyffyng hym in bourde and fcof.'²
The kyng feide as the knight gan kenne,³
"Drynk hayle," fmylynge on Rouewenne.
Ronewenne drank right as hure lyft,
And gaf the kyng, and fyn⁴ hym kift.
That was the firfte waffail in dede,
That now and evere the fame yede.⁵
Of that ' waffail ' men tolde grete tale,
And ufed ' waffail' when they were at th' ale.
And ' drynkhail' to them that drank,
Thus was waffail take to thank.

Ful often thus thys mayden 3yng⁶
Waffailed and kyfte ther the kyng.
Of body fche was ful avenaunt,⁷
Of fair colour, wyth fwet femblaunt.⁸
Hure atir⁹ ful wel hit byfemed,
Merveillyke¹⁰ the kyng fcheo quemed,¹¹
Out of mefure was he glad,
Opon that mayden he wax al mad.
The fend and dronkeneffe hit wrought,
Of that Payen¹² was al his thought.
As mefchaunce that tyme hym fpedde ;
He afked that Payen for to wedde ;
And Hengift wernde hym bot lyte,¹³
Bot graunted hure hym al fo tyt.

And again :—

"Un Latinier vieil ferant et henu
Molt fot de plet, et molt entrefnie fu."

And in the *Roman du Rou*, which will again be mentioned :—

"L'archevefque Franches a Jumeges ala,
A Rou, et a fa gent par Latinier parla."

We find it in Froiffart, tom. iv. c. 87, and in other ancient French writers. In the old Norman poem on the fubject of King Dermod's expulfion from his kingdom of Ireland, in the Lambeth library [and printed by M. Michel in 1837,] it feems more properly to fignify, in a limited fenfe, the *king's domeftic fecretary*.

"Parfon demeine Latinier
Que moi conta de luy l'hiftore," &c.

See Lyttelton's *Hift. Hen. II.* vol. iv. App. p. 270. We might here render it literally his Latinift, an officer retained by the king to draw up the public inftruments in Latin. As in *Domefdai-Book:* "Godwinus accipitrarius, Hugo Latinarius, milo portarius." *MS. Excerpt. penes me.* But in both the laft inftances the word may bear its more general and extenfive fignification. Camden explains Latimer by Interpreter. *Rem.* p. 158. See alfo p. 151, edit. 1674.

¹ efteems. ² fport, joke. ³ to [fhew.]
⁴ fince, afterwards. ⁵ went. ⁶ young.
⁷ handfome, gracefully fhaped, &c. ⁸ [appearance.—*Ellis.*]
⁹ attire. ¹⁰ marvelloufly. ¹¹ pleafed.
¹² pagan, heathen. ¹³ [refufed him but little.]

> And Hors his brother confented fone.
> Hire frendes feyd alle, hit was to done.
> They afkede the kyng to gyve hure Kent,
> In dowarye, to take of rent.
> Upon that mayde his herte fo kaft,
> What-fo they afked, the kyng mad faft.
> I wene the kyng tok hure that day,
> And wedded hure on Payens lay.[1]
> Of preft was ther no benifoun,[2]
> No meffe fongen, ne oryfoun.
> In fefyn the kyng had hure that nyght.
> Of Kent he gaf Hengift the ryght.
> The Erl that tyme that Kent held,
> Sir Gorogon, that bar the fcheld,
> Of that gyft no thyng he ne wyfte,[3]
> Til he was dryuen out wyth[4] Hengift.[5]

In the fecond part, [from Langtoft] the attack of Richard I. on a caftle held by the Saracens is thus defcribed :—

> The dikes were fulle wide that clofed the caftelle about,
> & depe on ilk a fide, with bankis hie without.
> Was ther non entre that to the caftelle gan ligge,[6]
> Bot a ftreite kauce,[7] at the end a drauht brigge.
> With grete duble cheynes drauhen ouer the gate,
> And fyfti armed fueynes,[8] porters at that ȝate.
> With flenges & magneles[9] thei kaſt[10] to kyng Richard;
> Our Criſten by parcelles kafted ageynward.[11]
> Ten fergeanz of the beft his targe gan him bere,
> That egre wer & preft to couere him & to were.[12]
> Himfelf as a Geant the cheynes in tuo hew,
> The targe was his warant,[13] that non tille him threw.
> Right unto the ȝate with the targe thei ȝede,
> Fightand on a ȝate, vndir him the flou his ftede.
> Ther for ne wild he feffe,[14] alone in to the caftele
> Thorgh tham alle wild preffe, on fote fauȝht he fulle wele.
> & whan he was withinne, fauȝt as a wilde leon,
> He fondred the Sarazins otuynne, & fauht as a dragon.
> Without the Criften gan crie, allas; R[ichard] is taken,
> Tho Normans were forie, of contenance gan blaken,
> To flo doun & to ftroye neuer wild thei ftint,
> Thei ne left for dede no noye,[15] ne for no wound no dynt,
> That in went alle ther pres, maugre the Sarazins alle,
> And fond R[ichard] on des fightand, & wonne the halle.[16]

From thefe paffages it appears that Robert of Brunne has fcarcely more poetry than Robert of Gloucefter. He has, however, taken care to acquaint his readers that he avoided high defcription, and

---

[1] in pagans' law; according to the heathenifh cuftom.
[2] benediction, bleffing.   [3] knew not.   [4] by.
[5] [ed. Furnivall, pp. 265-268. See the Temple MS. verfion in] Hearne's *Robert of Glo.* p. 695.
[6] lying.   [7] caufey.   [8] fwains, young men, fodiers.
[9] mangonels.   [10] caft.
[11] In Langtoft's French :—
> "Dis feriauntz des plus feres e de melz vanez,
> Devaunt le cors le Reis fa targe ount portez."
[12] ward, defend.   [13] guard, defence.
[14] "he could not ceafe."   [15] annoyance.   [16] *Chron.* ed. Hearne, pp. 182, 183.

that fort of phrafeology which was then ufed by the minftrels and harpers; that he rather aimed to give information than pleafure, and that he was more ftudious of truth than ornament. As he intended his chronicle to be fung, at leaft by parts, at public feftivals, he found it expedient to apologife for thefe deficiencies in the prologue; as he had partly done before in his prologue to [his *Handlyng Synne*, [or the *Manual of Sins*:

> I mad noght for no difours,[1]
> Ne for feggers, no harpours,
> Bot for the luf of fymple meñ,
> That ftrange Inglis cañ not keñ:[2]
> For many it ere[3] that ftrange Inglis
> In ryme wate[4] never what it is (l. 75-80).
> I made it not for to be prayfed,
> Bot at[5] the lewed meñ were ayfed (l. 83-4).[6]

He next mentions feveral forts of verfe or profody, which were then fafhionable among the minftrels, and have become long fince unknown:

> If it were made in ryme *couwée*,
> Or in *ftrangere* or *enterlacè*, (l. 85-6), &c.[7]

---

[1] tale-tellers, *Narratores*, Lat.: *Conteours*, Fr. *Segger* in the next line perhaps means the fame thing, *i.e.* Sayers. The writers either of metrical or of profe romances. See *Antholog. Fran.* p. 17, 1765, 8vo. Or *Difours* may fignify Difcourfe, *i.e.* adventures in profe. We have the " Devils difours," in *P. Plowman*, fol. xxxi. b. edit. 1550. *Difour* precifely fignifies a tale-teller at a feaft in Gower. *Conf. Amant.* lib. vii. fol. 155, a, edit. 1554. He is fpeaking of the coronation feftival of a Roman emperor:—

> " When he was gladeft at his mete,
> And every minftrell had plaide
> And every *diffour* had faide
> Which moft was pleafaunt to his ere."

Du Cange fays, that *Difeurs* were judges of the turney. *Difs. Joinv.* p. 179.
[2] know.   [3] *it ere*, there are.   [4] knew.   [5] that.   [6] eafed.
[7] The rhymes here called by Robert de Brunne *Couwée* [*verfus caudati*, final rhymes, equivalent to the *coda* in mufic] and *Enterlacée*, were undoubtedly derived from the Latin rhymers of that age, who ufed verfus *caudati et interlaqueati*. Brunne here profeffes to avoid thefe elegancies of compofition, yet he has intermixed many paffages in *Rime Couwée*. See his *Chronicle*, pp. 266, 273, &c. &c. [and Gueft's *Hiftory of Englifh Rhythms*.] Almoft all the latter part of his work from the Conqueft is written in rhyme *interlacée*, each couplet rhyming in the middle as well as the end. As thus, MSS. Harl. 1002:

> " Plaufus Græcorum | lux cæcis et via claudis
> Incola cælorum | virgo digniffima laudis."

The rhyme Bafton had its appellation from Robert Bafton, a celebrated Latin rhymer about the year 1315. The rhyme *ftrangere* means uncommon. See *Canterbury Tales*, vol. iv. p. 72, *feq. ut infra*. The reader, curious on this fubject, may receive further information from a MS. in the Bodleian library, in which are fpecimens of *Metra Leonina*, *criftata*, *cornuta*, *reciproca*, &c. MSS. Laud. K 3. 4to. In the fame library there is a very ancient MS. of Aldheim's Latin poem *De Virginitate et Laude Sanctorum*, written about the year 700, and given by Thomas Allen, with Saxon gloffes, and the text almoft in femi-faxon characters. Thefe are the firft two verfes:

> " Metrica tyrones nunc promant carmina cafti,
> Et laudem capiat quadrato carmine Virgo."

[But fee Wright's *Biog. Brit. Literaria*, A-S. period, 217.] Langbaine, in reciting

He adds that the old stories of chivalry had been so disguised by foreign terms, by additions and alterations, that they were now become unintelligible to a common audience: and particularly that the tale of *Sir Tristram*,[1] the noblest of all, was much changed from the original composition of its first author:

> I see in song in sedgeyng tale[2]
> Of Erceldoun, and of Kendale,
> Non tham says as thai tham wroght,[3]
> And in ther say[i]ng[4] it semes noght:
> That may thou here in Sir Tristram;[5]
> Over gestes* it has the steem,[6]

---

this MS. thus explains the *quadratum* carmen. "Scil. prima cujusque versus litera, per Acrostichidem, conficit versum illum *Metrica tyrones*. Ultima cujusque versus litera, ab ultimo carmine ordine retrogrado numerando, hunc versum facit:

"Metrica tyrones nunc promant carmina casti."

(Langb. MSS. v. p. 126.) MSS. Digb. 146. There is a very ancient tract, by one Mico, I believe called also Levita, on Prosody, *De Quantitate Syllabarum*, with examples from the Latin poets, perhaps the first work of the kind. Bib. Bodl. MSS. Bod. A 7. 9. See Hocker's *Catal. MSS. Bibl. Heidelb.* p. 24, who recites a part of Mico's Preface, in which he appears to have been a grammatical teacher of youth. See also Dacheri *Spicileg.* tom. ii. p. 300, b, edit. *ult.* [Mr. Wright has observed that the *ryme couwée* occurs both in heroic and elegiac verse.]

[1] [Sir W. Scott and others have endeavoured to prove that the English romance of Tristram was written by Thomas of Erceldoune; but the translator merely alludes to him at the commencement in a fanciful manner; and I think it, with Mr. Wright, most probable, that finding the name *Thomas* in the French original, and not understanding it, he was induced to take a character, then so famous, to add some popularity to the subject.—*Halliwell.* See *On the Legend of Tristan: its origin in myth, and its development in romance.* By E. T. Leith. Bombay, 1868, 8vo.—*F.* In all the former editions of Warton, eighteen pages were occupied by a vain discussion of the clearly erroneous opinion of Scott, that the romance, as he has (not very correctly) printed it, is the original cast of the story from the pen of Thomas of Erceldoune. In the edition of Warton, which appeared in 1840, Mr. Garnett thus sums up the evidence: "Upon the whole, then, it appears: 1. That the present *Sir Tristram* is a modernized copy of an old Northumbrian romance, which was probably written between A.D. 1260-1300; 2. That it is not, in the proper sense of the word, an original composition, but derived more or less directly from a Norman or Anglo-Norman source; 3. That there is no direct testimony in favour of Thomas of Erceldoune's claim to the authorship of it, while the internal evidence is, as far as it goes, greatly adverse to that supposition. It is, however, by no means improbable that the author availed himself of the previous labours of Erceldoune on the same theme."]

[2] "among the romances that are sung," &c.
[3] "none recite them as they were first written."
[4] "as they tell them." [5] "this you may see," &c. [6] esteem.

* Hearne says that Gests were opposed to Romance. *Chron. Langt.* Pref. p. 37. But this is a mistake. Thus we have the *Geste of kyng Horne*, a very old metrical romance. MSS. Harl. 2253, p. 70. Also in the Prologue of *Rychard Cuer de Lyon:*

> "King Richard is the best
> That is found in any *jeste.*"

And the passage in the text is a proof against his assertion. Chaucer, in the following passage, by Jestours, does not mean jesters in modern signification, but writers of adventures. *House of Fame*, v. 108:

> "And Jestours that tellen tales
> Both of wepyng and of game."

> Over alle that is or was,
> If men it fayd, as made Thomas (l. 93-100).
> Thai fayd in fo quante Inglis
> That many one[1] wate not what it is (l. 109-110).
> And forfoth I couth[e] noght
> So ftrange Inglis as thai wroght (l. 115-116).

On this account, he fays, he was perfuaded by his friends to write his *Chronicle* in a more popular and eafy ftyle, that would be better underftood:

> And men befoght me many a tyme
> To turne in bot in light[e] ryme.
> Thai fayd if I in ftrange it turne
> To here it manyon fuld fkurne[2]
> For it ere names fulle felcouthe[3]
> That ere not ufed now in mouth (l. 117-122).
> In the hous of Sixille I was a throwe[4]
> Danz Robert of Meltone,[5] that ye knowe,
> Did it wryte for felawes fake,
> Wheñ thai wild folace make[6] (l. 141-4).

[Thomas of[7]] Erceldoune and [Thomas of[8]] Kendal are mentioned, in fome of thefe lines of Brunne, as [writers of] old romances

---

In the *Houfe of Fame* he alfo places thofe who wrote "olde geftes," v. 425. It is however obvious to obferve from whence the prefent term *jeft* arofe. See Fauchet, *Rec.* p. 73. In *P. Plowman*, we have *Job's Jeftes*, fol. xlv. b:
> "Job the gentyl in his jeftes greatly wytneffeth."

That is, "Job in the account of his Life." In the fame page we have:
> "And japers and judgelers, and jangelers of jeftes."

That is, minftrels, reciters of tales. Other illuftrations of this word will occur in the courfe of the work. *Chanfons de geftes* were common in France in the thirteenth century among the [trouvères]. See *Mem. concernant les principaux monumens de l'Hiftoire de France: Mem. Lit.* xv. p. 582; by M. de Sainte Palaye. I add the two firft lines of a MS. entitled, *Art de Kalender par Rauf*, who lived 1256. Bibl. Bodl. J. b. 2. Th. (Langb. MSS. 5. 439):
> "De gefte ne voil pas chanter,
> Ne veilles eftoires el canter."

There is even *Gefta Paffionis et Refurrectionis Chrifti*, in many MSS. libraries. [The *chanfons de gefte*, as Mr. Wright has fhown, do not fupport Warton here, as they were poems founded on the real or fuppofed exploits of the earlier kings of France.]

[1] many a one. [2] fcorn. [3] ftrange. [4] a little while.
[5] "Sir Robert of Malton." It appears [hence that he caufed the work to be written.—Madden.]
[6] Pref. *Rob. Glouc.* pp. 57, 58.
[7] [Compare "as made Thomas," l. 100 of Manning's *Chronicle*, with line 94, "tale of Erceldoun and of Kendale," and with "I was at [Erceldoune:] with Tomas fpak y there," *Sir Triftram*, l. 1, &c.:

[8] "When Engle hadde þe lond al þorow,
> He gaf to Scardyng Scardeburghe;
> Toward þe northe, by þe fee fide,
> An hauene hit is, fchipes in to ryde.
> ffiayn highte his broþer, als feyþ þe tale
> þat Thomas made of Kendale;
> Of Scarthe & ffiayn, Thomas feys,
> What þey were, how þey dide, what weys."
>   Manning's *Chronicle*, part i. p. 514.]

or popular tales. Of the latter I can discover no traces in our ancient literature. As to the former, Thomas of Erceldoun or Ashelington is said to have written *Prophecies*, like those of Merlin. Leland, from the *Scalæ Chronicon*,[1] says that " William Banastre,[2] and Thomas Erceldoune, spoke words " yn figure as were the prophecies of Merlin." In the library of Lincoln cathedral there is a [poem, which is almost entitled to the name of a romance,] entitled, *Thomas of Erseldown*, [slightly imperfect,] which begins with an address [not found in the other MSS. of this piece]:

" Lordynges both great and small "—

[But several other MSS. copies of it are extant.[3] The Lincoln MS. has been printed.[4]] In the Bodleian library, among the theological works of John Lawern, monk of Worcester, and student in theology at Oxford about the year 1448, written with his own hand, a fragment of an English poem occurs, which begins thus:

Joly chepert of Askeldowne.[5]

[but is wholly unconnected, except in name, with Erceldoun.] In the British Museum a MS. English poem occurs, with this French title prefixed: *La Countesse de Dunbar, demanda a Thomas Essedoune quant la guere d'Escoce prendret fyn.*[6] This was probably our pro-

---

[1] An ancient French history or chronicle of England never printed, which Leland says was translated out of French rhyme into French prose. *Coll.* vol. i. p. ii. pag. 59, edit. 1770. It was probably written or reduced by Thomas Gray into prose. *Londinens. Antiquitat. Cant.* lib. i. p. 38. Others affirm it to have been the work of John Gray, an eminent churchman, about the year 1212. It begins, in the usual form, with the creation of the world, passes on to Brutus, and closes with Edward III.

[2] One Gilbert Banestre was a poet and musician. The *Prophesies* of *Banister of England* are not uncommon among MSS. In the *Scotch Prophesies*, printed at Edinburgh, [1603,] Banaster is mentioned as the author of some of them. " As Berlington's books and Banester tell us," p. 2. Again, " Beid hath brieved in his book and Banester also," p. 18. He seems to be confounded with William Banister, a writer of the reign of Edward III. Berlington is probably John Bridlington, an Augustine canon of Bridlington, who wrote three books of *Carmina Vaticinalia*, in which he pretends to foretell many accidents that should happen to England. MSS. Digb. Bibl. Bodl. 89 and 186. There are also *Versus Vaticinales* under his name, MSS. Bodl. NE. E. ii. 17, f. 21. He died, aged sixty, in 1379. He was canonised. There are many other *Prophetiæ*, which seem to have been fashionable at this time, bound up with those of the canon of Bridlington in MSS. Digb. 186.

[3] [MSS. Publ. Lib. Camb. Ff. v. 48 (printed by Halliwell in 1845); MS. Cotton. Vitell. E, x; MS. Lansd. 762; MS. Sloane 2578. Of these the first is damaged, the second is a copy of no great importance or antiquity, and the third and fourth are imperfect. A later transcript is in MS. Rawl. c. 258.]

[4] [Laing's *Remains of the Early Popular Poetry of Scotland*, 1822.]

[5] MSS. Bodl. 692, fol.

[" Joly chepte of Aschell downe
Can more on love than al the town."—*Price.*

Ritson could, of course, make out no more, because there is no more to make out, the leaf being torn off here."—*Madden.*]

[6] MSS. Harl. 2253, f. 127. It begins thus:

" When man as mad a kingge of a capped man
When mon is lever other monnes thynge then ys owen."

phefier Thomas of Erceldown. One of his predictions is mentioned in a Scotifh poem entitled [*ane new ʒeir gift*] written in the year 1562 by Alexander Scot.[1] One Thomas [of] Leirmouth, or [the] Rhymer, was alfo a prophetic bard, and lived at Erflingtoun, fometimes perhaps pronounced Erfeldoun. This is therefore probably the fame perfon. One who perfonates him, fays:

> In Erflingtoun I dwell at hame,
> Thomas Rymer men call me.

He has left vaticinal rhymes, in which he predicted the union of Scotland with England, about the year 1279.[2] Fordun mentions feveral of his prophecies concerning the future ftate of Scotland.[3]

Robert de Brunne [perhaps] tranflated into Englifh rhymes the treatife of Cardinal Bonaventura, his cotemporary,[4] *De cœna et paffione domini et pœnis S. Mariæ Virginis*, with the following title: *Medytaciuns of the Soper of our Lorde Jhefu, and alfo of hys Paffyun, and eke of the Peynes of hys fwete Modyr mayden Marye, the whiche made yn Latyn Bonaventure Cardynall.*[5] But I forbear to give further extracts from this writer, who appears to have poffeffed much more induftry than genius,[6] and cannot at prefent be read with much

---

[1] [Alex. Scot's *Poems*, ed. 1821, p. 5.]
[2] See *Scotch Prophecies*, [ed. 1680], pp. 11, 13, 18, 19, 36, viz. *The Prophefy of Thomas Rymer*. Pr. "Stille on my wayes as I went."
[3] Lib. x. cap. 43, 44. I think he is alfo mentioned by Spottifwood. See Dempft. xi. 810.
[4] He died 1272. Many of Bonaventure's tracts were at this time tranflated into Englifh. We have, "The Treatis that is kallid *Prickynge of Love*, made bi a Frere menour Bonaventure, that was Cardinall of the courte of Rome." Harl. MS. 2254, 1. f. 1. This book belonged to Dame Alys Braintwat "the worchypfull prioras of Dartforde." This is not an uncommon MS. [Bonaventura flourifhed in Italy, about the year 1270. The enormous magnificence of his funeral deferves notice more than any anecdote of his life; as it paints the high devotion of the times, and the attention formerly paid to theological literature. There were prefent Pope Gregory X., the emperor of Greece by feveral Greek noblemen his proxies, Baldwin II., the Latin eaftern emperor, James, king of Arragon, the patriarchs of Conftantinople and Antioch, all the cardinals, five hundred bifhops and archbifhops, fixty abbots, more than a thoufand prelates and priefts of lower rank, the ambaffadors of many kings and potentates, the deputies of the Tartars and other nations, and an innumerable concourfe of people of all orders and degrees. The fepulchral ceremonies were celebrated with the moft confummate pomp, and the funeral oration was pronounced by a future pope. Miræi *Auctar. Script. Eccles.* p. 72, edit. Fabric.
[5] MSS. Harl. 1701, f. 84. The firft line is,

"Almighti god in trinite."

[In the two beft MSS. known to us of Manning's complete *Handlyng fynne*, the *Medytaciuns* follow it, after a break. Mr. Bowes, of Streatham caftle, Durham, has a later MS. of the *Handlyng fynne*, not yet examined.—F. Caxton printed a compilation from the Latin of Bonaventura under the title of *Speculum vite Crifti*. See Blades, ii. 194-7.]
[6] [Sir F. Madden and Mr. Furnivall are of opinion that Warton has done fcanty juftice to De Brunne. They confider him the beft poet before Chaucer, anterior to 1330, and very fuperior to the later Hampole and Naffyngton, though not to the writer of *The Pearl* in the Early Englifh Alliterative Poems, edited by Mr. R. Morris for the Early Englifh Text Society in 1864, or the compofer of the allitera-

pleasure. Yet it should be remembered, that even such a writer as Robert de Brunne, uncouth and unpleasing as he naturally seems, and [partly] employed in turning the theology of his age into rhyme, contributed to form a style, to teach expression, and to polish his native tongue. In the infancy of language and composition, nothing is wanted but writers: at that period even the most artless have their use.

Robert [Grosseteste,] bishop of Lincoln,[1] who died in 1253, is said in some verses of Robert de Brunne, quoted above, to have been fond of the metre and music of the minstrels. He was most attached to the French minstrels, in whose language he [is said to have] left a poem of some length. This was translated into English rhyme probably about the reign of Edward [II. or III.] It is called by Leland *Chateau d'Amour*.[2] But in one of the Bodleian MSS. of this book we have the following title: *Romance par Mestre Robert Grosseteste*.[3] In another it is called, *Ce est la vie de D. Jhū de sa*

---

tive *Morte Arthure* in the Thornton MS., assuming that that spirited poem was written some seventy or eighty years before the date of the MS. it is in (1440 A.D.).]

[1] See Diss. ii.—The author and translator are often thus confounded in manuscripts. To an old English religious poem on the holy Virgin, we find the following title: *Incipit quidam cantus quem composuit frater Thomas de Hales de ordine fratrum minorum*, &c. MSS. Coll. Jes. Oxon. [29,] *supr. citat.* [It is hard to tell whether this de Hales is the same as Tanner assigns (by mistake) to the fourteenth century, or a different person.] But this is the title of our friar's original, a Latin hymn de B. Maria Virgine, improperly adopted in the translation. Thomas de Hales was a Franciscan friar, a doctor of the Sorbonne, and flourished about the year 1340. We shall see other proofs of this.

[2] *Script. Brit.* p. 285. [The English version was printed for the Philological Society.]

[3] MSS. Bodl. NE. D. 69. [It has been shown in a former note, that Grosseteste's claim to the authorship of the French *Manuel Peches*—at least to the work at present known by that name—cannot be made good]. The following extract from the *Chateau d'Amour*, ascribed to him by Leland and others, [shows that the poem was also ascribed to him in early times; for in it he is called " Saint Robert de Nichole " (the French name for Lincoln), just as he is called "Seynt Robert," whose surname is "Grosteft of Lynkolne," by Robert of Brunne in the *Handlyng Synne*, l. 4743-5, p. 64 above. Price, seemingly ignorant of *Nichole* meaning Lincoln, thought that St. Robert de Nichole could not be Grosseteste.]

> " Ici comence un escrit,
> Ke Seint Robert de Nichole fift.
> Romanze de romanze eft apelé,
> Tel num a dreit li eft affigné ;
> Kar de ceo livre la materie,
> Eft eftret de haut cleregie,
> E pur ceo ke il pafco (furpaffe) altre romanz
> Apelé eft romanz de romanz.
> Les chapitres ben conuz ferunt
> Par les titres ke fiverunt
> *Les titles ne voil pas rimer*
> Kar leur matiere ne volt fuffrer.
> Primis fera le prologe mis
> E puz les titles tuz affis."
> MSS. Reg. 20 B. xiv.

[It is just possible that both the present poem and the *Manuel Peche* are founded on similar works of Grosseteste written in the Latin language ; and that the tran-

humanite fet a ordine de Saint Robert Groffetefte ke fut eveque de Nichole;[1] and in this copy a very curious apology to the clergy is prefixed to the poem for the language in which it is written.[2] "Et quamvis lingua romana [romance] coram clericis faporem fuavitatis non habeat, tamen pro laicis qui minus intelligunt opufculum illud aptum eft."[3] This piece profeffes to treat of the creation, the redemption, the day of judgment, the joys of heaven, and the torments of hell: but the whole is a religious allegory, and under the ideas of chivalry the fundamental articles of Chriftian belief are reprefented. It has the air of a fyftem of divinity written by a troubadour. The poet, in defcribing the advent of Chrift, fuppofes that he entered into a magnificent caftle, which is the body of the immaculate virgin. The ftructure of this caftle is conceived with fome imagination, and drawn with the pencil of romance. The poem begins with thefe lines:

> Ki penfe ben, ben peut dire:
> Sanz penfer ne poet fuffife:
> De nul bon oure commencer
> Deu nos dont de li penfer
> De ki par ki, en ki, font
> Tos les biens ki font en el mond.

But I haften to the tranflation, which is more immediately connected with our prefent fubject, and has this title:

> Her bygenet a tretys that ys yclept *Caftel of Love*
> that bifcop Groftey3t made ywis for lewde mennes by-hove.[4]

Then follows the prologue or introduction, [from which an extract may fuffice, as the work has been printed three times:]

---

fcribers, either from ignorance, or a defire of giving a fictitious value to their own labours, have infcribed his name upon the copies. His *Templum Domini*, a copious fyftem of myftical divinity, abounding in pious raptures and fcholaftic fubtleties, may have afforded the materials for the former poem; and his treatife, *De feptem vitiis et remediis*—if we except the *Contes devots*, which Wadington may have gleaned from another fource—poffibly fupplied the doctrines of the latter. The title adopted by Leland and the Englifh tranflator has been taken from the following paffage of the French work:

> "En un chaftel bel e grant,
> Bien fourme et avenant,
> *Ceo eft le chaftel d'amour*,
> E de folaz e de focour."

Harl. MSS. No. 1121.—*Price*.]

[1] F 16, Laud. The word *Nicole* is perfectly French for *Lincoln*. See likewife MSS. Bodl. E. 4, 14. [A parliament was held at Nicole in 1300-1. Riley's *Chronicles of Old London*, p. 245, ed. 1863.—F.]

[2] In the hand-writing of the poem itfelf, which is very ancient.

[3] f. 1. So alfo in MSS. C. C. C. Oxon. 232. In MSS. Harl. 1121, 5. "[Ici demouftre] Roberd Groffetefte evefque de Nichole un tretis en Franceis, del commencement du monde," &c. f. 156. Cod. membran.

[4] Bibl. Bodl. MS. Vernon, f. 292. This tranflation [has been printed from a later copy in a MS. of the 14th century, differing greatly from the Vernon in its language and dialect, in private hands, by Mr. Halliwell, 1849, 4to. The Vernon MSS. and Add. MS. Brit. Mus. 22283, were edited for the Philological Society in 1864 by Mr. Weymouth.]

On Englifch[1] I chul mi refun fchowen
For him that con not i-knowen
Nouther French ne Latyn:
On Englifch I chulle tullen him
Wherfore the world was i-wrouht,
And aftur how he was bi-tauht,
Adam vre fader to ben his,
With al the merthe of paradys,
To wonen and welden to fuch ende
Til that he fcholde to heuene wende;
And hou fone he hit for-les
And feththen hou hit for-bouht wes
Thorw the hei3e kynges fone,
That here on eorthe wolde come,
For his fuftren that were to-boren,
And for a prifon that was forloren;
And hou he made as 3e fchul beeren
That heo i-cufte and fauht weren;
And to w3uche a Caftel he alihte, &c.

The moft poetical paffages of this poem [are thofe which defcribe the caftle. Of thefe we quote a few lines:]

This Caftel is fiker and feir abouten,[2]
And is al depeynted withouten
With threo heowes that wel beth fene,[3]
So is the foundement al grene,
That to the roche fafte lith.
Wel is that ther murthe i-fihth,
For the grenefchipe lafteth euere,
And his heuh ne leofeth neuere,
Seththen abouten that other heu3
So is inde and eke bleu.[4]
That the midel heu3 we clepeth ariht,
And fchyneth fo feire and fo bri3t.

The thridde heu3 an ouemaft
Ouer-wri3eth al and fo is i-caft
That withinnen and withouten
The caftel lihteth al abouten,
And is raddore then euere eny rofe fchal
That thuncheth as hit barnde[5] al.[6]
Withinne the Caftel is whit fchinynge
So[7] the fnow3 that is fneuwynge,
And cafteth that li3t fo wyde
After-long the tour and be-fyde,
That never cometh ther wo ne wou3,
Ac fwetneffe ther is euer i-nou3.

---

[1] [*Caftel off Loue*, edit. Weymouth, p. 3.]
[2] [Edit. Weymouth, p. 31.]
[3] [" Li chafteaus eft bel e bon
De hors depeint enuiron,
De iii. colurs diuerfement."—*Fr. Orig.*]
[4] " Si refte ynde fi blui."—*Fr. Orig.*   [5] burned, on fire.
[6] " Plus eft vermaille qui neft rofe
E piert vne ardante chofe."—*Fr. Orig.*
[7] as.

Amidde¹ the hei3e tour is fpringynge
A welle that euere is eornynge²
With foure ftremes that ftriketh wel,
And erneth vppon the grauel,
And fulleth the diches a-boute the wal;
Muche bliffe ther is ouer-al,
Ne dar he feche non other leche
That mai riht of this water cleche.

In³ thulke derworth feire tour
Ther ftont a trone with muche honour,
Of whit iuori, and feirore of liht
Then the fomeres day whon hee is briht,
With cumpas i-throwen, and with gin al i-do.
Seuene fteppes ther beoth ther-to, &c.
The⁴ foure fmale toures abouten,
That [witeth] the hei3e tour with-outen,
Foure hed thewes that aboute hire i-feoth,
Foure vertues cardinals [that] beoth, &c.
And⁵ whyche beoth the threo bayles 3et,
That with the carnels beth fo wel i-fet,
And i-caft with cumpas and walled abouten,
That witeth the hei3e tour with-outen?
Bote the inemafte bayle, I wot,
Bi-tokeneth hire holy maidenhod, &c.
The⁶ middel bayle, that wite 3e,
Bi-tokeneth hire holy chaftite
And feththen the [outemafte] bayle
Bi-tokeneth hire holy fpofayle, &c.
The feue [berbicans] abouten,
That with gret gin beon i-wrou3t withouten,
And witeth this Caftel fo wel,
With arwe and with qwarel,⁷
That beth the feuen vertues with winne
To ouercome the feuen dedly finne, &c.⁸

---

¹ " In mi la tur plus hauteine
   Eft furdant une funtayne
   Dunt iffent quater ruiffell.
   Ki bruinet par le gravel," &c.—*Fr. Orig.*

² running.

³ " En cele bel tur a bone
   A de yvoire un trone
   Ke plufa eiffi blanchor
   Ci en mi efte la beau jur
   Par engin eft compaffez," &c.—*Fr. Orig.*

⁴ [Edit. Weymouth, p. 37.]   ⁵ [*Ibid.* p. 38.]

   " Les treis bailles du chaftel
   Ki funt overt au kernel
   Qui a compas funt en virun
   E defendent le dungun."—*Fr. Orig.*

⁶ [*Ibid.*]

⁷ " Les barbicanes feet
   Kis hors de bailles funt fait,
   Ki bien gardent le chaftel,
   E de feete e de quarrel."—*Fr. Orig.*

⁸ [*Ibid.* 38-9.] Afterwards the fountain is explained to be God's grace: Charity is conftable of the caftle, &c. &c.

It was undoubtedly a great impediment to the cultivation and progressive improvement of the English language at these early periods, that the best authors chose to write in French. Many of Robert [Grosseteste's] pieces are indeed in Latin; yet where the subject was popular, and not immediately addressed to learned readers, he adopted the Romance or French language, in preference to his native English. Of this, as we have already seen, his *Chateau d'Amour* is sufficient proof; and his example and authority must have had considerable influence in encouraging the practice. Peter Langtoft not only compiled the large chronicle of England, above recited, in French, but even translated Herbert Boscam's Latin *Life of Thomas Becket* into French rhymes.[1] John [de] Hoveden, a native of London, doctor of divinity, and chaplain to Queen Eleanor, mother of Edward I. wrote in French rhymes a book entitled, *Rosarium de Nativitate, Passione, Ascensione, Jhesu Christi*.[2] Various other proofs have before occurred. [There is in] the Lambeth library [an imperfect] poem in [Anglo-] Norman verse on the subject of King Dermod's expulsion from Ireland and the recovery of his kingdom.[3] I could mention many others. Anonymous French pieces, both in prose and verse, and written about this time, are innumerable in our manuscript repositories.[4] Yet this fashion proceeded rather from necessity and

---

[1] Pits, p. 890. Append. He with great probability supposes him to have been an Englishman.

[2] MSS. Bibl. C. C. C. Cant. G. 16. where it is also called *The Nightingale*. Pr. "Alme fesse lit de peresse."

In this MS. the whole title is this: *Le Rossignol, ou la pensee Jehan de Hovedene clerc la roine d'Engleterre mere le roi Edward, de la naissance et de la mort et du relievement et de lascension Jesu Crist et de lassumption notre dame*. This MS. was written in the 14th century.

Our author, John [de] Hovenden, was also skilled in sacred music, and a great writer of Latin hymns. He died, and was buried, at Hoveden, 1275. Pits, p. 356, Bale, v. 79.

There is an old French metrical life of Tobiah, which the author, most probably an Englishman, says he undertook at the request of William, Prior of Kenilworth in Warwickshire. MSS. Jes. Coll. Oxon. 85, *supr. citat.*

"Le prior Gwilleyme me prie
De l'eglyse seynte Marie
De Kenelworth an Ardenne,
Ki porte le plus haute peyne
De charite, ke nul eglyse
Del reaume a devyse
Ke jeo liz en romaunz le vie
De kelui ki ont nun Tobie," &c.

[3] [MS. Lamb. 96. See Todd's *Cat.* 1812, p. 94. The poem, which wants beginning and end, has been printed by Michel, 1837, 12mo. An incorrect analysis of it, made by Sir George Carew, to whom it once belonged, is in Harris's *Hibernica*, 1757.] It was probably written about 1190. See Ware, p. 56, and compare Walpole's *Anecd. Paint.* i. 28, Notes. [The original Latin of this has been already noticed as a production of the reign of Edward I., to whose queen John de Hoveden was chaplain. In the Observations on the *Lai de Laustic*, the error of identifying an English translation of de Hoveden's tract with the lay is pointed out.]

[4] Among the learned Englishmen who now wrote in French, Tyrwhitt mentions Helis de Guincestre, or Winchester, a translator of Cato into French. (See vol. ii.

a principle of convenience, than from affectation. The vernacular English, as I have before remarked, was rough and unpolished: and although these writers possessed but few ideas of taste and elegance, they embraced a foreign tongue almost equally familiar, and in which they could convey their sentiments with greater ease, grace, and propriety. It should also be considered, that our most eminent scholars received a part of their education at the university of Paris. Another and a very material circumstance concurred to countenance this fashionable practice of composing in French. It procured them readers of rank and distinction. The English court, for more than two hundred years after the Conquest, was totally French: and our kings, either from birth, kindred, or marriage, and from a perpetual intercourse, seem to have been more closely connected with France than with England.[1] It was however fortunate that these French pieces were written, as some of them met with their translators who, perhaps, unable to aspire to the praise of original writers, at least by this means contributed to adorn their native tongue: and who very

---

sect. xxvii.) And Hue de Roteland [or rather, according to Sir F. Madden, Walter de Biblesworth] author of the Romance, in French verse, called *Ipomidon*. MSS. Cott. Vesp. A. vii. [Hugh] is supposed to have written a French Dialogue in metre, MSS. Bodl. 3904. *La pleinte par entre mis Sire Henry de Lacy Counte de Nichole, et Sire Wauter de Byblesworth pur la croiserie en la terre feinte*. And a French romantic poem on a knight called *Capanee*, perhaps Statius's Capaneus. MSS. Cott. Vesp. A vii. *ut supr.* It begins:

" Que bons countes viel entendre."

I have before hinted that it was sometimes customary to intermix Latin with French. As thus, MSS. Harl. 2253, f. 137, b. :

" Dieu roy de Mageste,
Ob personas trinas,
Nostre roy esa meyne
Ne perire sinas," &c.

Again, ibid. f. 76, where a lover, an Englishman, addresses his mistress who was of Paris:

" *Dum ludis floribus velut lacinia*,
Le dieu d'amour moi tient en tiel *Angustia*," &c.

Sometimes their poetry was half French and half English. As in a song to the holy virgin on our Saviour's passion. *Ibid.* f. 83.

" Mayden moder milde, oyez cel oreysoun,
From shome thou me shilde, e de ly mal feloun :
For love of thine childe me menez de tresoun,
Ich wes wod and wilde, ore su en prisoun," &c.

In the same MS. I find a French poem probably written by an Englishman, and in the year 1300, containing the adventures of Gilote and Johanne, two ladies of gallantry, in various parts of England and Ireland; particularly at Winchester and Pontefract, f. 66, b. The curious reader is also referred to a French poem, in which the poet supposes that a minstrel, *jugelour*, travelling from London, clothed in a rich tabard, met the king and his retinue. The king asks him many questions, particularly his lord's name and the price of his horse. The minstrel evades all the king's questions by impertinent answers; and at last presumes to give his majesty advice. *Ibid.* f. 107, b.

[1] [It is very certain that many French poems were written during this period by Englishmen; but it is probable that several were also composed by Normans.—Douce.]

probably would not have written at all, had not original writers, I mean their cotemporaries who wrote in French, furnished them with models and materials.

Hearne, to whose diligence even the poetical antiquarian is much obliged, but whose conjectures are generally wrong, imagines that the old English metrical romance, called *Rychard cuer de Lyon*, was written by Robert de Brunne. It is at least probable, that the leisure of monastic life produced many rhymers. From proofs here given we may fairly conclude, that the monks often wrote for the minstrels: and although our Gilbertine brother of Brunne chose to relate true stories in plain language, yet it is reasonable to suppose, that many of our ancient tales in verse containing fictitious adventures were written, although not invented, in the religious houses. The romantic history of *Guy Earl of Warwick* is expressly said, on good authority, to have been written by Walter of Exeter, a Franciscan friar of Carocus in Cornwall, about the year 1292.[1] The libraries of the monasteries were full of romances. *Bevis of Southampton*, in French, was in the library of the abbey of Leicester.[2] In that of the abbey of Glastonbury, we find *Liber de Excidio Trojæ, Gesta Ricardi Regis,* and *Gesta Alexandri Regis,* in the year 1247.[3] These were some of the most favourite subjects of romance, as I shall shew hereafter. In a catalogue of the library of the abbey of Peterborough are recited *Amys and Amelon,*[4] *Sir Tristram, Guy de*

---

[1] Carew's *Surv. Cornw.* p. 59, edit. *ut supr.* I suppose Carew means the metrical Romance of *Guy.* But Bale says that Walterw rote *Vita Guidonis,* which seems to imply a prose history. x. 78. [Gerard of Cornwall, a very obscure writer, in the eleventh chapter of his lost work, *De Gestis regum West-Saxonium,* introduced] Guy's history. Hearne has printed an *Historia Guidonis de Warwik: Append. ad Annal. Dunstaple,* num. xi. It was extracted from Girald. Cambrens. *Hist. Reg. West-Sax.,* capit. xi. by Girardus Cornubiensis. Lydgate's *Life of Guy,* never printed, is translated from this Girardus, as Lydgate himself informs us at the end. MSS. Bibl. Bodl. Laud. D 31, f. 64, Tit. *Here gynneth the liff of Guy of Warwyk:*

"Out of the Latyn made by the Chronycler
Called of old Girard Cornubyence:
Which wrote the dedis, with grete diligence,
Of them that were in Westsex crowned kynges," &c.

See Wharton, *Angl. Sacr.* i. p. 89.

[2] See *Registrum Librorum omnium et Jocalium in monasterio S. Mariæ de Pratis prope Leycestriam.* f. 132, b. MSS. Bibl. Bodl. Laud. I 75. This catalogue was written by Will. Charite, one of the monks, A.D. 1517, f. 139.

[3] Hearne's Joann. Glaston. *Catal. Bibl. Glaston.* p. 435. One of the books of Troy is called *bonus et magnus.* There is also *Liber de Captione Antiochiæ Gallice. legibilis,* ibid.

[4] The same Romance is in MSS. Harl.
[The Harl. MS. is a bad copy of about one half of the poem. This Romance was translated into German verse by Conrad of Würzburg, who flourished about the year 1300. He chose to name the heroes Engelhard and Engeldrud.—Weber. See Du Cang. *Gloss. Lat.* i. *Ind. Auctor,* p. 193. There is an old French Morality on this subject—" *Comment Amille tue ses deux enfans pour guerir Amis son compagnon,*" &c. Beauchamps, *Rech. Theatr. Fr.* p. 109. There is a French metrical romance, *Histoire d'Amys et Amilion,* MSS. Reg. 12, C xii. 9, and at Bennet College, Num. L. 1. It begins,

"Ki veut oir chauncoun damur."

Burgoyne, and *Gesta Osuelis* [*Otuelis*],¹ all in French: together with *Merlin's Prophecies, Turpin's Charlemagne,* and the *Destruction of Troy*.² Among the books given to Winchester college by the founder William of Wykeham, a prelate of high rank, about the year 1387, we have *Chronicon Trojæ*.³ In the library of Windsor college, in the reign of Henry VIII., were discovered, in the midst of missals, psalters and homilies, *Duo libri Gallici de Romances, de quibus unus liber de Rose, et alius difficilis materiæ.*⁴ This is the language of the king's commissioners, who searched the archives of the college: the first of these two French romances is perhaps [Guillaume de Lorris]'s *Roman de la Rose*. A friar, in *Pierce Plowman*, is said to be much better acquainted with the *Rimes of Robin Hood* and *Randal Erle of Chester* than with his Pater-noster.⁵ The monks, who very naturally sought all opportunities of amusement in their retired and confined situations, were fond of admitting the minstrels to their festivals, and were hence familiarised to romantic stories. Seventy shillings were expended on minstrels, who accompanied their songs with the harp, at the feast of the installation of Ralph abbot of Saint Augustin's at Canterbury, in the year 1309. At this magnificent solemnity, six thousand guests were present in and about the hall of the abbey.⁶ It was not deemed an occurrence unworthy to be recorded, that when Adam de Orleton, bishop of Winchester, visited his cathedral priory of Saint Swithin in that city, a minstrel named Herbert was introduced, who sang the *Song*

[In the Pipe-roll, 34 and 36 Hen. III. is mentioned, "liber magnus, *Gallico ydiomiate* scriptus, in quo continentur Gesta Antiochie et regum et etiam aliorum." —Mr. Wright's inform. Sir F. Madden conjectures this to have been a version of the *Antiocheis* of Joseph of Exeter. Mr. Wright also refers us to a very curious list of romances given by Guy de Beauchamp, Earl of Warwick, to the abbey of Bardesley, printed from the original deed in M. Michel's *Tristan*.

¹ There is a romance called *Otuel*, MSS. Bibl. Adv. Edinb. W 4, l. xxviii. I think he is mentioned in Charlemagne's story. He is converted to Christianity, and marries Charlemagne's daughter. [Analysed by Mr. Ellis: vol. ii. p. 324. It has been printed entire for the Abbotsford Club, with the romance of *Rowland and Vernagu*, 1836.

But as to the signification of the word *romance* in early documents, it is extremely difficult, after all, to come to any conclusion. In a Close-roll of 6 John (1205), *Romancium de historia Angliæ* evidently means merely a narrative of English history.]

² Gunton's *Peterb.* p. 108, *seq.* I will give some of the titles as they stand in the catalogue. *Dares Phrygius de Excidio Trojæ,* bis, p. 180. *Prophetiæ Merlini versifice,* p. 182. *Gesta Caroli secundùm Turpinum,* p. 187. *Gesta Æneæ post destructionem Trojæ,* p. 198. *Bellum contra Runcivallum,* p. 202. There are also the two following articles, viz., *Certamen inter regem Johannem et Barones, versifice,* per H. de Davench, p. 188. This I have never seen, nor know anything of the author. *Versus de ludo scaccorum,* p. 195.

³ Ex archivis Coll. Wint.

⁴ Dugd. *Mon.* iii. *Eccles. Collegiat.* p. 80.

⁵ Fol. xxvi. b, edit. 1550. [See the *Erles of Chestre* in the *Percy Folio*, Ballads and Romances.]

⁶ *Dec. Script.* p. 2011.

s. 2.   *of the old Englifh Abbeys and Colleges.*   97

of *Colbrond*, a Danifh giant, and the tale of *Queen Emma delivered from the ploughfhares*, in the hall of the prior Alexander de Herriard, in the year 1338. I will give this very curious article, as it appears in an ancient regifter of the priory: "Et cantabat Joculator quidam nomine Herebertus canticum Colbrondi, necnon Geftum Emme regine a judicio ignis liberate, in aula prioris."[1] In an annual accompt-roll of the Auguftine priory of Bicefter in Oxfordfhire, for the year 1431, the following entries relating to this fubject occur, which I choofe to exhibit in the words of the original: " Dona Prioris. Et in datis cuidam citharizatori in die fancti Jeronimi, viii. d. Et in datis alteri citharizatori in Fefto Apoftolorum Simonis et Jude cognomine Hendy, xii. d. Et in datis cuidam minftrallo domini le Talbot infra natale domini, xii. d. Et in datis miniftrallis domini le Straunge in die Epiphanie, xx. d. Et in datis duobus miniftrallis domini Lovell in craftino S. Marci evangelifte, xvi. d. Et in datis miniftrallis ducis Gloceftrie in Fefto nativitatis beate Marie, iii. s. iv. d." I muft add, as it likewife paints the manners of the monks, " Et in datis cuidam Urfario, iiii. d."[2] In the Prior's accounts of the Auguftine canons of Maxtoke in Warwickfhire, of various years in the reign of Henry VI., one of the ftyles or general heads is *De Joculatoribus et Mimis*. I will without apology produce fome of the particular articles, not diftinguifhing between *Mimi, Joculatores, Jocatores, Lufores,* and *Citharifta*, who all feem alternately, and at different times, to have exercifed the fame arts of popular entertainment: "Joculatori in feptimana S. Michaelis, iv. d. Citharifte tempore natalis domini et aliis jocatoribus, iv. d. Mimis de Solihull, vi. d. Mimis de Coventry, xx. d. Mimo domini Ferrers, vi. d. Luforibus de Eton, viii. d. Luforibus de Coventry, viii. d. Luforibus de Daventry, xii. d. Mimis de Coventry, xii. d. Mimis domini de Afteley, xii. d. Item iiii. mimis domini de Warewyck, x. d. Mimo ceco, ii. d. Sex mimis domini de Clynton. Duobus Mimis de Rugeby, x. d. Cuidam citharifte, vi. d. Mimis domini de Afteley, xx. d. Cuidam citharifte, vi. d. Citha-

---

[1] *Regiftr. Priorat. S. Swithini Winton.* MSS. Archiv. de Wolvefey Wint. Thefe were local ftories. Guy fought and conquered Colbrond, a Danifh champion, juft without the northern walls of the city of Winchefter, in a meadow to this day called Danemarch: and Colbrond's battle-axe was kept in the treafury of St. Swithin's priory till the Diffolution. Th. Rudb. apud Wharton, *Angl. Sacr.* i. 211. This hiftory remained in rude painting againft the walls of the north tranfept of the cathedral till within my memory. Queen Emma was a patronefs of this church, in which fhe underwent the trial of walking blindfold over nine red-hot ploughfhares. Colbrond is mentioned in the *Squyr of Lowe Degre*. [Hazlitt's *Pop. Poetry*, ii. 26:]

" Or els fo doughty of my hande
As was the gyaunte fyr Colbrande."

[See Turnbull's edit. of *Guy of Warwick*, 1840, Introd.]

[2] *Compotus dñi Ricardi Parentyn Prioris, et fratris Ric. Albon canonici, burfarii ibidem, de omnibus bonis per eofdem receptis et liberatis a craftino Michaelis anno Henrici Sexti poft Conqueftum octavo ufque in idem craftinum anno R. Henrici prædicti nono.* In Thefaurar. Coll. SS. Trin. Oxon. Bifhop Kennet has printed a Computus of the fame monaftery under the fame reign, in which three or four entries of the fame fort occur. *Paroch. Antiq.* p. 578.

II.   H

riſte de Coventry, vi. d. Duobus cithariſtis de Coventry, viii. d. Mimis de Rugeby, viii. d. Mimis domini de Buckeridge, xx. d. Mimis domini de Stafford, ii. s. Luſoribus de Coleſhille, viii. d." [1] Here we may obſerve, that the minſtrels of the nobility, in whoſe families they were conſtantly retained, travelled about the county to the neighbouring monaſteries; and that they generally received better gratuities for theſe occaſional performances than the others. Solihull, Rugby, Coleſhill, Eton or Nun-Eton, and Coventry, are all towns ſituated at no great diſtance from the priory.[2] Nor muſt I omit that two minſtrels from Coventry made part of the feſtivity at the conſecration of John, prior of this convent, in the year 1432, viz. "*Dat. duobus mimis de Coventry in die confecrationis prioris*, xii. d."[3] Nor is it improbable, that ſome of our great monaſteries kept minſtrels of their own in regular pay. So early as the year 1180, in the reign of Henry II., *Jeffrey the harper* received a corrody or

---

[1] *Ex orig. penes me.*

[2] In the ancient annual rolls of accompt of Winchefter College, there are many articles of this ſort. The few following, extracted from a great number, may ſerve as a ſpecimen. They are chiefly in the reign of Edward IV. viz. in the year 1481: "Et in ſol. miniſtrallis dom. Regis venientibus ad collegium xv. die Aprilis, cum 12*d*. folut. miniſtralis dom. Epiſcopi Wynton. venientibus ad collegium primo die junii, iiii *s*. iiii *d*.—Et in dat. miniſtralis dom. Arundell ven. ad Coll. cum viii *d*. dat. miniſtrallis dom. de Lawarr, ii *s*. iii *d*."—In the year 1483: "Sol. miniſtrallis dom. Regis ven. ad Coll. iii *s*. iiii *d*."--In the year 1472: "Et in dat. miniſtrallis dom. Regis cum viii *d*. dat. duobus Berewardis ducis Clarentie, xx *d*. Et in dat. Johanni *Stulto* quondam dom. de Warewyco, cum iiii *d*. dat. Thome Nevyle taborario.—Et in datis duobus miniſtrallis ducis Gloceſtrie, cum iiii *d*. dat. uni miniſtrallo ducis de Northumberlond, viii *d*. Et in datis duobus citharatoribus ad vices venient. ad collegium viii *d*."—In the year 1479: "Et in datis ſatrapis Wynton venientibus ad coll. feſto Epiphanie, cum xii *d*. dat. miniſtrallis dom. epiſcopi venient. ad coll. infra octavas epiphanie, iii *s*."—In the year 1477: "Et in dat. miniſtrallis dom. Principis venient. ad coll. feſto Aſcenſionis Domini, cum xx *d*. dat miniſtrallis dom. Regis, v *s*."—In the year 1464: " Et in dat. miniſtrallis comitis Kancie venient. ad Coll. in menſe julii, iiii *s*. iiii *d*."—In the year 1467 : "Et in datis quatuor mimis dom. de Arundell venient. ad Coll. xiii. die Febr. ex curialitate dom. Cuſtodis, ii *s*." —In the year 1466: "Et in dat. ſatrapis, [*ut ſupr*.] cum ii *s*. dat. iiii. interludentibus et J. Meke cithariſtæ eodem ffeſto, iiii *s*."—In the year 1484: "Et in dat. uni miniſtrallo dom. principis, et in aliis miniſtrallis ducis Gloceſtrie v. die julii, xx *d*." The minſtrels of the biſhop, of lord Arundel, and the Duke of Glouceſter, occur very frequently. In domo muniment. coll. prædict. in ciſta ex orientali latere.

In rolls of the reign of Henry VI. the counteſs of Weſtmoreland, ſiſter of cardinal Beaufort, is mentioned as being entertained in the college; and in her retinue were the minſtrels of her houſehold, who received gratuities. *Ex Rot. Comp. orig.*

In theſe rolls there is an entry, which ſeems to prove that the *Luſores* were a ſort of actors in dumb ſhow or maſquerade. *Rot. ann.* 1467. "Dat. luſoribus de civitate Winton. venientibus ad collegium in *apparatu* ſuo mens. julii, v *s*. vii *d*." This is a large reward. I will add from the ſame rolls, *ann.* 1479. "In dat. Joh. Pontiſbery and ſocio ludentibus in aula in die circumciſionis, ii *s*."

[3] *Ibid.* It appears that the Coventry-men were in high repute for their performances of this ſort. In the entertainment preſented to Queen Elizabeth at Kenilworth caſtle in 1575, the Coventry-men exhibited "their old ſtoriall ſheaw." Laneham's *Narrative*, &c. p. 32. Minſtrels were hired from Coventry to perform at Holy Croſſe feaſt at Abingdon, Berks, 1422. Hearne's *Lib. Nig. Scacc.* ii. p. 598. See an account of their play on Corpus Chriſti day, in Dugdale's *Monaſticon*, by Stevens, i. p. 138, and Hearne's *Fordun*, p. 1450, *ſub ann.* 1492.

annuity from the Benedictine abbey of Hide near Winchester;[1] undoubtedly on condition that he should serve the monks in the profession of a harper on public occasions. The abbeys of Conway and Stratflur in Wales respectively maintained a bard:[2] and the Welsh monasteries in general were the grand repositories of the poetry of the British bards.[3]

In the statutes of New College at Oxford, given about the year 1380, the founder, William of Wykeham, orders his scholars, for their recreation on festival days in the hall after dinner and supper, to entertain themselves with songs and other diversions consistent with decency: and to recite poems, chronicles of kingdoms, the wonders of the world, together with the like compositions, not misbecoming the clerical character.[4] The latter part of this injunction seems to be an explication of the former: and on the whole it appears that the *Cantilenæ*, which the scholars should sing on these occasions, were a sort of *Poemata* or poetical Chronicles, containing general histories of kingdoms.[5] It is natural to conclude that they preferred pieces of English history, [such as the *Brut* already described, of a somewhat amplified version of which (of the reign of Edward III.) some fragments occur among Hearne's MSS.][6]

Although we have taken our leave of Robert de Brunne, yet as the subject is remarkable, and affords a striking portraiture of ancient manners, I am tempted to transcribe that chronicler's description of the presents received by King Athelstane from the king of France; especially as it contains some new circumstances, and supplies the

---

[1] Madox, *Hist. Exchequer*, p. 251. Where he is styled, "Galfridus citharœdus."

[2] Powel's *Cambria*. *To the Reader*, pag. 1, edit. 1584.

[3] Evans's *Diss. de Bardis. Specimens of Welsh Poetry*, p. 92. Wood relates a story of two itinerant priests coming, towards night, to a cell of Benedictines near Oxford, where, on a supposition of their being mimes or minstrels, they gained admittance. But the cellarer, sacrist, and others of the brethren, hoping to have been entertained with their *gesticulatoriis ludicrisque artibus*, and finding them to be nothing more than two indigent ecclesiastics who could only administer spiritual consolation, and being consequently disappointed of their mirth, beat them and turned them out of the monastery.—*Hist. Antiq. Univ. Oxon.* i. 67. Under the year 1224.

[4] I will transcribe his words: "Quando ob dei reverentiam aut suæ matris, vel alterius sancti cujuscunque, tempore yemali, ignis in aula sociis ministratur; tunc scolaribus et sociis post tempus prandii aut cene liceat gracia recreationis in aula, in Cantilenis et aliis solaciis honestis, moram facere condecentem; et Poemata, regnorum Chronica, et mundi hujus Mirabilia, ac cetera que statum clericalem condecorant, seriosius pertractare."—*Rubric.* xviii. The same thing is enjoined in the statutes of Winchester College, *Rubr.* xv. I do not remember any such passage in the statutes of preceding colleges in either university. But this injunction is afterwards adopted in the statutes of Magdalene College, and thence, if I recollect right, was copied into those of Corpus Christi, Oxford.

[5] Hearne thus understood the passage: "The wise founder of New College permitted them [metrical chronicles] to be sung by the fellows and scholars upon extraordinary days."—Heming. *Cartul.* ii. Append. Numb. ix. § vi. p. 662.

[6] Given to him by Mr. Murray. See Heming, *Chartul.* ii. p. 654. And *Rob. Glouc.* ii. p. 731. Nunc MSS. Bibl. Bodl. Oxon. *Rawlins*, Cod. 4to. (E. Pr. 87.) [Ritson has printed these fragments entire in his *Metrical Romances*, 1802; and the editor could not perceive the advantage of quoting them to the extent that Warton, not knowing what they were, has done.]

defects of [the *Brut*]. It is from his verſion of Peter Langtoft's
chronicle above mentioned:

> At the feſte of oure lady the Aſſumpcion,
> Went the kyng fro London toward Abindon.
> Thider out of France, fro Charles kyng of fame,
> Com the duke of Boloyn, Adulphus was his name,
> & the duke of Burgoyn, Edmonde ſonne Reynere.
> The brouht kynge Athelſton preſent withouten pere:
> Fro Charles kyng ſanz faile thei brouht a gonfaynoun
> That Saynt Morice bare in batayle befor the legioun;
> & the ſcharp lance that thrilled Iheſu ſide;
> & a ſuerd of golde,—in the hilte did men hide
> Tuo of tho nayles that war thorh Jheſu fete
> Tached[1] on the croyce; the blode thei out lete;
> & ſom of the thornes that don were on his heued,
> & a fair pece that of the croyce leued,[2]
> That ſaynt Heleyn ſonne at the batayle wan
> Of the Soudan Aſkalone, his name was Madan.
> Than blewe the trumpes fulle loud & fulle ſchille,
> The kyng com in to the halle that hardy was of wille.
> Than ſpak Reyner, Edmunde ſonne, for he was meſſengere:
> ' Athelſtan, my lord, the gretes, Charles that has no pere;
> He ſends the this preſent, and ſais, he wille hym bynde
> To the thorh[3] Ilde thi ſiſtere, & tille alle thi kynde."
> Befor the meſſengers was the maiden brouht,
> Of body ſo gentill was non in erthe wrouht;
> No non ſo faire of face, ne non of ſpech ſo luſty.
> Scho granted befor tham all to Charles hir body:
> & ſo did the kyng, & alle the baronage,
> Mykelle was the richeſſe thei purveied [in] hir paſſage.[4]

[One of Hearne's fragments is added here, becauſe it defends and
explains the derivation of the name Ynglond from maiden Ynge, of
whom Robert Manning declares twice[5] that he had never heard. She
is the later repreſentative of Ronwen or Rowenna. This fragment]
begins with the martyrdom of Saint Alban, and paſſes on to the introduction of Waſſail, and to the names and diviſion of England:

> And now he ys alle ſo hole yſonde,
> As whan he was yleyde on grounde.
> And 3yf 3e wille not trow[6] me,
> Goth to Weſtmyſtere, and 3e mow ſe.
> In that tyme Seynt Albon
> For Goddys loue tholed[7] martirdome,
> And xl. 3ere with ſchame & ſchonde[8]
> Was drowen[9] oute of Englond.

---

[1] Tacked, faſtened.   [2] Remained.   [3] "Thee through."

[4] *Chron.* pp. 29, 30, [edit. 1810, *ut ſupr.*] Afterwards follows the combat of
Guy with "a hogge (huge) geant, hight Colibrant." As in our fragment, p. 31.
See Will. Malms. *Geſt. Angl.* ii. 6. The lance of Charlemagne is to this day ſhown
among the relics of St. Denis in France.—Carpentier, *Suppl. Gloſſ. Lat. Ducange.*
tom. ii. p. 994, edit. 1766.

[5] [*Chronicle,* Part i. pp. 265, 515.

> "Bot this lewed men ſey and ſynge,
> And telle that hit was mayden Inge.
> Wryten of Inge, no clerk may kenne,
> Bot of Hengiſte doughter, Ronewenne."]

[6] Believe.   [7] Suffered.   [8] Confuſion.   [9] Driven, drawn.

In that tyme wete¹ the welle,
Cam ferſt waſſayle & drynkehayl
In to this londe, with owte wene,²
Thurghe a mayde brygh³ and ſchene.⁴
Sche was cleput⁵ mayde ynge.
For hur many dothe rede & ſynge,
Lordyngys gent⁶ & free.
This lond hath hadde namys thre.
Ferſt hit was cleput Albyon
And ſyth,⁷ for Brute, Bretayne anon,
And now ynglond clepyd hit ys,
Aftir mayde ynge ywyſſe.
Thilke ynge fro Saxone was come,
And with here many a moder ſonne,
For gret hungure y underſtonde
ynge went oute of hure londe.
And thorow leue of oure kyng
In this lande ſche hadde reſtyng.
As meche lande of the kyng ſche bade,⁸
As with a hole hyde me my 3th⁹ ſprede,
The kyng graunted [t]he bonne:¹⁰
A ſtrong caſtel ſche made ſone,
And when the caſtel was al made,
The kyng to the mete ſche bade.¹¹
The kyng graunted here anone.
He wyſt not what thay wolde done.

* * *

And ſayde to ham¹² in this manere,
" The kyng to morrow ſchal ete here,
He and alle hys men,
Euer¹³ one of vs and one of them,
To geder ſchal ſitte at the mete.
And when thay haue al moſt yete,
I wole ſay waſſayle to the kyng,
And ſle hym with oute any leſyng.¹⁴
And loke that 3e in this manere
Eche of 3ow ſle his fere."¹⁵
And ſo ſche dede thenne,
Slowe the kyng and alle hys men.
And thus, thorowgh here queyntyſe,¹⁶
This londe was wonne in this wyſe.
Syth¹⁷ anon ſone an ſwythe¹⁸
Was Englond deled¹⁹ on fyue,
To fyue kynggys trewelyche,
That were nobyl and ſwythe ryche.
That one hadde alle the londe of Kente,
That ys free and ſwythe gente.
And in hys lond byſshopus tweye.
Worthy men where²⁰ theye.
The archebyſshop of Caunturbery,
And of Rocheſtere that ys mery.
The kyng of Eſſex of renon²¹

---

¹ know ye.	² doubt.	³ bright.
⁴ fair.	⁵ called.	⁶ gentle.
⁷ [afterwards.]	⁸ requeſted, deſired.	⁹ men might.
¹⁰ granted her requeſt.	¹¹ bid.	¹² them.
¹³ every.	¹⁴ lye.	¹⁵ companion.
¹⁶ ſtratagem.	¹⁷ after.	¹⁸ [quickly].
¹⁹ divided.	²⁰ were.	²¹ renown.

> He hadde to his portion
> Weſtſchire, Barkſchire,
> Souſſex, Southamptſhire.
> And ther-to Dorſetſhyre,
> All Cornewalle & Deuenſhire,
> All thys were of hys anpyre.[1]
> The kyng hadde on his hond
> Fyue Byſshopes ſtarke & ſtrong,
> Of Saluſbury was that on.[2]

As to the *Mirabilia Mundi*, mentioned in the ſtatutes of New College at Oxford, in conjunction with theſe *Poemata* and *Regnorum Chronica*, the immigrations of the Arabians into Europe and the Cruſades produced numberleſs accounts, partly true and partly fabulous, of the wonders ſeen in the eaſtern countries; which, falling into the hands of the monks, grew into various treatiſes under the title of *Mirabilia Mundi*. There were alſo ſome profeſſed travellers into the Eaſt in the dark ages, who ſurpriſed the weſtern world with their marvellous narratives which, could they have been contradicted, would not have been believed.[3] At the court of the grand Khan, perſons of all nations and religions, if they diſcovered any diſtinguiſhed degree of abilities, were kindly entertained and often preferred.

In the Bodleian Library we have a ſuperb vellum MS. [of Marco Polo, in French,] decorated with ancient deſcriptive paintings and illuminations, entitled, *Hiſtoire de Graunt Kaan et des Merveilles du Monde*.[4] The ſame work is among the royal MSS.[5] A [ſpurious] Latin epiſtle, ſaid to be tranſlated from the Greek by Cornelius Nepos, is an extremely common manuſcript, entitled, *De ſitu et Mirabilibus Indiæ*.[6]

---

[1] empire. [2] [Robert of Glouceſter, edit. 1810, 731-3.]

[3] The firſt European traveller who went far Eaſtward, is Benjamin, a Jew of Tudela in Navarre. He penetrated from Conſtantinople through Alexandria in Ægypt and Perſia to the frontiers of Tzin, now China. His travels end in 1173. He mentions the immenſe wealth of Conſtantinople, and ſays that its port ſwarmed with ſhips from all countries. He exaggerates in ſpeaking of the prodigious number of Jews in that city. He is full of marvellous and romantic ſtories. William de Rubruquis, a monk, was ſent into Perſic Tartary, and by the command of S. Louis, King of France, about the year 1245; as was alſo Carpini, by Pope Innocent IV. Marco Polo, a Venetian nobleman, travelled eaſtward into Syria and Perſia to the country conſtantly called in the dark ages Cathay, which proves to be the northern part of China. This was about the year [1280.] His book is [ſometimes] entitled *De Regionibus Orientis*. He mentions the immenſe and opulent city of Cambalu, undoubtedly Pekin. Hakluyt cites a friar, named Oderick, who tarvelled to Cambalu in Cathay, and whoſe deſcription of that city correſponds exactly with Pekin. Friar Bacon, about 1280, from theſe travels formed his geography of this part of the globe, as may be collected from what he relates of the Tartars. See Purchas, *Pilgr.* iii. 52, and Bac. *Op. Maj.* 228, 235.

[4] MSS. Bodl. F. 10 [264] ad calc. Cod. The handwriting is about the reign of Edward III. [1380-1400].

[5] MSS. Bibl. Reg. 19, D i. 3. [The royal MS. is a magnificent copy of the French tranſlation of Marco Polo's travels, which it affirms to have been made in the year 1298.—*Price*.]

[6] [Maittaire cites an edition of the Latin tranſlation as printed at Venice in 1499, but ſee Brunet, *dern.* edit. i. 163. The Greek has been often printed. Sir F. Madden refers to a Saxon tranſlation in Cotton. MS. Vitell. A. xv.]

It is from Alexander the Great to his preceptor Aristotle; and the Greek original was most probably drawn from some of the fabulous authors of Alexander's story.

There is a MS. containing *La Chartre que Prestre Jehan maunda a Fredewik l' Empereur de Mervailles de sa Terre*.[1] This was Frederic Barbarossa, emperor of Germany, or his successor, both of whom were celebrated for their many successful enterprises in the Holy Land before the year 1230. Prester John, a Christian, was emperor of India. I find another tract, *De Mirabilibus Terræ Sanctæ*.[2] A book of Sir John Mandeville, a famous traveller into the East about the year 1340, is under the title of *Mirabilia Mundi*.[3] His *Itinerary* might indeed have the same title.[4] [A copy of his famous book] in the Cotton Library is, "The Voiage and Travaile of Sir John Maundevile knight, which treateth of the way to Hierusaleme and of the *Marveyles of* Inde with other ilands and countryes;"[5] [but in the edition by Wynkyn de Worde in 1499 the title is somewhat more elaborate.][6] In the Cotton Library there is a piece with the title, *Sanctorum Loca, Mirabilia Mundi*, &c.[7] Afterwards the wonders of other countries were added : and when this sort of reading began to grow fashionable, Gyraldus Cambrensis composed his book *De Mirabilibus Hiberniæ*.[8] There is also another *De Mirabilibus Angliæ*,[9] [a very common MS., of which a copy is attached to Hearne's edition of *Robert of Gloucester*.] At length the superstitious

---

[1] MSS. Reg. 20, A xii. 3. And in Bibl. Bodl. MSS. Bodl. E 4. 3. "Literæ Joannis Presbiteri ad Fredericum Imperatorem," &c.

[2] MSS. Reg. 14, C xiii. 3.

[3] MSS. C. C. C. Cant. A iv. 69. We find *De Mirabilibus Mundi Liber*, MSS. Reg. 13, E ix. 5. And again, *De Mirabilibus Mundi et Viris illustribus Tractatus* 14, C vi. 3.

[4] His book is supposed to have been interpolated by the monks. Leland observes that Asia and Africa were parts of the world at this time, "Anglis de sola fere nominis umbra cognitas." *Script. Br.* p. 366. He wrote his *Itinerary* in French, English, and Latin. It extends to Cathay or China before mentioned. Leland says that he gave to Becket's shrine in Canterbury cathedral a glass globe enclosing an apple, which he probably brought from the East. Leland saw this curiosity, in which the apple remained fresh and undecayed. *Ubi supr.* Mandeville, on returning from his travels, gave to the high altar of St. Albans abbey church a sort of patera brought from Ægypt, [formerly] in the hands of an ingenious antiquary in London. He was a native of the town of St. Albans, and a physician. He says that he left many Mervayles unwritten, and refers the curious reader to [the] *Mappa Mundi*, chap. cviii, cix. A history of the Tartars became popular in Europe about the year 1310, written or dictated by Aiton, [kinsman to] a king of Armenia who, having traversed the most remarkable countries of the East, turned monk at Cyprus, and published his travels which, on account of the rank of the author, and his amazing adventures, gained great esteem. [A competent and critical edition of Sir John Mandeville's *Travels* is still a want. It has been long on the list of intended re-editions by the Early English Text Society.]

[5] [Printed in 1725, again in 1839, and thirdly in 1866.]

[6] [See *Handb. of E. E. Lit.* art. *Mandevile*.]   [7] Galb. A xxi. 3.

[8] It is printed among the *Scriptores Hist. Angl.* 1602, 692. Written about the year 1200. It was so favourite a title that we have even *De Mirabilibus Veteris et Novi Testamenti*. MSS. Coll. Æn. Nas. Oxon. Cod. 12, f. 190, a.

[9] Bibl. Bodl. MSS. C 6.

curiosity of the times was gratified with compilations under the comprehensive title of *Mirabilia Hiberniæ, Angliæ, et Orientis*.[1] But enough has been said of these infatuations. Yet the history of human credulity is a necessary speculation to those who trace the gradations of human knowledge. Let me add, that a spirit of rational enquiry into the topographical state of foreign countries, the parent of commerce and of a thousand improvements, took its rise from these visions.

[There is a French elegy on the death of Edward I. in 1307, written in the succeeding reign, and also an English version, which is supposed to be taken from it, as it is substantially identical. As the whole has been printed,[2] a specimen will probably be sufficient:]

> The messager to the pope com
>   And seyde that oure kynge was ded :[3]
> Ys dune hond the lettre he nom,
>   Y-wis his herte wes ful gret :
> The Pope himself the lettre redde,
>   And spec a word of gret honour.
> Alas, he seide, is Edward ded ?
>   Of Cristendome he ber the flour.
>
> The pope to is chaumbre wende
>   For del ne mihte he speke na more ;
> Ant after cardinals he sende
>   That muche couthen of Cristes lore.
> Both the lasse ant eke the more
>   Bed hem both rede ant synge :
> Gret deol me myhte se thore,
>   Many mon is honde wrynge.
>
> The pope of Peyters stod at is masse
>   With ful gret solempnete,
> Ther me cou the soule blesse :
>   Kyng Edward, honoured thou be :
> God leue thi sone come after the
>   Bringe to ende that thou hast bygonne,
> The holy crois y-mad of tre
>   So fain thou woldest hit han y-wonne, &c.[4]

---

[1] As in MSS. Reg. 13 D, i. 11. I must not forget that the *Polyhistor* of Julius Solinus appears in many MSS. under the title of Solinus *de Mirabilibus Mundi*. This was so favourite a book as to be translated into hexameters by some monk in the twelfth century, according to Voss. *Hist. Lat.* iii. p. 721.

[2] [Wright's *Political Songs*, 1839, 241-50.]

[3] He died in Scotland, July 7, 1307. The chronicles pretend that the Pope knew of his death the next day by a vision or some miraculous information. So Robert of Brunne, who recommends this tragical vent to those who "Singe and say in romance and ryme."—*Chron.* p. 340, edit. *u isupr.*:

> "The Pope the tother day wist it in tne court of Rome,
> The Pope on the morn bifor the clergi cam
> And tolde tham biforn, the floure of Cristendam
> Was ded and lay on bere, Edward of Ingeland.
> He said with hevy chere, in spirit he it fond."

He adds, that the Pope granted five years of pardon to those who would pray for his soul.

[4] MSS. Harl. 2253, f. 73. In [Mrs. Cooper's] *Muses Library*, 1737, there is an elegy on the death of Henry I., "wrote immediately after his death, the author

S. 2.   *Elegy on the Death of Edward I.*   105

That the Pope fhould here pronounce the funeral panegyric of Edward I. is by no means furprifing, if we confider the predominant ideas of the age. And in the true fpirit of thefe ideas, the poet makes this illuftrious monarch's achievements in the Holy Land his principal and leading topic. But there is a particular circumftance alluded to in thefe ftanzas, relating to the crufading character of Edward,[1] together with its confequences, which needs explanation. Edward, in the decline of life, had vowed a fecond expedition to Jerufalem; but finding his end approach, in his laft moments he devoted the prodigious fum of thirty thoufand pounds to provide one hundred and forty knights,[2] who fhould carry his heart into Paleftine. But this appointment of the dying king was never executed. Our elegift and the chroniclers impute the crime of withholding fo pious a legacy to the advice of the king of France, whofe daughter Ifabel was married to the fucceeding king. But it is more probable to fuppofe that Edward II. and his profligate minion Piers Gavefton diffipated the money in their luxurious and expenfive pleafures.

SECTION III.

E have feen, in the preceding fection, that the character of our poetical compofition began to be changed about the reign of the firft [or fecond] Edward: that either fictitious adventures were fubftituted by the minftrels in the place of hiftorical and traditionary facts, or reality difguifed by the mifreprefentations of invention; and that a tafte for ornamental and even exotic expreffion gradually prevailed over the rude fimplicity of the native Englifh phrafeology. This change, which with our language affected our poetry, had been growing for fome time, and among other caufes was occafioned by the introduction and increafe of the tales of chivalry.

The ideas of chivalry, in an imperfect degree, had been of old eftablifhed among the Gothic tribes. The fafhion of challenging to fingle combat, the pride of feeking dangerous adventures, and the

---

unknown," p. 4. [It has been remarked by Ritfon, that the elegy printed by Mrs. Cooper was the compofition of Fabyan the chronicler, who died in 1511: but then it is a tranflation from the original Latin, preferved by Knighton, of the twelfth century.—*Park*.]

[1] It appears that King Edward I. about the year 1271, took his harper with him to the Holy Land. This officer was a clofe and conftant attendant of his mafter: for when Edward was wounded with a poifoned knife at Ptolemais, the harper, *cithareda fuus*, hearing the ftruggle, rufhed into the royal apartment, and killed the affaffin. *Chron.* Hemingford, cap. xxxv. p. 591. (*V. Hiftor. Anglic. Scriptor.* vol. ii. 1687.) [After the king himfelf had flain the affaffin his harper had the fingular courage to brain a dead man with a trivet or *tripod*, for which act of heroifm he was juftly reprimanded by Edward.—*Ritfon*.]

[2] The poet fays eighty.

spirit of avenging and protecting the fair sex, seem to have been peculiar to the Northern nations in the most uncultivated state of Europe. All these customs were afterwards encouraged and confirmed by corresponding circumstances in the feudal constitution. At length the Crusades excited a new spirit of enterprise, and introduced into the courts and ceremonies of European princes a higher degree of splendour and parade, caught from the riches and magnificence of eastern cities.[1] These oriental expeditions established a taste for hyperbolical description, and propagated an infinity of marvellous tales, which men returning from distant countries easily imposed on credulous and ignorant minds. The unparalleled emulation with which the nations of Christendom universally embraced this holy cause, the pride with which emperors, kings, barons, earls, bishops, and knights, strove to excel each other on this interesting occasion, not only in prowess and heroism, but in sumptuous equipages, gorgeous banners, armorial cognisances, splendid pavilions, and other expensive articles of a similar nature, diffused a love of war and a fondness for military pomp. Hence their very diversions became warlike, and the martial enthusiasm of the times appeared in tilts and tournaments. These practices and opinions cooperated with the kindred superstitions of dragons,[2] dwarfs, fairies, giants, and enchanters, which the traditions of the Gothic scalds had already planted; and produced that extraordinary species of composition which has been called Romance.

Before these expeditions into the East became fashionable, the principal and leading subjects of the old fablers were the achievements of King Arthur with his knights of the round table, and of Charlemagne with his twelve peers. But in the romances written after the holy war, a new set of champions, of conquests and of countries were introduced. Trebizond took place of Roncevalles, and Godfrey of Bulloigne, Solyman, Nouraddin, the caliphs, the soldans, and the cities of Ægypt and Syria, became the favourite topics.[3] The

---

[1] I cannot help transcribing here a curious passage from old Fauchet. He is speaking of Louis the young king of France about the year 1150. "Le quel fut le premier roy de sa maison, qui monstra dehors ses richesses allant en Jerusalem. Aussi la France commença de son temps a s'embellir de bastimens plus magnifiques: prendre plaisir a pierrieres et autres delicatesses goustus en Levant par luy, ou les seigneurs qui avoient ja fait ce voyage. De sorte qu'on peut dire qu'il a este le premier tenant Cour de grand Roy: estant si magnifique, que sa femme, dedaignant la simplicité de ses predecesseurs, luy fit elever une sepulture d'argent, au lieu de pierre." *Recueil de la Lang. et Poes. Fr.* ch. viii. p. 76. edit. 1581. He adds, that a great number of French romances were composed about this period.

[2] See Kircher's *Mund. Subterran.* viii. § 4. He mentions a knight of Rhodes made grand master of the order for killing a dragon, 1345.

[3] [Though this passage has been the subject of severe animadversion, and characterized as containing nothing but " random assertion, falsehood and imposition," there are few of its positions which a more temperate spirit of criticism might not reconcile with the truth. The popularity of Arthur's story, anterior to the first Crusade, is abundantly manifested by the language of William of Malmesbury and Alanus de Insulis, who refer to it as a fable of common notoriety and general belief among the people. Had it arisen within their own days, we may be certain

troubadours of Provence, an idle and unsettled race of men, took up arms, and followed their barons in prodigious multitudes to the conquest of Jerusalem. They made a considerable part of the household of the nobility of France. Louis VII., king of France, not only entertained them at his court very liberally, but commanded a considerable company of them into his retinue, when he took ship for Palestine, that they might solace him with their songs during the dangers and inconveniences of so long a voyage.[1] The ancient chronicles of France mention *Legions de poetes* as embarking in this wonderful enterprise.[2] Here a new and more copious source of fabling was opened: in these expeditions they picked up numberless extravagant stories, and at their return enriched romance with an infinite variety of oriental scenes and fictions. Thus these later wonders in some measure supplanted the former: they had the recommendation of novelty, and gained still more attention, as they came from a greater distance.[3]

---

that Malmesbury, who rejected it as beneath the dignity of history, would not have suffered an objection so well founded as the novelty of its appearance to have escaped his censure; nor can the narrative of Alanus be reconciled with the general progress of traditionary faith—a plant of tardy growth—if we limit its first publicity to the period thus prescribed (1096-1142). With regard to Charlemagne and his peers, as their deeds were chaunted by Talliefer at the battle of Hastings (1066), it would be needless to offer further demonstrations of their early popularity; nor in fact does the accuracy of this part of Warton's statement appear to be called in question by the writer alluded to. It would be more difficult to define the degree in which these romances were superseded by similar poems on the achievements of the Crusaders; or, to use the more cautious language of the text, to state how far "Trebizond took place of Roncevalles." But it will be recollected that in consequence of the Crusades, the action of several romances was transferred to the Holy Land, such as Sir Bevis, Sir Guy, Sir Isumbras, the King of Tars, &c.: and that most of these were "favorite topics" in high esteem, is clear from the declaration of Chaucer, who catalogued them among the "romances of Pris." In short, if we omit the names of the caliphs, and confine ourselves to the Soldans—a generic name used by our early writers for every successive ruler of the East—and the cities of Egypt and Syria, this rhapsody, as it has been termed, will contain nothing which is not strictly demonstrable by historical evidence or the language of the old romancers. The Life of Godfrey of Boulogne was written in French verse by Gregory Bechada, about the year 1130. It is usually supposed to have perished; unless, indeed, it exist in a poem upon the same subject by Wolfram Von Eschenbach, who generally founded his romances upon a French or Provençal original.—*Price*.]

[1] Velley, *Hist. Fr.* sub an. 1178.

[2] Massieu, *Hist. Poes. Fr.* p. 105. Many of the troubadours, whose works now exist, and whose names are recorded, accompanied their lords to the holy war. Some of the French nobility of the first rank were troubadours about the eleventh century: and the French critics with much triumph observe, that it is the glory of the French poetry to number counts and dukes, that is sovereigns, among its professors, from its commencement. What a glory! The worshipfull company of Merchant-taylors in London, if I recollect right, boast the names of many dukes, earls, and princes, enrolled in their community. [Herbert's *Hist. of the 12 Livery-Companies*, ii. 384.] This is indeed an honour to that otherwise respectable society. But poets can derive no lustre from counts and dukes, or even princes, who have been enrolled in their lists; only in proportion as they have adorned the art by the excellence of their compositions.

[3] The old French historian Mezeray goes so far as to derive the origin of the French poetry and romances from the Crusades. *Hist.* pp. 416, 417. Geoffrey Vine-

In the mean time we should recollect that the Saracens or Arabians, the same people which were the object of the Crusades, had acquired an establishment in Spain about the ninth century: and that by means of this earlier intercourse many of their fictions and fables, together with their literature, must have been known in Europe before the Christian armies invaded Asia. It is for this reason the elder Spanish romances have professedly more Arabian allusions than any other. Cervantes makes the imagined writer of Don Quixote's history an Arabian. Yet, exclusively of their domestic and more immediate connection with this eastern people, the Spaniards from temper and constitution were extravagantly fond of chivalrous exercises. Some critics have supposed that Spain, having learned the art or fashion of romance-writing from their naturalised guests the Arabians, communicated it, at an early period, to the rest of Europe.[1]

It has been imagined that the first romances were composed in metre, and sung to the harp by the poets of Provence at festive solemnities: but an ingenious Frenchman, who has made deep researches into this sort of literature, attempts to prove that this mode of reciting romantic adventures was in high reputation among the natives of Normandy above a century before the troubadours of Provence, who are generally supposed to have led the way to the poets of Italy, Spain and France, and that it commenced about the year 1162.[2] If the critic means to insinuate, that the French troubadours acquired their art of versifying from these Norman bards, this reasoning will favour the system of those who contend that metrical romances lineally took their rise from the historical odes of the Scandinavian scalds; for the Normans were a branch of the Scandinavian stock. But Fauchet, at the same time that he allows the Normans to have been fond of chanting the praises of their heroes in verse, expressly pronounces that they borrowed this practice from the Franks or French.[3]

---

sauf says, that when King Richard I. arrived at the Christian camp before Ptolemais, he was received with *populares Cantiones*, which recited *Antiquorum Præclara Gesta. It. Hierosol.* cap. ii. p. 332, *ibid.*

[1] Huet in some measure adopts this opinion. But that learned man was a very incompetent judge of these matters. Under the common term Romance, he confounds romances of chivalry, romances of gallantry, and all the fables of the Provençal poets. What can we think of a writer who, having touched upon the gothic romances, at whose fictions and barbarisms he is much shocked, talks of the consummate degree of art and elegance to which the French are at present arrived in romances? He adds, that the superior refinement and politesse of the French gallantry has happily given them an advantage of shining in this species of composition. *Hist. Rom.* p. 138. But the sophistry and ignorance of Huet's Treatise has been already detected and exposed by a critic of another cast in the *Supplement to Jarvis's Preface*, prefixed to the Translation of *Don Quixote*.

[2] Mons. L'Eveque de la Ravaliere, in his *Revolutions de la Langue Françoise, à la suite des Poesies du Roi de Navarre.* [2 vols. 12mo., Paris, 1743.]

[3] " Ce que les Normans avoyent pris des François." *Rec.* liv. i. p. 70. edit. 1581. [Mr. Wright very properly animadverts on the temerity of seeking the origin of romance in any one source, or of tracing the progress of romance from one people to another, and illustrates his position by pointing out that, while there

William, Bishop of Ely.

It is not my business, nor is it of much consequence, to discuss this obscure point, which properly belongs to the French antiquaries. I therefore proceed to observe, that [William Bishop of Ely, chancellor to] our Richard I., who [was] a distinguished hero of the Crusades, a most magnificent patron of chivalry, and a Provençal poet,[1] invited to his [master's] court many minstrels or troubadours from France, whom he loaded with honours and rewards.[2] These

---

is no nation which has not probably borrowed some of its romantic literature from other nations, there is also none which has not a certain share of home-grown romance. He thinks that the Teutonic tribes possessed many of the *fabliaux*, before they were known to Western Europe.]

[1] See *Observations on Spenser*, i. § i. pp. 28, 29. And Mr. Walpole's *Royal and Noble Authors*, i. 5. See also Rymer's *Short View of Tragedy*, ch. vii. p. 73. [Guilhem le Breton,] one of the Provençal poets, said of Richard:—
"Coblas a teira faire adroitement
Pou voz oillez enten dompna gentiltz."
"He could make stanzas on the eyes of gentle ladies." Rymer, *ibid*. p. 74. There is a curious [but most probably apocryphal] story recorded by the French chroniclers concerning Richard's skill in the minstrel art. [Here, in all the editions, follows the absurd story of Blondel, which is not worth repeating, especially as it is to be found in so many books. It may, however, be worth while to refer the reader to M. de la Rue, *Essais sur les Jougleurs*, ii. 325-9, where Guillaume Blondel, an Anglo-Norman, is said to have been the real Blondel, and to have been rewarded with estates, which were restored to his descendant by Henry III.—Mr. Thoms' inform.] See also Fauchet, *Rec*. p. 93. Richard lived long in Provence, where he acquired a taste for their poetry.

[There is too much reason to believe the story of Blondel and his illustrious patron to be purely apocryphal. The poem published by Walpole is written in the Provençal language, and a Norman version of it is given by M. Sismondi, in his *Literature du Midi*, vol. i. p. 149. In which of these languages it was originally composed remains a matter of dispute among the French antiquaries.—*Price*.]

[2] "De regno Francorum cantores et joculatores muneribus allexerat." *Rog. Hoved*. Ric. i. p. 340. These gratuities were chiefly arms, clothes, horses, and sometimes money.

It appears to have been William bishop of Ely, chancellor to Richard I. who thus invited minstrels from France, whom he loaded with favours and presents to sing his praises in the streets. This passage is in a letter of Hugh bishop of Coventry, which see also in Hearne's *Benedictus Abbas*, vol. ii. p. 704, *sub ann*. 1191. It appears from this letter, that he was totally ignorant of the English language, *ibid*. p. 708. By his cotemporary Gyraldus Cambrensis he is represented as a monster of injustice, impiety, intemperance, and lust. Gyraldus has left these anecdotes of his character, which shew the scandalous grossness of the times. "Sed taceo quod ruminare solet, nunc clamitat Anglia tota, qualiter puella, matris industria tam coma quam cultu puerum professa, simulansque virum verbis et vultu, ad cubiculum belluæ istius est perducta. Sed statim ut exosi illius sexus est inventa, quanquam in se pulcherrima, thalamique thorique deliciis valde idonea, repudiata tamen est et abjecta. Unde et in crastino, matri filia, tam flagitiosi facinoris conscia, cum Petitionis effectu, terrisque non modicis eandem jure hæreditario contingentibus, virgo, ut venerat, est restituta. Tantæ nimirum intemperantiæ, et petulantiæ fuerat tam immoderatæ, quod quotidie in prandio circa finem, pretiosis tam potionibus quam cibariis ventre distento, virga aliquantulum longa in capite aculeum præferente pueros nobiles ad mensam ministrantes, eique propter multimodam qua fungebatur potestatem in omnibus ad nutum obsequentes, pungere vicissim consueverit: ut eo indicio, quasi signo quodam secretiore, quem fortius, inter alios, atque frequentius sic quasi ludicro pungebat," &c. &c. *De Vit. Galfrid. Archiepiscop. Ebor*. apud Whart. *Angl.*

poets imported into England a great multitude of their tales and songs; which before or about the reign of Edward II. became familiar and popular among our ancestors, who were sufficiently acquainted with the French language. The most early notice of a professed book of chivalry in England, as it should seem, appears under the reign of Henry III., and is a curious and evident proof of the reputation and esteem in which this sort of composition was held at that period. In the revenue roll of the twenty-first year of that king, there is an

---

Sacr. vol. ii. p. 406. But Wharton endeavours to prove, that the character of this great prelate and statesman in many particulars had been misrepresented through prejudice and envy. *Ibid.* vol. i. p. 632.

[Two metrical reliques by Richard I. were first printed in *La Tour ténébreuse*, &c. 1705. The first of these, in mixed *Romance* and Provençal, professes to be the veritable *chanson* of Blondel; the other is a love-song in Norman French. The sonnet cited by Mr. Walpole was exhibited with an English version in Dr. Burney's *History of Music*, but has since received a more graceful illustration from the pen of Mr. George Ellis, in the last edition of *Royal and Noble Authors.*—*Park.* The whole has been published by M. Raynouard, in the fourth volume of his *Choix des Poesies originales des Troubadours*, a volume which had not reached me when the note, to which this is a supplement, was sent to the press. Another poem by Richard I. will be found in the *Parnasse Occitanien*, Toulouse, 1819, a publication from which the following remark has been thought worth extracting: " Crescimbeni avait dit qu'il existait des poesies du roi Richard dans le manuscrit 3204; et la-dessus Horace Walpole le taxe d'inexactitude. Cependant le sirvente se trouve au fol. 170, Ro. et 171 Ro. C'est donc l'Anglois qui se trompe en disant : there is no work of King Richard."—*Price*. Mr. Thoms adds, that there may be some foundation for the statement in the preface to *La Tour Tenebreuse*, that the basis of the work was a MS. communicated by the then possessor, and called *Chronique et Fabliaux de la composition de Richard Roy d'Angleterre recueillis tot a nouvel et conjoints ensemblement, par le labour de Jean de Sorels l'an* 1308. These fabliaux are the two which Richard is alleged to have written during his imprisonment in La Tour Tenebreuse.]

It seems the French minstrels, with whom the Song of Roland originated, were famous about this period. Muratori cites an old history of Bologna, under the year 1288, by which it appears that they swarmed in the streets of Italy. " Ut Cantatores Francigenarum in plateis comunis ad cantandum morari non possent." On which words he observes, " Colle quale parole sembra verisimile, che sieno disegnati i cantatori del favole romanze, che spezialmente della Franzia erano portate in Italia." *Dissert. Antichit. Ital.* tom. ii. c. xxix. p. 16. He adds, that the minstrels were so numerous in France as to become a pest to the community, and that an edict was issued, about the year 1200, to suppress them in that kingdom. Muratori, in further proof of this point, quotes the above passage from Hoveden, which he [also] misapplies to our Richard I. But, in either sense, it equally suits his argument. In the year 1334, at a feast on Easter Sunday, celebrated at Rimini, on occasion of some noble Italians receiving the honour of knighthood, more than one thousand five hundred histriones are said to have attended. " Triumphus quidem maximus fuit ibidem, &c.—Fuit etiam multitudo Histrionum circa mille quingentos et ultra." *Annal. Cæsenat.* tom. xiv. *Rer. Italic. Scriptor.* col. 1141. But their countries are not specified. In the year 1227, at a feast in the palace of the archbishop of Genoa, a sumptuous banquet and vestments without number were given to the minstrels or Joculatores then present, who came from Lombardy, Provence, Tuscany, and other countries. Caffari *Annal. Genuens.* lib. vi. p. 449, D. *apud* tom. vi. *ut supr.* In the year 774, when Charlemagne entered Italy and found his passage impeded, he was met by a minstrel of Lombardy, whose song promised him success and victory. " Contigit Joculatorem ex Longobardorum gente ad Carolum venire, et Cantiunculam a se compositam, rotando in conspectu suorum, cantare." Tom. ii. p. 2, ut supr. *Chron. Monast. Noval.* lib. iii. cap. x. p. 717, D.

entry of the expense of silver clasps and studs for the king's great book of romances. This was in the year 1237. But I will give the article in its original dress: "Et in firmaculis hapsis et clavis argenteis ad magnum librum Romancis regis."[1] That this superb volume was in French, may be partly collected from the title which they gave it: and it is highly probable that it contained [some of the *Round Table* romances or the *Brut*. An earlier instance may be pointed out in the Close Rolls of King John, in 1205, where Reginald Cornhille is ordered to send to the king *Romancium de Historia Angliæ*.*q*] The victorious achievements of Richard I. were so famous in the reign of Henry III. as to be made the subject of a picture in the royal palace of Clarendon near Salisbury. A circumstance which likewise appears from the same ancient record, under the year 1246: "Et in camera regis subtus capellam regis apud Clarendon lambruscanda, et muro ex transverso illius cameræ amovendo et hystoria Antiochiæ in eadem depingenda cum duello regis Ricardi."[3] To these anecdotes we may add that in the Royal library at Paris there is, *Lancelot du Lac mis en François par [Walter Mapes,] du commandement d'Henri roi de Angleterre avec figures*;[4] and the same MS. occurs twice again in that library in three and in four volumes of the largest folio.[5] Which of our Henries it was who thus commanded the romance of *Lancelot au Lac* to be translated [out of Latin, as is pretended,] into French, is indeed uncertain: but most probably it was Henry [II.][6]

---

[1] *Rot. Pip. an.* 21, *Hen. III.* [Although Warton has himself stated frequently enough that the word *romance* in early writers need mean nothing but French, yet he is continually arguing on the supposition that it must mean romance in our present acceptation of the term. The above-mentioned book was not necessarily a book of romances. However, the following entry in the Close Roll of the 34th of the same reign (March 17) may refer to the same book, in which case it would seem to countenance Warton's supposition:—"De quodam libro liberato ad opus regine. Mandatum est fratri R. de Sanforde, magistro milicie Templi in Anglia, quod faciat habere Henrico de Warderoba, latori presencium, ad opus Regine, quendam librum magnum, qui est in domo sua Londoniis, Gallico ydiomate scriptum, in quo continentur Gesta Antiochie et regum et etiam aliorum." Teste ut supra.—*Wright.*]
[2] [Sir F. Madden's correction. It by no means follows that the contents of this book were romances of chivalry. Any collection of French pieces, especially in verse, would at this time be called romances; and this from the language, not the subject.—*Douce.*]
[3] *Rot. Pip. an.* 36, *Henr. III.* Richard I. performed great feats at the siege of Antioch in the Crusade. The Duellum was another of his exploits among the Saracens. Compare Walpole's *Anecd. Paint.* i. 10. Who mentions [the *Gesta Antiochiæ* above referred to]. He adds, that there was a chamber in the old palace of Westminster painted with this history in the reign of Henry III., and therefore called the Antioch Chamber: and another in the Tower.
[4] Cod. 6783, fol. max. See Montfauc. *Cat. MSS.* p. 785 a.
[5] The old *Guiron le Courtois* is said to be translated by "Luce chevalier seigneur du chasteau du Gal, [perhaps Sal., an abbreviation for Salisberi,] voisin prochain du Sablieres, par le commandement de tres noble et tres puissant prince M. le roy Henry jadis roy d'Angleterre."—*Bibl. Reg. Paris. Cod.* 7526.
[6] [With regard to the period when the prose romances of the *Round Table* were compiled, and whether by order of King Henry II. or III., has long been a subject of discussion; but the writers on it have generally been too little acquainted with the subject to attempt to draw any certain or reasonable conclusions. A recent

From an ingenious correspondent, who has not given me the honour of his name, and who appears to be well acquainted with the manners and literature of Spain, I have received the following notices relating to the Spanish Trovadores, of which other particulars may be seen in the old French history of Languedoc. "At the end of the second volume of Mayan's *Origines de la Lingua Espanola*, 1737, is an extract from a MS. entitled, *Libro de la Arte de Trovar, ò Gaya Sciencia, por Don Enrique de Villena*, said to exist in the library of the cathedral of Toledo, and perhaps to be found in other libraries of Spain. It has these particulars. The Trovadores had their origin at Toulouse, about the middle of the twelfth century. A Consistorio de la Gaya Sciencia was there founded by Ramon Vidal de Besalin, containing more than one hundred and twenty celebrated poets, and among these, princes, kings, and emperors. Their art was extended throughout Europe, and gave rise to the Italian and Spanish poetry, *servio el Garona de Hippocrene*. To Ramon Vidal de Besalin succeeded Jofre de Foxa, Monge negro, who enlarged the plan, and wrote what he called *Continuacion de trovar*. After him Belenguer de Troya came from Majorca, and compiled a treatise *de Figuras y Colores Rhetoricos*. And next Gul. Vedal of Majorca wrote *La Suma Vitulina*. To support the Gaya Sciencia at the poetical college of Toulouse, the King of France appropriated privileges and revenues: appointing seven Mantenedores, *que liciessen Leyes*. These constituted the Laws of Love, which were afterwards abridged by Guill. Moluier under the title *Tratado de las Flores*. Next Fray Ramon framed a system called Doctrinal, which was censured by Castilnon. From thence nothing was written in Spanish on the subject till the time of Don Enrique de Villena. So great was the credit of the Gay Science, that Don Juan, the first king of Arragon, who died 1393, sent an embassy to the king of France requesting that some Troubadours might be transmitted to teach this art in his kingdom. Accordingly two Mantenedores were dispatched from Toulouse, who founded a college for poetry in Barcelona, consisting of four Mantenedores, a cavalier, a master in theology, a master in laws, and an honourable citizen. Disputes about Don Juan's successor occasioned the removal of the college to Tortosa. But Don Ferdinand being elected king, Don Enrique de Villena was taken into his service; who restored the college, and was chosen principal. The subjects he proposed were sometimes the Praises of the Holy Virgin, of Arms, of Love, *y de buenas Costumbres*. An account of the ceremonies of their public acts then follows, in which

---

writer, however, M. Paulin Paris, in his account of the French MSS. preserved in the Bibliothèque du Roi, 8vo. Par. 1836, more critically considered the history of these remarkable compositions, and has produced a passage from the Chronicle of Helinand, (who brings down his work to the year 1204, and died in 1227,) which proves satisfactorily that the prose romance of the *Saint Graal* was composed in the twelfth century, a fact confirmed by the lines quoted by Warton from Fauchet. Now as Robert de Borron, who composed the *Saint Graal*, wrote also the romance of *Merlin* and the first part of *Lancelot*, we must necessarily refer the period of their composition to the reign of Henry II.—*M*.]

every compofition was recited, being written 'en papeles Damafquinos dediverfos colores, con letras de oro y de platau, et illuminaduras formofas, lo major qua cada una podio.' The beft performance had a crown of gold placed upon it; and the author, being prefented with a *joya* or prize, received a licence to *cantar y decir in publico*. He was afterwards conducted home in form, efcorted among others by two Mantenedores, and preceded by minftrels and trumpets, where he gave an entertainment of confects and wine."

There feems to have been a fimilar eftablifhment at Amfterdam, called Rhederiicker camer, or the Chamber of Rhetoricians, mentioned by Ifaacus Pontanus, who adds, "Sunt autem hi rhetores viri amœni et poetici fpiritus, qui lingua vernacula, aut profa aut verfa oratione, comœdias, tragœdias, fubindeque et mutas perfonas, et facta maiorum notantes, magna fpectantium voluptate exhibent."[1] In the preceding chapter, he fays that this fraternity of rhetoricians erected a temporary theatre at the folemn entry of Prince Maurice into Amfterdam in 1594, where they exhibited in dumb fhow the hiftory of David and Goliah.[2] Meteranus, in his Belgic hiftory, fpeaks largely of the annual prizes, affemblies, and contefts of the guilds or colleges of the rhetoricians in Holland and the Low Countries. They anfwered in rhyme queftions propofed by the Dukes of Burgundy and Brabant. At Ghent, in 1539, twenty of thefe colleges met with great pomp, to difcufs an ethical queftion, and each gave a folution in a moral comedy, magnificently prefented in the public theatre. In 1561, the rhetorical guild of Antwerp, called the Violet, challenged all the neighbouring cities to a decifion of the fame fort. On this occafion, three hundred and forty rhetoricians of Bruffels appeared on horfeback, richly but fantaftically habited, accompanied with an infinite variety of pageantries, fports and fhows. Thefe had a garland, as a reward for the fuperior fplendour of their entry. Many days were fpent in determining the grand queftions: during which there were feaftings, bonfires, farces, tumbling, and every popular diverfion.[3]

In Benet College Library at Cambridge, there is [part of] an Englifh poem on the Sangreal and [Merlin], containing forty thoufand verfes.[4] The MS. is imperfect both at the beginning and at the end.

---

[1] *Rer. et Urb. Amft.* lib. ii. c. xvi. p. 118, ed. 1611, fol.
[2] *Ibid.* c. xv. p. 117.
[3] *Belg. Hiftor. Vniverfal.* fol. 1597, lib. i. pp. 31, 32.
[4 MS. lxxx. Edited by F. J. Furnivall for the Roxburghe Club, 1862-6, 2 vols. The reader, who is defirous of forming more correct opinions upon the fubject, is referred to M. Raynouard's *Poefies des Troubadours* (*Lexique Roman*, 1838, i.) a work which has done more towards forming a juft underftanding of the merits of Provençal poetry, and the extent and value of Provençal literature, than any publication which has hitherto appeared. The mafs of evidence there adduced in favour of the early efforts of the Provençal mufe muft effectually filence every theory attempting to confine fong and romantic fiction to any particular age or country.—*Price.* Mr. R. Taylor alfo refers us to M. Rochegude's *Parnaffe Occitanien*, 1819, Mr. E. Taylor's *Lays of the Minnefingers*, 1825, and to De la Rue's *Hift. of Northern French Poetry.*]

The title at the head of the firſt page is *Acta Arthuri Regis*, written probably by Joceline, chaplain and ſecretary to Archbiſhop Parker. The narrative, which appears to be on one continued ſubject, is divided into books or ſections of unequal length. It is a tranſlation made from Robert [de] Borron's French romance[s of the *Saint Graal* and *Merlin*] by Henry Lonelich, Skinner, a name which I never remember to have ſeen among thoſe of the Engliſh poets. The diction is of the age of Henry VI. Borel, in his *Treſor de Recherches et Antiquitez Gauloiſes et Francoiſes*, ſays, "Il y'a un Roman ancien intitule le Conqueſte de Sangreall," &c. [In the recent edition of the *Saint Graal*] Robert [de] Borron's French [proſe] romance [is printed in parallel columns with Lonelich's tranſlation]. The diligence and accuracy of Mr. Naſmith have furniſhed me with the following tranſcript from Lonelich's tranſlation in Benet College Library:—

> Thanne paſſeth forth this ſtorye with al,
> That is cleped of ſom men Seynt Graal;
> Alſo the Sank Ryal iclepid it is
> Of mochel peple with owten mys.
>
> . . . . .
>
> Now of al this ſtorie have I mad an ende
> That is ſchwede of Celidoygne, and now forthere to wend,
> And of anothir brawnche moſt we begynne,
> Of the ſtorye that we clepen prophet Merlynne,
> Wiche that Maiſter Robert of Borrown
> Owt of Latyn it tranſletted hol and ſoun;
> Onlich into the langage of Frawnce
> This ſtorie he drowgh be adventure and chaunce;
> And doth Merlynne inſten with Sank Ryal,
> For the ton ſtorie the tothir medlyth withal,
> After the ſatting of the forſeid Robert
> That ſomtym is tranſletted in Middilerd.
> And I, as an unkonneng man trewely,
> Into Engliſch have drawen this ſtorye;
> And thowgh that to ȝow not pleſyng it be,
> Ȝit that ful excuſed ȝe wolde haven me
> Of my neclegence and unkonnenge,
> On me to taken ſwich a thinge,
> Into owre modris tonge for to endite,
> The ſwettere to ſowne to more and lyte,
> And more cler to ȝoure undirſtondyng
> Thanne owthir Frenſh other Latyn to my ſuppoſing.
> And therfore atte the ende of this ſtorye
> A pater noſter ȝe wolden for me preye,
> For me that Herry Lonelich hyhte;
> And greteth owre lady ful of myhte.
> Hartelich with an ave that ȝe hir bede,
> This proceſſe the bettere I myhte procede,
> And bringen this book to a good ende:
> Now thereto Jeſu Criſt grace me ſende,
> And than an ende there offen myhte be,
> Now good Lord graunt me for charite.
>
> . . . . .
>
> Thanne Merlyn to Blaſye cam anon,
> And there to hym he ſeide thus ſon:
> "Blaſye, thou ſchalt ſuffren gret peyne

> This ſtorye to an ende to bringen certeyne;
> And ʒit ſchall I ſuffren mochel more."
> How ſo, Merlyn, quod Blaſye there.
> " I ſhall be ſowht," quod Merlyne tho,
> " Owt from the weſt with meſſengeris mo,
> And they that ſcholen comen to ſeken me,
> They have maad ſewrawnce, I telle the,
> Me forto ſlen for any thing,
> This ſewrawnce hav they mad to her kyng.
> But whanne they me ſen, and with me ſpeke,
> No power they ſchol hav on me to ben awreke,
> For with hem hens moſte I gon,
> And thou into othir partyes ſchalt wel ſon,
> To hem that hav the holy veſſel
> Which that is icleped the Seynt Graal;
> And wete thow wel and ek forſothe,
> That thow and ek this ſtorye bothe
> Ful wel beherd now ſchall it be,
> And alſo beloved in many contre;
> And has that will knowen in ſertaygne
> What kynges that weren in grete Bretaygne
> Sithan that Chriſtendom thedyr was browht,
> They ſcholen hem fynde has ſo that it ſawht
> In the ſtorye of Brwttes book;
> There ſcholen ʒe it fynde and ʒe weten look,
> Which that Martyn de Bewre tranſlated here
> From Latyn into Romaunce in his manere.
> But leve me now of Brwttes book,
> And aftyr this ſtorye now lete us look.

After this latter extract, which is to be found nearly in the middle of the MS., [the romance of *Merlin* begins, and] the ſcene and perſonages of the poem are changed; and King Evalach, King Mordreins, Sir Naſciens, Joſeph of Arimathea, and the other heroes of the former part, give place to King Arthur, King Brangors, King Loth, and the monarchs and champions of the Britiſh line. In a paragraph, very ſimilar to the ſecond of theſe extracts, the following note is written in the hand of the text, " Henry Lonelich, Skynner, that tranſlated this boke out of Frenſhe into Englyſhe, at the inſtaunce of Harry Barton."

The *Queſt of the Sangreal*, as it is called, in which devotion and necromancy are equally concerned, makes a conſiderable part of King Arthur's romantic hiſtory, and was one grand object of the knights of the Round Table. He who achieved this hazardous adventure was to be placed there in the " ſiege perillous," or ſeat of danger. " When Merlyn had ordayned the rounde table, he ſaid, by them that be fellowes of the rounde table the truthe of the Sangreall ſhall be well knowne, &c.—They which heard Merlyn ſay ſoe, ſaid thus to Merlyn, Sithence there ſhall be ſuch a knight, thou ſhouldeſt ordayne by thy craft a ſiege that no man ſhould ſitte therein, but he onlie which ſhall paſſe all other knights.—Then Merlyn made the ſiege perillous," &c.[1] Sir Lancelot, "who is come but of the eighth degree from our Lord Jeſus Chriſt," is repreſented as the chief adventurer in this honourable expedition.[2] At a celebration of the

---

[1] [Malory's] *Mort d'Arthur*, B. xiv. c. 2. [2] *Ibid.* B. iii. c. 35.

feast of Pentecost at Camelot by King Arthur, the Sangreal suddenly enters the hall, "but there was no man might see it nor who bare it," and the knights, as by some invisible power, are instantly supplied with a feast of the choicest dishes.¹ Originally *Le Brut, Lancelot, Tristan,* and the *Saint Greal* were separate histories; but they were [subsequently brought into a certain degree of connection—perhaps at a very early date, and some confusion may also have arisen from the carelessness or ignorance of copyists]. The book of the *Sangreal,* a separate work, is referred to in *Morte Arthur.* "Now after that the quest of the *Sancgreall* was fulfylled, and that all the knyghtes that were lefte alive were come agayne to the Rounde Table, as the booke of the Sancgreall makethe mencion, than was there grete joye in the courte. And especiallie King Arthur and quene Guenever made grete joye of the remnaunt that were come home. And passynge glad was the kinge and quene of syr Launcelot and syr Bors, for they had been passynge longe awaye in the quest of the Sancgreall. Then, as the Frenshe booke sayeth, syr Lancelot," &c.² And again, in the same romance: "Whan syr Bors had tolde him [Arthur] of the adventures of the Sancgreall, such as had befallen hym and his felawes,—all this was made in grete bookes, and put in almeryes at Salisbury."³ The former part of this passage is almost literally translated from one in the French romance of *Tristan.*⁴ "Quant Boort ot conte laventure del Saint Graal teles com eles estoient avenues, eles furent mises en escrit, gardees en lamere de Salisbieres, *dont Mestre Galtier Map l'estrest a faist son livre du Saint Graal por lamor du roy Herri son sengor, qui fist lestoire tralater del Latin en romanz.*"⁵ In the Royal Library at Paris there is *Le Roman de Tristan et Iseult, traduit de Latin en François, par Lucas, Chevalier du Gast pres de Sarisberi, Anglois, avec figures.*⁶ And again,⁷ *Liveres de Tristan mis en François par Lucas chevalier sieur de chateau du Gat.*⁸ *Almeryes* in the English, and *l'Amere,* properly *aumoire* in the French, mean, I believe, *Presses, Chests,* or *Archives. Ambry,* in this sense, is not an uncommon old English word. From the second part of the first

---

¹ [Malory's] *Mort d'Arthur,* B. iii. c. 35. ² B. xviii. cap. 1.
³ B. xvii. c. 23. The romance says that King Arthur "made grete clerkes com before him that they should cronicle the adventures of these goode knygtes." [See *infra,* Section xi.]
⁴ Bibl. Reg. MSS. 20 D. ii. fol. antep.
⁵ See *infra,* sect. xxviii. note. [No doubt the "chastel de Gast prés de Salisberi" is referred to here as well as in the next paragraph; it appears to have been in the canton of St. Severe, in the department of Calvados.—De la Rue, *Essais sur les Bardes,* &c., vol. ii. p. 231, quoted by Sir F. Madden. See especially M. Paulin Paris's introduction to his *Romans de la Table Ronde mis en nouveau Langage,* Paris, 1868.—F.]
⁶ Montfauc. Catal. MSS. Cod. Reg. Paris, Cod. 6776, fol. max.
⁷ Cod. 6956, fol. max.
⁸ There is printed, *Le Roman du noble et vaillant Chevalier Tristan fils du noble roy Meliadus de Leonnoys, par Luce, chevalier, seigneur du chasteau de Gast.* Rouen, 1489, fol. [But see Brunet, *dern.* edit. v. 955. All the poems relating to this hero were collected by M. Michel, 3 vols. 12mo.]

French quotation which I have distinguished by italics, it appears that Walter Mapes,[1] a learned archdeacon in England, under the reign of Henry II., wrote a French *Sangreal*, which he translated from Latin, by the command of that monarch. Under the idea that Walter Mapes was a writer on this subject, and in the fabulous way, some critics may be induced to think, that the Walter, Archdeacon of Oxford, from whom Geoffrey of Monmouth professes to have received the materials of his history, was this Walter Mapes, and not Walter Calenius, who was also an eminent scholar, and an archdeacon of Oxford. Geoffrey says in his Dedication to Robert Earl of Gloucester, "Finding nothing said in Bede or Gildas of King Arthur and his successors, although their actions highly deserved to be recorded in writing, and are orally celebrated by the British bards, I was much surprised at so strange an omission. At length Walter, archdeacon of Oxford, a man of great eloquence, and learned in foreign histories, offered me an ancient book in the British or Armorican tongue which, in one unbroken story and an elegant diction, related the deeds of the British kings from Brutus to Cadwallader. At his request, although unused to rhetorical flourishes, and contented with the simplicity of my own plain language, I undertook the translation of that book into Latin."[2] Some writers suppose that Geoffrey pretended to have received his materials from Archdeacon Walter, by way of authenticating his romantic history. These notices seem to disprove that suspicion. In the year 1488, a French romance was published, in two magnificent folio volumes, entitled *Histoire de Roy Artus et des Chevaliers de la Table Ronde*. The first volume was printed at Rouen, the second at Paris. It contains in four detached parts the Birth and Achievements of King Arthur, the Life of Sir Launcelot, the Adventure of the Sangreal, and the Death of Arthur and his Knights. In the body of the work, this romance more than once is said to be written by Walter Map or Mapes, and by the command of his master King Henry. For instance:[3] "Cy fine Maistre Gualtier Map son traittie du Saint Graal." Again:[4] "Apres ce que Maistre Gualtier Map eut tractie des avantures du Saint Graal assez soufisamment, sicomme il luy sembloit, il fut ad adviz au roy Henry son seigneur, que ce quil avoit fait ne debuit soufrire sil ne racontoys la fin de ceulx dont il fait mention.—Et commence Maistre Gualtier en telle manier ceste derniere partie." This derniere partie treats of the death of King Arthur and his knights. At the end of the second tome there is this colophon: "Cy fine le dernier volume de La Table Ronde,

---

[1] [From a passage in the French romance of *Lancelot du Lac*, M. Roquefort is of opinion that there were two persons of this name. In that he is styled "messire Gautier Map qui fut chevalier le roi." But so much confusion prevails upon this subject, that it is almost impossible to name the author of any prose romance.—*Price*.]

[2] B. i. ch. i. See also B. xii. ch. xx.
[3] Tom. ii. sign. Dd i. end of *Partie du Saint Graal*.
[4] Tom. ii. ch. i. sign. D d ii. (*La derniere partie*).

faisant mencion des fais et proesses de monseigneur Launcelot du Lac et dautres plusieurs nobles et vaillans hommes ses compagnons. Compile et extraict precisement et au juste des vrayes histoires faisantes de ce mencion par tresnotable et tresexpert historien Maistre Gualtier Map," &c. The passage quoted above from the royal MS. in the British Museum, where King Arthur orders the adventures of the Sangreal to be chronicled, is thus represented in this romance: " Et quant Boort eut compte depuis le commencement jusques a la fin les avantures du Saint Graal telles comme il les avoit veues, &c. Si fist le roy Artus rediger et mettre par escript aus dictz clers tout ci que Boort avoit compte," &c.[1] At the end of the royal MS. at Paris,[2] entitled *Lancelot du Lac mis en François par Robert de Borron par le commandement de Henri roi d'Angleterre*, it is said that Messire Robert de Borron translated into French not only Lancelot, but also the story of the *Saint Graal:* " Li tout du Latin du *Gautier Mappe.*" The French antiquaries in this sort of literature are of opinion that the word Latin here signifies Italian, and that by this Latin of Gualtier Mapes we are to understand English versions of those romances made from the Italian language; [but such a notion seems scarcely deserving of serious discussion.] The French history of the *Sangreal*, printed at Paris in 1516, is said in the title to be translated from Latin into French rhymes, and from thence into French prose by Robert [de] Borron. This romance was reprinted in 1523.

[Malory's] *Morte Arthur*, finished in the year 1469, [is an abstract of certain old French Arthur romances.][3] But the matter of the whole is so much of the same sort, and the heroes and adventures of one story are so mutually and perpetually blended with those of another, that no real unity or distinction is preserved. It consists of twenty-one books. The first seven books treat of King Arthur. The eighth, ninth, and tenth, of Sir Tristram. The eleventh and twelfth, of Sir Lancelot.[4] The thirteenth of the Saingral, which is also called Sir Lancelot's book. The fourteenth, of Sir Percival. The fifteenth, again, of Sir Launcelot. The sixteenth, of Sir Gawaine. The seventeenth, of Sir Galahad. [But all the four last-mentioned books are also called the *historye of the holy Sancgreall.*] The eighteenth and nineteenth, of miscellaneous adventures. The two last, of

---

[1] Ibid. tom. ii. La Partie du Saint Graal, ch. *ult.* Just before it is said, " Le roy Artus fist venir les clercs qui les aventures aux chevallieres mettoient en escript" —as in *Mort d'Arthur.*

[2] Cod. 6783.

[3] [The only MS. exhibiting in French the story of *Balin and Balan*, which Sir Thomas Malory has in his English, (printed by Caxton in 1485,) is at present in the possession of Mr. Henry Huth. It is a folio volume on vellum, with initial letters, but no miniatures. Three or four leaves, including the first, are deficient. It exhibits in those parts where it covers the same ground as the English work, marked variations from the latter. This MS. is in preparation for the press by Mr. Furnivall.]

[4] But at the end, this twelfth book is called " the second booke of *Syr Trystram.*" And it is added, " But here is no reherfall of the thyrd booke [of *Sir Tristram.*"]

King Arthur and all the knights. Lwhyd mentions a Welsh Sangreall which, he says, contains various fables of King Arthur and his knights, &c.[1] *Morte Arthur* is often literally translated[2] from various and very ancient detached histories of the heroes of the round table, which I have examined; and on the whole, it nearly resembles Walter Map's romance above mentioned, printed at Rouen and Paris, both in matter and disposition.

I take this opportunity of observing, that a very valuable vellum fragment of *Le Brut*, of which the writing is uncommonly beautiful and of high antiquity, containing part of the story of Merlin and King Vortigern, covers a MS. of Chaucer's *Astrolabe*, presented, together with several Oriental MSS., to the Bodleian library by Thomas Hedges, of Alderton in Wiltshire; a gentleman possessed of many curious MSS. and Greek and Roman coins, and most liberal in his communications.

But not only the pieces of the French minstrels, written in French, were circulated in England about this time, but translations of these pieces were made into English which, containing much of the French idiom, together with a sort of poetical phraseology before unknown, produced various innovations in our style. These translations, it is probable, were enlarged with additions, or improved with alterations of the story. Hence it was that Robert de Brunne, as we have already seen, complained of strange and quaint English, of the changes made in the story of *Sir Tristram*, and of the liberties assumed by his cotemporary minstrels in altering facts and coining new phrases. Yet these circumstances enriched our tongue, and extended the circle of our poetry. And for what reason these fables were so much admired and encouraged, in preference to the languid poetical chronicles of Robert of Gloucester and Robert of Brunne, it is obvious to conjecture. The gallantries of chivalry were exhibited with new splendour, and the times were growing more refined. The Norman fashions were adopted even in Wales. In the year 1176, a splendid carousal, after the manner of the Normans, was given by a Welsh prince. This was Rhees ap Gryffyth king of South Wales, who at Christmas made a great feast in the castle of Cardigan, then called Aber-Teify, which he ordered to be proclaimed throughout all Britain; and to " which came many strangers, who were honourably received and worthily entertained, so that no man departed discontented. And among deeds of arms and other shewes, Rhees caused all the poets of Wales[3] to come thither; and provided chairs for them to be set in

---

[1] *Archæolog. Brit.* Tit. vii, p. 265, col. 2. [It is only a translation of Map's French *Queste del Saint Graal.*]

[2] [In Hoffmann's *Horæ Belgicæ*, 1830, according to Mr. R. Taylor, is an account of various Flemish versions of these romances.]

[3] In illustration of the argument pursued in the text we may observe, that about this time the English minstrels flourished with new honours and rewards. At the magnificent marriage of [Joan Plantagenet, grand-]daughter of Edward I., every king minstrel received xl. shillings. See Anstis, *Ord. Gart.* ii. p. 303; and Dugd. *Mon.* i. 355. In the same reign a multitude of minstrels attended the ceremony of knighting Prince Edward on the Feast of Pentecost. They entered the hall, while

his hall, where they should dispute together to try their cunning and gift in their several faculties, where great rewards and rich giftes were appointed for the overcomers.¹" Tilts and tournaments, after a long disuse, revived with superior lustre in the reign of Edward I. Roger [de] Mortimer, a magnificent baron of that reign, erected in his stately castle of Kenilworth a Round Table, at which he restored the rites of King Arthur. He entertained in this castle the constant retinue of one hundred knights and as many ladies, and invited thither adventurers in chivalry from every part of Christendom.² These fables were therefore an image of the manners, customs, mode of life, and favourite amusements, which now prevailed not only in France but in England, accompanied with all the decorations which fancy could invent, and recommended by the graces of romantic fiction. They complimented the ruling passion of the times, and cherished in a high degree the fashionable sentiments of ideal honour and fantastic fortitude.

Among Richard's French minstrels, the names only of three are recorded. I have already mentioned Blondel de Nesle. Fouquet of Marseilles³ and [Gauç]elme Fayditt,⁴ many of whose compositions

---

the king was sitting at dinner surrounded with the new knights. Nic. Trivet. *Annal.* p. 342, edit. Oxon. The whole number knighted was two hundred and sixty-seven. Dugd. *Bar.* i. 80, b. Robert de Brunne says this was the greatest royal feast since King Arthur's at Carleon, concerning which he adds, "thereof yit men *rime*," p. 332. In the wardrobe-roll of the same prince, under the year 1306, we have this entry: "Will. Fox et Cradoco socio suo cantatoribus cantantibus coram Principe et aliis magnatibus in comitiva sua existente apud London, &c. xx *s.*" Again, "Willo Ffox et Cradoco socio suo cantantibus in præsentia principis et al. Magnatum apud London de dono ejusdem dni per manus Johis de Ringwode, &c. 8 die jan. xx *s.*" Afterwards, in the same roll, four shillings are given, "Ministrallo comitissæ Mareschal. facienti menestralciam suam coram principe, &c. in comitiva sua existent. apud Penreth." *Comp. Garderob. Edw. Princip. Wall.* ann. 35 Edw .I. This I chiefly cite to shew the greatness of the gratuity. Minstrels were part of the establishment of the households of our nobility before the year 1307. Thomas Earl of Lancaster allows at Christmas cloth, or *vestis liberata*, to his household minstrels at a great expence, in the year 1314. Stow's *Surv. Lond.* p. 134, edit. 1618. See *supr.* Soon afterwards the minstrels claimed such privileges that it was thought necessary to reform them by an edict in 1315. See Hearne's *Append. Leland. Collectan.* vi. 36. Yet, as I have formerly remarked in Observations on Spenser's *Faerie Queene,* we find a person in the character of a minstrel entering Westminster-hall on horseback while Edward I. was solemnizing the feast of Pentecost as above, and presenting a letter to the king. See Walsing. *Hist. Angl. Franc.* p. 109.

¹ Powell's *Wales,* 237, edit. 1584. Who adds, that the bards of "Northwales won the prize, and amonge the musicians Rees's owne houshold men were counted best." Rhees was one of the Welsh princes who, the preceding year, attended the Parliament at Oxford, and were magnificently entertained in the castle of that city by Henry II. Lord Lyttelton's *Hist. Hen. II.* edit. iii. p. 302. It may not be foreign to our present purpose to mention here, that Henry II., in the year 1179, was entertained by Welsh bards at Pembroke castle in Wales, in his passage into Ireland. Powell, *ut supr.* p. 238. The subject of their songs was the history of King Arthur. See Selden on *Polyolb.* s. iii. p. 53.

² Drayton's *Heroic. Epist.* Mort. Isabel. v. 53. And Notes *ibid.* from Walsingham.

[³ Mr. Thoms refers us to Diez (*Leben und Werke der Troubadours,* s. 234-51) for

still remain, were also among the poets patronised and entertained in England by Richard. They are both celebrated and sometimes imitated by Dante and Petrarch. Fayditt, a native of Avignon, united the professions of music and verse; and the Provençals used to call his poetry *de bon mots e de bon son*. Petrarch is supposed to have copied, in his *Triomfo d'Amore*, many strokes of high imagination from a poem written by Fayditt on a similar subject; particularly in his description of the Palace of Love. But Petrarch has not left Fayditt without his due panegyric: he says that Fayditt's tongue was shield, helmet, sword, and spear.[1] He is likewise in Dante's *Paradiso*. Fayditt was extremely profuse and voluptuous. On the death of King Richard, he travelled on foot for nearly twenty years, seeking his fortune; and during this long pilgrimage he married a nun of Aix in Provence, who was young and lively, and could accompany her husband's tales and sonnets with her voice. Fouquet de Marseilles had a beautiful person, a ready wit, and a talent for singing; these popular accomplishments recommended him to the courts of King Richard, Raymond, count of Toulouse, and Beral de Baulx; where, as the French would say, *il fit les delices de cour*. He fell in love with Adelasia the wife of Beral, whom he celebrated in his songs. One of his poems is entitled, *Las complanchas de Beral*. On the death of all his lords, he received absolution for his sin of poetry, turned monk, and at length was made Archbishop of Toulouse.[2] But among the

---

an account of Fouquet. Twenty-five of his songs are extant, of which two are printed in Raynouard's *Lexique Romain*, i. 341-5).]

[⁴ See Raynouard, *Lexique*, ed. 1838, i. 368. Mr. Thoms remarks that the object of Fayditt's admiration and poetical ardour was Maria de Ventadour, daughter of Boso II. and wife of Ebles IV. Vicomte de Ventadour, "a lady of refined taste in poetry, and celebrated by the troubadours and their historians as the noblest of her sex." A considerable number of Fayditt's pieces is extant.]

[1] Triunf. Am. c. iv.

[2] See Beauchamps, *Recherch. Theatr. Fr.* 1735, pp. 7, 9. It was Jeffrey, Richard's brother, who patronised Jeffrey Rudell, a famous troubadour of Provence, who is also celebrated by Petrarch. This poet had heard, from the adventurers in the Crusades, the beauty of a Countess of Tripoli highly extolled. He became enamoured from imagination; embarked for Tripoli, fell sick in the voyage through the fever of expectation, and was brought on shore at Tripoly half expiring. The countess, having received the news of the arrival of this gallant stranger, hastened to the shore and took him by the hand. He opened his eyes, and, at once overpowered by his disease and her kindness, had just time to say inarticulately that, having seen her, he died satisfied. The countess made him a most splendid funeral, and erected to his memory a tomb of porphyry, inscribed with an epitaph in Arabian verse. She commanded his sonnets to be richly copied and illuminated with letters of gold; was seized with a profound melancholy, and turned nun. I will endeavour to translate one of the sonnets which he made on his voyage. *Yrat et dolent m'en partray,* &c. It has some pathos and sentiment, "I should depart pensive, but for this love of mine *so far away;* for I know not what difficulties I have to encounter, my native land being *so far away*. Thou who hast made all things, and who formed this love of mine *so far away*, give me strength of body, and then I may hope to see this love of mine *so far away*. Surely my love must be founded on true merit, as I love one *so far away!* If I am easy for a moment, yet I feel a thousand pains for her who is *so far away*. No other love ever touched my heart than this for her *so*

many French minstrels invited into England by Richard, it is natural to suppose, that some of them made their magnificent and heroic patron a principal subject of their compositions.¹ And this subject, by means of the constant communication between both nations, probably became no less fashionable in France; especially if we take into the account the general popularity of Richard's character, his love of chivalry, his gallantry in the Crusades, and the favours which he so liberally conferred on the minstrels of that country. We have a romance now remaining in English rhyme, which celebrates the achievements of this illustrious monarch. It is entitled *Richard Cuer de Lyon*, and was probably translated from the French about the [reign of Edward I.] That it was, at least, translated from the French, appears from the prologue:

> In Fraunce these rymes were wroht,
> Every Englyshe ne knew it not.

From which also we may gather the popularity of his story, in these lines:

> King Richard is the beste
> That is found in any geste.

[It was printed by W. de Worde in 1509 and 1528.]² That this romance, either in French or English, existed before the year 1300, is evident from its being cited by Robert of Gloucester, in his relation of Richard's reign:

> In Romance of him imade me it may finde iwrite.³

This tale is also mentioned as a romance of some antiquity among other famous romances, in the prologue of a voluminous metrical translation of Guido de Colonna, [wrongly] attributed to Lidgate.⁴

---

far away. A fairer than she never touched any heart, either near, or *far away*." Every fourth line ends with *du luench*. See Nostradamus, &c.

[The original poem, of which the above is only a fragment, will be found in the third volume of M. Raynouard's *Choix des Poesies Originales des Troubadours*. [*Lexique Roman*, 1838, i. 341.] The seeming inaccuracies of Warton's translation may have arisen from the varied readings of his original text. The fragment published by M. Sismondi differs essentially from the larger poem given by M. Raynouard.—Price.]

¹ Fayditt is said to have written a *Chant funèbre* on his death. Beauchamps, *ibid.* p. 10.

[For specimens of the poetry of Fouquet de Marseilles and Gauçelm Faidit the reader is referred to the first volume of M. Raynouard's excellent work already noticed. The second volume of the old edition contains a prose translation of Faidit's *Planh* on the death of Richard I.—Price.]

² There is a MS. copy of it in Caius College, Cambridge.
³ *Chron.* p. 487.
⁴ "Many speken of men that romaunces rede," &c.

> "Of Bevys, Gy, and Gawayne,
> Of Kyng Rychard, and Owayne,
> Of Tristram, and Percyvayle,
> Of Rowland ris, and Aglavaule,
> Of Archeroun, and of Octavian,
> Of Charles, and of Cassibelan,
> Of K[H]eveloke, Horne, and of Wade,
> In romances that of hem bi made

It is likewise frequently quoted by Robert de Brunne, who wrote much about the same time with Robert of Gloucester:

> Whan Philip tille Acres cam, litelle was his dede,
> The Romance fais gret sham who so that pas[1] will rede.
> The Romancer it sais Richard did make a pele.[2]—
> The Romance of Richard sais he wan the toun.[3]—

> That gestours dos of him gestes
> At mangeres and at great festes,
> Here dedis ben in remembraunce
> In many fair romaunce.
> But of the worthiest wyght in wede,
> That ever bystrod any stede,
> Spekes no man, ne in romaunce redes,
> Off his battayle ne of his dedes;
> Off that battayle spekes no man,
> There all prowes of knyghtes began,
> Thet was forsothe of the batayle
> Thet at Troye was saunfayle,
> Of swythe a fyght as ther was one, &c.
> For ther were in thet on side,
> Sixti kynges and dukes of pride.—
> And there was the best bodi in dede
> That ever yit wered wede,
> Sithen the world was made so ferre,
> That was Ector in eche werre," &c.

Laud. K 76 [595], f. 1, MSS. Bibl. Bodl. Cod. membr. [There is no authority, as Sir F. Madden has stated, for attributing this to Lydgate.] Whether this poem was written by Lidgate, I shall not enquire at present. I shall only say here, that it is totally different from either of Lidgate's two poems on the Theban and Trojan Wars; and that the manuscript, which is beautifully written, appears to be of the age of Henry VI.

By the way, it appears from this quotation that there was an old romance called *Wade*. Wade's *Bote* is mentioned in Chaucer's *Marchaunts Tale*, v. 940:

> "And eke these olde wivis, god it wote,
> They connin so much crafte in Wadis bote."

Again *Troil. Cress*. iii. 615:

> "He songe, she plaide, he tolde a tale of Wade."

Where, says the glossarist, "A romantick story, famous at that time, of one Wade, who performed many strange exploits, and met with many wonderful adventures in his boat *Guigelot*." Speght says that Wade's history was *long* and *fabulous*.

[The story of Wade is also alluded to in the following passage taken from the romance of Sir Bevis:

> "Swiche bataile ded neuer non
> Cristene man of flesch and bon—
> Of a dragoun thar beside,
> That Beues slough ther in that tide,
> Saue Sire Launcelot de Lake,
> He faught with a fur-drake,
> And Wade dede also,
> And neuer knightes boute thai to."—*Price*.

A personage of similar name occurs in the *Vilkina Saga* and in the *Scóp, or Gleeman's Tale*, l. 46. The English myth is referred to in the metrical *Morte Arthure*, edited by Halliwell, 1847, and again for the Early English Text Society. M. Michel has published a *brochure*, entitled *Wade: Lettre a M. Henri Ternaux-Compans, &c. sur une Tradition Angloise du Moyen Age*. Paris, 1837. 8vo.]

[1] Passus. Compare Percy's *Reliques*, ii. 66, 398, edit. 1767.
[2] Percy's *Rel.* ii. p. 157.   [3] *Ibid.*

> He tellis in the Romance fen Acres wonnen was
> How God gaf him fair chance at the bataile of Caifas.[1]—
> Sithen at Japhet was flayn fauelle his ftede
> The Romans tellis gret pas of his douhty dede.[2]—
> Soudan fo curteys never drank nö wyne,
> The fame the Romans fais that is of Richardyn.[3]
> In prifoun was he bounden, as the Romance fais,
> In cheynes and lede wonden, that hevy was of peis.[4]

I am not indeed quite certain, whether or no in fome of thefe inftances, Robert de Brunne may not mean his French original Peter Langtoft. But in the following lines he manifeftly refers to our romance of *Richard*, between which and Langtoft's chronicle he exprefsly makes a diftinction. And in the conclufion of the reign:

> I knowe no more to ryme of dedes of kyng Richard:
> Who fo wille his dedes all the fothe fe,
> The romance that men reden, ther is propirte.
> This that I have faid it is Pers fawe.[5]
> Als he in romance[6] lad, ther after gan I drawe.[7]

It is not improbable that both thefe rhyming chroniclers cite from the Englifh tranflation: if fo, we may fairly fuppofe that this romance was tranflated in the reign of Edward I. This circumftance throws the French original to a ftill higher period.

In the Royal Library at Paris there is *Hiftoire de Richard Roi d'Angleterre et de Maquemore d'Irlande en rime*.[8] Richard is the laft of our monarchs whofe achievements were adorned by fiction and fable. If not a fuperftitious belief of the times, it was an hyperbolical invention ftarted by the minftrels, which foon grew into a tradition, and is gravely recorded by the chroniclers, that Richard carried with him to the Crufades King Arthur's celebrated fword Caliburn, and that he prefented it as a gift or relic of ineftimable value, to Tancred King of Sicily, in the year 1191.[9] Robert of Brunne calls this fword a *jewel*.[10]

> And Richard at that time gaf him a faire juelle,
> The gude fwerd Caliburne which Arthur luffed fo well.[11]

---

[1] p. 175. [Warton's conjecture is perfectly correct in moft of thefe inftances. They contain allufions to circumftances which are unnoticed by Langtoft.—*Price*.]
[2] Percy's *Rel*. ii. p. 175. [3] *Ibid*. p. 188. [4] p. 198.
[5] "The words of my original Peter Langtoft." [6] In French.
[7] p. 205. Du Cange recites an old French MS. profe romance, entitled *Hiftoire de la Mort de Richard Roy d'Angleterre*. Glofs. Lat. Ind. Auct. i. p. cxci. [But this is upon the depofition of Richard II.] There was one, perhaps the fame, among the MSS. of Martin of Palgrave.
[8] Num. 7532. [An account of this hiftorical poem will be found in Mr. Strutt's *Regal Antiquities*. It relates entirely to the Irifh wars of Richard II. and the latter part of the reign of that unfortunate monarch.—*Price*. The poem is printed entire in *Archæologia*, xx.]
[9] In return for feveral veffels of gold and filver, horfes, bales of filk, four great fhips, and fifteen galleys, given by Tancred. Benedict. Abb. p. 642, edit. Hearne.
[10] *Jocale*. In the general and true fenfe of the word. Robert de Brunne, in another place, calls a rich pavilion a *jowelle*, p. 152.
[11] *Chron*. p. 153. [Sir F. Madden refers for an account of *Caliburne* to M. Michel's *Triftan*, lxxxv.]

Indeed the Arabian writer of the life of the Sultan Saladin mentions some exploits of Richard almost incredible. But, as Lord Lyttelton justly observes, this historian is highly valuable on account of the knowledge he had of the facts which he relates. It is from this writer we learn, in the most authentic manner, the actions and negotiations of Richard in the course of the enterprise for the recovery of the Holy Land, and all the particulars of that memorable war.[1]

But before I produce a specimen of Richard's English romance, I stand still to give some more extracts from its prologues, which contain matter much to our present purpose: as they have very fortunately preserved the subjects of many romances, perhaps metrical, then fashionable both in France and England. And on these therefore, and their origin, I shall take this opportunity of offering some remarks:

> Fele romanses men make newe
> Of good knyghtes strong and trewe:
> Of hey dedys men rede romance,
> Bothe in England and in Fraunce;
> Of Rowelond and of Olyver,
> And of everie Doseper,[2]
> Of Alysander and Charlemain,
> Of Kyng Arthor and of Gawayn;
> How they wer knyghtes good and curteys,
> Of Turpyn and of Ocier Daneys.
> Of Troye men rede in ryme,
> What werre ther was in olde tyme;
> Of Ector and of Achylles,
> What folk they flewe in that pres, &c.[3]

And again, in a second prologue, after a pause has been made by the minstrel in the course of singing the poem:

> Now hearkenes to my tale sothe,
> Though I swere yow an othe
> I wole reden romaunces non
> Of Paris,[4] ne of Ypomydone,
> Of Alisaundre, ne Charlemagne,
> Of Arthour, ne of sere Gawain,
> Nor of sere Launcelot the Lake,
> Of Beffs, ne Guy, ne sere Sydrake,
> Ne of Ury, ne of Octavian,
> Ne of Hector the strong man,
> Ne of Jason, neither of Hercules,
> Ne of Eneas, neither Achilles.[5]

---

[1] See *Hist. of Hen. II.* vol. iv. p. 361, App.
[2] Charlemagne's twelve peers. *Douze Pairs.* Fr.
[3] [The text has been corrected by Mr. Weber's edition of this romance, in his *Metrical Romances*, 1810.—*Price*.]
[4] [The old printed copy reads Pertonape,] perhaps Parthenope, or Parthenopeus.
[5] Line 6657. To some of these romances the author of the MSS. *Lives of the Saints*, written about the year 1[3]00, and cited above at large, alludes in a sort of prologue. See sect. i. *supr.*

> "Wel auht we loug Cristendom that is so dere y bou3t,
> With oure lordes herte blode that the spere hath y-fou3t.

Here, among others, some of the most capital and favourite stories of romance are mentioned, Arthur, Charlemagne, the Siege of Troy with its appendages, and Alexander the Great: and there are four authors of high esteem in the dark ages, Geoffry of Monmouth, Turpin, Guido di Colonna, and Callisthenes, whose books were the grand repositories of these subjects, and contained most of the traditionary fictions, whether of Arabian or classical origin, which constantly supplied materials to the writers of romance.

> Men wilnethe more yhere of batayle of kyngis,
> And of kny3tis hardy, that mochel is lesyngis.
> Of Roulond and of Olyvere, and Gy of Warwyk,
> Of Wawayen and Tristram that ne foundde here y-like.
> Who so loveth to here tales of suche thinge,
> Here he may y-here thyng that nys no lelynge,
> Of postoles and marteres that hardi kny3ttes were,
> And stedfast were in bataile and fledde no3t for no fere," &c.

The anonymous author of *The boke of Stories called Cursor Mundi*, translated from the French, seems to have been of the same opinion. His work [is a history of the two Testaments]: but in the prologue he takes occasion to mention many tales of another kind, which were more agreeable to the generality of readers. MSS. Laud, K 53, f. 177, Bibl. Bodl.

> "Men lykyn Jestis for to here
> And romans rede in divers manere:
> Of Alexandre the conquerour,
> Of Julius Cesar the emperour,
> Of Greece and Troy the strong stryf,
> Ther many a man lost his lyf:
> Of Brut, that baron bold of hand,
> The first conquerour of Englond;
> Of kyng Artour that was so ryche,
> Was non in hys tyme so ilyche:
> Of wonders that among his knyghts felle,
> And auntyrs dedyn, as men her telle,
> As Gaweyn and othir full abylle,
> Which that kept the round tabyll.
> How kyng Charles and Rowland sawght
> With Sarazins, nold thei be cawght;
> Of Trystram and Ysoude the swete,
> How thei with love first gan mete.
> Of kyng John and Isenbras,
> Of Ydoyne and Amadas.
> Stories of divers thynges,
> Of princes, prelates and kynges:
> Many songs of divers ryme,
> As Englissh, French, and Latyne, &c.
> This ylke boke is translate
> Into Englissh tong to rede
> For the love of Englissh lede,
> For comyn folk of England, &c.
> Syldyn yt ys for any chaunce
> Englissh tong preched is in Fraunce," &c.

See Montf. Par. MSS. 7540, and p. 123, *supr.* [Sir F. Madden cites other MSS. of the *Cursor Mundi* in the Bodleian, Adv. Lib. Edinb., at Göttingen, *et alibi*. The work is to be printed from MSS. in the Br. Mus. and at Cambridge by the Early English Text Society. Mr. Furnivall notes, that the MS. Cotton Vesp. A. iii. is the best in the Northern dialect: that at Trinity College, in a Midland one.]

But I do not mean to repeat here what has been already observed[1] concerning the writings of Geoffrey of Monmouth and Turpin. It will be sufficient to say at present, that these two fabulous historians recorded the achievements of Charlemagne and of Arthur: and that Turpin's history was artfully forged under the name of that archbishop about the year 1110, with a design of giving countenance to the Crusades from the example of so high an authority as Charlemagne, whose pretended visit to the holy sepulchre is described in the twentieth chapter.

As to the siege of Troy, it appears that both Homer's poems were unknown, at least not understood, in Europe from the abolition of literature by the Goths in the fourth century to the fourteenth. Geoffrey of Monmouth indeed, who wrote about the year 11[28], a man of learning for that age, produces Homer in attestation of a fact asserted in his history: but in such a manner as shows that he knew little more than Homer's name, and was but imperfectly acquainted with Homer's subject. Geoffrey says that Brutus, having ravaged the province of Aquitaine with fire and sword, came to a place where the city of Tours now stands, as Homer testifies.[2] But the Trojan story was still kept alive in two Latin pieces, which passed under the names of Dares Phrygius and Dictys Cretensis. Dares' history of the destruction of Troy, as it was called, which purports to have been translated from the Greek of Dares Phrygius into Latin prose by Cornelius Nepos, is a wretched performance, and was forged under those specious names in the decline of Latin literature.[3] Dictys Cretensis is a prose Latin history of the Trojan war, in six books, paraphrased about the reign of Dioclesian or Constantine by one Septimius from some Grecian history on the same subject, said to be discovered under a sepulchre by means of an earthquake in the city of Cnossus about the time of Nero, and to have been composed by Dictys, a Cretan and a soldier in the Trojan war. The fraud so frequently practised, of discovering copies of books in this extraordinary manner, in order to infer thence their high and indubitable antiquity, betrays itself. But that the present Latin Dictys had a Greek original, now lost, appears from the numerous grecisms with which it abounds, and from the literal correspondence of many passages with the Greek fragments of one Dictys cited by ancient authors. The Greek original was very probably forged under the

---

[1] See Diss. i.   [2] L. i. ch. 14.

[3] In the Epistle prefixed, the pretended translator Nepos says, that he found this work at Athens in the handwriting of Dares. He adds, speaking of the controverted authenticity of Homer, "De ea re Athenis judicium fuit, cum pro insano Homerus haberetur, quod deos cum hominibus belligerasse descripsit." In which words he does not refer to any public decree of the Athenian judges, but to Plato's opinion in his *Republic*. Dares, with Dictys Cretensis next mentioned in the text, was first printed at Milan in 1477. Mabillon says, that a manuscript of the Pseudo-Dares occurs in the Laurentian library at Florence, upwards of eight hundred years old. *Mus. Ital.* i. p. 169. This work was abridged by Vincentius Bellovacensis, a friar of Burgundy, about the year 1244. See his *Specul. Histor.* lib. iii. 63.

name of Dictys, a traditionary writer on the subject, in the reign of Nero, who is said to have been fond of the Trojan story.¹ On the whole, the work appears to have been an arbitrary metaphrase of Homer, with many fabulous interpolations. At length Guido di Colonna, a native of Messina in Sicily, a learned civilian, and no contemptible Italian poet, about the year 1260, engrafting on Dares and Dictys many new romantic inventions, which the taste of his age dictated, and which the connection between Grecian and Gothic fiction easily admitted, at the same time comprehending in his plan the Theban and Argonautic stories from Ovid, Statius, and Valerius Flaccus,² compiled a grand prose romance in Latin, containing fifteen books, and entitled in most manuscripts *Historia de Bello Trojano*.³ It was written at the request of Matteo di Porta, Archbishop of Salerno. Dares Phrygius and Dictys Cretensis seem to have been in some measure superseded by this improved and comprehensive history of the Grecian heroes, [for, of course, Colonna cannot be regarded as the first popularizer of the subject;] and from this period Achilles, Jason and Hercules were adopted into romance, and celebrated in common with Lancelot, Rowland, Gawain, Oliver, and other Christian champions, whom they so nearly resembled in the extravagance of their adventures.⁴ This work abounds with Ori-

---

¹ See Perizon. *Dissertat. de Dict. Cretens.* sect. xxix. Constantinus Lascaris, a learned monk of Constantinople, one of the restorers of Grecian literature in Europe near four hundred years ago, says that Dictys Cretensis in Greek was lost. This writer is not once mentioned by Eustathius, who lived about the year 1170, in his elaborate and extensive commentary on Homer.

² The *Argonautics* of Valerius Flaccus are cited in Chaucer's *Hypsipile and Medea*. "Let him reade the boke Argonauticon," v. 90. But Guido is afterwards cited as a writer on that subject, *ibid.* 97. [Only two MSS. appear to be known : in Queen's Coll. Oxford, and at Holkham. It seems to be almost open to question, whether Chaucer refers to Valerius Flaccus.]

³ It was first printed [at Cologne, 1477, and there are many later edits.] The work was finished, as appears by a note at the end, in 1287. It was translated into Italian by Philip or Christopher Ceffio, a Florentine, and this translation was first printed at Venice in 1481, 4to. It has also been translated into German. See Lambec. ii. 948. The purity of our author's Italian style has been much commended. For his Italian poetry, see Mongitor, *ubi. infra*, p. 167. Compare also, *Diar. Eruditcr. Ital.* xiii. 258. Montfaucon mentions, in the royal library at Paris, Le Roman de Thebes qui futracine de Troye la grande. *Catal. MSS.* ii. p. 923—198. [This *Roman de Thebes* is in reality one of those works on the story of the siege of Troy, engrafted either on that of Columna or on his materials.—*Douce.*]

⁴ Bale says, that Edward I. having met with our author in Sicily, in returning from Asia, invited him into England, xiii. 36. This prince was interested in the Trojan story, as we shall see below. Our historians relate, that he wintered in Sicily in the year 1270. *Chron. Rob. Brun.* p. 227. A writer quoted by Hearne, supposed to be John Stow the chronicler, says that "Guido de Columpna arriving in England at the commaundement of king Edward the Firste, made scholies and annotations upon Dictys Cretensis and Dares Phrigius. Besides these, he writ at large the Battayle of Troye." Heming. *Cartul.* ii. 649. Among his works is recited *Historia de Regibus Rebusque Angliæ.* It is quoted by many writers under the title of *Chronicum Britannorum*. He is said also to have written *Chronicum Magnum libri* xxxvi. See Mongitor. *Bibl. Sic.* i. 265.

[Eichhorn has stated these "Scholies" of Guido to have been published in the year 1216; a manifest mistake,—since it leaves seventy-one years between this

ental imagery, of which the subject was extremely susceptible. It has also some traits of Arabian literature. The Trojan horse is a horse of brass; and Hercules is taught astronomy and the seven liberal sciences. But I forbear to enter at present into a more par-

---

date and the period to which he assigns the first appearance of the *Historia Trojana*. But whatever may have been Guido's merit in thus affording a common text-book for subsequent writers, his work could have contained little of novelty, either in matter or manner, for his contemporaries; and it may be reasonably doubted, whether his labours extended beyond the humble task of reducing into prose the metrical compilations of his predecessors. It is true, this circumstance will not admit of absolute proof, till the several poems upon the Trojan story extant in our own and various continental libraries shall be given to the world; but the following notices of some of these productions, though scanty and imperfect, will perhaps justify the opinion which has been expressed. The history of the Anglo-Saxon kings by Geoffri Gaimar, a poet antecedent to Wace (1155), is but a fragment of a larger work, which the author assures us commenced with an account of Jason and the Argonautic expedition. This was doubtless continued through the whole cycle of Grecian fabulous history, till the siege of Troy connected Brutus, the founder of the British dynasty, with the heroes of the ancient world. The voluminous work of Benoit de Saint More (noticed by Warton below) is confessedly taken from Dares Phrygius and Dictys Cretensis, and is adorned with all those fictions of romance and chivalric costume, which these writers are supposed to have received from the interpolations of Guido. Among the romances enumerated by Melis Stoke, as the productions of earlier writers in Holland, and still (1300) held in general esteem, we find "The Conflict of Troy" (*De Stryd van Troyen*); and we know upon the authority of Jakob van Maerlant (1270), the translator of Vincent de Beauvais' *Speculum Historiale*, that this was a version of Benoit's poem. It is not so certain whence Conrad of Wurzburg, a contemporary of Guido, derived his German Ilias; but he professes to have taken it from a French original, and his poem, like Gaimar's, commences with Jason and the Argonautic expedition. Upon the same principle that Conrad conceived it necessary to preface his Ilias with the story of the Golden Fleece, his countryman Henry von Veldeck embraced the whole of the Trojan war, its origin and consequences, in his version of the Æneis. This, however, is usually believed to be a translation from the *Enide* of Chretien de Troyes; and, if the date (*ante* 1186) assumed for its appearance by Von der Hagen be correct, would place the French original in an earlier period than is given it by the French antiquaries. In the year 1210, Albrecht von Halberstadt published a metrical version of Ovid's *Metamorphoses*. See Von der Hagen's *Grundriss zur Geschichte der Deutschen Poesie*, Berlin, 1812; and Henrik van Wyn's *Historische Avondstonden*, Amsterdam, 1800.—*Price*.]

[Sir F. Madden refers us to Hoffmann's *Horæ Belgicæ*, 1830, p. 30. Mr. Wright speaks of a history of the siege of Troy in Latin prose, attributed to the eleventh century, and executed in France (Arundel MSS. Br. Mus. No. 375).]

[The popularity of the *Historia Trojana* in Britain is well attested by the number of versions of it in English that have come down to us. Besides Lydgate's *Troy Book* and the metrical version in the Bodleian Library, noticed by Warton, there is an Alliterative version in the Hunterian Museum, University of Glasgow, which the Early English Text Society is now publishing; and in a MS. copy of Lydgate in the University Library, Cambridge, there are two considerable fragments of another version by Barbour, author of the *Brus*, discovered by Mr. Bradshaw in 1866. These versions are independent translations from Guido de Colonna, belong to the end of the fourteenth and beginning of the fifteenth century, and must have been made within a period of fifty years. Probably the earliest was that by Barbour, then the Alliterative, then Lydgate's, and last of all, the Bodleian. Yet there is abundant evidence that Lydgate had read the Alliterative version, for many of his interpolations and renderings are the same as, or expansions of those given in that version; the same may be affirmed of the author of the Bodleian version. Indeed, it may be to the Alliterative version that the author refers as the

ticular examination of this hiftory, as it muft often occafionally be cited hereafter. I fhall here only further obferve in general, that this work is the chief fource from which Chaucer derived his ideas about the Trojan ftory; that it was profeffedly paraphrafed by Lydgate [between the years 1414 and 1420] into a prolix Englifh poem, called the *Boke of Troye*,[1] at the command of Henry V.; that it became the ground-work of a new compilation in French on the fame fubject ["out of dyuerce bookes of latyn"] by Raoul le Feure, chaplain to the Duke of Burgundy, in the year 1464 and partly tranflated into Englifh profe in the year 1471 by Caxton, under the title of the [recuyell of the hiftoryes of Troye,] at the requeft of Margaret, duchefs of Burgundy: and that from Caxton's book, afterwards modernifed, Shakefpeare [may have] borrowed his drama of *Troilus and Creffida*.[2]

Romana that the "fothe telles,"—a phrafe that occurs very frequently in the Alliterative verfion.

Befides thefe metrical renderings, the third book of Caxton's *Recuyell of the Hiftoryes of Troye*, is a profe tranflation of the greater portion of the *Hiftoria Trojana*, omitting the ftory of Jafon and Medea.

That the Bodleian MS. is probably a popular rendering of the Alliterative, compare the paffages given by Warton with thofe in the Early Englifh Text Society, vol. i. pp. 12*-15. All the paffages from the Bodleian MS. that I have compared, and they were many, fhow the fame peculiarities: fome of them are even more ftriking.—*Donaldfon*.]

[1] Who mentions it in a French as well as Latin romance: edit. 1555, fignat. B i. pag. 2:

"As in the latyn and the frenfhe yt is."

It occurs in French, MSS. Bibl. Reg. Brit. Mus. 16 F. ix. This MS. was probably written not long after the year 1300. In Lincoln's-inn Library there is a poem entitled *Bellum Trojanum*. Num. 150. Pr.

"Sithen god hade this worlde wroght."

[2] The weftern nations, in early times, have been fond of deducing their origin from Troy. This tradition feems to be couched under Odin's original emigration from that part of Afia which is connected with Phrygia. Afgard, or Afia's fortrefs, was the city from which Odin led his colony; and by fome it is called Troy. To this place alfo they fuppofed Odin to return after his death, where he was to receive thofe who died in battle, in a hall roofed with glittering fhields. See Bartholin. l. ii. cap. 8, pp. 402, 403. *feq*. This hall, fays the Edda, is in the city of Afgard, which is called the Field of Ida. Bartholin. *ibid*. In the very fublime ode on the Diffolution of the World, cited by Bartholinus, it is faid, that after the twilight of the gods fhould be ended, and the new world appear, "the Afæ fhall meet in the field of Ida, and tell of the deftroyed habitations." Barthol. l. ii. cap. 14, p. 597. Compare Arngrim. Jon. Crymog. l. i. c. 4, pp. 45, 46. See alfo Edda, fab. 5. In the proem to Refenius's Edda it is faid, "Odin appointed twelve judges or princes at Sigtune in Scandinavia, as at Troy; and eftablifhed there all the laws of Troy and the cuftoms of the Trojans." See Hickes, *Thefaur*. i. Differtat. Epift. p. 39. See alfo Mallet's *Hift. Dannem*. ii. p. 34. Bartholinus thinks that the compiler of the Eddic mythology, who lived A.D. 1070, finding that the Britons and Franks drew their defcent from Troy, was ambitious of affigning the fame boafted origin to Odin. But this tradition appears to have been older than the Edda. And it is more probable that the Britons and Franks borrowed it from the Scandinavian Goths, and adapted it to themfelves; unlefs we fuppofe that thefe nations, I mean the former, were branches of the Gothic ftem, which gave them a fort of inherent right to the claim. This reafoning

Proofs have been given in the two prologues just cited of the general popularity of Alexander's story, another branch of Grecian history famous in the dark ages. To these we may add the evidence of Chaucer:

> Alisaundres storie is so commune,
> That everie wight that hath discrecioune
> Hath herde somewhat or al of his fortune.[1]

In the *House of Fame*, Alexander is placed with Hercules.[2] I have already remarked that he was celebrated in a Latin poem by Gualtier de Chatillon, in the year 1212.[3] Other proofs will occur in their proper places.[4] The truth is, Alexander was the most eminent knight errant of Grecian antiquity. He could not therefore be long without his romance. Callisthenes, an Olynthian, educated under Aristotle with Alexander, wrote an authentic life of Alexander.[5] This history,

---

may perhaps account for the early existence and extraordinary popularity of the Trojan story among nations ignorant and illiterate, who could only have received it by tradition. Geoffrey of Monmouth took this descent of the Britons from Troy from the Welsh or Armoric bards, and they perhaps had it in common with the Scandinavian scalds. There is not a syllable of it in the authentic historians of England, who wrote before him; particularly those ancient ones, Bede, Gildas, and the uninterpolated Nennius. Henry of Huntingdon began his history from Cæsar; and it was only on further information that he added Brute. But this information was from a manuscript found by him in his way to Rome in the abbey of Bec in Normandy, [which, says Sir F. Madden, is, however, merely a copy of Geoffrey of Monmouth's Latin work.] H. Hunt. *Epistol. ad Warin.* MSS. Cantabr. Bibl. publ. cod. 251. I have mentioned in another place, that Witlaf, a king of the West Saxons, grants in his charter, dated A.D. 833, among other things to Croyland-abbey his robe of tissue, on which was embroidered " The destruction of Troy." *Obs. on Spenser's Fairy Queen,* i. sect. v. p. 176. This proves the story to have been in high veneration even long before that period: and it should at the same time be remembered, that the Saxons came from Scandinavia.

This fable of the descent of the Britons from the Trojans was solemnly alleged as an authentic and undeniable proof in a controversy of great national importance, by Edward I. and his nobility, without the least objection from the opposite party. It was in the famous dispute concerning the subjection of the crown of England to that of Scotland, about the year 1301. The allegations are in a letter to Pope Boniface, signed and sealed by the king and his lords. *Ypodigm. Neustr.* apud Camd. *Angl. Norman.* p. 492. Here is a curious instance of the implicit faith with which this tradition continued to be believed even in a more enlightened age, and an evidence that it was equally credited in Scotland.

[1] V. 656.   [2] V. 323.   [3] See Second Dissertation.

[4] In the reign of Henry I. the sheriff of Nottinghamshire is ordered to procure the queen's chamber at Nottingham to be painted with the History of Alexander. Madox, *Hist. Exch.* pp. 249-259. " Depingi facias historiam Alexandri undiquaque." In the Romance of Richard, the minstrel says of an army assembled at a siege in the Holy Land, sign. Q iii:

> " Covered is both mount and playne
> Kyng Alysaunder and Charlemayne
> He never had halfe the route
> As is the city now aboute."

By the way, this is much like a passage in Milton, *Par. Reg.* iii. 337:

> " Such forces met not, nor so wide a camp,
> When Agrican," &c.

[5] See *Recherch. sur la Vie et les Ouvrages de Callisthene.* Par M. l'Abbe Sevin.

which is frequently referred to by ancient writers, has been long since lost. But a Greek life of this hero, under the adopted name of Callisthenes, at present exists, and is no uncommon manuscript in good libraries.[1] It is entitled, Βιος Αλεξανδρου του Μακεδονος και Πραξεις. That is, *The Life and Actions of Alexander the Macedonian*.[2] This piece was written in Greek, being a translation from the Persic, by Simeon Seth, styled *Magister*, and protovestiary or wardrobe keeper of the Palace of Antiochus at Constantinople,[3] about the year 1070 under the Emperor Michael Ducas.[4] It was most probably very

---

Mem. de Lit. viii. p. 126, 4to. But many very ancient Greek writers had corrupted Alexander's history with fabulous narratives, such as Orthagoras, Onesicritus, &c.

[Julian Africanus, who lived in the third century, records the fable of Nectanabus, king of Egypt, the presumptive father of Alexander, who figures so conspicuously in the later romances. It is also presumed, that similar fictions were introduced into the poems of Arrian, Hadrian, and Soterichus. See *Görres Volksbücher*, p. 58, a translation of whose observations upon this subject will be found in the *Retrospective Review*, No. vi. For an account of Arabic, Turkish, and Persian versions of this story, see Herbelot, i. 144, and Weber's *Metrical Romances*, vol. i. xx.—Price.]

[1] Particularly Bibl. Bodl. Oxon. MSS. Barocc. Cod. xvii. And Bibl. Reg. Paris. Cod. 2064. See Montfauc. *Catal. MSS.* p. 733. See passages cited from this manuscript, in Steph. Byzant. Abr. Berckel. V. Βουκεφαλεια. Cæsar Bulenger de Circo, c. xiii. 30, &c. and Fabric. *Bibl. Gr.* xiv. 148, 149, 150. It is adduced by Du Cange, *Glossar. Gr.* ubi vid. tom. ii. *Catal. Scriptor.* p. 24.

[2] Undoubtedly many smaller histories now in our libraries were formed from this greater work.

[3] Πρωτοβεςιαριος, *Protovestiarius.* See Du Cange, *Constantinop. Christ.* lib. ii. § 16. n. 5. Et ad Zonar. p. 46.

[4] Allat. de Simeonibus, p. 181. And Labb. *Bibl. nov. MSS.* p. 115. Simeon Seth translated many Persic and Arabic books into Greek. Allat. *ubi supr.* p. 182, *seq.* Among them he translated from Arabic into Greek, about the year 1100, for the use of or at the request of the Emperor Alexius Comnenus, the celebrated Indian Fables now commonly called the *Fables of Bidpay*. This work he entitled, Στεφανιτης και Ιχηλατης, and divided it into fifteen books. It was printed at Berlin, A.D. 1697, under the title, Συμεων Μαγιςρυ και φιλοσοφυ του Σηθ Κυλιλε και Διμνη. These are the names of two African or Asiatic animals, called in Latin *Thoes,* a sort of [jackall,] the principal interlocutors in the fables. Sect. i-ii. This curious monument of a species of instruction peculiar to the Orientals is upwards of two thousand years old. It has passed under a great variety of names. Khosru a king of Persia, in whose reign Mahomet was born, sent his physician named Burzvisch into India, on purpose to obtain this book, which was carefully preserved among the treasures of the kings of India, and commanded it to be translated out of the Indian language into the ancient Persic. Herbelot. *Dict. Oriental.* p. 456. It was soon afterwards turned into Syriac, under the title *Calaileg* and *Damnag.* Fabric. *Bibl. Gr.* vi. p. 461. About the year of Christ 750, one of the caliphs ordered it to be translated from the ancient Persic into Arabic, under the name *Kalila ve Damna.* Herbel. *ubi supr.* In the year 920, the Sultan Ahmed, of the dynasty of the Samanides, procured a translation into more modern Persic: which was soon afterwards put into verse by a celebrated Persian poet named Roudeki. Herbel. *ibid.* Fabric. *ibid.* p. 462. About the year 1130, the Sultan Bahram, not satisfied with this Persian version, ordered another to be executed by Nasrallah, the most eloquent man of his age, from the Arabic text of Mocanna: and this Persian version is what is now extant under the title *Kalila ve Damna.* Herbel. *ibid.* See also Herbel. p. 118. But as even this last-mentioned version had too many Arabic idioms and obsolete phrases, in the reign of Sultan Hosein Mirza, it was thrown into a more modern and intelligible style, under the name of *Anuar Soheli.* Fraser's *Hist. Nadir-Shah. Catal. MSS.* pp. 19, 20. Nor must it

soon afterwards translated from the Greek into Latin, and at length from thence into French, Italian, and German.[1] The Latin trans-

---

be forgotten, that about the year 1100, the Emir Sohail, general of the armies of Hussain, Sultan of Khorassan of the posterity of Timur, caused a new translation to be made by the Dr. Hussien Vaez, which exceeded all others in elegance and perspicuity. It was named *Anwair Sohaili*, Splendor *Canopi*, from the Emir who was called after the name of that star. Herbel. pp. 118, 245. It would be tedious to mention every new title and improvement which it has passed through among the eastern people. It has been translated into the Turkish language both in prose and verse; particularly for the use of Bajazet II. and Solyman II. Herbel. p. 118. It has been translated also into Hebrew by Rabbi Joel: and into Latin, under the title *Directorium Vitæ humanæ*, by Johannes of Capua [about 1480.] From thence [in 1498] it got into Castilian: and from the Spanish was made an Italian version, printed at Ferrara, A.D. 1583, viz. *Lelo Damno* [for *Calilah u Damnah*] *del Governo de regni, sotto morali*, &c. A second edition appeared at Ferrara in 1610, viz. *Philosophia morale del doni*, &c. But there was an Italian edition at Venice, under the last-mentioned title, with old rude cuts, 1552. From the Latin version [also] it was translated into German, by the command of Ebelhard first Duke of Wirtenberg: and this translation was printed at Ulm [1485. There are several later editions by David Sahid d'Ispahan which appeared at Paris in 1644, of which Gilbert Gaulmin is believed to have been in great part the author.] But this is rather a paraphrase, and was reprinted in Holland. See Starchius, *ubi supr. præf.* § 19, 20, 22. Fabric. *ubi supr.* p. 463, *seq.* Another translation was printed at Paris, viz. *Contes et Fables Indiennes de Bidpai et De Lokman traduits d'Ali Tchelchi-Bengalek auteur Turc, par M. Galland* [1724, and again, 1778.] Fabricius says, that Mons. Galland had procured a Turkish copy of this book four times larger than the printed copies, being a version from the original Persic, and entitled *Humagoun Nameh*, that is, *The royal* or *imperial book*, so called by the Orientals, who are of opinion that it contains the whole art of government. See Fabric. *ubi supr.* p. 465. Herbel. p. 456. A translation into English from the French of the four first books was printed at London in 1747, under the title of *Pilpay's Fables;* [but all the earlier English versions are singularly indifferent. The best translation is that by Eastwick in 1854.] As to the name of the author of this book, Herbelot says that Bidpai was an Indian philosopher, and that his name signifies the merciful physician. See Herbelot, pp. 206, 456, and *Bibl. Lugdun. Catal.* p. 301. [Sir Wm. Jones, who derives this name from a Sanscrit word, interprets it the beloved or favourite physician.—Price.] Others relate, that it was composed by the Brahmins of India, under the title *Kurtuk Dumnik*. Fraser, *ubi supr.* p. 19. It is also said to have been written by Isame fifth king of the Indians, and translated into Arabic from the Indian tongue three hundred years before Alexander the Macedonian. Abraham Ecchelens, *Not. ad Catal. Ebed Jesu*, p. 87.—The Indians reckon this book among the three things in which they surpass all other nations, *viz.* "Liber Culila et Dimna, ludus Shatangri, et novem figuræ numerariæ." Saphad. *Comment. ad Carm. Tograi.* apud Hyde, *prolegom. ad lib. de lud. Oriental.* d. 3. Hyde intended an edition of the Arabic version. *Præfat. ad lib. de lud. Oriental.* vol. ii. 1767, edit. ad calc. I cannot forsake this subject without remarking, that the Persians have another book, which they esteem older than any writings of Zoroaster, entitled *Javidan Chrad*, that is, *æterna Sapientia.* Hyde *Præfat. Relig. Vet. Persarum.* This has been also one of the titles of Bidpai's Fables.
See Wolfii *Bibl. Hebr.* i. 468, ii. 931, iii. 350, iv. 934.
[The Indian origin of these fables is now placed beyond the possibility of dispute. Mr. Colebrooke has published a Sanscrit version of them, under the title of *Hitopadesa*, and they have been translated, from the same language, by Sir Wm. Jones and Dr. Wilkins.—*Price.* See *supra.*]

[1] Casaub. *Epist. ad Jos. Scaliger.* 402, 413. Scalig. *Epist. ad Casaubon*, 113, 115; who mentions also a translation of this work from the Latin into Hebrew, by one who adopted the name of Jos. Gorionides, called Pseudo-Gorionides. This Latin history was translated into German by John Hartlieb Moller, a German

lation was printed at Cologne in 1489.[1] [Among Rawlinson's books at Oxford is a MS. copy of the *Gesta Alexandri Metricé Composita*, which once belonged to Hearne.] It is said to have been [written in Greek by Æsopus, and to have been thence turned into Latin] by Julius Valerius:[2] suppositious names, which seem to have been forged by the artifice, or introduced through the ignorance, of scribes and librarians. This Latin translation, however, is of high antiquity in the middle age of learning: for it is quoted by Giraldus Cambrensis, who flourished about the year 1190.[3] About the year 1236, the substance of it was thrown into a long Latin poem, written in elegiac verse[4] by Aretinus Quilichinus.[5] This fabulous narrative of Alexander's life and achievements is full of prodigies and extravagances.[6] But we should remember its origin. The Arabian books

---

physician, at the command of Albert Duke of Bavaria, and published August. Vindel. A.D. 1478, fol. [This edition was preceded by two others from the press of Bämler, dated 1472 and 1473. These and the Strasburg edition of 1488 call the translator Dr. John Hartlieb of Munich.—*Price*.] See Lambecc. lib. ii. *de Bibl. Vindobon*, p. 949. Labbe mentions a fabulous history of Alexander, written, as he says, in 1217, and transcribed in 1455. Undoubtedly this in the text. Londinensis quotes "pervetustum quendam librum manuscriptum de actibus Alexandri." Hearne's T. Caius *ut infr.* p. 82. See also pp. 86, 258.

[1] Lenglet mentions *Historia fabulosa incerti authoris de Alexandri Magni præliis*, 1494. He adds, that it is printed in the last edition of Cæsar's Commentaries by Grævius in octavo. *Bibl. des Romans*, ii. pp. 228, 229, edit. Amst. Compare Vogt's *Catalogus librorum rarior*, p. 24, edit. 1753. Montfaucon says this history of Callisthenes occurs often in the royal library at Paris, both in Greek and Latin: but that he never saw either of them printed. *Cat. MSS*. ii. p. 733, 2543. I think a life of Alexander is subjoined to an edition of Quintus Curtius in 1584 by Joannes Monachus.

[2] Du Cange *Glossar. Gr.* v. Εβελλινος. Jurat. ad Symmach. iv. 33. Barth. Adversar. ii. 10, v. 14. [Sir F. Madden has shown that the work of Julius Valerius, which is said to have been taken from the Greek of Æsopus, is entirely different from the ordinary Latin prose narratives of the Life of Alexander. It was published by Mai, Frankf. 1818, 8vo., with a second piece called *Itinerarium Alexandri*, from MSS. in the Ambrosian library, at Milan, of the twelfth century.]

[3] Hearne, T. Caii *Vindic. Antiquit. Acad. Oxon.* tom. ii. Not. p. 802, who thinks it a work of the monks. "Nec dubium quin monachus quispiam Latine, ut potuit, scripserit. Eo modo, quo et alios id genus fœtus parturiebant scriptores aliquot monastici, e fabulis quas vulgo admodum placere sciebant."—*Ibid.*

[4] A Greek poem on this subject will be mentioned below, written in politic verses, entitled Αλεξανδρευς ὁ Μακιδων.

[5] Labb. *Bibl. Nov. MSS*. p. 68. Ol. Borrich. *Dissertat. de Poet.* p. 89.

[6] The writer relates that Alexander, inclosed in a vessel of glass, dived to the bottom of the ocean for the sake of getting a knowledge of fishes and sea monsters. He is also represented as soaring in the air by the help of gryphons. At the end, the opinions of different philosophers are recited concerning the sepulchre of Alexander. Nectabanos, a magician and astrologer, king of Egypt, is a very significant character in this romance. He transforms himself into a dragon, &c. Compare Herbelot. *Bibl. Oriental.* p. 319, b. *seq.* In some of the MSS. of this piece which I have seen, there is an account of Alexander's visit to the trees of the sun and moon: but I do not recollect this in the printed copies. Undoubtedly the original has had both interpolations and omissions. Pseudo-Gorionides above mentioned seems to hint at the groundwork of this history of Alexander in the following passage: "Cæteras autem res ab Alexandro gestas, et egregia ejus facinora ac quæcunque demum perpetravit, ea in libris Medorum et Persarum,

abound with the most incredible fictions and traditions concerning Alexander the Great, which they probably borrowed and improved from the Persians. They call him Escander. If I recollect right, one of the miracles of this romance is our hero's horn. It is said, that Alexander gave the signal to his whole army by a wonderful horn of immense magnitude, which might be heard at the distance of sixty miles, and that it was blown or sounded by sixty men at once.[1] This is the horn which Orlando won from the giant Jatmund, and which, as Turpin and the Islandic bards report, was endued with magical power, and might be heard at the distance of twenty miles. Cervantes says, that it was bigger than a massy beam.[2] Boiardo, Berni and Ariosto have all such a horn: and the fiction is here traced to its original source. But in speaking of the books which furnished the story of Alexander, I must not forget that Quintus Curtius was an admired historian of the romantic ages. He is quoted in the *Policraticon* of John of Salisbury, who died in the year 1181.[3] Eneas Sylvius relates, that Alphonsus IX., king of Spain in the thirteenth century and a great astronomer, endeavoured to relieve himself from a tedious malady by reading the Bible over fourteen times, with all the glosses; but not meeting with the expected success, he was cured by the consolation he received from once reading Quintus Curtius.[4] Peter Blesensis, [or Peter of Blois,] Archdeacon of London, a student at Paris about the year 1150, mentioning the books most common in the schools, declares that he profited much by frequently looking into this author.[5] Vincentius Bellovacensis, cited above, a writer of the thirteenth century, often quotes Curtius in his *Speculum Historiale*.[6] He was also early translated into French. Among the royal MSS. in the British Museum, there is a fine copy of a French translation of this classic, adorned with elegant old paintings and illuminations, entitled, *Quinte Curse Ruf, des faiz d'Alexandre, ix. liv. translate par Vasque de Lucene Portugalois. Escript par la main de Jehan du Chesne, a Lille*.[7] It

---

atque apud Nicolaum, Titum, et Strabonem; et in libris nativitatis Alexandri, rerumque ab ipso gestarum, quos Magi ac Ægyptii eo anno quo Alexander decessit, composuerunt, scripta reperies." Lib. ii. c. 12-22, [Lat. Vers.] p. 152, edit. Jo. Frid. Briethaupt.

[1] It is also in a MS. entitled *Secreta Secretorum Aristotelis*, lib. 5. MSS. Bodl. D. 1, 5. This treatise, ascribed to Aristotle, was anciently in high repute. It is pretended to have been translated out of Greek into Arabic or Chaldee by one John, a Spaniard; thence into Latin by Philip, a Frenchman; at length into English verse by Lydgate: under whom more will be said of it. [The Latin is dedicated to Guido Vere de Valentia, Bishop of Tripoli.—*Madden*.]

[2] See *Observat. Fair. Qu.* i. § v. p. 202.
[3] viii. 18.   [4] Op. p. 476.
[5] Epist. 101. *Frequenter inspicere historias Q. Curtii*, &c.
[6] iv. 61, &c. Montfaucon, I think, mentions a MS. of Q. Curtius in the Colbertine library at Paris 800 years old. See Barth. ad Claudian. p. 1165. Alexander Benedictus, in his history of Venice, transcribes whole pages from this historian. I could give other proofs.
[7] 17 F i. Brit. Mus. And again, 20 C. iii. and 15 D. iv. [Sir F. Madden refers to M. Paris's Cat. of the MSS. of the Bibl. Imper. 1836, Noes, 6727-9.]

was made in 1468. But I believe the Latin tranflations of Simeon Seth's romance on this fubject were beft known and moft efteemed for fome centuries.

The French, to refume the main tenor of our argument, had written metrical romances on moft of thefe fubjects before or about the year 1200. Some of thefe feem to have been formed from profe hiftories, enlarged and improved with new adventures and embellifhments from earlier and more fimple tales in verfe on the fame fubject. Chreftien of Troyes wrote *Le Romans du Graal*, or the adventures of the Sangraal, which included the deeds of King Arthur, Sir Triftram, Lancelot du Lac, and the reft of the knights of the round table, before 1191. There is a paffage in a coeval romance, relating to Chreftien, which proves what I have juft advanced, that fome of thefe hiftories previoufly exifted in profe:—

> Chriftians qui entent et paine
> A rimoyer le meillor conte,
> Par le commandement le Conte,
> Qu'il foit contez in cort royal
> Ce eft li contes del Graal
> Dont li quens li bailla le livre.[1]

Chreftien alfo wrote the romance of *Sir Percival*, which belongs to the fame hiftory.[2] Godfrey de Ligny, a cotemporary, finifhed a romance begun by Chreftien, entitled *La Charette* [or Du Chevalier a la Charette], containing the adventures of Launcelot. [This has been printed of late years.] Fauchet affirms, that Chreftien abounds with

---

[1] *Apud* Fauchet, *Rec.* liv. ii. x. p. 99, who adds, "Je croy bien que Romans que nous avons ajourdhuy imprimez, tels que Lancelot du Lac, Triftan, et autres, font refondus fus les vielles profes et rymes et puis refraichis de language."

[The *Roman du Saint Graal* is afcribed to an anonymous *Trouvere* by M. Roquefort, who denies that it was written by Chretien de Troyes. On the authority of the *Cat. de la Valliere*, he alfo attributes the firft part of the profe verfion of this romance to Luces du Gaft, and the continuation only to Robert de Borron. Of de Borron's work entitled *Enfierrement de Merlin ou Roman de St. Graal*, there is a metrical verfion MS. 110. 1987 fonds de l'abbaye St. Germain. See *Poefie Françaife dans les xii. et xiii. Siècles.*—Price.]

The oldeft MSS. of romances on thefe fubjects which I have feen are the following. They are in the royal MSS. of the Britifh Mufeum. *Le Romanz de Triftran*, 20 D. ii. This was probably tranfcribed not long after the year 1200.—*Hiftoire du Lancelot ou S. Graal*, ibid. iii. Perhaps older than the year 1200. Again, *Hiftoire du S. Graal, ou Lancelot*, 20 C. vi. 1. Tranfcribed foon after 1200. This is imperfect at the beginning. The fubject of Jofeph of Arimathea bringing a veffel of the Sangral, that is [the holy difh or veffel] into England, is of high antiquity. It is thus mentioned in *Morte Arthur*. "And then the old man had an harpe, and he fung *an olde fonge* how Jofeph of Arimathy came into this lande." B. iii. c. 5.

[2] Fauchet, p. 103. [*Perceval le galloys, le qui acheua les aduëtures du Sâict Graal, auec aulchuns faictz belliqueulx du noble cheualier Gauuaï, &c.*], *tranflatees de rime de l'ancien auteur.*—[Chretien de Troyes. Printed at Paris, 1530, folio. This writer at his death left the ftory unfinifhed. It was refumed by Gautier de Denet, and concluded by Meffenier. See Roquefort *ut fup.* p. 194.—*Price.*]

In the royal library at Paris is *Le Roman de Perfeval le Galois, par Creftien de Troyes*. In verfe, fol. Mons. Galland thinks there is another romance under this title, *Mem. de Lit.* iii. p. 427, feq. 433, 8vo. The author of which he fuppofes may be Rauol de Biavais, mentioned by Fauchet, p. 142. Compare Lenglet, *Bibl. Rom.*

beautiful inventions.¹ But no story is so common among the earliest French poets as Charlemagne and his Twelve peers. In the British Museum we have an old French MS. containing the history of Charlemagne, translated into prose from Turpin's Latin. The writer declares, that he preferred a sober prose translation of this authentic historian, as histories in rhyme, undoubtedly very numerous on this subject, looked so much like lies.² His title is extremely curious: *Ci comence l'Estoire que Turpin le Ercevesque de Reins fit del bon roy Charlemayne, coment il conquist Espaigne, e delivera des Paens. Et pur ceo qe Estoire rimee semble mensunge, est ceste mis in prose, folun le Latin qe Turpin mesmes fist, tut ensi cume il le vist et vist.*³

Ogier the Dane makes a part of Charlemagne's history, and, I believe, is mentioned by Archbishop Turpin. But his exploits have been recorded in verse by Adenez, an old French poet, not mentioned by Fauchet, author of the two metrical romances of [Berthe] and *Cleomades*, under the name of *Ogier le Danois*, in the year 1270. This author was master of the musicians, or, as others say, heralds at arms, to the Duke of Brabant. Among the royal

---

p. 250. The author of this last-mentioned Percevall, in the exordium, says that he wrote, among others, the romances of Eneas, Roy Marc, and Uselt le Blonde : and that he translated into French, Ovid's *Art of Love*. [The French romance of *Perceval* is preserved in a MS. in the College of Arms, No. 14.—*Madden*. The English translation is preserved in a MS. in Lincoln Cathedral Library, and is included in Mr. Halliwell's *Thornton Romances*, 1844.]

¹ P. 105, *ibid*. [Perhaps the same, says Ritson, with *Les romans de Chevalier à l'épée, ou L'Histoire de Lancelot du Lac*. To the same romance-writer are attributed, *Du Chevalier à Lion, du prince Alexandre, d'Erec*, with others that are now lost.—*Park*. M. Roquefort's catalogue of Chretien's works still extant contains : *Perceval, le Chevalier au Lion, Lancelot du Lac, Cliget* (Cleges ?), *Guillaume d'Angleterre*, and *Erec et Enide*. The latter probably gave rise to the opinion, that Chretien translated the Æneid, and which has been adopted from Von der Hagen.—*Price*.]

² There is a curious passage to this purpose in an old French prose romance of *Charlemagne*, written before the year 1200. "Baudouin Comte de Hainau trouva a Sens en Bourgongne le vie de Charlemagne: et mourant la donna a sa sour Yolond Comtesse de S. Pol, qui m'a prie que je la mette en *Roman sans ryme*. Parce que tel se delitera el Roman qui del Latin n'ent cure ; et par le Roman sera mielx gardee. Maintes gens en ont ouy conter et chanter, mais n'est ce *mensonge* non ce qu'ils en disent et chantent cil conteour ne cil jugleor. Nuz contes rymes n'en est vrais : tot mensonge ce qu'ils dient." Liv. quatr. [Sir F. Madden notes that this is the same as that of Turpin, and refers to M. Paris's Cat. of the MSS. in the national library at Paris, pp. 211-20. There is certainly no conclusive testimony in favour of the composition of the translation between 1178 and 1205, though Sir F. M. positively declares, that it "must be limited between these dates." He mentions that it was Yoland Countess of St. Pol, who caused the metrical story of Guillaume de Palerme to be translated into French. This is our *William and the Werwolf*, edited by Sir F. M. 1832, and more recently by the Early Text Society.]

³ MSS. Harl. 273, f. 86. There is a very old metrical romance on this subject, *ibid*. MSS. Harl. 527, l. f. 1. [*Ogier le Dannois duc de Dannemarche* was printed at Paris about 1498; and at Troyes in 1608, were printed, *Histoire de Morgant le geant*, and *Histoire des nobles Provesses et Vaillances de Gallien restauré*.—*Park*. See also M. Michel's edit. of *Charlemagne*, 1836, from Royal MS. 16 E. viii. 7, written in the twelfth century.]

MSS. in the Museum we have a poem, *Le Livre de Ogeir de Dannemarche*.[1] The French have likewise illustrated this champion in Leonine rhyme. And I cannot help mentioning that they have in verse *Visions of Oddegir the Dane in the kingdom of Fairy*, "Visions d'Ogeir le Danois au Royaume de Faerie en vers François," printed at Paris in 1548.[2]

On the Trojan story the French have an ancient poem, at least not posterior to the thirteenth century, entitled *Roman de Troye*, written by Benoit de Sainct More. As this author appears not to have been known to the accurate Fauchet, nor la Croix du Maine, I will cite the exordium, especially as it records his name, and implies that the piece [was] translated from the Latin, and that the subject was not then common in French:

> Cette estoire n'est pas usée,
> N'en gaires livres n'est trouvée:
> La retraite ne fut encore
> Mais Beneoit de sainte More,
> L'a translaté, et fait et dit,
> Et a sa main les mots ecrit.

He mentions his own name again in the body of the work, and at the end:—

> Je n'en fait plus ne plus en dit;
> Beneoit qui c'est Roman fit.[3]

Du Cange enumerates a metrical MS. romance on this subject by Jaques Millet, entitled *De la Destruction de Troie*.[4] Montfaucon, whose extensive inquiries nothing could escape, mentions Dares Phrigius translated into French verse, at Milan, about the twelfth century.[5] We find also, among the royal MSS. at Paris, Dictys Cretensis translated into French verse.[6] To this subject, although almost equally belonging to that of Charlemagne, we may also refer a French romance in verse, written by Philipes Mousques, canon and chancellor of the church of Tournay. It is, in fact, a chronicle of France: but the author, who does not choose to begin quite so high as Adam and Eve, nor yet later than the Trojan war, opens his history with the rape of Helen, passes on to an ample description of the siege of

---

[1] 15 E. vi. 4.
[The title of Adenez' poem is *Les Enfances d'Ogier-le-Danois*, a copy of which is preserved among the Harl. MSS. No. 4404. His other poem, noticed in the text, is called *Le Roman de Pepin et de Berthe*. See *Cat. Valliere*, No. 2734. The life of Ogier contained in the royal MS. embraces the whole career of this illustrious hero; and is evidently a distinct work from that of Adenez. Whether it be the same version alluded to in the French romance of *Alexander*, where the author is distinguished from the "conteurs batards" of his day, is left to more competent judges.—*Price*. For an account of the modern printed edition of these and other romances of the same cycle, see Brunet, *dern. edit. art. Roman*.]

[2] There is also *L'Histoire du preux Meurvin fils d'Ogier le Danois*, Paris, 1539 and 1540. [Of this there is an English version, Lond. 1612, 4to.]

[3] See Galland *ut supr*. p. 425. [For an account of Benoit de Saint More's poem, the reader is referred to the 12th vol. of the *Archæologia*, and to the modern edition of the original.]

[4] Gloss. *Lat. Ind. Aut*. p. cxiii.   [5] *Monum. Fr*. i. 374.

[6] See Montf. *Catal. MSS*. ii. p. 1669.

Troy, and through an exact detail of all the great events which succeeded conducts his reader to the year 1240. This work comprehends all the fictions of Turpin's Charlemagne, with a variety of other extravagant stories dispersed in many professed romances. But it preserves numberless curious particulars, which throw considerable light on historical facts. Du Cange has collected from it all that concerns the French emperors of Constantinople, which he has printed at the end of his entertaining history of that city.

It was indeed the fashion for the historians of these times to form such a general plan as would admit all the absurdities of popular tradition. Connection of parts and uniformity of subject were as little studied as truth. Ages of ignorance and superstition are more affected by the marvellous than by plain facts, and believe what they find written without discernment or examination. No man before the sixteenth century presumed to doubt that the Francs derived their origin from Francus, a son of Hector; that the Spaniards were descended from Japhet, the Britons from Brutus, and the Scots from Fergus. Vincent de Beauvais, who lived under Louis IX. of France, and who, on account of his extraordinary erudition, was appointed preceptor to that king's sons, very gravely classes archbishop Turpin's Charlemagne among the real histories, and places it on a level with Suetonius and Cæsar. He was himself an historian, and has left a large history of the world, fraught with a variety of reading, and of high repute in the middle ages; but edifying and entertaining as this work might have been to his cotemporaries, at present it serves only to record their prejudices, and to characterise their credulity.[1]

Hercules and Jason, as I have before hinted, were involved in the Trojan story by Guido di Colonna, and hence became familiar to the romance writers.[2] The Hercules, the Theseus, and the Amazons of Boccaccio, hereafter more particularly mentioned, came from this source. I do not at present recollect any old French metrical romances on these subjects, but presume that there are many. Jason seems to have vied with Arthur and Charlemagne; and so popular was his expedition to Colchos, or rather so firmly believed, that in honour of so respectable an adventure a duke of Burgundy instituted the order of the Golden Fleece in the year 1468. At the same time his chaplain Raoul le Feure illustrated the story which gave rise to this magnificent institution, in a prolix and elaborate history, afterwards translated by Caxton.[3] But I must not forget, that

---

[1] He flourished about 1260.

[2] The Trojomanna Saga, a Scandic manuscript at Stockholm, seems to be posterior to Guido's publication. It begins with Jason and Hercules, and their voyage to Colchos: proceeds to the rape of Helen, and ends with the siege and destruction of Troy. It celebrates all the Grecian and Asiatic heroes concerned in that war. Wanl. *Antiquit. Septentr.* p. 315, col. 1.

[3] See *Observat. on Spenser's Fairy Queen,* i. § v. p. 176, *seq.* Montfaucon mentions *Medeæ et Jasonis Historia a Guidone de Columna.* Catal. MSS. Bibl. Coislin. ii. p. 1109.—818.

among the royal manuscripts in the Museum, the French romance of *Hercules* occurs in two books, enriched with numerous ancient paintings.[1] [It was, at a later date, reduced into a chap-book. *Parthenope* is, of course, the hero of the romance of that name, inserted in Le Grand's collection, and of which the English versions have been lately printed.][2] *Ypomedon* has also christened a tale of chivalry, to be noticed hereafter.

The conquests of Alexander the Great were celebrated by one Simon, in old [French], about the twelfth century. This piece thus begins:

> Chanson voil dis per ryme et per Leoin
> Del fil Filippe lo roy de Macedoin.

An Italian poem on Alexander, called *Trionfo Magno*, was presented to Leo X. by Dominicho Falugi Ancifeno, in the year 1521. Crescimbeni says it was copied from a Provençal romance.[3] But one of the most valuable pieces of the old French poetry is on the subject of this victorious monarch, entitled *Roman d' Alexandre*. It has been called the second poem now remaining in the French language, and was written about the year 1200. It was confessedly translated from the Latin; but it bears a nearer resemblance to Simeon Seth's romance than to Quintus Curtius. It was the confederated performance of four writers who, as Fauchet expresses himself, were *associez en leur* jouglerie.[4] Lambert li Cors, a learned

---

[1] 17 E. ii. [This romance of *Hercules* commences with an account of Uranus or Cælum, and terminates with the death of Ulysses by his son Telegonus. The mythological fables with which the first part abounds, are taken from Boccaccio's *Genealogia Deorum*; and the third part, embracing the destruction of Troy by the Greeks under Agamemnon, professes to be a translation from *Dictys of Greece and Dares of Troy*. The Pertonape of the text is evidently Partonepex de Blois (see Le Grand, *Fabliaux*, tom. iv. p. 261, and *Notices des Manuscrits*, tom. ix.), and Ypomedon the hero whom Warton dignifies with the epithet of Childe Ippomedone.—*Price*.]

[2] [*The Old English Versions of Partenope of Blois*. Edited by the Rev. W. E. Buckley. Roxburghe Club, 1862. There is a modern paraphase in verse by Mr. W. S. Rose.]

[3] *Istor. Volg. Poes.* i. iv. p. 332. In the royal manuscripts there is a French poem entitled *La Vengeaunce du graunt Alexandre*, 19 D. i. 2, Brit. Mus. I am not sure whether it is not a portion of the French *Alexander*, mentioned below, written by Jehan li Nivelois [Venelais].

[4] Fauchet, Rec. p. 83. [The order in which Fauchet has classed Lambert li Cors and Alexander of Paris, and which has also been adopted by M. Le Grand, is founded on the following passage of the original poem:

> " La verité d l'istoire si com li roys la fist
> Un clers de Chastiaudun Lambers li Cors li mist
> Qui du Latin la trait et en roman la fist. . . . .
> Alexandre nous dit qui de Bernay fu nez
> Et de Paris refu se surnoms appelles
> Qui or a les siens vers o les Lambert melles."

MM. de la Ravalliere and Roquefort have considered Alexander as the elder writer; apparently referring (*Alexandre nous dit*) to Lambert li Cors. But the last line in this extract clearly confirms M. Le Grand's arrangement. The date assigned by M. Roquefort for its publication is 1184. Jehan li Venelais wrote *Le Testament d'Alexandre*; and Perot de Saint Cloot, *La Vengeaunce d'Alexandre*. Mr. Douce has enumerated eleven French poets, who have written on the subject

civilian, began the poem; and it was continued and completed by Alexandre de Paris, Jean le [Venelais], and [Perot] de Saint [Cloot],[1] The poem is closed with Alexander's will. This is no imagination of any of our three poets, although one of them was a civil lawyer. Alexander's will, in which he nominates successors to his provinces and kingdoms, was a tradition commonly received, and is mentioned by Diodorus Siculus and Ammianus Marcellinus.[2] [This work has never been edited.][3] It is voluminous; and in the Bodleian library at Oxford is a vast folio MS. of it in vellum, which is of great antiquity, richly decorated, and in high preservation.[4] The margins and initials exhibit not only fantastic ornaments and illuminations exquisitely finished, but also pictures executed with singular elegance, expressing the incidents of the story, and displaying the fashion of buildings, armour, dress, musical instruments,[5] and other particulars appropriated to the times. At the end we read this hexameter, which points out the name of the scribe [of that portion, which contains a Scotish metrical romance of Alexander, an addition of the fifteenth century]:[6]

Nomen scriptoris est Thomas plenus amoris.

Then follows the date of the year in which the transcript was completed, viz. 1338. Afterwards there is the name and date of the illuminator, in the following colophon, written in golden letters: *Che livre fu perfais de la enluminiere an xviii°. jour davryl par Jehan de grise l'an de grace m.ccc.xliiii.*[7] Hence it may be concluded, that the illuminations and paintings of this superb manuscript, which were most probably begun as soon as the scribe had finished his part, took up six years: no long time, if we consider the attention of an artist to ornaments so numerous, so various, so minute, and so laboriously touched. It has been supposed that before the appearance

---

of Alexander or his family: and Mr. Weber observes, that several others might be added to the list. See Weber's *Metrical Romances* (who notices various European versions), *Notices des Manuscrits du Roi*, t. v.; *Catalogue de la Valliere*, t. ii.—*Price*. Sir F. Madden refers us also to De la Rue, *Essais*, &c. ii. 341-56, and supplies us with the name of Thomas of Kent, an Anglo-Norman (not mentioned by Mr. Price or by Mr. Wright) as one of the continuators of the romance of *Alexander*.]

[1] Fauchet, *ibid.* Mons. Galland mentions a French romance in verse, unknown to Fauchet, and entitled *Roman d'Athys et de Prophylias*, written by one Alexander, whom he supposes to be this Alexander of Paris. *Mem. Lit.* iii. p. 429, edit. Amst. [This conjecture is confirmed by M. Roquefort, *ubi supr.* p. 118.—*Price*.] It is often cited by Carpentier, Suppl. Cang.

[2] See Fabric. *Bibl. Gr.* c. iii. l. viii. p. 205.   [3] [Sir F. Madden's inform.]

[4] MSS. Bodl. B 264, fol.

[5] The most frequent of these are organs, bagpipes, lutes, and trumpets.

[6] [Sir F. Madden's inform. He adds, that another portion of the *Alexander* is in MS. Ashmole, 44. The Rev. J. S. Stevenson edited the Alliterative Romances of Alexander for the Roxburghe Club in 1849. In it he printed the alliterative fragments from Bodl. MS. 264, and Ashmole 44 (ab. 1450 A.D.) The far earlier alliterative fragment in MS. Greaves 60 was printed by Mr. Skeat in his edit. of *William of Palerne*, Early English Text Society, 1867.]

[7] [Bishop Warburton had] a most beautiful French manuscript on vellum of *Mort d'Arthur*, ornamented in the same manner. It was a present from Vertue the engraver.

of this poem, the *Romans*, or those pieces which celebrated Gests, were constantly composed in short verses of six or eight syllables: and that in this *Roman d'Alexandre* verses of twelve syllables were first used. It has therefore been imagined, that the verses called *Alexandrines*, the present French heroic measure, took their rise from this poem; Alexander being the hero, and Alexander the chief of the four poets concerned in the work. That the name, some centuries afterwards, might take place in honour of this celebrated and early effort of French poetry, I think very probable; but that verses of twelve syllables made their first appearance in this poem, is a doctrine which, to say no more, from examples already produced and examined is at least ambiguous.[1] In this poem Gadifer, hereafter mentioned, of Arabian lineage, is a very conspicuous champion:

> Gadifer fu moult preus, d'un Arrabi lignage.

A rubric or title of one of the chapters is, "Comment Alexander fuit mys en un vesal de vooire pour veoir le merveiles," &c. This is a passage already quoted from Simeon Seth's romance, relating Alexander's expedition to the bottom of the ocean, in a vessel of glass, for the purpose of inspecting fishes and sea monsters. In another place from the same romance, he turns astronomer, and soars to the moon by the help of four gryphons. The caliph is frequently mentioned in this piece; and Alexander, like Charlemagne, has his twelve peers.

These were the four reigning stories of romance: on which perhaps English pieces, translated from the French, existed before or about the year 1300. But there are some other English romances mentioned in the prologue of *Richard Cuer du Lyon*, which we likewise probably received from the French in that period, and on which I shall here also enlarge.

Beuves de Hanton, or *Sir Bevis de Southampton*, is a French romance of considerable antiquity, although the hero is not older than the Norman conquest. It is alluded to in our English romance on this story, which will again be cited, and at large:

> Forth thei yode, *so saith the boke*.[2]

And again more expresly,

> Under the bridge wer sixty belles,
> Right as the *Romans* telles.[3]

The *Romans* is the French original. It is called the Romance of *Beuves de Hanton*, by Pere Labbe.[4] The very ingenious Monsieur de la Curne de sainte Palaye mentions an ancient French romance in prose, entitled *Beufres de Hanton*.[5] Chaucer mentions Bevis, with other famous romances, but whether in French or English is uncer-

---

[1] See Pref. *Le Roman de la Rose*, par Mons. L'Abbé Lenglet, i. p. xxxvi.
[2] Signat. P ii. [*Bevis of Hamton* was edited from the Auchinleck MS. for the Maitland Club, 1838, 4to.]
[3] Signat. E iv.
[4] *Nov. Bibl.* p. 334, edit. 1652.
[5] *Mem. Lit.* xv. 582, 4to.

tain.¹ *Beuves of Hantonne* was printed at [Troyes as early as 1489].²
Afcapart was one of his giants, a character³ in very old French
romances. Bevis lived at Downton in Wiltfhire. Near Southampton
is an artificial hill called Bevis Mount, on which was probably a
fortrefs; [and within the town there is a gate which ftill retains his
name].⁴ It is pretended that he was Earl of Southampton. His
fword is fhown in Arundel caftle. This piece was evidently written
after the Crufades; as Bevis is knighted by the King of Armenia,
and is one of the generals at the fiege of Damafcus.

Guy Earl of Warwick is recited as a French romance by Labbe.⁵
In the Britifh Mufeum a metrical hiftory in very old French appears,
in which Felicia, or Felice, is called the daughter of an earl of
Warwick, and Guido, or Guy, of Warwick is the fon of Seguart
the earl's fteward. The manufcript is at prefent imperfect.⁶ Montfaucon mentions among the royal manufcripts at Paris, *Roman de
Guy et Beuves de Hanton*. The latter is the romance laft mentioned.
Again, *Le Livre de Guy de Warwick et de Harold d'Ardenne*.⁷ This
Harold d'Arden is a diftinguifhed warrior of Guy's hiftory, and
therefore his achievements fometimes form a feparate romance: as
in the royal MSS. of the Britifh Mufeum, where we find *Le Romant
de Herolt Dardenne*.⁸ In the Englifh romance of Guy, mentioned

---

¹ *Rim. Thop.* [Mr. Wright refers to a good MS. of Bevis, in Caius Coll. Camb.; but the editor does not obferve any fuch MS. in Smith's Cat. 1849.]

² [The earlieft printed copy of this romance that I have met with, is in Italian, and printed at Venice, 1489, 4to. Other editions in the fame language are, Venice, 1562, 1580, 12mo.; Milan, 1584, 4to.; Piacenza, 1599, 12mo.; French editions, Paris, folio, no date, by Verard; *Ibid.* 4to., no date, by Bonfons. I have been informed from refpectable authority, that this romance is to be found in Provençal poetry, among the MSS. of Chriftina, queen of Sweden, now in the Vatican library, and that it appears to have been written in 1380. See likewife *Bibl. de du Verdier*, tom. iii. p. 266.—*Douce.* For an account of the Englifh editions, fee *Handb. of E. E. Lit.*, art. Bevis and Additions, *ibid.*]

³ Selden's Drayton, *Polyolb.* s. iii. p. 37.

⁴ [*Bevis* feems long to have retained its popularity, fince Wither thus complained of the fale it had about the year 1627. "The ftationers have fo peftered their printing houfes and fhopps with fruitleffe volumes, that the auncient and renowned authors are almoft buried among them as forgotten; and at laft you fhall fee nothing to be fould amongft us, but Currantos, Beavis of Hampton, or fuch trumpery." *Scholler's Purgatory*, (circa 1625).—*Park.* Sir F. Madden and fome other gentlemen, in the year 1833, opened the tumulus at the bottom of the vale of Pugh Dean, about a mile from Arundel caftle, but found no remains of the hero. The tradition is, that Bevis threw his fword, fix feet long, from the walls of the caftle into the valley, and there appointed to be buried.]

⁵ *Ubi fupr.*

⁶ MSS. Harl. 3775, 2. [Other copies are in Corpus Chrifti Coll. Camb. and in the College of Arms.—*Madden.*]

⁷ Catal. MSS. p. 792. Among the Benet manufcripts there is *Romanz de Gui de Warwyk*, Num. l. It begins,
"Puis cel tems ke deus fu nez."
This book belonged to Saint Auguftin's abbey at Canterbury. With regard to the preceding romance of Bevis, the Italians had *Buovo d'Antona*, undoubtedly from the French, before 1348. And Lhuyd recites in Welfh, *Yftori Boun o Hamtun*. *Archæol.* p. 264.

⁸ 15 E. vi. 8. [This romance might be called with more propriety an epifode in

at large in its proper place, this champion is called, *Syr Heraude of Arderne*.[1] At length this favourite subject formed a large prose romance, entitled *Guy de Warwick, Chevalier d' Angleterre, et de la belle fille Felix samie*, and printed at Paris [March 12, 1525-6]. Chaucer mentions Guy's story among the *Romaunces of Pris*:[2] and it is alluded to in the Spanish romance of *Tirant lo Blanch*, or *Tirante the White*, supposed to have been written not long after the year 1430.[3] This romance was composed, or perhaps enlarged, after the Crusades, as we find that Guy's redoubted encounters with Colbrond the Danish giant, with the monster of Dunsmore-heath, and the dragon of Northumberland, are by no means equal to some of his achievements in the Holy Land, and the trophies which he won from the Soldan under the command of the Emperor Frederick.

The romance of *Sidrac*, entitled in the French version [*La fontaine de toutes sciéces du philosophe Sydrach*], appears to have been very popular, from the present frequency of its MSS. [both in French and English.] But it is rather a romance of Arabian philosophy than of chivalry. It is a system of natural knowledge, and particularly treats of the virtues of plants. Sidrac, the philosopher of this system, was astronomer to an eastern king. He lived eight hundred and forty-seven years after Noah, of whose book of astronomy he was possessed.

He converts Bocchus, an idolatrous king of India, to the Christian faith, by whom he is invited to build a mighty tower against the invasions of a rival king of India. But the history, no less than the subject of this piece, displays the state, nature and migrations of literature in the dark ages. After the death of Bocchus, Sidrac's book fell into the hands of a Chaldean renowned for piety. It then successively becomes the property of King Madian, Naaman the Assyrian, and Grypho, archbishop of Samaria. The latter had a priest named Demetrius, who brought it into Spain, and here it was translated from the Greek into Latin. This translation is said to be made at Toledo by Roger of Palermo, a minorite friar, in the 13th century. A king of Spain then commanded it to be translated from Latin into Arabic, and sent it as a most valuable present to Emir Elmomenim, lord of Tunis. It was next given to Frederick II., emperor of Germany, famous in the Crusades. This work, which is of considerable length, was translated into English verse, and will be mentioned on that account again. Sidrac is recited as an eminent philosopher, with Seneca and King Solomon, in the *Marchaunts Second tale*, ascribed to Chaucer.[4]

It is natural to conclude that most of these French romances were

---

the life of Raynbrun, Guy's son. It recounts the manner in which he released Herolt d'Ardenne from prison, and the return of both to their native country. It has the merit of being exceedingly short, and states, among other matter, that Herolt was born at Walmforth in England.—*Price*.]

[1] Sign. L ii. *vers*. [2] *Rim. Thop*. [3] Percy's *Ball*. iii. 100.
[4] v. 1932. There is an old translation of *Sidrac* into Dutch, MSS. Marshall, Bibl. Bodl. 31, fol. [King Bocchus or Boccus seems to have been rather a popular character in our own early literature. See *Handb. of E. E. Lit*. p. 43.]

current in England, either in the French originals, which were well underſtood at leaſt by the more polite readers, or elſe by tranſlation or imitation, as I have before hinted, when the romance of *Richard Cuer de Lyon*, in whoſe prologue they are recited, was tranſlated into Engliſh. That the latter was the caſe as to ſome of them, at leaſt, we ſhall ſoon produce actual proofs. A writer, who has conſidered theſe matters with much penetration and judgment, obſerves, that probably from the reign of our Richard I. we are to date that remarkable intercommunication and mutual exchange of compoſitions, which we diſcover to have taken place at ſome early period between the French and Engliſh minſtrels; the ſame ſet of phraſes, the ſame ſpecies of characters, incidents, and adventures, and often the identical ſtories, being found in the metrical romances of both nations.[1] From cloſe connection and conſtant intercourſe, the traditions and the champions of one kingdom were equally known in the other: and although Bevis and Guy were Engliſh heroes, yet on theſe principles this circumſtance by no means deſtroys the ſuppoſition, that their achievements, although perhaps already celebrated in rude Engliſh ſongs, might be firſt wrought into romance by the French;[2] and it ſeems probable, that we continued for ſome time this practice of borrowing from our neighbours. Even the titles of our oldeſt romances, ſuch as [*Sir Pleyndamour*, mentioned by Chaucer in the *Rime of Sir Thopas*, but not at preſent known under ſuch a title],[3] *Sir Triamour*,[4]

---

[1] Percy's *Eſs. on Anc. Eng. Minſtr.* p. 12, [attached to his edit. of the *Reliques*.]

[2] Dugdale relates, that in the reign of Henry IV., about the year 1410, a lord Beauchamp, travelling into the Eaſt, was hoſpitably received at Jeruſalem by the Soldan's lieutenant: "Who hearing that he was deſcended from the famous Guy of Warwick, *whoſe ſtory they had in books of their own language*, invited him to his palace and, royally feaſting him, preſented him with three precious ſtones of great value, beſides divers cloaths of ſilk and gold given to his ſervants." Baron. i. p. 243, col. 1. This ſtory is delivered on the credit of John Rouſe, the traveller's cotemporary. Yet it is not ſo very improbable that Guy's hiſtory ſhould be a book among the Saracens, if we conſider, that Conſtantinople was not only a central and connecting point between the eaſtern and weſtern world, but that the French in the thirteenth century had acquired an eſtabliſhment there under Baldwin earl of Flanders: that the French language muſt have been known in Sicily, Jeruſalem, Cyprus, and Antioch, in conſequence of the conqueſts of Robert Guiſcard, Hugo le Grand, and Godfrey of Bulloigne: and that pilgrimages into the Holy Land were exceſſively frequent. It is hence eaſy to ſuppoſe, that the French imported many of their ſtories or books of this ſort into the Eaſt; which being thus underſtood there, and ſuiting the genius of the Orientals, were at length tranſlated into their language. It is remarkable, that the Greeks at Conſtantinople, in the twelfth century and ſince, called all the Europeans by the name of Franks, as the Turks do to this day. See Seld. [Note on Drayton's] *Polyolb.* § viii. p. 130. [Buſbec, in the third letter of his Embaſſy into Turkey, mentions that the Georgians in their ſongs make frequent mention of Roland, whoſe name he ſuppoſes to have paſſed over with Godfrey of Bulloigne.—*Douce*.]

[3] [The editor merely throws out the ſuggeſtion that *Pleyndamour* is merely another form of *Plenus Amoris*, and that Thomas Plenus Amoris purports to have been the writer or tranſcriber of an early Scotiſh romance on the ſubject of Alexander, above mentioned. Sir Blandamour is one of the characters in the *Faerie Queene*.]

[4] [Edited by Mr. Halliwell for the Percy Society, 1846.]

Sir Eglamour of Artois,[1] La Mort d'Arthur, with many more, betray their French extraction. It is likewise a presumptive argument in favour of this assertion, that we find no prose romances in our language before Caxton translated from the French the History of Troy, the Life of Charlemagne, the Histories of Jason, Paris and Vyenne,[2] [Morte d'Arthur,] and other prose pieces of chivalry: by which, as the profession of minstrelsy decayed and gradually gave way to a change of manners and customs, romances in metre were at length imperceptibly superseded, or at least grew less in use as a mode of entertainment at public festivities.

Various causes concurred, in the mean time, to multiply books of

---

[1] In our English *Syr Eglamour of Artoys*, there is this reference to the French, from which it was translated. Sign. E. i.

"His own mother there he wedde,
In Romaunce as we rede."

Again, fol. ult.

"In Romaunce this cronycle ys."

The authors of these pieces often refer to their original. Just as Ariosto mentions Turpin for his voucher. [Halliwell's *Thornton Romances*, Camd. Soc. 1844.]

[2] [A short prose tale of chivalry, an English version of which was printed by Caxton in 1485. See Roxburghe Library reprint, 1868, Pref. But to what is there said may now be added that in the French language there are no fewer than three independent versions of this story, all derived from an at present undiscovered Provençal original. 1. The MS. No. 7534 in the Bibliothèque Imperiale, at Paris, printed in 1835. 2. A MS. in large 4to. on paper, with the prologue of Pierre de la Sippade dated, not 1459, as in the Paris copy, but 1432, a very important variation, since in the Paris MS. Sippade is made (as it would seem falsely) to represent that he did not translate the work out of the Provençal till 1459. 3. An abridged version, of which there were several early-printed editions in 4to., of which one, now before me, has thirty-two leaves, with woodcuts, and is in two columns. This last was Caxton's original; and he has followed the French text very closely. There must have been impressions of the shorter story in type before 1485, therefore; but the earliest editions cited by Brunet are without note of the year. The copy, mentioned above as having the date 1432 to the Prologue, differs likewise materially in the arrangement of the text, and, to a certain extent, in the conduct of the story. In the old library of the Dukes of Burgundy,[1] according to an inventory taken about 1467, No. 2291 of the MSS. was *Le Roman de Paris et de la belle Vienne traduit de provençal en françois, par Pierre de la Ceppède Marseillois*, sur papier, avec miniatures.

Mr. Price observes: Its early and extensive popularity is manifested by the prologue to the Swedish version, made by order of Queen Euphemia, in the second month of the year 1308. This refers to a German original, executed at the command of the Emperor Otho (1197-1208); but this again was taken from a foreign (Wälsche) source.]

But I must not omit here that Du Cange recites a metrical French romance in MS., *Le Roman de Girard de Vienne*, written by Bertrand le Clerc. *Gloss. Lat.* i. Ind. Auct. p. cxciii. Madox has printed the names of several French romances found in the reign of Edward III., among which one on this subject occurs. *Formul. Anglic.* p. 12. Compare *Observations on Spenser's Fairy Queen*, vol. ii. § viii. p. 43. Among the royal MSS. in the British Museum, there is in verse *Histoire de Gyrart de Vienne et de ses freres*, 20 D. xi. 2. This MS. was perhaps written before the year 1300. [It is on vellum, in two columns. It appears to be the romance quoted by Du Cange.]

---

[1] [Blades, *Life and Typogr. of W. Caxton*, i. 278.]

chivalry among the French, and to give them a superiority over the English, not only in the number but in the excellence of those compositions. Their barons lived in greater magnificence. Their feudal system flourished on a more sumptuous, extensive, and lasting establishment. Schools were instituted in their castles for initiating the young nobility in the rules and practice of chivalry. Their tilts and tournaments were celebrated with a higher degree of pomp; and their ideas of honour and gallantry were more exaggerated and refined.

We may add, what indeed has been before incidentally remarked, that their troubadours were the first writers of metrical romances. But by what has been here advanced, I do not mean to insinuate without any restrictions, that the French entirely led the way in these compositions. Undoubtedly the Provençal bards contributed much to the progress of Italian literature. Raimond IV. of Arragon, count of Provence, a lover and a judge of letters, about the year 1220, invited to his court the most celebrated of the songsters who professed to polish and adorn the Provençal language by various sorts of poetry.[1] Charles I., his son-in-law, and the inheritor of his virtues and dignities, conquered Naples, and carried into Italy a taste for the Provençal literature. This taste prevailed at Florence especially, where Charles reigned many years with great splendour, and where his successors resided. Soon afterwards the Roman court was removed to Provence.[2] Hitherto the Latin language had only been in use. The Provençal writers established a common dialect; and their example convinced other nations that the modern languages were no less adapted to composition than those of antiquity.[3] They introduced a love of reading, and diffused a general and popular taste for poetry, by writing in a language intelligible to the ladies and the people. Their verses, being conveyed in a familiar tongue, became the chief amusement of princes and feudal lords, whose courts had now begun to assume an air of greater brilliancy; a circumstance which necessarily gave great encouragement to their profession, and by rendering these arts of ingenious entertainment universally fashionable, imper-

---

[1] Giovan. Villani, *Istor.* l. vi. c. 92.

[2] Villani acquaints us, that Brunetti Latini, Dante's master, was the first who attempted to polish the Florentines by improving their taste and style. He died in 1294. See Villan. *ibid.* l. ix. c. 135. [That Brunetti did not write his *Tesoro* in Provençal we have his own authority, and the evidence of the work itself:—Et se aucuns demandoit pourquoi chis livre est escrit en roumans selon la raison de France, pour chou que nous sommes Ytalien je diroie que ch'est pour chou que nous sommes en France; l'autre pour chou que la parleure en est plus delitable et plus commune a toutes gens. Notices des Manuscripts, t. v. p. 270.--*Price.*]

[3] Dante designed at first that his *Inferno* should appear in Latin. But finding that he could not so effectually in that language impress his satirical strokes and political maxims on the laity or illiterate, he altered his mind, and published that piece in Italian. Had Petrarch written his *Africa*, his Eclogues, and his prose compositions in Italian, the literature of his country would much sooner have arrived at perfection. [Mr. R. Taylor refers to Rossetti's *Spirito Antipapale*, 1832.]

ceptibly laid the foundation of polite literature. From these beginnings it were easy to trace the progress of poetry to its perfection, through John de Meun in France, Dante in Italy, and Chaucer in England.

This praise must undoubtedly be granted to the Provençal poets. But in the mean time, to recur to our original argument, we should be cautious of asserting, in general and undiscriminating terms, that the Provençal poets were the first writers of metrical romance: at least we should ascertain, with rather more precision than has been commonly used on this subject, how far they may claim this merit. I am of opinion that there were two sorts of French troubadours, who have not hitherto been sufficiently distinguished. If we diligently examine their history, we shall find that the poetry of the first troubadours consisted in satires, moral fables, allegories, and sentimental sonnets. So early as the year 1180, a tribunal, called the Court of Love, was instituted both in Provence and Picardy, at which questions in gallantry were decided. This institution furnished eternal matter for the poets, who threw the claims and arguments of the different parties into verse, in a style that afterwards led the way to the spiritual conversations of Cyrus and Clelia.[1] Fontenelle does not scruple to acknowledge, that gallantry was the parent of French poetry.[2] But to sing romantic and chivalrous adventures was a very different task, and required very different talents. The troubadours, therefore, who composed metrical romances, form a different species, and ought always to be considered separately. And this latter class seems to have commenced at a later period, not till after the Crusades had effected a great change in the manners and ideas of the western world. In the meantime I hazard a conjecture. Giraldi Cinthio supposes that the art of the troubadours, commonly called the Gay Science, was first communicated from France to the Italians, and afterwards to the Spaniards.[3] This, perhaps, may be true; but at the same time it is highly probable, as the Spaniards had their *Juglares* or convivial bards very early, as from long connection they were immediately and intimately acquainted with the fictions of the Arabians, and as they were naturally fond of chivalry, that the troubadours of Provence in great measure caught this turn of fabling from Spain. To mention no other obvious means of intercourse in an affair of this nature, the communication was easy through the ports of Toulon and Marseilles, by which the two nations carried on from early times a constant commerce. Even the French critics themselves universally allow that the Spaniards, having learned rhyme from the Arabians, through this very channel conveyed it to Provence. Tasso preferred *Amadis de Gaul*, a romance originally written in [Portugal] by Vasco Lobeyra before the year 1300,[4] to

---

[1] This part of their character will be insisted upon more at large when we come to speak of Chaucer.
[2] *Theatr. Fr.* p. 13.   [3] Apud Huet. *Orig. Rom.* p. 108.
[4] Nic. Antonius, *Bibl. Hispan. Vet.* tom. ii. l. viii. c. 7, num. 291.

the most celebrated pieces of the Provençal poets.[1] But this subject [has received illustration from several writers to whom we may refer, Sainte Palaye,[2] Millot,[3] Fauriel,[4] Paulin Paris,[5] Paul Meyer, Gaston Paris, &c.]

SECTION IV.

VARIOUS matters suggested by the Prologue of *Richard cuer de Lyon*, cited in the last section, have betrayed us into a long digression, and interrupted the regularity of our annals. But I could not neglect so fair an opportunity of preparing the reader for those metrical tales which, having acquired a new cast of fiction from the Crusades and a magnificence of manners from the increase of chivalry, now began to be greatly multiplied, and as it were professedly to form a separate species of poetry. I now therefore resume the series, and proceed to give some specimens of the English metrical romances which appeared before or about the reign of Edward II.: and although most of these pieces continued to be sung by the minstrels in the halls of our magnificent ancestors for some [time] afterwards, yet, as their first appearance may most probably be dated at this period, they properly coincide in this place with the tenor of our history. In the mean time, it is natural to suppose, that by frequent repetition and successive changes of language during many generations, their original simplicity must have been in some degree corrupted. Yet some of the specimens are extracted from manuscripts written in the reign of Edward III. Others indeed from printed copies, where the editors took great liberties in accommodating the language to the times. However, in such as may be supposed to have suffered most from depravations of this sort, the substance of the ancient style still remains, and at least the structure of the story. On the whole, we mean to give the reader an idea of those popular heroic tales in verse, professedly written for the harp, which began to be multiplied among us about the beginning of the fourteenth century. We will begin with the romance of *Richard cuer de Lyon*, already mentioned.

The poem opens with the marriage of Richard's father, Henry II. with the daughter of Carbarryne, a king of Antioch. But this is only a lady of romance. Henry married Eleanor, the divorced

---

[1] *Disc. del Poem. Eroic.* l. ii. pp. 45, 46.
[2] [*Memoires sur l'ancienne Chevalerie*, 1781, 3 vols. 12mo.]
[3] [*Histoire Litteraire des Troubadours*, 1774, 3 vols. 12mo. An abridged English version appeared in 1807. See Brunet, *dern. edit.* v. 65.]
[4] [*Histoire de la Poesie Provençale*, 1847-8, 3 vols. 8vo.]
[5] *Li Romans de Garin le Loherain, publié pour la première fois, et precedé de l'examen du système de M. Fauriel sur les romans Carlovingiens*, 1833-5, 2 vols. 12mo. It may be worth while to add Bishop Hurd's *Letters on Chivalry and Romance*, 1762, 8vo.]

queen of Louis of France. The minstrels could not conceive any thing less than an Eastern princess to be the mother of this magnanimous hero:

> His barons hym fedde[1]
> That he graunted a wyff to wedde.
> Haftely he fente hys fondes
> Into many dyuerfe londes,
> The feyrefte wyman that wore on liff
> Men wolde[2] bringe hym to wyff.[3]

The meffengers or ambaffadors, in their voyage, meet a ship adorned like Cleopatra's galley:

> Swylk on ne feygh they never non ;
> All it was whyt of huel-bon,
> And every nayl with gold begrave :
> Off pure gold was the ftave ;[4]
> Her maft was [of] yvory ;
> Off famyte the fayl wytterly.
> Her ropes wer off tuely fylk,
> Al fo whyt as ony mylk.
> That noble fchyp was al withoute
> With clothys of golde fprede aboute ;
> And her loof[5] and her wyndas[6]
> Off afure forfothe it was.
>   In that fchyp ther wes i-dyght
> Knyghts and ladyys of mekyll myght ;
> And a lady therinne was,
> Bryght as the funne thorugh the glas.
> Her men aborde gunne to ftonde,
> And fefyd that other with her honde,
> And prayde hem for to dwelle
> And her counfayl for to telle :
> And they graunted with all fkylle
> For to telle al at her wylle :
> "Swo wyde landes we have went[7]
> For kyng Henry us has fent,

---

[1] [redde, *advifed*.]   [2] [fholde.]

[3] [The prefent text has been taken from the edition of this romance by Mr. Weber, who followed a manufcript of no very early date in Caius College library, Cambridge. The variations between this and the early printed editions confift principally in the ufe of a more antiquated phrafeology, with fome trifling changes of the fenfe. The moft important of thefe are given in the notes below. Mr. Ellis, who has analyfed this romance (vol. ii. p. 186), conceives the fable in its prefent form to have originated with the reign of Edward I. ; and that the extravagant fictions it contains were grafted by fome Norman minftrel upon an earlier narrative, more in unifon with Richard's real hiftory. Of the ftory in its uncorrupted ftate, he confiders a fragment occurring in the Auchinlech MS. to be an Englifh tranflation ; and as this document was "tranfcribed in the minority of Edward III." the following declaration of Mr. Weber may not exceed the truth : —"There is no doubt that our romance exifted before the year 1300, as it is referred to in the Chronicles of Robert of Gloucefter and Robert de Brunne; and as thefe rhymefters wrote for mere Englifh readers, it is not to be fuppofed that they would refer them to a French original."—*Price*.]

[4] [fklave, *rudder : clavus*.]

[5] [loft, *deck*. Sir F. Madden refers for an explanation of this word to Michel's *Triftan*, Gloff. under *Lof*. and to his own edit. of Laʒamon's *Brut*, 1847, i. 335, where the word is tranflated *luff*.]

[6] [wyndlace.]   [7] ["To dyverfe londes do we wende."]

For to feke hym a qwene
The fayrefte that myghte fonde bene."
Upros a kyng off a chayer
With that word they fpoke ther.
The chayer was [of] charboncle fton,
Swylk on ne fawgh they never non:
And tuo dukes hym befyde,
Noble men and mekyl off pryde,
And welcomed the meffangers ylkone.
Into that fchyp they gunne gone. . . .
They fette trefteles and layde a borde;
Cloth of fylk theron was fprad,
And the kyng hymfelve bad,
That his doughter were forth fette,
And in a chayer before hym fette.
Trumpes begonne for to blowe;
Sche was fette forth in a throwe[1]
With twenty knyghtes her aboute
And moo off ladyes that wer ftoute. . .
Whenne they had nygh i-eete,
Adventures to fpeke they nought forgeete.
The kyng ham tolde, in hys refoun
It com hym thorugh a vyfyoun,
In his land that he cam froo,
Into Yngelond for to goo;
And his doughtyr that was fo dere
For to wende bothe in fere,[2]
" In this manere we have us dyght
Into that lande to wende ryght."
Thenne aunfweryd a meffanger,
Hys name was callyd Bernager,
" Forther wole we feke nought
To my lord fhe fchal be brought."

They foon arrive in England, and the lady is lodged in the Tower of London, one of the royal caftles:

The meffangers the kyng have tolde
Of that ladye fayr and bold,
Ther he lay in the Tour
Off that lady whyt fo flour.
Kyng Henry gan hym fon dyght,
With erls, barons, and manye a knyght,
Agayn the lady for to wende:
For he was curteys and hende.
The damyfele on lond was led,
And clothes of gold before her fpred,
And her fadyr her beforn
With a coron off gold icorn;
The meffangers be ylk a fyde
And menftralles with mekyl pryde
Kyng Henry lyght in hyyng
And grette fayr that uncouth kyng. . .

---

[1] immediately. [In an ancient Provençal poem, of which M. de Sainte Palaye has given fome account in his *Mémoires fur l'ancienne Chevalerie*, tom. ii. p. 160, a mafter gives the following inftructions to his pupil, " Ouvrez a votre cheval par des coupes redoublés, la route qu'il doit tenir, et que fon portrail foit garni de beaux grelots ou fonnettes bien rangées; car ces fonnettes reveillent merveilleufement le courage de celui qui le monte, et repandent devant lui la terreur."—*Douce*.]

[2] company.

> To Weſtemenſtre they wente in fere
> Lordyngs and ladys that ther were.
> Trumpes begonne for to blowe,
> To mete[1] they wente in a throwe, &c.[2]

The firſt of our hero's achievements in chivalry is at a ſplendid tournament held at Saliſbury. Clarendon, near Saliſbury, was one of the king's palaces:[3]

> Kyng Rychard gan hym dyſguyſe
> In a ful ſtrange queyntyſe.[4]
> He cam out of a valaye
> For to ſe of theyr playe,
> As a knyght aventurous:
> Hys atyre was orgolous:[5]
> Al togyder cole black
> Was hys horſe withoute lacke;
> Upon hys creſt a raven ſtode,
> That yaned[6] as he wer wode.
> He bare a ſchafte that was grete and ſtrong,
> It was fourtene foot long;
> And it was grete and ſtout,
> One and twenty ynches about.[7]
> The fyrſt knyght that he there mette,
> Ful egyrly he hym grette
> With a dente amyd the ſchelde;
> His hors he bar doun in the felde, &c.[8]

A battle-axe which Richard carried with him from England into the Holy Land is thus deſcribed:

> King Richard, I underſtond,
> Or he went out of Englond,

---

[1] to dinner.   [2] line 135.
[3] In the pipe-rolls of this king's reign I find the following articles relating to this ancient palace, which has been already mentioned incidentally. *Rot. Pip.* 1 *Ric. I.* "Wiltes.—Et in cariagio vini Regis a Clarendon uſque Woodeſtoke, 34*s*. 4*d*. per Br. Reg. Et pro ducendis 200 m. [marcis] a Sareſburia uſque Briſtow, 7*s*. 4*d*. per Br. Reg. Et pro ducendis 2500 libris a Sareſburia uſque Gloceſtriam, 26*s*. 10*d*. per Br. Reg. Et pro tonellis et clavis ad eoſdem denarios. Et in cariagio de 4000 marcis a Sarum uſque Suthanton, et pro tonellis et aliis neceſſariis, 8*s*. et 1*d*. per Br. Reg." And again in *Rot. Pip.* 30 *Hen. III.* "Wilteſcire.—Et in una marcelſia ad opus regis et reginæ apud Clarendon cum duobus intercluſoriis et duabus cameris privatis, hoſtio veteris aulæ amovendo in porticu, et de eadem aula camera facienda cum camino et feneſtris, et camera privata, et quadam magna coquina quadrata, et aliis operationibus, contentis in Brevi, inceptis per eundem Nicolaum et non perfeɛtis, 526*l*. 16*s*. 5*d*. ob. per Br. Reg." Again, *Rot. Pip.* 39 *Hen. III.* "Sudhamt.—*Comp. Novæ foreſtæ.* Et in triginta miliaribus ſcindularum [ſhingles] faciend. in eadem foreſta et cariand. eaſdem uſque Clarendon ad domum regis ibidem cooperiandam, 6*l*. et 1 marc. per Br. Reg. Et in 30 mill. ſcindularum faciend. in eadem, et cariand. uſque Clarendon, 11*l*. 10*s*." And again, in the ſame reign, the canons of Ivy-church receive penſions for celebrating in the royal chapel there. *Rot. Pip.* 7 *Hen. III.* "Wiltes.—Et canonicis de monaſterio ederoſo miniſtrantibus in Capella de Clarendon. 35*l*. 7*d*. ob." Stukeley is miſtaken in ſaying this palace was built by King John.
[4] See Du Cange, *Gl. Lat.* Cointiſe.
[5] proud, pompous.   [6] yawned.
[7] It is "One and twenti inches aboute." So Dr. Farmer's MS., purchaſed from Mr. Martin's library. See *ſupr.* This is in Engliſh.
[8] line 267.

> Let him make an axe[1] for the nones,
> To breke therwith the Sarafyns[2] bones.
> The head was wrought right wele;
> Therin was twenty pounde of ftele;
> And when he came into Cyprus lond,
> The ax he tok in his hond.
> All that he hit, he all to-frapped;
> The griffons[3] away faft rapped;
> Natheles many he cleaved,
> And their unthanks ther by-lived;
> And the prifoun when he cam to,
> With his ax he fmot right tho,
> Dores, barres, and iron chains, &c.[4]

This formidable axe is again mentioned at the fiege of Acon or Acre, the ancient Ptolemais:

> Kyng Rychard aftyr, anon ryght,
> Toward Acres gan hym dyght;
> And as he faylyd toward Surreye,[5]
> He was warnyd off a fpye,
> Howe the folk off the hethene lawe
> A gret cheyne hadden i-drawe
> Over the havene of Acres fers,
> And was feftnyd to two pelèrs,
> That noo fchyp ne fcholde in-wynne,[6]
> Ne they nought out that wer withynne.
> Therfore fevene yer and more
> Alle Cryftene kynges leyen thore,
> And with gret hongyr fuffryd payne,
> For lettyng off that ilke chayne.
> Kyng Richard herd that tydyng;
> For joye hys herte beganne to fprynge,
> And fwor and fayde in his thought,
> 'That ylke chayne fcholde helpe hem nought
> A fwythe ftrong galeye he took,
> And[7] Trenchemer,[8] fo fays the book,

---

[1] Richard's battle-axe is alfo mentioned by [de] Brunne, and on this occafion, *Chron.* p. 159.

[2] The Crufades imported the phrafe Jeu Sarrazionois, for any fharp engagement, into the old French romances.—Thus in the *Roman d'Alexandre*, MSS. Bibl. Bodl. *ut fupr.* P. 1.

"Tholomer le regrette et le plaint en Grijois,
Et dift que s'il cuffent o culz telz vingt et trois,
Il nous euffent fet un Jeu Sarrazionois."

[3] The Byzantine Greeks are often called Griffones by the hiftorians of the middle ages. See Du Cange *Gloff. Ville-Hard.* p. 363. See alfo Rob. [de] Brun. *Chron.* pp. 151, 157, 159, 160, 165, 171, 173. Wanley fuppofes that the Griffin in heraldry was intended to fignify a Greek or Saracen, whom they thus reprefented under the figure of an imaginary eaftern monfter, which never exifted but as an armorial badge.

[4] line 2196.   [5] Syria.

[6] So Fabyan, of Rofamond's bower: "that no creature, man or woman, myght *wynne* to her," *i. e.* go in, by contraction, Win. *Chron.* vol. i. p. 320, col. i. edit. 1533. [þinnan A.-S. to labour, ftrive at, and hence attain to by labour.—*Price.*]

[7] Rob. [de] Brun. *Chron.* p. 170.

"The kynge's owne galeie he cald it *Trencthemere.*"

[8] ["*Trenchemere*, fo faith the boke.—
The galey yede as fwift
As ony fowle by the lyfte."]

>Steryd the galey ryght ful evene,
>Ryght in the myddes off the havene.
>Wer the maryners faughte or wrothe,
>He made hem fayle and rowe bothe;
>And kynge Rychard, that was fo good,
>With hys axe in forefchyp ftood.
>And whenne he com the cheyne too,
>With hys ax he fmot it in two,[1]
>That all the barouns, verrayment,
>Sayde it was a noble dent;
>And for joye off this dede
>The cuppes faft abouten yede,[2]
>With good wyn, pyement and clarré;
>And faylyd toward Acres cyté.
>Kyng Richard, oute of hys galye,
>Cafte wylde-fyr into the fkeye,
>And fyr Gregeys into the fee,
>And al on fyr wer thê.
>Trumpes yede in hys galeye,
>Men mighte it here into the fkye,
>Taboures and hornes Sarezyneys,[3]
>The fee brent all off fyr Gregeys.[4]

This *fyr Gregeys*, or Grecian fire, feems to be a compofition belonging to the Arabian chemiftry. It is frequently mentioned by the Byzantine hiftorians, and was very much ufed in the wars of the middle ages, both by fea and land. It was a fort of wild-fire, faid to be inextinguifhable by water, [but innocuous againft vinegar prepared in a certain manner,] and chiefly ufed for burning fhips, againft which it was thrown in pots or phials by the hand. In land engagements it feems to have been difcharged by machines conftructed on purpofe. The oriental Greeks pretended that this artificial fire was invented by Callinicus, an architect of Heliopolis, under Conftantine; and that Conftantine prohibited them from communicating the manner of making it to any foreign people. It was, however, in common ufe among the nations confederated with the Byzantines; and Anna Comnena has given an account of its ingredients,[5] which were bitumen, fulphur, and naphtha. It is called *feu gregois* in the French chronicles and romances. Our minftrel, I believe, is fingular in faying that Richard fcattered this fire on Saladin's fhips: many monkifh hiftorians of the holy war, in defcribing the fiege of Acon, relate that it was employed on that occafion and many others by the Saracens againft the Chriftians.[6] Procopius, in his hiftory of the Goths, calls it *Medea's Oil*, as if it had been a preparation ufed in the forceries of that enchantrefs.[7]

---

[1] Thus R. de Brunne fays, "he fondred the Sarazyns otuynne." p. 574. [But *fondred* feems to be a mif-reading for *fondred*, parted or clove.]
[2] went.   [3] [fhalmys, *fhawms*.]   [4] line 2593.
[5] See Du Cange, *Not. ad. Joinvil.* p. 71. And *Gl. Lat.*, V. *Ignis Græcus.*
[6] See more particularly *Chron.* Rob. [de] Brun. p. 170. And Benedict. Abb. p. 652. And Joinv. *Hift.* L. pp. 39, 46, 52, 53, 62, 70.
[7] iv. 11.

The quantity of huge battering rams and other military engines, now unknown, which Richard is said to have transported into the Holy Land, was prodigious. The names of some of them are given in another part of this romance.[1] It is an historical fact, that Richard was killed by the French from the shot of an arcubalist, a machine which he often worked skilfully with his own hands: and Guillaume le Breton, a Frenchman, in his Latin poem called *Philippeis*, introduces Atropos making a decree that Richard should die by no other means than by a wound from this destructive instrument, the use of which, after it had been interdicted by the Pope in the year 1139, he revived, and is supposed to have shown the French in the Crusades:[2]

> [Ginnes?] he hadde on wondyr wyse;
> Mang[o]neles[3] off gret queintyse;[4]
> Arwblast bowe, and[5] with gynne
> The Holy Lond[e] for to wynne.
> Ovyr al othyr wyttyrly,
> A melle[6] he hadde off gret maystry;

---

[1] "Twenty grete gynnes for the nones
Kynge Richard sent for to cast stones," &c.

Among these were the Mategriffon and the Robynet. Sign. N. iii. The former of these is thus described. Sign. E. iiii.:

> "I have a castell I understonde
> Is made of tembre of Englonde
> With syxe stages full of tourelles
> Well flouryshed with cornelles," &c.

See Du Cange *Not. Joinv.* p. 68, Mategryffon is the Terror or plague of the Greeks. Du Cange, in his [*Histoire de Constantinople sous les empereurs Français,*] mentions a castle of this name in Peloponesus. Benedict says that Richard erected a strong castle, which he called Mate-gryffon, on the brow of a steep mountain without the walls of the city of Messina in Sicily. Benedict. Abb. p. 621, ed. Hearn. sub. ann. 1190. Robert de Brunne mentions this engine from our romance. *Chron.* p. 157:

> "The romancer it sais Richarde did make a pele,
> On kastelle wise allwais wrought of tre ful wele.—
> In schip he ded it lede, &c. . . . . .
> His pele from that dai forward he cald it Mate-griffon."

Pele is a house [a castle, fortification]. Archbishop Turpin mentions Charlemagne's wooden castles at the siege of a city in France, cap. ix.

[2] See Carpentier's *Suppl. Du Cange*, Lat. Gl. tom. i. p. 434. And Du Cange, *ad Ann. Alex.* p. 357.

[3] See *supr.* It is observable that *Manganum*, Mangonell, was not known among the Roman military machines, but existed first in the Byzantine Greek Μάγγανον, a circumstance which seems to point out its inventors, at least to shew that it belonged to the oriental art of war. It occurs often in the Byzantine Tactics, although at the same time it was perhaps derived from the Latin *Machina:* yet the Romans do not appear to have used in their wars so formidable and complicated an engine, as this is described to have been in the writers of the dark ages. It was the capital machine of the wars of those ages. Du Cange, in his [*Constantinople sous les empereurs Français*] mentions a vast area at Constantinople in which the machines of war were kept. p. 155.

[4] See *supr.* [5] [made.] [6] mill.

In myddys a schyp for to stand ;
Swylke on sawgh nevyr man in land :
Four[e] sayles wer theretoo,
Yelew and grene, red and bloo.
With canevas layd wel al about,
Ful schyr withinne and eke without ;
Al withinne ful off feer,
Of torches maad with wex ful cleer ;
Ovyrtwart and endelang,
With strenges of wyr the stones hang ;[1]
Stones that deden never note,
Grounde they never whete, no grote,
But rubbyd as they wer wood,
Out of the eye ran red blood.[2]
Beffore the trowgh there stood on ;
Al in blood he was begon,
And hornes grete upon his hede ;
Sarezynes theroff hadde gret drede.[3]

The last circumstance recalls a fiend-like appearance drawn by Shakespeare ; in which, exclusive of the application, he has converted ideas of deformity into the true sublime, and rendered an image terrible, which in other hands would have probably been ridiculous :—

> Methought his eyes
> Were two full moons ; he had a thousand noses,
> Horns whelk'd and wav'd like the enridged sea,
> It was some fiend——[4]

---

[1] [With spryngelles of fyre they dyde honde.]—Espringalles, Fr. Engines. See Du Cange, *Gl. Lat.* Spingarda, Quadrellus. And Not. Joinv. p. 78. Perhaps he means pellets of tow dipped in the Grecian fire, which sometimes were thrown from a sort of mortar. Joinville says, that the Greek fire thrown from a mortar looked like a huge dragon flying through the air, and that at midnight the flashes of it illuminated the Christian camp, as if it had been broad day. When Louis's army was encamped on the banks of the Thanis in Ægypt, says the same curious historian, about the year 1249, they erected two *chats chateils*, or covered galleries, to shelter their workmen, and at the end of them two *befrois*, or vast moveable wooden towers, full of crossbow men, who kept a continual discharge on the opposite shore. Besides eighteen other new-invented engines for throwing stones and bolts. But in one night, the deluge of Greek fire ejected from the Saracen camp utterly destroyed these enormous machines. This was a common disaster ; but Joinville says, that his pious monarch sometimes averted the danger, by prostrating himself on the ground, and invoking our Saviour with the appellation of *Beau Sire*, pp. 37, 39.

[2] This device is thus related by Robert of Brunne, *Chron.* pp. 175-176 :

> "Richard als suithe did raise his engyns
> The Inglis wer than blythe, Normans and Petevyns :
> In bargeis and galeis he set mylnes to go,
> The sailes, as men sais, som were blak and blo,
> Som were rede and grene, the wynde about them blewe.
> The stones were of Rynes, the noyse dreadfull and grete ;
> It affraied the Sarazins ; as leven the fyre out schete.
> The noyse was unride," &c.

Rynes is the river Rhine, whose shores or bottom supplied the stones shot from their military engines. The Normans, a barbarous people, appear to have used machines of immense and very artificial construction at the siege of Paris in 885. See the last note. And *Vit. Saladin.* per Schultens, pp. 135, 141, 167, &c.

[3] Line 2631.   [4] King Lear, iv. vi. [Dyce's edit. 1868, vii. 324.]

At the touch of this powerful magician, to speak in Milton's language, "The griesly terror grows tenfold more dreadful and deform."

The moving castles described by our minstrel, which seem to be so many fabrics of romance, but are founded in real history, afforded suitable materials for poets who deal in the marvellous. Accordingly they could not escape the fabling genius of Tasso, who has made them instruments of enchantment, and accommodated them with great propriety to the operations of infernal spirits.

At the siege of Babylon, the soldan Saladin sends King Richard a horse. The messenger says:

> Thou sayest thy God is ful of myght:
> Wylt thou graunt, with spere and scheeld,
> Derayè the ryghtè in the feeld,
> With helm, hawberk and brondes bryght
> On strong[e] stedes, good and lyght,
> Whether is off more powèr
> Jesu or Jubyter?
> And he sente thé to say this,
> Yiff thou wilt have an hors [of] hys?
> In alle the landes ther thou hast gon,
> Swylk on say thou nevyr non!
> Favel off Cypre, ne Lyard off Prys,[1]
> Are nought at nede as that he is;
> And, yiff thou wylt, this selve day
> It shall be brought thè to asay.'
> Quoth kyng Richard: "Thou sayest wel;
> Swylke an hors, by Seynt Mychel,

---

[1] Horses belonging to Richard, "Favel of Cyprus and Lyard of Paris." Robert de Brunne mentions one of these horses, which he calls [Fauuel]. *Chron.* p. 175:

> "Sithen at Japhet was slayn [Fauuel] his stede,
> The Romans telles gret pas ther of his douhty dede."

This is our romance, viz. Sign. Q. iii.:

> "To hym gadered every chone
> And slewe Favell under hym,
> Tho was Richard wroth and grym."

This was at the siege of Jaffa, as it is here called. Favell of Cyprus is again mentioned, Sign. O. ii.:

> "Favell of Cyprus is forth fet
> And in the sadell he hym sett."

Robert of Brunne says that Saladin's brother sent King Richard a horse. *Chron.* p. 194:

> "He sent to King Richard a stede for curteisie
> On of the best reward that was in paemie."

In the wardrobe-roll of Prince Edward, afterwards Edward II., under the year 1272, the masters of the horse render their accounts for horses purchased, specifying the colours and prices with the greatest accuracy. One of them is called "Unus equus *favellus* cum stella in fronte," &c. Hearne's *Joann. de Trokelowe.* Præf. p. xxvi. Here *favellus* is interpreted by Hearne to be *honeycomb*. I suppose he understands a dappled or roan horse. But *favellus*, evidently an adjective, is barbarous Latin for *falvus* or *fulvus*, a dun or light yellow, a word often used to express the colour of horses and hawks. See Carpentier, Suppl. Du Cange, *Lat. Glos.* V. *Favellus*, tom. ii. p. 370. It is hence that King Richard's horse is called Favel. From which word [Fauvel] in Robert de Brunne is a corruption.

I wolde have to ryde upon.
Bydde hym fende that hors to me;
I fchal afaye, what that he be.
Yiff he be trufty, withoute fayle
I kepe non othir in batayle."
The meffanger thenne home wente,
And tolde the Sawdon in prefente,
Hou kyng Richard wolde hym mete.
The rych[e] Sawdon, al fo fkete,
A noble clerk he fente for thenne
A maftyr negromacien,[1]
That conjuryd as [I] you telle,
Thorwgh the feendes craft off helle,
Twoo ftrongè feendes off the eyr
In lykneffe off twoo ftedes feyr,
Lykè bothe of hewe and here;
As they faydè that wer there,
Never was ther feen non flyke.
That on was a merè lyke,
That other a colt, a noble ftede,
Wher he wer in ony nede,
Was nevyr kyng ne knyght[2] fo bolde,
That, whenne the damè neyghè[3] wolde,
Scholde hym holde agayn hys wylle,
That he ne woldè renne her tylle,[4]
And knele adoun, and foukè[5] hys dame:
That whyle, the Sawdon [thought] with fchame,
Scholde Kyng Richard foone aquelle.
All thus an aungyl gan hym telle,
That cam to hym aftyr mydnyght;
And fayd "Awake, thou Goddes knyght!
My lord[6] dos thè to undyrftande,
Thè fchal com an hors to hande;
Fayr he is off body pyght;
Betraye thè yiff the Sawdon myght.
On hym to ryde have thou no drede,
He fchal thè help[en] at thy nede."

The angel then gives King Richard feveral directions about managing this infernal horfe, and a general engagement enfuing, between the Chriftian and Saracen armies:—[7]

To lepe to hors thenne was he dyght;
Into the fadyl or he leep,
Off many thynge he took keep.
Hys men him brought al that he badde.
A quarry tree off fourty foote
Before hys fadyl anon dyd hote

---

[1] necromancer.   [2] his rider.   [3] neigh.
[4] go to her.   [5] fuck.   [6] God.
[7] In which the Saracen line extended twelve miles in length, and
"The grounde myght unnethe be fene
For bryght armure and fperes kene."
Again
"Lyke as fnowe lyeth on the mountaynes
So were fulfylled hylles and playnes
With hauberkes bryght and harneys clere
Of trompettes, and tabourere."

Faste that men scholde it brace, &c.
Hymself was rychely begoo
From the crest unto the too.¹
He was armyd wondyr weel,
And al with plates off good steel;
And ther aboven, an hawberk;
A schafft wrought off trusty werk;
On his schuldre a scheeld off steel,
With three lupardes² wrought ful weel.
An helme he hadde off ryche entayle;
Trusty and trewè hys ventayle;
On hys crest a douvè whyte
Sygnyfycacioun off the Holy Spryte:
Upon a croys the douvè stood,
Off goldè wrought ryche and good.
God³ hymself, Mary and Jhon,
As he was naylyd the roode upon,⁴
In sygne off hym for whom he faught,
The sperè-hed forgatt he naught:
Upon hys spere he wolde it have,
Goddes hygh name theron was grave.
Now herkenes what oth they swore,
Ar they to the batayle wore:
Yiff it were soo, that Richard myght
Sloo the Sawdon in feeld with fyght,
Hee and alle hys scholde gon,
At her wylle everilkon,
Into the cytè off Babylone;
And the kyngdom of Massidoyne
He scholde have undyr his hand:
And yiff the Sawdon off that land
Myghte sloo Richard in that feeld
With swerd or spere undyr scheeld,
That Cristene men scholde goo
Out off that land for ever moo,
And Sarezynes have her wylle in wolde.
Quod kyng Richard: "Thertoo I holde!
Thertoo my glove, as I am knyght!"
They ben armyd and wel i-dyght.
Kyng Richard into the sadyl leep;
Who that wolde, theroff took keep,
To see, that fyght was ful fayr.
The stede[s] ran ryght with gret ayr,⁵
Al so harde as they myght dure,
Aftyr her feet sprong the fure,
Tabours beten, and trumpes blowe;
Ther myghte men see in a throwe,
How kyng Richard, the noble man,
Encounteryd with the Sawdan,
That cheef was told off Damas.⁶
Hys trust upon hys merè was.
Therfoore, as the booke⁷ telles,

---

¹ from head to foot.   ² leopards.   ³ Our Saviour.
⁴ "As he died upon the cross." So in [the fragmentary version of the *Brut*.] cited by Hearne, *Gloss. Rob. Br.* p. 634.

"Pyned under Ponce Pilat,
Don on the rod after that."

⁵ ire.   ⁶ See Du Cange, *Joinv.* p. 87.   ⁷ The French romance.

Hys crouper heeng al ful off belles,[1]
And his peytrel [2] and his arſoun [3]
Three myle myghte men here the ſoun.
The mere gan nygh, her belles to ryng
For grete pryde, withoute leſyng,
A brod fawchoun to hym he bar,
For he thought that he wolde thar
Have ſlayn kyng Richard with treſoun,
Whenne hys hors had knelyd doun,
As a colt that ſcholde ſouke.
And he was war off that pouke :[4]
Hys [5] eeres with wax wer ſtoppyd faſt,
Therfore was he nought agaſt.
He ſtrook the feend that undyr hym yede,
And gaff the Sawdon a dynt off dede.
In his blaſoun, verrayment,
Was i-paynted a ſerpent.
With the ſpere, that Richard heeld,
He beor him thorwgh and undyr the ſcheeld,
None off hys armes myghtè laſte ;
Brydyl and peytrel al to-braſt ;
Hys gerth and hys ſteropes alſoo ;
The merè to the grounde gan goo.
Mawgry him, he garte hym ſtaupe [6]
Bakward ovyr hys meres croupe ;
The feet toward the fyrmament.
Behynd the Sawdon the ſpere out went.
He leet hym lye upon the grene ;[7]
He prekyd the feend with ſpores [8] kene ;
In the name off the Holy Goſt,
He dryves into the hethene hooſt,

---

[1] Anciently no perſon ſeems to have been gallantly equipped on horſeback, unleſs the horſe's bridle or ſome other part of the furniture was ſtuck full of ſmall bells. Vincent of Beauvais, who wrote about 1264, cenſures this piece of pride in the knights-templars. They have, he ſays, bridles embroidered, or gilded, or adorned with ſilver, " Atque in pectoralibus campanulas infixas magnum emittentes ſonitum, ad gloriam eorum et decorem." Hiſt. lib. xxx. cap. 85. Wicliffe, in his *Trialoge*, inveighs againſt the prieſts for their "fair hors, and jolly and gay ſadeles, and bridles ringing by the way," &c. Lewis's *Wickliffe*, p. 121. Hence Chaucer may be illuſtrated, who thus deſcribes the ſtate of a monk on horſeback. *Prol. Cant. Tales*, v. 170 :

" And when he rode, men might his bridell here
 Gingling in a whiſtling wind as clere,
 And eke as lowde, as doth the chapell bell."

That is, becauſe his horſe's bridle or trappings were ſtrung with bells.

[2] The breaſt-plate, or breaſt-band of a horſe. *Poitral*, Fr. *Pectorale*, Lat. Thus Chaucer, of the Chanones Yemans horſe. *Chan. Yem. Prol.* v. 575 :

" About the paytrell ſtoode the fome ful hie."

[3] The ſaddle-bow. " Arcenarium extencellatum cum argento," occurs in the wardrobe rolls, ab an. 21 ad an. 23 Edw. III. Membr. xi. This word is not in Du Cange or his *Supplement*.

[4] [And he was ware of that ſhame.]   [5] The colt's ears.

[6] [Maugre her heed, he made her ſeche
 The grounde, withoute more ſpeche.]

[7] [Ther he fell dede on the grene.]   [8] ſpurs.

> And al fo foone as he was come,
> He brak afunder the fcheltrome; [1]
> For al that ever before hym ftode
> Hors and man to erthe yode,
> Twenty foot on every fyde, &c.
> Whenne they of Fraunce wyfte,
> That the mayftry hadde the Chryfte,
> They wer bolde, her herte they tooke;
> Stedes prekyd, fchaufftes fchooke.[2]

Richard arming himfelf is a curious Gothic picture. It is certainly a genuine picture, and drawn with fome fpirit: as is the fhock of the two necromantic fteeds, and other parts of this defcription. The combat of Richard and the Soldan, on the event of which the Chriftian army got poffeffion of the city of Babylon, is probably the Duel of King Richard, painted on the walls of a chamber in the royal palace of Clarendon. The foldan is reprefented as meeting Richard with ["A faucon brode," or a broad falchion,] in his hand. Tabour, a drum, a common accompaniment of war, is mentioned as one of the inftruments of martial mufic in this battle with characteriftical propriety. It was imported into the European armies from the Saracens in the holy war. The word is conftantly written tabour, not tambour, in Joinville's *Hiftory of Saint Louis*, and all the elder French romances. Joinville defcribes a fuperb bark or galley belonging to a Saracen chief, which he fays was filled with fymbols, tabours, and Saracen horns.[3] Jean d'Orronville, an old French chronicler of the life of Louis, duke of Bourbon, relates that the king of France, the king of Thrafimere, and the king of Bugie, landed in Africa according to their cuftom with cymbals, kettledrums, tabours,[4] and whiftles.[5] Babylon, here faid to be befieged by King Richard, and fo frequently mentioned by the romance writers and the chroniclers of the Crufades, is Cairo or Bagdat. Cairo and Bagdat, cities of recent foundation, were perpetually confounded with Babylon, which had been deftroyed many centuries before, and was fituated at a confiderable diftance from either. Not the leaft enquiry was made in the dark ages concerning the true fituation of places, or the difpofition of the country in Paleftine,

---

[1] *Schiltron.* I believe, foldiers drawn up in a circle. Rob. de Brunne ufes it in defcribing the battle of Fowkirke, *Chron.* p. 305:

"Ther Scheltron fone was fhad with Inglis that wer gode."

Shad is *feparated.* [Scheltron, *turma clipeata*, a troop armed with fhields. See Jamiefon's *Etymol. Scott. Dict.*—*Price.*]

[2] Line 5642.

[3] *Hiftoire de S. Loys*, p. 30. The original has "Cors Sarazinois." See alfo pp. 52, 56. And Du Cange's Notes, p. 61.

[4] [Roquefort, who cites the fame paffage, calls Glais a mufical inftrument, without defining its peculiar nature.—*Price.*]

[5] Cap. 76. Nacaires is here the word for kettle-drums. See Du Cange, *ubi fupr.* p. 59. Who alfo from an old roll "de la chambre des Comptes de Paris" recites, among the houfehold muficians of a French nobleman, "Meneftrel du Cor Sarazinois," *ib.* p. 60. This inftrument is not uncommon in the French romances.

although the theatre of so important a war; and to this neglect were owing, in a great measure, the signal defeats and calamitous distresses of the Christian adventurers, whose numerous armies, destitute of information, and cut off from every resource, perished amidst unknown mountains and impracticable wastes. Geography at this time had been but little cultivated. It had been studied only from the ancients: as if the face of the earth and the political state of nations had not, since the time of those writers, undergone any changes or revolutions.

So formidable a champion was King Richard against the infidels, and so terrible the remembrance of his valour in the holy war, that the Saracens and Turks used to quiet their froward children only by repeating his name. Joinville is the only writer who records this anecdote. He adds another of the same sort. When the Saracens were riding, and their horses started at any unusual object, " ils disoient a leurs chevaulx en les picquant de l'esperon: et cuides tu que ce soit le Roy Richart?"[1] It is extraordinary that these circumstances should have escaped Malmesbury, Matthew Paris, [Benedictus Abbas], Langtoft, and the rest of our old historians, who have exaggerated the character of this redoubted hero by relating many particulars more likely to be fabulous, and certainly less expressive of his prowess.

SECTION V.

HE romance of *Sir Guy* which [probably in one of its earlier casts, as exhibited in the Auchinleck MS.] is enumerated by Chaucer among the " Romances of pris," affords a series of fictions customary in pieces of this sort, concerning the [adventures of the hero both in England and abroad.[2] The following is the description of the first meeting of Guy and Felice, his future wife:[3]

---

[1] *Hist. de S. Loys*, pp. 16, 104. Who had it from a French MS. chronicle of the holy war. See Du Cange's Notes, p. 45.

[2] [See *The Romances of Sir Guy of Warwick, and Rembrun his Son. Now first edited from the Auchinleck MS.* (by W. B. D. D. Turnbull). Edinburgh: Printed for the Abbotsford Club. MDCCCXL. In the Preface the Editor has given an account of the various MSS. and printed editions of the romance, and has printed at length a fragment of an otherwise unknown English version in the possession of Sir Thomas Philipps.] The [old printed] copy of Sir Guy is a considerable volume in quarto. My edition is without date, " Imprynted at London in Lothbury by Wylliam Copland," with rude wooden cuts. It runs to Sign. Ll. iii. [An imperfect copy is in Garrick's Collection, vol. K. 9, and a perfect one was in Heber's library, Cat. pt. iv. 961. A fragment of this romance belonged to Dr. Farmer, and afterwards to Mr. Douce, which Ritson in his MS. Cat. of Engl. Romances, states to have been printed by W. de Worde, about 1495. In the possession of Mr. Staunton of Longbridge House, co. Warw. is a larger fragment of thirty-six leaves, printed in a thinner letter than W. de Worde's, with wood-cuts, which I

> "It was opon a Pentecoft day y-teld
> Therl a gret feft held
> At Warwike in that cite
> That than was y-won to be
> Thider cam men of miche might
> Erls and barouns bothe aplight
> Leuedis and maidens of gret mounde
> That in the lond wer y-founde
> Eueriche maiden ches hir loue
> Of knightes that wer thider y-come
> And euerich knight his leman
> Of that gentil maiden wiman
> When thai were fro chirche y-come
> Ther alight mani a noble gome
> Therl to the mete was fett
> Gij ftode forn him in that flett
> That was the fteward fone
> Therl to ferue it was his wone
> To him he cleped Gij
> And him hete and comandi
> That he in to chaumber went

---

fhould feel inclined to afcribe to Pynfon. Ritfon mentions alfo an edition by John Cawood.—*Madden.*

It feems to be older than the *Squyr of lowe degree,* in which it is quoted. Sign. a. iii.:

"Or els fo bolde in chivalrie
As was fyr Gawayne or fyr Gie."

The two beft MSS. are at Cambridge, MSS. Bibl. Publ. Mor. 690, 33, and MSS. Coll. Caii, A 8, from which text it has now been given.

An analyfis of this romance will be found in the "Specimens" of Mr. Ellis, who is of opinion that "the tale in its prefent ftate has been compofed from the materials of at leaft two or three if not more romances. The firft is a moft tirefome love ftory which, it may be prefumed, originally ended with the marriage of the fond couple. To this it fhould feem was afterwards tacked on a feries of frefh adventures, invented or compiled by fome pilgrim from the Holy Land; and the hero of this legend was then brought home for the defence of Athelftan and the deftruction of Colbrand." Mr. Ritfon, in oppofition to Dugdale, who regarded Guy as an undeniably hiftorical perfonage, has laboured to prove that "no hero of this name is to be found in real hiftory," and that he was "no more an Englifh hero than Amadis de Gaul or Perceforeft." Mr. Ellis, on the other hand, conceives the tale "may poffibly be founded on fome Saxon tradition," and that though the name in its prefent form be undoubtedly French, yet as it bears fome refemblance to Egil, the name of an Icelandic warrior, who "contributed very materially to the important victory gained by Athelftan over the Danes and their allies at Brunanburgh," he thinks "it is not impoffible that this warlike foreigner may have been transformed by fome Norman monk into the pious and amorous Guy of Warwick." This at beft is but conjecture, nor can it be confidered a very happy one. Egil himfelf (or his namelefs biographer) makes no mention of a fingle combat on the occafion in which he had been engaged; and the fact, had it occurred, would have been far too interefting, and too much in unifon with the fpirit of the times, to have been paffed over in filence. In addition to this, the fubftitution of Guy for Egil is againft all analogy, on the transformation of a Northern into a French appellation. The initial letters in Guy, Guyon, and Guido, are the reprefentatives of the Teutonic W, and clearly point to fome cognomen beginning with the Saxon Wig, *bellum.*—*Price.*]

³ [In the prefent edition extracts from the Auchinleck MS., as printed in 1840, have been fubftituted for Warton's quotations from Copland's modernized and altered text.]

And grete wele that maiden gent
And that he fchuld that ich day
Serue wele that feir may
　　Gij him anfwerd freliche
Sir Ichil wel bletheliche
In a kirtel of filk he gan him fchrede
Into chaumber wel fone he zede
The kirtel bicom him fwithe wel
To amenden theron was neuer a del
The maidens biheld him feir an wel
For that he was fo gentil
Gij on his knes fone him fett
And on hir fader half he hir grett
And feyd he was thider fent
To ferue hir to hir talent
Felice anfwerd than to Gij
Bieus amis molt gramerci
And feththe fche afked him in the plas
Whennes he cam and what he was
Mi fader he feyd hat Suward
That is thi fader fteward
That with him me hath y-held
And forth y-brought God him foryeld
Artow fche feyd Suward fone
That of al godenes hath the wone
Gij ftode ftille and feyd nought
With that was the water forth brought
Thai fett hem to mete anon
Erl baroun fweyn and grom[1]

We fhall next give the account of the knighthood of our hero:[2]

It was at the holy Trinite
Therl dubbed Sir Gij the fre
And with him tventi god gomis
Knightes and riche baroun fonis
Of cloth of Tars and riche cendel
Was he dobbeing euerich adel
The pauis al of fow and griis
The mantels weren of michel priis
With riche armour and gode ftedes
The beft that wer in lond at nedis
Alder beft was Gij y-dight
Thei he wer an emperour fone aplight
So richeliche dubbed was he
Nas no fwiche in this cuntre
With riche ftedes wel erninde
Palfreys courfours wele bereinde
No was ther noither fweyn no knaue
That ought failed that he fchuld haue
　　How is Sir Gij dobbed to knight
Feir he was and michel of might
To Felice went Sir Gij
And gret her wel curteyflie
And feyd Ichaue don aftow feydeft me to
For the Ichaue fuffred miche wo
Arme for the Ichaue vnderfong
The to fe me thought long

[1] [Ed. 1840, pp. 3-5.]　　[2] [Ibid. p. 22.]

>   Thou art me bothe leue and dere
>   Ich am y-comen thi wille to here.

A knight, who goes under the name of Amis of the Mountain, is introduced into this romance, and in the fequel, where the later adventures of Guy's fon, Rembrun, are related, the fame character is defcribed as fuffering a captivity in a myfterious and inacceffible caftle, from which, however, Rembrun fucceeds in delivering him. Here is a picture of Rembrun's journey in fearch of the caftle:

>   Amorwe Rembroun aros erly
>   And armede him ful haftely
>   For to winne pris
>   A gode ftede he beftrod
>   And forth a wente withoute abod
>   To the foreft Y wis
>
>   Heraud with him go wolde
>   Ac he feide that he ne fcholde
>   For non fkines nede
>   And he dradde of him ftrangliche
>   And betaughte him God in heuen riche
>   And in is wey a yede
>   Heraud blefte and he gan gon
>   The merkes ftake a pafed anon
>   That was wel vnrede
>   Al the dai a tok the pas
>   Til it noun apafed was
>   Ridand vpon is ftede
>
>   An hille he fegh before him there
>   Gates theron maked were
>   Forth right he rod in
>   The gate agen anon was fpered
>   Tho was Rembroun fore afered
>   And fafte bleffede him
>   Nought he ne fegh boute the fterneffe
>   Half a mile a rod Y wiffe
>   The wai was therk and dim
>   He rod afe fafte afe a mighte
>   Thanne he fegh more lighte
>   Be a water is brim
>
>   To the water he com fone thas
>   A riuer be a launde ther was
>   Thar he gan to lighte
>   Faire hit was y-growe with gras
>   A fairer place neuer nas
>   That he fegh with fighte
>   On that place was a paleis on
>   Swich ne fegh he neuer non
>   Ne of fo meche mighte
>   The walles were of criftal
>   The heling was of fin ruwal
>   That fchon fwithe brighte
>
>   The reftes al cipres be
>   That fwote fmal caften he
>   Ouer al aboute
>   The refins wer of fin coral
>   Togedre iuned with metal
>   Withinne and ek withoute
>   On the front ftod a charbokel fton

Ouer al the contre it schon
 Withouten eni doute
Postes and laces that ther were
Of iaspe gentil that was dere
 Al of one soute

The paleis was beloken al
Aboute with a marbel wal
 Of noble entaile
Upon eueriche kernal
Was ful of speres and of springal
 And stoutliche enbataile
Withoute the gate stod a tre
With foules of mani kines gle
 Singande withoute faile
The water was so sterne and grim
Mighte no man come therin
 Boute he hadde schip to saile

Rembroun dorste nought pasy
With is spere a gan it prouy
 How dep hit was beside
He thoughte on is fader fot hot
The stede in the side a smot
 And in he gan to ride
Ouer is helm the water is gon
He nolde haue be ther for eighte non
 Swich aunter him gan betide
Er he vp of the water ferde
A fond it was thretti mete yerde
 Se dep he gan doun glide

Thanne he thoughte on Ihesu Crist
His hors was wel swithe trist
 And quikliche swam to londe
His fet fastnede on the grounde
Rembroun was glad in that stounde
 And thankede Gode sonde
In to the pales he him dede
He helde the estes of that stede
 For no man a nolde wonde
Ac wimman ne man fand he non there
That with him speke or consort bere
 Naither sitte ne stonde

And tharof war a is
Into a chaumber a goth Y wis
 A knight a se alone
A-grette him with wordes fre
And seide sire God with the be
 That sit an hegh in trone
Sire a sede tel thow me
Gif this pales thin owen be
 Ich bidde the a bone
And gif thow ert her in prisoun dight
Tel hit me so wel thow might
 To me now make the mone]

Afterwards, the knight of the mountain directs Raynburne to find a wonderful sword which hung in the hall of the palace. With this weapon Raynburne attacks and conquers the Elvish knight; who buys his life, on condition of conducting his conqueror over the perilous ford, or lake, above defcribed, and of delivering all the captives confined in his fecret and impregnable dungeon.

[A] romance of the *Squire of Low Degree*[1] is alluded to by Chaucer in the *Rime of Sir Topas*;[2] [and it is probably the fame as that which was inferted by Ritfon in his *Ancient Romancees*, and more recently in a new collection of a fomewhat fimilar character. What feems to be the original edition, and from the appearance of the types, was printed by W. de Worde, is entitled oddly enough : " Here begynneth Undo your Dore," which correfponds exactly with the reading in the colophon of a later impreffion by W. Copland : " Thus endeth vndo your doore ; otherwife called the fquyer of lowe degre." But only a fragment of the former has yet been found.] The princefs is thus reprefented, in her clofet adorned with painted glafs, liftening to the fquire's complaint.[3]

> That lady herde his mournyng alle,
> Ryght vnder the chambre wall :
> In her oryall[4] there fhe was,
> Clofed well with royall glas,

---

[1] [Printed twice, firft, as it is fuppofed, by W. de Worde, under a different title (fee *Handb. of E. E. Lit.* art. SQUYR OF LOWE DEGRE), and fecondly by W. Copland. Warton's extracts were, in all the preceding editions, moft inaccurate. See the romance in *Remains of E. Pop. Poetr. of England*, 1864-6, ii.] I have never feen it in MS. [Ritfon characterizes it as a "ftrange and whimfical but genuine Englifh performance." On Warton's opinion, "that it is alluded to by Chaucer in the *Rime of Sir Topas*," he remarks ; "as Lybeaus Difconus [Le Bel Inconnu] one of the romancëes enumeratëed by Chaucer, is alluded to in the Squyr of lowe degre, it is not probablely, allfo, of his age." But the Lybeaus Difconus, referred to in this romance, is evidently a different verfion of the ftory from that printed by Mr. Ritfon [and from a different text by the Early Englifh Text Society] ; and the quotation, if it prove anything, would rather fpeak for the exiftence of a more ancient tranflation now unknown. Befides, Mr. Ritfon himfelf has fupplied us with an argument ftrongly favouring Warton's conjecture. For if, as he obferves, the Squyr of lowe degre be the only inftance of a romance containing any fuch impertinent digreffions or affected enumerations of trees, birds, &c. as are manifeftly the object of Chaucer's fatire, the natural inference would be—in the abfence of any evidence for its more recent compofition—that this identical romance was intended to be expofed and ridiculed by the poet. At all events, Copland's editions with their modern phrafeology are no ftandard for determining the age of any compofition ; and until fome better arguments can be adduced than thofe already noticed, the ingenious fuppofition of Dr. Percy—for by him it was communicated to Warton—may be permitted to remain in full force.—*Price.*]

[2] See *Obfervations on the Fairy Queen*, i. § iv. p. 139.

[3] Sign. a. iii.

[4] An Oriel feems to have been a recefs in a chamber, or hall, formed by the projection of a fpacious bow-window from top to bottom. *Rot. Pip.* an. 18. Hen. III. [A.D. 1234.] "Et in quadam capella pulchra et decenti facienda ad caput Orioli camere regis in caftro Herefordie, de longitudine xx. pedum." This Oriel was at the end of the king's chamber, from which the new chapel was to begin. Again, in the caftle of Kenilworth. *Rot. Pip.* an. 19. Hen. III. [A.D. 1235.] "Et in uno magno Oriollo pulchro et competenti, ante oftium magne camere regis in caftro de Kenilworth faciendo, vil. xvis. ivd. per Brev. regis."

The etymologifts have been puzzled to find the derivation of an oriel-window. A learned correfpondent fuggefts, that Oriel is Hebrew for Lux mea, or Dominus illuminatio mea. [See a note to the *Squyr of Low Degre* (R. *of the E. P. Poetry of England* ii. 27, *ad finem*).]

> Fulfylled it was with ymagery,
> Euery wyndowe by and by
> On eche syde had there a gynne,
> Sperde[1] with many a dyuers pynne.
> A none that lady fayre and fre
> Undyd a pynne of yueré,
> And wyd the windowes she open set,
> The sunne shone in at her closet.
> In that arber fayre and gaye
> She saw where that sqyre lay, &c.

I am persuaded to transcribe the following passage, because it delineates in lively colours the fashionable diversions and usages of ancient times. The king of Hungary endeavours to comfort his daughter with these promises, after she had fallen into a deep and incurable melancholy from the supposed loss of her paramour:

> To morowe ye shall on hunting fare ;
> And ryde, my doughter, in a chare,
> It shalbe couered with veluet reede
> And clothes of fyne golde al about your heid,
> With damske, white and asure blewe
> Well dyapred[2] with lyllyes newe ;

---

[1] Closed, shut. In *P. Plowman*, of a blind man, "unsparryd his eine, *i. e.* opened his eyes.

[2] Embroidered, diversified. So Chaucer, of a bow, *Rom. R.* v. 934.

> "And it was painted wel and thwitten
> And ore all diapred, and written," &c.

Thwitten is twisted, wreathed. The following instance from Chaucer is more to our purpose. *Knight's Tale*, v. 2160:

> "Upon a stede bay, trappid in stele,
> Coverid with cloth of gold diaprid wele."

This term, which is partly heraldic, occurs in the Provisor's rolls of the Great-wardrobe, containing deliveries for furnishing rich habiliments at tilts and tournaments, and other ceremonies. "Et ad faciendum tria harnesia pro Rege, quorum duo de velvetto albo operato cum garteriis de blu et diasprez per totam campedinem cum wodehouses." *Ex comp. J. Coke Clerici, Provisor Magn. Garderob.* ab ann. xxi. Edw. III. de 23 membranis. ad ann. xxiii. memb. x. I believe it properly signifies embroidering on a rich ground, as tissue, cloth of gold, &c. This is confirmed by Peacham. "Diapering is a term in drawing.—It chiefly serveth to counterfeit cloth of gold, silver, damask, branched velvet, camblet, &c." *Compl. Gent.* p. 345. Anderson, in his *History of Commerce*, conjectures that Diaper, a species of printed linen, took its name from the city of Ypres in Flanders, where it was first made, being originally called *d'ipre*. But that city and others in Flanders were no less famous for rich manufactures of stuff; and the word in question has better pretensions to such a derivation. Thus, "rich cloth embroidered with raised work" we called *d'ipre*, and from thence Diaper; and to do this, or any work like it, was called to diaper, whence the participle. Satin of Bruges, another city of Flanders, often occurs in inventories of monastic vestments, in the reign of Henry VIII: and the cities of Arras and Tours are celebrated for their tapestry in Spenser. All these cities, and others in their neighbourhood, became famous for this sort of workmanship before 1200. The Armator of Edward III., who finishes all the costly apparatus for the shows above mentioned, consisting, among other things, of a variety of the most sumptuous and ornamented embroideries on velvet, satin, tissue, &c. is John of Cologn. Unless it be Colonia in Italy, *Rotul. prædict.* memb. viii. memb. xiii. "Quæ omnia ordinata fuerunt per gar-

> Your pomelles fhalbe ended with gold,
> Your chaynes enameled many a folde;
> Your mantel of ryche degre,
> Purpyl palle and armyne fre;
> Jennettes of fpayne that ben fo wyght
> Trapped to the ground with veluet bright;
> Ye fhall have harp, fautry, and fonge,
> And other myrthés you amonge;
> Ye fhal haue rumney and malmefyne,
> Both ypocraffe and vernage wyne,
> Mountrofe and wyne of greke,
> Both algrade and refpice eke,
> Antioche and baftarde,
> Pyment[1] alfo and garnarde;

---

derobarium competentem, de precepto ipfius Regis: et facta et parata per manus Johīs de Colonia, Armatoris ipfius domini noftri Regis." Johannes de Strawefburgh [Strafburgh] is mentioned as *broudator regis*, i.e. of Richard II. in Anftis, *Ord. Gart.* i. 55. See alfo ii. 42. I will add a paffage from Chaucer's *Wife of Bath*, v. 450:

> "Of cloth-making fhe had fuch a haunt,
> She paffid them of *Ipre* and of *Gaunt*."

"Cloth of Gaunt," *i.e.* Ghent, is mentioned in the *Romaunt of the Rofe*, v. 574. Bruges was the chief mart for Italian commodities, about the thirteenth century. In the year 1318, five Venetian galeaffes, laden with Indian goods, arrived at this city in order to difpofe of their cargoes at the fair. L. Guic. *Defcr. di Paefi Bafs.* p. 174. Silk manufactures were introduced from the Eaft into Italy, before 1130. Giannon. *Hift. Napl.* xi. 7. The crufades much improved the commerce of the Italian ftates with the Eaft in this article, and produced new artificers of their own. But to recur to the fubject of this note. Diaper occurs among the rich filks and ftuffs in the French *Roman de la Rofe*, where it feems to fignify Damafk, v. 21867:

> "Samites, *dyaprés*, camelots."

I find it likewife in the *Roman d'Alexandre*, written about 1200. MSS. Bodl. fol. i. b. col. 2:

> "*Dyapres* d'Antioch, famis de Romanie."

Here is alfo a proof that the Afiatic ftuffs were at that time famous; and probably Romanie is Romania. The word often occurs in old accounts of rich ecclefiaftical veftments. Du Cange derives this word from the Italian *diafpro*, a jafper, a precious ftone which fhifts its colours. V. Diafprus. In Dugdale's *Monafticon* we have *diafperatus*, diapered. "Sandalia cum caligis de rubeo fameto *diafperato* breudata cum imaginibus regum," tom. iii. 314 and 321.

[1] Sometimes written *pimeate*. In the romance of *Syr Bevys*, a knight juft going to repofe takes the ufual draught of *pimeate;* which mixed with fpices is what the French romances call *vin du coucher*, and for which an officer, called Efpicier, was appointed in the old royal houfehold of France. Sig. m. iii. :

> "The knight and fhe to chamber went:
> With *pimeate* and with fpifery,
> When they had dronken the wyne."

See Carpentier, *Suppl. Gloff. Lat. du Cange*, tom. iii. p. 842. So Chaucer, *Leg. Dido*. v. 185:

> "The fpicis parted, and the wine agon,
> Unto his chamber he is lad anon."

Froiffart fays, among the delights of his youth, that he was happy to tafte:

> "Au couchier, pour mieulx dormir,
> Efpeces, clairet, et rocelle."

Mem. Lit. x. 665. Lidgate, of Tideus and Polimite in the palace of Adraftus at Thebes. *Stor. Theb.* p. 634, edit. Chauc. 1687:

Wyne of Greke and muscadell,
Both claré, pyment, and rochell,
The reed your stomake to defye
And pottes of osey sett you by.
You shall haue venison ybake,[1]
The best wylde foule y[t] may be take.
A lese of grehound[2] with you to streke,
And hert and hynde and other lyke,
Ye shalbe set at such a tryst
That hert and hynde shall come to your fyst.
Your dyseafe to dryue you fro,
To here the bugles there yblow.
Homward thus shall ye ryde,
On haukyng by the ryuers syde,
With Goshauke and with gentyll fawcon,
With Egle horne and merlyon.
Whan you come home your men amonge,
Ye shall haue reuell, daunces and songe:
Lytle chyldren, great and smale,
Shall syng, as doth the nyghtyngale,
Than shal ye go to your euensong
With tenours and trebles a mong,
Threscore of copes of damaske bryght
Full of perles th[e]y shalbe pyght:—

"gan anon repaire
To her lodging in a ful stately toure;
Assigned to hem by the herbeiour.
And aftir spicis plenty and the wine
In cuppis grete wrought of gold ful fyne,
Without tarrying to bedde straightes they gone," &c.

Chaucer has it again, *Squ. T.* v. 311, p. 62, and *Mill. T.* v. 270, p. 26:
"He sent her *piment*, methe, and spicid ale."

Some orders of monks are enjoined to abstain from drinking *pigmentum*, or *piment*. Yet it was a common refection in the monasteries. It is a drink made of wine, honey, and spices. "Thei ne could not medell the geste of Bacchus to the clere honie; that is to say, they could not make ne *piment* ne claré." Chaucer's *Boeth.* p. 371, a. Urr. *Clarre* is clarified wine. In French *Clarey*. Perhaps the same as piment, or hypocrass. See *Mem. Lit.* viii. p. 674, 4to. Compare Chauc. *Sh. T.* v. 2579. Du Cange, *Gloss. Lat.* v. Pigmentum. Species. and *Suppl. Carp.* and *Mem. sur l'anc. Chevalerie,* i. pp. 19, 48. I must add, that πιγμεντάριος, or πιμμεντάριος, signified an Apothecary among the middle and lower Greeks. See Du Cange, *Gl. Gr.* in voc. i. 1167, and ii. *Append. Etymolog. Vocab. Ling. Gall.* p. 301, col. 1. In the register of the Bishop of Nivernois, under the year 1287, it is covenanted, that whenever the bishop shall celebrate mass in St. Mary's abbey, the abbess shall present him with a peacock and a cup of piment. Carpentier, *ubi supr.* vol. iii. p. 277. [Sir F. Madden refers us also to Weber's *Met. Rom.* note on Alisaunder, l. 4178, and Roquefort, *Histoire de la vie priveé des François,* iii. pp. 65-8.]

[1] Chaucer says of the Frankelein, *Prol.* v. 345:
"Withoutin *bake mete* never was his house."

And in this poem, signat. B. iii:
"With birds in *bread ybake,*
The tele, the duck and drake."

[2] In a MS. of Froissart full of paintings and illuminations, there is a representation of the grand entrance of Queen Isabel of England into Paris, in the year 1324. She is attended by a greyhound who has a flag, powdered with fleurs de lys, bound to his neck. Montf. *Monum. Fr.* ii. p. 234.

Your sensours shalbe of Golde,
Endent with asure many a folde :
Your quere nor organ songe shall wante
With countre note and dyscant.
The other halfe on orgayns playeng,
With yonge chyldren full fayre syngyng.
Then shall ye go to your suppere,
And sytte in tentes in grene arbere,
With clothes of aras pyght to the grounde,
With saphyres set and dyamonde.—
An hundreth knyghtes truly tolde
Shall play with bowles in alayes colde,
Your disease to driue awaie :
To se the fishes in poles plaie ;—
To a draw brydge than shall ye,
The one halfe of stone, the other of tre,
A barge shall mete you full ryght,
With xxiiii ores full bryght,
With trompettes and with claryowne,
The fresshe water to rowe vp and downe.—
Than shal ye, doughter, aske the wyne,
With spices that be good and fyne :
Gentyll pottes, with genger grene,
With dates and deynties you betwene.
Forty torches brenynge bryght
At your brydges to brynge you lyght.
Into your chambre they shall you brynge
With muche myrthe and more lykyng.—
Your blankettes shall be of fustyane,
Your shetes shall be of clothe of rayne :[1]
Your head shete shall be of pery pyght,[2]
With dyamondes set and rubyes bryght.

---

[1] cloth, or linen, of Rennes, a city in Brittany. Chaucer, *Dr.* v. 255.

"And many a pilowe, and every bere
Of clothe of raynes to slepe on softe,
Him thare not nede to turnin ofte."

Tela de Raynes is mentioned among habits delivered to knights of the garter, 2 Rich. ii. Anstis, *Ord. Gart.* i. 55.

Cloth of Rennes seems to have been the finest sort of linen. In [one of the *Coventry Mysteries*, edited by Mr. Halliwell, 1841, there is a passage, supposed by Mr. Collier to have been interpolated towards the close of the 15th century, in which] a Galant, one of the retainers to the group of the Seven Deadly Sins, is introduced with the following speech :

"Hof, Hof, Hof, a frysch new galaunt !
Ware of thryft, ley that a doune :
What mene ye, syrrys, that I were a marchaunt,
Because that I am new com to toun ?
With praty . . . . wold I fayne round,
I have a *shert* of *reyns* with sleves peneaunt,
A lase of sylke for my lady Constant—
I woll, or even, be shaven for to seme yong," &c.

So also in Skelton's *Magnificence*, a Morality written [about 1500], f. xx. b :

"Your skynne, that was wrapped in *shertes of raynes*,
Nowe must be storm ybeten."

[2] "Inlaid with jewels." Chaucer, *Kn. T.* v. 2938 :

"And then with cloth of gold and with *perie*."

And in numberless other places.

> Whan you are layde in bedde fo fofte,
> A cage of Golde fhal hange a lofte
> With longe peper fayre burnning,
> And cloues that be fwete fmellyng,
> Frankenfence and olibanum,
> That whan ye flepe the tafte may come,
> And yf ye no reft may take,
> All night minftrelles for you fhall wake.[1]

Syr Degoré, [or *L'Egaré, the Strayed One*,] is a romance perhaps belonging to the fame period.[2] After his education under a hermit, Sir Degore's firft adventure is againft a dragon. This horrible monfter is marked with the hand of a mafter:"[3]

> Degore went furth his waye,
> Through a foreft halfe a daye :
> He herd no man, nor fawe none,
> Tyll yt paft the hygh none,
> Then herde he grete ftrokes falle,
> That yt made grete noyfe with alle,
> Full fone he thoght that to fe,
> To wete what the ftrokes myght be:
> There was an erle, both ftout and gaye,
> He was com ther that fame daye,
> For to hunt for a dere or a do,
> But hys houndes were gone hym fro.
> Then was ther a dragon grete and grymme,
> Full of fyre and alfo venymme,
> Wyth a wyde throte and tufkes grete,
> Uppon that knygte faft gan he bete.
> And as a lyon then was hys feete,
> Hys tayle was long, and full unmeete :
> Betwene hys head and hys tayle
> Was xxii fote withouten fayle ;
> Hys body was lyke a wyne tonne,
> He fhone ful bryght agaynft the funne :
> Hys eyen were bright as any glaffe,

---

[1] Sign. D ii. *feq*. [In Warton's original text, fcarcely a line, which he quoted, was without feveral blunders in orthography and fenfe, and the obfervation applies equally to the editions of 1824 and 1840.] At the clofe of the romance it is faid that the king, in the midft of a great feaft which lafted forty days, created the fquire king in his room; in the prefence of his twelve lords. See what I have obferved concerning the number twelve, Introd. Difs. i.

[2] [There are three old printed editions ; See *Handb. of E. E. Lit. Art.* DEGORÉ. The Auchinleck copy, noticed below by Mr. Price, has been printed three times, once in 1817, by Mr. Utterfon; for the Abbotsford Club, with the cuts from De Worde's ed. 1849; and in Mr. Laing's *Antient Englifh Poetry*, 1857.] There is a manufcript of it among Bifhop More's at Cambridge, Bibl. Publ. 690, 36.

[This romance is analyfed by Mr. Ellis in his "Specimens." From a fragment of it preferved in the Auchinleck MS. it is clear that the poem in its prefent form is an unfkilful *rifacimento* of an earlier verfion, fince the writer was even ignorant of the true mode of pronouncing the hero's name. Throughout Copland's edition—with one exception—it is a word of two fyllables, rhyming with "before ;" but in p. 135 of the reprint we obtain its true accentuation as exhibited in the Auchinleck MS. :

> "As was the yonge knyght Syr Degoré,
> But none wyft what man was he."

The name is intended to exprefs, as the author tells us (line 230), "a thing (or perfon) almoft loft," *Dégaré* or *Lígaré*.—PRICE.]

[3] Sign. B. ii.

> His fcales were hard as any braffe;
> And therto he was necked lyke a horfe,
> He bare hys hed up wyth grete force:
> The breth of hys mouth that did out blow
> As yt had been a fyre on lowe.
> He was to loke on, as I you telle,
> As yt had bene a fiende of helle.
> Many a man he had fhent,
> And many a horfe he had rente.

As the minftrel profeffion became a fcience, and the audience grew more civilized, refinements began to be ftudied, and the romantic poet fought to gain new attention, and to recommend his ftory, by giving it the advantage of a plan. Moft of the old metrical romances are, from their nature, fuppofed to be incoherent rhapfodies. Yet many of them have a regular integrity, in which every part contributes to produce an intended end. Through various obftacles and difficulties one point is kept in view, till the final and general cataftrophe is brought about by a pleafing and unexpected furprife. As a fpecimen of the reft, and as it lies in a narrow compafs, I will develop the plan of the fable now before us, which preferves at leaft a coincidence of events, and an uniformity of defign.

[A king of England has a beautiful daughter, who is wooed by many fuitors; but none can win her, becaufe none can perform the neceffary condition by unhorfing her father in a jouft. At laft, when fhe has accompanied her father to an abbey near a foreft to attend mafs, on the anniverfary of his wife's death, fhe feparates herfelf unintentionally from her companions, lofes her way in the foreft, and is met by a knight, who deflowers her. He leaves in her charge, as a token, his fword. The princefs has a fon, who is fecretly carried by one of her attendants to a hermit's cottage, and left at the door in a cradle with £30 under his head, a pair of gloves,[1] which muft fit the girl whom he marries, and a requeft that whoever finds him, will have him chriftened. The foundling is chriftened Sir Degoré [L'Egaré] by the hermit, and educated by him. When he is twenty years of age he is allowed to return to his mother, and takes the gloves, which were difcovered in his cradle. Having refcued an earl from a dragon, armed with nothing but an oak-fapling, he is invited to his deliverer's houfe. The earl offers him his daughter in marriage, but Degoré, mindful of the gloves, afks to fee all the ladies. The gloves fit none of them.

His next adventure is with a king, who has offered his daughter and half his lands to any knight who can unhorfe him at the tournament. Degoré fucceeds, and marries the princefs, without calling to mind the gloves, which ought to have been tried firft. His wife

---

[1] Gloves were anciently a coftly article of drefs, and richly decorated. They were fometimes adorned with precious ftones. *Rot. Pip. an.* 53. *Henr.* iii. [A. D. 1267.] "Et de i. pectine auri cum lapidibus pretiofis ponderant. xliiis. et iiid. ob. Et de ii. paribus chirothecarum cum lapidibus." This golden comb, fet with jewels, realifes the wonders of romance.

turns out to be his own mother; but neither is aware of the fact until it is time to retire, when Degoré mentions his case, and insists on trying the gloves as a preliminary.¹ The princess puts on the gloves, and then declares herself to be his mother. There is hereupon great rejoicing. Degoré is made known to the king as his daughter's son; and when the knight demands who and where his father is, she can only give him the pointless sword she had received as a token from her seducer. He swears that he will not sleep till he has found the person. He meets with an extraordinary adventure at a castle, and afterwards sallying forth, he encounters a knight richly armed, with whom he fights, till the knight, seeing that his sword has no point, discovers Degoré to be his son by that sign, and the contest ceases. His father and mother are married, and Degoré espouses the lady whom he had met at the castle, and whom he had delivered from a giant. The incident of the mother marrying her son also occurs in *Sir Eglamore of Artois*.]

The romance of *King Robert of Sicily* begins and proceeds thus:²

> Pryncis, that be prowde in prese,
> I wylle [telle] that that ys no lees.
> Yn Cysylle was a nobulle kynge,
> Fayre and stronge, and some dele ȝinge;
> He had a brodur in grete Rome,
> That was pope of alle Cryftendome;
> Of Almayne hys odur brodur was emperowre,
> Thorow Cryftendome he had honowre.
> The kynge was calde kynge Roberd,
> Never man in hys tyme wyfte hym aferde.
> He was kynge of grete valowre,
> And also callyd conquerowre;
> Nowhere in no lande was hys pere,
> Kynge nor dewke, ferre nor nere,
> And also he was of chevalrye the flowre:
> And hys odur brodur was emperowre.
> Hys own brodur in ȝorthe Godes generalle vykere,
> Pope of Rome, as ye may here;
> Thys pope was callyd pope Urbane:
> For hym lovyd bothe God and man;
> The emperowre was callyd Valamownde,
> A ftrawnger warreowre was none founde
> After hys brodur, the kyng of Cysyle,
> Of whome y thynke to speke a whyle.
> The kynge thoght he had no pere
> For to acownte, nodur far nor nere,
> And thorow hys thoght he had a pryde,
> For he had no pere, he thoȝt, on no fyde.

---

¹ All the romances have such an obstacle as this. They have all an enchantress, who detains the knight from his queft by objects of pleafure; and who is nothing more than the Calypfo of Homer, the Dido of Virgil, and the Armida of Taffo.

² MS. Vernon, *ut fupr.* Bibl. Bodl. f. 299. It is also in Caius College Camb. MSS. Clafs. E 174. 4. and Bibl. Publ. Cambr. MSS. More, 690. 35. [printed in Halliwell's *Nugæ Poeticæ*, 1844, 8vo.] and Brit. Mus. MSS. Harl. 525. 2. f. 35. [Printed privately by Utterfon, 1839, 8vo. The extracts in this edition have been copied from the text given from a collation of the Publ. Lib. Camb. and Harl. MSS. in *Remains of the Early Popular Poetry of England*, 1864-6, i.]

And on a nyght of seynt Johan,
Thys kynge to the churche come,
For to here hys evynsonge;
Hys dwellynge thoȝt he there to longe,
He thoght more of worldys honowre,
Then of Cryste hys saveowre.
In *magnificat* he harde a vers,
He made a clerke hym hyt reherse
In the langage of hys owne tonge:
For in Laten wyte he not what they songe.
The verse was thys, as y telle the,
Deposuit potentes de sede,
Et exaltavit humiles.
Thys was the verse withowten lees:
The clerke seyde anon ryght:
Syr, soche ys Godys myght,
That he make may hye lowe,
And lowe hye in a lytylle throwe.
God may do, withowten lye,
Hys wylle in the twynkelyng of an ye,
The kyng seyde than with thoȝt unstabulle:
Ye synge thys ofte, and alle ys a fabulle,
What man hath that powere
To make me lowear and in dawngere?
I am flowre of chevalrye;
Alle myn enmyes y may dystroye.
Ther levyth no man in no lande,
That my myght may withstande;
Then ys yowre songe a songe of noght.
Thys arrowre had he in hys thoght,
And in hys thoght a slepe hym toke
In hys closet, so seyth the boke.
When evynsonge was alle done,
A kynge, hym lyke, owte can come,
And alle men with hym can wende,
And kynge Roberd lefte behynde.
The newe kynge was, y yow telle,
Godys aungelle, hys pryde to felle;
The aungelle in the halle yoye made,
And alle men of hym were glade.
Kynge Roberd wakenyd that was in the kyrke:
Hys men he thoȝt now for to wyrke,
For he was lefte there allone,
And merke nyght felle hym upon.
He began to crye upon hys men,
But there was none that answeryd then,
But the sexten at the ende
Of the kyrke, and to hym can wende,
And seyde: lurden, what doyst thou here?
Thou art a thefe or thefeys fere;
Thou art here sykerlye
Thys churche to robbe with felonye.
He seyde: fals thefe and fowle gadlyng,
Thou lyest falsely; y am thy Kynge.
Opyn the churche dore anon,
That y may to my pales gone.
The sexten went welle than,
That he had be a wode man,
And of hym he had farlye,
And wolde delyver the churche in hye,

>   And openyd the dore ry3t fone in hafte.
>   The kyng began to reaue owte fafte,
>   As a man that was nere wode,
>   And at hys pales 3ate he ftode,
>   And callyd the porter: gadlyng, begone,
>   And bad hym come fafte, and hye hym foone.

When admitted, he is brought into the hall, where the angel, who had affumed his place, makes him *the fool of the hall*, and clothes him in a fool's coat. He is then fent out to lie with the dogs; in which fituation he envies the condition of thofe dogs, which in great multitudes were permitted to remain in the royal hall. At length the Emperor Valemounde fends letters to his brother King Robert, inviting him to vifit, with himfelf, their brother the pope at Rome. The angel, who perfonates King Robert, welcomes the meffengers, and clothes them in the richeft apparel, fuch as could not be made in the world:

>   The aungelle welcomyd the meffengerys,
>   And clad them alle in clothys of pryfe,
>   And furryd them with armyne;
>   Ther was never 3yt pellere half fo fyne;
>   And alle was fet with perrye,
>   Ther was never no better in cryftyante';
>   Soche clothyng and hyt were to dyght,
>   Alle cryften men hyt make ne myght,
>   Where foche clothys were to felle,
>   Nor who them made, no man can telle.
>   On that wondyrd alle that bande,
>   Who wro3t thofe clothys with any hande.
>   The meffengerys went with the kynge
>   To grete Rome, withowte lefynge;
>   The fole Roberd with hym went
>   Clad in a fulle fympulle garmente,
>   With foxe tayles riven alle ahowte;
>   Men myght hym knowe in alle the rowte.
>   A babulle he bare agenfte hys wylle,
>   The aungelles hefte to fulfylle.

Afterwards they return in the fame pomp to Sicily, where the angel, after fo long and ignominious a penance, reftores King Robert to his royalty.

Sicily was conquered by the French in the eleventh century,[1] and

---

[1] There is an old French romance, *Robert le Diable*, often quoted by Carpentier in his *Supplement to Du Cange*, and a French Morality, without date or name of the author: [" Cy commence un miracle de Noftre dame, de Robert le dyable, fils du duc de Normandie, a qui il fut enjoint pour fes mesfaiz quil feift le fol fans parler, et depuis or Noftre Seignor mercy de li, et efpoufa la fille de lempereur."] Beauchamp's *Rech. Theat. Fr.* p. 109. [Printed at Rouen, 1836, 8vo.

The French profe romance of *Robert le Diable*, printed in 1496, is extant in the collection called *Bibliothèque Bleue*. It has been tranflated into other languages: among the reft into Englifh. The Englifh verfion was [twice] printed by Wynkyn de Worde, [and is reprinted in Thom's *Early Profe Romances*, 1828 and 1858]. The title of one of the chapters is, "How God fent an aungell to the hermyte to fhewe him the penaunce that he fholde gyve to Robert for his fynnes."—"Yf that Robert wyll be fhryven of his fynnes, he muft kepe and counterfeite the wayes of a fole and be as he were dombe," &c. There is an old Englifh Morality on this tale,

this tale might have been originally got or written during their possession of that island, which continued through many monarchies.¹ But Sicily, from its situation, became a familiar country to all the western continent at the time of the Crusades, and consequently soon found its way into romance, as did many others of the Mediterranean islands and coasts, for the same reason. Another of them, Cilicia, has accordingly given title to an ancient tale called *The King of Tars*, touched with a rude but expressive pencil, from which I shall give some extracts: "Her bigenneth of the Kyng of Tars, and of the

---

under the very corrupt title of *Robert Cicyll*, which was represented at the High-Cross in Chester in 1529. There is a MS. of the poem on vellum in Trinity College library at Oxford (MSS. Num. lvii.).

[*Robert of Cicyle* and *Robert the Devil*, though not identical, are clearly members of the same family, and this poetic embodiment of their lives is evidently the offspring of that tortuous opinion so prevalent in the middle ages, and which time has mellowed into a vulgar adage, that "the greater the sinner the greater the saint." The subject of the latter poem was doubtlessly Robert the sixth duke of Normandy, who became an early object of legendary scandal; and the transition to the same line of potentates in Sicily was an easy effort when thus supported. The romantic legend of "Sir Gowther" published in the *Select Pieces of Early Popular Poetry*, [1817], is only a different version of Robert the Devil with a change of scene, names, &c.—*Price*.

That the subject of the legend of Robert the Devil was Robert the sixth duke of Normandy, is treated by some writers as a matter of much uncertainty, although Mr. Price appears to have entertained no doubt of it. In the *Revue de Rouen* for March, 1836, M. Pothier observes: "Setting out with the scarcely plausible opinion, that all the personages of semi-historic romance must have their type and representative in history, they have set themselves to investigate what real pattern the fabulous Robert the Devil could have been modelled after. As the chronicle [of Normandy], the drama, and the romance agree in making him the son of a duke of Normandy, it has been thence concluded that he must himself have been duke of Normandy; and comparisons have been instituted of his legend with the history of the two or three Roberts that the whole ducal lineage furnishes. Yet neither chroniclers nor poets had ever dreamt of creating, of their own mere authority, Robert the Devil duke of Normandy: the chronicle makes him die at Jerusalem; the romance, in a hermitage near Rome; and the miracle makes him marry the emperor's daughter, and then of course succeed his father-in-law, agreeably to the external law of all seekers of adventures, from the paladins of the round table down to the renowned Knight of the Sorrowful Countenance." According to the later version of the Bibliotheque Bleue, Robert brings his wife into Normandy, ascends the ducal throne, and having lived a good prince, dies laden with honours and with years, leaving the duchy to *his son Richard-sans-Peur*, whose marvellous history has also been recounted by the writers of romance."—*Taylor*.

See also remarks on this subject in *Remains of the Early Popular Poetry of England*, 1864-6, i. 264-9.]

¹ A passage in Fauchet, speaking of rhyme, may perhaps deserve attention here. " Pour le regard de *Siciliens*, je me tiens presque asseure, que Guillaume Ferrabrach frère de Robert Guischard et autres seigneurs de Calabre et Pouille enfans de Tancred François-Normand, l'ont portee aux païs de leur conqueste, estant une coustume des gens de deça chanter, avant que combattre, les beaux faits de leurs ancestres, composez en vers." *Rec.* p. 70. Boccaccio's *Tancred*, in his beautiful tale of *Tancred and Sigismunda*, was one of these Franco-Norman kings of Sicily. Compare *Nouv. Abreg. Chronol. Hist. Fr.* pag. 102, edit. 1752. [Also Gibbon, ch. lvi.—*Anon.*]

Soudan of Dammias,[1] how the Soudan of Dammias was criftened thoru Godis gras:"[2]

> Herkeneth now, bothe olde and ȝyng,
> For Maries love, that fwete thyng:
> How a werre bigan
> Bitwene a god Criftene kyng,
> And an hethene heyȝe lordyng,
> Of Damas the Soudan.
> The kyng of Taars hedde a wyf,
> The feirefte that mighte bere lyf,
> That eny mon telle can:
> A doughter thei hadde hem bitween,
> That heore[3] riȝte heir fcholde ben;
> White fo[4] fether of fwan:
> Chaaft heo[5] was, and feir of chere,
> With rode[6] red fo blofme on brere,
> Eyyen[7] ftepe and gray,
> With lowe fchuldres and whyte fwere;[8]
> Hire to feo[9] was gret preyere
> Of princes pert in play.
> The word[10] of hire fprong ful wyde
> Feor and ner, bi vche a fyde:
> The Soudan herde fay;
> Him thoughte his herte wolde breke on five
> Bot he mihte have hire to wyve,
> That was fo feir a may;
> The Soudan ther he fat in halle;
> He fente his meffagers fafte withalle,
> To hire fader the kyng.
> And feide, hou fo hit ever bifalle,
> That mayde he wolde clothe in palle
> And fpoufen hire with his ryng.
> "And elles[11] I fwere withouten fayle
> I fchull[12] hire winnen in pleyn battayle
> With mony an heiȝ lordyng," &c.

The Soldan, on application to the King of Tarfus for his daughter, is refufed; and the meffengers return without fuccefs. The Soldan's anger is painted with great characteriftical fpirit:

> The Soudan fat at his des,
> I-ferved of his furfte mes;
> Thei comen into the halle
> To fore the prince proud in pres:
> Heore tale thei tolden withouten lees,
> And on heore knees gunne falle:

---

[1] Damafcus.

[2] MS. Vernon. Bibl. Bodl. f. 304. It is alfo in Bibl. Adv. Edinb. W 4, 1, Num. iv. In five leaves and a half.

[This romance will be found in Mr. Ritfon's Collection, vol. ii. from whofe tranfcript the prefent text has been corrected. On the authority of Douglas's verfion of the *Æneid* and Ruddiman's Gloffary, he interprets "Tars" to mean Thrace; but as the ftory is one of pure invention, and at beft but a romantic legend, why not refer the Damas and Tars of the text to the Damafcus and Tarfus of Scripture? —*Price.*]

[3] their.　　[4] as.　　[5] fhe.　　[6] [complexion.]
[7] eyes.　　[8] neck.　　[9] fee.　　[10] The report of her.
[11] [elfe.]　　[12] fhall.

And feide, "Sire, the king of Tars
Of wikked wordes nis not fcars,
  Hethene hound¹ he doth the² calle;
And er his doughtur he give the tille,³
Thyn herte blode he wol fpille
  And thi barouns alle."
Whon the Soudan this iherde,
As a wod man he ferde:
  His robe he rente adoun;
He tar the her⁴ of hed and berd,
And feide he wold her wiue with fwerd,
  Beo his lord feynt Mahoun.
The table adoon riȝt he fmot,
In to the floore foot hot,⁵
  He lokede as a wylde lyoun;
Al that he hitte he fmot doun riȝt,
Bothe fergaunt and kniȝt,
  Erl and eke baroun.
So he ferde forfothe a pliȝt,
Al a day and al a niȝt,
  That no man miȝte him chafte:⁶
A morwen whon hit was day liȝt,
He fent his meffagers ful riȝt,
  After his barouns in hafte:
[That thai com to his parlement,
For to heren his jugement
  Bothe left and maft.
When the parlement was pleyner,
Tho bifpac the Soudan fer,
  And feyd to hem in haft.]⁷
"Lordynges," he feith, "what to rede?"⁸
Me is don a grete myfdede,
  Of Taars the Criften kyng;
I bed him bothe lond and lede
To have his douhter in worthli wede,
  And fpoufe hire with my ryng.
And he feide withouten fayle:
Arft he wolde me fle in batayle
  And mony a gret lordynge.
Ac fertes⁹ he fchal be forfwore,
Or to wrothe hele¹⁰ that he was bore,

---

¹ A phrafe often applied to the Saracens. So, in *Syr Bevys*, fig. C ii b:
  "To fpeke with an *hethene hounde*."
² thee.   ³ "Before his daughter is given to thee."
⁴ "tore the hair."
⁵ ftruck, ftamped. [Sir F. Madden fays, that this is ftill in ufe in Ireland to denote *anger* or *hafte*.]
⁶ check.
⁷ [The lines within brackets were inferted by Mr. Ritfon from the Auchinleck MS.—*Price*.]
⁸ "what counfel fhall we take?"
⁹ But certainly.
¹⁰ Lofs of health or fafety. Malediction. So R. of Brunne, *Chron.* apud Hearne's *Rob. Glouc.* pp. 737, 738:
  "Morgan did after confeile,
  And wrought him felfe to *wrotherheile*."
Again:
  "To zow al was a wikke confeile,
  That ze felle fe full *wrotherheile*."

Bote he hit therto¹ bryng.
Therefore, lordynges, I have after ow sent
For to come to my parliment,
    To wite of ȝow counsayle.
And alle onswerde with gode entent
Thei wolde be at his comaundement
    Withouten eny fayle.
And whon thei were alle at his heste,
The Soudan made a wel gret feste
    For love of his batayle;
The Soudan gedred an oste unryde²
With Sarazyns of muchel pryde,
    The kyng of Taars to assayle.
Whon the kyng hit herde that tyde,
He sent about on vche a syde,
    Alle that he miȝte of seende;
Gret werre tho bigan to wrake
For the mariage ne most be take
    Of that mayden heende.³
Batayle thei sette uppon a day,
Withinne the thridde day of May,⁴
    Ne longer nolde thei leende.⁵
The Soudan com with gret power,
With helm briȝt and feir baneer,
    Uppon that kyng to wende.
The Soudan ladde an huge ost,
And com with much pruyde and cost,
    With the kyng of Tars to fiȝte.
With him mony a Sarazyn feer;⁶
Alle the feldes feor and neer,
    Of helmes leomede⁷ liȝte.
The kyng of Tars com also
The Soudan batayle for to do
    With mony a Cristene kniȝe;
Either ost gon othur assayle:
Ther bigon a strong batayle,
    That grislych was of siȝt.
Threo hethene ayein twey Cristene men,
And falde hem doun in the fen,
    With wepnes stif and goode:
The steorne Sarazyns in that fiȝt,
Slowe vr Cristen men doun riȝt,
    Thei fouhte as heo weore woode.
The Soudan ost in that stounde
Feolde the Cristene to the grounde,
    Mony a freoly foode;
The Sarazyns withouten fayle
The Cristens culde⁸ in that battayle,
    Nas non that hem withstoode.
Whon the king of Tars sauȝ that fiȝt
Wodde he was for wrathe⁹ apliȝt;
    In honde he hent a spere,

---

¹ to that issue.   ² [numerous.]
³ [courteous. A general term expressive of personal and mental accomplishments.—*Price*.]
⁴ [Respecting the selection of this period for a contest, see a suggestion in *Rem. of the E. P. Poetr. of Engl.* 1864-6, ii. 109.]
⁵ tarry.   ⁶ companion.   ⁷ shone.
⁸ killed.   ⁹ wraþþe. *Orig.*

And to the Soudan he rode ful riʒt
With a dunt[1] of much miʒt,
   Adoun he gon him bere :
The Soudan neigh he hedde i-lawe,
But thritti thoufent of hethene lawe
   Coomen him for to were ;
And broughten him ayeyn upon his ftede,
And holpe him wel in that nede,
   That no mon miʒt him dere.[2]
Whon he was brouʒt uppon his ftede,
He fprong, as fparkle doth of glede,[3]
   For wrathe and for envye.
Alle that he hutte he made hem blede,
He ferde as he wolde a wede,[4]
   Mahoun help, he gan crye.
Mony an helm ther was unweved,
And mony a bacinet[5] to-cleved,
   And fadeles mony emptye ;
Men miʒte fe uppon the feld
Moni a kniʒt ded under fcheld
   Of the Criften cumpagnie.
Whon the kyng of Taars faugh hem fo ryde,
No lengor there he nolde abyde,
   Bote fley[6] to his oune citè :
The Sarazyns that ilke tyde
Slough adoun bi vche fyde
   Vr Criftene folk fo fre.
The Sarazyns that tyme fauns fayle
Slowe vre Criftene in battayle,
   That reuthe hit was to fe ;
And on the morwe for heore[7] fake
Truwes thei gunne togidere take,[8]
   A moneth and dayes thre.
As the kyng of Tars fat in his halle,
He made ful gret deol[9] withalle,
   For the folk that he hedde i-lore :[10]
His douʒter com in riche palle.
On kneos heo[11] gon biforen him falle,
   And feide with fyking fore :
Fader, heo feide, let me beo his wyf,
That ther be no more ftryf, &c.

To prevent future bloodfhed, the princefs voluntarily declares fhe is willing to be married to the Soldan, although a Pagan: and notwithftanding the king her father peremptorily refufes his confent, and refolves to continue the war, with much difficulty fhe finds means to fly to the Soldan's court, in order to produce a fpeedy and lafting reconciliation by marrying him:

   To the Soudan heo[11] is i-fare ;
He com with mony an heiʒ lordyng,
For to welcom that fwete thyng,
   Ther heo com in hire chare :[12]
He cufte[13] hire wel mony a fithe,
His joye couthe no man kithe,[14]

---

[1] *dint*, wound, ftroke.   [2] hurt.   [3] coal, fire-brand.
[4] as if he was mad.   [5] helmet.   [6] flew.
[7] their.   [8] They began to make a truce together.
[9] dole, grief.   [10] loft.   [11] fhe.   [12] chariot.   [13] kift.   [14] know.

> Awei was al hire care.
> Into chambre heo was led,
> With riche clothes heo was cled,
>   Hethene as thauȝ heo were.[1]
> The Soudan ther he fat in halle,
> He comaundede his kniȝtes alle
>   That mayden for to fette,
> In cloth of riche purpil palle,
> And on hire hed a comeli calle:
>   Bi the Soudan heo was fette.
> Unfemli was hit for to fe
> Heo that was fo bright of ble,
>   To habbe[2] fo foule a mette,[3] &c.

They are then married, and the wedding is folemnized with a grand tournament, which they both view from a high tower. She is afterwards delivered of a fon, which is fo deformed as to be almoft a monfter. But at length fhe perfuades the Soldan to turn Chriftian; and the young prince is baptized, after which ceremony he fuddenly becomes a child of moft extraordinary beauty. The Soldan next proceeds to deftroy his Saracen idols:

> He hente a ftaf with herte grete,
> And al his goddes he gan to bete,
>   And drouȝ hem alle adoun;
> And leyde on, til that he con fwete,
> With fterne ftrokes and with grete,
>   On Jovyn[4] and Plotoun,
> On Aftrot and fire Jovin,
> On Tirmagaunt and Apollin,
>   He brak hem fcolle and croun;
> On Tirmagaunt, that was heore brother,
> He lafte no lym hole with other,
>   Ne on his lord feynt Mahoun, &c.

The Soldan then releafes thirty thoufand Chriftians, whom he had long detained prifoners. As an apoftate from the pagan religion, he is powerfully attacked by feveral neighbouring Saracen nations: but he folicits the affiftance of his father-in-law, the king of Tars; and they, joining their armies, in a pitched battle defeat five Saracen kings, Kenedoch, Lefyas, king of Taborie, Merkel, Cleomadas, and Membrok. There is a warmth of defcription in fome paffages of this poem, not unlike the manner of Chaucer. The reader muft have already obferved that the ftanza refembles that of Chaucer's *Rime of Sir Topas*.[5]

---

[1] as if fhe had been a heathen, one of that country.   [2] have.   [3] mate.

[4] I know not if by *fire Jovyn* he means Jupiter, or the Roman emperor called Jovinian, againft whom Saint Jerom wrote, and whofe hiftory is in the *Gefta Romanorum*, c. 59. He is mentioned by Chaucer as an example of pride, luxury, and luft. *Somp. T.* v. 7511. Verdier (in v.) recites a *Moralité* on Jovinian, with nineteen charaƈters, printed at Lyons, from an ancient copy in 1584, 8vo, with the title *L'Orgueil et préfomption de l'Empereur Jovinian*. [Compare *fupra*, vol. i. p. 255, and fee Brunet, *dern.* edit. iii. 1885.] But Jovyn being mentioned here with Plotoun and Apollin, feems to mean Jove or Jupiter; and the appellation *fire* perhaps implies father, or chief, of the heathen gods.

[5] The romance of *Sir Libeaux* or *Lybius Difconius* [printed by Ritfon], is in this

[Of the romance of *Ypotis*,[1] mentioned by Chaucer, there are four copies preserved in the British Museum,[2] and three at Oxford.[3] Though mentioned by Chaucer along with *Horn Child*, *Sir Bevis*, and *Sir Guy*, it has but little in common with those romances of Price. It professes to be "a tale of holy writ," and the work of St. John the Evangelist. The scene is Rome. A child, named Ypotis, appears before the Emperor Adrian, saying that he is come to teach men God's law; whereupon the emperor proceeds to interrogate him as to what is God's law, and then of many other matters, not in any captious spirit, but with the utmost reverence and faith. He asks questions about heaven, Adam's sin, the Trinity, the creation, Sins, why men should fast on Friday, and other subjects; and at last he asks the wondrous child who has solved all his queries whether he is a wicked angel or a good:

> þe child onswerde with milde mood:
> "I am he þat þe wrouhte
> And also þat þe deore abougte."
> þe child wente to heuene þo
> To þe stude þat he com fro.
> þe Emperour kneled on þe grounde
> And þonked God, þat blisful stounde
> He bi com good. In alle wyse
> Lyuede & diyede in Godes seruise.

And so, with a second ascription of itself to Saint John as its author, the work ends. There is a little tract in prose on the same legend from the press of Wynkyn de Worde.

The editor of the *Catalogue of the Ashmolean MSS.* suggests that the origin of this curious dialogue is to be found in those spurious pieces relating to the philosopher Secundus, &c., which are described by Fabricius.[4] What little is known of Secundus is given by Philostratus, in his *Vitæ Sophistarum*. He was an Armenian sophist, who flourished about A.D. 100. Suidas confounds him with the younger Pliny; his words are, ὅς ἐχρημάτισε πλήνιος. Vincent of Beauvais made him known to the Middle Ages, or at least extended the knowledge of him, by recording the wonderful taciturnity he was said to have preserved, and also certain answers in writing given to the Emperor Hadrian.[5] Besides this conversation between the Emperor Hadrian and Secundus, Fabricius gives a similar altercation

---

stanza. MSS. Cott. Cal. A 2, f. 40. [The *Beau Disconu, Bel Inconnu*, or rather *Li Biaus Desconneus* was written by Renals de Biauju, and a MS. of the original French is in the possession of the Duc d'Aumale. But the English versions are not a literal translation of the Duc d'Aumale's French copy, and therefore there must have been formerly a somewhat different text, or the English author took unacknowledged liberties with the poem. The title of the original French is: "Le Bel Inconnu, ou Giglain fils de Messire Gauvain et de la Fee aux Blanches Mains, Poeme de la Table Ronde, par Renauld de Beaujeu, Poete du XIII⁰. siecle. Publié d'après le MS. unique, par C. Hippeau. Paris, 1860, 8vo.]

[1] [Communicated by Mr. J. W. Hales.]
[2] Arundel MSS. No. 140, addit. MSS. No. 22283; Cott. MSS. Calig. A. ii. and Titus A. xxvi.
[3] Vernon MS. 140; Ashm. Nos. 61 and 750.
[4] *Bibl. Græc.* tom. xiii.   [5] See *Spec. Hist.* x. 70, 71.

between that same emperor and Epictetus. But indeed between these pieces and *Ypotis* there is no likeness whatever, except that the form is catechetical, and that the questions are put in the mouth of the same imperial figure. Secundus's answers are not answers, but mere accumulations of epigrams, mere rhetorical bouquets. He is asked what are κόσμος, ὠκεανος, θεός, ἡμέρα, ἥλιος, &c., and replies in each case with a series of elaborate metaphors. Thus, to the question, τί ἐστι γυνη; the response of the oracle is, ἀνδρὸς ἐπιθύμιον, συνεστιώμενον θηρίον, συγκοιμω μένη λέαινα . . . . . ἀνθρωπόποιον ὑπούργημα, ζῶον πονηρον, ἀναγκαῖον κακόν. Whereas in *Ypotis* the questions are all answered with the wish, not to air tropes and similes, but to convey information. In fact, *Ypotis* is a very curious medieval catechism. It is evidently the work of some sober-minded ecclesiastical instructor—of some monastic Pinnock of the thirteenth or fourteenth century. The statements contained in it concerning the seven elements of which Adam was composed, the list of the sins committed by him, the description of the seven heavens and the nine celestial orders, the thirteen reasons for fasting on Friday—all these things formed part of what was once held to be highly important knowledge, to impart which in a form easy to remember, and to invest with a certain personal interest, was the object of the versifier, who produced *Ypotis*.

For the name I venture to suggest that it is a corruption of the Greek Ὑποστασις, or rather, perhaps, Ὑποστατης. The former was a common word with the Greek ecclesiastical writers for a person of the Trinity; the latter is used by them for a creator.]

Ipomydon is mentioned among the romances in the Prologue of *Richard Cuer de Lyon*; in an ancient copy of the British Museum, it is called *Syr Ipomydon*, a name borrowed from the Theban war, and transferred here to a tale of the feudal times.[1] This piece is derived from a French original. Our hero Ippomedon is son of Ermones king of Apulia, and his mistress is the fair heiress of Calabria. About the year 1230, William Ferrabras[2] and his brethren, sons of Tancred the Norman, and well known in the history of the Paladins, acquired the signories of Apulia and Calabria. But our English romance seems to be immediately translated from the French; for Ermones is called king of *Poyle* or Apulia, which in French is *Pouille*. I have transcribed some of the most interesting passages.[3]

Ipomydon, although the son of a king, is introduced waiting in his father's hall, at a grand festival. This servitude was so far from being dishonourable, that it was always required as a preparatory step to knighthood:

> Every yere the kyng wold
> At Whytsontyde a fest hold

---

[1] MSS. Harl. 2252, 44, f. 54. [In Heber's library was a printed copy deficient of sheet A, which had been part of the collection bequeathed to Lincoln Cathedral by Dean Honeywood. It was from the press of W. de Worde.]
[Printed in Mr. Weber's collection of Metrical Romances, whose text has been substituted for Warton's. It has also been analysed by Mr. Ellis.—*Price*.]
[2] *Bras de fer*. Iron arm.   [3] MSS. f. 55.

Off dukis, erlis, and barons,
Many there come frome dyvers townes,
Ladyes, maydens, gentill and fre,
Come thedyr from ferre contrè:
And grette lordis of ferre lond
Thedyr were prayd by fore the hond.[1]
When all were come togedyr than
There was joy of mani a man;
Full riche I wote were hyr feruice,
For better might no man devyſe.
Ipomydon that day ſervyd in halle,
All ſpake of hym bothe grete and ſmalle,
Ladies and maydens by helde hym on,
So godely a man they had ſene none:
Hys feyre chere in halle theym ſmert
That mony a lady ſmote throw the hert.
And in there hertis they made mone
That there lordis ne were ſuche one.
After mete they went to pley,
All the peple, as I you ſey;
Some to chambre, and ſome to boure,
And ſome to the hye towre;[2]
And ſome in the halle ſtode
And ſpake what hem thought gode:
Men that were of that cite[3]
Enquered of men of other cuntrè, &c.

Here a converſation commences concerning the heireſs of Calabria: and the young Prince Ipomydon immediately forms a reſolution to viſit and to win her. He ſets out in diſguiſe:

Now they go furth on her way,
Ipomydon to hys men gan ſay,
That ther be none of hem alle,
So hardy by his name hym calle,
Whereſo thei wend ferre or nere,
Or over the ſtrange ryvere;
" Ne man telle what I am,
What I ſchall be, ne whens I cam."
All they granted hys commandement,
And forthe they went with one aſſent.
Ipomydon and Tholomew
Robys had on and mantillis new,
Of the richeſt that myght bee,
Ther nas ne ſuche in that cuntrèe:
For many was the ryche ſtone
That the mantillis were uppon.
So longe there weys they have nome[4]
That to Calabre they ar come:
They come to the caſtelle yate
The porter was redy there at,
The porter to theme they can calle
And prayd hym go into the halle

---

[1] before-hand.
[2] In the feudal caſtles, where many perſons of both ſexes were aſſembled, who did not know how to ſpend the time, it is natural to ſuppoſe that different parties were formed, and different ſchemes of amuſement invented. One of theſe was to mount to the top of one of the higheſt towers in the caſtle.
[3] The Apulians.   [4] [taken.]

And say thy lady[1] gent and fre,
That come ar men of ferre contrèe,
And if it plese hyr we wold hyr prey,
That we might ete with hyr to day.
The porter seyd full cortesly
" Your errand to do I am redy."
The lady to hyr mete was sette,
The porter come and feyre hyr grette,
"Madame," he sayd, "God you save,"
Atte your gate gestis ye have,
Strange men all for to see
Thei aske mete for charytè."
The lady comaundith sone anon
That the gates were undone,
" And bryng theym all byfore me
For wele at ese shall they bee."
They toke hyr pagis hors and alle,
These two men went into the halle.
Ipomydon on knees hym sette,
And the lady feyre he grette:
" I am a man of strange contrè
And pray you yff your will to [so] be
That I myght dwelle with you to-yere
Of your norture for to lere,[2]
I am come frome ferre lond;
For speche I here bi fore the hand
That your norture and your servyse
Ys holden of so grete empryse.
I pray you that I may dwelle here
Some of your servyse to lere."
The lady by held Ipomydon,
Hym semyd wele a gentilmon,
She knew non suche in hyr lande,
So goodly a man and wele farand;[3]
She saw also by his norture
He was a man of grete valure:
She cast full sone in hyr thoght
That for no servyse come he noght;
But it was worship hyr unto
In feir servyse hym to do.
She sayd, Syr, welcome ye be,
And all that comyn be with the;
Sithe ye have had so grete travayle,
Of a servise ye shall not fayle:

---

[1] She was lady, by inheritance, of the signory. The female feudatories exercised all the duties and honours of their feudal jurisdiction in person. In Spenser, where we read of the *Lady of the Castle*, we are to understand such a character. See a story of a *Comtesse*, who entertains a knight in her castle with much gallantry. *Mem. sur l'Anc. Chev.* ii. 69. It is well known that anciently in England ladies were sheriffs of counties. [Margaret, countess of Richmond, was a justice of peace. Sir W. Dugdale tells us that Ela, widow of William, earl of Salisbury, executed the sheriff's office for the county of Wilts in different parts of the reign of Henry III. (See *Baronage*, vol. i. 177.) From Fuller's *Worthies* we find that Elizabeth, widow of Thomas Lord Clifford, was sheriffess of Westmoreland for many years, and from Pennant's *Scottish Tour* we learn that for the same county Anne, the celebrated Countess of Dorset, Pembroke and Montgomery, often sat in person as sheriffess.—*Park*.]
[2] learn.   [3] handsome.

In thys contre ye may dwelle here
And at your will for to lere,
Of the cuppe ye shall serve me
And all your men with you shal be,
Ye may dwelle here at youre wille,
But[1] your beryng be full ylle.
Madame, he sayd, grantmercy,
He thankid the lady cortesly.
She comandyth hym to the mete,
But or he satte in ony sete,
He saluted theym grete and smalle,
As a gentillman shuld in halle;
All they sayd sone anone,
They saw nevyr so goodli a mon,
Ne so light, ne so glad,
Ne non that so ryche atyre had:
There was non that sat nor yede,[2]
But they had marvelle of hys dede,[3]
And sayd, he was no lytell syre,
That myght shew suche atyre.
Whan they had ete, and grace sayd,
And the tabyll away was leyd;
Upp than aroos Ipomydon,
And to the botery he went anon,
Ant [dyde] hys mantille hym aboute;
On hym lokyd all the route,
Ant every man sayd to other there,
" Will ye se the proude squeer
Shall serve[4] my ladye of the wyne,
In hys mantell that is so fyne?"
That they hym scornyd wist he noght:
On othyr thyng he had his thoght.
He toke the cuppe of the botelere,
And drewe a lace of sylke ful clere,
Adowne than felle hys mantylle by,
He prayd hym for hys curtesly,
That lytelle yifte[5] that he wolde nome
Tille efte sone a better come;
Up it toke the botelere.
Byfore the lady he gan it bere,
And prayd the lady hertely
To thanke hym of his cortessye;
All that was tho in the halle
Grete honowre they spake hym alle.
And sayd he was no lytelle man
That such yiftys yiffe kan.
There he dwellyd many a day,
And servid the lady wele to pay.
He bare hym on so feyre manere
To knyghtes, ladyes, and squyere,
All lovyd hym that com hym by,
For he bare hym so cortesly.
The lady had a cosyne that hight Jason,
Full well he lovyd Ipomydon;
Where that he yede in or oute,
Jason went with hym aboute.

---

[1] unless. [2] walked. [3] behaviour.
[4] " who is to serve." [5] *i. e.* his mantle.

The lady lay, but she slept noght,
For of the squyere she had grete thoght;
How he was feyre and shape wele,
Body and armes, and every dele:
Ther was non in al hir land
So wel besemyd dougty of hand.
But she kowde wete for no case,
Whens he come ne what he was,
Ne of no man cowde enquere
Other than the strange squyere.
She hyr bythought on a quentyse,
If she myght know in ony wyse,
To wete whereof he were come.
Thys was hyr thoght all and some:
She thought to wode hyr men to tame[1]
That she myght knowe hym by his game.
On the morow, whan it was day,
To hyr men than gan she say,
" To morrow whan it is day lyght,
Loke ye be all redy dight,
With youre houndis more and lesse,
In the forrest to take my grese,
And there I will myself be
Youre game to byhold and see."
Ipomydon had houndis thre
That he broght frome his contrè;
When they were to the wode gone,
This lady and hyr men ichone,
And with hem her houndis ladde,
All that ever any howndis hadde.
Sir Tholomew foryate he noght,
His maistres howndis thedyr he broght,
That many a day ne had ronne ere,
Full wele he thoght to note hem there.
Whan they come to the laund on hight,
The quenys pavylon there was pight,
That she myght se of the best
All the game of the forèst,
The wandlessours went throw the forèst,
And to the lady broght many a best,[2]
Herte and hynde, buk and doo,
And othir bestis many moo.
The howndis that were of gret prise
Pluckid downe dere all at a tryse;
Ipomydon with his houndis thoo
Drew downe bothe buk and doo;
More he tok with houndis thre
Than all that othyr compaigne.
There squyres undyd hyr dere,
Iche man on his owne manere:
Ipomydon a dere yede unto,
Full konnyngly gan he it undo;
So feyre that venyson he gan to dight,
That bothe hym byheld squyer and knight:
The lady lokyd oute of her pavyloun,
And saw hym dight the venyson.
There she had grete deyntè
And so had all that dyd hym see:

.[1] [tane or tan, A.-S. to *lure* or *entice*.]   [2] beast.

> She faw all that he downe droughe
> Of huntyng fhe wift be cowde ynoughe
> And thoght in hyr herte then
> That he was come of gentillmen:
> She bad Jafon hyr men to calle:
> Home they paffyd grete and fmalle:
> Home they come fone anone,
> This lady to hyr mete gan gone,
> And of venery[1] had hyr fille
> For they had take game at wille.

He is afterwards knighted with great folemnity:

> The heraudes gaff the child[2] the gree,
> A m. pownde he had to fee,
> Mynftrellys had yiftes of golde
> And fourty dayes thys feft was holde.[3]

The metrical romance entitled *La Mort Arthure*, preferved in the fame repofitory, is fuppofed by the learned and accurate Wanley to be a tranflation from the French: he adds, that it is not perhaps older than the times of Henry VII.[4] But as it abounds with many Saxon words, and feems to be quoted in *Syr Bevys*, I have given it a place here.[5] Notwithftanding the title and the exordium which promife the hiftory of Arthur and the Sangreal, the exploits of Sir Lancelot du Lak, king of Benwike, his intrigues with Arthur's queen Geneura, and his refufal of the beautiful daughter of the Earl of Afcalot, form the greateft part of the poem. At the clofe, the repentance of Lancelot and Geneura, who both affume the habit of religion, is introduced. The writer mentions the Tower of London. The following is a defcription of a tournament performed by fome of the knights of the Round Table:[6]

> Tho to the caftelle gon they fare,
>   To the ladye fayre and bryht:
> Blithe was the ladye thare,
>   That they wold dwelle with hyr that nyght.
> Haftely was there foper yare[7]
>   Off mete and drinke rychely dight;
> On the morow gon they dine and fare
>   Both Launcelott and that other knight.

---

[1] [hunting, game.]   [2] Ipomydon.   [3] MS. f. 61. b.
[4] MSS. Harl. 2252. 49. f. 86. Pr. "Lordinges that are leffe and deare." [Edited by F. J. Furnivall for the Roxburghe Club, 1864. The late Mr. Ritfon was of opinion that [this romance] was verified from the profe work of the fame name written by Malory and printed by Caxton; in proof of which he contended that the ftyle is marked by an evident affectation of antiquity. But in truth it differs moft effentially from Malory's work, which was a mere compilation, whilft this follows with tolerable exactnefs the French romance of *Lancelot*; and its phrafeology, which perfectly refembles that of Cheftre and other authors of the fifteenth century, betrays no marks of affectation.—*Ellis*. A new edition of Caxton's *Morte Arthur* has fince been publifhed by Mr. Southey.—*Price*. The Early Englifh Text Society alfo propofes to republifh Caxton's edit. Southey's fo-called edition, 1817, was a mere bookfeller's fpeculation, with a very elaborate, but fomewhat difcurfive introduction by the nominal editor. An imperfect copy feems to have been employed, and the deficiencies fupplied from a later text.]
[5] Signat. K ii b.   [6] MS. f. 89. b.   [7] ready.

Whan they come in to the feld
  Myche there was of game and play,
Awhile they hovid¹ and byheld
  How Arthurs knightis rode that day,
Galehodis² party bygan to held³
  On fote his knightis ar led away.
Launcelott ftiff was undyr fcheld,
  Thinkis to helpe yif that he may.
Befyde hym come than fir Ewayne,
  Breme⁴ as eny wilde bore;
Launcellott fpringis hym ageyne,⁵
  In rede armys that he bore:
A dynte he yaff with mekill mayne,
  Sir Ewayne was unhorfid thare,
That alle men wente⁶ he had ben flayne
  So was he woundyd wondyr fare.⁷
Sir Boerte thoughte no thinge good,
  When Syr Ewaine unhorfid was;
Forthe he fpringis, as he were wode,
  To Launcelot withouten lees:
Launcellot hyte hym on the hode,
  The nexte way to grounde he chefe:
Was none fo ftiff agayne hym ftode
  Ffule thynne he made the thikkeft prees.⁸
Sir Lyonelle beganne to tene,⁹
  And haftely he made hym bowne,¹⁰
To Launcellott, with herte kene,
  He rode with helme and fword browne;
Launcellott hitte hym as I wene,
  Throughe the helme in to the crowne:
That evyr after it was fene
  Bothe hors and man there yod adoune.
The knightis gadrid to gedir thare
  And gan with crafte, &c.

I could give many more ample fpecimens of the romantic poems of thefe namelefs minftrels, who probably flourifhed before or about the reign of Edward II.¹¹ But it is neither my inclination nor inten-

---

[¹ tarried.—Sir F. Madden's corr.]   ² Sir Galahad's.
³ [heel, *i. e.* give way.—Sir F. Madden's note.]   ⁴ fierce.
⁵ againft.   ⁶ weened.   ⁷ fore.   ⁸ crowd.
⁹ be troubled.   ¹⁰ ready.
¹¹ *Octavian* is one of the romances mentioned in the Prologue to *Richard Cuer de Lyon*, above cited. [An imperfect copy of an early printed edition, fuppofed to be from W. Copland's prefs, was fold amongft Mr. Heber's books.] In the Cotton MSS. there is the metrical romance of *Octavian imperator*, but it has nothing of the hiftory of the Roman emperors. Pr. "Jhefu pat was with fpere yftonge." Calig. A. 12. f. 20. It is a very fingular ftanza. In Bifhop More's manufcripts at Cambridge, there is a poem with the fame title, but a very different beginning, viz. "Lytyll and mykyll olde and younge." Bibl. Publ. 690. 30.—[This romance has been edited by Mr. Halliwell for the Percy Society.] The Emperor *Octavyen*, perhaps the fame, is mentioned in Chaucer's *Dreme*, v. 368. Among Hatton's MSS. in Bibl. Bodl. we have a French poem, *Romaunce de Otheuien Empereur de Rome.* Hyper. Bodl. 4046. 21. [Of which Conybeare printed an Englifh epitomized verfion, 1809, 8vo.]

In the fame line of the aforefaid Prologue, we have the romance of *Ury*. This is probably the father of the celebrated Sir Ewaine or Yvain, mentioned in the *Court Mantel.* (*Mem. Anc. Cheval.* ii. p. 62.)

tion to write a catalogue, or compile a miscellany. It is not to be expected that this work should be a general repository of our ancient poetry. I cannot however help observing, that English literature and English poetry suffer[ed], while so many pieces of this kind still remain[ed] concealed and forgotten in our manuscript libraries. They contain in common with the prose-romances, to most of which indeed

> "Li rois pris par la destre main
> L'amiz monseignor Yvain
> Qui au roi Urien fu filz,
> Et bons chevaliers et hardiz,
> Qui tant ama chiens et oisiaux."

Specimens of the English *Syr Bevys* may be seen in Percy's *Reliques*, iii. 216, 217, 297, edit. 1767, and *Observations on the Fairy Queen*, § ii. p. 50. It is in manuscript at Cambridge, Bibl. Publ. 690. 30, and Coll. Caii. A 9. 5. And MSS. Bibl. Adv. Edinb. W 4. 1. Num. xxii.

It is in this romance of *Syr Bevys*, that the knight passes over a bridge, the arches of which are hung round with small bells. Signat. E iv. This is an oriental idea. In the *Alcoran* it is said, that one of the felicities in Mahomet's paradise will be to listen to the ravishing music of an infinite number of bells, hanging on the trees, which will be put in motion by the wind proceeding from the throne of God. Sale's *Koran*, Prelim. Disc. p. 100. In the enchanted horn, as we shall see hereafter, in *le Lai du Corn*, the rim of the horn is hung round with a hundred bells of a most musical sound.

We shall have occasion, in the progress of our poetry, to bring other specimens of these compositions. See *Obs. on Spenser's Fairy Queen*, ii. 42, 43.

I must not forget here, that Sir Gawaine, one of Arthur's champions, is celebrated in a separate romance. [In MS. Rawlinson, C. 86, is *The Wedding of Sir Gawayne*, a later copy of which, mutilated, occurs in the Percy MS. Sir F. Madden, who included the Rawlinson copy in his *Sir Gawayne*, 1839, observes: "It is, unquestionably, the original of the mutilated poem in the Percy folio, and is sufficiently curious to render its insertion in the Appendix an object of interest." It is called *The weddynge of Sr Gawen & Dame Ragnell*, and begins:

> "Lythe and listenyth the lif of a lord riche
> The while that he lyvid was none hym liche."]

Dr. Percy has printed the *Marriage of Sir Gawayne*, which he believes to have furnished Chaucer with his *Wife of Bath*, *Reliques*, i. 11. It begins, "Kinge Arthur liues in merry Carliele." [This is printed in Sir F. Madden's *Sir Gawayne*, 1839.] I think I have somewhere seen a romance in verse entitled, *The Turke and Gawaine*. [This romance occurs in the recently edited *Percy MS*. Many important romances altogether omitted and probably unseen by Warton and his editors, might be mentioned here, such as *Blonde of Oxford and Jehan of Dammartin*, edited for the Camden Society, 1858; *Sir Generides*, recently edited for the Roxburghe Club by Mr. Furnivall (a ballad-poem on the same subject is in a MS. in the library of Trinity College, Cambridge; and of the longer narrative fragments printed with the types of W. de Worde are extant); *The Romans of Partenay or Melusine*, Early English Text Society, 1866; and *Torrent of Portugal*, printed from the Chetham MS. 1842, 8vo. *Torrent of Portugal*, which, from a small fragment with his types remaining, seems to have been printed by Pynson in the early part of the sixteenth century, is a very dull and puerile performance. It appears to be in heroic fiction what *Jack the Giant Killer* is in the romance of the nursery. How far Jack may have owed his existence to his grander and more imposing prototype, it is not easy to say. We see in *Torrent of Portugal* a curiously vague use of geographical terms connected with America; possibly the story, in its present shape, was not composed long before it came from Pynson's press.]

they gave rise, amusing images of ancient customs and institutions not elsewhere to be found, or at least not otherwise so strikingly delineated: and they preserve, pure and unmixed, those fables of chivalry which formed the taste, and awakened the imagination, of our elder English classics. The antiquaries of former times overlooked or rejected these valuable remains, which they despised as false and frivolous, and employed their industry in reviving obscure fragments of uninstructive morality or uninteresting history. But in the present age we are beginning to make ample amends: in which the curiosity of the antiquarian is connected with taste and genius, and his researches tend to display the progress of human manners, and to illustrate the history of society.

As a further illustration of the general subject and 'many particulars of this section and the three last, I will add a new proof of the reverence in which such stories were held, and of the familiarity with which they must have been known, by our ancestors. These fables were not only perpetually repeated at their festivals, but were the constant objects of their eyes. The very walls of their apartments were clothed with romantic history. Tapestry was anciently the fashionable furniture of our houses, and it was chiefly filled with lively representations of this sort. The stories are still preserved of the tapestry in the royal palaces of Henry VIII.;[1] which I will here give without reserve, including other subjects, as they happen to occur, equally descriptive of the times. In the tapestry of the Tower of London, the original and most ancient seat of our monarchs, there are recited "Godfrey of Bulloign, the three kings of Cologne, the emperor Constantine, saint George, king Erkenwald,[2] the history of Hercules, Fame and Honour, the Triumph of Divinity, Esther and Ahasuerus, Jupiter and Juno, saint George, the eight Kings, the ten Kings of France, the Birth of our Lord, Duke Joshua, the rich history of king David, the seven Deadly Sins, the rich history of the Passion, the Stem of Jesse,[3] our Lady and Son, king Solomon, the

---

[1] "The seconde part of the Inventorye of our late sovereigne lord kyng Henry the Eighth, conteynynge his guardrobes, houshold stuff," &c. &c. MSS. Harl. 1419, fol. The original. [The account which followed here in all the former edits. of the furniture in Henry VIII.'s palace at Greenwich, did not seem to be any part of the subject; but at any rate it is to be found much more full and accurate in the *Retrospective Review*, second series, i. 132-6.]

[2] So in the record. But he was the third bishop of St. Paul's, London, son of King Offa, and a great benefactor to St. Paul's church, in which he had a most superb shrine. He was canonised. Dugdale, among many other curious particulars relating to his shrine, says that in the year 1339 it was decorated anew, when three goldsmiths, two at the wages of five shillings by the week, and one at eight, worked upon it for a whole year. *Hist. St. Paul's*, p. 21. See also p. 233.

[3] This was a favourite subject for a large gothic window. This subject also composed a branch of candlesticks thence called a *jesse*, not unusual in the ancient churches. In the year 1097, Hugo de Flori, abbot of St. Aust. Canterb., bought for the choir of his church a great branch-candlestick. "Candelabrum magnum in choroæneum quod *jesse* vocatur in partibus emit transmarinis." Thorn, *Dec. Script.* col. 1796. About the year 1330, Adam de Sodbury, abbot of Glastonbury,

Woman of Canony, Meleager, and the Dance of Maccabre."[1] At Durham-place we find the "Citie of Ladies,[2] the tapestrie of Thebes and of Troy, the City of Peace, the Prodigal Son,[3] Esther, and other pieces of Scripture." At Windsor castle the "siege of Jerusalem, Ahasuerus, Charlemagne, the siege of Troy, and *hawking and hunting*."[4] At Nottingham castle, "Amys and Amelion."[5] At Woodstock manor, the "tapestrie of Charlemagne."[6] At the More, a palace in Hertfordshire, "king Arthur, Hercules, Astyages, and Cyrus." At Richmond, the "arras of Sir Bevis, and Virtue and Vice fighting."[7] Many of these subjects are repeated at Westminster, Greenwich, Oatlands, Bedington in Surrey, and other royal seats, some of which are now unknown as such.[8] Among the rest we have also Hannibal, Holofernes, Romulus and Remus, Æneas, and Susannah.[9] I have mentioned romances written on many of these

gave to his convent "Unum dorsale laneum *le Jesse*." Joan. Glaston, edit. Hearne, p. 265. That is, a piece of tapestry embroidered with the *stem of Jesse*, to be hung round the choir, or other parts of the church, on high festivals. He also gave a tapestry of this subject for the abbot's hall. *Ibid.* And I cannot help adding, what indeed is not immediately connected with the subject of this note, that he gave his monastery, among other costly presents, a great clock, "processionibus et spectaculis insignitum," an organ of prodigious size, and eleven bells, six for the tower of the church, and five for the clock tower. He also new-vaulted the nave of the church, and adorned the new roof with beautiful paintings. *Ibid.*

[1] f. 6. In many churches of France there was an ancient shew of mimicry, in which all ranks of life were personated by the ecclesiastics, who all danced together, and disappeared one after another. It was called *Dance Maccabre*, and seems to have been often performed in St. Innocent's at Paris, where was a famous painting on this subject, which gave rise to Lydgate's poem under the same title. See Carpent. *Suppl. du Cange*, Lat. Gl. ii. p. 1103. More will be said of it when we come to Lydgate.

[2] A famous French allegorical romance [by Christine de Pise. An English translation appeared in 1521].

[3] A picture on this favourite subject is mentioned in Shakespeare. And in Randolph's *Muses Looking-glass*. "In painted cloth the story of the Prodigal." *Dodsl. Old Pl.* vi. 260.

[4] f. 298. [5] f. 364. [6] f. 318. [7] f. 346.

[8] Some of the tapestry at Hampton-court, described in this inventory, is to be seen still in a fine old room, now remaining in its original state, called the Exchequer. [In an inventory of the effects of King Henry V. several pieces of tapestry are mentioned, with the subjects of the following romances, viz. Bevis of Hampton, Octavian, Gyngebras (?) Hawkyn namtelet, l'arbre de jeonesse, Farman (*i. e.* Pharamond), Charlemayn, Duke Glorian, Elkanus le noble, Renaut, Trovis roys de Coleyn, &c. See Rolls of Parl. *sub anno* 1423.—Douce. These *Rolls* are not very correctly printed, and the editor suspects some errors in the preceding list.]

[9] Montfaucon, among the tapestry of Charles V. king of France, in the year 1370, mentions, Le tappis *de la vie du saint Theseus*. Here the officer who made the entry calls Theseus a saint. *The seven Deadly Sins, Le saint Graal, Le graunt tappis de Neuf Preux, Reyne d'Ireland*, and *Godfrey of Bulloign. Monum. Fr.* iii. 64. The *neuf preux* are the Nine Worthies. Among the stores of Henry VIII. we have, "two old stayned clothes of the ix worthies for the greate chamber," at Newhall in Essex, f. 362. These were pictures. Again, at the palace of Westminster in "the little study called the Newe Librarye," which I believe was in Holbein's elegant Gothic gatehouse, there is, "Item, xii pictures of men on horsebacke of enamelled stuffe of the Nyne Worthies, and others upon square tables." f. 188. MSS. Harl. 1419, *ut supr.*

subjects, and shall mention others. In the romance of Syr Guy, that hero's combat with the dragon in Northumberland is said to be represented in tapestry in Warwick castle:

> In Warwike the truth shall ye see
> In arras wrought ful craftely.[1]

This piece of tapestry appears to have been in Warwick castle before the year 1398. It was then so distinguished and valued a piece of furniture, that a special grant was made of it by Richard II. in that year, conveying " that suit of arras hangings in Warwick castle, which contained the story of the famous Guy earl of Warwick," together with the castle of Warwick, and other possessions, to Thomas Holland, earl of Kent;[2] and in the restoration of forfeited property to this lord after his imprisonment, these hangings are particularly specified in the patent of Henry IV., dated 1399. When Margaret, daughter of Henry VII., was married to James IV. of Scotland in 1503, Holyrood House at Edinburgh was splendidly decorated on that occasion; and we are told in an ancient record, that the " hanginge of the queenes grett chammer represented the ystory of Troye toune." Again, " the king's grett chammer had one table, wer was satt hys chammerlayn, the grett sqyer, and many others, well served; the which chammer was haunged about with the story of Hercules, together with other ystorys."[3] And at the same solemnity, " in the hall wher the qwenes company wer satt in lyke as in the other, an wich was haunged of the history of Hercules," &c.[4] A stately chamber in the castle of Hesdin in Artois was furnished by a duke of Burgundy with the story of Jason and the Golden Fleece, about the year 1468.[5] The affecting story of Coucy's Heart, which [may have given] rise to an old metrical English romance entitled, the *Knight of Courtesy and the Lady of Faguel*, was woven in tapestry in Coucy castle in France.[6] I have seen an ancient suite of arras, containing Ariosto's Orlando and Angelica, where at every group the story was all along illustrated with short rhymes in romance or old French. Spenser sometimes dresses the superb bowers of his fairy castles with this sort of historical drapery.

---

[1] Signat. Ca 1. Some, perhaps, may think this circumstance an innovation or addition of later minstrels. A practice not uncommon.

[2] Dugd. *Bar.* i. p. 237.

[3] Leland. *Coll.* vol. iii. p. 295, 296. *Opuscul.* edit. 1770.   [4] *Ibid.*

[5] See *Obs. Fair. Qu.* i. p. 177.

[6] Howell's *Letters,* xx. § vi. B. i. This is a true story, about the year 1180. Fauchet relates it at large from an old authentic French chronicle; and then adds, " Ainsi finerint les amours du Chastelain du Couci et de la dame de Faiel." Our Castellan, whose name is [Raoul] de Couci, was famous for his *chansons* and chivalry, but more so for his unfortunate love, which became proverbial in the old French romances. See Fauch. *Rec.* pp. 124, 128. [The Knight of Curtesy and the Fair Lady of Faguel has been reprinted by Mr. Ritson, vol. iii. p. 193. See *Memoires Historiques sur Raoul de Courcy.* Paris, 1781.—Price. See *Remains of the E. P. Poetry of Engl.* ii. 65.6; the romance is also included in that collection. Ritson's text is not accurate. The French story of *Le Chatelain de Coucy et la dame de Fayel* was printed at Paris, 1829, 8vo. ; but it has very little in common with the English romance.]

S. 5.   *Ancient Tapestry and Hangings.*   195

In Hawes's *Paſtime of Pleaſure* [1517,] the hero of the piece ſees all his future adventures diſplayed at large in the ſumptuous tapeſtry of the hall of a caſtle. I have before mentioned the moſt valuable and perhaps the moſt ancient work of this ſort now exiſting, the entire ſeries of Duke William's deſcent on England, preſerved in the church of Bayeux in Normandy, and intended as an ornament of the choir on high feſtivals. Bartholinus relates that it was an art much cultivated among the ancient Iſlanders, to weave the hiſtories of their giants and champions in tapeſtry.[1] The ſame thing is recorded of the old Perſians; and this furniture is ſtill in high requeſt among many Oriental nations, particularly in Japan and China.[2] It is well known, that to frame pictures of heroic adventures in needle-work was a favourite practice of claſſical antiquity.

[The following liſt compriſes all the known Engliſh Romances relating to Charlemagne.[3]

1. *Roland.* All that remains of this is a fragment[4] of a poem, probably written in the thirteenth century. It is not ſtrictly alliterative, but abounds with alliteration. An analyſis and ſome extracts furniſhed by Mr. Thos. Wright are printed at the end of M. Michel's edition of *La Chanſon de Roland.* The whole of the fragment will probably be publiſhed by the Early Engliſh Text Society. It relates the treachery of Gwynylon (the French *Ganelon* or *Guenelon*), and the beginning of the fight at Roncevaux. In deſcribing Gwynylon's treachery the poet has derived one remarkable circumſtance, not from the French *Roland*, but from the Chronicle of the pſeudo-Turpin. M. Paris is miſtaken, however, in ſuppoſing that he does not include Turpin in the number of the combatants at Roncevaux.[5] He ſays expreſſly (leaf 384):

> vnto Roulond then went the princ*is* xij
> 'Olyu*er* and Rog*er* and Aubry hym-ſelue
> Richard and Rayn*er* that redy was eu*er*
> tirry and turpyn all redy wer.

The following deſcription of the "ſtrange weather" that happened in France while the battle was going on may ſerve as a ſpecimen of the ſtyle of the poem, which is remarkably vigorous:

> — while our folk fought to-gedur
> ther fell in Fraunce A ſtrau*n*g wedur
> A gret derk myſt in the myd-day-tym
> thik and clowdy and euyll wedur thene
> and thiknes of ſterris and thond*er* light
> the erthe dynnyd doillfully to wet

---

[1] *Antiquit. Dan.* lib. i. 9, p. 51.
[2] In the royal palace of Jeddo, which overflows with a profuſion of the moſt exquiſite and ſuperb eaſtern embelliſhments, the tapeſtry of the emperor's audience-hall is of the fineſt ſilk, wrought by the moſt ſkilful artificers of that country, and adorned with pearls, gold, and ſilver. *Mod. Univ. Hiſt.* B. xiii. c. ii. vol. ix. p. 83. (Not. G.) edit. 1759.
[3] [Communicated by Mr. Shelly, of Plymouth.]
[4] [Lanſd. MS. 388, leaf 381 to 395.]
[5] [*Hiſt. Poét de Charlemagne,* p 155, note.]

> Foulis fled for fere it was gret wond*er*
> bowes of trees *t*hen breftyn afond*er*
> beft ran to bank*is* And cried full fore
> they durft not abid in the mor
> ther was no man but he hid his hed
> And thought not but to dy in *t*hat fted
> the wekid wedur laftid full long
> from the mornying to the euynfong
> then Rofe a clowd euyn in the weft
> as red as blod wit*h*-outon reft
> It fhewid doun on the erthe & *t*her did fhyn
> So many doughty men as died *t*hat tym.

2. *Otuwel.* This is alfo incomplete. Ellis has given an analyfis of it;[1] and the poem was printed from the Auchinleck MS. for the Abbotsford Club in 1836. Its date is fuppofed to be not later than 1330. Ellis has completed the ftory, as he fays, from another MS. then in the poffeffion of Mr. Fillingham, in which, however, M. Gafton Paris has recognized a portion of a cyclic poem, to which he gives the title of *Charlemagne and Roland*, and which I will next defcribe. Our Otuwel is the French *Otinel*.[2] Otuwel or Otinel, the hero of the poem, comes as the ambaffador of the Saracen king Garfie (Garfile), to fummon Charles to pay homage to his mafter, and to abjure the Chriftian faith; but by a miracle he is himfelf converted, and "forfakes all his gods." He is then betrothed to Belecent, the daughter of Charles, and marches with Charles and his "duzze peres" (douze pairs) to fight againft Garfie in Lombardy. Garfie is taken prifoner, and led to Charles by Otuwel, who is rewarded—according to the French Romances, for here our fragment ends—with the hand of Belecent and the crown of Lombardy.

3. *Charlemagne and Roland.* This is the title which, according to M. Paris,[3] ought to be given to a poem which we poffefs only in fcattered fragments. The poem belongs probably to the beginning of the fourteenth century. M. Paris divides it into four parts. 1ft. Charlemagne's Journey to the Holy Land according to the Latin legend. 2nd. The beginning of the war in Spain after the firft chapters of Turpin's *Chronicle*. 3rd. Otuwel, but a different verfion from that defcribed above. 4th. The end of Turpin's hiftory. The firft and fecond parts confift of the poem in the Auchinleck MS., printed for the Abbotsford Club under the title of *Roland and Vernagu*, and analyfed by Ellis as *Roland and Ferragus*.[4] The ftory of the firft part, as related in this poem, fhould rather be defcribed as Charles's vifit to the emperor "Conftanfious," and that of the fecond part, which begins on page 15 of the Abbotsford [Club] edition, as the combat of Roland and Vernagu. The concluding lines of this fecond part connect it with the third:

> To Otuel alfo yern
> That was a farrazin ftern
> Ful fone this word fprong.

---

[1] *Specimens of Early Engl. Metr Romances* (ed. 1811), vol. ii. p. 324.]
[2] *Les Anciens Poetes de la France*, tom. i.]
[3] *Hift. Poét. de Charlem.* liv. 1, ch. viii.]   [4 Vol. ii. 302.]

This third and the fourth part are comprised in Mr. Fillingham's MS., which we know only from Ellis's analyſis. It contains, according to Ellis, about 11,000 lines, and relates not only the ſtory of Otuwel (the third part of the poem), but alſo the conqueſt of Spain, the deceit of Ganelon, the fight at Roncevaux, the defeat of the Saracens by Charles,[1] and the puniſhment of Ganelon, which form the fourth part. The poem concludes as follows:—

> Here endeth Otuel, Roland, and Olyuere,
> And of the twelve duſſypere.

It is worth while remarking how entirely the meaning of the title given to the peers has been loſt by the Engliſh poets. Here we read of "the *twelve duſſypere*" (les douze pairs), and in other places we find each ſingle knight called "a dozeper," while in the Aſhmole MS. of Sir Ferumbras the word becomes "doth*theper."

4. *Ferumbras*. We have two verſions of this romance; one of them the Farmer MS. analyzed by Ellis,[2] and now in the library

---

[1] [*La Conqueſte que fit le grand roi Charlemaigne et Eſpaignes* ne doit pas être confondue avec la compilation de David Aubert. Ce livre eſt le même que celui qui porte le nom de *Fierabras* ...... Sous le nom de *Fierabras* M. Brunet indique une édition de 1478; ſous le titre de la *Conquête de Charlemagne* il n'en connaît pas avant 1501, mais la Bibliothèque Impériale en poſſède une de 1486. Cy finiſt Fierabras. Imprimée a Lyon par Pierre de Sainĉte Lucye diĉt le Prince. Lan de grace MCCCCLXXXVI. Le vii jour de Septembre. Toutefois le titre au moins et les trois feuillets qui ſuivent cet explicit ſont poſtérieurs. Au reſte l'ouvrage eſt diviſé en trois livres, et la traduĉtion en proſe de *Fierabras* ne forme que le ſecond; l'enſemble a la prétention d'être une hiſtoire de Charlemagne. Elle y eſt même précédée d'un abrégé de l'hiſtoire de France depuis Clovis, groſſièrement conforme aux chroniques. Puis vient l'éloge de Charlemagne et un ſommaire de ſon règne; on raconte enſuite le voyage à Jéruſalem d'après la légende latine—tel eſt le contenu du premier livre. Le troiſième comprend le récit de la guerre d'Eſpagne d'après Turpin. L'auteur nous a donné lui-même des renſeignements ſur ſes ſources. Il nous apprend d'abord qu'il a écrit ſur la demande de meſſire Henry Bolomier, chanoine de Lauſanne, grand admirateur de Charlemagne. "Selon les matières que j'ay peu amaſſer, j'ay ordonné ceſtuy livre; car je n'ay eu intencion de déduyre la matière que je ne aye eſté informé par pluſieurs livres et principallement par ung qui eſt intitulé le *Mirouer hyſtorial*, et auſſi par les cronicques qui font mention de l'oeuvre ſuyvante." Il eſt fort probable que ces *cronicques*, vaguement déſignées, n'ont jamais été conſultées par notre auteur, qui trouvait dans le *Speculum hiſtoriale* de Vincent de Beauvais tout ce dont il parle, ſauf le *Fierabras;* auſſi dit-il au début du ſecond livre: "Ce que j'ay deſſus eſcript, je l'ay prins en ung moult autentique livre, lequel ſe nomme le Mirouer hyſtorial, et auſſi es croniques anciennes, et l'ay tranſlaté de latin en françoys; et la matière ſuyvante que fera le ſecond livre eſt d'ung romant faiĉt en l'ancienne façon, ſans grande ordonnance, dont j'ay eſté incité à le réduyre en proſe par chapitres ordonnez. Et eſt appellé celluy livre ſelon aulcuns *Fierabras*." On voit que le travail auquel le compilateur s'eſt livré, "ſelon la capacité de ſon petiĉt engin," n'etait pas fort difficile: il a ſimplement mis en mauvaiſe proſe françaiſe le latin de Vincent de Beauvais et les vers de *Fierabras*. Son ouvrage n'en a pas moins eu dès ſon apparition un ſuccès immenſe, qui d'ailleurs n'eſt pas épuiſé; car on le réimprime encore à Epinal et à Montbéliard, de plus en plus défiguré dans chaque édition ſucceſſive, et de temps à autre un peu rajeuni.—Gaſton Paris (*Hiſt. Poët de Charlemagne*, livre i. chap. iv. § iv. pp. 97-8-9).]

[2] [Vol. ii. p. 369.]

of Sir Thomas Phillipps; the other a fragment[1] of great length, which will shortly be printed by the Early English Text Society. They both belong probably to the end of the fourteenth century. The original of the romance is the French Fierabras.[2] I give parallel extracts from the French and the two English versions. There is a Provençal as well as a French version of the romance, and I would suggest the enquiry whether the poem analyzed by Ellis does not follow this Provençal version, or rather perhaps the lost French original of which the French editors have shown the Provençal version to be a translation. They agree at any rate in brevity, though they both give a long introduction, which the existing French version omits. The Ashmole MS. is imperfect at the beginning and at the end; but it appears generally to follow very nearly the story of the existing French version, though it is much more diffuse, the remaining fragment containing about 10,450 lines, while the entire French poem contains only 6219. Both the English versions agree, however, in some little particulars which the French omits; *e. g.* the mention of Richard blessing himself in the extracts I give. Our fragment begins, like the French poem, with the relation of a long combat between Oliver and Ferumbras (Fierabras, *ferri brachium*), the son of the admiral (anirans, *Arab.* amir) Balan, who in the Farmer MS. is strangely called Laban. Ferumbras is vanquished, and embraces the Christian faith; but Oliver is surprised by the Saracens, and made prisoner, with four other peers. The rest of the peers are sent by Charles to demand the surrender of their companions, but are thrown into the same dungeon. They are, however, protected by Florippe, the daughter of Balan, and after many battles are at length delivered by Charlemagne. Balan refuses baptism, but Florippe is baptized, and here the Ashmole MS. ends, being imperfect; but the other versions relate the marriage of Florippe to Guy de Bourgoyne, and the division of the kingdom of Spain between him and Ferumbras.

With the Ashmole MS. is preserved its ancient vellum cover, made out of portions of two Latin documents, one relating to the Vicarage of Columpton, and the other to the chapel of Holne and parish of "Bukfastleghe." This cover, however, is chiefly remarkable, because it contains what is evidently part of the first draft of the poem, written in the same hand as the MS. itself. The following extracts from both will show how the poet corrected his verses:

DRAFT.
So sturne strokes thay araȝte
eyther til other the whyle
That al the erthe about quaȝte
men miȝt hure a mvle
They wer so fers on hure mod
And eger on hure fiȝte
That eyther of hem thoȝte god
to slen other if he miȝt.

---

[1] [Ashm. MS. 33.]   [2] [*Les Anciens Poetes de la France*, tom. iv.]

MS.

So fterne ftrokes thay arauȝte
  eyther til other with ftrenghthe
That al the erthe ther ofte quaȝte
  a myle and more on lenghthe
They weren fo eger bothe of mod
  And eke fo fers to fiȝte
That eyther of hem than thoȝte god
  to fle other if he miȝte.[1]

The poem is written in the Southern dialect, but it contains a remarkably large admixture of Northern forms, words occurring fometimes in two forms in lines clofe together, if not in the fame line. Thus we find *ich* and *I*, *a* and *he*, *heo* and *fche*, *hy* and *thay* (the latter moft frequently), and *thilke* and *this*, *to* and *til*, *prykyng* and *prykande*, *vafte* and *fafte*, and fo forth, the former being the Southern, the latter the Northern form. The Southern infinitive in *y* (ftill ufed occafionally in Devonfhire) continually occurs: *e. g.* *maky*, *afky*, *graunty*, *robby*, *wivy* (to wed), &c. On the whole one would be inclined to fuppofe that the poem was written in the South (perhaps in the diocefe of Exeter) by a fouthern man, who had, however, lived in the North fufficiently long to become familiar with northern forms. But a more careful examination (in preparation for the Early Englifh Text Society's edition) will very likely lead to our being better informed concerning the character and hiftory of this moft interefting MS.

From *Fierabras, Chanfon de Gefte*, edited from MSS. of the xiv. and xv. centuries by MM. A. Krœber and G. Servois (Paris, 1860). The extract begins with line 4354, p. 132 of this edition:

  RICHARS refgarde l'yaue, qui moult fait à douter;
  Se eft grande et hideufe que il n'i offe entrer.
  Plus toft cuert que fajete, quaint on le lait aler;
  Ne barge ne galie n'i puent abiter;
  La rive en eft moult haute, bien fait à redouter.
  Richars de Normendie fe prinft à refgarder,
  Efcortrement commence Jhefu à reclamer:
  "Glorieus fire pere, qui te laifas pener

---

[1] [Refpecting the early Englifh profe life of Charles the Great, from the prefs of Caxton, M. Gafton Paris remarks: "Au quinzième fiècle, le célèbre imprimeur Caxton publia un livre intitulé, 'The lyf of Charles the Great,' &c. Cette *Vie de Charles le Grand*, qui eft à préfent d'une rareté exceffive, a été généralement regardée comme une compilation faite par Caxton; on a loué le difcernement qu'il avait montré dans la choix de fes fources, et on a remarqué qu'il avait donné un beau rôle au duc de Normandie, Richard fans peur, évidemment par patriotifme. Voy. *Revue britannique* [Britifh Review?] Mars, 1844. On lui a fait honneur furtout des fentiments exprimés dans la préface, adreffée *à un de fes amis particuliers*, Henri Bolomyer, chanoine de Laufanne. Mais ce nom fuffit pour nous faire voir que Caxton avait fimplement traduit, et, comme il le dit lui-même, *réduit en anglais* le livre des *Conqueftes de Charlemagne* ou de *Fierabras*. . . . Quant au rôle de Richard fans peur, il fe trouvait auffi développé dans le livre français, qui l'avait pris lui-même dans le poëme de *Fierabras*."—*Hiftoire Poétique de Charlemagne*, livre i. chap. viii. p. 157.]

" En la crois benéoite pour ton pule fauver,
" Garifiés hui mon cors de mort et d'afoler,
" Que je puiffe Karlon mon meffage conter."
Or oiés quel vertu Diex i vaut demonftrer
Por le roi Karlemaine, qui tant fait à douter.
Ançois que on éuft une liuée alé,
Véiffiés fi Flagot engroifier et enfler,
Que par defous la rive commence à feronder.
Atant es vous . 1 . cerf, que Diex i fift aler,
Et fu blans comme nois, biaus fu à refgarder.
Devant le ber Richart fe prent à demonftrer,
Devant lui eft tantoft eus en Flagot entrés.
Li dus voit Sarrazins après lui aroutés;
S'il ot paour de mort ne fait à demander.
Après le blance biffe comme[n] cha à errer,
Tout ainfi com ele vait, lait le ceval aler;
Et li ciers vait devant, qui bien f'i fot garder,
D'autre part à la rive fe prent à ariver.

From the *Romance of Ferumbras*, analyzed by Ellis, who has modernized the fpelling :

> When Richard faw there was no gate
>   But by Flagote the flood,
> His meffage would he not let ;
>   His horfe was both big and good.
> He kneeled, befeeching God, of His grace,
>   To fave him fro mifchief :
> A white hind he faw anon in that place,
>   That fwam over to the cliff.
> He bleffed him in Goddis name,
>   And followed the fame way,
> The gentil hind that was fo tame,
>   That on that other fide gan play.

From the *Romance of Ferumbras* (Afhmole MSS. 33). The following paffage begins on fol. 52 :

> ¶ Now y-come ys he to *th*e ryuere
>   By fyde a treo *and* a ftod hi*m* *th*ere
>   *Th*at water to by holde
>   *And* faw *th*e ryuer was dup *and* brod
>   And ran away as he were wod
>   Ys herte gan waxe colde
> ¶ Richard tok herte *and th*enche gan
>   *Th*at nedelich a moft entrye *th*an
>   In *and* paffe *th*at ryuere
>   Ou*th*er he mofte turn agee
>   And figte agayn al *th*at maygne
>   *Th*at after hi*m* come there
>   To ihe*f*u *th*a*n*ne he had a bone
>   Lord *th*at madeft funne mone
>   Lond *and* water cler
>   Kep me *th*ys day fra*m* my fone
>   *And* if y *th*ys ryuer potte me one
>   *Th*at y ne a-drenche her
>   *And* fuch grace *th*ow me fende
>   *Th*at y may fafe to Charlis wende
>   *And* telle hy*m* my porpos
>   So *th*at he may come wy*th* focour

And delyuery ys barons of hon*our* [Fol. 523.]
    That ligge*th* among *thy* fos
¶ Nad he nog*t tha*t word ful fpeke
Er *that that* cam an hert for*th* reke
    As wyt afe melkys fom
Rygt euene by-fore duk Rychard
The hert hym wente to watre-ward
    And fayre by-fore hym fwom
Wa*n*ne *the* duk *that* wonder y-feg
And *the* farfyns *that tho* wer come wel neg
    Wi*th* boft *and* noyfe gret
Wi*th* is rigt honde *than* bleffede he hym
And *thog the* ryuere were ftyf *and* grym
    Wy*th* bo*the* hors in a fchet
Ys ftede was an hors of prys
And bar *the* knigt at al dyuys
    Swy*m*mynge wi*th* ys felawe
The hert *that* was fo fair of figt
Ouer *the* Ryuer fwam ful rigt
    And Ry*ch*ard do*th* after-drawe.

SECTION VI.

LTHOUGH much poetry began to be written about the reign of Edward II., yet I have found only [two] Englifh poet[s] of that reign whofe name[s] ha[ve] defcended to pofterity.[1] [One] is Adam Davy or Davie. He may be placed about the year 1312. I can collect no circumftances of his life, but that he was marfhal of Stratford-le-bow near London.[2] He has left feveral poems never printed, which are almoft as forgotten as his name. Only one manufcript of thefe pieces now remains, which feems to be coeval with its author.[3] They are, *Vifions, The Battell of Jerufalem, The Legend of Saint Alexius, Scripture hiftories, of fifteen toknes before the day of Judgement,* [and] *Lamentations of Souls.*[4]

In the *Vifions,* which are of the religious kind, Adam Davie draws this picture of Edward II. ftanding before the fhrine of Edward the Confeffor in Weftminfter Abbey at his coronation. The lines have a ftrength arifing from fimplicity:

---

[1] Robert de Brunne, above mentioned, lived, and wrote fome of his pieces, in this reign; but he more properly belongs to the laft.

[2] This will appear from citations which follow.

[3] MSS. Bibl. Bodl. Laud. 622 *olim* I 74, fol. 26 *b.* It has been much damaged. [All the extracts have now been collated with the original MS.—a procefs which was found highly neceffary.]

[4] In the MS. there is alfo a piece in profe, entitled, *The Pylgrymages of the holi land,* f. 65, 66. It begins: "Qwerr foever a cros ftandyth ther is a forʒivenes of payne." I think it is a defcription of the holy places, and it appears at leaft to be of the hand-writing of the reft.

To oure lorde Ihefu crift in heuene
Ich to day fhawe myne fweuene,¹
þat ich mette² in one niȝth,
Of a kniȝth of mychel miȝth :
His name is ihote³ fir Edward þe kynge,
Prince of Wales Engelonde the faire þinge ;
Me mette þat he was armed wel,
Boþe wiþ yrne *and* wiþ ftel,
And on his helme that was of ftel,
A Coroune of golde bicom hym wel.
Bifore þe fhryne of Seint Edward he ftoode,
Myd glad chere *and* mylde of mood.⁴

Moft of thefe Vifions are compliments to the king. Our poet then proceeds thus :

Anoþer fweuene me mette on a tiwes niȝth⁵
Bifore the fefte of Allehalewen of þat ilke kniȝth,
His name is nempned³ here bifore,
Bliffed be þe tyme þat he was bore, [&c.]
Of fir Edward oure derworþ⁶ kynge
Ich mette of hym anoþere fair metynge, [&c.]
Me pouȝth he rood vpon an Affe,
And þat ich take god to witneffe ;
Y-wonden he was in a Mantel gray,
Toward Rome he nom⁷ his way,
Vpon his heuede fate an gray hure,
It femed hym wel a mefure ;
He rood wiþouten hofe *and* fho,
His wone was nouȝth fo forto do ;
His fhankes femeden al blood-rede,
Myne herte wop⁸ for grete drede ;
Als a pilgryme he rood to Rome,
And þider he com wel fwiþe fone.
Þe þrid fweuene me mette a niȝth
Rigth of þat derworþe kniȝth :
Þe Wedenyfday a niȝth it was
Nexte þe day of feint lucie bifore criftenmeffe, [&c.]
Me pouȝth þat ich was at Rome,
And þider ich com fwiþe fone,
The Pope *and* fir Edward oure kynge
Boþe hij⁹ hadden a newe dubbynge, [&c.]
Ihefus crift ful of grace
Graunte oure kynge in euery place
Maiftrie of his wiþerwynes
And of alle wicked Sarafynes.
Me met a fweuene on worþinge¹⁰ niȝth
Of þat ilche derworþe kniȝth,
God ich it fhewe *and* to witneffe take
And fo fhilde me fro fynne *and* fake.
In-to an chapel ich com of oure lefdy,¹¹
Ihefus crift hire leue¹² fon ftood by,

---

¹ dream.
² thought, dreamed. In the firft fenfe, we have *me mette* in Chaucer, *Non. Pr T.* v. 1013. And below.
³ named.   ⁴ fol. 26 b.   ⁵ twelfth-night.
⁶ dear-worthy.   ⁷ took.   ⁸ wept.
⁹ they.   ¹⁰ [on worthing nyth.—*Park.*]   ¹¹ lady.
¹² dear.

On rode¹ he was an louelich Man,
Als þilke þat on rode was don
He vnneiled² his honden two, [&c.]
Adam þe marchal of ſtretforde atte bowe
Wel ſwiþe wide his name is yknowe
He hymſelfe mette þis metynge,
To witneſſe he takeþ Iheſu heuene kynge,
On wedenyſday³ in clene leinte⁴
A voice me bede I ne ſhulde nouȝth feinte,
Of þe ſweuenes þat her ben write
I ſhulde ſwiþe don⁵ my lorde kynge to wite, [&c.]
Þɛ þurſday next þe berynge⁶ of oure leſdy
Me þouȝth an Aungel com ſir Edward by, [&c.]
Ich telle ȝou forſoþe wiþouten les,⁷
Als god of heuene maide marie to moder ches,⁸
Þe Aungel com to me Adam Dauy *and* ſede
Bot þou Adam ſhewe þis þee worþe wel yuel mede, [&c.]
Who-ſo wil ſpeke myd me Adam þe marchal
In ſtretforþe bowe he is yknowe *and* ouere al,
Ich ne ſhewe nouȝth þis forto haue mede
Bot for god Almiȝtties drede.

There is a very old proſe romance, both in French and Italian, on the ſubject of the *Deſtruction of Jeruſalem.*⁹ It is tranſlated from a Latin work in five books, very popular in the middle ages, entitled, *Hegeſippus de Bello Judaico et Excidio Urbis Hieroſolymitanæ Libri quinque.* This is a licentious paraphraſe of a part of Joſephus's Jewiſh hiſtory, made about the fourth century: and the name Hegeſippus is moſt probably corrupted from Joſephus, perhaps alſo called Joſippus. The paraphraſt is ſuppoſed to be Ambroſe of Milan, who flouriſhed in the reign of Theodoſius.¹⁰ On the ſubject of Veſpaſian's ſiege of Jeruſalem, as related in this book, our poet Adam

---

¹ croſs. ² unnailed.
³ Wodenis day. Woden's day, *i.e. Wedneſday.* ⁴ Lent.
⁵ [Swithe don to wite, *quickly let him know.—Ritſon.*]
⁶ Chriſtmas-day. ⁷ lies.
⁸ "As ſure as God choſe the Virgin Mary to be Chriſt's mother."
⁹ In an ancient inventory of books, all French romances, made in England in the reign of Edward III., I find the romance of *Titus and Veſpaſian.* Madox, *Formul. Anglican.* p. 12. See alſo Scipio Maffei's *Traduttori Italiani,* p. 48. Creſcimbeni (*Volg. Poeſ.* vol. i. l. 5, p. 317), does not ſeem to have known of this romance in Italian. Du Cange mentions *Le Roman de la Priſe de Jeruſalem par Titus,* in verſe, *Gloſſ. Lat.* i. *Ind. Auct.* p. cxciv. A metrical romance on this ſubject is in Royal MS. 16 E viii. 2, Brit. Muſ. [and has been printed by M. Michel, as already mentioned, 1836, 12mo. But it merely relates to the mythical expedition of Charlemagne to Jeruſalem]. There is an old French play on this ſubject, acted in 1437. It was printed in 1491, fol. Beauchamps, *Rech. Fr. Theat.* p. 134. [This is probably the ſame as Le Vengeance et Deſtruction de Iheruſalem par perſonages executée par Veſpaſien et ſon filz Titus, contenant en ſoy pluſieurs chronicques Rommaines tant du regne de Neron Empereur que de pluſieurs aultres belles hyſtoires. Printed at Paris, 1510, 4to, for Jehan Trepparel.—*Douce. The Dyſtruccyon of Iheruſalem by Waſpaȝyan and Tytus,* of which there are two old printed edits. appears to be a paraphraſe of the French.]
¹⁰ He mentions Conſtantinople and New Rome: and the provinces of Scotia and Saxonia. From this work the Maccabees ſeem to have got into romance. It was firſt printed at Paris, fol. 1511. Among the Bodleian MSS. there is a moſt beautiful copy of this book, believed to be written in the Saxon times.

Davie has left a poem entitled the *Battell of Jerusalem*.¹ It begins thus:

>   þE BATAILE OF JERUſaLeM.
>   Liſtneþ alle þat beþ alyue,
>   boþe criſten Men *and* wyue :
>   I wil ȝou telle a wond*er* cas,
>   hou Iheſus criſt bihated was,
>   Of þe lewes felle *and* kene,
>   þat was *on* hem ſiþþe iſene,
>   Goſpelles I d*ra*we to witneſſe
>   of þis mat*ere* mo*re and* leſſe, &c.²

In the courſe of the ſtory, Pilate challenges our Lord to ſingle combat. This ſubject will occur again.

Davie's *Legend of ſaint Alexius the confeſſor, ſon of Euphemius*, is tranſlated from Latin, and begins thus :

[The line preceding is this :

> *Here endeþ the vengeaunce of goddes deth.*]

>   Alle þat willen here in ryme,
>   Hou gode Men in olde tyme,
>   Loueden god Almiȝth ;
>   þat weren riche, of grete valoure,
>   Kynges ſones and Emperoure
>   Of bodies ſtronge *and* liȝth ;
>   Ȝee habbeþ yherd*e* ofte in geſte,
>   Of holy men maken feſte
>   Boþe day *and* niȝth,
>   Forto haue þe ioye in heuene
>   (Wiþ Aungels ſong*e, and* mery ſteuene,)
>   þ*ere* blis is brode *and* briȝth :
>   To ȝou alle heiȝe *and* lowe
>   þe riȝth ſoþe to biknowe
>   Ȝoure ſoules forto ſaue, [&c.]³

Our author's *Scripture Hiſtories* want the beginning. Here they begin with Joſeph, and end with Daniel :

>   For þritty pens⁴ þai ſolde*n* þat childe
>   þe ſeller hiȝth Judas,
>   þo⁵ Ruben com hom *and* myſſed hy*m*
>   Sori ynoȝ he was.⁶

His *Fifteen Toknes*⁷ *before the Day of Judgment* are taken from the prophet Jeremiah :

---

¹ The latter part of this poem appears detached, in a former part of our MS. with the title *The Vengeaunce of Goddes Death*, viz. fol. 1. This latter part begins with theſe lines :
>   "And at þe ſourty dayes ende,
>   Whider I wolde he bad me wende,
>   Vpon þe mount of Olyuete," [&c.

An imperfect copy, ſays Mr. Furnivall, is in Addit. MS. Brit. Mus. 10,036, and another, wanting only one ſheet, is in the poſſeſſion of the Earl of Cardigan. See alſo Addit. MS. 10,269.]

² MS. *ut ſupr.* f. 71 b.
³ *Ibid.* f. 21 b. ⁴ Thirty pence.
⁵ [The capital "þ" in this MS. is always written thus: " Iþ".]
⁶ MS. *ut ſupr.* f. 65. ⁷ Tokens.

> Þe firſt ſigne per aƷeins, as oure lord hym-ſelf ſede,
> Hungere ſchal on erþe be, treccherie, and falſhede,
> Batailes, and litel loue, ſekeneſſe and haterede,
> And þe erþe ſchal quaken, þat vche man ſchal drede:
> Þe mone ſchal turne to blood, þe ſunne to derkhede, &c.[1]

Another of Davie's poems may be called the *Lamentation of Souls*. But the ſubject is properly a congratulation of Chriſt's advent, and the lamentation of the ſouls of the fathers remaining in limbo, for his delay:

> OF ioye and bliſſe is my ſonge, care to bileue,[2]
> And to herie hym amonge þat al oure ſorouȝ ſchal reue,
> Ycome he is þat ſwete dew, þat ſwete hony drope,
> Iheſus kynge of alle kynges, to whom is al oure hope:
> Bicome he is oure broþer, whare was he ſo longe?
> He it is and non oþer, þat bouȝth vs ſo ſtronge:
> Oure broþer we mowe[3] hym clepe wel, ſo ſeiþ hym-ſelf ilome.[4]

My readers will be perhaps ſurpriſed to find our language improve ſo ſlowly, and will probably think, that Adam Davie writes in a leſs intelligible phraſe than many more ancient bards already cited. His obſcurity, however, ariſes in great meaſure from obſolete ſpelling, a mark of antiquity which I have here obſerved in exact conformity to a manuſcript of the age of Edward II., and which in the poetry of his predeceſſors, eſpecially the minſtrel-pieces, has been often effaced by multiplication of copies and other cauſes. In the meantime it ſhould be remarked, that the capricious peculiarities and even ignorance of tranſcribers often occaſion an obſcurity, which is not to be imputed either to the author or his age.[5]

[The ſame volume with Adam Davie's poems (fol. 27 b), and therefore ſometimes, but wrongly aſcribed to him, has a production without any author's name, of the ſame period, entitled] the *Life of Alexander*, which deſerves to be publiſhed entire on many accounts. It ſeems to be founded chiefly on Simeon Seth's romance above mentioned; but many paſſages are alſo copied from the French *Roman d'Alexandre*, a poem in our author's age perhaps equally popular both in England and France. It is a work of conſiderable length.[6] I will firſt give ſome extracts from the Prologue:

---

[1] MS. *ut ſupr.* f. 70 b.   [2] Leave.   [3] May.   [4] MS. *ut ſupr.* f. 71.

[5] Chaucer in *Troilus and Creſſida* mentions "the grete diverſite in Engliſh, and *in writing of our tongue.*" He therefore prays God, that no perſon would *miſwrite*, or *miſſe-metre* his poem. Lib. *ult.* v. 1792, *ſeq.*

[6] [In attributing this romance to Davie [in his original edition] Warton has followed the authority of Tanner, who was probably led into the miſtake by finding it bound up with the remaining works of this "poetic marſhall." We are indebted to Mr. Ellis for detecting—upon the force of internal evidence—this miſappropriation of a very ſpirited compoſition to the inſipid author of the Legend of Saint Alexius. It has ſince been publiſhed from a tranſcript of the Lincoln's-Inn MS. made by Mr. Park, and forms the firſt volume in Mr. Weber's collection.—Price. The text, conformably with Price's own opinion, has now been taken from the Laud MS. in preference to that preſerved at Lincoln's-Inn, and printed by Weber.]

Diuers is þis middellerrde
To lewed Men *and* to lerede,[1]
Byſyneſſe, care and ſorouȝ
Is myd Man vche morowȝe [&c.]
Naþeles, wel fele *and* fulle
Roeþ y-founde in herte *and* ſhulle
Þat hadden leuer a Ribaudye
Þan here of god, oi þer ſeint Marie;
Oiþer to drynke a Copful ale,
Þan to heron any gode tale:
Swiche ich wolde were oute-biſhett;
For certeyn lich, it were nett.
For hire ne haeþ wille ich woot welbb
Bot in þe gute *and* in þe barel.[2]

[The writer] thus deſcribes a ſplendid proceſſion made by Olympias:

In þis tyme faire *and* Iolyſe[3]
Olympyas, þat faire wŷfe
Wolde make a riche feſte
Of kniȝttes *and* leſdyes honeſte,
Of Burgeys *and* of Iugelers
And of Men of vche meſters,[4]
For Men ſeiþ by north *and* ſouth
Wymmen beeþ, euere ſelcouþ;
Mychel ſhe deſireþ to ſhewe hire body
Her faire here, her face rody,
To haue looſ[5] *and* ek praiſynge:
And al is folye by heuene kynge
So dude þe dame Olympyas
Forto ſhowe hire gentyl face.
She hete Marſhales, *and* kniȝhtes
Greiþe hem to ryde onon riȝttes
And leuedyes *and* damoyſele
Quyk hem greiþed þouſandes fele,
In faire atyre, in dyuers queyntiſe
Many þere roode on riche wiſe.
A Mule, alſo whyte ſo mylke
Wiþ ſadel of gold, ſambu of ſylke
Was y-brouȝth to þe quene
Myd many belle of ſyluer ſhene
Yfaſtned on Orfreys[6] of mounde
Þat hengen doune to neiȝ grounde.
Forþ ſhe ferdeu[7] myd her rote
A þouſande leſdyes of riche ſoute.

---

[1] Leg. *lerd.* learned.
[2] The work begins thus:

WHilom clerkes wel ylerede
On þre dizttin þis Middel erde,
And clepid hit in here maiſtrie,
Europe, Affryke, and Aſyghe:
At Aſyghe al ſo muchul ys
As Europe, and Affryk, I wis, &c.

And ends with this diſtich:

Aliſaunder! me reowith thyn endyng
That thou n'adeſt dyghed in criſtenyng.

[3] Jolly.   [4] Of each, or every, profeſſion, trade, ſort.   [5] Praiſe.
[6] Embroidered work, cloth of gold. *Auriſrigium*, Lat.   [7] Fared: went.

A fperuer¹ þat was honefte
So fat on þe lefdyes fyfte :
Foure trumpes toforne² hire belew :
Many Man þat day hire knew :
An hundreþ houfande *and* ek moo
Alle alouten hire vnto.
Al þe toun by-honged was³
Azeins⁴ þe lefdy Olympyas.⁵
Orgues, Chymbes, vche man*ere* glee⁶
Was dryuen azein þat leuedy free.
Wiþouten þees tounes Murey :
Was arered vche man*er* pley ;⁷
Þere was knizttes tourneying*e*
Þere was maydens Carolyng*e*
Þere was Champions fkirmyng*e*,⁸
Of hem of oþ*er* alfo wreftlyng*e*
Of lyons chace, of bere baityng*e*.
A bay of bore⁹ of bole flatyng*e*.¹⁰
Al þe Cite was by-honge
Wiþ Riche Samytes *and* pelles¹¹ longe
Dame Olympias amonge this pres¹²
Sengle rood,¹³ al Mantel-les.—
And naked heued in one coroune
She rood þorouz out*e* al þe tou*n*.
Here zelewe her¹⁴ was faire atired*e*
Mid riche ftrenges of golde wyred*e*
It helyd her*e* abouten al¹⁵
To her*e* gentale Myddel fmal
Brizth *and* fhene was her face¹⁶
Eu*ery* fairehede¹⁷ in hir was.¹⁸

---

¹ fparrow-hawk ; a hawk. ² before.
³ "hung with tapeftry." We find this ceremony practifed at the entrance of Lady Elizabeth, queen of Henry VII. into the city of London.—"Al the ftrets ther whiche fhe fhulde paffe by wer clenly dreffed and befene with cloth, of tappeftrye and arras, and fome ftreetes as Chepe, hanged with riche clothes of golde, velvettes and filkes." This was in the year 1481. Leland, *Coll.* iv. *Opufcul.* p. 220, edit. 1770.
⁴ "againft her coming."
⁵ See the defcription of the tournament in Chaucer, *Knight's Tale,* where the city is hanged with cloth of gold. v. 2570.
⁶ "organs, timbrels, all manner of mufic."
⁷ "all forts of fports." ⁸ fkirmifhing.
⁹ "baying or bayting of the boar."
¹⁰ *flaying bulls,* bull-feafts. [Sir F. Madden fays, bull-*baiting*.] Chaucer fays that the chamber of Venus was painted with "white *bolis* grete." *Compl. of Mars and Ven.* v. 86.
¹¹ fkins. ¹² crowd; company. ¹³ rode fingle.
¹⁴ yellow hair. ¹⁵ "covered her all over."
¹⁶ line 155. ¹⁷ beauty.
¹⁸ John Gower, who lived an hundred years after our author, hath defcribed the fame proceffion. *Confefs. Amant.* lib. vi. [ed. 1857, iii. 62-3.]

"But in that citee thanne was
The quene, whiche Olimpias
Was hote, and with folempnite
The fefte of her nativite
As it befell, was than holde ;
And for her luft to be beholde,
And preifed of the people about,
She fhop her for to riden out,

Much in the same strain the marriage of Cleopatra is described:

  Þhoo þis message was hom y-come
  Þere was many a bliþe gome
  Of Olyue *and* of muge floures
  Weren strywed halle *and* boures:
  Wiþ Samytes *and* Baudekyns
  Weren curtyned þe gardyns.
  Alle þe Innes of þe tou*n*
  Hadden litel foyfou*n*,[1]
  Þat day þat com Cleopatras;
  So mychel poeple wiþ hir was.
  She rood on a Mule, white so mylk*e*;
  Her herneys was gold beten fylk*e*
  Þe prince hire led*e* of Candas,
  And of Sydoyne Sir Ionathas,
  Ten þoufande barons hir co*m*me myde,
  And to chirche wiþ hire ryde.
  Yfpoufed fhe is *and* fet on deys:
  Nov gynneþ geft of g*re*t nobléys:
  At þe feft was harpyng*e*,
  And pipyng*e and* tabouryng*e*,
  And fitelyng*e a*nd tru*m*pyng*e*.[2]

We have frequent opportunities of observing, how the poets of these times engraft the manners of chivalry on ancient classical history. In the following lines Alexander's education is like that of Sir Tristram. He is taught tilting, hunting, and hawking:

  Now can Alifaundre of fkirmyng*e*
  As of ftedes derayeyng*e*,

  At after-mete all openly.
  Anone were alle men redy,
  And that was in the month of may
  This lufty quene in good array
  Was fet upon a mule white
  To fene it was a great delite
  The joie that the citee made.
  With frefshe thinges and with glade
  The noble town was al behonged;
  And every wight was fore alonged
  To fe this lufty ladie ride.
  There was great merth on alle fide,
  Where as fhe paffeth by the ftrete
  There was ful many a tymbre bete,
  And many a maide carolende.
  And thus through out the town pleinde
  This quene unto the pleine rode
  Where that fhe hoved and abode
  To fe diverfe games pley,
  The lufty folk jouft and tourney.
  And fo forth every other man
  Which pleie couth, his pley began,
  To plefe with this noble quene."

Gower continues this ftory, from a romance mentioned above, to fol. 140.
 [1] provifion.
 [2] line 1023; f. 32 of MS. Laud.

> Vpon ſtedes of Juſtuynge,
> And wiþ ſwerdes turneyeinge,
> Of aſſailynge and defendynge.
> In grene woode *and* of huntynge
> And of Ryuer of haukynge :[1]
> Of bataile *and* of alle þinge.[2]

In another place Alexander is mounted on a ſteed of Narbonne,[3] and, amid the ſolemnities of a great feaſt, rides through the hall to the high table. This was no uncommon practice in the ages of chivalry :[4]

> He lepeþ vp myd ydone
> On a ſtede of Nerebone;
> He daſsheth forþ vpon þe londe
> þe riche coroune on his honde,
> Of Nicholas þat he wan :
> Biſide hy*m* rideþ many a gentil man.
> To þe paleys he comeþ ryde
> And fyndeþ þis feſte *and* al þis pride
> Forþ gooþ Aliſaundre, ſaun<u>z</u> fable
> Riȝth vnto þe heiȝe table.[5]

His horſe Bucephalus, who even in claſſical fiction is a horſe of romance, is thus deſcribed:

> An horne in the forhed amydwarde
> þat wolde perce a ſhelde harde.[6]

To which theſe lines may be added:

> ALiſaunder ariſen is
> And ſitteþ on his deys I wys
> His dukes *and* his barou*n*s ſaunz doute
> Stondeþ *and* ſitteþ hym aboute.[7]

The two following extracts are in a ſofter ſtrain, and not inelegant for the rude ſimplicity of the times:

> Mery is þe blaſt of þe ſtyuoure[8]
> Mery is þe touchynge of þe harpoure ;[9]

---

[1] Chaucer, *R. of Sir Thop.* v. 3245:
"He couth hunt al the wild dere,
And ride an *hawkyng by the rivere.*"
And in the *Squyr of low degree* [*Rem. of the E. P. Poet. of Engl.* ii. 52]:
"—— Shall ye *ryde*
On *haukyng by the ryuers ſide.*"
Chaucer, *Frankleins Tale,* v. 1752:
"Theſe fauconers upon a faire rivere
That with the hawkis han the *heron* ſlaine."

[2] f. 30 *b.* MS. Laud.

[3] [The Lincoln's Inn MS. reads "faire bone," which is probably the correcter verſion.—*Price.*]

[4] See *Obſervations on the Fairy Queen,* i. § v. p. 146.

[5] line 1075, (ll. 1074-83 Laud. MS. f. 32.)

[6] ll. 692, 3; f 30 *b.*

[7] line 3966; (ll. 3954-7, f. 45 *b.*)

[8] [The editor thinks that Mr. Halliwell is ſcarcely correct in defining this to be a kind of bagpipe. Mr. Herbert Coleridge (*Gloſſary,* 1859, *in voce*) is ſurely nearer the truth in deſcribing it as a ſort of *trumpet,* Fr. *eſtive.* In the preſent paſſage it ſtands for a trumpeter, or, at leaſt, a perſon blowing a *ſtive.*]

[9] This poem has likewiſe, in the ſame vein, the following well-known old rhyme, which paints the manners, and is perhaps the true reading, line 1163:

> Swete is þe smellynge of þe floure
> Swete yit is in maydens boure
> Appel swete bereþ fair[1] coloure
> Of trewe loue is swe (*sic*) amoure.

Again:

> In tyme of May, þe niȝttyngale
> In wood makeþ mery gale;
> So don þe foules grete *and* smale
> Summe on hylles, *and* summe in dale.[2]

Much the same vernal delights, clothed in a similar style, with the addition of knights turneying and maidens dancing, invite King Philip on a progress; he is entertained on the road with hearing tales of ancient heroes:

> Mery tyme it is in may
> Þe foules syngeþ her lay;
> Þe kniȝttes loueþ þe *turnay*
> Maydens so dauncen *and* þay play.
> Þe kynge forþ rideþ his Iournay
> Now hereþ geste of grete noblay.[3]

Our author thus describes a battle:[4]

> Alisaunder tofore is ride
> And many a gentil kniȝth hy*m* myde
> Ac, forto gadre his meignè free
> He abideþ vnder a tree.
> Fourty þousande of shyualerie
> He takeþ in his compaignye.
> He dassheþ hy*m* forþ þan fastwarde:
> And þe oþer comen afterwarde:
> He seeþ his kniȝttes, in Meschief
> He takeþ it gretlich a greef.
> He taked Bulcyphal[5] by þe side;
> So a swalewe he gynneþ forþ glide.
> A duke of Perce sone he mette
> And wiþ his launce he hy*m* grette;
> He perceþ his breny and cleueþ his shelde,
> Þe herte tokerneþ þe yrne chelde:
> Þe duke fel doune to þe grounde
> And starf quykly in þat stounde.
> Alisaunder aloude þan seiede,

> "Swithe mury hit is in halle
> When the *burdes wawen alle.*"

And in another place we have:

> "Mury hit is in halle to here the harpe;
> The mynstrall syngith, theo jogolour carpith."—l. 5990.

Here, by the way, it appears, that the minstrels and juglers were distinct characters. So Robert de Brunne, in describing the coronation of King Arthur, apud Anstis, *Ord. Gart.* i. p. 304:

> "*Jogeleurs* wer ther inouȝ
> That wer queitise for the drouȝ,
> *Mynstrels* many with dyvers glew," &c.

And Chaucer mentions "*minstrels* and *eke joglours.*"—*Rom. R.* v. 764. But they are often confounded or made the same.

[1] line 2571; (ll. 2566-71, f. 39.)
[2] line 2546; (ll. 2542-5, f. 39).
[3] line 5210; (ll. 5194-9, f. 51).
[4] line 3776; (ll. 3764-3853, ff. 44 b, 45).
[5] Bucephalus.

Oþere tol neuere ich ne paiede :
Ʒute ȝee shullen of myne paie
Or ich gon more Assaie !
Anoþer launce in honde he hente ;
Aȝein þe prince of Tyre he wente,
He smoote hym þorouȝ þe breeste þare
And out of sadel ouere croupe hym bare ;
And I sigge forsoþe þinge
He braake his nek in þe fallynge.
Oxeatre, wiþ mychel wonder
Antiochum hadde hym vnder,
And wiþ swerd wolde his heuede
From his body habbe yreuede.
He seiz Alisaunder þe gode gome
Towardes hym swiþe come
He lete his pray and fleiz on hors
Forto saue his owen cors.
Antiochus on stede lep
Of none woundes ne tooke he kep ;
And eke he hade foure sorde
Alle ymade wiþ speres orde.[1]
Þolomeus and alle hise felawen [2]
Of þis socour so weren wel fawen.
Alisaunder made a cry hardy
Ore tost, a ly ! a ly !
Þere þe kniȝttes of Achaye
Iusted wiþ hem of Arabye ;
Þoo [3] of Rome, wiþ hem of Mede
Many londe wiþ oþere þede
Egipte iusted wiþ hem of Tyre
Symple kniȝth wiþ riche syre ;
Þere nas foreȝifte ne for berynge ;
bituene vauasoure [4] ne kynge,
Tofore, men miȝtten and byhynde
Cunteke [5] seke and cuntek fynde.
Wiþ Perciens fouȝtten þe gregeys ; [6]
Þere roos cry and grete honteys.
Hy kidden [7] þat hy neren merce
Hy braken speres alto slice :
Þere miȝth kniȝth fynde his pere,
Þere les many his destrere :
Þere was quyk in litel þrawe,[8]
Many gentil kniȝth yslawe ;
Many Arme, many heued,[9]
Sone from þe body reued :
Many gentil lauedy [10]
Þere lese quyke her amy. [11]
Þere was many maym ykede
Many fair pensel biblede.[12]
Þere was swerdes lik lakynge [13]
Þere was speres baþinge.[14]

---

[1] point.   [2] fellows.   [3] they.   [4] servant ; subject.   [5] strife.
[6] Greeks.   [7] [shewed.]   [8] short time.   [9] head.   [10] lady.
[11] paramour.   [12] "many a rich banner, or flag, sprinkled with blood."
[13] clashing. [This phrase is one of frequent occurrence in Anglo-Saxon poetry, and bears a very different import from that given by Mr. Weber : sweord-lac, A.-S. gladiorum ludus, from lacan, to play.—*Price*.]
[14] [Bathyng is the same as *Beating* ; but perhaps the true word is Bateing=*Fluttering*.]

> Boþe kynges þere, saunȝ doute
> Beeþ in dasshet wiþ al her route ;
> Þe on to don men of hym speke
> Þe oþere his harmes forto wreke.
> Many londes neiȝ and ferre
> Lesen her lorde in þat werre.
> Þe erþe quaked of her rydynge
> Þe weder¹ þicked of her crieynge
> Þe blood of hem þat weren yslawe
> Ran by flodes to þe lowe, &c.²

I have already mentioned Alexander's miraculous horn :³

> He blew an horne quyke, saunȝ doute⁴
> His folke com swiþe aboute :
> And hem he seide wiþ voice clere,
> Ich bidde, frendes, þat ȝe me here !
> Alisaunder is comen in þis londe
> Wiþ stronge knniȝttes, wiþ miȝtty of honde.

Alexander's adventures in the deserts among the Gymnosophists, and in India, are not omitted. The authors, whom he quotes for his vouchers, shew the reading and ideas of the times :⁵

> Þoo Alisaunder wente þorouȝ deserte
> Many wondres he seiȝ aperte⁶
> Whiche he dude wel descryue
> By gode clerkes in her lyue
> By Aristotle his maister þat was
> Better clerke siþen non nas.
> He was wiþ hym and seiȝ and wroote
> Alle þise wondres, (god it woote)
> Salomon þat al þe werlde þorouȝ ȝede
> In sooþ witnesse helde hym myde.
> Ysidre⁷ also, þat was so wys
> In his bokes telleþ þis.
> Maister eustroge bereþ hym witnesse
> Of þe wondres more and lesse.
> Seint Jerome, ȝee shullen y-wyte
> Hem haþ also in booke y-write ;
> And Magestene, þe gode clerke
> Haþ made þerof mychel werke.
> Denys þat was of gode memorie
> It sheweþ al in his booke of storie ;
> And also Pompie⁸ of Rome lorde,
> Duke it writen euery worde.
> Beheldeþ me þerof no fynder ;⁹
> Her bokes ben my shewer
> And þe lyf of Alisaunder
> Of whom fleȝ so riche sklaunder.

---

¹ weather, sky.   ² (l. 3843, f. 45.)
³ [It is most probable that Warton interpreted this passage of Alexander's horn : though the context plainly shews that it was Darius who blew it.—*Price.*]
⁴ (l. 3848, f. 45.)   ⁵ line 4772.   ⁶ saw openly.
⁷ *Isidore.* He means, I suppose, Isidorus Hispalensis, a Latin writer of the seventh century.
⁸ He means Justin's Trogus Pompeius the historian, whom he confounds with Pompey the Great.
⁹ "don't look on me as the inventor."

Ȝif ȝee willeþ ȝiue listnynge
Now ȝee shullen here gode þinge
In somers tyde þe day is longe;
Foules syngeþ *and* makeþ songe
Kynge Alisaunder y-wente is,
Wiþ dukes, Erles, *and* folke of pris,
Wiþ many kniȝth *and* douȝtty Men,
Toward the Cité of facen;
After kynge Porus þat flowen[1] was
Into the Cité of Bandas:
He wolde wende þorouȝ deserte
Þise wondres to seen aperte.
Gyoures he name[2] of þe londe
Fyue þousande I vnderstonde
Þat hem shulden lede riȝth,[3]
Þorouȝ deserte by day *and* niȝth.
Þe Gyoures loueden þe kynge nouȝth
And wolden haue hym bicauȝth:
Hy ledden hy*m* þerfore als I fynde
In þe straungest peryl of ynde.
Ac, so ich fynde in the booke
Hy were*n* asshreynte in her crooke.
Now rideþ Alisaunder wiþ his Oste,
Wiþ mychel pride *and* mychel booste;
Ac ar hy comen to Castel, oiþer tou*n*
Hy shullen speken anoþere lessou*n*.
Lordynges, also I fynde
At Mede so bigynneþ ynde:
Forsoþe ich woote, it stretcheth ferreste,
Of alle the londes in þe Este,
And oþ þe souþ half sikerlyke
To þe cee takeþ of Affryke;
And þe norþ half to a mountayne,
Þat is ycleped Caucasayne.[4]
Forsoþe ȝee shullen vnderstonde
Twyes is Somer in þe londe
And neuermore wynter ne chelen.[5]
Þat londe is ful of al wele;
Twyes hy gaderen fruyte þere
And wyne *and* Corne in one ȝere.
In þe londe als I fynde, of ynde
Ben Cités fyue þousynde;
Wiþouten ydles *and* Castels,
And Boroughȝ tounes swiþe feles.[6]
In þe londe of ynde þou miȝth lere
Nyne þousynde folk of selcouþ[7] man*er*e
Þhat þer non is oþer yliche;
Ne helde þou it nouȝth ferliche
Ac by þat þou vnderstonde þe gestes
Boþe of Men *and* eke of beestes, [&c.][8]

Edward II. is said to have carried with him to the siege of Stirling Castle a poet named Robert Baston.[9] He was a Carmelite friar of

---

[1] fled. [2] took. [3] strait. [4] Caucasus.
[5] chill, cold. [6] very many. [7] uncommon. [8] [l. 4831, f. 49 b.]
[9] [Winstanley, in his *Account of the Englisȟ Poets*, 1687, has introduced the name of BASTON, and has quoted the opening of his involuntary eulogium on Scotland and her king:

Scarborough; and the king intended that Baston, being an eye-witness of the expedition, should celebrate his conquest of Scotland in verse. Holinshed, an historian not often remarkable for penetration, mentions this circumstance as a singular proof of Edward's presumption and confidence in his undertaking against Scotland: but a poet seems to have been a stated officer in the royal retinue when the king went to war.[1] Baston, however, appears to have been chiefly a Latin poet, and therefore does not properly fall into our series. At least his poem on the siege of Stirling Castle is written in monkish Latin hexameters:[2] and our royal bard, being taken prisoner in the expedition, was compelled by the Scots, for his ransom, to write a panegyric on Robert Brus, which is composed in the same style and language.[3] Bale mentions his *Poemata et Rhythmi, Tragœdiæ et Comœdiæ vulgares*.[4] Some of these indeed appear to have been written in English: but no English pieces of this author now remain. In the meantime, the bare existence of dramatic compositions in England at this period, even if written in the Latin tongue, deserve notice in investigating the progress of our poetry. I must not pass over a Latin [dialogue in verse], written about the year [1367]. This [dialogue] is thus entitled in the Bodleian MS.: *De Babione et Croceo domino Babionis et Viola filiastra Babionis quam Croceus duxit invito Babione, et Pecula uxore Babionis et Fodio suo*, &c.[5] It is

---

"In dreery verse my Rymes I make,
Bewailing whilest such Theme I take."

which appears to be Winstanley's own rendering of the opening lines.]

[1] Leland. *Script. Brit.* p. 338. Holinsh. *Hist.* ii. pp. 217, 220. Tanner mentions, as a poet of England, one Gulielmus Peregrinus, who accompanied Richard I. into the Holy Land, and sang his achievements there in a Latin poem, entitled *Odoeporicon Ricardi Regis*, lib. i. It is dedicated to Hurbert, archbishop of Canterbury, and Stephen Turnham, a captain in the expedition. He flourished about A.D. 1200. *Bibl.* p. 591. See Voss. *Hist. Lat.* p. 441. He is called "poeta per eam ætatem excellens." See Bale, iii. 45. Pits. 266. See Leland *Script. Brit.* p. 228. And a note in the editor's first Index, under Gulielmus de Canno.

[2] It is extant in Fordun's *Scoti-Chron.* c. xxiii. l. 12.

[3] Leland. *ut supr.* And MSS. Harl. 1819. Brit. Mus. See also Wood, *Hist. Ant. Univ. Oxon.* i. p. 101.

[4] Tanner, p. 79.

[5] Arch. B. 52. [In the Cotton MS. Titus A. xx. the several parts of the dialogue are distinguished by initial capitals; and on the opposite side stand marginal notices of the change of person. Thus: "Babio, Violæ; Viola, Babioni; Fodius, Babioni; Babio, Croceo." The *Geta* [by Vitalis Blesensis], noticed below, and also occurring in the Cotton MS., is founded on the ancient fable of Jupiter's intrigue with Alcmena, [and is a mediæval version of the *Geta* of Plautus.] It is in the same style of dialogue with Babio, and has similar marginal directions; such as "Jupiter Alcmenæ; Alcmena Jovi," The line quoted by Warton occurs in what may be called the Prologue. The Cotton MS. affords no clue as to the date of these singular productions, [but Mr. Wright has shown the extreme probability that they belong to the middle of the thirteenth century.] It contains a farrago of rhythmical pieces from the time of Gualo (1160) to Baston and perhaps later. But in France such pieces appear to have been current during the twelfth century. Du Boulay has noticed a tragedy *de Flaura et Marco*, and a comedy called *Alda*, written by [Matthæus Vindocinensis].—Price. "Three manuscripts are known of this poem. One is in the Cotton MS. Titus, A. xx, which, amongst a vast mass of

written in long and short Latin verses. The story is in Gower's *Confessio Amantis*. Whether Gower had it from this performance I will not enquire. It appears at least that he took it from some previous book.

> I find write of Babio,
> Which had a love at his menage,
> Ther was no fairer of her age,
> And highte Viola by name, &c.
> And had affaited to his honde
> His servant, the which Spodius
> Was hote, &c.
> A freshe a free a frendly man, &c.
> Which Croceus by name hight, &c.[1]

There is nothing dramatic in the structure of this nominal comedy; and it has certainly no claim to that title, only as it contains a familiar and comic story carried on with much scurrilous satire intended to raise mirth. But it was not uncommon to call any short poem, not serious or tragic, a comedy. In the Bodleian MS. which comprehends [the *Babio*] just mentioned, there follows [the] *Geta*: this is in Latin long and short verses,[2] and has no marks of dialogue.[3] In the library of Corpus Christi College at Cambridge is a piece entitled *Comedia ad monasterium de Hulme ordinis S. Benedicti Diocef. Norwic. directa ad Reformationem sequentem, cujus data est primo die Septembris sub anno Christi 1477, et a morte Joannis Fastolfe militis eorum benefactoris*[4] *precipui 17, in cujus monasterii ecclesia humatur.*[5] This is nothing more than a satirical ballad in Latin; yet some allegorical personages are introduced, which, however, are in no respect accommodated to scenical representation. About the reign of Edward IV. one Edward Watson, a scholar in grammar at Oxford, is permitted to proceed to a degree in that faculty, on condition that within two years he would write one hundred verses in praise of the university, and also compose a comedy.[6] The nature and subject of Dante's *Commedia*, as it is styled, are well known.[7] The comedies

---

Anglo-Latin poetry of the twelfth, thirteenth, and fourteenth centuries, contains also a copy of the *Geta*. . . . The two other MSS. of the Babio are preserved in the Bodleian Library."—*Wright*.]

[1] [Gower's *C. F.* ed. Pauli, ii. 288-9.]
[2] Carmina composuit, voluitque placere poeta. [The best edition of the *Geta* of Vitalis *Blesensis* is in Mr. Wright's volume of *Early Mysteries*, &c. 1838, 8vo. p. 79 *et seqq*.]
[3] f. 121.
[4] In the episcopal palace at Norwich is a curious piece of old wainscot brought from the monastery of Hulme at the time of its dissolution. Among other antique ornaments are the arms of Sir John Falstaff, their principal benefactor. This magnificent knight was also a benefactor to Magdalene College in Oxford. He bequeathed estates to that society, part of which were appropriated to buy liveries for some of the senior scholars. But this benefaction, in time, yielding no more than a penny a week to the scholars who received the liveries, they were called, by way of contempt, *Falstaff's Buckram-men*.
[5] *Miscell. M.* p. 274.
[6] *Hist. Antiq. Univ. Oxon.* ii. 4, col. 2.
[7] [In the dedication of his Paradiso to Can della Scala, Dante thus explains his own views of Tragedy and Comedy: "Est comœdia genus quoddam poeticæ nar-

ascribed to Chaucer are probably his *Canterbury Tales*. We learn from Chaucer's own words, that tragic tales were called *Tragedies*. In the Prologue to the *Monkes Tale*:

> Tregedis is to sayn a certeyn storie,
> As olde bookes maken us memorie,
> Of hem that stood in greet prosperite,
> And is y-fallen out of heigh degre, &c.¹

Some of these, the monk adds, were written in prose, others in metre. Afterwards follow many tragical narratives, of which he says:

> *Tragidies* first wol I tell
> Of which I have an hundred in my cell.

Lidgate further confirms what is here said with regard to comedy as well as tragedy:

> My maister Chaucer with fresh *comedies*,
> Is dead, alas! chief poet of Britaine:
> That whilom made ful piteous *tragedies*.²

The stories in the *Mirror for Magistrates* are called tragedies, so late as the sixteenth century. Bale calls his play or Mystery of *God's Promises*, which appeared about the year 1538, a tragedy.

I must however observe here that dramatic entertainments, representing the lives of saints and the most eminent scriptural stories, were known in England for more than [a century] before the reign of Edward II. These spectacles they commonly styled miracles. I have already mentioned the play of Saint Catharine, acted at Dunstable about the year 1110.³ [Two of the oldest miracle-plays in the *English* language are perhaps the *Harrowing of Hell*⁴ and the *Incredulity of St. Thomas*, the latter of which was exhibited by the Scriveners' Guild at York.⁵ The *Harrowing of Hell* exists in a MS. which may

---

rationis ab omnibus aliis differens. Differt ergo in materia a tragœdia per hoc, quod tragœdia in principio est admirabilis et quieta, in fine sive exitu fœtida et horribilis. . . . . Comœdia vero inchoat asperitatem alicujus rei, sed ejus materiam prospere terminatur.' Similiter differunt *in modo loquendi*." He has also expatiated upon the distinctive styles peculiar to such compositions in his treatise, *De vulgari Eloquentia;* though his precepts when opposed to his practice have proved a sad stumbling-block to the critics: " Per Tragœdiam superiorem stylum induimus, per Comœdiam inferiorem. . . . . Si tragice canenda vicentur, tum adsumendum est vulgare illustre. Si vero comice, tum quandoque mediocre, quandoque humile vulgare sumatur." Lib. ii. c. iv.—*Price*.]

¹ v. 85. See also, *ibid.* v. 103, 786, 875.
² Prol. F. Pr. v. i. See also Chaucer's *Troil. and Cr.* v. 1785, 1787.
³ Dissertation ii. [The earliest examples of such compositions now known are three plays written in France by Hilarius, an Englishman, and disciple of the famous Abelard, the subjects of which are the Raising of Lazarus, a miracle of St. Nicholas, and the History of Daniel; they were written early in the twelfth century—*Wright*. There is an edition of them at Paris, 1838, 8vo.]

[Perhaps the plays of Rosvvitha, a nun of Gandersheim in Lower Saxony, who lived towards the close of the tenth century, afford the earliest specimens of dramatic composition, since the decline of the Roman Empire. They were professedly written for the benefit of those Christians who, abjuring all other heathen writers, were irresistibly attracted by the graces of Terence, to the imminent danger of their

be nearly coeval with the performance itself; of the other piece we have apparently only a copy made at a much later date.] William Fitz-Stephen, a writer of the twelfth century, in his *Description of London*, relates that " London, for its theatrical exhibitions, has holy plays, or the representation of miracles wrought by confessors, and of the sufferings of martyrs."⁶ These pieces must have been in high vogue at our present period; for Matthew Paris, who wrote about the year 1240, says that they were such as " Miracula vulgariter

---

spiritual welfare and the certain pollution of their moral feelings. Rofwitha appears to have been impressed with a hope, that by contrasting the laudable chastity of Christian virtue, as exhibited in her compositions, with what she is pleased to term the lewd voluptuousness of the Grecian females, the Catholic world might be induced to forget the ancient classic, and to receive with avidity an orthodox substitute, combining the double advantage of pleasure and instruction. How far her expectations were gratified in this latter particular, it is impossible to say; but we can easily conceive, that the almost total obliviscence of the Roman author during the succeeding ages must have surpassed even her sanguine wishes. It does not appear that these dramas were either intended for representation, ór exhibited at any subsequent period. They have been published twice: by Conrad Celtes in 1501, and Leonhard Schurzfleisch in 1707. They have also been analysed by Gottsched in his Materials for a History of the German Stage. Leip. 1757.—Pez (in his *Thesaur. Noviss. Anecd.* vol. ii. p. iii. f. 185) has published an ancient Latin Mystery, entitled *De Adventu et Interitu Antichristi*, which he acknowledges to have copied from a manuscript of the twelfth century. It approaches nearer to the character of a pageant, than to the dramatic cast of the later mysteries. The dumb-show appears to have been considerable, the dialogue but occasional; and ample scope is given for the introduction of pomp and decoration. The passages to be declaimed are written in Latin rhyme. Lebeuf also mentions a Latin Mystery written so early as the time of Henry I. of France (1031—1061). In this Virgil is associated with the prophets who come to offer their adorations to the new-born Messiah; and at the conclusion he joins his voice with theirs in singing a long Benedicamus. A fragment of what may be a German translation of the same mystery, copied from a manuscript of the thirteenth century, will be found in Dieterich's *Specimen Antiquitatum Biblicarum*, p. 122. But here Virgil appears as an acknowledged heathen; and he is only admitted with the other prophets from his supposed predictions of the coming Messiah contained in his *Pollio*. In conformity with this opinion, Dante adopted him as his guide in the *Inferno.—Price*. Mr. Price's assertion as to the almost total obliviscence of Terence in the middle ages is not founded on fact. No classic author is oftener quoted by monkish writers, and in the British Museum alone there are above thirty MSS. copies written between the tenth and fifteenth centuries.—*Madden*.]

⁴ [Edited from Harl. MS. 2253 by Mr. Halliwell, 1840, 8vo, and from the Auchinleck MS. by Mr. Laing (*Owain Miles and other Pieces of Ancient English Poetry*, 1837, 8vo).]

⁵ [Printed in Croft's *Excerpta Antiqua*, 1797, and again by Collier, *Camden Miscellany*, iv.]

⁶ " Lundonia pro spectaculis theatralibus, pro ludis scenicis, ludos habet sanctiores, representationes miraculorum quæ sancti confessores operati sunt, seu representationes passionum quibus claruit constantia martyrum." Stow's *Survey of London*, p. 480, edit. 1599. The reader will observe, that I have construed *sanctiores* in a positive sense. [But here Warton merely follows Pegge in his translation of Fitz-Stephen: neither states a reason. See Collier's *Hist. of E. D. P.* i. 2, *note*.] Fitz-Stephen mentions at the end of his tract, " Imperatricem Matildem, Henricum regem tertium, et beatum Thomam, &c." p. 483. [Fitz-Stephen is speaking of Henry the younger, son of Henry II. and grandson to the Empress Matilda, who was crowned king in the lifetime of his father, and is expressly styled Henricus Tertius by Matthew Paris, William of Newbury, and several other of our early historians.—*Ritson*.]

appellamus."[1]   And we learn from Chaucer, that in his time Plays of Miracles were the common refort of idle goffips in Lent:

> Therefore made I my vifitations,
> To prechings eke and to pilgrimagis,
> To Plays of Miracles, and mariagis, &c.[2]

---

[1] *Vit. Abbat.* ad calc. *Hift.* p. 56, edit. 1639.

[William de Wadington (who poffibly was a contemporary of Matthew Paris) has left a violent tirade againft this general practice of acting miracles. As it contains fome curious particulars relative to the manner in which they were conducted, and the places felected for exhibiting them, an extract from it may not be out of place here:

> " Une autre folie apert
> Unt les fols clers cuntrové;
> Qe miracles funt apelé.
> Lur faces unt la deguife,
> Par vifers li forfene,
> Qe eft defendu en decree;
> Tant eft plus grant lur peché.
> Fere poent reprefentement,
> Mes qe ceo feit chaftement.
> En office de feint eglife
> Quant hom fet la, Deu fervife.
> *Cum Ihu Crift le fiz Dee,*
> *En fepulcre efteit pofé;*
> *Et la refurrectiun:*
> Par plus aver devociun.
> Mes fere foles affemblez,
> En les rues des citez,
> Ou en cymiters apres mangers,
> Quant venent les fols volonters,
> Tut dient qe il le funt pur bien:
> Crere ne les devez pur rien,
> Qe fet feit pur le honur de Dee.
> E iuz del Deable pur verité.
> Seint Yfidre me ad teftimonie,
> Qe fut fi bon clerc lettré.
> Il dit qe cil qe funt fpectacles,
> Cum lem fet en miracles,
> Ou iuʒ qe vus nomames einʒ,
> Burdiz ou turnemens,
> Lur baptefme unt refufez,
> E Deu de ciel reneiez, &c.
> Ke en lur iuz fe delitera,
> Chevals ou harneis les apreftera,
> Vefture ou autre ournement,
> Sachez il fet folement.
> Si veftemens ferent dediez,
> Plus grant daffez eft le pechez.
> Si prefte ou clerc le uft prefte,
> Bien duft eftre chauftie;
> Car facrilege eft pur verité.
> E ki par vanite les verrunt,
> De lur fet partaverunt."
>   Harl. MS. 273, f. 141.—*Price.*

This has been printed by Mr. Furnivall in his edition of Robert de Brunne's *Handlyng Synne*, Roxburghe Club, 1862.]

[2] *Prol. Wif. B.* v. 555.

This is the genial *Wife of Bath*, who amuses herself with these fashionable diversions, while her husband is absent in London, during the holy season of Lent. And in Pierce the Plowman's *Crede*, a friar Minorite mentions the miracles as not less frequented than markets or taverns:

> We haunten no tavernes, ne hobelen abouten,
> Att markets and Miracles we medeley us never.[1]

Among the plays usually represented by the guild of Corpus Christi at Cambridge, on that festival, *Ludus filiorum Israelis* was acted in the year 1355.[2] Our drama seems hitherto to have been almost entirely confined to religious subjects, and these plays were nothing more than an appendage to the specious and mechanical devotion of the times. I do not find expressly, that any play on a profane subject, either tragic or comic, had as yet been exhibited in England. Our very early ancestors scarce knew any other history than that of their religion. Even on such an occasion as the triumphant entry of a king or queen into the city of London, or other places, the pageants were almost entirely Scriptural.[3] I likewise find in the wardrobe-rolls of Edward III., 1348, an account of the dresses, *ad faciendum Ludos domini regis ad ffestum Natalis domini celebratos apud*

---

[1] Signat. A iii b, edit. 1561.

[2] Masters' *Hist. C. C. C. C.* p. 5, vol. i. What was the antiquity of the *Guary-Miracle*, or *Miracle-Play* in Cornwall, has not been determined. In the Bodleian library are three Church interludes, written on parchment. [Bodley, 791.] In the same library there is also another, written on paper in the year 1611. Arch. [N. 219.] Of this last there is a translation in the British Museum. MSS. Harl. 1867, 2. It is entitled the *Creation of the World*, [and bears traces of an obligation on the part of the compiler to the earlier production printed by Norris—the *Origo Mundi*.] It is called a Cornish play or opera, and said to be written by Mr. William Jordan. The translation into English was made by John Keigwin of Mousehole in Cornwall, at the request of Trelawney, Bishop of Exeter, 1691. Of this William Jordan I can give no account. [Mr. Davies Gilbert published the *Creation of the World* in 1827, 8vo., and more recently, Mr. Edwin Norris has edited from the Bodleian MS. the three Cornish Dramas, *Origo Mundi, Passio Domini Nostri*, and *Resurrectio Domini Nostri*, 1859, 2 vols. 8vo. Mr. Gilbert also edited the poem of *Mount Calvary* in 1826, 8vo.; but his text is very bad both there and in the *Creation*. See Mr. Norris's remarks and explanations in his Appendix, ii. 439 *et seqq*. I fear that Mr. Norris's own text is not very trustworthy. In the library of Mr. C. Wynne, at Peniarth, Montgomeryshire, is another Cornish play, unknown to Gilbert and Norris.]

In the British Museum there is an ancient Cornish poem on the death and resurrection of Christ. It is on vellum, and has some rude pictures. The beginning and end are lost. The writing is supposed to be of the fifteenth century. MSS. Harl. 1782, 4to. [This is the poem on *Mount Calvary* already referred to, but three other copies are known.] See the learned Lwhyd's *Archæol. Brit.* p. 265. And Borlase's *Cornwall, Nat. Hist.* p. 295, edit. 1758.

[3] When our Hen. VI. entered Paris in 1431, in the quality of King of France, he was met at the gate of Saint Denis by a Dumb Shew, representing the birth of the Virgin Mary and her marriage, the adoration of the three kings, and the parable of the sower. This pageant indeed was given by the French: but the readers of Holinshed will recollect many instances immediately to our purpose. See Monstrelet *apud* Fonten. *Hist. Theatr.* ut supr. p. 37.

Guldeford, for furnishing the plays or sports of the king, held in the castle of Guildford at the feast of Christmas.[1] In these Ludi, says my record, were expended eighty tunics of buckram of various colours, forty-two visors of various similitudes, that is, fourteen of the faces of women, fourteen of the faces of men with beards, fourteen of heads of angels, made with silver; twenty-eight crests,[2] fourteen mantles embroidered with heads of dragons: fourteen white tunics wrought with heads and wings of peacocks, fourteen heads of swans with wings, fourteen tunics painted with eyes of peacocks, fourteen tunics of English linen painted, and as many tunics embroidered with stars of gold and silver.[3] In the *Wardrobe* rolls of Richard II. there is also an entry which seems to point out a sport of much the same nature [in 1389, 12 Rich. II.] "Pro xxi *coifs* de tela linea pro hominibus de lege contrafactis pro ludo regis tempore natalis domini anno xii."[4] That is, "for twenty-one linen coifs for counterfeiting men of the law in the king's play at Christmas." It will be sufficient to add here on the last record, that the serjeants at law at their creation anciently wore a cap of linen, lawn, or silk, tied under the chin: this was to distinguish them from the clergy who had the tonsure. Whether in both these instances we are to understand a dumb-shew, or a dramatic interlude with speeches, I leave to the examination of those who are professedly making enquiries into the history of our stage from its rudest origin. But that plays on general subjects were no uncommon mode of entertainment in the royal palaces of England, at least at the commencement of the fifteenth century, may be collected from an old memoir of shews and ceremonies exhibited at Christmas, in the reign of Henry VII. in the palace of Westminster. It is in the year 1489. "This cristmas I saw no disguysings, and but *right few* Plays. But ther

---

[1] Comp. J. Cooke, Provisoris Magnæ Garderob. *ab ann.* 21 Edw. [III.] *ad ann.* 23. Memb. ix.

[2] I do not perfectly understand the Latin original in the place, viz. " xiiij *Crestes* cum tibiis reversatis et calceatis, xiiij *Crestes* cum montibus et cuniculis." Among the stuffs are "viii pelles de Roan." In the same wardrobe rolls, a little above, I find this entry, which relates to the same festival. " Et ad faciendum vi pennecellos pro tubis et clarionibus contra Festum natalis domini, de syndone, vapulatos de armis regis quartellatis." Membr. ix.

[3] Some perhaps may think, that these were dresses for a Masque at court. If so, Holinshed is mistaken in saying, that in the year 1512, " on the daie of Epiphanie at night, the king with eleven others were disguised after the manner of Italie called a maske, *a thing not seen before in England.* They were apparalled in garments long and broad wrought all with gold, with visors and caps of gold," &c. *Hist.* vol. iii. p. 812, 2, 40. Besides, these maskings most probably came to the English, if from Italy, through the medium of France. Holinshed also contradicts himself: for in another place he seems to allow their existence under our Henry IV., A. D. 1400. "The conspirators ment upon the sudden to have set upon the king in the castell of Windsor, under colour of a *maske* to *mummerie*," &c. *ibid.* p. 515, b. 50. Strype says there were Pageaunts exhibited in London when Queen Eleanor rode through the city to her coronation, in 1236. And for the victory over the Scots by Edward I. in 1298. *Anec. Brit. Topograph.* p. 725, edit. 1768.

[4] Comp. Magn. Garderob. an. 14 Ric. II. f. 198. b.

was an abbot of Mifrule, that made much fport, and did right well his office." And again, "At nyght the kynge, the qweene, and my ladye the kynges moder, cam into the Whitehall, and ther hard a Play."[1]

As to the religious dramas, it was cuftomary to perform this fpecies of play on holy feftivals in or about the churches. In the regifter of William of Wykeham, bifhop of Winchefter, under the year 1384, an epifcopal injunction is recited, againft the exhibition of *Spectacula* in the cemetery of his cathedral.[2] Whether or no thefe were dramatic *Spectacles*, I do not pretend to decide.[3] In feveral of our old fcriptural plays, we fee fome of the fcenes directed to be reprefented *cum cantu et organis*, a common rubric in the miffal. That is, becaufe they were performed in a church where the choir affifted. There is a curious paffage in Lambarde's *Topographical Dictionary* written about 1570, much to our purpofe, and which I am therefore tempted to tranfcribe:[4]—"In the Dayes of ceremonial religion, they ufed at *Wytney* (in Oxfordfhire) to fet foorthe yearly in maner of a Shew, or Enterlude, the Refurrection of our Lord, &c. For the which Purpofe, and the more lyvely thearby to exhibite to the Eye the hole Action of the Refurrection, the Prieftes garnifhed out certain fmalle Puppets, reprefentinge the Parfons of *Chrifte*, the Watchmen, *Marie*, and others; amongeft the which, one bare the Parte of a wakinge Watcheman, who (efpiinge *Chrift* to arife) made a continual Noyce, like to the Sound that is caufed by the Metinge of two Styckes, and was therof comonly called *Jack Snacker of Wytney*. The like Toye I my felfe (beinge then a Childe,) once faw in *Poules* Churche at *London*, at a Feaft of *Whitfuntyde*; wheare the comynge downe of the *Holy Goft* was fet forthe by a white Pigion, that was let to fly out of a Hole, that yet is to be fene in the mydft of the Roofe of the great Ile, and by a longe Cenfer, which defcendinge out of the fame Place almoft to the verie Grounde, was fwinged up and downe at fuche a Lengthe, that it reached with thone Swepe almoft to the Weft Gate of the Churche, and with the

---

[1] Leland, *Coll.* iii. *Append.* p. 256, edit, 1770.

[2] *Regiftr.* lib. iii. f. 88. "Canere Cantilenas, ludibriorum *fpectacula* facere, faltationes et alios ludos inhoneftos frequentare, choreas," &c. So in Statut. Eccles. Nannett. A. D. 1405. No "mimi vel joculatores, ad *monftra larvarum* in ecclefia et cemeterio," are permitted. Marten. *Thefaur. Anecd.* iv. p. 993. And again, "Joculatores, hiftriones, faltatrices, in ecclefia, cemeterio, vel porticu.—nec aliquæ choreæ." Statut. *Synod Eccles. Leod.* A.D. 1287, *apud* Marten. *ut fupr.* 846. Fontenelle fays, that anciently among the French, comedies were acted after divine fervice in the church-yard. "Au fortir du fermon ces bonnes gens alloient a la *Comedie*, c'eft a dire, qu'ils changeoint de Sermon."—*Hift. Theatr.* ut fupr. p. 24. But thefe were fcriptural comedies, and they were conftantly preceded by a Benedicite, by way of prologue. The French ftage will occur again below.

[3] ["Had he (Warton) feen the paffage in the *Manuel de Peché*, where *Miracles* are exprefsly called *Spectacles*, his doubt (as to the nature of thefe *Spectacula*) would have been removed. The author of the French original is very particular in ftating to what performances he refers."—*Collier*.]

[4] 1730, 459. [Warton's tranfcript was full of errors in the orthography, although he muft have copied from the ed. of 1730.]

other to the Quyre Staires of the fame; breathinge out over the whole Churche and Companie a moft pleafant Perfume of fuch fwete Thinges as burned thearin; withe the like doome Shewes alfo, they ufed every whear to furnifhe fondrye Partes of their Churche Service, as by their Spectacles of the Nativitie, Paffion, and Afcenfion" &c.

This practice of acting plays in churches, had at laft grown to fuch an enormity, and was attended with fuch inconvenient confequences, that in the reign of Henry VIII., Bonner, bifhop of London, iffued a proclamation to the clergy of his diocefe, dated 1542, prohibiting " all maner of common plays, games, or interludes to be played, fet forth, or declared, within their churches, chapels," &c.[1] This fafhion feems to have remained even after the Reformation, and when perhaps profane ftories had taken place of religious.[2] Archbifhop Grindal, in the year 1563, remonftrated againft the danger of interludes: complaining that players " did, efpecially on holy days, fet up bills inviting to their play."[3] From this ecclefiaftical fource of the modern drama, plays continued to be acted on Sundays fo late as the reign of Elizabeth, and even till that of Charles I., by the chorifters or finging-boys of Saint Paul's Cathedral in London, and of the royal chapel.

It is certain that thefe *Miracle-plays* were the earlieft of our dramatic exhibitions. But as thefe pieces frequently required the introduction of allegorical characters, fuch as Charity, Sin, Death, Hope, Faith, or the like, and as the common poetry of the times, efpecially among the French, began to deal much in allegory, at length plays were formed entirely confifting of fuch perfonifications. Thefe were called *Moralities*. The miracle-plays, or *Myfteries*, were totally deftitute of invention or plan: they tamely reprefented ftories according to the letter of fcripture, or the refpective legend. But the Moralities indicate dawnings of the dramatic art; they contain fome rudiments of a plot, and even attempt to delineate characters, and to paint manners. Hence the gradual tranfition to real hiftorical perfonages was natural and obvious. It may be alfo obferved, that many licentious pleafantries were fometimes introduced in thefe religious reprefentations. This might imperceptibly lead the way to fubjects entirely profane and to comedy, and perhaps earlier than is imagined. In a Myftery[4] of the *Maffacre of the Holy Innocents*, part of the fubject of a facred drama given by the Englifh fathers at the famous council of Conftance in the year 1417,[5] a

---

[1] Burnet, *Hift. Ref.* i. Coll. Rec. p. 225.
[2] From a puritanical pamphlet entitled *The [fecond and] third Blaft of Retrait from Plaies*, &c. 1580, p. 77 [*Englifh Drama & Stage*, 1869, p. 134.] Where the author fays, the players are " permitted to publifh their mamettree in euerie Temple of God, and that through England," &c. This abufe of acting plays in churches is mentioned in the canon of James I., which forbids alfo the profanation of churches by court-leets, &c. The canons were given in the year 1603.
[3] Strype's *Grindal*, p. 82.
[4] [Ancient Myfteries from the Digby MSS., 1835.]
[5] L'Enfant, ii. 440.

low buffoon of Herod's court is introduced, desiring of his lord to be dubbed a knight, that he might be properly qualified to *go on the adventure* of killing the mothers of the children of Bethlehem. This tragical business is treated with the most ridiculous levity. The good women of Bethlehem attack our knight-errant with their spinning-wheels, break his head with their distaffs, abuse him as a coward and a disgrace to chivalry, and send him home to Herod as a recreant champion with much ignominy. It is in an enlightened age only that subjects of scripture history would be supported with proper dignity. But then an enlightened age would not have chosen such subjects for theatrical exhibition.[1] It is certain that our ancestors intended no sort of impiety by these monstrous and unnatural mixtures. Neither the writers nor the spectators saw the impropriety, nor paid a separate attention to the comic and serious part of these motley scenes; at least they were persuaded that the solemnity of the subject covered or excused all incongruities. They had no just idea of decorum, consequently but little sense of the ridiculous: what appears to us to be the highest burlesque, on them would have made no sort of impression. We must not wonder at this, in an age when courage, devotion, and ignorance composed the character of European manners; when the knight, going to a tournament, first invoked his God, then his mistress, and afterwards proceeded with a safe conscience and great resolution to engage his antagonist. In these Mysteries I have sometimes seen gross and open obscenities. In a play of *the Old and New Testament*,[2] Adam and

---

[1] [Even what may be called *the vices* of literature have their favourable side; for, if in our early drama from the Mysteries downward, there had not been the uncouth vernacular diction, the gross anachronisms, the ribaldry, and the totally unartistic construction, which we see, those remains would never have possessed the interest in our eyes, which under the circumstances they have, as storehouses of information upon many points connected with ancient manners and opinions.]

[2] MSS. Harl. 2013, &c. Exhibited at Chester in the year 1327, at the expense of the different trading companies of the city. *The Fall of Lucifer* by the Tanners. *The Creation* by the Drapers. *The Deluge* by the Dyers. *Abraham, Melchisedech, and Lot* by the Barbers. *Moses, Balak, and Balaam* by the Cappers. *The Salutation* and *Nativity* by the Wrightes. *The Shepherds feeding their flocks by night* by the Painters and Glaziers. *The three Kings* by the Vintners. *The Oblation of the three Kings* by the Mercers. *The Killing of the Innocents* by the Goldsmiths. *The Purification* by the Blacksmiths. *The Temptation* by the Butchers. *The last Supper* by the Bakers. *The Blindmen and Lazarus* by the Glovers. *Jesus and the Lepers* by the Corvesarys. *Christ's Passion* by the Bowyers, Fletchers, and Ironmongers. *Descent into Hell* by the Cooks and Innkeepers. *The Resurrection* by the Skinners. *The Ascension* by the Taylors. *The election of S. Mathias, Sending of the holy ghost, &c.* by the Fishmongers. *Antechrist* by the Clothiers. *Day of Judgment* by the Websters. The reader will perhaps smile at some of these combinations. This is the substance and order of the former part of the play:—God enters creating the world: he breathes life into Adam, leads him into Paradise, and opens his side while sleeping. Adam and Eve appear naked and *not ashamed*, and the old serpent enters lamenting his fall. He converses with Eve. She eats of the forbidden fruit and gives part to Adam. They propose, according to the stage-direction, to make themselves *subligacula a foliis quibus tegamus Pudenda*. Cover their nakedness with leaves, and converse with God. God's curse. The serpent *exit* hissing. They are driven from Paradise by four angels and the cherubim with a flaming sword. Adam appears digging the ground, and Eve spinning.

Eve are both exhibited on the stage naked, and conversing about their nakedness: this very pertinently introduces the next scene, in which they have coverings of fig-leaves. This extraordinary spectacle was beheld [at Chester] by a numerous assembly of both sexes with great composure: they had the authority of scripture for such a representation, and they gave matters just as they found them in the third chapter of Genesis. It would have been absolute heresy to have departed from the sacred text in personating the primitive appearance of our first parents, whom the spectators so nearly resembled in simplicity: and if this had not been the case, the dramatists were ignorant what to reject and what to retain.

["The original date and the authorship of the Chester plays," says Mr. Wright, "have been subjects of considerable discussion. My own impression, from the phraseology and forms of words, which may frequently be discovered in the blunders of the modern scribes, is that the original manuscript from which they copied was of the earlier part of the fifteenth or of the end of the fourteenth century." The transcript from which the edition superintended by Mr. Wright is printed, appears to have been made late in the reign of Elizabeth.[1] Besides the Coventry and Chester series, and the other miscellaneous productions of the same class in the Digby and other MSS., there were the York and Towneley or Widkirk Mysteries. The former, in fact, have had a most unfortunate destiny in being secreted by successive owners. It is to be regretted that they were not secured, when they occurred for sale about twenty years ago, for the national library, since only one of the York series, the Scriveners' Play, exists in a duplicate copy. The Towneley plays, however, which are also known only in one MS. (and that not entirely perfect), have been published.][2]

In the meantime, profane dramas seem to have been known in France at a much earlier period.[3] Du Cange gives the following

---

Their children Cain and Abel enter: The former kills his brother. Adam's lamentation. Cain is banished, &c.

[The *Chester Mysteries* have been published entire by T. Wright, Esq., 2 vols. 8vo. 1843-7. Mr. Wright observes: "The traditions adopted or imagined by some old Chester antiquaries, which carried the composition of these plays so far back as the mayoralty of John Arneway (1268 to 1270), and the supposition of Warton that they were the productions of Ralph Higden the chronicler, appear to me too improbable to deserve our serious consideration, unless they were founded on more authentic statements, or on more substantial arguments."]

[1] [Mr. Whitley Stoke edited for the Philological Society (1860-1) *The Play of the Sacrament*, which he terms a middle-English "drama." A pageant called *The Salutation of Gabriel*, was exhibited at Edinburgh in 1503, at the nuptials of James IV. and the Princess Margaret.]

[2] [By the Surtees Society, 1836, 8vo.]

[3] At Constantinople it seems that the stage flourished much under Justinian and Theodora, about the year 540. For in the Basilical codes we have the oath of an actress μη αναχωρειν της πορνειας. Tom. vii. p. 682, edit. Fabrot. Græco-Lat. The ancient Greek fathers, particularly Saint Chrysostom, are full of declamation against the drama, and complain that the people heard a comedian with much more pleasure than a preacher of the Gospel.

picture of the king of France dining in public before the year 1300. During this ceremony, a fort of farces or drolls feems to have been exhibited. All the great officers of the crown and the houfehold, fays he, were prefent. The company was entertained with inftrumental mufic of the minftrels, who played on the kettle-drum, the flageolet,[1] the cornet, the Latin cittern, the Bohemian flute, the trumpet, the Moorifh cittern, and the fiddle. Befides there were "des FARCEURS, des jougleurs, et des plaifantins, qui divertiffeoient les compagnies par leur faceties et par leur COMEDIES, pour l'entretien." He adds, that many noble families in France were entirely ruined by the prodigious expenfes lavifhed on thofe performers.[2] The annals of France very early mention buffoons among the minftrels at thefe folemnities; and more particularly that Louis le Debonnaire, who reigned about the year 830, never laughed aloud, not even when, at the moft magnificent feftivals, players, buffoons, minftrels, fingers, and harpers, attended his table.[3] In fome conftitutions given to a cathedral church in France, in the year 1280, the following claufe occurs: " Nullus SPECTACULIS aliquibus quæ aut in *Nuptiis* aut in *Scenis* exhibentur, interfit."[4] Where, by the way, the word *Scenis* feems to imply fomewhat of a profeffed ftage, although the eftablifhment of the firft French theatre is dated not before the year 1398.[5] The play of *Robin and Marian* is faid to

---

[1] I believe, a fort of pipe. This is the French word, viz. Demy-canon. See Carpent. Du Cange, *Gl. Lat.* i. p. 760.
[2] *Differtat. Joinv.* p. 161. [3] *Ibid.*
[4] Montfauc. *Cat. Manufcrip.* p. 1158. See alfo Marten. *Thefaur. Anecd.* tom. iv. p. 506. *Stat. Synod.* A.D. 1468. " Larvaria ad Nuptias," &c. Stow, in his *Survey of London*, mentions the practice of acting plays [mafques] at weddings.
[5] [A modern French antiquary (M. Roquefort) has claimed a much higher antiquity for the eftablifhment or rather origin of the French ftage; though upon principles, it muft be allowed, which have a decided tendency to confound all diftinctions between the feveral kinds of poetic compofition. The beautiful tale of Aucaffin and Nicolette is the corner-ftone upon which this theory repofes, and as the narrative is interfperfed with fong, feems to have induced a belief, that the recitations were made by a fingle Trouvere, and the poetry chaunted by a band of attendant minftrels. Admitting this to be the cafe—yet for it no authority is offered—the approximation to dramatic compofition is as remote as when left in the hands of a folitary declaimer. Upon this ground every ballad or romantic tale, which is known to have been accompanied by mufic and the voice, might be ftyled " a monument of theatric art;" and by analogy the rhapfodifts of Greece, who fang the *Iliad* at the public games, might be faid to have " enacted the plays" of Homer. Nor is the argument in favour of the *Jeux-partis* or fuch fabliaux as the *deux Bordeors ribauds*, in any degree more admiffible. In all thefe pieces there is nothing more than a fimple interchange of opinion, whether argumentative or vituperative, without pretenfion to incident, fable, or development of character. Indeed, if a multiplicity of interlocutors would alone conftitute a drama, the claim of Wolfram von Efchenbach to be the founder of the German ftage (as fome of his countrymen have maintained) would be undeniable. In his *Krieg auf Wartburg*, a fingular monument of early (1207) improvifatorial fkill, the declaimers in the firft part are fix and in the fecond three Mafter or Minne-fingers. But this poem, like the *Tenfons* of the Troubadours, is a mere trial of poetical ingenuity, and bears a ftrong refemblance both in matter and manner to the *Torneyamens* of the fame writers. That it was not confidered a play in earlier

have been performed by the schoolboys of Angiers, according to annual custom, in the year 1392.[1] A royal carousal given by Charles V. of France to the emperor Charles IV. in the year 1378, was closed with the theatrical representation of the *Conquest of Jerusalem by Godfrey of Bulloign*, which was exhibited in the hall of the royal palace.[2] This indeed was a subject of a religious tendency; but not long afterwards, in the year 1395, perhaps before, the interesting story of *Patient Grisel* appears to have been acted at Paris. This piece still remains, and is entitled *Le Mystere de Grisildis marquise de Saluce*.[3] For all dramatic pieces were indiscriminately called *Mysteries*, whether a martyr or a heathen god, whether Saint Catharine or Hercules was the subject.

In France the religious *Mysteries*, often called *Piteaux*, or *Pitoux*, were certainly very fashionable and of high antiquity: yet from any written evidence I do not find them more ancient than those of the English. In the year 1384, the inhabitants of the village of Aunay, on the Sunday after the feast of Saint John, played the *Miracle* of Theophilus, "ou quel Jeu avoit un personnage de un qui devoit getter d'un canon."[4] In the year 1398, some citizens of Paris met

times, is clear from an illumination published by Docen, where the actors in this celebrated contest are represented seated and singing together, and above them is this decisive inscription: "Hie krieget mit sange, Herr walther von der vogilweide," &c. *Here bataileth in song*, &c. However, should this theory obtain, Solomon, bishop of Constance in the tenth century, will perhaps rank as the earliest dramatist at present known: Metro primus et coram Regibus plerumque pro ludicro *cum aliis certator*. Ekkehardus *de Casibus S. Galli*, p. 49.—Price.]

[1] The boys were *deguisiez*, says the old French record: and they had among them *un Fillette desguisée*. Carpent. *ubi supr.* v. *Robinet Pentecoste*. Our old character of *Mayd Marian* may be hence illustrated. It seems to have been an early fashion in France for schoolboys to present these shews or plays. In an ancient MS. under the year 1477, there is mentioned "Certaine MORALITE, ou FARÇE, que les escolliers de Pontoise avoit fait, *ainsi qu'il est de coustume*." Carpent. *ubi supr.* v. *Moralitas*. The *Mystery of the old and new Testament* is said to have been represented in 1424 by the boys of Paris placed like statues against a wall, without speech or motion, at the entry of the duke of Bedford, regent of France. See J. de Paris, p. 101. And Sauval, *Ant. de Paris*, ii. 101. [*Le Jeu de Robin et de Marion*, the piece alluded to in the text, has been analysed by M. le Grand in the second volume of his *Fabliaux et Contes*. It is there called *Le Jeu du Berger et de la Bergere*, and by him attributed to Adan de la Hale, nicknamed le Boçu d'Arras. In this he is followed by M. Meon, the editor of Barbazan's *Fabliaux*, who also ascribes to the same author a play called *Le Jeu du Mariage*. M. Roquefort catalogues *Robin et Marion* among the works of Jehan Bodel d'Arras, the author of three plays called *Le Jeu de Pelerin, Le Jeu d'Adam ou de la Feuillée, Le Jeu de St. Nicholas*; and a mystery called *Le Miracle de Theophile*. This latter may be the same referred to below. Adan de la Hale appears to have lived in the early part of the thirteenth century (Roquefort, p. 103), and Jehan Bodel during the reign of Saint Louis (1226-70). These perhaps are the earliest specimens extant of anything resembling dramatic composition in the French language.—Price.]

[2] Felib. tom. ii. p. 681. [The thirteenth century romance (on this subject) was published by M. Hippeau of Caen; Paris, 1868, 8vo.—F.]

[3] [Printed at Paris about 1550, 4to, 20 leaves. See Brunet, *dern.* edit. iii. 1968-9.]

[4] Carpentier, Suppl. Du' Cange, *Lat. Gl.* v. *Ludus*. [The story of a man who sold himself to the devil, and was redeemed by the virgin to whom he had recom-

at Saint Maur to play the *Paſſion of Chriſt*. The magiſtrates of Paris, alarmed at this novelty, publiſhed an ordonnance, prohibiting them to repreſent " aucuns jeux de perſonages ſoit de vie de ſaints ou autrement," without the royal licence, which was ſoon afterwards obtained.[1] In the year 1486, at Anjou, ten pounds were paid towards ſupporting the charges of acting the *Paſſion of Chriſt*, which was repreſented by maſks, and, as I ſuppoſe, by perſons hired for the purpoſe.[2] The chaplains of Abbeville, in the year 1455, gave four pounds and ten ſhillings to the players of the Paſſion;[3] [and at Angiers, about the ſame period, Jean Michel's very curious *miſtere de la paſſion ieſu Criſt* was performed; it was ſubſequently exhibited at Paris in 1507; and the old editions of it are tolerably numerous]. But the French *Myſteries* were chiefly performed by the religious communities, and ſome of their Fetes almoſt entirely conſiſted of a dramatic or perſonated ſhew. At the *Feaſt of Aſſes*, inſtituted in [commemoration of the Flight into Egypt,] the clergy walked on Chriſtmas-day in proceſſion, habited to repreſent the prophets and others. Moſes appeared in an alb and cope, with a long beard and rod. David had a green veſtment. Balaam with an immenſe pair of ſpurs, rode on a wooden aſs, which incloſed a ſpeaker. There were alſo ſix Jews and ſix Gentiles. Among other characters the poet Virgil was introduced as a gentile prophet and a tranſlator of the Sibylline oracles. They thus moved in proceſſion, chanting verſicles, and converſing in character on the nativity and kingdom of Chriſt, through the body of the church, till they came into the choir. Virgil ſpeaks ſome Latin hexameters during the ceremony, not out of his fourth eclogue, but wretched monkiſh lines in rhyme. This feaſt was, I believe, early ſuppreſſed. In the year 1445, Charles VII. of France ordered the maſters in theology at Paris to forbid the miniſters of the collegiate[4] churches to celebrate at Chriſtmas the

---

mended himſelf, occurs in a collection of miracles put in verſe by Guatier de Quenſi, a French poet of the thirteenth century, from whoſe work and others of the ſame kind an abridgment was printed at Paris in the beginning of the ſixteenth century. This was made by Jean le Comte, a friar minor. Quenſi's work is among the Harl. MSS. No. 4400.—*Douce*. It is alſo the legend of the *Knyght and his Wyfe* (*Rem. of the Early Pop. P. of Engl.* i. 16, *et ſeqq*. and Brunet, *ut ſupr*. 1979).]

[1] Beauchamps, *ut ſupr*. p. 90. This was the firſt theatre of the French: the actors were incorporated by the king, under the title of the *Fraternity of the Paſſion of our Saviour*. Beauch. *ibid*. See above, ſect. ii. The *Jeu de perſonages* was a very common play of the young boys in the larger towns, &c. Carpentier, *ut ſupr*. v. *Perſonagium*, and *Ludus Perſonag*. [But almoſt all the old French miracle-plays purport to have been *jeux de perſonnages*.] At Cambray mention is made of the ſhew of a boy *larvatus cum maza in collo* with drums, &c. Carpent. *ibid*. v. *Kalendæ Januar*.

[2] "Decem libr. ex parte nationis, ad onera ſupportanda hujus Miſterii." Carpent. *ut ſupr*. v. *Perſonagium*.

[3] [Brunet, *ut ſupr*. 1971.] Carpent. *ut ſupr*. v. *Ludus*. He adds, from an ancient Computus, that three ſhillings were paid by the miniſters of a church, in the year 1537, for parchment for writing *Ludus Reſurrectionis Domini*.

[4] Marten. *Anecd*. tom. i. col. 1804. See alſo Belet. *De Divin. Offic*. cap. 72. And Guſſanvill. *poſt. Not. ad Petr. Bleſens*. Felibien confounds *La Fete de Fous et la*

Feast of Fools in their churches, where the clergy danced in masques and antic dresses, and exhibited "plusieurs mocqueries spectacles publics, de leur corps deguisements, farces, rigmereis," with various enormities shocking to decency. In France as well as England it was customary to celebrate the feast of the boy-bishop. In all the collegiate churches of both nations, about the feast of St. Nicholas,[1] or the Holy Innocents, one of the children of the choir, completely apparelled in the episcopal vestments, with a mitre and crosier, bore the title and state of bishop, and exacted canonical obedience from his fellows, who were dressed like priests. They took possession of the church, and performed all the ceremonies and offices,[2] the mass excepted, which might have been celebrated by the bishop and his prebendaries.[3] In the statutes of the archiepiscopal cathedral of Tulles, given in the year 1497, it is said, that during the celebration of the festival of the boy-bishop, "Moralities were presented, and shews of Miracles, with farces and other sports, but compatible with

---

Fete de Sotise. The latter was an entertainment of dancing called *Les Saulties*, and thence corrupted into *Soties* or *Sotise.* See *Mem. Acad. Inscript.* xvii, 225, 226, and Probat. *Hist. Antissiodor.* p. 310. Again, the *Feast of Fools* seems to be pointed at in Statut. Senonens. A.D. 1445. Instr. tom. xii. *Gall. Christian.* Coll. 96. "Tempore divini servitii larvatos et monstruosos vultus deferendo, cum vestibus mulierum, aut lenonum, aut histrionum, choreas in ecclesia et choro ejus ducendo," &c. With the most immodest spectacles. The nuns of some French convents are said to have had *Ludibria* on Saint Mary Magdalene's and other festivals, when they wore the habits of seculars, and danced with them. Carpent. *ubi supr.* v. *Kalenda.* There was the office of the *Rex Stultorum* in Beverley church, prohibited 1391. Dugd. *Mon.* iii. Append. 7. [In the Constitutions of Robert Grossetefte, bishop of Lincoln, is the following prohibition : " Execrabilem etiam consuetudinem quæ consuevit in quibusdam ecclesiis observari de faciendo Festo Stultorum speciali authoritate rescripti Apostolici penitus inhibemus ; ne de domo orationis fiat domus ludibrii," &c. See Brown *Fascicul. rerum expetendarum*, ii. 412. And in his 32nd Letter, printed in the same collection, ii. 331, after reciting that the house of God is not to be turned into a house of buffoonery, &c. he adds : " Quapropter vobis mandamus in virtute obedientiæ firmiter injungentes, quatenus Festum Stultorum, cum sit vanitate plenum et voluptatibus spurcum, Deo odibile et dæmonibus amabile, de cætero in ecclesia Lincoln. die venerandæ solennitatis circumcisionis Domini nullatenus permittatis fieri."— *Douce.*]

[1] [This feast was probably celebrated on St. Nicholas's day, on account of his being the patron saint of children. See his legend, printed at Naples, 1645, 4to.— *Douce.* See also *Popular Antiquities of Great Britain*, by Hazlitt, i. 232-40.]

[2] In the statutes of Eton College, given 1441, the *Episcopus Puerorum* is ordered to perform divine service on Saint Nicholas's day. Rubr. xxxi. In the statutes of Winchester College, given 1380, *Pueri*, that is, the boy-bishop and his fellows, are permitted on Innocents'-day to execute all the sacred offices in the chapel, according to the use of the church of Sarum. Rubr. xxix. This strange piece of religious mockery flourished greatly in Salisbury cathedral. In the old statutes of that church there is a chapter De Episcopo Choristarum : and their Processionale gives a long and minute account of the whole ceremony, edit. 1555.

[3] This ceremony was abolished by a proclamation, no later than 33 Hen. VIII. MSS. Cott. Tit. B 1, f. 208. In the inventory of the treasury of York cathedral, taken in 1530, we have " Item una mitra parva cum petris pro episcopo puerorum," &c. Dugd. *Monast.* iii. 169, 170. See also 313, 314, 177, 279. See also Dugd. *Hist. S. Paul's*, pp. 205, 206, where he is called Episcopus Parvulorum. And Anstis *Ord. Gart.* ii. 309, where, instead of Nihilensis, read Nicolensis, or Nicolatensis.

decorum. After dinner they exhibited, without their mafks, but in proper dreffes, fuch farces as they were mafters of, in different parts of the city."[1] It is probable that the fame entertainments attended the folemnifation of this ridiculous feftival in England:[2] and from this fuppofition fome critics may be inclined to deduce the practice of our plays being acted by the choir-boys of St. Paul's church and the chapel royal, which continued, as I before obferved, till Cromwell's ufurpation. The Englifh and French ftages mutually throw light on each other's hiftory. But perhaps it will be thought, that in fome of thefe inftances I have exemplified in nothing more than farcical and gefticulatory reprefentations. Yet even thefe traces fhould be attended to. In the meantime we may obferve upon the whole, that the modern drama had no foundation in our religion, and that it was raifed and fupported by the clergy. The truth is, the members of the ecclefiaftical focieties were almoft the only perfons who could read, and their numbers eafily furnifhed performers: they abounded in leifure, and their very relaxations were religious.

I did not mean to touch upon the Italian ftage. But as fo able a judge as Riccoboni feems to allow that Italy derived her theatre from thofe of France and England, by way of an additional illuftration of the antiquity of the two laft, I will here produce one or two Miracle-Plays, acted much earlier in Italy than any piece mentioned by that ingenious writer or by Crefcimbeni. In the year 1298, on "the feaft of Pentecoft, and the two following holidays, the reprefentation of the *Play of Chrift*, that is, of his paffion, refurrection, afcenfion, judgment, and the miffion of the holy ghoft, was performed by the clergy of Civita Vecchia, 'in curia domini patriarchæ Auftriæ civitatis honorifice et laudabiliter.'"[3] And again, "In 1304, the chapter of Civita Vecchia exhibited a play of the creation

---

[1] *Statut. Eccles. Tullens.* apud Carpent. *Suppl. Lat. Gl. Du Cang.* v. *Kalendæ.*

[2] It appears that in England the boy-bifhop with his companions went about to different parts of the town; at leaft vifited the other religious houfes. As in *Rot. Comp. Coll. Winton.* A.D. 1461. "In Dat. epifcopo Nicolatenfi." This I fuppofe was one of the children of the choir of the neighbouring cathedral. In the ftatutes of the collegiate church of S. Mary Ottery, founded by Bifhop Grandifon in 1337, there is this paffage: "Item ftatuimus, quod nullus canonicus, vicarius, vel fecundarius, pueros choriftas in fefto fanctorum Innocentium extra Parochiam de Otery trahant, aut eis licentiam vagandi concedant."—cap. 50, *MS. Regiftr. Priorat. S. Swithin. Winton.* quat. 9. In the wardrobe-rolls of Edward III. an. 12, we have this entry, which fhews that our mock-bifhop and his chapter fometimes exceeded their adopted clerical commiffion, and exercifed the arts of fecular entertainment. "Epifcopo puerorum ecclefiæ de Andeworp cantanti coram domino rege in camera fua in fefto fanctorum Innocentium, de dono ipfius dom. regis. xiii *s.* vi *d.*"

[3] *Chron. Forojul.* in Append. ad *Monum. Eccl. Aquilej.* p. 30, col. 1. [An earlier record of the exhibition of thefe miracle-plays in Italy will be found in the *Catalogo de' Podefte di Padova:* "In queft anno (1243) fu fatta la rapprefentazion della Paffione e Refurreccione di Chrifto nel Pra della Valle." Muratori, *Script. Rer. Ital* v. 8, p. 365.—The chief object of the Compagna del Confalone inftituted at Rome in the year 1264, was to reprefent the Myfteries, "della Paffione del Redentore." Tirabofchi, vol. iv. p. 343.—*Price.*]

of our firſt parents, the annunciation of the Virgin Mary, the birth of Chriſt, and other paſſages of ſacred ſcripture." [1] In the mean time, thoſe critics, who contend for the high antiquity of the Italian ſtage, may adopt theſe inſtances as new proofs in defence of that hypotheſis.

This ſhow of the BOY-BISHOP, not ſo much for its ſuperſtition as its levity and abſurdity, had been formerly abrogated by King Henry VIII. fourteen years before, in the year 1542, as appears by a "Proclamation deuiſed by the Kings Maieſty by the advys of his Highneſs Counſel the xxii day of Julie, 33 Hen. viij, commanding the Feaſts of ſaint Luke, ſaint Mark, ſaint Marie Magdalene, Inuention of the Croſſe, and ſaint Laurence, which had been abrogated, ſhould be nowe againe celebrated and kept holie days," of which the following is the concluding clauſe. "And where as heretofore dyuers and many ſuperſtitious and chyldyſh obſeruances have be vſed, and yet to this day are obſerued and kept, in many and ſundry partes of this realm, as vpon ſaint Nicholas,[2] ſaint Catharine,[3] ſaint Clement,[4] the holie Innocents, and ſuch like,[5] Children [boys]

---

[1] *Ibid.* p. 30, col. 1. It is extraordinary that the Miracle-plays, even in the churches, ſhould not ceaſe in Italy till the year 1660.

[2] In Barnaby Googe's *Popiſh Kingdom*, 1570, a tranſlation from Naogeorgus's *Regnum Antichriſti*, fol. 55 :—
"Saint Nicholas monie vſde to give to maydens ſecretlie,
Who that be ſtill may vſe his wonted liberalitie:
The mother all their children on the Eeve do cauſe to faſt,
And when they euerie one at night in ſenſeleſſe ſleepe are caſt,
Both apples, nuts and payres they bring, and other thinges beſide,
As cappes, and ſhoes, and petticoates, wich ſecretly they hide,
And in the morning found, they ſay, that 'this Saint Nicholas brought,'" &c.

I have already given traces of this practice in the colleges of Wincheſter and Eton. To which I here add another. *Regiſtr. Coll. Wint. ſub ann.* 1427. "Crux deaurata de cupro [copper] cum Baculo, pro Epiſcopo puerorum." But it appears that the practice ſubſiſted in common grammar-ſchools. "Hoc anno, 1464, in feſto ſancti Nicolai non erat Epiſcopus Puerorum in ſchola grammaticali in civitate Cantuariæ ex defectu Magiſtrorum, viz. J. Sidney et T. Hikſon," &c. *Lib. Johannis Stone, Monachi Eccles. Cant. ſc. De Obitibus et aliis Memorabilibus ſui cœnobii ab anno* 1415, *ad annum* 1467. MS. C.C.C.Q. 8. The abuſes of this cuſtom in Wells Cathedral are mentioned ſo early as Decemb. 1. 1298. *Regiſtr. Eccl. Wellens.*

[3] The reader will recollect the old play of Saint Catharine, *Ludus Catharinæ*, exhibited at Saint Albans Abbey in 1160. Strype ſays, in 1556, "On Saint Katharines day, at ſix of the clock at night, S. Katharine went about the battlements of S. Paul's church accompanied with fine ſinging and great lights. This was ſaint Katharine's Proceſſion." *Eccl. Mem.* iii. 309. ch. xxxix. Again, her proceſſion in 1553 is celebrated with five hundred great lights, round Saint Paul's ſteeple, &c. *Ibid.* p. 51. ch. v. And p. 57. ch. v.

[4] Among the church-proceſſions revived by Queen Mary, that of S. Clement's church, in honour of this ſaint, was by far the moſt ſplendid of any in London. Their proceſſion to Saint Paul's in 1557 "was made very pompous with fourſcore banners and ſtreamers, and the waits of the city playing, and threeſcore prieſts and clarkes in copes. And divers of the Inns of Court were there, who went next the prieſts," &c. Strype, *ubi ſupr.* iii. 337, ch. xlix.

[5] In the Synodus Carnotenſis, under the year 1526, it is ordered, "In feſto ſancti Nicholai, Catharinæ, Innocentium, aut alio quovis die, prætextu recreationis, ne Scholaſtici, Clerici, Sacerdoteſve, ſtultum aliquod aut ridiculum faciant in

be ſtrangelie decked and apparayled, to counterfeit Prieſts, Biſshopes, and Women, and ſo be ledde with Songes and Dances from houſe to houſe, bleſſing the people, and gathering of money; and Boyes do ſinge maſſe, and preache in the pulpitt, with ſuch other vnfittinge and inconuenient vſages, rather to the deryſyon than anie true glorie of God, or honor of his ſayntes: The Kynges maieſtie therefore, myndinge nothing ſo moche as to aduance the true glory of God without vain ſuperſtition, wylleth and commandeth, that from henceforth all ſvch ſvperſtitious obſeruations be left and clerely extinguiſhed throwout all this his realme and dominions, for-as moche as the ſame doth reſemble rather the vnlawfull ſuperſtition of gentilitie, than the pvre and ſincere religion of Chriſte." With reſpect to the diſguiſings of theſe young fraternities, and their proceſſions from houſe to houſe with ſinging and dancing, ſpecified in this edict, in a very mutilated fragment of a Computus, or annual Accompt-roll, of Saint Swithin's Cathedral Priory at Wincheſter, under the year 1441, a diſburſement is made to the ſinging-boys of the monaſtery, who, together with the choriſters of Saint Elizabeth's collegiate chapel near that city, were dreſſed up like girls, and exhibited their ſports before the abbeſs and nuns of Saint Mary's Abbey at Wincheſter, in the public refectory of that convent, on Innocents' day.[1] " Pro Pueris Eleemoſynariæ una cum Pueris Capellæ ſanctæ Elizabethæ, ornatis more puellarum, et ſaltantibus, cantantibus, et ludentibus, coram domina Abbatiſſa et monialibus beatæ Mariæ virginis, in aula ibidem in die ſanctorum Innocentium."[2] Again, in a fragment of an Accompt of the Cellarer of Hyde Abbey at Win-

---

eccleſia. Denique ab eccleſia ejiciantur veſtes fatuorum perſonas ſcenicas agentium." See Bochellus, *Decret. Eccles. Gall.* lib. iv. Tit. vii. C. 43. 44. 46. p. 586. Yet theſe ſports ſeem to have remained in France ſo late as 1585. For in the Synod of Aix, 1585, it is enjoined, " Ceſſent in die Sanctorum Innocentium ludibria omnia et pueriles ac theatrales luſus." Bochell, *ibid.* C. 45. p. 586. A Synod of Tholouſe, an. 1590, removes plays, ſpectacles, and *hiſtrionum circulationes* from churches and their cemeteries. Bochell, *ibid.* lib. iv. tit. 1. c. 98, p. 560.

[1] In the Regiſter of Wodeloke Biſhop of Wincheſter, the following is an article among the injunctions given to the nuns of the convent of Rumſey in Hampſhire, in conſequence of an epiſcopal viſitation, under the year 1310. "Item prohibemus, ne cubent in dormitorio pueri maſculi cum monialibus, vel foemellæ, nec per moniales ducantur in Chorum, dum ibidem divinum officium celebratur." fol. 134. In the ſame regiſter theſe injunctions follow in a literal French tranſlation, made for the convenience of the nuns.

[2] *MS. in Archiv. Wulves, apud Winton.* It appears to have been a practice for itinerant players to gain admittance into the nunneries, and to play Latin myſteries before the nuns. There is a curious canon of the council of Cologne, in 1549, which is to this effect. "We have been informed that certain Actors of Comedies, not content with the ſtage and theatres, have even entertained the nunneries, in order to recreate the nuns, *ubi virginibus commoveant voluptatem*, with their profane, amorous, and *ſecular* geſticulations. Which ſpectacles or plays, although they conſiſted of ſacred and pious ſubjects, can yet notwithſtanding leave little good, but on the contrary much harm, in the minds of the nuns, who behold and admire the outward geſtures of the performers, and underſtand not the words. Therefore we decree, that henceforward no plays, *Comediae*, ſhall be admitted into the convents of nuns," &c. *Sur. Concil.* tom. iv. p. 852. Binius, tom. iv. p. 765.

chester, under the year 1490. "In larvis et aliis indumentis Puerorum visentium Dominum apud Wulsey, et Constabularium Castri Winton, in apparatu suo, necnon subintrantium omnia monasteria civitatis Winton, in Festo sancti Nicholai."[1] That is, "In furnishing masks and dresses for the boys of the convent, when they visited the bishop at Wulvesey-palace, the constable of Winchester-castle, and all the monasteries of the city of Winchester, on the festival of saint Nicholas." As to the divine service being performed by children on these feasts, it was not only celebrated by boys, but there is an injunction given to the Benedictine nunnery of Godstowe in Oxfordshire by Archbishop Peckham, in the year 1278, that on Innocents' day, the public prayers should not any more be said in the church of that monastery per parvulas, that is, by little girls.[2]

The ground-work of this religious mockery of the boy-bishop, which is evidently founded on modes of barbarous life, may perhaps be traced backward at least as far as the year 867.[3] At the Constantinopolitan synod under that year, at which were present three hundred and seventy-three bishops, it was found to be a solemn custom in the courts of princes, on certain stated days, to dress some layman in the episcopal apparel, who should exactly personate a bishop both in his tonsure and ornaments: as also to create a burlesque patriarch, who might make sport for the company.[4] This scandal to the clergy was anathematized. But ecclesiastical synods and censures have often proved too weak to suppress popular spectacles, which take deep root in the public manners, and are only concealed for a while, to spring up afresh with new vigour.

After the form of a legitimate stage had appeared in England, mysteries and miracles were also revived by Queen Mary, as an appendage of the papistic worship:

En, iterum crudelia retro
Fata vocant![5]

In the year 1556 a goodly stage-play of the *Passion of Christ* was

---

[1] MS. *Ibid.* See *supr*.

[2] Harpsfield, *Hist. Eccl. Angl.* p. 441, edit. 1622.

[3] Or, 870. [See Mr. Strutt's *Sports and Pastimes of the People of England.—Price.*]

[A tract explaining the origin and ceremonial of the Boy-bishop was printed [by John Gregory] in 1649 with the following title: "*Episcopus puerorum in die Innocentium;* or a Discoverie of an ancient Custom in the church of Sarum, making an anniversarie Bishop among the Choristers." This tract was written in explanation of a stone monument still remaining in Salisbury Cathedral, representing a little boy habited in episcopal robes, with a mitre upon his head, a crosier in his hand, &c. and the explanation was derived from a chapter in the ancient statutes of that church entitled *De Episcopo Choristarum*. See a long account of the *Boy Bishop*, in Hawkins's *History of Music*, vol. ii.—*Park*. See *Handb. of E. E. Lit.* art. *Episcopus Puerorum.*]

[4] Surius, *Concil.* iii. 529. 539. Baron. *Annal.* Ann. 869. § 11. See *Concil.* Basil. num. xxxii. The French have a miracle play, *Beau Miracle de S. Nicolas,* to be acted by twenty-four personages, printed at Paris, for Pierre Sergeant, in quarto, without date, Bl. lett. [Compare Brunet, iii. 1742-3.]

[5] Virgil, *Georg.* iv. 495.

presented at the Grey-Friars in London, on Corpus-Christi day, before the lord mayor, the privy-council, and many great estates of the realm.[1] Strype also mentions, under the year 1557, a stage-play at the Grey-Friars, of the *Passion of Christ*, on the day that war was proclaimed in London against France, and in honour of that occasion.[2] On Saint Olave's day in the same year, the holiday of the church in Silver-street which is dedicated to that saint, was kept with much solemnity. At eight of the clock at night began a stage-play of goodly matter, being the miraculous history of the life of that saint,[3] which continued four hours, and was concluded with many religious songs.[4]

Many curious circumstances of the nature of these miracle-plays appear in a roll of the churchwardens of Bassingborne in Cambridgeshire, which is an account of the expenses and receptions for acting the play of *Saint George* at Bassingborne, on the feast of Saint Margaret in the year 1511. They collected upwards of four pounds in twenty-seven neighbouring parishes for furnishing the play. They disbursed about two pounds in the representation. These disbursements are to four minstrels, or waits, of Cambridge for three days, v s. vj d. To the players, in bread and ale, iij s. ij d. To the garnement-man for garnements, and propyrts,[5] that is, for dresses, decorations, and implements, and for play-books, xx s. To John Hobard, brotherhoode preeste, that is, a priest of the guild in the church, for the play-book, ij s. viij d. For the crofte, or field in which the play was exhibited, j s. For propyrte-making, or furniture, j s. iv d. "For fish and bread, and to setting up the stages, iv d." For painting three fanchoms and four tormentors, words which I do not understand, but perhaps phantoms and devils. . . . The rest was expended for a feast on the occasion, in which are recited, "Four chicken for the gentilmen, iv d." It appears from the *Coventry Plays* that a temporary scaffold only was erected for these performances; and Chaucer says of Absolon, a parish-clerk,

---

[1] MSS. Cotr. Vitell. E. 5. Strype. See *Life of Sir Thomas Pope*, Pref. p. xii.
[2] Eccl. Mem. vol. iii. ch. xlix.
[3] Strype, *ibid.* p. 379. With the religious pageantries, other ancient sports and spectacles also, which had fallen into disuse in the reign of Edward VI., began to be now revived. As thus, "On the 30th of May was a goodly May-game in Fenchurch-street, with drums, and guns, and pikes, with the Nine Worthies who rid. And each made his speech. There was also the morice-dance, and an elephant and castle, and the lord and lady of the May appeared to make up this show." Strype, *ibid.* 376, ch. xlix.
[4] Ludovicus Vives relates that it was customary in Brabant to present annual plays in honour of the respective saints to which the churches were dedicated; and he betrays his great credulity in adding a wonderful story in consequence of this custom. *Not. in Augustin. De Civit. Dei*, lib. xii. cap. 25, C.
[5] The property-room is yet known at our theatres. ["Malone (Shakespeare by Boswell, iii. 25), following Warton, has remarked upon the use of the word *properties* in the reign of Henry VIII., but we here (in the *Castle of Perseverance*) find it employed, and in the same sense of furniture, apparel, &c., a century earlier."—Collier.]

and an actor of King Herod's character in thefe dramas, in the *Miller's Tale:*

> And for to fhew his lightneffe and maiftry
> He playith Herawdes on a fcaffald hie.[1]

Scenical decorations and machinery[2] which employed the genius and invention of Inigo Jones, in the reigns of the firft James and Charles, feem to have migrated from the mafques at court to the public theatre. In the inftrument here cited, the prieft who wrote the play, and received only two fhillings and eight pence for his labour, feems to have been worfe paid in proportion than any of the other perfons concerned. The learned Oporinus, in 1547, publifhed in two volumes a collection of religious interludes, which abounded in Germany. They are in Latin, and not taken from legends, but from the Bible.

The Puritans were highly offended at thefe religious plays now revived.[3] But they were hardly lefs averfe to the theatrical repre-

---

[1] *Mill. T.* v. 275. Mr. Steevens and Mr. Malone have fhown that the accommodations in our early regular theatres were but little better. That the old fcenery was very fimple, may partly be collected from an entry in a Computus of Winchefter College, under the year 1579, viz. *Comp. Burs. Coll. Winton.* A. D. 1573. Eliz. xvº.—"Cuftos Aulæ. Item, pro diverfis expenfis circa Scaffoldam erigendam et deponendam, et pro Domunculis de novo compofitis cum carriagio et recarriagio *ly joyftes*, et aliorum mutuatorum ad eandem Scaffoldam, cum vj *linckes* et jº [uno] duodeno candelarum, pro lumine expenfis, tribus noctibus in Ludis comediarum et tragediarum, xxv s. viij d." Again in the next quarter, " Pro vij *ly linckes* deliberatis pueris per M. Informatorem [the fchoolmafter] pro Ludis, iij s." Again, in the laft quarter, " Pro removendis Organis e templo in Aulam et præparandis eifdem erga Ludos, v s." By Domunculis I underftand little cells of board, raifed on each fide of the ftage, for dreffing-rooms, or retiring places. Strype, under the year 1559, fays that after a grand feaft at Guildhall, " the fame day was a fcaffold fet up in the hall for a play." *Ann. Ref.* i. 197, edit. 1725.

[2] [Dr. Afhby fuggefts that fome diftinction fhould perhaps be made between fcenery and machinery; and it may probably be ceded that fcenic decoration was firft introduced.—*Park.*]

[3] A very late fcripture-play is *The Hiftory of Jacob and Efau*, 1568. But this play had appeared in Queen Mary's reign, " An enterlude vpon the hiftory of Jacobe and Efawe," &c. Licenfed to Henry Sutton in 1557. *Regiftr. Station.* A. fol. 23, a. It is certain, however, that the fafhion of religious interludes was not entirely difcontinued in the reign of Queen Elizabeth; for I find licenfed to T. Hackett, in 1561, " A newe enterlude of the ij fynnes of Kynge Dauyde." *Ibid.* fol. 75, a. [For other pieces of the fame nature, fee *Handb. of E. E. Lit.* 1867, arts. *Plays, Wager,* &c. The "enterlude of the fynnes of Kynge Dauyde" is not known, unlefs it was the *ballad* reprinted by Chappell (*Roxburghe Ballads,* vol. i. part ii.)] Ballads on Scripture fubjects are now innumerable. Peele's *David and* [*Bethfabe*] is a remain of the fafhion of Scripture-plays. I have mentioned the play of *Holofernes* acted at Hatfield in 1556. *Life of Sir Thomas Pope,* p. 87. In 1556 was printed " A ballet intituled the hiftorye of Judith and Holyfernes." *Regiftr.* ut fupr. fol. 154, b. And Regiftr. B. fol. 227. In Hearne's *Manufcript Collectanea* there is a licence, dated 1571, from the queen, directed to the officers of Middlefex, permitting one John Swinton Powlter, " to have and ufe fome playes and games at or uppon nine feverall fondaies," within the faid county. "And becaufe greate reforte of people is lyke to come thereunto, he is required, for the prefervation of the peace and for the fake of good order, to take with him four or five difcreet and fubftantial men of thofe places where the games fhall be put in practice, to fuperintend duringe the contynuance of the games or playes." Some of

fentation of the Chriſtian than of the Gentile ſtory: yet for different reaſons. To hate a theatre was a part of their creed, and therefore plays were an improper vehicle of religion. The heathen fables they judged to be dangerous, as too nearly reſembling the ſuperſtitions of popery.[1]

In this tranſient view of the origin and progreſs of our drama, which was incidentally ſuggeſted by the mention of Baſton's ſuppoſed comedies, I have treſpaſſed upon future periods. But I have chiefly done this for the ſake of connection, and to prepare the mind of the reader for other anecdotes of the hiſtory of our ſtage, which will occur in the courſe of our reſearches, and are reſerved for their reſpective places. I could have enlarged what is here looſely thrown together, with many other remarks and illuſtrations: but I was unwilling to tranſcribe from the collections of thoſe who have already treated this ſubject with great comprehenſion and penetration, and eſpecially from the author of the Supplement to the Tranſlator's Preface of Jarvis's *Don Quixote*.[2] I claim no other merit from this digreſſion, than that of having collected ſome new anecdotes relating to the early ſtate of the Engliſh and French ſtages, the original of both which is intimately connected, from books and manuſcripts not eaſily found, nor often examined. Theſe hints may perhaps prove of ſome ſervice to thoſe who have leiſure and inclination to examine the ſubject with more preciſion.

SECTION VII.

DWARD III. was an illuſtrious example and patron of chivalry. His court was the theatre of romantic elegance. I have examined the annual rolls of his wardrobe, which record various articles of coſtly ſtuffs delivered occaſionally for the celebration of his tournaments; ſuch as ſtandards, pennons, tunics, capariſons, with other ſplendid furniture of the ſame ſort: and it appears that he commanded theſe ſolemnities to be kept, with a magnificence ſuperior to that of former ages, at Lichfield, Bury, Guilford, Eltham, Canterbury, and twice at Windſor, in little more than the ſpace of one year.[3] At his tri-

---

the exhibitions are then ſpecified, ſuch as "Shotinge with the brode arrowe, The lepping for men, The pitchynge of the barre," and the like. But then follows this very general clauſe, "With all ſuche other games, as haue at anye time heretofore or now be lycenſed, uſed, or played." *Coll. MSS. Hearne*, tom. lxi. p. 78. One wiſhes to know whether any interludes, and whether religious or profane, were included in this inſtrument.

[1] [Oppoſite ſects, as Romaniſts and Proteſtants, often adopt each other's arguments. See Bayle's *Dict.*—*Aſhby*.]

[2] [This ſubject is reſumed in Sect. 34.]

[3] *Comp. J. Cooke, Proviſoris Magn. Garderob.* ab ann. 21 Edw. III. ad ann. 23, *ſupr. citat.* I will give, as a ſpecimen, this officer's accompt for the tournament

umphant return from Scotland, he was met by two hundred and thirty knights at Dunstable, who received their victorious monarch with a grand exhibition of these martial exercises. He established in the castle of Windsor a fraternity of twenty-four knights, for whom he erected a round table, with a round chamber still remaining, according to a similar institution of King Arthur.[1] Anstis treats the notion, that Edward in this establishment had any retrospect to King Arthur, as an idle and legendary tradition.[2] But the fame of Arthur was still kept alive, and continued to be an object of veneration long afterwards: and however idle and ridiculous the fables of the round table may appear at present, they were then not only universally known, but firmly believed. Nothing could be more natural to such a romantic monarch, in such an age, than the renovation of this most ancient and revered institution of chivalry. It was a prelude to the renowned order of the garter, which he soon afterwards founded at Windsor, during the ceremonies of a magnificent feast, which had been proclaimed by his heralds in Germany, France, Scotland, Burgundy, Hainault, and Brabant, and lasted fifteen days.[3] We must not try the modes and notions of other ages, even if they have arrived to some degree of refinement, by those of our own. Nothing is more probable, than that this latter foundation of Edward III. took its rise from the exploded story of the garter of the Countess of Salisbury.[4] Such an origin is interwoven with the manners and ideas of the times.

---

at Canterbury. " Et ad faciendum diversos apparatus pro corpore regis et suorum pro hastiludio Cantuariensi, an. reg. xxii. ubi Rex dedit octo hernesia de syndone ynde facta, et vapulata de armis dom. Stephani de Cosyngton militis, dominis principibus comiti Lancastriæ, comiti Suffolciæ, Johanni de Gray, Joh. de Beauchamp, Roberto Maule, Joh. Chandos, et dom. Rogero de Beauchamp. Et ad faciendum unum harnesium de bokeram albo pro rege, extencellato cum argento, viz. tunicam et scutum operata cum dictamine Regis,

' Hay Hay the wythe swan
By Godes soule I am thy man.'

Et croparium, pectorale, testarium, et arcenarium extencellata cum argento. Et ad parandum i. tunicam Regis, et i. clocam et capuciam cum c. garteris paratis cum boucles, barris, et pendentibus de argento. Et ad faciendum unum dublettum pro Rege de tela linea habente, circa manicas et fimbriam, unam borduram de panno longo viridi operatam cum nebulis et vineis de auro, et cum dictamine Regis, *It is as it is.*" Membr. xi. [A.D. 1349.]

[1] Walsing. p. 117.   [2] *Ord. Gart.* ii. 92.
[3] Barnes, i. ch. 22, p. 292. Froissart, c. 100. Anstis, *ut supr.*
[4] Ashmole proves, that the orders of the Annunciada, and of the Toison d'Or, had the like origin. *Ord. Gart.* pp. 180, 181. Even in the ensigns of the order of the Holy Ghost, founded so late as 1578, some love-mysteries and emblems were concealed under ciphers introduced into the blasonry. See Le Laboureur, *Contin. des Mem. de Castelnau,* p. 895. "Il y eut plus de mysteres d'amourettes que de religion," &c. But I cannot in this place help observing, that the fantastic humour of unriddling emblematical mysteries, supposed to be concealed under all ensigns and arms, was at length carried to such an extravagance, at least in England, as to be checked by the legislature. By a statute of Queen Elizabeth, a severe penalty is laid, "on all fond phantastical prophecies upon or by the occasion of any arms, fields, beastes, badges, or the like things accustomed in arms, cognisaunces, or signetts," &c. *Statut.* c. Eliz. ch. 15, A.D. 1564.

Their attention to the fair sex entered into every thing. It is by no means unreasonable to suppose, that the fantastic Collar of SS., worn by the knights of this Order, was an allusion to her name. Froissart, an eye-witness, and well acquainted with the intrigues of the court, relates at large the king's affection for the countess, and particularly describes a grand carousal which he gave in consequence of that attachment.[1] The first festival of this order was not only adorned by the bravest champions of Christendom, but by the presence of Queen Philippa, Edward's consort, accompanied by three hundred ladies of noble families.[2] The tournaments of this stately reign were constantly crowded with ladies of the first distinction, who sometimes attended them on horseback, armed with daggers, and dressed in a succinct soldier-like habit or uniform prepared for the purpose.[3] In a tournament exhibited at London, sixty ladies on palfries appeared, each leading a knight with a gold chain. In this manner they paraded from the Tower to Smithfield.[4] Even Philippa, a queen of singular elegance of manners,[5] partook so much of the heroic spirit which was universally diffused, that just before an engagement with the king of Scotland, she rode round the ranks of the English army encouraging the soldiers, and was with some difficulty persuaded or compelled to relinquish the field.[6] The Countess of Montfort is another eminent instance of female heroism in this age. When the strong town of Hennebond, near Rennes, was besieged by the French, this redoubted amazon rode in complete armour from street to street on a large courser, animating the garrison.[7] Finding from a high tower that the

---

[1] *Ubi supr.* [In *Notes and Queries,* from time to time, a good deal of information has been printed on this subject. See General Indices.]

[2] They soon afterwards regularly received robes, with the knights companions, for this ceremony, powdered with garters. Ashmol. *Ord. Gart.* 217, 594. And Anstis, ii. 123.

[3] Knyghton, *Dec. Script.* p. 2597.

[4] Froissart *apud.* Stow's *Surv. Lond.* p. 718, edit. 1616. At an earlier period, the growing gallantry of the times appears in a public instrument. It is in the reign of Edward I. Twelve jurymen depose upon oath the state of the king's lordship at Woodstock: and among other things it is solemnly recited, that Henry II. often resided at Woodstock, "pro amore cujusdam mulieris nomine Rosamunda." Hearne's *Avesbury,* Append. 331.

[5] And of distinguished beauty. Hearne says, that the statuaries of those days used to make Queen Philippa a model for their images of the Virgin Mary. *Gloss. Rob.* [*de*] *Brun.* p. 349. He adds, that the holy virgin, in a representation of her assumption was constantly figured young and beautiful; and that the artists before the Reformation generally "had the most beautiful women of the greatest quality in their view, when they made statues and figures of her." *Ibid.* p. 550.

[6] Froissart, i. c. 138.

[7] Froissart says, that when the English proved victorious, the countess came out of the castle, and in the street kissed Sir Walter Manny the English general, and his captains, one after another, twice or thrice, *comme noble et valliant dame.* On another like occasion, the same historian relates, that she went out to meet the officers, whom she kissed and sumptuously entertained in her castle, i. c. 86. At many magnificent tournaments in France, the ladies determined the prize. See *Mem. anc. Cheval,* i. p. 175, *seq.* p. 223, *seq.* An English squire, on the side of the French, captain of the castle of Beaufort, called himself *le Poursuivant d' amour,* in 1369. Froissart, l. i. c. 64. In the midst of grand engagements between the French and English armies,

whole French army was engaged in the assault, she issued, thus completely accoutred, through a convenient postern at the head of three hundred chosen soldiers, and set fire to the French camp.¹ In the mean time riches and plenty, the effects of conquest, peace and prosperity, were spread on every side; and new luxuries were imported in great abundance from the conquered countries. There were few families, even of a moderate condition, but had in their possession precious articles of dress or furniture: such as silks, fur, tapestry, embroidered beds, cups of gold, silver, porcelain and crystal, bracelets, chains, and necklaces, brought from Caen, Calais, and other opulent foreign cities.² The increase of rich furniture appears in a foregoing reign. In an act of Parliament of Edward I.³ are many regulations, directed to goldsmiths, not only in London, but in other towns, concerning the sterling alloy of vessels and jewels of gold and silver, &c.; and it is said, " Gravers or cutters of stones and seals shall give every one their just weight of silver and gold." It should be remembered, that about this period Europe had opened a new commercial intercourse with the ports of India.⁴ No fewer than eight sumptuary laws, which had the usual effect of not being observed, were enacted in one session of parliament during this reign.⁵ Amid these growing elegances and superfluities, foreign manners, especially of the French, were perpetually increasing; and the native simplicity of the English people was perceptibly corrupted and effaced. It is not quite uncertain that masques had their beginning in this reign. These shews, in which the greatest personages of the court often bore a part, and which arrived at their height in the reign of Henry VIII., encouraged the arts of address and decorum, and are symptoms of the rise of polished manners.⁶

In a reign like this, we shall not be surprised to find such a poet as Chaucer, with whom a new era in English poetry begins, and on whose account many of these circumstances are mentioned, as they serve to prepare the reader for his character, on which they throw no inconsiderable light.

But before we enter on so ample a field, it will be perhaps less embarrassing, at least more consistent with our prescribed method,

---

when perhaps the interests of both nations are vitally concerned, Froissart gives many instances of officers entering into separate and personal combat to dispute the beauty of their respective mistresses. *Hist.* l. ii. ch. 33, 43. On this occasion an ingenious French writer observes, that Homer's heroes of ancient Greece are just as extravagant: who, in the heat of the fight, often stop on a sudden, to give an account of the genealogy of themselves or their horses. *Mem. anc. Cheval.* ubi supr. Sir Walter Manny, in 1343, in attacking the castle of Guigard, exclaims, "Let me never be beloved of my mistress, if I refuse this attack," &c. Froissart, i. 81.

¹ Froissart, i. c. 80. Du Chesne, p. 656. Mezeray, ii. 3, p. 19, *seq.*
² Walsing. *Ypodigm.* 121, *Hist.* 159. ³ A.D. 1300, Edw. I. *an.* 28, cap. xx.
⁴ Anderson, *Hist. Comm.* i. p. 141. ⁵ *Ann.* 37 Edw. III. cap. viii. *seq.*
⁶ This spirit of splendour and gallantry was continued in the reign of his successor. See the genius of that reign admirably characterized, and by the hand of a master, in Bishop Lowth's *Life of Wykeham*, p. 222. See also Holinsh. *Chron.* sub ann. 1399, p. 508, col. 1.

if we previously display the merits of two or three poets, who appeared in the former part of the reign of Edward III., with other incidental matters.

The first of these is Richard [Rolle, of] Hampole, [near Doncaster, commonly called Richard Hampole, who is said to have been a hermit] of the Order of Saint Augustine. He was a doctor of divinity, and lived a solitary life near the nuns of Hampole, four miles from Doncaster in Yorkshire.[1] The neighbourhood of this female society could not withdraw our recluse from his devotions and his studies. He [died] in the year 1349.[2] His Latin theological tracts, both in prose and verse, in which Leland justly thinks he has displayed more erudition than eloquence, are numerous. His principal pieces of English rhyme are a *Paraphrase of part of the Book of Job*, of the *Lord's Prayer*, and of the *seven penitential Psalms*, and the *Pricke of Conscience*. But our hermit's poetry, which indeed from these titles promises but little entertainment, has no tincture of sentiment, imagination, or elegance. The following verses are extracted from the *Pricke of Conscience*, one of the most common manuscripts in our libraries, and I prophesy that I am its last transcriber.[3] But I must observe first that this piece is divided into seven parts. I. Of man's nature. II. Of the world. III. Of death. IV. Of purgatory. V. Of the day of judgment. VI. Of the torments of hell. VII. Of the joys of heaven.[4]

---

[1] Wharton, App. ad Cave, p. 75. *Sæcul. Wickley.*

[2] [Of the Black Death of 1348, no doubt.—F. The fact of not finding MSS. older than the fourteenth century would seem to show that Hampole compiled the *Pricke of Conscience* but a few years before his death (A.D. 1349).—*Morris.*]

[3] [*The Pricke of Conscience*, notwithstanding Warton's prediction to the contrary, has been edited by Richard Morris, 1863, 8vo., his text being chiefly taken from Cotton. MS. Galba, E. ix.; an imperfect copy of the poem in Canterbury cathedral library exhibits, I am informed by Mr. Furnivall, dialectic changes, as *ho* for *wha*, *to* for *till*, *schal* for *sal*, &c. The ensuing extracts are from edit. Morris, pp. 11-12. In the *Archæologia*, vol. xix. pp. 314-335, 4to. 1821, is a long analysis of Hampole's poem, by Mr. J. B. Yates, illustrated by extracts; in which the writer advocates with very doubtful success the poetical talent of the recluse against the opinion of Warton. But it is somewhat remarkable, that previous to the publication of Mr. Yates's paper, a pamphlet of limited circulation (only fifty copies having been printed), written by W. J. Walter, appeared, 8vo. London, 1816, pp. 17, under the title of *An Account of a MS. of ancient English Poetry, entitled Clavis Scientiæ, or Bretayne's Skyll-kay of Knawing, by John de Dageby, monk of Fountains Abbey.* This MS. in reality, is only one of the numerous copies existing of Hampole's *Pricke of Conscience*, somewhat altered and abbreviated, with some lines added at the conclusion by the scribe John de Dageby, whose name appears in the colophon. Mr. Walter gives a copious analysis of the work; and, like his successor Mr. Yates, is inclined to place the author much higher in the scale of poets than Warton's critique would justify.—*Madden.* The MS. was subsequently sold to the British Museum.]

[4] Stimulus Conscientiæ *thys boke ys namyd.* MS. Ashmol. fol. No. 41. There is much transposition in this copy. In MS. Digb. Bodl. 87, it is called *The Key of knowing.* Princ.

" The miȝt of the fader admiti
The wisdom of the sone al witti."

[Mr. Corser's MS. adds an eighth part of the state of the world after doomsday; it

Here bygynnes the firſt part
That es of mans wrechednes.
Firſt whan God made al thyng of noght,
Of the fouleſt matere man he wroght
That was of erthe; for twa ſkyls to halde;
The tane es forthy that God walde
Of foul matere, mak man in deſpite
Of Lucifer that fel als tyte
Til helle, als he had ſynned thurgh pryde,
And of alle that with him fel that tyde;
For thai ſuld have than the mare ſhenſhepe,
And the mare ſorow when thai tuk kepe,
That men of ſwa foul matere ſuld duelle
In that place fra whilk thai felle.
The ather ſkille es this to ſe;
For man ſuld here the meker he
Ay, when he ſeſe and thynkes in thoght,
Of how foul mater he is wroght;
For God, thurgh his gudnes and his myght,
Wold, that then that place in heven bright
Was made voyde thurgh the ſyn of pryde,
It war filled ogayne on ilka ſyde
Thurgh the vertu of mekenes,
That euen contrary til pride es;
Than may na man thider come
Bot he that meke es, and boghſome;
That proves the goſpelle that ſays us,
How God ſayd till his diſciples thus :

Niſi efficiamini ſicut parvulus, non intrabitis in regnum celorum.

Bot yhe, he ſayde, be als a childe,
That es to ſay, bathe meke and mylde,
Yhe ſal noght entre, be na way
Hevenryke that ſal laſt ay, &c.

In the Bodleian library I find three copies of the *Pricke of Conſcience* very different from that which I have juſt cited. In theſe this poem is given to Robert Groſſeteſte, biſhop of Lincoln, above mentioned.[1] With what probability, [we need not] inquire; but I haſten to give a ſpecimen. I will premiſe, that the language and handwriting are of conſiderable antiquity, and that the lines are here much longer. The poet is deſcribing the future rewards and puniſhments of mankind :[1]

The goode ſoule ſchal have in his herynge
Gret joye in hevene and grete lykynge;

---

is the end of the fifth in edit. Morris, with additions.—F. But all theſe texts are decidedly very inferior to the MS. in the Northern dialect ſelected by Dr. Morris.]

[1] Compare Tanner, *Bibl.* p. 375, col. 1, and p. 374, col. 1, notes. MSS. Aſh. 52, pergamen. 4to. Laud. K. 65, pergamen. And G. 21. And MSS. Digb. 14 [and 87. The former begins :]

"The miȝt of the fader of hevene
The wit of his ſon with his giftes ſevene."

[Other copies are in Royal MS. Br. Mus. 18 A v; Harl. MS. 2261; Add. MS. 11,305. See MS. Aſhmol. 60 (Catalogue, p. 306, col. 1), and MSS. 41 and 52.—F.]

For hi schulleth yhere the aungeles song,
And with hem hi schulleth¹ synge ever among,
With delitable voys and swythe clere,
And also with that hi schullen have [there]
All other maner of ech a melodye,
Off well lykyng noyse and menstralsye,
And of al maner tenes² of musike,
The whuche to mannes herte³ migte like,
Withoute eni maner of travayle,
The whuche schal never cesse ne fayle:
And so schil⁴ schal that noyse bi, and so swete,
And so delitable to smale and to grete,
That al the melodye of this worlde heer
That ever was yhuryd ferre or neer
Were therto bote⁵ as sorwe⁶ and care
To the blisse that is in hevene well zare.⁷

Of the contrarie of that blisse.

Wel grete sorwe schal the synfolke⁸ bytyde,
For he schullen yhere in ech a syde⁹
Well gret noyse that the feondes¹⁰ willen make,
As thei al the worlde scholde alto schake;
And alle the men lyvynge that migte hit yhure,
Scholde here wit¹¹ loose, and no lengere alyve dure.¹²
Thanne hi¹³ schulleth for sorwe here hondes wringe,
And ever weilaway hi schullethe be cryinge, &c.
The gode men schullethe have worschipes grete,
And eche of them schal be yset in a riche sete,
And ther as kynges be ycrownid fayre,
And digte with riche perrie¹⁴ and so ysetun¹⁵ in a chayre,
And with stones of vertu and precioufe of choyse,
As David [thus sayth¹⁶] to god with a mylde voyse,
  Posuisti, domine, super caput eorum, &c.
"Lorde," he seyth, "on his heved thou settest wel arigt
A coronne of a pretious ston richeliche ydigt."
[Ac¹⁷] so fayre a coronne nas never non ysene,
In this worlde on kynges hevede,¹⁸ ne on quene:
For this coronne is the coronne of blisse,
And the ston is joye whereof hi schilleth never misse, &c.
The synfolke schulleth, as I have afore ytold,
Ffele outrageous hete, and afterwards to muche colde;
For now he schullethe freose, and now brenne,¹⁹
And so be ypyned that non schal other kenne,²⁰
And also be ybyte with dragonnes felle and kene,
The whuche schulleth hem destrye outrigte and clene,
And with other vermyn and bestes felle,
The whiche beothe nougt but fendes of helle, &c.

We have then this description of the New Jerusalem:

[¹ Not Hampole's version; I cannot find this in edit. Morris. See it, slightly altered, in Add. MS. 11,305, leaf 119, *verso*.]
² tunes. ³ beorte. W. ⁴ shrill. ⁵ but.
⁶ sorrow. ⁷ prepared. ⁸ sinners. ⁹ either side.
¹⁰ devils. ¹¹ senses. ¹² remain. ¹³ they.
¹⁴ precious stones. ¹⁵ seated. ¹⁶ thy said. W. ¹⁷ and. W.
¹⁸ Head. ¹⁹ This is the Hell of the monks, which Milton has adopted.
²⁰ know.

> This citie is yſet on an hei hille,
> That no ſynful man may therto tille:[1]
> The whuche ich likne to beril clene,
> [Ac[2]] ſo fayr berel may non be yſene.
> Thulke hyl is nougt elles to underſtondynge
> Bote holi thugt, and deſyr brennynge,
> The whuche holi men hadde heer to that place,
> Whiles hi hadde on eorthe here lyves ſpace;
> And I likne, as ymay ymagene in my thougt,
> The walles of hevene, to walles that were ywrougt
> Of all maner preciouſe ſtones yſet yfere,[3]
> And yſemented with gold brigt and clere;
> Bot ſo brigt gold, ne non ſo clene,
> Was in this worlde never yſene, &c.
> The wardes of the cite of hevene brigt
> I likne to wardes that wel were ydygt,
> And clenly ywrougt and ſotely enteyled,
> And on ſilver and gold clenly anamayled,[4] &c.
> The torettes[5] of hevene grete and ſmale
> I likne to the torrettes of clenc criſtale, &c.

I am not, in the mean time, quite convinced that any MS. of the *Pricke of Conſcience* in Engliſh belongs to Hampole. That this piece is a tranſlation from the Latin appears from theſe verſes:

> Therefore this boke is in Englis drawe
> Of fele[6] matters that bene unknawe
> To lewed men that are unkonande,[7]
> That con no latyn undirſtonde.[8]

---

[1] come.   [2] and. W.   [3] together.   [4] aumayled.
[5] turrets.   [6] many.   [7] ignorant.
[8] MSS. Digb. *ut ſupr.* 87, *ad princip.* [Mr. Ritſon conceived this paſſage " by no means concluſive of a Latin original," and inferred that it might " be nothing more than [Hampole's] reaſon for preferring Engliſh to Latin." Lydgate, however, conſidered Hampole as a tranſlator only:

> " In perfit living which paſſeth poyſie
> Richard hermite contemplative of ſentence
> *Drough in Engliſhe*, the Pricke of Conſcience."—*Bochas*, f. 217, b.

And this opinion is confirmed by the expreſs acknowledgment of the King's MS.

> " Now have I firſte as I undertoke
> Fulfilled the ſevene materes of this boke,
> *And oute of Latyn I have hem idrawe*,
> The whiche to ſom man is unknawe,
> And namely to lewed men of Yngelonde
> That konneth no thinge but Engliſhe undirſtonde.
> *And therfor this tretys oute drawe I wolde*
> In Engliſhe that men undirſtonde hit ſholde,
> And prikke of conſcience is this tretys yhote, &c.
> For the love of our Lord Jeſu Chriſt now
> Praieth ſpecially for hym that hit oute drow,
> And alſo for hym that this boke hath iwrite here,
> Whether he be in water, other in londe ferre or nere."

Indeed it would be difficult to account for the exiſtence of two Engliſh verſions, eſſentially differing in metre and language; though generally agreeing in matter, unleſs we aſſume a common Latin original. Which of theſe is Hampole's tranſlation, can only be decided by inſpecting a copy once in the poſſeſſion of Dr. Monro; and which Hampole " left to the ſociety of Friers-minors at York, after his and his brother's death." No manuſcript, which has fallen under the Editor's notice,

S. 7.   *The Poem a Translation.*   243

The Latin original in prose, entitled *Stimulus Conscientiæ*,[1] was most probably written by Hampole: and it is not very likely that he should translate his own work. The author and translator were easily confounded. As to the copy of the English poem given to Bishop Groseteste, he could not be the translator, to say nothing more, if Hampole wrote the Latin original. On the whole, whoever was the author of the two translations, at least we may pronounce with some certainty, that they belong to the reign of Edward III.

---

makes mention of Hampole in the text; nor has he been able to discover any shadow of authority for attributing to this sainted bard, the pieces numbered from 6 to 16 in Mr. Ritson's *Bibliographia Poetica.*—Price.]

[1] In the Cambridge MS. of Hampole's *Paraphrase on the Lord's Prayer*, above mentioned, containing a prolix description of human virtues and vices, at the end this remark appears. "Explicit quidam tractatus super Pater noster *secundum* Ric. Hampole qui obiit A.D. MCCCLXXXIV." [But the true date of his death is in another place, viz. 1349.]   MSS. More, 215, Princ.

"Almighty God in trinite
In whom is only personnes thre."

The *Paraphrase on the Book of Job*, mentioned also before, seems to have existed first in Latin prose under the title of *Parvum Job*. The English begins thus:

"Lieff lord my soul thou spare."

In Bibl. Bodl. MSS. Laud. F 77. 5, &c. &c. It is a paraphrase of some Excerpta from the book of Job. The *seven penitential Psalms* begin thus:

"To goddis worschippe that dere us bougt."

MSS. Bodl. Digb. 18. Hampole's *Expositio in Psalterium* is not uncommon in English. [Copies are in Corpus Christi College, Cambridge, and at Eton College.—F.] It has a preface in English rhymes in some copies, in praise of the author and his work. Pr. "This blessyd boke that hire." MSS. Laud. F 14, &c. Hampole was a very popular writer. Most of his many theological pieces seem to have been translated into English soon after they appeared: and those pieces abound among our MSS. Two of his tracts were translated by Richard Misyn, prior of the Carmelites at Lincoln, about the year 1435. The *Incendium Amoris* at the request of Margaret Hellingdon a recluse. Princ. "To the askynge of thi desire." And *De Emendatione Vitæ*. "Tarry thou not to oure." They are in the translator's own handwriting in the library of C.C.C. Oxon. MSS. 237. I find other ancient translations of both these pieces. Particularly, *The Pricke of Love after Richard Hampol treting of the three degrees of love*. MSS. Bodl. Arch. B. 65, f. 109. As a proof of the confusions and uncertainties attending the works of our author, I must add, that we have a translation of his tract *De Emendatione* under this title: *The form of perfyt living, which holy Richard the hermit wrote to a recluse named Margarete*. MS. Vernon. But Margarete is evidently the recluse, at whose request Richard Misyn, many years after Hampole's death, translated the *Incendium Amoris*. These observations, to which others might be added, are sufficient to confirm the suspicions insinuated in the text. Many of Hampole's Latin theological tracts were printed very early at Paris and Cologne.

[In 1866, Mr. Perry edited some of his English Prose Treatises for the Early English Text Society. See Mr. Perry's Preface.]

SECTION VIII.[1]

N this section we shall proceed to give some account of the poem which is commonly called the *Vision of Piers the Plowman*, with several extracts from the best edition. The remarks of our earlier antiquaries upon the subject are frequently misleading; and in the following sketch the reader's attention will often be most invited to those points on which preceding writers have gone most widely astray.

The title of the poem has been constantly misunderstood. In the MSS. it is *Dialogus de Petro Plowman*, and is divided into two sections; the former being *Visio Willelmi de Petro Plowman*, and the latter *Visio ejusdem* [or *Vita*] *de Dowel, Dobet, et Dobest*; from which it follows that the author's name was *William*, and that "Piers Plowman" is the subject of the poem. Yet it is quite usual, in nearly all text books, to speak of *Piers Plowman's Vision* as though Piers Plowman were the author's name! But this mistake is made even by Spenser, in his epilogue to the *Shepheard's Calendar*, where he alludes to Chaucer under the name of Tityrus, and next speaks of "the Pilgrim that the Ploughman playde awhyle." Let it be noted that the term "Piers Plowman's Vision" is sheer nonsense, because the words "*of* Piers the Plowman" mean "*concerning* Piers the Plowman," *of* not being here the sign of a possessive case.

This blunder is frequently doubled by confusing the "VISION" with an imitation of it by another author, which will be considered in the next section.

The name of the author of the VISION is not certainly known, but all accounts agree in giving him the name of LANGLAND, whilst numerous allusions in the poem concur with the Latin title in assigning to him the Christian name of WILLIAM. There are two notices of him, in handwriting of the fifteenth century. The one, discovered on the flyleaf of a MS. of the poem in Trinity College, Dublin, by Sir F. Madden, is as follows, "Memorandum, quod Stacy de Rokayle, pater *Willielmi de Langlond*, qui Stacius fuit generosus, et morabatur in Schipton vnder Whicwode [about 4 miles from Burford, co. Oxford] tenens domini le Spenser in comitatu Oxon. qui predictus Willielmus fecit librum qui vocatur Perys Ploughman." The other is on the flyleaf of a MS. (numbered cxxx) now in the possession of Lord Ashburnham, which says—"Robert or william langland made pers ploughman;" beneath which is added, in the handwriting of John Bale—"Robert Langlande, natus in comitatu Salopie in villa Mortimers Clybery in the Clayland and within viij miles of Malvern hills, scripsit piers ploughman," &c.

[[1] Communicated by the Rev. W. W. Skeat, whose text and remarks have been for the most part substituted for those of Warton and his earlier editors.]

It has commonly been assumed that we know very little more about the author than this; but the internal evidence of his poem really reveals much more, quite enough, in fact, to give us a clear conception of him. But it is necessary first to give some account of the poem itself, and to correct the common notion which assigns to it the date 1362, as if it were most of it written all at once.

The poem assumes at least five shapes in the various MSS., of which more than forty are still extant. Two of these are due to errors of copyists, but it is clear that three of these forms are due to the author himself, and that he rewrote his poem, not once only, but twice, and that rather long intervals intervened between the first and second, and between the second and third, versions.

(A). The *first* version, which is by much the shortest, and written with great rapidity and vigour, consists of a prologue and twelve Passus. It may be called the A-text, or the "Vernon" text, as the best copy of it exists in the Vernon MS. in the Bodleian library, and it has been published by the Early English Text Society, with the title—"The Vision of William concerning *Piers [the] Plowman*, together with *Vita de Dowel, Dobet, et Dobest, secundum Wit et Resoun*, by William Langland, A. D. 1362."[1] None of these MSS. contains the twelfth Passus, except the University Coll. MS., which preserves only eighteen lines of it; but there is one *complete* copy in the Bodleian library, viz. MS. Rawl. Poet. 137, in which the twelfth Passus begins at fol. 40. The date 1362 was suggested by Tyrwhitt, who observed with great sagacity and justice, that the "Southwestern wind on a Saturday at even," which the author refers to as a recent event, was certainly the terrible storm of Saturday, Jan. 15, 1361-2, which is noticed by many writers, and in particular, is thus recorded by Thorn, apud Decem Scriptores: "A. D. MCCCLXII. 15 die Januarii, circa horam *vesperarum*, ventus vehemens notus australis Africus tantâ rabie erupit," &c.[2] Mention is made in the same passage of the poem (p. 52) of "these pestilences," *i. e.* the pestilences of 1348-1349, and 1361-1362. This version consists of about 2567 lines.

(B). Not foreseeing the popularity which his poem was destined to enjoy, the author resorted to the not uncommon device of killing himself off, in the concluding lines of the earliest version, where he says:

> "Wille[3] wiste thurgh inwit[4] · thou wost wel the sothe,
> That this speche was spedelich · and sped him wel faste,
> And wroughthe that here is wryten[5] · and other werkes bothe

---

[1] [Edited from the "Vernon" MS., collated with MS. R. 3. 14 in the library of Trinity College, Cambridge, MS. Harl. 875 and 6041, the MS. in University College, Oxford, MS. Douce, 323, &c.: by the Rev. W. W. Skeat; London, 1867.]

[2] [Cf. Walsingham, ed. H. T. Riley, vol. i. p. 296, Fabyan's Chronicle, ed. Ellis, p. 475, Hardyng's Chronicle, ed. Ellis, p. 330.]

[3] [*i. e.* William, the author himself.] [4] [conscience.]

[5] [*i.e.* the Vision of Do-wel; the "other werkes" refer to the Vision of Piers the Plowman, properly so called.]

Of *peres the plowman* · and mechel puple¹ alſo ;
And whan this werk was wrought · ere wille² myghte aſpie,
Deth delt him a dent³ · and drof him to the erthe,
And [he] is cloſed vnder clom⁴ · criſt haue his ſoule !"

And ſo the matter reſted for nearly fifteen years. But the grief of the whole nation at the death of the Black Prince, the diſquieting political events of 1377, the laſt year of Edward III., the diſſatisfaction of the commons with the conduct of the Duke of Lancaſter, rouſed our poet, as it rouſed other men. Then it was that, taking his text from Eccleſiaſticus, x. 16, *Væ terræ ubi rex puer eſt*, he compoſed his famous verſion of the well-known fable of the rats wiſhing to bell the cat, a fable which has never been elſewhere told ſo well or ſo effectively. Then it was that, taking advantage of his now more extenſive acquaintance with Scripture, and his familiarity with the daily ſcenes of London life, he rewrote and added to his poem till he had trebled the extent of it, and multiplied the number of his Latin quotations by ſeven. The additions are, moſt of them, exceedingly good, and diſtinguiſhed by great freedom and originality of thought ; indeed, we may ſay that, upon the whole, the " B-text " is the beſt of the three, and the beſt ſuited for giving us a fair idea of the author's peculiar powers. The complete text compriſes the two Viſions, viz. of Piers Plowman, and of Do-wel, Do-bet, and Do-beſt ; the former conſiſting of a Prologue and ſeven Paſſus, and the latter of three Prologues and ten Paſſus, viz. a Prologue and ſix Paſſus of Do-wel, a Prologue and three Paſſus of Do-bet, and a Prologue and 1 Paſſus of Do-beſt. But in many (perhaps all) of the MSS. the diſtinctions between the component parts are not much regarded, and in ſome there is no mention of Do-wel, Do-bet, and Do-beſt whatever, but the whole is called *Liber* (or *Dialogus*) *de petro plowman*, and made to conſiſt of a Prologue and *twenty* Paſſus. Not to go into further details, it is neceſſary to add that there are two perfect MSS. of it which are of ſpecial excellence, and which do not greatly vary from each other ; from one of theſe, MS. Trin. Coll. Camb. B. 15, 17, Mr. Wright printed his well-known and convenient edition of the whole poem, and the other, MS. Laud 581, forms the baſis of the text publiſhed by the Early Engliſh Text Society in 1869. Other good MSS. of this verſion are Rawl. Poet. 38 (which contains ſome extra lines), MS. Dd. 1. 17, in the Cambridge Univerſity library, MS. 79 in Oriel College, Oxford, &c.

The B-text was alſo printed by Robert Crowley, in 1550, from a very good MS. Indeed, Crowley printed three impreſſions of it in the ſame year, the firſt and ſcarceſt being the moſt correct, and the third (called " ſecond " impreſſion on the title-page) being the worſt. Crowley's edition was very incorrectly reprinted by Owen Rogers in 1561.

The third verſion was probably not compoſed till 1380 or even later, or, ſtill more probably, it contains additions and reviſions made

---

¹ [much people.] ² [*i. e.* William, the author himſelf.]
³ [dint, blow.]   ⁴ [loam, clay.]

at various periods later than 1378. Throughout these the working of the same mind is clearly discernible, but there is a tendency to diffuseness and to a love for theological subtleties. It is of still greater length, containing a Prologue and nine Passus of *Piers the Plowman*, a Prologue and six Passus of *Do-wel*, a Prologue and three Passus of *Do-bet*, and a Prologue and one Passus of *Do-best*; or, according to the shorter notation, a Prologue and twenty-two Passus. It may be remarked that the short poem of *Do-best* stands almost exactly the same in both the B and C versions.

An edition of this text was printed (very incorrectly) by Dr. Whitaker, in 1813, from a MS. now belonging to Sir Thomas Phillipps.[1]

We may safely date the A-text about A.D. 1362, the B-text about A.D. 1377, and the C-text about A.D. 1380. To assume the date 1362 for all three is to introduce unnecessary confusion.

Besides this extraordinary work, with its three varying editions, I hold that we are indebted to the same author for a remarkable poem on the *Deposition of Richard II.* of course written in 1399, and which has been twice printed by Mr. Wright, the more convenient edition being that published for the Camden Society in 1838. This is not the place to discuss a question of some difficulty, and concerning which a careful reader may form an opinion for himself, and can come, I think, to no other conclusion. It is true that Mr. Wright has expressed a different opinion, but he was misled by a marginal note in his MS. to which he attached some importance.[2]

Returning to the author, we may now piece together the following account of him, which is probably true, and, at any rate, rests chiefly upon his own statements. At the time of writing the B-text of *Do-wel*, he was forty-five years of age, and he was therefore born

---

[1] [For further information concerning the MSS. see the prefaces to the Early English Text Society's edition, and a pamphlet also published by the same society, with the title—"Parallel Extracts from twenty-nine MSS. of Piers Plowman," &c.: ed. Skeat, 1866.]

For general remarks upon the poem, see the same prefaces; Mr. Wright's preface to his edition of 1842, reprinted in 1856; Professor Morley's *English Writers*, vol. i.: Marsh's *Lectures on the Origin and History of the English Language*, 8vo., 1862, p. 296, &c.; and a fine passage in Dean Milman's *History of Latin Christianity*, vol. vi. p. 536, ed. 1855. Respecting Whitaker's edit. 1813, to extracts from which the former editors of Warton very uselessly, as the present writer thinks, devoted several pages, Mr. Wright has observed: "Dr. Whittaker was not well qualified for this undertaking; he also laboured under many disadvantages; he had access to only three manuscripts, and those not very good ones; and he has not chosen the best text even of these. Unless he had some reason to believe that the book was originally written in a particular dialect, he ought to have given a preference to that among the oldest manuscripts, which presents the purest language."]

[2] [See his edition (Camd. Soc.) p. vi., where "liber hic" should have been printed "liber homo," an error which vitiates the whole argument. The unique copy of this poem is found in MS. Ll. 4. 14. in the Cambridge University library, where it follows a copy of *Piers the Plowman*, and is in the same handwriting with it, though that of course proves but little. I argue from internal evidence, of which I can adduce a great deal.]

about A.D. 1332, probably at Cleobury Mortimer. His father and his friends put him to school (possibly in the monastery at Great Malvern), made a *clerk* or scholar of him, and taught him what holy writ meant. In 1362, at the age of about thirty, he wrote the A-text of the poem, without any thought of continuing or enlarging it. In this he refers to Edward III. and his son the Black Prince, to the murder of Edward II., to the great pestilences of 1348 and 1361, to the treaty of Bretigny in 1360, and Edward's wars in Normandy, and also most particularly to the great storm of wind which took place on Saturday evening, Jan. 15th, 1361-2.[1] This version of the poem he describes as having been partly composed in May, whilst wandering on Malvern Hills, which are thrice mentioned in the part rightly called *Piers the Plowman*. In the introduction or prologue to *Do-wel*, he describes himself as wandering about all the summer till he met with two Minorite Friars, with whom he discoursed concerning *Do-wel*. It was probably not long after this that he went to reside in London, with which he already had some acquaintance; there he lived in Cornhill, with his wife Kitte and his daughter Calote, for many long years.[2] In 1377, he began to expand his poem into the B-text, wherein he alludes to the accession of Richard II. in the words—"ȝif I regne any while,"[3] and also explicitly to the dearth in the dry month of April, 1370, when Chichester was mayor; a dearth due to the excessive rains in the autumn of 1369. Chichester was elected in 1369 (probably in October) and was still mayor in 1370. In Riley's *Memorials of London*, p. 344, he is mentioned as being mayor in that very month of April in that very year in the words—"Afterwards, on the 25th day of April in the year above-mentioned, it was agreed by John de Chichestre, Mayor," &c. It is important to insist upon this, because the MS. followed by Mr. Wright, in company with many inferior ones, has a corrupt reading which turns the words—"A þousand and thre hondreth · tweis *thretty* and ten" into "twice *twenty* and ten," occasioning a great difficulty, and misleading many modern writers and readers, since the same mistake occurs in Crowley's edition. Fortunately, the Laud MS. 581 and MS. Rawl. Poet. 38 set us right here, and all difficulty now vanishes; for it is easily ascertained that Chichester was mayor in 1369-70, and at no other time, having never been re-elected. Stow and other old writers have the right date. In the C-text, written at some time after 1378, the poet represents himself as still in London, and in the commencement of Passus v. (also called Passus vi, as in Whitaker) gives us several particulars concerning himself, wherein he alludes to his own tallness, saying that he is too "long" to stoop low, and he has also some remarks concerning the sons of freemen which imply that he

---

[1] [That is, the year 1362, which was formerly called 1361, when the year was supposed not to begin till March. See, for these allusions, B-text, Pass. iii. 186, 188; iv. 45; and v. 14.]
[2] [C-Text, Pass. v.]   [3] [B. iv. 177.]

was himself the son of a franklin or freeman, and born in lawful wedlock. He wore the clerical tonsure, probably as having taken minor orders, and earned a precarious living by singing the *placebo*, *dirige*, and "seven psalms" for the good of men's souls; for, ever since his friends died who had first put him to school, he had found no kind of life that pleased him except to be in "these long clothes," and by help of such (clerical) labour as he had been bred up to he contrived not only to live "*in* London, but *upon* London" also. The supposition that he was married (as he says he was) may, perhaps explain why he never rose in the church. He has many allusions to his extreme poverty. Lastly, in the deposition of Richard II. he describes himself as being in Bristol in the year 1399, when he wrote his last poem. This poem is but short, and in the only MS. wherein it exists, terminates abruptly in the middle of a page, and it is quite possible that it was never finished. This is the last trace of him, and he was then probably about sixty-seven years of age, so that he may not have long survived the accession of Henry IV. In personal appearance, he was so tall that he obtained the nickname of "Longe Wille," as he tells us in the line:

"I have lyued in londe," quod I · "my name is Longe wille."[1]

This nickname may be paralleled from Mr. Riley's *Memorials of London*, p. 457, where we read of John Edward, "otherwise called Longe Jack," under the date 1382. In Passus xv. (B-text) he says that he was loath to reverence lords or ladies, or persons dressed in fur, or wearing silver ornaments; he never would say "God save you" to serjeants whom he met, for all of which proud behaviour, then very uncommon, people looked upon him as a fool. It requires no great stretch of imagination to picture to ourselves the tall gaunt figure of Long Will in his long robes and with his shaven head, striding along Cornhill, saluting no man by the way, minutely observant of the gay dresses to which he paid no outward reverence. It ought also to be observed how very frequent are his allusions to lawyers, to the law-courts at Westminster, and to legal processes. He has a mock-charter, beginning with the ordinary formula *Sciant præsentes et futuri*, a form of making a will, and in one passage (B-text, Pass. xi.) he speaks with such scorn of a man who draws up a charter badly, who interlines it, or leaves out sentences, or puts false Latin in it, that I think we may fairly suppose him to have been conversant with the writing out of legal documents, and to have eked out his subsistence by the small sums received for doing so. The various texts are so consistent, that we may well suppose him to have been his own scribe in the first instance. Indeed, there are some reasons for supposing the MS. *Laud Misc.* 581 to be an autograph copy.

Wood confuses Langland with John Maluerne, a continuation of

---

[1] [See Wright's edition, p. 304, where "quod *I*" is printed "quod *he*," an error which a collation of many MSS. has removed. It is very curious that the words *londe*, *longe*, and *wille* in this line form *Wille Longelonde* when read backwards.]

the *Polychronicon*, who is said to have been a fellow of Oriel, and was certainly a prior of the Benedictine monastery at Worcester.

The poem itself contains a series of distinct visions, which the author imagines himself to have seen, while he was sleeping, after a long ramble on Malverne-hills in Worcestershire. It is a satire on the vices of almost every profession; but particularly on the corruptions of the clergy, and the absurdities of superstition. These are ridiculed with much humour and spirit, couched under a strong vein of allegorical invention.

But it is untrue that Langland adopts the style of the Anglo-Saxon poets, as has been well shown by Mr. Marsh who, in the passage already referred to, thus refutes this notion:

"The Vision of the Ploughman furnishes abundant evidence of the familiarity of its author with the Latin Scriptures, the writings of the fathers, and the commentaries of Romish expositors, but exhibits very few traces of a knowledge of romance literature. Still the proportion of Norman-French words, or at least of words which, though of Latin origin, are French in form, is quite as great as in the works of Chaucer.[1] The familiar use of this mixed vocabulary, in a poem evidently intended for the popular ear, and composed by a writer who gives no other evidence of an acquaintance with the literature of France, would, were other proof wanting, tend strongly to confirm the opinion I have before advanced, that a large infusion of French words had been not merely introduced into the literature, but incorporated into the common language of England; and that only a very small proportion of those employed by the poets were first introduced by them.

"The poem, if not altogether original in conception, is abundantly so in treatment. The spirit it breathes, its imagery, the turn of thought, the style of illustration and argument it employs, are *as remote as possible from the tone of Anglo-Saxon poetry*, but exhibit the characteristic moral and mental traits of the Englishman as clearly and unequivocally as the most national portions of the works of Chaucer or of any other native writer."

The whole poem is in alliterative verse, not because Langland wished here again to "imitate the Anglo-Saxon style," but because that rhythm was more thoroughly English than any other kind, and familiar to most Englishmen, especially in the northern and western parts. Neither did the necessity of finding similar initial letters cramp his expression, as Warton intimated; for it is clear that Langland was often careless about his alliteration, and wrote with great ease, sacrificing sound to sense in every case of perplexity. It ought further to be noticed that the poem is something more than a satire; the author, dreaming like another Bunyan, sees his ideal type of excellence in the shape of Piers the Ploughman, and his chief

---

[1] [The Prologue to Piers the Plowman and the first 420 lines of Chaucer's Prologue alike contain 88 per cent. of Anglo-Saxon words. See Marsh, *Lectures on English;* 1st Series, p. 124.]

aim is to develop the whole hiſtory of the religious life of man, ſo that Piers anſwers in ſome ſenſe to Bunyan's "Chriſtian," though he is ſtill more like "Greatheart." In fact, Piers is ſpoken of under ſeveral aſpects. At one time he is the honeſt and utterly truthful labourer, whoſe ſtrong common ſenſe can give good advice to his betters; at another, he is identified with the human nature of Chriſt; and again, he repreſents the whole Chriſtian church in its primitive and beſt condition. At all times he is the imperſonation of the ſpiritual part of human nature which ever wars againſt evil, but which can never wholly triumph in this world. Unleſs this be kept in view, the poem indeed ſeems wanting in unity.

The ſatire is conducted by the agency of ſeveral allegorical perſonages, ſuch as Avarice, Bribery, Simony, Theology, Conſcience, &c. There is much imagination in the following picture, which is intended to repreſent human life and its various occupations:

> Thanne gan I to meten · a merueilouſe ſweuene,[1]
> That I was in a wilderneſſe · wiſt I neuer where;
> As I bihelde in-to þe eſt · an hiegh to þe ſonne,
> I ſeigh a toure on a toft · trielich ymaked;
> A depe dale binethe · a dongeon þere-Inne,
> With depe dyches & derke · and dredful of ſight.
> A faire felde ful of folke · fonde I there bytwene,
> Of alle maner of men · þe mene and þe riche,
> Worchyng and wandryng · as þe worlde aſketh.
> Some putten hem to þe plow · pleyed ful ſelde,
> In ſettyng and in ſowyng · ſwonken ful harde,
> And wonnen that waſtours · with glotonye deſtruyeth.
> And ſome putten hem to pruyde, &c.

The following extracts from Paſſus viii-x. (Text B.) are not only ſtriking ſpecimens of our author's allegorical ſatire, but contain much ſenſe and obſervation of life, with ſome ſtrokes of poetry:

> Thus yrobed in ruſſet · I romed aboute
> Al a ſomer ſeſoun · for to ſeke dowel,[2]
> And frayned[3] ful oft · of folke þat I mette,
> If ani wiȝte wiſte · where dowel was at Inne,[4]
> And what man he miȝte be · of many man I axed.
> ¶ Was neuere wiȝte, as I went · þat me wiſſe couthe[5]
> Where þis lede lenged[6] · laſſe ne more;
> ¶ Tyl it bifel on a fryday · two freres I mette,
> Maiſtres of þe Menoures[7] · men of grete witte.
> I hailſed hem hendely[8] · as I hadde lerned,
> And preyed hem *par* charitee · ar þei paſſed forther,
> If þei knewe any contre · or coſtes, as þei went,
> Where þat dowel dwelleth · doth me to wytene.[9]
> ¶ For þei ben men on þis molde · þat moſte wyde walken,
> And knowen contrees, and courtes · and many kynnes places,[10]
> Bothe prynces paleyſes · and pore mennes cotes,
> And do-wel and do-yuel · where þei dwelle bothe.
> ¶ "Amonges vs," *quod* þe Menours · "þat man is dwellyng*e*,
> And euere hath, as I hope · and euere ſhal her*e*-after."

---

[1] B-text; Prol. ll. 11-22 (ed. Skeat).
[2] [Do-well.] [3] [inquired.] [4] [lived.] [5] [could inform me.]
[6] [lingered, dwelt.] [7] [Friars Minors.] [8] [ſaluted them civilly.]
[9] [know.] [10] [Places of many a kind; *i.e.* many ſorts of places.]

¶ "Contra," quod I as a clerke · and comſed to diſputen,
And ſeide hem ſothli, "*ſepcies · in die cadit iuſtus;*
Seuene ſythes,[1] ſeith þe boke · ſynneth þe riȝtful.
And who-ſo ſynneth," I ſeyde · "doth yuel, as me þinketh,
And dowel and do-yuel · mow nouȝt dwelle togideres.
Ergo, he nys nauȝt alway · amonge ȝow freres;
He is otherwhile ellis where · to wiſſe þe peple."
¶ "I ſhal ſey þe, my ſone" · ſeide þe frere þanne,
"How ſeuene ſithes þe ſad man[2] · on þe day ſynneth;
By a forbiſene,"[3] quod þe frere · "I ſhal þe faire ſhewe.
¶ Lat Brynge a man in a bote · amydde a brode water,
Þe wynde and þe water · and the bote waggynge
Maketh þe man many a tyme · to falle and to ſtonde;
For ſtonde he neuere ſo ſtyf · he ſtombleth ȝif he moeue;
Ac ȝit is he ſauf and ſounde · and ſo hym bihoueth,
For ȝif he ne ariſe þe rather · and rauȝte to þe ſtiere;
Þe wynde wolde, wyth þe water · þe bote ouerthrowe;
And þanne were his lyf loſte · þourgh laccheſſe[4] of hym-ſelf.
¶ And þus it falleth," quod þe frere · "bi folke here on erthe;
Þe water is likned to þe worlde · þat wanyeth and wexeth,
Þe godis of þis grounde aren like · to þe grete wawes,
Þat as wyndes and wederes · walweth aboute.
Þe bote is likned to owre body · þat brutel is of kynde,
Þat þorugh þe fende and þe fleſshe · and þe frele worlde
Synneth þe ſadman · a day, ſeuene ſythes.
¶ Ac dedly ſynne doth he nouȝt · for dowel hym kepith,
And þat is charite þe champioun · chief help aȝein ſynne;
For he ſtrengtheth man to ſtonde · and ſtereth mannes ſoule,
And þowgh þi body bow · as bote doth in þe water,
Ay is þi ſoule ſauf · but if þi-ſelf wole
Do a dedly ſynne · and drenche ſo þi ſoule;
God wole ſuffre wel þi ſleuthe · ȝif þi-ſelf lyketh.
For he ȝaf þe to ȝeresȝyue · to ȝeme wel þi-ſelue,
And þat is witte and fre wille · to euery wyȝte a porcioun,
To fleghyng foules · to fiſſches & to beſtes.
Ac man hath moſte þerof · and moſte is to blame,
But if he worche wel þer-with · as dowel hym techeth."
¶ "I haue no kynde knowyng," quod I · "to conceyue alle ȝowre wordes,
Ac if I may lyue and loke · I ſhal go lerne bettere."
"I bikenne þe cryſt, quod he · þat on þe croſſe deyde."
And I ſeyde, "þe ſame · ſaue ȝow fro myſchaunce,
And ȝiue ȝow grace on þis grounde · good men to worthe."
¶ And þus I went wide-where · walkyng myne one,
By a wilde wildernesse · and bi a wode-ſyde.
Bliſſe of þo briddes · abyde me made,
And vnder a lynde[5] vppon a launde · lened I a ſtounde,[6]
To lythe[7] þe layes · þe louely foules made.
Murthe of her mouthes · made me þere to ſlepe;
Þe merueilloufeſt meteles · mette me[8] þanne
Þat euer dremed wyȝte · in worlde, as I wene.
¶ A moche man, as me þouȝte · and lyke to my-ſelue
Come and called me · by my kynde[9] name.
"What artow," quod I þo · "þat þou my name knoweſt?"
"Þat þou woſt wel," quod he · "and no wyȝte bettere."

---

[1] [times.] [2] [ſober, good man.] [3] [ſimilitude, example.]
[4] [lazineſs.] [5] [lime-tree.] [6] [a while]
[7] [liſten to.] [8] [I dreamed.]
[9] [own; *i.e.* Chriſtian name of "Will."]

¶ "Wote I what þow art?" · "þought," feyde he þanne,
"I haue fuwed[1] þe þis feuene 3ere · fey þow me no rather?"
¶ "Art þow thought?" quod I þo · "þow coutheſt me wiſſe
Where þat dowel dwelleth · and do me þat to knowe?"
¶ "Dowel and dobet · and dobeſt þe thridde," quod he,
"Aren three faire vertues · and beth nau3te fer to fynde.
Who-ſo is trewe of his tonge · and of his two handes,
And þorugh his laboure or þorugh his londe · his lyflode wynneth,[2]
And is truſti of his tailende[3] · taketh but his owne,
And is nou3t dronkenlew[4] ne dedeignous · dowel hym folweth.
Dobet doth ry3t þus · ac he doth moche more;
He is as low as a lombe · and loueliche of ſpeche,
And helpeth alle men · after þat hem nedeth;
þe bagges and þe bigurdeles · he hath to-broken[5] hem alle,
þhat þe Erl auarous · helde, and his heires;
And þus with Mammonaes moneie · he hath made hym frendes,
And is ronne in-to Religioun · and hath rendred[6] þe bible,
And precheth to the poeple · ſeynt Poules wordes,
    Libenter ſuffertis inſipientes, cum ſitis ipſi ſapientes,
'And ſuffreth þe vnwiſe · with 3ow for to libbe,
And with gladde wille doth hem gode · for ſo god 3ow hoteth.'
¶ Dobeſt is aboue bothe · and bereth a biſſchopes croſſe,
Is hoked on þat one ende · to halie[7] men fro helle.
A pyke is on þat potente[8] · to pulte adown þe wikked,
þat wayten any wikkedneſſe · dowel to tene.
And dowel and dobet · amonges hem ordeigned
To croune one to be kynge · to reule hem bothe;
þat 3if dowel or dobet · did a3ein dobeſt,
þanne ſhal þe kynge come · and caſten hem in yrens,
And but if dobeſt bede for hem · þei to be þere for euere.
¶ Thus dowel and dobet · and dobeſt þe thridde,
Crouned one to be kynge · to kepen hem alle,
And to reule þe Reume · bi her[9] thre wittes,
And none other-wiſe · but as þei thre aſſented."
¶ I thonked thou3t þo · þat he me þus tau3te;
"Ac 3ete ſauoureth me nou3t þi ſeggyng · I coueite to lerne
How dowel, dobet, and dobeſt · don amonges þe peple."
¶ "But witte conne wiſſe þe," quod þou3t · where þo[10] thre dwelle;
Ellis wote I none þat can · þat now is alyue."
¶ þou3te and I thus · thre days we 3eden,[11]
Diſputyng vppon dowel · day after other,
And ar we were ywar · with witte gan we mete.
He was longe and lene · liche to none other,
Was no pruyde on his apparaille · ne pouerte noyther,
Sadde of his ſemblaunt · and of ſoft chiere.
I dorſte meue no matere · to make hym to iangle,
But as I bad þou3t þo · be mene bitwene,
And put forth ſomme purpos · to prouen his wittes,
What was dowel fro dobet · and dobeſt fram hem bothe.
¶ þanne þou3t in þat tyme · ſeide þiſe wordes,
"Where dowel, dobet · and dobeſt ben in londe,
Here is wille wolde ywyte · yif witte couthe teche hym,
And whether he be man or [no] man · þis man fayne wolde aſpye,
And worchen as þei thre wolde · þis is his entente."

---

[1] [followed.]   [2] [earns.]
[3] [The Oriel MS. has *tayling*, i.e. dealing, reckoning.]   [4] [drunken.]
[5] [broken in pieces.]   [6] [tranſlated.]   [7] [hale, draw.]
[8] [ſtaff.]   [9] [their.]   [10] [thoſe.]
[11] [went, travelled.]

Passus IX. (B-text).

"Sire dowel dwelleth," quod witte · "nouȝt a day hennes,
In a castel þat kynde¹ made · of foure kynnes þinges;
Of erthe and eyre is it made · medled togideres,
With wynde and with water · witterly² enioyned.
Kynde hath closed þere-Inne · craftily with-alle,
A lemman³ þat he loueth · like to hym-selue,
Anima she hatte · ac enuye hir hateth,
A proude pryker of Fraunce · *prynceps huius mundi*,
And wolde winne hir awey · with wyles, and he myȝte.
¶ Ac kynde knoweth þis wel · and kepeth hir þe bettere,
And hath do hir with sire dowel · is duke of þis marches.
Dobet is hir damoisele · sire doweles douȝter,
To serue this lady lelly⁴ · bothe late and rathe.⁵
Dobest is aboue bothe · a bisschopes pere;
Þat he bit, mote be do⁶ · he reuleth hem alle;
Anima þat lady · is ladde bi his lerynge.
¶ Ac þe constable of þat castel · þat kepeth al þe wacche,
Is a wys kniȝte with-al · sire Inwitte he hatte,
And hath fyue feyre sones · bi his first wyf;
Sire sewel and saywel · and herewel þe hende,
Sire worche-wel-wyth-þine-hande · a wiȝte man of strengthe,
And sire godfrey gowel · gret lordes for sothe.
Þise fyue ben sette · to saue þis lady *anima*,
Tyl kynde come or sende · to saue hir for euere."
¶ "What kynnes thyng is kynde," quod I · "canstow me telle?"
¶ "Kynde," quod witte, "is a creatour · of alle kynnes þinges;
Fader and fourmour⁷ · of al þat euere was maked;
And þat is þe gret god · þat gynnynge had neuere,
Lorde of lyf and of lyȝte · of lysse and of peyne.
Angeles and al þing · aren at his wille.
Ac man is hym moste lyke · of marke⁷ and of schafte;
For þorugh þe worde þat he spake · wexen forth bestes,
   Dixit, & facta sunt;
¶ And made man likkest · to hym-self one,
And Eue of his ribbe-bon · with-outen eny mene.
For he was synguler hym-self · and seye *faciamus*,
As who seith, 'more mote here-to · þan my worde one;
My myȝte mote helpe · now with my speche.'
Riȝte as a lorde sholde make lettres · and hym lakked parchemyn,
Þough he couth write neuere so wel · ȝif he had no penne,
Þe lettre[s] for al þe lordship · I leue were neuere ymaked.
¶ And so it semeth bi hym · as þe bible telleth,
   Þere he seyde, *dixit, & facta sunt;*
He moste worche with his worde · and his witte shewe.
And in þis manere was man made · þorugh myȝte of god almiȝti,
With his worde and werkemanschip · and with lyf to laste.
And þus god gaf hym a goost⁸ · of þe godhed of heuene,
And of his grete grace · graunted hym blisse,
And þat is lyf þat ay shal last · to al his lynage after.
And þat is þe castel þat kynde made · *caro* it hatte,
And is as moche to mene · as man with a soule;
And þat he wrouȝt with werke · and with worde bothe,
Þorugh myȝte of þe maieste · man was ymaked.

---

¹ [nature.]   ² [verily, truly.]   ³ [lover.]
⁴ [loyally.]   ⁵ [early.]   ⁶ [What he bids, must be done.]
⁷ [form, fashion.]   ⁸ [spirit.]

¶ Inwit and alle wittes · closed ben þer-inne,
For loue of þe lady *anima* · þat lyf is ynempned ;[1]
Ouer al in mannes body · he walketh and wandreth,
Ac in þe herte is hir home · and hir moste[2] reste.
Ac Inwitte is in þe hed · and to the herte he loketh,
What *anima* is lief or loth[3] · he lat[4] hir at his wille ;
For after þe grace of god · þe gretteft is Inwitte.

* * * * * * *

PASSUS X. (B-TEXT.)

Thanne hadde witte a wyf · was hote dame ftudye,
Þat lene was of lere · and of liche bothe.
She was wonderly wroth · þat witte me þus tauȝte,
And al ftarynge dame ftudye · fternelich feyde,
"Wel artow wyſe," quod ſhe to witte · "any wyfdomes to telle
To flatereres or to folis · þat frantyk ben of wittes!"
And blamed hym and banned hym · and badde hym be ftylle,
With fuche wife wordes · to wiffen any fottes ;
And feyde, "*noli mittere*, man · margerye perlis
Amanges hogges, þat han · hawes at wille.
þei don but dryuele þer-on · draffe[5] were hem leuere[6]
Þan al þe *pre*cious perre · þat in paradys wexeth.[7]
I fey it bi fuche," quod ſhe · "þat fheweth bi her werkes,
Þat hem were leuer[6] londe · and lordfhip on erthe,
Or riccheffe or rentis · and refte at her wille,
Þan alle þe fothe fawes · þat falamon feyde euere.
¶ Wifdome and witte now · is nouȝt worth a carfe,[8]
But if it be carded with coueytife[9] · as clotheres kemben here wolle.
Who-fo can contreue deceytes · an confpire wronges,
And lede forth a loue-day[10] · to latte with treuthe ;
He þat fuche craftes can · to confeille is clepid ;
þei lede lordes with lefynges · and bilyeth treuthe.
¶ Iob þe gentel · in his geftes witneffeth,
Þat wikked men, þei welden · þe welthe of þis worlde,
And þat þei ben lordes of eche a londe · þat oute of lawe libbeth ;

Quare impij viuunt ? bene eft omnibus, qui preuaricantur & inique agunt ?

¶ Þe fauter feyth þe fame · bi fuche þat don ille,

Ecce ipfi peccatores habundantes ; in feculo optinuerunt diuicias.

'Lo !' feith holy letterrure · 'whiche lordes beth þis fhrewes !'
Þilke þat god mofte gyueth · lefte good þei deleth,
And mofte vnkynde to þe comune · þat mofte catel weldeth ;[11]

Que perfecifti, deftruxerunt ; iuftus autem quid fecit !

Harlotes for her harlotrye · may haue of her godis,
And iaperes and iogeloures[12] · and iangelers of geftes.
¶ Ac he þat hath holy writte · ay in his mouth,
And can telle of Tobye · and of þe twelue apoftles,
Or prechen of þe penaunce · þat pilat wrouȝt
To Ihefu þe gentil · þat Iewes to-drowe :—
Litel is he loued · þat fuche a leffoun fcheweth,
Or daunted or drawe forth · I do it on god hym-felf !

---

[1] [named.]   [2] [greateft, chief.]   [3] [unwilling.]   [4] [leadeth.]
[5] [dregs, refufe ; ufed by Chaucer.]
[6] [dearer to them ; *i.e.* they would rather have.]   [7] [grows.]
[8] [Some MSS. have *kerfe*, i. e. a water-crefs.]   [9] [covetoufnefs.]
[10] [A day for the amicable fettlement of differences was called a *love-day*.]
[11] [wields ; *i.e.* poffeffes.]   [12] [jugglers.]

¶ But þo¹ þat feynen hem folis · and with faityng² libbeth,
Aȝein þe lawe of owre lorde · and lyen on hem-felue,
Spitten and fpewen · and fpeke foule wordes,
Drynken and dryuelen · and do men for to gape,
Lickne men and lye on hem · þat leneth hem no ȝiftes,
Þei conne³ namore mynftralcye · ne mufyke, men to glade,
Than Munde þe mylnere · of *multa fecit deus!*
Ne were here vyle harlotrye · haue god my treuthe,
Shulde neuere Kyng ne kniȝt · ne chanoun of feynt Poules
Ȝyue hem to her ȝereſȝiue · þe ȝifte of a grote!
¶ Ac murthe and mynftralcye · amonges men is nouthe
Leccherye, lofengerye,⁴ · and lofeles tales;
Glotonye and grete othes · þis murthe þei louieth.
¶ Ac if þei carpen⁵ of cryft · þis clerkis and þis lewed,
Atte mete in her murthes · whan mynftralles ben ftille,
Þanne telleth þei of þe trinite · a tale other tweyne,
And bringen forth a balled refoun · and taken Bernard⁶ to witneffe,
And putten forth a prefumpfioun · to preue þe fothe.
Þus þei dryuele at her deyfe⁷ · þe deite to knowe,
And gnawen god with þe gorge⁸ · whan her gutte is fulle.
¶ Ac þe careful⁹ may crye · and carpen atte ȝate,
Bothe afyngred¹⁰ and a-thurft · and for chele¹¹ quake;
Is none to nymen hym nere · his noye¹² to amende,
But hoen on hym as an hounde · and hoten hym go þennes.
Litel loueth he þat lorde · þat lent hym al þat bliffe,
Þat þus parteth with þe pore · a parcel whan hym nedeth.
Ne were mercy in mene men · more þan in riche,
Mendinantȝ meteles¹³ · miȝte go to bedde.
God is moche in þe gorge · of þife grete mayftres,
Ac amonges mene men · his mercy and his werkis;
And fo feith þe fauter · I haue yfeye it ofte,
    *Ecce audiuimus eam in effrata, inuenimus eam in campis
      filue.*
Clerkes and other kynnes men · carpen of god fafte,
And haue hym moche in þe mouthe · ac mene men in herte.
¶ Freres and faitoures · han founde fuche queftiouns
To plefe with proude men · fithen þe peftilence tyme,
And prechen at feint poules · for pure enuye of clerkis,
Þat folke is nouȝte fermed in þe feith · ne fre of her goodes,
Ne fori for her fynnes · fo is pryde waxen
In religioun in alle þe rewme · amonges riche & pore,
Þat prayeres haue no power · þe peftilence to lette.
And ȝette þe wrecches of þis worlde · is none ywar bi other,
Ne for drede of þe deth · withdrawe nouȝt her pryde,
Ne beth plentyuous to þe pore · as pure charite wolde,
But in gayneffe and in glotonye · for-glotton her goode hem-felue,
And breken nouȝte to þe beggar · as þe boke techeth,
    Frange efurienti panem tuum, &c.
And þe more he wynneth and welt · welthes & riccheffe,
And lordeth in londes · he laffe good he deleth.
¶ Thobye telleth ȝow nouȝt fo · take hede, ȝe riche,
How þe boke bible · of hym bereth witneffe:
    *Si tibi fit copia, habundanter tribue; fi autem exiguum,
      illud impertiri ftude libenter:—*
Who-fo hath moche, fpene manliche · fo meneth Thobie,

---

¹ [thofe.]   ² [deceit.]   ³ [know.]   ⁴ [flattery.]
⁵ [fpeak.]   ⁶ [St. Bernard.]   ⁷ daïs, high table.   ⁸ [throat.]
⁹ [poor.]   ¹⁰ [very hungry.]   ¹¹ [cold.]   ¹² [trouble.]
¹³ [Beggars fupperlefs.]

And who-fo litel weldeth · reule him þer-after ;
For we haue no *lettre* of owre lyf · how longe it fhal dure.
Suche leffou*n*es lordes fhulde · louie to here,
And how he my3te moft meyne · manliche fynde.
¶ Nou3t to fare as a fitheler or a frere · for to feke feftes,
Homelich at other mennes houfes · and hatyen her owne.
Elyng¹ is þe halle · vche daye in þe wyke,
Þere þe lorde ne þe lady · liketh nou3te to fytte.
Now hath vche riche a reule² · to eten bi hym-felue
In a pryue parloure · for pore mennes fake,
Or in a chambre with a chymneye · and leue þe chief halle,
Þat was made for meles · men to eten Inne ;
And al to fpare to fpille · þat fpende fhal an other.
¶ And whan þat witte was ywar · what dame ftudye tolde,
He bicome fo confus · he couth nou3te loke,
And as doumbe as deth · and drowe hym arrere³ ;
¶ And for no carpyng I couth after · ne knelyng to þe grounde,
I my3te gete no greyne · of his grete wittis,
But al laughyng he louted · and loked vppon ftudye,
In figne þat I fhulde · bifeche hir of grace.
¶ And whan I was war of his wille · to his wyf gan I loute,
And feyde, "mercy, madame · 3owre man fhal I worthe,
As longe as I liue · bothe late & rathe,
Forto worche 3owre wille · þe while my lyf dureth,
With þat 3e kenne me kyndely · to knowe what is dowel."
¶ "For þi mekeneffe, man," quod fhe · " and for þi mylde fpeche,
I fhal kenne þe to my cofyn · þat clergye is hoten.⁴
He hath wedded a wyf · with-Inne his fyx monethes,
Is fybbe⁵ to þe feuene artz · fcripture is hir name.
Þei two, as I hope · after my techyng,
Shullen wiffen þe to dowel · I dar it vndertake."
¶ Þanne was I alfo fayne⁶ · as foule⁷ of faire morwe,
And gladder þan þe gleman⁸ · þat golde hath to 3ifte,
And axed hir þe heighe weye · where þat clergye⁹ dwelte,
" And telle me fome token," quod I · " for tyme is þat I wende."
¶ " Axe þe heighe waye," quod fhe · " hennes to fuffre-
Bothe-wel-&-wo · 3if þat þow wolt lerne,
And ryde forth by ricchelle · ac reft þow nau3t þerinne,
For if þow coupleft þe þer-with · to clergye comeftow neuere.
¶ And alfo þe likeroufe launde · þat leccherye hatte,
Leue hym on þi left halue · a large myle or more,
Tyl þow come to a courte · kepe-wel-þi-tonge-
Fro-lefynges-and-lither¹⁰-fpeche- and-likeroufe-drynkes.
Þanne fhaltow fe fobrete · and fympleté-of-fpeche,
Þat eche wi3te be in wille · his witte þe to fhewe,
And þus fhaltow come to clergye · þat can many þinges.
¶ Saye hym þis figne · I fette hym to fcole,
And þat I grete wel his wyf · for I wrote hir many bokes,
And fette hir to fapience · and to þe fauter glofe.
Logyke I lerned hir · and many other lawes,
And alle þe mufou*n*s in mufike · I made hir to knowe.
¶ Plato þe poete · I put hym fyrfte to boke,
Ariftotle and other moo · to argue I tau3te.
Grammer for gerles · I garte firft wryte,
And bette hem with a baleis · but if þei wolde lerne.

---

¹ [ftrange, deferted. Henry VIII. in a letter to Anne Bullen fpeaks of his *Ellengnefs* fince her departure. Hearne's *Avefbury*, p. 360.] ² [cuftom.]
³ back. ⁴ named. ⁵ akin. ⁶ glad.
⁷ bird. ⁸ harper. ⁹ learning. ¹⁰ wanton, bad.

Of alkinnes craftes · I contreued toles,
Of carpentrie, of kerueres · and compaſſed maſouns,
And lerned hem leuel and lyne · þough I loke dymme.
¶ Ac theologie hath tened me · ten ſcore tymes,
The more I muſe þere-Inne · þe miſtier it ſemeth,
And þe depper I deuyne · þe derker me it þinketh ;
It is no ſcience for ſothe · forto ſotyle Inne ;
A ful lethy þinge it were · ȝif þat loue nere.
Ac for it let beſt by loue · I loue it þe bettre ;
For þere þat loue is leder · ne lacked neuere grace, &c.]

The artifices and perſuaſions of the monks to procure donations to their convents are thus humorouſly ridiculed, in a ſtrain which ſeems to have given riſe to Chaucer's *Sompnour's Tale* :—

Thanne he aſſoilled hir ſone · and ſithen he ſeyde,
"We han a wyndowe a wirchyng · wil ſitten vs ful heigh ;
Woldeſtow glaſe þat gable · and graue þere-inne þi name,
Siker ſholde þi ſoule be · heuene to haue." [B. iii. 47.][1]

Covetiſe or Covetouſneſs is thus drawn in the true colours of ſatirical painting.

And þanne cam coueytiſe · can I hym nouȝte deſcryue,
So hungriliche and holwe · ſire Heruy hym loked.
He was bitelbrowed · and baberlipped alſo,
With two blered eyghen · as a blynde hagge ;
And as a letheren purs · lolled his chekes,
Wel ſydder þan his chyn · þei chiueled for elde ;
And as a bondman of his bacoun · his berde was bidraueled.
With an hode on his hed · a louſi hatte aboue,
And in a tauny tabarde[2] · of twelue wynter age,
Al totorne and baudy · and ful of lys crepynge ;
But if þat a lous couthe · haue lopen þe bettre,
She ſholde nouȝte haue walked on þat welche · ſo was it thredebare.
"I haue ben coueytouſe," quod þis caityue · "I biknowe it here ;
For ſome tyme I ſerued · Symme atte Stile,

---

[1] Theſe, and the following lines, are plainly copied by Chaucer, viz. :—
"And I ſhall cover your kyrke, and your cloiſture do maken."
Chaucer, *Sompn. T.* v. 399, Morris edit. But with new ſtrokes of humour.

"' Yif me than of thy good to make our cloyſter,'
Quod he, 'for many a muſcle and many an oyſter
Hath ben oure foode, our cloyſter to arreyſe,
Whan other men han ben ful wel at eyſe ;
And yit, God wot, unnethe the foundement
Parformed is, ne of oure pavyment
Is nought a tyle yit withinne our wones ;
Bi God, we owe yit fourty pound for ſtones.' "

So alſo in the *Ploughman's Crede*, hereafter mentioned, l. 396, a friar ſays—

"So that thou mowe amenden our hous · with money other elles,
With ſom katell, other corne · or cuppes of ſiluer."

And again, l. 123—

"And mighteſtou amenden vs · with money of thyn owne,
Thou ſholdeſt enely bifore Criſt · in compas of gold,
In the wide windowe · weſtwarde · wel nighe in the myddell."

That is, "your figure ſhall be painted in glaſs, in the middle of the weſt window," &c. But of this paſſage hereafter.

[2] tabard. A coat.

And was his prentis yplizte · his profit to wayte.
Firſt I lerned to lye · a leef other tweyne,
Wikkedlich to weye · was my furſt leſſou*n*.
To Wy¹ and to Wyncheſtre² I went to þe faire,

---

¹ Wy is probably Weyhill in Hampſhire, where a famous fair ſtill ſubſiſts.

² Anciently, before many flouriſhing towns were eſtabliſhed, and the neceſſaries or ornaments of life, from the convenience of communication and the increaſe of provincial civility, could be procured in various places, goods and commodities of every kind were chiefly ſold at fairs, to which, as to one univerſal mart, the people reſorted periodically, and ſupplied moſt of their wants for the enſuing year. The diſplay of merchandiſe, and the conflux of cuſtomers at theſe principal and almoſt only emporia of domeſtic commerce, was prodigious; and they were often held on open and extenſive plains. One of the chief of them ſeems to have been that of St. Giles's hill or down near Wincheſter, to which our poet here refers. It was inſtituted and given as a kind of revenue to the biſhop of Wincheſter by William the Conqueror, who by his charter permitted it to continue for three days. But in conſequence of new royal grants, Henry III. prolonged its continuance to ſixteen days. Its juriſdiction extended ſeven miles round, and comprehended even Southampton, then a capital trading town: and all merchants who ſold wares within that circuit forfeited them to the biſhop. Officers were placed at a conſiderable diſtance, at bridges and other avenues of acceſs to the fair, to exact toll of all merchandiſe paſſing that way. In the meantime all ſhops in the city of Wincheſter were ſhut. In the fair was a court called the pavilion, at which the biſhop's juſticiaries and other officers aſſiſted, with power to try cauſes of various ſorts for ſeven miles round: nor among other ſingular claims could any lord of a manor hold a court-baron within the ſaid circuit without licence from the pavilion. During this time the biſhop was empowered to take toll of every load or parcel of goods paſſing through the gates of the city. On Saint Giles's eve the mayor, bailiffs, and citizens of the city of Wincheſter delivered the keys of the four city gates to the biſhop's officers who, during the ſaid ſixteen days, appointed a mayor and bailiff of their own to govern the city, and alſo a coroner to act within the ſaid city. Tenants of the biſhop, who held lands by doing ſervice at the pavilion, attended the ſame with horſes and armour, not only to do ſuit at the court there, but to be ready to aſſiſt the biſhop's officers in the execution of writs and other ſervices. But I cannot here enumerate the many extraordinary privileges granted to the biſhop on this occaſion, all tending to obſtruct trade and to oppreſs the people. Numerous foreign merchants frequented this fair; and it appears that the juſticiaries of the pavilion, and the treaſurer of the biſhop's palace of Wolveſey, received annually for a fee, according to ancient cuſtom, four baſins and ewers of thoſe foreign merchants who ſold brazen veſſels in the fair, and were called *mercatores diaunteres*. In the fair ſeveral ſtreets were formed, aſſigned to the ſale of different commodities, and called the Drapery, the Pottery, the Spicery, &c. Many monaſteries in and about Wincheſter had ſhops or houſes in theſe ſtreets, uſed only at the fair, which they held under the biſhop, and often let by leaſe for a term of years. One place in the fair was called *Speciarium Sancti Swythini*, or the Spicery of Saint Swithin's monaſtery. In the revenue rolls of the ancient biſhops of Wincheſter, this fair makes a grand and ſeparate article of reception, under this title: *Feria. Computus Feriæ ſancti Egidii*. But in the revenue roll of biſhop Will. of Waynflete [an. 1471], it appears to have greatly decayed: in which, among other proofs, I find mention made of a diſtrict in the fair being unoccupied, "*Ubi homines Cornubiæ ſtare ſolebant*." From whence it likewiſe appears that different counties had their different ſtations. The whole reception to the biſhop this year from the fair amounted only to 45*l*. 18*s*. 5*d*. Yet this ſum, ſmall as it may ſeem, was worth upwards of 400*l*. Edward I. ſent a precept to the ſheriff of Hampſhire to reſtore to the biſhop this fair, which his eſcheator Malcolm de Harlegh had ſeized into the king's hands, without command of the treaſurer and barons of the exchequer, in the year 1292. *Regiſtr. Joh. de Pontiſſara, Epiſc. Wint.* fol. 195. After the charter of Henry III. many kings by charter confirmed this

With many manere marchandife · as my Maiftre me hi3te;
Ne had þe grace of gyle · ygo amonge my ware,
It had be vnfolde þis feuene 3ere · fo me god helpe!
    Thanne drowe I me amonges draperes · my donet[1] to lerne,
To drawe þe lyfer alonge · þe lenger it femed;
Amonge þe riche rayes · I rendred a leffoun, &c. [B. v. 188.]

---

fair with all its privileges to the bifhops of Winchefter. The laft charter was of Henry VIII. to Bifhop Richard Fox and his fucceffors, in the year 1511. But it was followed by the ufual confirmation-charter of Charles II. In the year 1144, when Brian Fitz-count, lord of Wallingford in Berkfhire, maintained Wallingford Caftle, one of the ftrongeft garrifons belonging to Maud the emprefs, and confequently fent out numerous parties for contributions and provifions, Henry de Blois, bifhop of Winchefter, enjoined him not to moleft any paffengers that were coming to his fair at Winchefter, under pain of excommunication. *Omnibus ad feriam meam venientibus*, &c. *MSS. Dodfworth*, vol. 89, fol. 76, Bibl. Bodl. This was in King Stephen's reign. The laft of Richard I., in the year 1194, the king grants to Portfmouth a fair lafting for fifteen days, with all the privileges of Saint Giles's fair at Winchefter. Anders. *Hift. Com.* i. 197. In the year 1234, the eighteenth of Henry III., the fermier of the city of Winchefter paid twenty pounds to Ailward chamberlain of Winchefter Caftle, to buy a robe at this fair for the king's fon, and divers filver implements for a chapel in the caftle. Madox, *Exch.* p. 251. It appears from [the *Northumb. Houfh. Book*], that the ftores of his lordfhip's houfe at Wrefille, for the whole year, were laid in from fairs. "He that ftandes charged with my lordes houfe for the houll yeir, if he may poffible, fhall be at all Faires where the groice emptions fhall be boughte for the houfe for the houlle yeire, as wine, wax, beiffes, multons, wheite, and maltie," p. 407. This laft quotation is a proof that fairs ftill continued to be the principal marts for purchafing neceffaries in large quantities, which now are fupplied by frequent trading towns: and the mention of "beiffes" and "multons," which were falted oxen and fheep, fhews that at fo late a period they knew but little of breeding cattle. Their ignorance of fo important an article of hufbandry is alfo an evidence that in the reign of Henry VIII. the ftate of population was much lower among us than we may imagine.

In the ftatutes of Saint Mary Ottery's college in Devonfhire, given by Bifhop Grandifon the founder, the ftewards and facrift are ordered to purchafe annually two hundred pounds of wax for the choir of the college, at this fair. "Cap. lxvii.—Pro luminaribus vero omnibus fupradictis inveniendis, etiam ftatuimus, quod fenefcalli fcaccarii per vifum et auxilium facrifte, omni anno, in nundinis Wynton, vel alibi apud Toryngton et in partibus Barnftepol, ceram fufficientem, quam ad ducentas libras æftimamus pro uno anno ad minus faciant provideri." Thefe ftatutes were granted in the year 1338. MS. apud Regiftr. Priorat. S. Swithin. Winton. In Archiv. Wolves. In the accompts of the Priories of Maxtoke in Warwickfhire, and of Bicefter in Oxfordfhire, under the reign of Henry VI., the monks appear to have laid in yearly ftores of various yet common neceffaries, at the fair of Sturbridge in Cambridgefhire, at leaft one hundred miles diftant from either monaftery. It may feem furprifing, that their own neighbourhood, including the cities of Oxford and Coventry, could not fupply them with commodities neither rare nor coftly, which they thus fetched at a confiderable expence of carriage. It is a rubric in fome of the monaftic rules *De Euntibus ad Nundinas*. See Dugd. Mon. Angl. ii. p. 746. It is hoped the reader will excufe this tedious note, which at leaft developes ancient manners and cuftoms.

[1] Leffon. Properly a *Grammar*, from *Ælius Donatus* the grammarian. *Teftam. L.* p. 504, b. edit. Urr. "No paffef to vertues of this Margarite, but therin al my *donet* can I lerne." In the ftatutes of Winchefter-college, [written about 1386,] grammar is called "Antiquus donatus," *i. e.* the *old donat*, or the name of a fyftem of grammar at that time in vogue, and long before. The French have a book entitled "*Le Donnet, traité de grammaire, baillé a feu roi Charles* viii." Among Rawlinfon's MSS. at Oxford, I have feen *Donatus optimus noviter compi-*

Attack on the Prelacy.

Our author, who probably could not get preferment, thus inveighs against the luxury and diversions of the prelates of his age:

> Ac now is religiou*n* a ryder [1] a rowmer bi stretes,
> A leder of louedayes [2] · and a londe-bugger,
> A priker on a palfray · fro maner*e* to maner*e*,
> An heep of houndes at his ers · as he a lorde were. [1]
> And but if his knaue knele · þat shal his cuppe brynge,
> He loureth on hym and axeth hym · who tau3te hym curteisye ? [3]

There is great picturesque humour in the following lines:

---

latus, a manuscript on vellum, given to Saint Alban's, by John Stoke, abbot, in 1450. In the introduction, or *lytell Proheme*, to Dean Colet's *Grammatices Rudimenta*, we find mention made of "certayne introducyons into latyn speche called *Donates*," &c. Among the books written by Bishop Pecock, there is the *Donat into christian religion*, and the *Folower to the Donat*. Lewis's *Pecock*, p. 317. I think I have before observed, that John of Basing, who flourished in the year 1240, calls his Greek Grammar *Donatus Græcorum*. Pegge's *Weseham*, p. 51. Wynkyn de Worde printed *Donatus ad Anglicanarum scholarum usum*. [But see *Handb. of E. E. Lit*. art. *Children*.] Cotgrave (in v.) quotes an old French proverb, " Les diables estoient encores *a leur Donat, The devils were but yet in their grammar*."

[1] Walter de Suffield, bishop of Norwich, bequeaths by will his pack of hounds to the king in 1256. Blomefield's *Norf.* ii. 347. See Chaucer's *Monkes Prol.* v. 165. This was a common topic of satire. It occurs again, fol. xxvii. a. See [the] *Testament of Love*, p. 492, col. ii. Urr. The archdeacon of Richmond, on his visitation, comes to the priory of Bridlington in Yorkshire, in 1216, with ninety-seven horses, twenty-one dogs, and three hawks, Dugd. *Mon*. ii. 65.

[2] [love-days.]

[3] B. x. 306. The following prediction, although a probable conclusion, concerning a king, who after a time would suppress the religious houses, is remarkable. I imagined it was foisted into the copies, in the reign of Henry VIII. But it is in [all the] MSS. of this poem [which exhibit the *second* version, many of which are] older than the year 1400.

> " ¶ Ac þere shal come a kyng · and confesse 3ow religiouses,
> And bete 3ow as þe bible telleth · for brekynge of 3owre reule,
> And amende monyales · monkes and chanouns—
> ¶ And þanne Freres in her*e* freitour*e* · shal fynden a keye
> Of costantynes coffres · in which is þe catel
> Þat Gregories god-children · han yuel dispended.
> ¶ And þanne shal þe abbot of Abyndoun · and alle [his] issu for euere
> Haue a knokke of a kynge · and incurable þe wounde." [B. x. 317.]

Again, where he alludes to the knights-templers, lately suppressed :

> " Men of holy kirke
> Shul tourne as templeres did, *the tyme approcheth faste*."
> [B. xv. 507.]

This, I suppose, was a favourite doctrine in Wickliffe's discourses. I cannot help taking notice of a passage in *Piers Plowman*, which shews how the reigning passion for chivalry infected the ideas and expressions of the writers of this period. The poet is describing the crucifixion, and speaking of the person who pierced our Saviour's side with a spear. This person our author calls a knight, and says that he came forth " with his spere in hand, and justed with Jesus." Afterwards for doing so base an act as that of wounding a dead body, he is pronounced a disgrace to knighthood : and [this " champioun chiualer, chief knyght of yow alle " is declared to have yielded himself recreant. B. xviii. 99.] This knight's name is Longis, and he is blind ; but receives his sight from the blood which springs from our Saviour's side. This miracle is recorded in the *Golden Legend*. He is called Longias, " A blinde knight men ycallid Longias," in Chaucer, *Lam. Mar. Magd*. v. 177.

> Hunger in haſte þo · hent waſtour bi þe mawe,
> And wronge hym ſo bi þe wombe · þat bothe his eyen wattered;
> He buffeted þe Britoner · aboute þe chekes,
> þat he loked like a lanterne · al his lyf after.[1]

And in the following, where the Vices are repreſented as converted and coming to confeſſion, among which is the figure of Envy:

> Of a freres frokke · were þe forſleues.
> And as a leke hadde yleye · longe in þe ſonne,
> So loked he with lene chekes · lourynge foule. [B. v. 81.]

It would be tedious to tranſcribe other ſtrokes of humour, with which this poem abounds. Before one of the Viſions the poet falls aſleep, while he is bidding his beads. In another he deſcribes Antichriſt, whoſe banner is borne by Pride, as welcomed into a monaſtery with ringing of bells, and a ſolemn congratulatory proceſſion of all the monks as marching out to meet and receive him.[2]

Theſe images of mercy and truth are in a different ſtrain:

> Out of þe weſt coſte · a wenche, as me thouȝte,
> Cam walkynge in þe wey · to-helle-ward ſhe loked.
> Mercy hiȝt þat mayde · a meke þynge with-alle,
> A ful benygne buirde · and boxome of ſpeche.
> Her ſuſter, as it ſemed · cam ſoftly walkynge,
> Euene out of þe eſt · and weſtward ſhe loked.
> A ful comely creature · treuth ſhe hiȝte,
> For þe vertue þat hir folwed · aferd was ſhe neuere.
> Whan þis maydenes mette · mercy and treuth,
> Eyther axed other · of þis grete wonder,
> Of þe dyne & of þe derkneſſe, &c.[3]

The imagery of Nature, or Kinde, ſending forth his diſeaſes from the planets, at the command of Conſcience, and of his attendants Age and Death, is conceived with ſublimity:

> Kynd Conſcience tho herde · and cam out of the planets,
> And ſent forth his foreioures · feures & fluxes,
> Coughes, and cardiacles · crampes, and tothaches,
> Rewmes, & radegoundes · and roynouſe ſcalles,
> Byles, and bocches · and brennyng agues;
> Freneſyes, & foule yueles · forageres of kynde,
> Hadde yprykked and prayed · polles of peple,
> þat largelich a legioun · leſe her lyf ſone.
> ¶ There was—" harrow and help! · here cometh kynde,
> With deth þat is dredful · to vndone vs alle!"
> ¶ The lorde that lyued after luſt · tho alowde cryde
> After conforte, a knyghte · to come and bere his banere
> ¶ Elde þe hore · he was in þe vauntwarde,
> And bare þe banere bifor deth · by riȝte he it claymed.
> Kynde come after · with many kene ſores,
> As pokkes and peſtilences · and moche poeple ſhente;
> So kynde þorw corupciouns · kulled ful manye.
> ¶ Deth cam dryuende after · and al to douſt paſshed
> Knyges & knyȝtes · kayſeres and popes;
> Many a louely lady · and lemmanes of knyghtes
> Swouned and ſwelted · for ſorwe of dethes dyntes.
> ¶ Conſcience of his curteiſye · to kynde he biſouȝte,
> To ceſſe & ſuffre · and ſee where þei wolde

---

[1] [B. text; vi. 176.]   [2] [B. xx. 57.]   [3] [B. xviii. 113.]

Leue pryde pryuely · and be parfite criftene.
¶ And kynde ceffed tho · to fe þe peple amende.[1]

Thefe lines at leaft put us in mind of Milton's *Lazarhoufe*:[2]

> . . . . . Immediately a place
> Before his eyes appeared, fad, noifome, dark:
> A lazar-houfe it feem'd, wherein were laid
> Numbers of all difeas'd: all maladies
> Of gaftly fpafm, or racking torture, qualms
> Of heart-fick agony, all feverous kinds,
> Convulfions, epilepfies, fierce catarrhs,
> Inteftine ftone, and ulcer, cholic pangs,
> Demoniac phrenzy, moping melancholy,
> And moon-ftruck madnefs, pining atrophy,
> Marafmus, and wide-wafting Peftilence:
> Dropfies and afthma, and joint-racking rheum.
> Dire was the toffing! Deep the groans! Defpair
> Tended the fick, bufy from couch to couch;
> And over them triumphant Death his dart
> Shook, but delay'd to ftrike, &c.

At length Fortune or Pride fends forth a numerous army led by Luft, to attack Confcience.

> And gadered a gret hofte · al agayne CONSCIENCE:
> This LECHERYE leyde on · with a laughyng chiere,
> And with pryue fpeche · and peynted wordes,
> And armed hym in ydelneffe · and in hiegh berynge.
> He bare a bowe in his hande · and manye blody arwes,
> Weren fethered with faire bihefte · and many a falfe truthe.[3]

Afterwards Confcience is befieged by Antichrift and feven great giants, who are the feven capital or deadly fins: and the affault is made by Sloth, who conducts an army of more than a thoufand prelates.

It is not improbable, that Langland here had his eye on the old French *Roman d'Antechrift*, a poem written by Huon de Meri, about the year 1228. The author of this piece fuppofes that Antichrift is on earth, that he vifits every profeffion and order of life, and finds numerous partifans. The Vices arrange themfelves under the banner of Antichrift, and the Virtues under that of Chrift. Thefe two armies at length come to an engagement, and the battle ends to the honour of the Virtues, and the total defeat of the Vices. The banner of Antichrift has before occurred in our quotations from Longland. The title of Huon de Meri's poem deferves notice. It is [*Le*] *Turnoyement de l' Antechrift*. Thefe are the concluding lines:

> Par fon droit nom a peau cet livre
> Qui trefbien s'avorde a l' efcrit
> Le *Tournoiement de l'Antechrift*.

The author appears to have been a monk of St. Germain des Pres, near Paris.[4] This allegory is much like that which we find in the old dramatic Moralities. The theology of the middle ages abounded with conjectures and controverfies concerning Antichrft, who at a very early period was commonly believed to be the Roman pontiff.[5]

---

[1] [B. xx. p. 372, edit. Skeat.] [2] *Par. L.* ii. 475. [3] [B. xx. 112.]
[4] [See fome account of this poem in Mr. Wright's *St. Patrick's Purgatory.*]
[5] See this topic difcuffed with fingular penetration and perfpicuity, by Dr. Hurd. in *Twelve Sermons Introductory to the Study of the Prophecies*, 1772, p. 206, *feq*.

SECTION IX.

TO the *Vision of [William concerning] Pierce Plowman* has been commonly annexed a poem called *Pierce the Plowman's Crede*.[1] The author, in the character of a plain uninformed person, pretends to be ignorant of his creed, to be instructed in the articles of which, he applies by turns to the four orders of Mendicant friars. This circumstance affords an obvious occasion of exposing in lively colours the tricks of those societies. After so unexpected a disappointment, he meets one Pierce or Peter, a ploughman, who resolves his doubts, and teaches him the principles of true religion. In a copy of the [edition of the] *Crede*, [printed in 1561], presented to me by the Bishop of Gloucester, and once belonging to Mr. Pope, the latter in his own hand has inserted the following abstract of its plan. " An ignorant plain man having learned his Pater-noster and Ave-Mary, wants to learn his creed. He asks several religious men of the several orders to teach it him. First a friar Minor, who bids him beware of the Carmelites, and assures him they can teach him nothing, describing their faults, &c. but that the friars Minors shall save him, whether he learns his creed or not. He goes next to the friars Preachers, whose magnificent monastery he describes: there he meets a fat friar, who declaims against the Augustines. He is shocked at his pride, and goes to the Augustines. They rail at the Minorites. He goes to the Carmelites: they abuse the Dominicans, but promise him salvation, without the creed, for money. He leaves them with indignation, and finds an honest poor Ploughman in the field, and tells him how he was disappointed by the four orders. The ploughman answers with a long invective against them."

The language of the *Crede* is less embarrassed and obscure than that of the *Vision*. But before I proceed to a specimen, it may not

---

[1] The first edition [was printed by Reynold Wolfe in 1553.] It was reprinted, and added to Rogers's, or the fourth, edition of the *Vision*, 1561. It was evidently written after the year 1384. Wickliffe died in that year, and he is mentioned as no longer living, in signat.—C ii. edit. 1561 [l. 528]. Walter Britte or Brithe, a follower of Wickliffe, is also mentioned [l. 657] signat. C iii. [The *Crede* is in no sense an appendage to the *Vision*, but upon a totally different plan. The proper sequel to the *Vision* is the piece called the *Deposition of Richard II*., probably also by Langland. But *Pierce the Plowman's Crede* is by another author, a professed follower of Wickliffe, written about A.D. 1394, in order to discredit the four orders of Mendicant Friars. The only points of connection with the *Vision* are the title, which was imitated from it; the rhythm, and the fact that some have thought fit to print both poems in one volume, to the intense confusion of hasty students, who mix the two together in a most unscholarly fashion.—*Skeat*.] Britte is placed by Bale in 1390. Cent. vi. 94. See also Fuller's *Worth*. p. 8, *Wales*, [and Pref. to edit. Skeat.] The reader will pardon this small anticipation for the sake of connection.

be perhaps improper to prepare the reader, by giving an outline of the conſtitution and character of the four orders of Mendicant friars, the object of our poet's ſatire: an enquiry in many reſpects connected with the general purport of this hiſtory, and which, in this place at leaſt, cannot be deemed a digreſſion, as it will illuſtrate the main ſubject, and explain many particular paſſages, of the *Plowman's Crede*.[1]

Long before the thirteenth century, the monaſtic orders, as we have partly ſeen in the preceding poem, in conſequence of their ample revenues, had degenerated from their primitive auſterity, and were totally given up to luxury and indolence. Hence they became both unwilling and unable to execute the purpoſes of their eſtabliſhment: to inſtruct the people, to check the growth of hereſies, or to promote in any reſpect the true intereſts of the church. They forſook all their religious obligations, deſpiſed the authority of their ſuperiors, and were abandoned without ſhame or remorſe to every ſpecies of diſſipation and licentiouſneſs. About the beginning therefore of the thirteenth century, the condition and circumſtances of the church rendered it abſolutely neceſſary to remedy theſe evils, by introducing a new order of religious, who being deſtitute of fixed poſſeſſions, by the ſeverity of their manners, a profeſſed contempt of riches, and an unwearied perſeverance in the duties of preaching and prayer, might reſtore reſpect to the monaſtic inſtitution, and recover the honours of the church. Theſe were the four orders of mendicant or begging friars, commonly denominated the Franciſcans, the Dominicans, the Carmelites, and the Auguſtines.[2]

Theſe ſocieties ſoon ſurpaſſed all the reſt, not only in the purity of their lives, but in the number of their privileges and the multitude of their members. Not to mention the ſucceſs which attends all novelties, their reputation aroſe quickly to an amazing height. The popes, among other uncommon immunities, allowed them the liberty of travelling wherever they pleaſed, of converſing with perſons of all ranks, of inſtructing the youth and the people in general, and of hearing confeſſions, without reſerve or reſtriction: and as on theſe occaſions, which gave them opportunities of appearing in public and conſpicuous ſituations, they exhibited more ſtriking marks of gravity and ſanctity than were obſervable in the deportment and conduct of the members of other monaſteries, they were regarded with the

---

[1] And of ſome perhaps quoted above from the *Viſion*. ["Of the creed there does not appear to exiſt any manuſcript older than the firſt printed edition."—*Wright*. But ſee Mr. Skeat's notice of a MS. in Trin. Coll. Camb. which, though a late tranſcript, is obviouſly exactly copied from a MS. of the firſt half of the fifteenth century.]

[2] The Franciſcans were often ſtyled friars-minors, or minorites, and greyfriars: the Dominicans, friars-preachers, and ſometimes black-friars; the Carmelites, white-friars; and the Auſtins, grey-friars. The firſt eſtabliſhment of the Dominicans in England was at Oxford in 1221; of the Franciſcans, at Canterbury. Theſe two were the moſt eminent of the four orders. The Dominican friary at Oxford ſtood in an iſland on the ſouth of the city, ſouth-weſt of the Franciſcan friary, the ſite of which is hereafter deſcribed.

highest esteem and veneration throughout all the countries of Europe.

In the mean time they gained still greater respect, by cultivating the literature then in vogue with the greatest assiduity and success. Giannone says, that most of the theological professors in the university of Naples, newly founded in the year 1220, were chosen from the Mendicants.¹ They were the principal teachers of theology at Paris, the school where this science had received its origin.² At Oxford and Cambridge respectively, all the four orders had flourishing monasteries. The most learned scholars in the university of Oxford, at the close of the thirteenth century, were Franciscan friars: and long after this period, the Franciscans appear to have been the sole support and ornament of that university.³ Hence it was that Bishop Hugh de Balsham, founder of Peter-house at Cambridge, orders in his statutes given about the year 1280, that some of his scholars should annually repair to Oxford for improvement in the sciences.⁴ That is, to study under the Franciscan readers. Such was the eminence of the Franciscan friary at Oxford, that the learned Bishop Groseteste, in the year 1253, bequeathed all his books to that celebrated seminary.⁵ This was the house in which the renowned Roger Bacon was educated; who revived in the midst of barbarism, and brought to a considerable degree of perfection, the knowledge of mathematics in England, and greatly facilitated many modern discoveries in experimental philosophy.⁶ The same fraternity is likewise said to have stored their

---

¹ *Hist. Nap.* xvi. 3.
² See Boul. *Hist. Academ. Paris*, iii. pp. 138, 240, 244, 248, &c.
³ This circumstance in some degree roused the monks from their indolence, and induced the greater monasteries to procure the foundation of small colleges in the universities for the education of their novices. At Oxford the monks had also schools which bore the name of their respective orders : and there were schools in that university which were appropriated to particular monasteries. Kennet's *Paroch. Ant.* p. 214. Wood, *Hist. Ant. Univ. Oxon.* i. 119. Leland says, that even in his time at Stamford, a temporary university, the names of halls inhabited by the novices of Peterborough, Sempringham, and Vauldrey abbeys, were remaining. *Itin.* vi. p. 21. And it appears, that the greater part of the proceeders in theology at Oxford and Cambridge, just before the Reformation, were monks. But we do not find that, in consequence of all these efforts, the monks made a much greater figure in literature. In this rivalry which subsisted between the mendicants and the monks, the latter sometimes availed themselves of their riches: and with a view to attract popularity, and to eclipse the growing lustre of the former, proceeded to their degrees in the universities with prodigious parade. In the year 1298, William de Brooke, a Benedictine of St. Peter's abbey at Gloucester, took the degree of doctor in divinity at Oxford. He was attended on this important occasion by the abbot and whole convent of Gloucester, the abbots of Westminster, Reading, Abingdon, Evesham, and Malmesbury, with one hundred noblemen and esquires, on horses richly caparisoned. These were entertained at a sumptuous feast in the refectory of Gloucester college. But it should be observed, that he was the first of the Benedictine order that attained this dignity. Wood, *Hist. Ant. Univ. Oxon.* i. 25, col. 1. See also Dugdale, *Mon.* [edit. Stevens,] i. 70.
⁴ " De scholaribus emittendis ad universitatem Oxonie pro doctrina." Cap. xviii.
⁵ Leland. *Script. Brit.* p. 283. This house stood just without the city walls, near Little-gate. The garden called Paradise was their grove or orchard.
⁶ It is probable that the treatises of many of Bacon's scholars and followers, col-

valuable library with a multitude of Hebrew manuscripts, which they purchased of the Jews on their banishment from England.[1] Richard de Bury, Bishop of Durham, author of *Philobiblon*, and the founder of a library at Oxford, is prolix in his praises of the Mendicants for their extraordinary diligence in collecting books.[2] Indeed it became difficult in the beginning of the fourteenth century to find any treatise in the arts, theology, or canon law, commonly exposed to sale: they were all universally bought up by the friars.[3] This is mentioned by Richard Fitzralph, archbishop of Armagh, in his discourse before the Pope at Avignon in 1357; he was their bitter and professed antagonist, and adds, without any intention of paying them a compliment, that all the Mendicant convents were furnished with a "grandis et nobilis libraria."[4] Sir Richard Whittington built the library of the Grey Friars in London, which was one hundred and twenty-nine feet long, and twelve broad, with twenty-eight desks.[5] About the year 1430, one hundred marks were paid for transcribing the profound Nicholas de Lyra, in two volumes, to be chained in this library.[6] Leland relates that Thomas Wallden, a learned Carmelite, bequeathed to the same library as many MSS. of approved authors, written in capital Roman characters, as were then estimated at more than two thousand pieces of gold.[7] He adds that this library even in his time exceeded all others in London for multitude of books and antiquity of copies.[8] Among many other instances which might be given of the learning of the Mendicants, there is one which greatly contributed to establish their literary character. In the eleventh century, Aristotle's philosophy had been condemned in the university of Paris as heretical. About a hundred years afterwards, these prejudices began to subside; and new translations of Aristotle's writings were published in Latin by our countryman Michael Scotus, and others, with more attention to the original Greek, at least without the pompous and perplexed

---

lected by Thomas Allen in the reign of James I. still remain among the MSS. of Sir Kenelm Digby in the Bodleian library.

[1] Wood, *ubi supr.* 1, 77, col. 2.
[2] *Philobibl.* cap. v. This book was written in 1344.
[3] Yet I find a decree made at Oxford, where these orders of friars flourished so greatly, in the year 1373, to check the excessive multitude of persons selling books in the university without licence. *Vet. Stat. Univ. Oxon.* D. fol. 75. Archiv. Bodl.
[4] MSS. Bibl. Bodl. Propositio coram papa, &c. And MSS. C.C.C. Oxon. 182. Propositio coram, &c. See a translation of this Sermon by Trevisa, MSS. Harl. 1900, 2. See f. 11. See also Browne's *append. Fascic. Rer. expetend. fugiend.* ii. p. 466. I believe this discourse has been printed twice or thrice at Paris. In which, says the archbishop, there were thirty thousand scholars at Oxford in my youth, but now (1357) scarce six thousand. At Bennet in Cambridge, there is a curious MS. of one of Fitzrauf's Sermons, in the first leaf of which there is a drawing of four devils, hugging four mendicant friars, one of each of the four orders, with great familiarity and affection. MSS. L. 16. This book belonged to Adam Eston, a very learned Benedictine of Norwich, and a witness against Wickliffe at Rome, where he lived the greatest part of his life, in 1370.
[5] Stow's *Surv. Lond.* p. 255, edit. 1599.
[6] Stow, *ibid.* p. 256, Dugd. *Monast.* [ed. Stevens] i. 112.   [7] Aurei.
[8] *Script. Brit.* p. 441, and *Collectan.* iii. p. 52.

circumlocutions which appeared in the Arabic versions hitherto used. In the mean time sprang up the Mendicant orders who, happily availing themselves of these new translations, and making them the constant subject of their scholastic lectures, were the first who revived the doctrines of this philosopher, and acquired the merit of having opened a new system of science.[1] The Dominicans of Spain were accomplished adepts in the learning and language of the Arabians; and were employed by the kings of Spain in the instruction and conversion of the numerous Jews and Saracens who resided in their dominions.[2]

The buildings of the Mendicant monasteries, especially in England, were remarkably magnificent, and commonly much exceeded those of the endowed convents of the second magnitude. As these fraternities were professedly poor, and could not from their original institution receive estates, the munificence of their benefactors was employed in adorning their houses with stately refectories and churches: and for these and other purposes they did not want address to procure abundance of patronage, which was facilitated by the notion of their superior sanctity. It was fashionable for persons of the highest rank to bequeath their bodies to be buried in the friary churches, which were consequently filled with sumptuous shrines and superb monuments.[3] In the noble church of the Grey friars in London, finished in the year 1325, but long since destroyed, four queens, besides upwards of six hundred persons of quality, were buried, whose beautiful tombs remained till the dissolution.[4] These interments imported considerable sums of money into the mendicant

---

[1] See Joann. Laun. *de varia Aristotel. Fortun. in Acad. Paris*, p. 78, edit. 1662.

[2] R. Simon's *Lett. Chois.* tom. iii. p. 112. They studied the arts of popular entertainment. The Mendicants, I believe, were the only religious in England who acted plays. The *Creation of the World*, annually performed by the Grey friars at Coventry, is still extant. And they seem to have been famous abroad for these exhibitions. De la Flamma, who flourished about the year 1340, has the following curious passage in his chronicle of the Visconti of Milan, published by Muratori. In the year 1336, says he, on the feast of Epiphany, the first feast of the three kings was celebrated at Milan by the convent of the friars Preachers. The three kings appeared crowned on three great horses, richly habited, surrounded by pages, body-guards, and an innumerable retinue. A golden star was exhibited in the sky, going before them. They proceeded to the pillars of S. Lawrence, where King Herod was represented with his scribes and wife men. The three kings ask Herod where Christ should be born: and his wise men having consulted their books, answer him at Bethlehem. On which, the three kings with their golden crowns, having in their hands golden cups filled with frankincense, myrrh, and gold, the star still going before, marched to the church of S. Eustorgius with all their attendants, preceded by trumpets and horns, apes, baboons, and a great variety of animals. In the church, on one side of the high altar, there was a manger with an ox and an ass, and in it the infant Christ in the arms of his mother. Here the three kings offer their gifts, &c. The concourse of the people, of knights, ladies, and ecclesiastics, was such as never before was beheld, &c. *Rer. Italic. Scriptor.* tom. xii. col. 1017. D. This feast in the ritual is called The feast of the Star. Joann. Episcop. Abrinc. *de Offic. Eccl.* p. 30.

[3] Their churches were esteemed more sacred than others.

[4] Weev. *Fun. Mon.* p. 388.

focieties. It is probable that they derived more benefit from cafual charity, than they would have gained from a regular endowment. The Francifcans indeed enjoyed from the popes the privilege of diftributing indulgences, a valuable indemnification for their voluntary poverty.[1]

On the whole, two of thefe Mendicant inftitutions, the Dominicans and the Francifcans, for the fpace of nearly three centuries appear to have governed the European church and ftate with an abfolute and univerfal fway; they filled, during that period, the moft eminent ecclefiaftical and civil ftations, taught in the univerfities with an authority which filenced all oppofition, and maintained the difputed prerogative of the Roman pontiff againft the united influence of prelates and kings, with a vigour only to be paralleled by its fuccefs. The Dominicans and Francifcans were, before the Reformation, exactly what the Jefuits have been fince. They difregarded their monaftic character and profeffion, and were employed not only in fpiritual matters, but in temporal affairs of the greateft confequence; in compofing the differences of princes, concluding treaties of peace, and concerting alliances; they prefided in cabinet councils, levied national fubfidies, influenced courts, and managed the machinery of every important operation and event, both in the religious and political world.

From what has been here faid, it is natural to fuppofe that the Mendicants at length became univerfally odious. The high efteem in which they were held, and the tranfcendent degree of authority which they had affumed, only ferved to render them obnoxious to the clergy of every rank, to the monafteries of other orders, and to the univerfities. It was not from ignorance, but from a knowledge of mankind, that they were active in propagating fuperftitious notions, which they knew were calculated to captivate the multitude, and to ftrengthen the papal intereft; yet at the fame time, from the vanity of difplaying an uncommon fagacity of thought and a fuperior fkill in theology, they affected novelties in doctrine, which introduced dangerous errors, and tended to fhake the pillars of orthodoxy. Their ambition was unbounded, and their arrogance intolerable. Their increafing numbers became, in many ftates, an enormous and unwieldy burthen to the commonwealth. They had abufed the powers and privileges which had been intrufted to them; and the common fenfe of mankind could not long be blinded or deluded by the palpable frauds and artifices, which thefe rapacious zealots fo notorioufly practifed for enriching their convents. In England, the univerfity of Oxford refolutely refifted the perpetual encroachments of the Dominicans;[2] and many of our theologifts attacked all the four orders with great vehemence and feverity. Exclufively of the jealoufies and animofities which naturally fubfifted between four rival inftitutions, their vifionary refinements and love of difputation introduced

---

[1] See Baluz. *Mifcellan.* tom. iv. 490, vii. 392.
[2] Wood, *ut fupr.* i. 150, 154, 196.

among them the most violent dissensions. The Dominicans aimed at popularity by an obstinate denial of the immaculate conception. Their pretended sanctity became at length a term of reproach, and their learning fell into discredit. As polite letters and general knowledge increased, their speculative and pedantic divinity gave way to a more liberal turn of thinking and a more perspicuous mode of writing. Bale, who was himself a Carmelite friar, says that his order, which was eminently distinguished for scholastic erudition, began to lose their estimation about the year 1460. Some of them were imprudent enough to engage openly in political controversy; and the Augustines destroyed all their repute and authority in England by seditious sermons, in which they laboured to supplant the progeny of Edward IV., and to establish the title of the usurper Richard.[1] About the year 1530, Leland visited the Franciscan friary at Oxford, big with the hopes of finding in their celebrated library, if not many valuable books, at least those which had been bequeathed by the learned bishop Grosseteste. The delays and difficulties, with which he procured admittance into this venerable repository, heightened his curiosity and expectations. At length, after much ceremony, being permitted to enter, instead of an inestimable treasure, he saw little more than empty shelves covered with cobwebs and dust.[2]

After so prolix an introduction, I cannot but give a large quotation from our *Crede*, the humour and tendency of which will now be easily understood; especially as this poem is so curious and lively a picture of an order of men who once made so conspicuous a figure in the world:[3]

> For first y fraynede þe freres · and þey me fulle tolden,
> Þat all þe frute of þe fayþ · was in here foure ordres,
> And þe cofres of cristendam · & þe keye boþen,
> And þe lok [of beleve · lyeth] loken in her hondes.

---

[1] Newcourt, *Repert*. i. 289.

[2] Leland describes this adventure with some humour. "Contigit ut copiam peterem videndi bibliothecam Franciscanorum, ad quod obstreperunt asini aliquot, rudentes nulli prorsus mortalium tam sanctos aditus et recessus adire, nisi Gardiano et sacris sui collegii baccalariis. Sed ego urgebam, et principis diplomate munitus, tantum non coegi, ut sacraria illa aperirent. Tum unus e majoribus asinis multa subrudens tandem fores ægre referavit. Summe Jupiter! quid ego illic inveni? Pulverem autem inveni, telas aranearum, tineas, blattas, situm denique et squallorem. Inveni etiam et libros, sed quos tribus obolis non emerem."—*Script. Brit.* p. 286.

[3] [The British Museum contains but one MS. (King's MSS. 18. B. xvi.) of the *Crede*, and that of no early date. It agrees closely in orthography and matter with the printed copy, and is perhaps not much older.—Price. There is another MS. in the library of Trinity College, Cambridge. Both MSS., as well as the old printed edition, are evidently derived from one and the same older MS., now lost, of the early part of the fifteenth century. The Trinity MS. is a very faithful transcript, and far more correct than the Museum copy; both the MSS. copies are more correct than the printed edition. The *Crede*, as printed by Warton and his editors, has now been adjusted to the *Early English Text Society's* edition, 1867, ed. by Rev. W. W. Skeat.]

Þanne [wende] y to wyten · & wiþ a whiȝt y mette,
A Menoure in a morrow-tide · & to þis man I faide,
"Sire, for grete god[e]s loue · þe graiþ þou me telle,
Of what myddelerde man · miȝte y beft lerne
My Crede? For I can it nouȝt · my kare is þe more;
& þerfore, for Criftes loue · þi councell y praie.
A Carm me haþ y-couenaunt · þe Crede me to teche;
But for þou knoweft Carmes well · þi counfaile y afke."
Þis Menour loked on me · and lawȝyng he feyde,
"Leue Criften man · y leue þat þou madde!
Whouȝ fchulde þei techen þe God · þat con not hemfelue?
Þei ben but jugulers · and iapers, of kynde,
Lorels and Lechures · & lemmans holden;
Neyþer in order ne out · but vn-neþe lybbeþ,
And byiapeþ þe folke · wiþ geftes of Rome!
It is but a faynt folk · i-founded vp-on iapes,
Þei makeþ hem Maries men¹ · (fo þei men tellen),
And lieþ on our Ladie · many a longe tale.
And þat wicked folke · wymmen bi-traieþ,
And bigileþ hem of her good · wiþ glauerynge wordes,
And þerwiþ holden her hous · in harlotes werkes.
And, fo faue me God! · I hold it gret fynne
To ȝyuen hem any good · fwiche glotones to fynde,
To maynteyne fwiche maner men · þat mychel good deftruyeþ.
Ȝet feyn they in here futilte · to fottes in townes,
Þei comen out of Carmeli² · Crift for to followen,
& feyneþ hem with holynes · þat yuele hem bifemeþ.
Þei lyuen more in lecherie · and lieth in her tales
Þan fuen any god liife; · but [lurken] in her felles,
[And] wynnen werldliche god · & waften it in fynne.
And ȝif þei couþen her crede · oþer on Crift leueden,
Þei weren nouȝt fo hardie · fwich harlotri vfen.
Sikerli y can nouȝt fynden · who hem firft founded,
But þe foles foundeden hem-felf · freres of the Pye,
And maken hem mendynauns · & marre þe puple.
But what glut of þo gomes · may any good kachen,
He will kepen it hym-felf · & cofren it fafte,
And þeiȝ his felawes fayle good · for him he may fteruen.
Her money may bi-queft · & teftament maken,
And no obedience bere · but don as [hem] lufte.
[And] ryȝt as Robertes men³ raken aboute,
At feires & at ful ales · & fyllen þe cuppe,
And precheþ all of pardon · to plefen the puple.

---

¹ The Carmelites, fometimes called the brethren of the Bleffed Virgin, were fond of boafting their familiar intercourfe with the Virgin Mary. Among other things, they pretended that the Virgin affumed the Carmelite habit and profeffion: and that fhe appeared to Simon Sturckius, general of their order, in the thirteenth century, and gave him a folemn promife, that the fouls of thofe Chriftians who died with the Carmelite fcapulary upon their fhoulders fhould infallibly efcape damnation.

² The Carmelites pretended that their order was originally founded on Mount Carmel where Elias lived: and that their firft convent was placed there, within an ancient church dedicated to the Virgin Mary in 1121.

³ Robartes men, or Roberdfmen, were a fet of lawlefs vagabonds, notorious for their outrages when *Pierce Plowman* was written, that is, about the year [1362]. The ftatute Edw. III. (*an. reg.* 5. c. xiv.) fpecifies "divers manflaughters, felonies, and robberies, done by people that be called *Roberdefmen*, Waftours, and drawlatches." And the ftatute (*an. reg.* 7. c. v.) ordains, that the ftatute of King Edward concerning *Roberdfmen* and *Drawlacches* fhall be rigoroufly obferved.

Her pacience is all pafed · & put out to ferme,
And pride is in her pouerte · þat litell is to preifen.
And at þe lulling of oure Ladye · þe wymmen to lyken,
And miracles of mydwyves · & maken wymmen to wenen
Þat þe lace of oure ladie fmok · liʒteþ hem of children.
Þei ne prechen nouʒt of Powel · ne penaunce for fynne,
But all of mercy & menfk · þat Marie maie helpen.
Wiþ fterne ftaues and ftronge · þey ouer lond ftrakeþ
Þider as her lemmans liggeþ · and lurkeþ in townes,
(Grey grete-hedede quenes · wiþ gold by þe eiʒen),
And feyn, þat here fuftren þei ben · þat foiourneþ aboute;
And þus about þey gon · & godes folke by-traieþ.
It is þe puple þat Powel · preched of in his tyme;
He feyde of fwich folk · þat fo aboute wente,
' Wepyng, y warne ʒow · of walkers aboute;
It beþ enemyes of þe cros · þat crift opon þolede.
Swiche flomerers in flepe · flauþe is her ende,
And glotony is her God · wiþ g[l]oppyng of drynk,[1]
And gladnes in glees · & gret ioye y-maked;
In þe fchendyng of fwiche · fchall mychel folk lawʒe.'
Þerfore, frend, for þi feyþ · fond to don betere,
Leue nouʒt on þo lofels · but let hem forþ pafen,
For þei ben fals in her feiþ · & fele mo oþere."
" Alas! frere," quaþ I þo · " my purpos is i-failed,
Now is my counfort a-caft! · canftou no bote,
Where y myʒte meten wiþ a man · þat myʒte me [wiffen]
For to conne my Crede · Crift for to folwen?"
" CERTEYNE, felawe," quaþ þe frere · " wiþ-outen any faile.
Of all men opon mold · we Menures moft fcheweþ
Þe pure Apoftell[e]s life · wiþ penance on erþe,
And fuen hem in fauntite · & fuffren well harde.
We haunten none tauernes · ne hobelen abouten;
At marketts & myracles · we medleþ vs nevere;
We hondlen no money · but menelich faren,
And haven hunger at [the] meate · at ich a mel ones.
We hauen forfaken the worlde · & in wo lybbeþ.
In penaunce & pouerte · & precheþ þe puple,
By enfample of oure life · foules to helpen;
And in pouertie praien · for all oure parteners
Þat ʒyueþ vs any good · god to honouren,
Oþer bell oþer booke · or breed to our fode,
Oþer catell oþer cloþ · to coveren wiþ our bones,
Money or money-worthe; · here mede is in heven.
For we buldeþ a burwʒ · a brod and a large,
A Chirche and A Chapaile · with chambers a-lofte,
Wiþ wide windowes y-wrouʒt · & walles well heye,
Þat mote bene portreid and paynt · & pulched ful clene [2]
Wiþ gaie glittering glas · glowing as þe fonne.
And myʒteftou amenden vs · wiþ money[3] of þyn owne,
Þou chuldeft cnely bifore Crift · in compas of gold
In þe wide windowe weftwarde · wel niʒe in the myddell,[4]
And feynt Fraunces him-felf · fchall folden the in his cope,

---

[1] In the *Liber Pœnitentialis* there is this injunction, " Si monachus per ebrietatem *vomitum fecerit*, triginta dies *pœniteat*." MSS. James V. 237, Bibl. Bodl.

[2] Muft be painted and beautifully adorned. *Mote* is often ufed in Chaucer for muft.

[3] If you would help us with your money.

[4] Your figure kneeling to Chrift fhall be painted in the great weft window. This was the way of reprefenting benefactors in painted glafs. See *fupr*.

And presente the to the trynitie · and praie for thy synnes;
Þi name schall noblich ben wryten · & wrouȝt for the nones,
And, in remembrance of þe · y-rade þer for euer.[1]
And, broþer, be þou nouȝt aferd; · [bythenk in] thyn herte,
Þouȝ þou conne nouȝt þi Crede · kare þou no more.
I schal asoilen þe, syre · & setten it on my soule,
And þou maie maken þis good · þenk þou non oþer."
"SIRE," y saide, "in certaine · y schal gon & asaye;"—
And he sette on me his honde · & asoilede me clene,
And þeir y parted him fro · wiþ-outen any peine,
In couenant þat y come aȝen · Crist he me be-tauȝte.
Þanne saide y to my-self · "here semeþ litel trewþe!
First to blamen his broþer · and bacbyten him foule,
Þeire-as curteis Crist · clereliche saide,
'Whow myȝt-tou in thine broþer eiȝe · a bare mote loken,
And in þyn owen eiȝe · nouȝt a bem toten?
See fyrst on þi-self · and siþen on anoþer,
And clense clene þi syȝt · and kepe well þyn eiȝe,
And for anoþer mannes eiȝe · ordeyne after.'
And also y sey coueitise · catel to fongen,
Þat Crist haþ clerliche forboden · & clenliche destruede,
And saide to his sueres · forsoþe on þis wise,
'Nouȝt þi neiȝbours good · couet yn no tyme.'
But charite & chastete · ben chased out clene,
But Crist seide, 'by her fruyt · men shall hem ful knowen.'"
Þanne saide y, "certeyn, sire · þou demest full trewe!"
Þanne þouȝt y to frayne þe first · of þis foure ordirs,
And presede to þe prechoures · to proven here wille.
[Ich] hiȝede to her house · to herken of more;
And whan y cam to þat court · y gaped aboute.
Swich a bild bold, y-buld · opon erþe heiȝte
Say i nouȝth in certeine · siþþe a longe tyme.
Y ȝemede vpon þat house · & ȝerne þeron loked,
Whouȝ þe pileres weren y-peynt · and pulched ful clene,
And queyntlei i-coruen · wiþ curiouse knottes,
Wiþ wyndowes well y-wrouȝt · wide vp o-lofte.
And þanne y entrid in · and even-forþ went,
And all was walled þat wone · þouȝ it wid were,
Wiþ posternes in pryuytie · to pasen when hem liste;
Orcheȝardes and erberes · euesed well clene,
And a curious cros · craftly entayled,
Wiþ tabernacles y-tiȝt · to toten all abouten.
Þe pris of a plouȝ-lond · of penyes so rounde
To aparaile þat pyler · were pure lytel.
Þanne y munte me forþ · þe mynstre to knowen,
And a-waytede a woon · wonderlie well y-beld,
Wiþ arches on eueriche half · & belliche y-corven,
Wiþ crochetes on corners · wiþ knottes of golde,
Wyde wyndowes y-wrouȝt · y-written full þikke,
Schynen wiþ schapen scheldes[2] · to schewen aboute,

---

[1] Your name shall be written in our table of benefactors for whose souls we pray. This was usually hung up in the church. Or else he means, Written in the windows, in which manner benefactors were frequently recorded.
Most of the [later] printed copies read *praid*. Hearne, in a quotation of this passage, reads *yrad*. *Gul. Newbrig.* p. 770. He quotes [the] edition of 1553. "Your name shall be richly written in the windows of the church of the monastery which men will read there for ever." This seems to be the true reading [unquestionably.]

[2] That is, coats of arms of benefactors painted in the glass. So in an ancient

Wiþ merkes of marchauntes[1] · y-medled bytwene,
Mo þan twenty and two · twyes y-noumbred.
Þer is none heraud þat haþ · half fwich a rolle,
Riȝt as a rageman · haþ reckned hem newe.
Tombes opon tabernacles · tyld opon lofte,
Houfed[2] in hirnes · harde fet abouten,
Of armede alabauftre · clad for þe nones,
[Made vpon marbel · in many maner wyfe,
Knyghtes in her conifantes[3] · clad for þe nones,]

roll in verfe, exhibiting the defcent of the family of the lords of Clare in Suffolk, preferved in the Auftin friary at Clare, and written in the year 1356.

"Dame Mault, a lady full honorable
Borne of the Ulfters, as fheweth ryfe
Hir armes of glaffe in the eaftern gable.
———— So conjoyned be
Ulftris armes and Gloceftris thurgh and thurgh,
As fhewith our Wyndowes in houfes thre,
Dortur, chapiter-houfe, and fraitour, which fhe
Made out the grounde both plancher and wall."

Dugdale cites this roll, *Mon. Angl.* i. p. 535. As does Weever, who dates it in 1460. *Fun. Mon.* p. 734. But I could prove this fafhion to have been of much higher antiquity.

[1] By merkes of merchauntes we are to underftand their fymbols, ciphers, or badges, drawn or painted in the windows. [A great variety of them may be feen in *Current Notes*.] Of this paffage I have received the following curious explication from Mr. Cole, rector of Blechley in Bucks, a learned antiquary in the heraldic art. "Mixed with the arms of their founders and benefactors ftand alfo the marks of tradefmen and merchants, who had no Arms, but ufed their Marks in a Shield like Arms. Inftances of this fort are very common. In many places in Great Saint Mary's church in Cambridge fuch a Shield of Mark occurs: the fame that is to be feen in the windows of the great fhop oppofite the Conduit on the Market-hill, and the corner houfe of the Petty Curry. No doubt, in the reign of Henry VII., the owner of thefe houfes was a benefactor to the building, or glazing Saint Mary's church. I have feen like inftances in Briftol cathedral; and the churches at Lynn are full of them."—In an ancient fyftem of heraldry in the Britifh Mufeum, I find the following illuftration, under a fhield of this fort. "Theys be none armys, bvt a Marke as Marchaunts vfe, for every mane may take hyme a Marke, but not armys, without an herawde or purcyvaunte." MSS. Harl. 2259, 9, fol. 110.

[2] Hurnes, interpreted, in the fhort Gloffary to the *Crede*, Caves, that is, in the prefent application, niches, arches. See *Glofs. Rob. Glouc.* p. 660, col. i. Hurn, is angle, corner. From the Saxon pẏnn, Angulus. Chaucer, *Frankel. T.* v. 393.

"Seeken in every halke [nook], and every herne."

And again, *Chan. Yem. Prol.* ver. 105.

"Lurking in hernes and in lanes blynde."

Read the line, thus pointed.

"Houfed in hurnes hard fet abouten."

The fenfe is therefore: "The tombs were within lofty-pinnacled tabernacles, and enclofed in a multiplicity of thick-fet arches." Hard is clofe, or thick. This conveys no bad idea of a Gothic fepulchral fhrine.

[3] In their proper habiliments. In their cognifances, or furcoats of arms. So again, fignat. C ii b.

"For though a man in her minftre a maffe wolde heren,
His fight fhall alfo byfet on fondrye workes,
The pennons, and the poinells, and pointes of fheldes
Withdrawen his devotion and dufken his harte."

That is, the banners, atchievements, and other armorial ornaments, hanging over the tombs.

All it femed feyntes · y-facred open erþe;
And louely ladies y-wrouȝt · leyen by her fydes
In many gay garmentes · þat weren gold-beten.
Þouȝ þe tax of ten ȝer · were trewly y-gadered,
Nolde it nouȝt maken þat hous · half, as y trowe.
Þanne kam I to þat cloifter · & gaped abouten
Whouȝ it was pilered and peynt · & portred well clene,
All y-hyled wiþ leed · lowe to þe ftones,
And y-paued wiþ peynt til · iche poynte after oþer;
Wiþ kundites of clene tyn · clofed all aboute,
Wiþ lauoures of latun · louelyche y-greithed.
I trowe þe gaynage of þe ground · in a gret fchire
Nolde aparaile þat place · oo poynt til other ende.
Þanne was þe chaptire-hous wrouȝt · as a greet chirche,
Coruen and couered · and queyntliche entayled;
Wiþ femlich felure · y-fet on lofte;
As a Parlement-hous · y-peynted aboute.[1]

---

[1] That they painted the walls of rooms, before tapeftry became fafhionable, I have before given inftances, *Obfervat. Spens.* vol. ii. § p. 232. I will here add other proofs. In an old French romance on the *Miracles of the Virgin*, liv. i. Carpent. *Suppl. Lat. Gl. Du Cang.* v. *Lambroiffare.*

"Lors mouftiers tiennent ors et fales,
Et lor cambres, et lor grans fales,
Font lambroiffier, paindre et pourtraire."

Gervafius Dorobernenfis, in his account of the burning of Canterbury Cathedral in the year 1174, fays, that not only the beam-work was deftroyed, but the ceiling underneath it, or concameration called cœlum, being of wood beautifully painted, was alfo confumed. "Cœlum inferius egregie depictum," &c. p. 1289. *Dec. Script.* 1652. And Stubbes, *Actus Pontif. Eboracenfium,* fays that Archbifhop Aldred, about 1060, built the whole church of York from the prefbytery to the tower, and "fuperius opere pictorio quod Cœlum vocant auro multiformiter intermixto, mirabili arte conftruxit." p. 1704. *Dec. Script.* ut fupr. There are many inftances in the pipe-rolls. The roof of the church of Caffino in Italy is ordered to be painted in 1349, like that of St. John Lateran at Rome. *Hift. Caffin.* tom. ii. p. 545, col. i. Dugdale has printed an ancient French record, by which it appears that there was a hall in the caftle of Dover called Arthur's hall, and a chamber called Geneura's chamber. *Monaft.* ii. 2. I fuppofe, becaufe the walls of thefe apartments were refpectively adorned with paintings of each. Geneura is Arthur's queen. In the pipe-rolls, Hen. III., we have this notice, A.D. 1259. "Infra portam caftri et birbecanam, etc. ab exitu Cameræ Rofamundæ ufque capellam fancti Thomæ in Caftro Wynton." *Rot. Pip. Hen. III.* an. 43.—This I once fuppofed to be a chamber in Winchefter caftle, fo called becaufe it was painted with the figure or fome hiftory of fair Rofamond. But a Rofamond-chamber was a common apartment in the royal caftles, perhaps in imitation of her bower at Woodftock, literally nothing more than a chamber, which yet was curioufly conftructed and decorated, at leaft in memory of it. The old profe paraphraft of the Chronicle of Robert of Gloucefter fays, "Boures hadde the Rofamonde a bout in Engelonde, which this kynge [Hen. II.] for hir fake made: atte Waltham bifhopes, in the caftelle of Wynchefter, atte park of Fremantel, atte Marteleſton, atte Woodeftoke, and other fele [many] places." *Chron.* edit. Hearne, 479. This paffage indeed feems to imply, that Henry II. himfelf provided for his fair concubine a bower, or chamber of peculiar conftruction, not only at Woodftock, but in all the royal palaces: which, as may be concluded from the pipe-roll juft cited, was called by her name. Leland fays, that in the ftately caftle of Pickering in Yorkfhire, "in the firft court be a foure Toures, of the which one is caullid Rofamundes Toure." *Itin.* fol. 71. Probably becaufe it contained one of thefe bowers or chambers. Or, perhaps we fhould read Rofamundes Boure. Compare Walpole's *Anecd. Paint.* i. pp. 10, 11.

Þanne ferd y into fraytour · and fond þere an oþer,
An halle for an heyȝ kinge · an housholde to holden,
Wiþ brode bordes aboute · y-benched wel clene,
Wiþ windowes of glas · wrouȝt as a Chirche.
Þanne walkede y ferrer · & went all abouten,
And seiȝ halles full hyȝe · & houses full noble,
Chambers wiþ chimneyes · & Chapells gaie ;
And kychens for an hyȝe kinge · in castells to holden,
And her dortour y-diȝte · wiþ dores ful stronge ;
Fermery and fraitur · with fele mo houses,
And all strong ston wall · sterne opon heiþe,
Wiþ gaie garites & grete · & iche hole y-glased ;
[And oþere] houses y-nowe · to herberwe þe queene.
And ȝet þise bilderes wilne beggen · a bagg-ful of wheate
Of a pure pore man · þat maie oneþe paie
Half his rente in a ȝer · and half ben behynde !
Þanne turned y aȝen · whan y hadde all y-toted,
And fond in a freitour · a frere on a benche,
A greet cherl & a grym · growen as a tonne,
Wiþ a face as fat · as a full bledder,
Blowen bretfull of breþ · & as a bagge honged
On boþen his chekes, & his chyn · wiþ a chol lollede,
As greet as a gos eye · growen all of grece ;
Þat all wagged his fleche · as a quyk myre.
His cope þat biclypped him · wel clene was it folden,
Of double worstede y-dyȝt · doun to þe hele ;
His kyrtel of clene whiȝt · clenlyche y-sewed ;
Hyt was good y·now of ground · greyn for to beren.
I haylsede þat herdeman · & hendliche y saide,
"Gode syre, for Godes loue · canstou me graiþ tellen
To any worþely wiȝt · þat [wissen] me couþe
Whou y schulde conne my Crede · Crist for to folowe,
Þat leuede lelliche him-self · & lyuede þerafter,
Þat feynede non falshede · but fully Crist suwede ?
For sich a certeyn man · syker wold y trosten,
Þat he wolde telle me þe trewþe · and turne to none oþer.
And an Austyn þis ender daie · egged me faste ;
Þat he wolde techen me wel · he plyȝt me his treuþe,
And seyde me, 'serteyne · syþen Crist died
Oure ordir was [euelles] · & erst y-founde.' "
"Fyrst, felawe !" quaþ he · " fy on his pilche !
He is but abortijf · eked wiþ cloutes !
He holdeþ his ordynaunce · wiþe hores and þeues,
And purchaseþ hem pryuileges · wiþ penyes so rounde ;
It is a pur pardoners craft · proue & asaye !
For haue þei þi money · a moneþ þerafter,
Certes, þeiȝ þou come aȝen · he nyl þe nouȝt knowen.
But, felawe, our foundement · was first of þe oþere,
And we ben founded fulliche · wiþ-outen fayntise ;
And we ben clerkes y-cnowen · cunnynge in scole,
Proued in procession · by processe of lawe.
Of oure ordre þer beþ · bichopes wel manye,
Seyntes on sundry stedes · þat suffreden harde ;
And we ben proued þe prijs · of popes at Rome,
And of gretest degre · as godspelles telleþ."

I must not quit our Ploughman without observing, that some other satirical pieces anterior to the Reformation bear the adopted name of *Piers the Plowman*. Under the character of a ploughman the religious are likewise lashed in a poem written in apparent imitation of

Langland's *Vision*, and [falsely] attributed to Chaucer. I mean the *Plowman's Tale*.[1] The measure is different, and it is in rhyme. But it has Langland's alliteration of initials; as if his example had, as it were, appropriated that mode of versification to the subject, and the supposed character which supports the satire.[2] All these poems [or rather, the *Crede* and the *Tale*] were, for the most part, founded on the doctrines newly broached by Wickliffe:[3] who maintained, among other things, that the clergy should not possess estates, that the ecclesiastical ceremonies obstructed true devotion, and that Mendicant friars, the particular object of our *Plowman's Crede*, were a public and insupportable grievance. But Wickliffe, whom Mr. Hume pronounces to have been an enthusiast, like many other reformers, carried his ideas of purity too far, and, as at least it appears from the two first

---

[1] [In the] *Plowman's Tale* this Crede is alluded to, v. 3005:
"And of *Freris* I have *before*
Told in a making of a *Crede*;
And yet I could tell worse and more."

This passage at least brings the *Plowman's Tale* below the *Crede* in time. But some have thought, very improbably, that this Crede is *Jack Upland*. [Internal evidence clearly shows that the author of the *Plowman's Tale* was also author of the *Crede*, as he claims to have been. In imitation of Langland, he named one of his poems the *Plowman's Crede*, and the other the *Plowman's Tale*. The probable date of the former is A. D. 1394, and of the latter A. D. 1395.]

[2] It is extraordinary that we should find in this poem one of the absurd arguments of the puritans against ecclesiastical establishments, v. 2253:
"For Christ made no cathedralls,
Ne with him was no Cardinalls."
But see what follows, concerning Wickliffe.

[3] It is remarkable, that they touch on the very topics which Wickliffe had just published in his *Objections of Freres*, charging them with fifty heresies. As in the following: "Also Freres buildin many great churches, and costy wast houses and cloisteres, as it wern casteles, and that withouten nede," &c. Lewis's *Wickliff*, p. 22. I will here add a passage from Wickliffe's tract entitled *Why poor Priests have no Benefices*. Lewis, App. Num. xix. p. 289. "And yet they [lords] wolen not present a clerk able of kunning of god's law, but a kitchen clerk, or a penny clerk, or wife in building castles, or worldly doing, though he kunne not reade well his sauter," &c. Here is a manifest piece of satire on Wykeham, bishop of Winchester, Wickliffe's cotemporary; who is supposed to have recommended himself to Edward III. by rebuilding the castle of Windsor. This was a recent and notorious instance. But in this appointment the king probably paid a compliment to that prelate's singular talents for business, his activity, circumspection, and management, rather than to any scientific and professed skill in architecture which he might have possessed. It seems to me that he was only a supervisor or comptroller on this occasion. It was common to depute churchmen to this department, from an idea of their superior prudence and probity. Thus John, the prior of St. Swithin's at Winchester in 1280, is commissioned by brief from the king to supervise large repairs done by the sheriff in the castle of Winchester and the royal manor of Wolmer. MS. *Registr. Priorat.* Quat. 19, fol. 3. The bishop of S. David's was master of the works at building King's College. Hearne's *Elmh.* p. 353. Alcock, bishop of Ely, was comptroller of the royal buildings under Henry VII. Parker's *Hist. Cambr.* p. 119. He, like Wykeham, was a great builder, but not therefore an architect. Richard Williams, dean of Lichfield, and chaplain to Henry VIII. bore the same office. MSS. Wood, Lichfield, D. 7. Ashmol. Nicholas Townley, clerk, was master of the works at Cardinal College. MS. Twyne, 8, f. 351. See also Walpole, *Anecd. Paint.* i. p. 40.

of these opinions, under the design of destroying superstition, his undistinguishing zeal attacked even the necessary aids of religion. It was certainly a lucky circumstance that Wickliffe quarrelled with the Pope. His attacks on superstition at first probably proceeded from resentment. Wickliffe, who was professor of divinity at Oxford, finding on many occasions not only his own province invaded, but even the privileges of the university frequently violated by the pretensions of the Mendicants, gratified his warmth of temper by throwing out some slight censures against all the four orders, and the popes their principal patrons and abettors. Soon afterwards he was deprived of the wardenship of Canterbury hall by the Archbishop of Canterbury, who substituted a monk in his place. Upon this he appealed to the Pope, who confirmed the archiepiscopal sentence, by way of rebuke for the freedom with which he had treated the monastic profession. Wickliffe, highly exasperated at this usage, immediately gave a loose to his indignation, and without restraint or distinction attacked in numerous sermons and treatises not only the scandalous enormities of the whole body of monks, but even the usurpations of the pontifical power itself, with other ecclesiastical corruptions. Having exposed these palpable abuses with a just abhorrence, he ventured still farther, and proceeded to examine and refute with great learning and penetration the absurd doctrines which prevailed in the religious system of his age: he not only exhorted the laity to study the Scriptures, but translated the Bible into English for general use and popular inspection. Whatever were his motives, it is certain that these efforts enlarged the notions of mankind, and sowed those seeds of a revolution in religion, which were quickened at length and brought to maturity by a favourable coincidence of circumstances, in an age when the increasing growth of literature and curiosity naturally led the way to innovation and improvement. But a visible diminution of the authority of the ecclesiastics, in England at least, had been long growing from other causes. The disgust which the laity had contracted from the numerous and arbitrary encroachments both of the court of Rome and of their own clergy, had greatly weaned the kingdom from superstition; and conspicuous symptoms had appeared, on various occasions, of a general desire to shake off the intolerable bondage of papal oppression.

SECTION X.

ANGLAND'S peculiarity of ſtyle and verſification ſeems to have had many imitators. One of theſe is a nameleſs author on the faſhionable hiſtory of Alexander the Great: and his poem on this ſubject is inſerted at the end of the beautiful Bodleian copy of the French *Roman d'Alexandre*, before mentioned, with this reference:[1] *Here ſayleth a proſſeſſe of this romaunce of Alixaunder the whiche proſſeſſe that ſayleth ye ſchulle ſynde at the ende of thys boke ywrete in Engeliche ryme.* It is imperfect, and begins and proceeds thus:[2]

> *How Alexander partyd thennys.*[3]
> When this weith at his wil weduring hadde,
> Ful rathe rommede he rydinge thederre;
> To Oridrace with his oſt Alixandre wendus:
> There wilde contre was wiſt, and wondurful peple,
> That weren proved ful proude, and prys of hem helde;
> Of bodi went thei bare withoute any wede,
> And had grave on the ground many grete cavys;
> There here wonnynge was wynturus and fomerus.
> No ſyte nor no ſur ſtede ſothli thei ne hadde,
> But holus holwe in the grounde to hide hem inne;
> The proude Genoſophiſtiens[4] were the gomus called,

---

[1] It is in a different hand, yet with Saxon characters. See ad calc. cod. f. 209. It has miniatures in water colours. [See Mr. Skeat's *Eſſay on Alliterative Poetry* in the third volume of the lately-edited Percy folio MS. (1868).— F.]

[2] There is a poem in the [Bodleian library,] complete in the former part, which is [certainly] the ſame. [Sir F. Madden aſſigns the former to the reign of Henry VI. That gentleman alſo informs us that in the Bodleian is a fragment of anothers and quite different alliterative romance of Alexander, compoſed, he believe, by the perſon who wrote the Engliſh alliterative romance of *William and the Werwolf*, ed. 1832.] MSS. Aſhm. 44. It has twenty-ſeven paſſus, and begins thus:

> "Whener folker faſtid and fed, fayne wolde thei her
> Some farand thing," &c.

[3] [Printed in Weber's collection, 1810.] At the end are theſe rubrics, with void ſpaces, intended to be filled:

> "How Alexandre remewid to a flood that is called Phiſon."
> "How king Duidimus ſente lettres to king Alexandre."
> "How Duidimus enditid to Alexaundre of here levyng."
> "How he ſpareth not Alexandre to telle hym of hys governance."
> "How he telleth Alexandre of his maumetrie."
> "How Alexandre ſente aunſwere to Duidimus by lettres."
> "How Duidimus ſendyd an anſwere to Alexandre by lettre."
> "How Alexandre ſente Duidimus another lettre."
> "How Alexandre pight a pelyr of marbyl ther."

[The laſt of theſe rubrics only is followed by a void ſpace in the Bodleian copy; the former being filled up with ſuch verſification as is given in Mr. Warton's text, which led Ritſon to conſider it a much earlier compoſition than Piers Plowman.— *Park.*]

[4] Gymnoſophiſts.

Now is that name to mene the nakid wife.
Wan the kiddefte of the cavus, that was kinge holde,
Hurde tydinge telle and toknynge wifte,
That Alixaundre with his oft atlede thidirre,
To beholden of hom hure hieʒeft prynce,
Than waies of worfhipe wittie and quainte
With his lettres he let to the lud fende.
Thanne fouthte thei fone the forefaide prynce,
And to the fchamlefe fchalk fchewen hur lettres.
Than rathe let the rink reden the fonde,
That newe tythingeit tolde in this wife :
The gentil Geneofophiftians, that gode were of witte,
To the emperour Alixandre here aunfweris wreten.
That is worfchip of word worthi to have,
And is conquerer kid in contres manie.
Us is fertefyed, feg, as we foth heren
That thou haft ment with thi man amongis us ferre
But yf thou kyng to us come with caere to fiʒte
Of us getift thou no good, gome, we the warne.
For what richeffe, rink, us might you us bi-reve,
Whan no wordliche wele is with us founde ?
We ben fengle of us filfe, and femen ful bare,
Nouht welde we nowe, but naked we wende,
And that we happili her haven of kynde
May no man but God maken us tine.
Thei thou fonde with thi folke to fighte with us alle,
We fchulle us kepe on cauʒt our cavus withinne.
Nevere werred we with wiʒth upon erthe ;
For we ben hid in oure holis or we harme laache.
Thus faide fothli the fonde that thei fente hadde,
And al fo cof as the king kende the fawe,
New lettres he let the ludus bitake,
And with his fawes of foth he fikerede hem alle,
That he wolde faire with his folke in a faire wife,
To b¹holden here home, and non harme wurke.
So hath the king to hem fente, and fithen with his peple,
Kaires cofti til hem, to kenne of hure fare.
But whan thai fieu the feg with fo manye ryde,
Thei war agrifen of hys grym, and wende gref tholie ;
Faft heiede thei to holis, and hidden there,[1]
And in the cavus hem kept from the king fterne, &c.

Another piece, written in Langland's manner, is entitled, [*The Deftruction of Jerufalem*]. This was a favourite fubject, as I have before obferved, drawn from the Latin hiftorical romance, which paffes under the name of *Hegefippus de Excidio Hierufalem:*

In Tyberyus tyme the trewe emperour[2]

---

[1] [In the Bodleian Library, MS. Greaves 60, is a fragment of another alliterative romance on the fubject of Alexander, totally different from the former one, and which I have good grounds to believe was compofed by the fame poet who wrote the Englifh alliterative romance of *William and the Werwolf*, edited by me for the Roxburghe Club, in 1832.—M.]

[2] [The prefent text has been collated with the Cott. MS. Calig. A. ii. The orthographical differences between this and the Laud MS. are numerous though not important. All its readings improving the fenfe have been adopted ; though this perhaps would have been wholly fuperfluous, had the original tranfcript been correctly made.—*Price*.]

Syr Sefar hym [felf fefed ¹] in Rome
Whyl Pylot was provoſt under that prynce ryche
And [jewes ²] juſtice alfo in Judens londis
Herode under his empire as heritage wolde
King of Galile was ycallid, whan that Criſt deyad
They ³ Sefar fakles wer, that oft fyn hatide
Throw Pilet pyned he was and put on the rode
A pyler was down pyȝt ⁴ upon the playne erthe
His body [bowndone ⁵] therto beten with fcourgis,
Whippes of [wherebole ⁶] bywent his white fides
Til he al on rede blode ran as rayn on the ſtrete;
[Sith ⁷] ſtockyd hym an a ſtole with ſtyf menes hondis,
Blyndfelled hym as a be and boffetis hym raȝte
Ȝif you be a prophete of pris, prophecie, they fayde
Which man her aboute [bolled ⁸] the laſte,
A ſtrange thorn crown was thraſte on his hed
[They ⁹] caſten [up a grete] cry [that hym on] cros flowen,
For al the harme that he had, haſted he noȝt
On hym the vyleny to venge that hys venys broſten,
Bot ay taried on the tyme, ȝif they [turne ¹⁰] wolde
Gaf [hem ¹¹] fpace that him fpilede they [hit fpedde ¹²] lyte
[Fourty wynter ¹³] as y fynde, and no fewer, &c.¹⁴

Notwithſtanding what has been fuppofed above, it is not quite cer-

---

¹ fuls fayfed.   ² fewen.
³ This is the orthography obferved for both *though* and *they*. It occurs again below: "they it," though it.
⁴ pygt was don.   ⁵ bouden.
⁶ quyrbole;—which might have ſtood, fince it only deſtroys the alliteration to the eye.
⁷ Warton read "Such;" the Cotton MS. "And fythen fette on a fete;" whence the genuine reading of the Laud MS. was obvious.
⁸ bobette, Cot. MS.
⁹ ... caſten hym with a cry and on a crofs flowen.
¹⁰ tone, which if intended for atone (like dure for endure, fperſt for difperfed, &c.) might be allowed to ſtand. The probability is that it is an erroneous tranſcript for torne.
¹¹ he.   ¹² he fpedde.
¹³ Yf aynt was. Perhaps: xl. wynterit was, &c.
¹⁴ Laud... 22, MSS. Bibl. Bodl. Ad calc. "Hic tractatur bellum Judaicum apud Jerufalem," f. 19, b. It is alfo in Brit. Mus. Cot. MSS. *Calig.* A. ii. fol. 109-123. Gyraldus Cambrenfis fays, that the Welſh and Engliſh ufe alliteration "in omni fermone exquifito." *Defcript. Cambr.* cap. xi. p. 889. O'Flaherty alfo fays of the Iriſh, "Non parva eſt apud nos in oratione elegantiæ fchema, quod Paromæon, *i. e. Affimile*, dicitur: quoties multæ dictiones, ab eadem litera incipientes, ex ordine collocantur." *Ogyg.* part iii. 30, p. 242. [An objection has been taken to the antiquity of the Welſh poetry, from its fuppofed want of alliteration. But this is not the cafe. For the alliteration has not been perceived by thofe ignorant of its conſtruction, which is to make it in the middle of words, and not at the beginning, as in this inſtance:

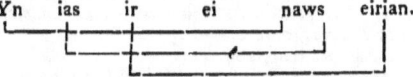

Yn   ias   ir   ei   naws   eirian.

This information was imparted to Mr. Douce by the ingenious Edward Williams, the Welſh bard.—*Park.* See alfo, fays Sir F. Madden, Conybeare's *Illuſtr. of Anglo-Saxon Poetry*, (1826) Introduction.]

tain that Langland was the firſt who led the way in this ſingular ſpecies of verſification. His *Viſion* was written on a popular ſubject, and [was formerly] the only poem, compoſed in this capricious ſort of metre, which [exiſted in print]. It is eaſy to conceive how theſe circumſtances contributed to give him the merit of an inventor on this occaſion.

Percy has exhibited ſpecimens of two or three other poems belonging to this claſs.[1] One of theſe is entitled *Death and Life:* it conſiſts of two hundred and twenty-nine lines, and is divided into two parts or *Fitts*. It begins thus:

> Chriſt, chriſten king, that on the croſſe tholed,
> Hadd paines & paſſyons to deffend our ſoules;
> Give us grace on the ground the greatlye to ſerve
> For that royall red blood that rann from thy ſide.

The ſubject of this piece is a *Viſion*, containing a conteſt for ſuperiority between *Our lady Dame Life*, and the *ugly fiend Dame Death:* who with the ſeveral attributes and concomitants are perſonified in a beautiful vein of allegorical painting. Dame Life is thus forcibly deſcribed:

> Shee was brighter of her blee then was the bright ſonn:
> Her rudd redder then the roſe that on the riſe hangeth:
> Meekely ſmiling with her mouth, & merry in her lookes;
> Ever laughing for love, as ſhee like wold:
> & as ſhe came by the bankes, the boughes eche one
> They lowted to that Ladye & layd forth their branches;
> Bloſſomes and burgens breathed full ſweete,
> Flowers flouriſhed in the frith where ſhee forth ſtepedd,
> And the graſſe that was gray greened belive.

The figure of Death follows, which is equally bold and expreſſive. Another piece of this kind, alſo quoted by Dr. Percy, is entitled *Chevelere Aſſigne*, or *De Cigne*, that is, *Knight of the Swan*.[2] Among the Royal MSS. in the Britiſh Muſeum, there is a French metrical romance on this ſubject, entitled *L'Yſtoire du Chevalier au Signe*,[3] [of which *Le Chevelere Aſſigne* is an abridgment]. Our Engliſh poem begins thus:[4]

---

[1] *Eſſay on the Metr. of P. P. Vis.* p. 8, *ſeq*. [The poem is printed in Biſhop Percy's folio MS. 1868, vol. iii.—F.]

[2] MS. Cotton. Caligula, A. 2. Printed by Mr. E. V. Utterſon, for the Roxburghe Club, 1820, and again by Mr. H. H. Gibbs for the Early Engliſh Text Society, 1868, with a ſeries of photographs from a very curious ivory-caſket in the editor's family, containing various illuſtrations of the ſtory.]

[3] 15 E. vi. 9. fol. And in the Royal library at Paris, MS. 7192. *Le Roman du Chevalier au Cigne en vers.* Montf. Cat. MSS. ii. p. 789. [There are ſix romance sin the cycle. M. Paullin Paris has edited *Le Chanſon d'Antioche*. See *Hiſtoire Litteraire de la France*, tome 22.—F.]

[4] See MSS. Cott. Calig. A. ii. f. 109. 123.
[The celebrated Godfrey of Bullogne was ſaid to have been lineally deſcended from the Chevalier au Cigne. *Melanges d'une Gr. Biblioth*. vol. v, c. iii. p. 148. The tradition is ſtill current in the Duchy of Cleves, and forms one of the moſt intereſting pieces in Otmar's Volkſſagen. It muſt have obtained an early and general circulation in Flanders; for Nicolaes de Klerc, who wrote at the com-

Alle-weldynge god whenne it is his wylle,
Wele he wereth his werke with his owne honde:
For ofte harmes were hente · that helpe we ne myȝte;
Nere the hyȝnes of hym that lengeth in heuene
For this, &c.

This alliterative meafure, unaccompanied with rhyme, and including many peculiar Saxon idioms appropriated to poetry, remained in ufe fo low as the fixteenth century. In [the newly-edited Percy MS.] there is one of this clafs called *Scottifh Feilde*, containing a very circumftantial narrative of the battle of Flodden fought in 1513.

[There is alfo an Englifh romance in profe, entitled *The Knight of the Swanne*, of which there feems to have been an edition by W. de Worde in 1512. It is a tranflation by Robert Copland, the induftrious typographer, of chapters 1-38 of a French romance entitled "La Genealogie avecques les Geftes & Nobles Faitz darmes du tres preux & renomme prince Godeffroy de Boulion & de fes cheualereux freres Baudouin et Euftace: yffus & defcendus de la très noble & illuftre lignée du vertueux Chevalier au Cyne." *The Knight of the Swanne* was reprinted by William Copland about 1560, and it is included in a modern collection.][1]

In fome of the earlieft of our fpecimens of old Englifh poetry,[2] we have long ago feen that alliteration was efteemed a fafhionable and favourite ornament of verfe. For the fake of throwing the fubject into one view, and further illuftrating what has been here faid concerning it, I choofe to cite in this place a very ancient hymn to the Virgin Mary, where this affectation profeffedly predominates.[3]

I.

Hail beo yow[4] Marie, moodur and may,
Mylde, and meke, and merciable;

---

mencement of the 14th century (1318), thus refers to it in his *Brabandfche Yeeften:*

"Om dat van Brabant die Hertoghen
Voormaels dicke fyn beloghen
Alfe dat fy quamen metten Swane
Daar by hebbics my genomen ane
Dat ic die waerheit wil out decken
Ende in Duitfche Rime vertrecken,

i.e. becaufe *formerly* the dukes of Brabant have been much belied, to wit, *that they came with a Swan*, I have undertaken to difclofe the truth, and to propound it in Dutch Rhyme. See Van Wynut *fupra,* p. 270. The French romance upon this fubject, confifting of about 30,000 verfes, was begun by one Renax or Renaux, and finifhed by Gandor de Douay.—*Price.*]

[1] [Thoms' *Early Profe Romances,* 1828, iii.]
[2] See fect. i.
[3] Among the Cotton MSS. there is an [Early Englifh] alliterative hymn to the Virgin Mary. *Ner.* A. xiv. f. 240, cod. membran. 8vo. "On ȝoꝺ ureifun to ure lefdi." That is, *A good prayer to our lady.*

"Criſteſ milꝺe moꝺer ꝛeÿnꞇe Marie
Miner hueꞃ leonie, mi leoue leꝼꝺi."

[4] See fome pageant-poetry, full of alliteration, written in the reign of Henry VII., Leland, *Coll.* iii. App. 180, edit. 1770.

Heyl folliche fruit of fothfaſt fay,
Agayn vche ſtryf ſtudefaſt and ſtable !
Heil ſothfaſt foul in vche a fay,
Undur the ſon is non ſo able.
Heil logge that vr lord in lay,
The formaſt that never was founden in fable,
Heil trewe, trouthfull, and tretable,
Heil cheef i choſen of chaſtite,
Heil homely, hende, and amyable
To preye for us to thi ſone ſo fre ! AVE.

II.

Heil ſtern, that never ſtinteth liht ;
Heil buſh, brennyng that never was brent ;
Heil rihtful rulere of everi riht,
Schadewe to ſchilde that ſcholde be ſchent.
Heil, bleſſed be yowe bloſme briht,
To trouthe and truſt was thine entent ;
Heil mayden and modur, moſt of miht,
Of all miſcheves and amendement ;
Heil ſpice ſprong that never was ſpent,
Heil trone of the trinitie ;
Heil ſoiene[1] that god us ſone to ſent
Yowe preye for us thi ſone fre ! AVE.

III.

Heyl hertely in holineſſe,
Heyl hope of help to heighe and lowe,
Heyl ſtrength and ſtel of ſtabylneſſe,
Heyl wyndowe of hevene wowe,
Heyl reſon of rihtwyſneſſe,
To vche a caityf comfort to knowe,
Heyl innocent of angerneſſe,
Vr takel, vr tol, that we on trowe,
Heyl frend to all that beoth fortth flowe
Heyl liht of love, and of bewte,
Heyl brihter then the blod on ſnowe,
Yow preye for us thi ſone ſo fre ! AVE.

IV.

Heyl mayden, heyl modur, heyl martir trowe,
Heyl kyndly i knowe confeſſour,
Heyl evenere of old lawe and newe,
Heyl buildor bold of criſtes bour,
Heyl roſe higeſt of hyde and hewe,
Of all ffruytes feireſt fflour,
Heyl turtell truſtieſt and trewe,
Of all trouthe thou art treſour,
Heyl puyred princeſſe of paramour,
Heyl bloſme of brere brihteſt of ble,
Heyl owner of eorthly honour,
Yowe preye for us thi ſone ſo fre ! AVE, &c.

V.

Heyl hende, heyl holy empereſſe,
Heyle queene corteois, comely, and kynde,
Heyl diſtruyere of everi ſtriſſe,
Heyl mender of everi monnes mynde,
Heil bodi that we ouht to bleſſe,
So feythful frend may never mon fynde,

---

[1] F. Seyen. *Scyon.*

Heil levere and lovere of largeneſſe
Swete and ſweteſt that never may ſwynde,
Heil botenere of everie bodi blynde,
Heil borgun brihtes of all bounte,
Heyl trewore then the wode bynde,
Yow preye for us thi ſone ſo fre! AVE.

VI.

Heyl modur, heyl mayden, heyl hevene quene,
Heyl gatus of paradys,
Heyl ſterre of the ſe that ever is ſene,
Heyl riche, royall, and ryhtwys,
Heyl burde i bleſſed mote yowe bene,
Heyl perle of al perey the pris,
Heyl ſchadewe in vche a ſchour ſchene,
Heyl fairer thae that flour de lys,
Heyl cher choſen that never nas chis
Heyl chef chamber of charite
Heyl in wo that ever was wis
Yowe preye for us thi ſone ſo fre! Ave, &c. &c.[1]

Theſe rude ſtanzas remind us of the Greek hymns aſcribed to Orpheus, which entirely conſiſt of a cluſter of the appellations appropriated to each divinity.

SECTION XI.

ALTHOUGH this work is profeſſedly confined to England, yet I cannot paſs over [a Scotiſh poet] of this period who ha[s] adorned the Engliſh language by a ſtrain of verſification, expreſſion, and poetical imagery, far ſuperior to [his] age; and who conſequently deſerve[s] to be mentioned in a general review of the progreſs of our national poetry. [His name] is John Barbour, archdeacon of Aberdeen. He was educated at Oxford; and Rymer has printed an inſtrument for his ſafe paſſage into England, in order to proſecute his ſtudies in that univerſity, in the years 1357 and 1365.[2] David Bruce, king of Scotland, gave him a penſion for life, as a reward for his poem called the [*Brus*]. It was printed at [Edinburgh about 1570,[3] and often afterwards].[4]

---

[1] MS. Vernon. f. 122. In this manuſcript are ſeveral other pieces of this ſort. The Holy Virgin appears to a prieſt who often ſang to her, and calls him her *joculator*. MSS. James, xxvi. p. 32.

[2] *Fœd.* vi. 31, 478.

[3] Tanner, *Bibl.* p. 73. [See our *Liſt of Early Engliſh Poems*, ſupra. Mr. Henry Bradſhaw aſſigns to Barbour two works hitherto unknown to have been by him: 1. Fragments of a *Troy-Book*, mixed up with ſome copies of Lydgate's *Troy-book*; 2. Nearly 40,000 lines of *Lives of Saints* (MSS. Camb. Univ. and Queen's Coll. Oxford).—F.]

[4] [Mr. D. Laing has a copy, wanting the title, of a 4to edit., which he aſſigns to this date. Extracts have now been taken from Mr. Skeat's new edition for the Early Engliſh Text Society, of which only Part I. (ten books) has yet appeared, 1870.

[The following is the account of the battle of Methven, near Perth, and the firſt diſcomfiture of King Robert :] [1]

On at*h*ir ſyd *th*us war *th*ai yhar,[2]
And till aſſemble[3] all redy war.
*Th*ai ſtraucht *th*ar ſper*is*, on at*h*ir ſyd,
And ſwa ruydly gan Samyn[4] ryd,
*Th*at ſper*is* [all] to-fruſchyt[5] war,
And feyle men dede, and woundyt ſar ;
*Th*e blud owt at *th*ar byrnys[6] breſt.
For *th*e beſt, and *th*e worthieſt,
*Th*at wilfull war to wyn honour,
Plungyt in *th*e ſtalwart ſtour,
And rowt*is* ruyd about *th*aim dang.[7]
Men myc*h*t haiff ſeyn in-to *th*at thrang
Knyc*h*t*is* tha*t* wyc*h*t and hardy war,
Wndyr horſs feyt defoulyt *th*ar ;
Sum woundyt, and ſum all ded :
*Th*e greſs woux[8] off *th*e blud all rede,
And *th*ai, tha*t* held on horſs, in hȳ[9]
Swappyt owt ſwerd*is* ſturdyly ;
And ſwa fell ſtrakys gave and tuk,
*Th*at all the renk[10] about *th*aim quouk.
*Th*e bruyſſis folk full hardely
Schawyt *th*ar gret chewalry :
And he him-ſelff, atour *th*e lave,[11]
Sa hard and hewy dynt*is* gave,
*Th*at quhar he come *th*ai maid hi*m* way.
His folk *th*aim put in hard aſſay,
To ſtynt[12] *th*ar fais mekill myc*h*t,
*Th*at *th*en ſo fayr had off *th*e fyc*h*t,
*Th*at *th*ai wan feild ay mar & mar :
*Th*e king*is* ſmall folk ner wencuſyt ar.
And quhen *th*e king his folk has ſene
Begyn to faile, for propyr tene,[13]
Hys aſſenȝhe[14] gan he cry ;
And in *th*e ſtour ſa hardyly
He ruſchyt, *th*at all *th*e ſemble[15] ſchuk :
He all till-hewyt[16] *th*at he our-tuk ;
And dang on *th*aim quhill he myc*h*t drey.[17]
And till his folk he cr*i*yt hey ;
"On *th*aim ! On *th*aim ! *th*ai feble faſt !
*Th*is bargane neu*ir* may lang*ar* laſt ! "
And wi*th* *th*at word ſa wilfully
He dang on, and ſa hardely,
*Th*at quha had ſene him in *th*at fyc*h*t
Suld hald him for A douchty knyc*h*t.
Bot thoc*h*t[18] he wes ſtout and hardy,

In all the preceding editions of Warton, the account of Blind Harry's *Wallace* has been improperly inſerted in the preſent ſection ; it has now been transferred to its correct place.]

[1] [Skeat's ed. pp. 38-42. "On the 19th June, 1306, the new king was completely defeated near Methven by the Engliſh Earl of Pembroke (Sir Aymer de Valence.)"—Scott's *Tales of a Grandfather*.]

[2] [ready.]   [3] [to encounter.]   [4] [together.]
[5] [all broken in pieces ; the word *all* is ſupplied from Hart's edition, 1616.]
[6] [breaſt-plates.]   [7] [dealt ſtern ſtrokes about them.]
[8] [graſs became.]   [9] [haſte.]   [10] [ring ; Hart prints *rinke*.]
[11] [above the reſt.]   [12] [ſtop.]   [13] [very grief.]   [14] [battle-cry.]
[15] [aſſembly.]   [16] [hewed in pieces.]   [17] [hold out.]   [18] [though.]

And othir als off his cumpany,
Thar mycht na worschip thar awailʒe,¹
For thar small folk begouth to failʒe,
And fled all skalyt² her and thar.
Bot the gude, at enchaufyt³ war
Off Ire, abade and held the stour
To conquyr thaim endles honour.
And quhen schir Amer⁴ has sene
The small folk fle all bedene,⁵
And sa few abid to fycht,
He releyt⁶ to him mony A knycht;
And in the stour sa hardyly
He ruschyt with hys chewalry,
That he ruschyt⁷ his fayis Ilkane.
Schir Thomas Randell⁸ thar wes tane,
That then wes A ʒoung bacheler;
And schir Alexander fraseyr;
And schir dauid the breklay,
Inchmertyne, and hew de le hay,
And somerweil,⁹ and othir ma;
And the king him-selff alsua
Wes set in-till full hard assay,
Throw schir philip the mowbray,¹⁰
That raid till him full hardyly,
And hynt hys rengʒe,¹¹ and syne gan cry
"Help! help! I have the new-maid king!"
With that come gyrdand, in A lyng,¹²
Crystall off Seytoun,¹³ quhen he swa
Saw the king sesyt with his fa;
And to philip sic rout he raucht,¹⁴
That thocht he wes of mekill maucht,
He gert him galay¹⁵ disyly;
And haid till erd gane fullyly,
Ne war he hynt him by his sted;
Then off his hand the brydill yhed;¹⁶
And the king his enssenʒe¹⁷ gan cry,
Releyt¹⁸ his men that war him by,
That war sa few that thai na mycht
Endur the fors mar off the fycht.
Thai prikyt then out off the press;
And the king, that angry wes,
For he his men saw fle him fra,
Said then: "lordingis, sen It is swa
That vre¹⁹ rynnys agane ws her,
Gud Is we pass off thar daunger,²⁰
Till god ws send eftsonys grace:
And ʒeyt may fall, giff thai will chace,
Quyt thaim torn²¹ but sum-dele we sall."
To this word thai assentyt all,
And fra thaim walopyt²² owyr mar.

---

¹ [avail.]   ² [dispersed.]   ³ [good ones, that enraged.]
⁴ [Sir Aymer de Valence.]   ⁵ [quickly.]   ⁶ [rallied.]
⁷ [overthrew.]   ⁸ [Randolph.]
⁹ [Sir David Barclay, Inchmartin, Hugh de la Haye, and Somerville.]
¹⁰ [Philip de Mowbray.]   ¹¹ [caught his rein.]
¹² [charging in a direct line.]   ¹³ [Sir Christopher Seton.]   ¹⁴ [blow he gave.]
¹⁵ [made him stagger.]   ¹⁶ [went.]   ¹⁷ [war-cry.]   ¹⁸ [rallied.]   ¹⁹ [fortune.]
²⁰ [out of their power to harm.]   ²¹ [requite them a turn.]   ²² [galloped.]

> *Th*ar fayis alſua wery war,
> *Th*at off *th*aim all *th*ar chaſſyt nane:
> Bot wi*th* priſoneris, *th*at *th*ai had tane,
> Ryc*h*t to *th*e toune¹ *th*ai held *th*ar way,
> Ryc*h*t glaid and Ioyfull off *th*ar pray.

[As a further ſpecimen of the poem, the opening of the deſcription in the fifth book of Bruce's " hanſaling in Carrik, at his firſt arriuing" may be ſufficient:]²

> This wes in were,³ quhen vynt*ir*-tyde
> Vith his blaſtis, hydwiſs to byde,
> Wes ourdriffin;⁴ and byrdis ſmale,
> As thriſtill and *th*e nychtingale,
> Begouth⁵ rycht meraly to ſyng,
> And for to mak in *th*air ſynging
> Syndry notis, and ſound*is* ſere,⁶
> And melody pleaſande to here.
> And *th*e treis begouth to ma
> Burgeonys⁷ and bryc*h*t blwmys alſua,
> To vyn *th*e heling of *th*ar hevede,⁸
> *Th*at vikkit vynt*ir* had *th*ame revede;
> And al grewis⁹ begouth to ſpryng.

[To the latter half of the fifteenth century we muſt refer another Scotiſh writer, Andrew of Wyntown, who compoſed the *Original Chronicle of Scotland*. Wyntown was born in all probability at the cloſe of the fourteenth, or beginning of the fifteenth century; but the exact date is wanting. It is difficult to allow that he ſaw the light during the reign of David II. (1329-71), ſince Dunbar, in his *Lament for the Makaris*, compoſed moſt probably not earlier than the year 1500, ſeems to refer to this author as one whom he had known, and who at that time had not been very long deceaſed.¹⁰ A tolerably copious account of Wyntoun and his writings is readily acceſſible elſewhere;¹¹ and his *Original Chronicle of Scotland* has been printed entire by Macpherſon.]¹²

About the preſent period, hiſtorical romances of recent events ſeem to have commenced. Many of theſe appear to have been written by heralds.¹³ In the library of Worceſter college at Oxford, there is a poem in French, reciting the achievements of Edward the Black Prince, who died in the year 1376. It is in the ſhort verſe of romance, and was written by the prince's herald, who attended cloſe by his perſon in all his battles, according to the eſtabliſhed mode of thoſe times. This was Chandos Herald, frequently mentioned in Froiſſart. In this piece, which is of conſiderable length, the names

---

¹ [Perth.]   ² [Skeat's edit. p. 105.]   ³ [ſpring.]   ⁴ [overpaſt.]
⁵ [began.]   ⁶ [various.]   ⁷ [buds.]
⁸ [to get the covering of their head. *Hevede* is clearly the reading, though ſpelt *hede* in the Cambridge, and *hewid* in the Edinburgh MS.]
⁹ [growing things; the Edinb. MS. has *greſſys*, graſſes.]
¹⁰ [Works by Laing, 1834, i. 213.]
¹¹ [Irving's *Hiſtory of Scotiſh Poetry*, edit. 1861, chap. v.]
¹² [1795, 2 vols. ſarge 8vo. A new edition by Dr. Laing has been promiſed.]
¹³ See Le Pere Meneſtrier, *Cheval. Ancien*. c. v. p. 225.

of the Englishmen are properly spelled, the chronology exact, and the epitaph,[1] forming a sort of peroration to the narrative, the same as was ordered by the prince in his will.[2] This poem, indeed, may seem to claim no place here, because it happens to be written in the French language: yet, exclusive of its subject, a circumstance I have mentioned, that it was composed by a herald, deserves particular attention, and throws no small illustration on the poetry of this era. There are several proofs which indicate that many romances of the fourteenth century, if not in verse, at least those written in prose, were the work of heralds. As it was their duty to attend their masters in battle, they were enabled to record the most important transactions of the field with fidelity. It was customary to appoint none to this office but persons of discernment, address, experience, and some degree of education.[3] At solemn tournaments they made

---

[1] It is a fair and beautiful MS. on vellum. It is an oblong octavo, and formerly belonged to Sir William Le Neve Clarencieux herald. [It has been edited by the Rev. H. O. Coxe, M.A. the present keeper of Bodley, for the Roxburghe Club, 1842.]

[2] The hero's epitaph is frequent in romances. In the French romance of [*Le Petit Jean de*] *Saintre*, written about this time, his epitaph is introduced.

[3] Le Pere Menestrier, *Cheval Ancien.* ut supr. p. 225, ch. v. "Que l'on croyoit avoir *l'Esprit*," &c. Feron says that they gave this attendance in order to make a true report. *L'Instit. des Roys et Herauds*, p. 44, a. See also Favin. p. 57. See a curious description, in Froissart, of an interview between the Chandois-herald, mentioned above, and a marshal of France, where they enter into a warm and very serious dispute concerning the *devices d'amour* borne by each army. Liv. i. ch. 161.

[A curious collection of German poems, evidently compiled from these heraldic registers, was formerly discovered in the library of Prince Sinzendorf. The reader will find an account of them and their author Peter Suchenwirt (who lived at the close of the fourteenth century) in the 14th volume of the *Vienna Annals of Literature (Jahrbücher der Literatur*, Wien, 1821). They are noticed here for their occasional mention of English affairs. The life of Burkhard v. Ellerbach recounts the victory gained by the English at the battle of Cressy; in which this terror of Prussian and Saracen infidels was left for dead on the field, "the blood and the grass, the green and the red, being so completely mingled in one general mass," that no one perceived him. Friedrich v. Chreuzpeckh served in Scotland, England, and Ireland. In the latter country he joined an army of 60,000 (!) men, about to form the siege of a town called Trachtal (?); but the army broke up without an engagement. On his return thence to England, the fleet in which he sailed fell in with a Spanish squadron, and destroyed or captured six-and-twenty of the enemy. These events occurred between the years 1332-36. Albrecht v. Nürnberg followed Edward III. into Scotland, and appears to have been engaged in the battle of Halidown-hill. But the "errant knight" most intimately connected with England was Hans v. Traun. He joined the banner of Edward III. at the siege of Calais, during which he was engaged in cutting off some supplies sent by sea for the relief of the besieged. He does ample justice to the valour and heroic resistance of the garrison, who did not surrender till their stock of leather,[1] rope and similar materials,—which had long been their only food,—was exhausted. Rats were sold at a crown each. In the year 1356 he attended the Black Prince in the campaign which preceded the battle of Poictiers; and on the morning of that eventful fight, Prince Edward honoured him with the important charge of bearing the English standard. The battle is described with considerable animation. The hostile armies advanced

---

[1] [The original reads "schuch, sil, chvnt und hewt;" the two last I interpret "kind und haut."]

an essential part of the ceremony. Here they had an opportunity of observing accoutrements, armorial distinctions, the number and appearance of the spectators, together with the various events of the turney, to the best advantage: and they were afterwards obliged to compile an ample register of this strange mixture of foppery and ferocity.[1] They were necessarily connected with the minstrels at public festivals, and thence acquired a facility of reciting adventures. A learned French antiquary is of opinion, that anciently the French heralds, called Hiraux, were the same as the minstrels, and that they sung metrical tales at festivals.[2] They frequently received fees or largess in common with the minstrels.[3] They travelled into different countries, and saw the fashions of foreign courts, and foreign tournaments. They not only committed to writing the process of the lists, but it was also their business, at magnificent feasts, to describe the number and parade of the dishes, the quality of the guests, the brilliant dresses of the ladies, the courtesy of the knights, the revels, disguisings, banquets, and every other occurrence most observable in the course of the solemnity. Spenser alludes expressly to these heraldic details, where he mentions the splendour of Florimel's wedding:

---

on foot, the archers forming the vanguard. "This was not a time," says the poet, "for the interchange of chivalric civilities, for friendly greetings and cordial love: no man asked his fellow for a violet or a rose;* and many a hero, like the ostrich, was obliged to digest both iron and steel, or to overcome in death the sensations inflicted by the spear and the javelin. The field resounded with the clash of swords, clubs, and battle-axes; and with shouts of Nater Dam and Sand Jors." But Von Traun, mindful of the trust reposed in him, rushed forward to encounter the standard-bearer of France: "He drove his spear through the vizer of his adversary—the enemy's banner sank to the earth never to rise again—Von Traun planted his foot upon its staff; when the king of France was made captive, and the battle was won." For his gallantry displayed on this day Edward granted him a pension of a hundred marks. He is afterwards mentioned as being intrusted by Edward III. with the defence of Calais during a ten weeks' siege; and at a subsequent period as crossing the channel, and capturing a (French?) ship, which he brought into an English port and presented to Edward.—*Price*. The Poems were published at Vienna in 1827 by Primisser under the title: Peter Suchenwirt *Werke aus dem vierzehuten Jahr-hunderte*. With an introduction, notes, and a glossary. See also Hormayr's *Taschenbuch für die vaterlandische Geschichte*. Vienna, 1828.—*Rye*.]

[1] "L'un des principaux fonctions des Herauts d'armes etoit se trouver au jousts, &c. ou ils gardoient les ecus pendans, recevoient les noms et les blasons des chevaliers, en tenoient registre, et en composoient recueils," &c. Menestr. *Orig. des Armoir*. p. 180. See also p. 119. These registers are mentioned in Perceforest, xi. 68, 77.

[2] Carpentier, *Suppl. Du-Cang. Gloss. Lat.* p. 750, tom. ii.

[3] Thus at St. George's feast at Windsor we have, "Diversis heraldis et ministrallis," &c. Ann. 21 Ric. ii. 9 Hen. vi. apud Anstis, *Ord. Gart.* i. 56, 108. And again, *Exit. Pell. M. ann.* 22 *Edw.* iii. "Magistro Andreæ Roy Norreys, [a herald,] Lybekin le Piper, et Hanakino filio suo, et sex aliis menestrallis regis in denariis eis liberatis de dono regis, in subsidium expensarum suarum, lv. *s.* iv. *d.*"—*Exit. Pell. P. ann.* 33 *Edw.* ii. "Willielmo Volaunt regi heraldorum et ministrallis existentibus apud Smithfield in ultimo hastiludio de dono regis, x *l.*" I could give many other proofs.

---

* [So I interpret "umb veyal (veilchen) noch umb rosen."]

> To tell the glorie of the feaſt that day,
> The goodly ſervyſe, the devicefull ſights,
> The bridegromes ſtate, the brides moſt rich aray,
> The pride of Ladies, and the worth of knights,
> The royall banquet, and the rare delights,
> Were worke fit for an herauld, not for me : [1]—

I ſuſpect that Chaucer, not perhaps without ridicule, glances at ſome of theſe deſcriptions, with which his age abounded ; and which he probably regarded with leſs reverence, and read with leſs edification, than did the generality of his cotemporary readers :

> What ſchuld I telle of the realté [2]
> Of this mariage, or which cours goth biforn,
> Who bloweth in a trompe or in an horn ?

Again, in deſcribing Cambuſcan's feaſt :

> Of which if I ſchal tellen al tharray, [3]
> Than wold it occupie a ſomeres day ;
> And eek it needith nought for to devyſe
> At every cours the ordre and the ſervyſe.
> I wol nat tellen of her ſtraunge ſewes,
> Ne of her ſwannes, ne here heroun-ſewes.

And at the feaſt of Theſeus, in the *Knight's Tale* :

> The mynſtralcye, the ſervyce at the feſte, [4]
> The grete yiftes to the moſt and leſte,
> The riche aray of Theſeus paleys,
> Ne who ſat firſt ne laſt upon the deys,
> What ladies fayreſt ben or beſt daunſynge,
> Or which of hem can daunce beſt or ſynge,
> Ne who moſt felyngly ſpeketh of love ;
> What haukes ſitten on the perche above,
> What houndes lyen in the floor adoun :
> Of al this make I now no mencioun.

In the *Flower and the Leaf*, the [author] has deſcribed in eleven long ſtanzas the proceſſion to a ſplendid tournament, with all the prolixity and exactneſs of a herald.[5] The ſame affectation, derived from the ſame ſources, occurs often in Arioſto.

It were eaſy to illuſtrate this doctrine by various examples. The famous French romance of [Le Petit Jean de] *Saintre* was evidently the performance of a herald. [Jean de] Saintre, the knight of the piece, was a real perſon, and, according to Froiſſart, was taken priſoner at the battle of Poitiers in 1356.[6] But the compiler confounds chronology, and aſcribes to his hero many pieces of true hiſtory belonging to others. This was a common practice in theſe books. Some authors have ſuppoſed that this romance appeared before the year 1380.[7] But there are reaſons to prove, that it was written by Antony de la Sale, a Burgundian, author of a book of Ceremonies, from his name very quaintly entitled *La Sallade*, and

---

[1] *F. Q.* v. iii. 3 [edit. Morris, 1869, p. 306.]
[2] [Morris's *Chaucer*, ii. 191, ver. 605.]
[3] [*Ibid.* ii. 356, ver. 55.]
[4] [*Ibid.* ii. 68, ver. 1339.]
[5] From ver. 204 to ver. 287.
[6] Froiſſart, *Hiſt.* i. p. 178.
[7] Byſshe, *Not. in Upton. Milit. Offic.* p. 56. Meneſtrier, *Orig. Arm.* p. 23.

frequently cited by our learned antiquary Selden.¹ This Antony came into England to see the solemnity of the queen's coronation in the year 1445.² I have not seen any French romance which has preserved the practices of chivalry more copiously than this of *Saintre*. It must have been an absolute master-piece for the rules of tilting, martial customs, and public ceremonies prevailing in its author's age. In the library of the [College] of Arms, there remains a very accurate description of a feast of Saint George, celebrated at Windsor in 1471.³ It appears to have been written by the herald Blue-Mantle Pursuivant. Menestrier says, that Guillaume Rucher, herald of Henault, has left a large treatise, describing the tournaments annually celebrated at Lisle in Flanders.⁴ In the reign of Edward IV., John Smarte, a Norman, garter king at arms, described in French the tournament held at Bruges, for nine days, in honour of the marriage of the duke of Burgundy with Margaret the king's daughter.⁵ There is a French poem [on the siege of the Castle of Karlaverock in the year] 1300.⁶ This was [probably, however, the production of Walter of Exeter, whom Carew supposes to have written the original Latin prose romance of *Guy of Warwick*.] The author thus describes the banner of John of Brittany, [nephew of the duke]:

> Baniere avoit cointe et paree
> De or et de azur eschequeree
> Au rouge ourle o iaunes lupars
> Dermine estoit la quarte pars.⁷

The pompous circumstances of which these heraldic narratives

---

¹ *Tit. Hon.* p. 413, &c.   ² Anst. *Ord. Gart.* ii. 321.
³ MSS. Offic. Arm. M. 15, fol. 12, 13.
⁴ "Guillaume Rucher, heraut d'armes du titre de Heynaut, a fait un gros volume des rois de l'Epinette a Lisle en Flanders ; c'est une ceremonie, ou un feste, dont il a decrit les joustes, tournois, noms, armoiries, livrees, et equipages de divers seigneurs, qui se rendoient de divers endroits, avec le catalogues de rois de cette feste." Menestr. *Orig. des Armoir*, p. 64.
⁵ See many other instances in MS. Harl. 69, entit. *The Booke of certaine Triumphes*. See also Appendix to the [last] edition of Leland's *Collectanea*.
⁶ MSS. Cott. [Caligula, A xviii. *The Siege of Carlaverock*, in the xxviii Edward I, A. D. MCCC : &c., from a MS. in the handwriting of Robert Glover the herald. Edited by H. N. Nicolas, Lond. 1828, 4to. In some copies the plates of arms are coloured. A reprint of the poem, with the roll of arms emblazoned, appeared in 1860, from which text the present extract has been taken, that of Warton being incorrect. The piece itself is also inserted from a collation of the two known copies in the *Antiquarian Repertory*, edit. 1807, iv. 469. See also Black's *Illustrations of Ancient State and Chivalry*, 1840, and *A Booke of Precedence*, &c. edit. Furnivall, 1869. The British Museum has quite lately (Dec. 1870) acquired a curious volume of French and Latin pieces on this subject.]
⁷ The bishop of Gloucester [says Warton] has most obligingly condescended to point out to me another source, to which many of the romances of the fourteenth century owed their existence. Montfaucon, in his *Monumens de la Monarchie Françoise*, has printed the "Statuts de l'Ordre du Saint Esprit au droit desir ou du Noeud etabli par Louis d'Anjou roi de Jerusalem et Sicile en 1352-3-4," tom. ii. p. 329. This was an annual celebration " au Chastel de l'Euf enchanti du merveilleux peril." The castle, as appears by the monuments which accompany these statutes, was built at the foot of the obscure grot of the enchantments of Virgil. The statutes are as extraordinary as if they had been drawn up by Don Quixote himself, or his assessors, the curate and the barber. From the seventh chapter we learn that

consisted, and the minute prolixity with which they were displayed, seemed to have infected the professed historians of this age. Of this there are various instances in Froissart, who had no other design than to compile a chronicle of real facts. I will give one example out of many. At a treaty of marriage between our Richard II. and Isabel daughter of Charles V. king of France, the two monarchs, attended with a noble retinue, met and formed several encampments in a spacious plain, near the castle of Guynes. Froissart expends many pages in relating at large the costly furniture of the pavilions, the riches of the side-boards, the profusion and variety of sumptuous liquors, spices, and dishes, with their order of service, the number of the attendants, with their address and exact discharge of duty in their respective offices, the presents of gold and precious stones made on both sides, and a thousand other particulars of equal importance, relating to the parade of this royal review.[1] On this account, Caxton, in his exhortation to the knights of his age, ranks Froissart's history, as a book of chivalry, with the romances of Lancelot and Percival, and recommends it to their attention, as a manual equally calculated to inculcate the knightly virtues of courage and courtesy.[2] This indeed was in an age when not only the courts of princes, but the castles of barons, vied with one another in the lustre of their shews; when tournaments, coronations, royal interviews, and solemn festivals, were the grand objects of mankind. Froissart was an eyewitness of many of the ceremonies which he describes. His passion seems to have been that of seeing magnificent spectacles, and of hearing reports concerning them.[3] Although a canon of two churches, he passed his life in travelling from court to court, and from castle to castle.[4] He thus, either from his own observation or the credible information of others, easily procured suitable materials for a history, which professed only to deal in sensible objects, and those of the most splendid and conspicuous kind. He was familiarly known to two kings of England and one of Scotland.[5] But the court which he

---

the knights who came to this yearly festival at the *chatel de l'euf*, were obliged to deliver in writing to the clerks of the chapel of the castle their yearly adventures. Such of these histories as were thought worthy to be recorded, the clerks are ordered to transcribe in a book, which was called " Le livre des avenements aux chevaliers, &c. Et demeura le dit livre toujours en la dicte chapelle." This sacred register certainly furnished from time to time ample materials to the romance-writers. And this circumstance gives a new explanation to a reference which we so frequently find in romances : I mean, that appeal which they so constantly make to some authentic record. [Warton's episcopal informant was, of course, his friend Warburton.]

[1] See Froissart's *Cronycle*, translated by Lord Berners, 1523, vol. ii. f. 242.

[2] [*Book of the ordre of chyualry or knyghthode* (circâ 1484).]

[3] His father was a painter of armories. This might give him an early turn for shews. See Sainte-Palaye, *Mem. Lit.* tom. x. p. 664, edit. 4to.

[4] He was originally a clerk of the chamber to Philippa, queen of Edward III. He was afterwards canon and treasurer of Chimay in Henault, and of Lisle in Flanders; and chaplain to Guy earl of Castellon. Labor. *Introd. a l'Hist. de Charles VI.* p. 69. Compare also Froissart's *Chron.* ii. f. 29, 305, 319. And Bullart, *Academ. des Arts et des Scienc.* i. p. 125, 126.

[5] *Cron.* ii. f. 158, 161.

most admired was that of Gaston, Comte de Foix, at Orlaix in Bearn; for, as he himself acquaints us, it was not only the most brilliant in Europe, but the grand centre for tidings of martial adventures.[1] It was crowded with knights of England and Arragon. In the meantime it must not be forgotten that Froissart, who from his childhood was strongly attached to carousals, the music of minstrels, and the sports of hawking and hunting,[2] cultivated the poetry of the troubadours, and was a writer of romances.[3] This turn, it must be confessed, might have some share in communicating that romantic cast to his history which I have mentioned. During his abode at the court of the Comte de Foix, where he was entertained for twelve weeks, he presented to the earl his collection of the poems of the duke of Luxemburg, consisting of sonnets, balades, and virelays. Among these was included a romance, composed by himself, called *Meliade[s] or The Knight of the Sun of Gold.* Gaston's chief amusement was to hear Froissart read this romance[4] every evening after supper.[5] At his introduction to Richard II. he presented that brilliant monarch with a book beautifully illuminated, engrossed with his own hand, bound in crimson velvet, and embellished with silver bosses, clasps, and golden roses, comprehending all the matters of Amours and Moralities, which in the course of twenty-four years he had composed.[6] This was in 1396. When he left

---

[1] *Cron.* ii. f. 30. This was in 1381.
[2] See *Mem. Lit.* ut supr. p. 665.
[3] Speaking of the death of King Richard, Froissart quotes a prediction from the old French prose romance of Brut, which he says was fulfilled in that catastrophe, liv. iv. c. 119. Froissart will be mentioned again as a poet.
[4] I take this opportunity of remarking, that romantic tales or histories appear at a very early period to have been read as well as sung at feasts. So Wace in the *Roman du Rou*, in the British Museum, above mentioned:

"Doit l'en les vers et les regestes
Et les estoires *lire* as festes."

[5] Froissart brought with him for a present to Gaston Comte de Foix four greyhounds, which were called by the romantic names of Tristram, Hector, Brut, and Roland. Gaston was so fond of hunting, that he kept upwards of six hundred dogs in his castle. Sainte-Palaye, *ut supr.* pp. 676, 678. He wrote a treatise on hunting, printed [about 1507. See Brunet, *dern.* edit. art. *Phebus.*] In illustration of the former part of this note, Crescimbeni says, "Che in molte nobilissime famiglie Italiane, ha 400 e più anni, passarono` i nomi de' *Lancillotti*, de' *Tristami*, de *Galvani*, di *Galeotti*, delle [Isoulde], delle *Genevre*, e d'altri cavalieri, à dame in esse Tavola Roitonda operanti," &c. *Istor. Volg. Poes.* vol. i. lib. v. p. 327.
[6] I should think that this was his romance of *Meliadus.* Froissart says, that the king at receiving it asked him what the book treated of. He answered *d'Amour.* The king, adds our historian, seemed much pleased at this, and examined the book in many places, for he was fond of reading as well as speaking French. He then ordered Richard Crendon, the chevalier in waiting, to carry it into his privy chamber, *dont il me fit bonne chere.* He gave copies of the several parts of his chronicle, as they were finished, to his different patrons. Le Laboureur says, that Froissart sent fifty-six quires of his *Roman au Croniques* to Guillaume de Bailly, an illuminator; which, when illuminated, were intended as a present to the king of England. *Hist.* ch. vi. En *la vie de Louis duc d'Anjou,* p. 67, *seq.* See also *Cron.* i. iv. c. i.—iii. 26. There are two or three fine illuminated copies of Froissart

England the fame year,[1] the king fent him a maffive goblet of filver, filled with one hundred nobles.[2]

As we are approaching to Chaucer, let us here ſtand ſtill, and take a retroſpect of the general manners. The tournaments and carouſals of our ancient princes, by forming ſplendid aſſemblies of both ſexes, while they inculcated the moſt liberal ſentiments of honour and heroiſm, undoubtedly contributed to introduce ideas of courteſy, and to encourage decorum. Yet the national manners ſtill retained a great degree of ferocity, and the ceremonies of the moſt refined courts in Europe had often a mixture of barbariſm which rendered them ridiculous. This abſurdity will always appear at periods when men are ſo far civilized as to have loſt their native ſimplicity, and yet have not attained juſt ideas of politeneſs and propriety. Their luxury was inelegant, their pleaſures indelicate, their pomp cumberſome and unwieldy. In the meantime it may ſeem ſurpriſing that the many ſchools of philoſophy which flouriſhed in the middle ages ſhould not have corrected and poliſhed the times. But as their religion was corrupted by ſuperſtition, ſo their philoſophy degenerated into ſophiſtry. Nor is it ſcience alone, even if founded on truth, that will poliſh nations. For this purpoſe, the powers of imagination muſt be awakened and exerted, to teach elegant feelings, and to heighten our natural ſenſibilities. It is not the head only that muſt be informed, but the heart muſt alſo be moved. Many claſſic authors were known in the thirteenth century, but the ſcholars of that period wanted taſte to read and admire them. The pathetic or ſublime ſtrokes of Virgil would be but little reliſhed by theologiſts and metaphyſicians.

---

among the Royal MSS. in the Britiſh Muſeum. Among the ſtores of Henry VIII. at his manor of Beddington in Surrey, I find the faſhionable reading of the times exemplified in the following books, *viz.* " *Item*, a great book of parchment written and lymned with gold of graver's work *De confeſſione Amantis*, with xviii. other bookes, Le premier volume de Lancelot, Froiſſart, Le grant voiage de Jeruſalem, Enguerain de Monſtrellet," &c. MSS. Harl. 1419, f. 382. Froiſſart was here properly claſſed.

[1] Froiſſart ſays, that he accompanied the king to various palaces, "A Elten, a Ledos, a Kinkeſtove, a Cenes, a Certeſée et a Windſor." This is, Eltham, Leeds, Kingſton, Chertſey, &c. *Cron.* liv. iv. c. 119, p. 348. The French are not much improved at this day in ſpelling Engliſh places and names.

Perhaps by *Cenes*, Froiſſart means Shene, the royal palace at Richmond.

[2] *Cron.* f. 251, 252, 255, 319, 348. Bayle, who has an article on Froiſſart, had no idea of ſearching for anecdotes of Froiſſart's life in his *Chronicle*. Inſtead of which, he ſwells his notes on this article with the contradictory accounts of Moreri, Voſſius, and others, whoſe diſputes might have been all eaſily ſettled by recurring to Froiſſart himſelf, who has interſperſed in his hiſtory many curious particulars relating to his own life and works.

SECTION XII.

THE most illustrious ornament of the reign of Edward III. and of his successor Richard II. was Geoffrey Chaucer, a poet with whom the history of our poetry is by many supposed to have commenced, and who has been pronounced, by a critic of unquestionable taste and discernment, to be the first English versifier who wrote poetically.[1] He was born [about] the year [1340, and was probably in his youth a page of Elizabeth, wife of Prince Lionel, third son of Edward III.]:[2] but the liveliness of his parts, and the native gaiety of his disposition, soon recommended him to the patronage of a magnificent monarch, and rendered him a very popular and acceptable character in the brilliant court which I have above described. In the meantime he added to his accomplishments by frequent tours into France and Italy, which he sometimes visited under the advantages of a public character. Hitherto our poets had been persons of a private and circumscribed education, and the art of versifying, like every other kind of composition, had been confined to recluse scholars. But Chaucer was a man of the world; and from this circumstance we are to account, in great measure, for the many new embellishments which he conferred on our language and our poetry. The descriptions of splendid processions and gallant carousals with which his works abound are a proof that he was conversant with the practices and diversions of polite life. Familiarity with a variety of things and objects, opportunities of acquiring the fashionable and courtly modes of speech, connections with the great at home, and a personal acquaintance with the vernacular poets of foreign countries, opened his mind, and furnished him with new lights.[3] In Italy he [is said to have met] Petrarch, at the wedding of Violante, daughter of Galeazzo, duke of Milan, with the duke of Clarence; and it is [even alleged] that Boccaccio was of the party.[4] Although Chaucer had undoubtedly studied the works of these celebrated writers, and particularly of Dante, before this, yet it seems likely that these excursions gave him a new relish for their compositions, and enlarged his knowledge of the Italian fables. His travels likewise enabled him to cultivate the Italian and [French] languages with

---

[1] Johnson's *Diction*. Pref. p. 1.

[2] [*New Facts in the Life of Geoffrey Chaucer*, by E. A. Bond, *Fortnightly Rev.*, Aug. 15, 1866.]

[3] The earl of Salisbury, beheaded by Henry IV., could not but patronize Chaucer. I do not mean for political reasons. The earl was a writer of verses, and very fond of poetry. On this account his acquaintance was much cultivated by the famous Christina of Pisa, whose works, both in prose and verse, compose so considerable a part of the old French literature. She used to call him, "Gracieux chevalier, aimant dictiez, et lui-meme gracieux dicteur." See M. Boivin, *Mem. Lit.* tom. ii. p. 767, *seq.* 4to.

[4] Froissart was also present. *Vie de Petrarque*, 1766, iii. 772. I believe Paulus Jovius is the first who mentions this anecdote. *Vit. Galeas.* ii. p. 152.

the greatest success, and induced him to polish the asperity, and enrich the sterility of his native versification with softer cadences, and a more copious and variegated phraseology. [This attempt was] authorized by the recent and popular examples of Petrarch in Italy and [Jean de Meun and others] in France.[1] The revival of learning in most countries appears to have first owed its rise to translation. At rude periods the modes of original thinking are unknown, and the arts of original composition have not yet been studied. The writers, therefore, of such periods are chiefly and very usefully employed in importing the ideas of other languages into their own. They do not venture to think for themselves, nor aim at the merit of inventors, but they are laying the foundations of literature; and while they are naturalizing the knowledge of more learned ages and countries by translation, they are imperceptibly improving the national language. This has been remarkably the case, not only in England, but in France and Italy. [To mention only a few instances: Laʒamon translated and enlarged Wace; Robert of Brunne translated William of Waddington, Wace, and Langtoft; and] in the year 1387, John Trevisa, canon of Westbury in Gloucestershire and a great traveller, not only finished a translation of the Old and New Testaments at the command of his munificent patron, Thomas Lord Berkley,[2] but also translated Higden's *Polychronicon* and other Latin pieces.[3] But these translations would have been alone insufficient to have produced or sustained any considerable revolution in our language: the great work was reserved for Gower and Chaucer. Wickliffe had also translated the Bible;[4] and in other respects his attempts to bring about a reformation in religion at this time proved beneficial to English literature. The orthodox divines of this period generally wrote in Latin: but Wickliffe, that his arguments might

---

[1] [Not Alain Chartier, as Warton says; for Alain Chartier was born at Bayeux not later than 1395, and did not compose his first work till after the battle of Agincourt (25 Oct. 1415); it was *Le Livre des Quatre Dames*. He was sent to Scotland on an embassy in June or July, 1428. See *Memoires de la Société des Antiquaires de Normandie*, tome xxviii. and *Revue Critique*, Aug. 28, 1869.—F. The example of Chartier could not have been, consequently, of much service to our Chaucer!]

[2] See Wharton, *Append. Cav.* p. 49.

[3] Such as Bartholomew Glanville *De Proprietatibus Rerum*, lib. xix. and Vegetius *De Arte Militari*. MSS. Digb. 233. Bibl. Bodl. In the same manuscript is Ægidius Romanus *De Regimine Principum*, a translation by [Occleve. It was edited for the Roxburghe Club, by Mr. T. Wright, 1860.] He also translated some pieces of Richard Fitzralph, archbishop of Armagh. See *supr.* He wrote a tract, prefixed to his version of the *Polychronicon*, on the utility of translations: *De Utilitate Translationum, Dialogus inter Clericum et Patronum*. See more of his translations in MSS. Harl. 1900. I do not find his *English Bible* in any of our libraries, nor do I believe that any copy of it now remains. Caxton mentions it in the preface to his edition of the English *Polychronicon*. See Lewis's *Wickliffe*, p. 66, 329, and Lewis's *History of the Translations of the Bible*, p. 66.

[4] It is observable that he made his translation from the vulgate Latin version of Jerom. See MS. Cod. Bibl. Coll. Eman. Cant. 102. [There is nothing in the MS. to warrant the statement in the former editions as to the work having been finished in 1383, which date is simply added in a note written in a second hand.—Madden.]

be familiarized to common readers and the bulk of the people, was obliged to compose in English his numerous theological treatises against the papal corruptions. Edward III. while he perhaps intended only to banish a badge of conquest, greatly contributed to establish the national dialect, by abolishing the use of the Norman tongue in the public acts and judicial proceedings, as we have before observed, and by substituting the natural language of the country. But Chaucer manifestly first taught his countrymen to write English, and formed a style by naturalizing words from the [Langue d'Oye],[1] at that time the [richest] dialect of any in Europe, and the best adapted to the purposes of poetical expression.

It is certain that Chaucer abounds in classical allusions; but his poetry is not formed on the ancient models. He appears to have been an universal reader, and his learning is sometimes mistaken for genius; but his chief sources were the French and Italian poets. From these originals two of his capital poems, the *Knight's Tale*,[2] and the *Romaunt of the Rose* [if his] are imitations or translations. The first of these is taken from Boccaccio. [Chaucer, out of the 2250 lines of his *Knight's Tale*, has translated 270 (less than one-eighth) from the 9054 of Boccaccio's original: 374 more lines

---

[1] The ingenious editor of the *Canterbury Tales* treats the notion, that Chaucer imitated the Provençal poets, as totally void of foundation. He says, "I have not observed in any of his writings a single phrase or word, which has the least appearance of having been fetched from the South of the Loire. With respect to the manner and matter of his compositions, till some clear instance of imitation be produced, I shall be slow to believe, that in either he ever copied the poets of Provence; with whose works, I apprehend, he had very little, if any acquaintance," vol. i. *Append. Pref.* p. xxxvi. I have advanced the contrary doctrine, at least by implication: and I here beg leave to explain myself on a subject materially affecting the system of criticism that has been formed on Chaucer's works. I have never affirmed that Chaucer imitated the Provençal bards; although it is by no means improbable that he might have known their tales. But as the peculiar nature of the Provençal poetry entered deeply into the substance, cast, and character, of some of those French and Italian models, which he is allowed to have followed, he certainly may be said to have copied, although not immediately, the *matter* and *manner* of these writers. I have called his *House of Fame* originally a Provençal composition. I did not mean that it was written by a Provençal troubadour: but that Chaucer's original was compounded of the capricious mode of fabling, and that extravagant style of fiction, which constitute the essence of the Provençal poetry. As to the *Flower and the Leaf*, which Dryden pronounces to have been composed *after their manner*, it is framed on the old allegorising spirit of the Provençal writers, refined and disfigured by the fopperies of the French poets in the fourteenth century. The ideas of these fablers had been so strongly imbibed, that they continued to operate long after Petrarch had introduced a more rational method of composition.

[2] Chaucer alludes to some book whence this tale was taken, more than once, viz. v. 1. "Whilom, as *olde stories* tellin us." v. 1465. "As *olde bookes* to us saine, that all *this storie telleth more plain*." v. 2814. "Of soulis fynd I nought in this *registre*." That is, this history, or narrative. See also v. 2297. In the *Legend of good women*, where Chaucer's works are mentioned, is this passage, v. 420.

"And al the love of Palamon and Arcite
Of Thebis, *though the storeis known lite*."

[The last words seem to imply that it had not made itself very popular.—*Tyrwhitt*.]

bear a general likeness to the Italian poets, and 132 more, a slight likeness.¹]

Boccaccio was the disciple of Petrarch: and although principally known and deservedly celebrated as a writer or inventor of tales, he was by his cotemporaries usually placed in the third rank after Dante and Petrarch. But Boccaccio having seen the Platonic sonnets of his master Petrarch, in a fit of despair committed [a portion of his own] to the flames,² except [only certain pieces, of which perhaps] his good taste had taught him to entertain a more favourable opinion, [one] thus happily rescued from destruction [was formerly] so little known even in Italy, as to have left its author but a slender proportion of that eminent degree of poetical reputation which he might have justly claimed from so extraordinary a performance. It is an heroic poem, in twelve books, entitled *La Teseide*, and written in the octave stanza, called by the Italians *ottava rima*, which Boccaccio adopted from the old French chansons, and here first introduced among his countrymen.³ It was printed at Ferrara, but with some deviations from the original, and even misrepresentations of the story, in 1475.⁴ [It was reprinted without date in 4to, and again in 1528. The poem has also been translated into Italian and French prose.]

Whether Boccaccio was the inventor of the story of this poem [seems rather doubtful]. It is certain that Theseus was an early hero of romance.⁵ He was taken from that grand repository of the Grecian heroes, the *History of Troy*, [composed from various materials] by Guido de Colonna. In the royal library at Paris there is a MS. entitled, *Roman de Theseus et de Gadifer*.⁶ Probably, this is the French romance, [printed at Paris in two folio volumes in 1534.⁷] Gadifer, with whom Theseus is joined in this ancient tale, written probably by a troubadour of Picardy, is a champion in the oldest French romances.⁸ He is mentioned frequently in the *Roman d'Alexandre*. In the romance of *Perceforrest*, he is called king of Scotland, and said to be crowned by Alexander the Great.⁹ [But this Theseus, as Mr. Douce has pointed out, is a different person altogether from the classical hero, being the son of Floridas, king of

---

¹ [*Temporary Preface*, by F. J. F., pp. 104-5.]
² Goujet, *Bibl. Fr.* tom. vii. p. 328.
³ See Crescimbeni *Istor. Volgar. Poes.* vol. i. l. i. p. 65.
⁴ [See the correct title in Brunet, last edit. i. 1016-17. A purer text of the poem appeared in 1819, 8vo, in which it was taken from a MS. The *Theseid* forms vol. 9 of the collected edit. of Boccaccio, published at Florence, 1827-31, 13 vols. 8vo.]
⁵ In Lydgate's *Temple of Glas*, among the lovers painted on the wall is Theseus killing the Minotaur. I suppose from Ovid, or from Chaucer's *Legend of Good Women*. Bibl. Bodl. MSS. Fairfax, 16.
⁶ MSS. Bibl. Reg. Paris. tom. ii. 974. E.
⁷ [See the full and correct title in the last edition of Brunet, v. 808. There was a later edition about 1550.]
⁸ The chevaliers of the courts of Charles V. and VI. adopted names from the old romances, such as Lancelot, Gadifer, Carados, &c. *Mem. Anc. Cheval.* i. p. 340.
⁹ [See Brunet, dern. edit. in v. *Perceforest*. This tedious story was printed at Paris in 1528, in six folio volumes, usually bound in three.]

Cologne, in the year 682.] There is in the same library a MS. called by Montfaucon *Historia Thesei in lingua vulgari*, in ten books.[1] The Abbé Goujet observes, that there is in some libraries of France an old French translation of Boccaccio's *Theseid*, from which Anna de Graville formed the French poem of *Palamon and Arcite*, at the command of Queen Claude, wife of Francis I., about the year 1487. Either the translation used by Anna de Graville, or her poem, is perhaps the second of the MSS. mentioned by Montfaucon. Boccaccio's *Theseid* has also been translated into Italian prose by Nicolas Granuci, and printed at Lucca in 157[9].[2] In the *Dedication* to this work, which was printed about one hundred years after the Ferrara edition of the *Theseide* appeared, Granucci [wrongly and even ignorantly, as we are much inclined to think], mentions Boccaccio's work as a translation from the barbarous Greek poem cited below.[3] Boccaccio himself mentions the story of Palamon and Arcite. This may seem to imply that the story existed before his time: unless he artfully intended to recommend his own poem on the subject by such an allusion. It is where he introduces two lovers singing a portion of this tale :—" Dioneo e Fiametta gran pezza canterono insieme d'Arcite e di Palamone."[4] By Dioneo Boccaccio represents himself; and by Fiametta, his mistress, Mary of Arragon, a natural daughter of Robert, king of Naples.

I confess I am of opinion, that Boccaccio's *Theseid* is [to a great extent] an original composition [though based on, and improved from, the *Thebais* of Statius]. But there is a Græco-barbarous poem extant on this subject, which, if it could be proved to be antecedent in point of time to the Italian poem, would degrade Boccaccio to a mere translator on this occasion. It is a matter that deserves to be examined at large, and to be traced with accuracy.

This Greek poem is [by no means so well] known as Boccaccio's. It is entitled Θησευς και Γαμοι της Εμηλιας. It was printed at Venice in 1529.[5] It is often cited by Du Cange in his Greek glossary under the title, *De Nuptiis Thesei et Æmiliæ*. The heads of the chapters are adorned with rude wooden cuts of the story. I once suspected that Boccaccio, having received this poem from some of his learned friends among the Grecian exiles, who being driven from Constantinople took refuge in Italy about the fourteenth century, translated it into Italian. Under this supposition, I was indeed surprised to find

---

[1] Bibl. MSS. *ut supr.*

[2] [But see Brunet, i. 1017.] The *Theseid* has also been translated into French prose, 1597, 12mo.—[*Ibid.*] Jeanne de la Fontaine translated into French verse this poem. She died 1536. Her translation was never printed. It is applauded by Joannes Secundus, *Eleg.* xv.

[3] *Dedicaz.* fol. 5. " Volendo far cosa, que non sio stata fatta da loro, pero mutato parere mi dicoli a ridurre in prosa questo Innamoramento, Opera di M. Giovanni Boccaccio, quale egli transporto dal Greco in ottava rima per compiacere alla sua Fiametta," &c. See Sloane MS. 1614. Brit. Mus.

[4] *Giorn.* vii. Nov. 10, p. 348, edit. 1548. Chaucer himself alludes to this story, *Bl. Kn.* v. 369. Perhaps on the same principle.

[5] A MS. of it is in the Royal Library at Paris, Cod. 2569. Du Cange, *Ind. Auct. Gloss. Gr. Barb.* ii. p. 65, col. 1.

the ideas of chivalry and the ceremonies of a tournament minutely described, in a poem which appeared to have been written at Constantinople. But this difficulty was soon removed, when I recollected that the [Latins, in which name we include the French, Flemings, Italians, and] Venetians, had been in possession of that city for more than one hundred years, Baldwin, earl of Flanders, having been elected emperor of Constantinople in 1204.[1] Add to this, that the word, τερνεμεντον, a tournament, occurs in the Byzantine historians.[2] From the same communication likewise, I mean the Greek exiles, I fancied Boccaccio might have procured the stories of several of his tales in the *Decameron:* as, for instance, that of *Cymon and Iphigenia*, where the names are entirely Grecian, and the scene laid in Rhodes,

---

[1] About which period it is probable that the anonymous Greek poem, called the *Loves of Lybister and Rhodamna*, was written. This appears by the German name Frederic, which often occurs in it, and is grecised, with many other German words. In a MS. of this poem which Crusius saw, were many paintings and illuminations; where, in the representation of a battle, he observed no guns, but javelins and bows and arrows. He adds, "et musicæ testudines." It is written in the iambic measure mentioned below. It is a series of wandering adventures with little art or invention. Lybister, the son of a Latin king, and a Christian, sets forward accompanied with an hundred attendants in search of Rhodamna, whom he had lost by the stratagems of a certain old woman skilled in magic. He meets Clitophon son of a king of Armenia. They undergo various dangers in different countries. Lybister relates his dream concerning a partridge and an eagle; and how from that dream he fell in love with Rhodamna daughter of Chyses a pagan king, and communicated his passion by sending an arrow, to which his name was affixed, into a tower, or castle, called Argyrocastre, &c. See Crusius, *Turko-Græcia*, p. 974. But we find a certain species of erotic romances, some in verse and some in prose, existing in the Greek empire, the remains and the dregs of Heliodorus, Achilles Tatius, Xenophon the Ephesian, Charito, Eustathius or Eumathius, and others, about or rather before the year 1200. Such are the *Loves of Rhodante and Dosicles*, by Theodorus Prodromus, who wrote about the year 1130. This piece was imitated by Nicetas Eugenianus in the *Loves of Charicell and Drosilla*. See Labb. *Bibl. Nov. Manuscript.* p. 220. *The Loves of Callimachus and Chrysorrhoe*, *The Erotic history of Hemperius*, *The history of the Loves of Florius and Platzaflora*, with some others, all by anonymous authors, and in Græco-barbarous iambics, were written at Constantinople, [and were probably translations from another language.] See Nessel. i. p. 342-343. Meurs. *Gloss. Gr. Barb.* v. Βαινν. And Lambecc. v. p. 262, 264.

[2] As also Τερις, *Hastiludium*. Fr. *Tournoi*. And Τουρνευιν, *hastiludio contendere*. Johannes Cantacuzenus relates, that when Anne of Savoy, daughter of Amadeus, the fourth earl of Savoy, was married to the Emperor Andronicus, junior, the Frankish and Savoyard nobles, who accompanied the princess, held tilts and tournaments before the court at Constantinople; which, he adds, the Greeks learned of the Franks. This was in 1326. *Hist. Byzant.* l. i. cap. 42. But Nicetas says, that when the Emperor Manuel [Comnenus] made some stay at Antioch, the Greeks held a solemn tournament against the Franks. This was about 1160. *Hist. Byzant.* l. iii. cap. 3. Cinnamus observes, that the same Emperor Manuel altered the shape of the shields and lances of the Greeks to those of the Franks. *Hist.* lib. iii. Nicephorus Gregoras, who wrote about the year 1340, affirms that the Greeks learned this practice from the Franks. *Hist. Byzant.* l. x. p. 339, edit. fol. Genev. 1615. The word Καβαλλαριοι, knights, chevaliers, occurs often in the Byzantine historians, even as early as Anna Comnena, who wrote about 1140. *Alexiad*, lib. xiii. p. 411. And we have in J. Cantacuzenus, "την Καβαλαριον παρειχε τιμην:"—He conferred the honour of Knighthood. This indeed is said of the Franks. *Hist.* ut supr. l. iii. cap. 25. And in the Greek poem now under consideration, one of the titles is, "Πως εποιησεν ὁ Θησευς τους δυο Θηβαιους Καβαλαριους:"—How Theseus dubbed the two Thebans knights. Lib. vii. signatur ynii fol. vers.

Cyprus, Crete, and other parts of Greece belonging to the imperial territory.[1] But, to say no more of this, I have at present no sort of doubt of what I before asserted, that Boccaccio is the writer and inventor of this piece. Our Greek poem is in fact a literal translation from the Italian *Theseid*. The writer has translated the prefatory epistle addressed by Boccaccio to the *Fiametta*. It consists of twelve books, and is written in Boccaccio's octave stanza, the two last lines of every stanza rhyming together. The verses are of the iambic kind, and something like the *Versus Politici*, which were common among the Greek scholars a little before, and long after, Constantinople was taken by the Turks in 1453. It will readily be allowed, that the circumstance of the stanzas and rhymes is very singular in a poem composed in the Greek language, and is alone sufficient to prove this piece to be a translation from Boccaccio. I must not forget to observe, that the Greek is extremely barbarous, and of the lowest period of that language.

It was a common practice of the learned and indigent Greeks, who frequented Italy and the neighbouring states about the fifteenth and sixteenth centuries, to translate the popular pieces of Italian poetry, and the romances or tales most in vogue, into these Græco-barbarous iambics.[2] *Pastor Fido* was thus translated. The romance of *Alexander the Great* was also translated in the same manner by Demetrius Zenus, who flourished in 1530, under the title of Αλεξανδρευς ὁ Μακεδων, and printed at Venice in 1529.[3]

In the very year, and at the same place, when and where our Greek poem on Theseus, or Palamon and Arcite, was printed, *Apollonius of Tyre*, another famous romance of the middle ages, was translated in the same manner, and entitled Διηγησις ὡραιωτατη Απολλωνιου του εν Τυρω[4] ρημαδα.[5] The story of King Arthur they also reduced into the same language. The French history or [rather] romance

---

[1] Giorn. v. Nov. 1.
[2] That is *versus politici* above mentioned, a sort of loose iambic. See Langius, *Philologia Græco-barbara*. Tzetzes's Chiliads are written in this versification. See Du Cange, *Gl. Gr.* ii. col. 1196.
[3] Crus. *ut supr.* pp. 373, 399.
[4] That is, Rythmically, poetically, *Gr. Barb.*
[5] Du Cange mentions, "Μεταγλωττισμα απο Λατινικης εις Ρωμαικην διηγησις πολληπαθους Απολλωνιου του Τυρου." *Ind. Auct. Gloss. Gr. Barb.* ii. p. 36, col. h. Compare Fabricius, *Bibl. Gr.* vi. 821. First printed at Venice [in 1534. See Brunet, i. 350-1, where other editions are quoted.] In the works of Velserus there is *Narratio Eorum quæ Apollonio regi acciderunt*, &c. He says it was first written by some Greek author. Velseri Op. p. 697, edit. 1682. The Latin is in Bibl. Bodl. MSS. Laud, 39.—Bodl. F. 7, and F. 11.45. In the preface, Velserus, who died 1614, says that he believes the original in Greek still remains at Constantinople, in the library of Manuel Eugenicus. Montfaucon mentions a noble copy of this romance, written in the xiii[th]. century, in the royal library at Paris. Bibl. MSS. p. 753. Compare MSS. Langb. Bibl. Bodl. vi. p. 15. *Gesta Apollonii*, &c. There is a [version] in [Anglo-]Saxon of the romance. Wanley's Catal. *apud* Hickes, ii. 146, [printed by Thorpe, 1834, 8vo.] See Martin. Crusii *Turco Græc.* p. 209, edit. 1594. Gower recites many stories of this romance in his *Confessio Amantis*. He calls Apollonius "a yonge, a freshe, a lustie knight." See lib. viii. fol. 175, b.—185, a. But he refers to Godfrey of Viterbo's *Pantheon*, or universal Chronicle, called also *Me-*

S. 12.   *of Latin, Italian, and other Originals.*   303

of *Bertrand du Guefcelin,* printed at Abbeville in 1487,[1] and that of *Belifaire* or *Belifarius,* they rendered in the fame language and metre, with the titles Διηγησις εξαιρετος Βελθανδρου του Ρωμαιου,[2] and Ἱστορικη εξηγησις περι Βελλισαριου, &c.[3] Boccaccio himfelf, in the *Decameron,*[4]

---

moriæ Sæculorum, partly in profe, partly verfe, from the creation of the world to the year 1186. The author died in 1190.
  " — A Cronike in daies gone
  The which is cleped Panteone," &c.
fol. 175, a. [There is a fragment of 140 lines of a fifteenth-century Englifh verfe tranflation of this romance in MS. Douce 216.—F. Another is in the poffeffion of Sir Thomas Philipps. Neither has any connection with the Englifh (profe) verfion of *Apollonius of Tyre,* executed by Robert Copland, and printed in 1510. The Duke of Devonfhire's copy of the latter, purchafed at the Roxburghe fale in 1812, feems to be unique. It has been lately (1870) reprinted in facfimile by Afhbee. Refpecting *Apollonius of Tyre,* fee the prefent work *infra,* Collier's *Shakefpeare's Library,* 1843, and Halliwell's *New Boke about Shakefpeare and Stratford-on-Avon,* 1850, where the Philipps fragment is printed for the firft time. It formerly belonged to Dr. Farmer.] The play called *Pericles Prince of Tyre,* attributed to Shakefpeare, is taken from this ftory of Apollonius as told by Gower, who fpeaks the prologue. It exifted in Latin before the year 900. See Barth. *Adverfar.* lviii. cap. i.   Chaucer calls him " of Tyre Apolloneus" (*Prol. Man. L. Tale,* ver. 82), and quotes from this romance:
  " How that the curfed kyng Anteochus
  Byreft his doughter of hir maydenhede,
  That is fo horrible a tale as man may reede,
  Whan he hir threw upon the pament."
[But Shakefpeare is alfo fuppofed to have been indebted to Lawrence Twyne's compilation: "The Patterne of painefull Aduentures," firft publifhed probably in 1576, and reprinted from a later ed. in the firft vol. of *Shakefpeare's Library,* 1843.] In the Britifh Mufeum there is *Hiftoire d'Apollin roy de Thir*. MSS. Reg. 20 C. ii. 2. With regard to the French editions of this romance, [the oldeft is probably that of Geneva, *fine ulla nota,* folio. See Brunet, i. 351. Thofe of 1530 and *fans date* (Paris, Jehan Boufont) are later, curtailed, and of courfe lefs valuable.]   At length the ftory appeared in a modern drefs by M. le Brun, under the title of *Avantures d'Apollonius de Thyr,* printed in 1710, and again the following year. In the edition of the *Gefta Romanorum,* printed at Rouen in 1521, and containing 181 chapters, [as well as in that of 1488 and others,] the hiftory of Apollonius of Tyre occurs, ch. 153. This is the firft of the additional chapters.
  [1] At the end of *Le Triumphe des neuf Preux:* that is, *The Nine Worthies*. [Compare Brunet, i. 44, with *ibid.* ii. 869.]
  [2] See Du Cange, *Gl. Gr. Barb.* ii. *Ind. Auctor.* p. 36, col. b. This hiftory contains Beltrand's or Bertrand's amours with Χρυσατζα, Chryfatfa, the king of Antioch's daughter.
  [3] See Lambecc. *Bibl. Cæfar.* lib. v. p. 264. It is remarkable that the ftory of *Date obolum Belifario* is not in Procopius, but in this romance. Probably Vandyck got this ftory from a modernized edition of it, called *Bellifaire ou le Conquerant,* Paris, 1643. It, however, is faid in the title-page to be taken from Procopius. It was written by [François de Grenaille, fieur de Chateaunieres.]
  [4] They fometimes applied their Greek iambics to the works of the ancient Greek poets. Demetrius Zenus, above mentioned, tranflated Homer's Βατραχομυομαχια; and Nicolaus Lucanus the *Iliad.* The firft was printed at Venice, and afterwards reprinted by Crufius, *Turco-Græc.* p. 373; the latter was alfo printed at Venice, 1526. This Zenus is faid to be the author of the Γαλιωμυομαχια, or *Battle of the Cats and Mice.* See Crus. *ubi fupr.* 396, and Fabric. *Bibl. Gr.* i. 264, 223. [But the true writer was Theodorus Prodronus.— *Rye.*]   On account of the Græcobarbarous books, which began to grow common, chiefly in Italy about the year 1520, Sabius above-mentioned, the printer of many of them, publifhed a Græco-barbarous lexicon at Venice, 1527: [*Introduttorio nuovo intitolato Corona preciofa,* &c. See Brunet, *dern.* edit. v. 7, and *ibid.* ii. 293.] It is a mixture of

mentions the story of Troilus and Cressida in Greek verse, which I suppose had been translated by some of the fugitive Greeks with whom he was connected, from a romance on that subject, many ancient copies of which now remain in the libraries of France.[1] The story of *Florius and Platzflora*, a romance which Ludovicus Vives with great gravity condemns under the name of *Florian and Blanca-Flor*, as one of the pernicious and unclassical popular histories current in Flanders about the year 1523,[2] of which there are old editions in French, Spanish,[3] and perhaps Italian, is likewise extant very early in Greek iambics, most probably as a translation into that language.[4] I could give many others, but I hasten to lay before my readers some specimens both of the Italian and the Greek *Palamon and Arcite*:[5] only premising that both have about a thousand verses

---

modern and ancient Greek words, Latin and Italian. It was reprinted at Venice [in 1543, of which there was a re-issue in] 1546.

[1] See *Le Roman de Troylus*, [a prose French copy of the *Filostrato*, in *Nouvelles Françoises du XIVme Siècle*, 1858,] and Montfaucon, *Bibl. MSS.* p. 792, 793, &c. &c. There is, "L'Amore di Troleo et Griseida, ove si tratta in buone parte la Guerra di Troja," d'Angelo Leonico, Ven. 1553, in octave rhyme.

[2] Lud. Viv. *de Christiana Femina*, lib. i. cap. *cui tit. Qui non legendi Scriptores*, &c. He lived at Bruges. He mentions other romances common in Flanders, *Leonela and Canamor, Curias and Florela*, and *Pyramus and Thisbe*.

[3] *Flores y Blancaflor*. En Alcala, 1512, 4to. See Brunet's remarks, ii. 1300. This Spanish version was translated into French, under the title:] *Histoire Amoreuse de Flores et de Blanchefleur*, traduite de l'Espagnol par Jacques Vincent. Paris, 1554, 8vo. *Florimont et Passeroze*, traduite de l'Espagnol en prose Françoise, Lyon, 15—, 8vo. There is a French edition at Lyons, 1571 ; it was, perhaps, originally Spanish. [Compare Brunet, ii. 1307.]

The translation of *Flores and Blanca[f]lore* in Greek iambics might also be made in compliment to Boccaccio. Their adventures make the principal subject of his *Philocopo*: but the story existed long before, as Boccaccio himself informs us, lib. i., edit. [1827-31.] Flores and Blancaflore are mentioned as illustrious lovers by Matfres Eymengau de Bezers, a poet of Languedoc, in his *Breviari d'Amor*, dated 1288. MSS. Reg. 19 C. i. fol. 199. This tale was probably enlarged in passing through the hands of Boccaccio. [The two different versions of the French thirteenth century romance of *Florice and Blancheflore* (Bibl. Imperiale, No. 6987; Paulin-Paris, vol. 3, pp. 215-16) have been printed at Berlin in 1844, and at Paris in 1856. Read in the latter M. du Méril's excellent introduction. Several MSS. of the English version are extant. There is a copy in the Auchinleck MS. printed in *Antient English Poetry*, 1857; in Cotton. MS. Vitellius, D, 111, printed by Early Engl. Text Society (with *King Horn*), 1866; and at Cambridge, printed (probably very badly) in Hartshorne's *Ancient Metrical Tales*, 1829. The Cotton. MS. is sadly mutilated.—F.]

[A German romance on this subject was translated by Konrad Flecke from the French of Robert d'Orleans, in the early part of the thirteenth century. The subject is referred to at an earlier period by several Provençal poets, and this, coupled with the theatre of its events, makes Warton's conjecture extremely probable that it is of Spanish origin.—*Price*. For the fullest account of the bibliography of this popular romance see Hoffmann's *Horæ Belgicæ*, 1830, part 3. See also art. *Assenede* in the *Dict. Soc. Useful Knowledge.—Rye*.]

[4] [Dr. Wagner is editing a Middle-Greek *Floris* for the Philological Society.—F.]

[5] [Warton was indebted, he tells us, to Mr. Stanley for the use of the Greek *Theseus*, printed at Venice in 1529, with woodcuts. Another copy was at that time in the hands of Ramsay the painter. The first edition of the original Italian, Ferrara, 1475, folio, was in Dr. Askew's collection. Consul Smith's copy was bought for King George III. Another copy is at Althorp, and a fourth sold at

in each of the twelve books, and that the two firſt books are introductory; the firſt containing the war of Theſeus with the Amazons, and the ſecond that of Thebes, in which Palamon and Arcite are taken priſoners. Boccaccio thus deſcribes the Temple of Mars:

> Ne' campi tracii ſotto i cieli iberni
> Da tempeſta continova agitati
> Dove ſchieré di nembi ſempiterni
> Da venti or qua ed or la traſmutati
> In varii luoghi ne guazzori verni
> E d' acqua globi per freddo aggroppati
> Gittati ſono, e neve tuttavia,
> Che 'n ghiaccio a mano a man' s' indura e cria:
>
> E 'n una ſelva ſteril di robuſti
> Cerri, dov' eran folti ed alti molte,
> Nodoſi ed aſpri, rigidi e vetuſti,
> Che d' ombra eterna ricuoprono il volto
> Del triſto ſuolo, e in fra gli antichi fuſti,
> Da ben mille furor ſempre ravvolto
> Vi ſi ſentia grandiſſimo romore,
> Ne v' era beſtia encora nè paſtore
>
> In queſta vide la ca' dello iddio
> Armipotente, e queſta è edificata
> Tutta d' acciaio ſplendido e pulio,
> Dal quale era dal ſol riveiberata
> La luce, che aborriva il luogo rio:
> Tutta di ferro era la ſtretta entrata
> E le porte eran d' eterno diamante
> Ferrate d' ogni parte tutte quante,
>
> E le colonne di ferro cuſtei
> Vide, che l' edificio ſoſtenieno
> Li gl' Impeti dementi parve a lei
> Veder, che fier fuor della uſcieno,
> Ed il cieco Peccare, ed ogni Omei
> Similemente quivi ſi vedieno;
> Videvi l' Ire roſſe come fuoco,
> E la Paura pallida in quel loco.
>
> E con gli occulti ferri i Tradimenti
> Vide, e le Inſidie con giuſta apparenza:
> Li Diſcordia ſedeva, e ſanguinenti
> Ferri avie in mano, e d' ogni differenza;
> E tutti i luoghi pareano ſtrepenti
> D' aſpre minacce e di crudele intenza:
> E 'n mezzo il loco la Virtù triſtiſſima
> Sedie di degne lode poveriſſima.
>
> Videvi ancora l' allegro Furore,
> E oltre a ciò con volto ſanguinoſo
> La Morte armata vide e lo Stupore;
> Ed ogni altare quivi era copioſo
> Di ſangue ſol nelle battaglie fuore
> De' corpi uman cacciato, e luminoſo
> Era ciaſcun di fuoco tolto a terre
> Arſe e disfatte per le triſte guerre.
>
> Ed era il tempio tutto iſtoriato[1]

Hibbert's ſale in 1829 for £160. See Dibdin's *Biblioth. Spencer.* iv. 84, and Brunet, i. 1015-16.]

[1] Thus, Στορισματα means paintings, properly hiſtory-paintings, and Ιϛοριν, and

Da fottil mano e di fopra e d' intorno
E ciò che pria vi vide difegnato
Eran prede di notte e di giorno
Tolti alle terre, e qualunque isforzato
Fu era quivi in abito muforno:
Vedevanfi le genti incatenate,
Porti di ferro e fortezze fpezzate

Videvi ancor le navi bellatrici,
I vôti carri, e li volti guaftati,
E li miferi pianti ed infelici,
Ed ogni forza cogli afpetti elati,
Ogni fedita ancor fi vedea lici:
E fangui colle terre mefcolati:
E 'n ogni loco nell' afpetto fiero
Si vedea Marte torbido ed altiero, &c.¹

The Temple of Venus has thefe imageries:

Poi vide preffo a fè paffar Bellezza
Senz' ornamento alcun sè riguardando,
E vide gir con lei Piacevolezza,
E l' una e l' altra feco commendano;
Poi con lor vide ftarfi Giovinezza
Deftra ed adorna molto fefteggiando:
E d' altra parte vide il folle Ardire
Lufinghe e Ruffianie infieme gire.

E 'n mezzo il loco in fu alte colonne
Di rame vide un tempio, al qual d' intorno
Danzando giovinetti vide e donne,
Qual da sè belle: e qual d' abito adorno,
Difcinte e fcalze, in capelli e gonne,
Che in quefto folo difpendeano il giorno:
Poi fopra il tempio vide volitare
Paffere molte e columbe rucchiare.

Ed all' entrata del tempio vicina
Vide che fi fedeva pianamente
Madonna Pace, e in mano una cortina
'Nanzi alla porta tenea lievemente:
Appreffo a lei in vifta affai tapina
Pacienza fedea difcretamente,

ἀνιςοριζιν, is to *paint*, in barbarous Greek. There are various examples in the Byzantine writers. In middle Latinity *Hiftoriographus* fignifies literally a painter. Perhaps our hiftoriographer royal was originally the king's illuminator. Ἱςοριογραφος μουσιατωρ occurs in an infcription publifhed by Du Cange, *Differtat. Joinv.* xxvii. p. 319. Where μουσιατωρ implies an artift who painted in mofaic work called μουσαιον, or μουσιον, *mufivum*. In the Greek poem before us Ἱςοριτας is ufed for a painter, lib. ii.:

Εκ την παρουσαν την ζωην ολεποικειν ὁ Ἱςοριτας.

In the middle Latin writers we have *depingere hiftorialiter*, to paint with hiftories or figures, viz. "Forinfecus dealbavit illud [delubrum,] intrinfecus autem *depinxit hiftorialiter*." Dudo, *De Act. Norman.* l. iii. p. 153. Dante ufes the Italian word before us in the fame fenfe. Dante, *Purgat*. Cant. x.:

"Quivi era hiftoriata l'alta gloria
Del Roman Principe."

Ἱςορια frequently occurs, fimply for picture or reprefentation in colours. Nilus Monach. lib. iv. *Epift.* 61. Και ἱςοριας πτηνων και ἑρπετων και βλαςηματαν. "Pictures of birds, ferpents, and plants." And in a thoufand other inftances.

¹ L. vii. [Ed. 1827-31, ix. 221-3. In all the former editions, the extract, as well as that which fucceeds, was fo disfigured by errors, as to be abfolutely unintelligible.]

> Pallida nell' aspecto; e d' ogni parte
> D' intorno a lei vide Promesse ad arte.
> Poi dentro al tempio entrata, di sospiri
> Vi senti un tumulto, che girava
> Focoso tutto di caldi disiri:
> Questo gli altari tutti aluminaua
> Di nuove fiamme nate di martiri,
> De' qua' ciascun di lagrime grondava,
> Mosse da una dona cruda e ria,
> Che vide li, chiamata Gelosia. &c.[1]

It is highly probable that Boccaccio learned many anecdotes of Grecian history and Grecian fable, not to be found in any Greek writer now extant, from his preceptors Barlaam, Leontius, and others, who had lived at Constantinople, while the Greek literature was yet flourishing. Some of these are perhaps scattered up and down in the composition before us, which contains a considerable part of the Grecian story; and especially in his Treatise of the Genealogies of the Gods.[2] Boccaccio himself calls his master Leontius an inexhaustible archive of Grecian tales and fables, although not equally conversant with those of the Latins.[3] He confesses that he took many things in his book of the genealogies of the gods from a vast work entitled *Collectivum*, now lost, written by his cotemporary Paulus Perusinus, the materials of which had in great measure been furnished by Barlaam.[4] We are informed also, that Perusinus made

---

[1] [*Ibid.* pp. 230-1.] Some of these stanzas are thus expressed in the Græco-barbarous translation:

> Εἰς τοῦτον ἴδε τοῦ θεοῦ, τὸν οἶκον τὸν μεγάλον,
> ἀπαρμάτα πολλὰ σκληρὰ, κτισμένος ἦτον ὅλος.
>
> Ὁ λόλαμπρος γὰρ ἦτοναι, ἐλαμπεν ὡς τὸν ἥλιον,
> ὅταν ὁ ἥλιος ἔκρουε, ἀστραπτεν ὡς τὸ φέγγος.
>
> Ὁ τόπος ὅλος ἔλαμπεν, ἐκτὴν λαμπρότητάντου,
> τὸ ἔμπατου ὁλοσίδηρον, καὶ τὰ στενώματάτου.
>
> Ἀπὸ διαμάντη πόρτεστου, ἦσαν καὶ τὰ καρφία,
> σιδερομέναις δυνατά, ἀπάπασαν μιρία.
>
> Κολώναις ἦσαν σιδηρὲς, πολλὰ χοντρὲς μεγάλαις,
> ἀπάνωτους ἐβάστεναν, ὅλον τὸν οἶκον κεῖνον.
>
> Ἐκεῖδι τὴν βουρκότιταν, τὸν λογισμὸν ἐκείνων,
> ὁπέκτην πόρταν βγένασι, ἄγροι καὶ θυμομένοι.
>
> Καὶ τὴν τυφλὴ τὴν ἁμαρτίαν καὶ τὸ οὐαὶ καὶ ὄχου
> ἐκεῖσι ἐφανώντησαν, ὅμοιον σὰν καὶ τ' ἄλλα.
>
> Καὶ ταῖς ὀργαῖς ἐσκείθηκεν, κόκιναις ὡς φωτία,
> τὸν φόβον εἶδε λόχλομον, ἐκεῖσε σμίαν μιρία.
>
> Μετὰ κοιφὰ τὰ σίδερα, εἶδε δημηγορσίαις,
> καὶ ταῖς φαλσίαις παυγίνονται, καὶ μοιάζουν δικαιοσούνες.
>
> Ἐκεῖτον ἀσυπηβασία, μεταῖς διαφωνίαις,
> ἐβάσα εἰς τὸ χέρητης, σίδερα ματομένα.
>
> Ὅλος ὁ τόπος ἔδειχνε, ἄγριος καὶ χολιασμένος,
> ἀγρίους γὰρ φοβερισμοὺς, κιωμότατην μαλέαν.
>
> Μέσα τον τόπον τοῦτονε, ἡ χάρνα τυχεμένη,
> ἐκάθετον ὁ πόπρεπε, νὰ ἔναι παιχεμίνη.

[2] In fifteen books. First printed in 1481, fol. And in Italian by Betussi, Venet. 1553. In French at Paris, 1531, fol. In the interpretation of the fables he is very prolix and jejune.

[3] *Geneal. Deor.* lib. xv. cap. vi.

[4] "Quicquid apud Græcos inveniri potest, adjutorio Barlaæ arbitror collegisse." —*Ibid.*

use of some of these fugitive Greek scholars, especially Barlaam, for collecting rare books in that language. Perusinus was librarian, about the year 1340, to Robert, king of Jerusalem and Sicily, and was the most curious and inquisitive man of his age for searching after unknown or uncommon manuscripts, especially histories and poetical compositions, and particularly such as were written in Greek. I will beg leave to cite the words of Boccaccio, who records this anecdote.[1] By the *Historiæ* and *Poetica Opera*, [mentioned below as] brought from Constantinople by Barlaam, undoubtedly works of entertainment, and perhaps chiefly of the romantic and fictitious species, I do not understand the classics. It is natural to suppose that Boccaccio, both from his connections and his curiosity, was no stranger to these treasures: and that many of these pieces, thus imported into Italy by the dispersion of the Constantinopolitan exiles, are only known at present through the medium of his writings. It is certain that many oriental fictions found their way into Europe by means of this communication.

Boccaccio borrowed the story of Titus and Gesippus from the *Gesta Romanorum*, or from the second fable of Alphonsus. There is another Latin history of these two friends, a translation from [the eighth novel of the tenth day of the *Decameron*,] by Bandello, and printed at Milan in 1509. An exceedingly scarce book.[2]

I take this opportunity of pointing out another source of Boccaccio's *Tales*. Friar Philip's story of the *Goose*, or of the young man who had never seen a woman, in the prologue to the fourth day of the *Decameron*, is taken from a spiritual romance, called the *History of Barlaam and Josaphat*. This fabulous narrative, in which Barlaam is a hermit and Josaphat a king of India, is supposed to have been originally written in Greek by Johannes Damascenus. The Greek is no uncommon manuscript.[3] It was from the old Latin translation, which is mentioned by Vincent of Beauvais, that it became a favourite in the dark ages. The Latin, which is also a common manuscript, was printed so early as the year 1470. It has often appeared in French. A modern Latin version was published at Paris in 1577. The legendary historians, who believed everything, and even Baronius, have placed Barlaam and Josaphat in their catalogues of confessors. Saint Barlaam and Saint Josaphat occur in the *Metrical Lives of the Saints*.[4] This history seems to have been composed by an oriental Christian: and, in some manuscripts, is said to have been brought by a monk of Saint Saba into the holy city from Ethiopia. Among the Baroccian MSS. Cod. xxi. there was an office in Greek for these two supposed saints.

In passing through Chaucer's hands, this poem has received many new beauties. Not only those capital fictions and descriptions, the

---

[1] "Et, si usquam curiosissimus fuit homo in perquirendis, jussu etiam principis, peregrinis undecunque libris, *Historiis et Poeticis* operibus, iste fuit. Et ob id, singulari amicitiæ Barlæ conjunctus, quæ a Latinis habere non poterat eo medio innumera exhausit a Græcis."—*Geneal. Deor.* lib. xv. cap. vi.

[2] [See, for the correct title, *Brunet*, i. 636.]   [3] See MSS. Laud. C. 72.

[4] MSS. Bodl. 72, fol. 288, b, [Vernon MS., &c.]

temples of Mars, Venus, and Diana, with their allegorical paintings, [but also] the figures of Lycurgus and Emetrius with their retinue, are so much heightened by the bold and spirited manner of the British bard, as to strike us with an air of originality. Boccaccio's situations and incidents respecting the lovers are often inartificial and unaffecting. In the Italian poet, Emilia walking in the garden and singing is seen and heard first by Arcite, who immediately calls Palamon. They are both equally, and at the same point of time, captivated with her beauty; yet without any expressions of jealousy, or appearance of rivalry. But in Chaucer's management of the commencement of this amour, Palamon by seeing Emilia first acquires an advantage over Arcite, which ultimately renders the catastrophe more agreeable to poetical justice. It is an unnatural and unanimated picture which Boccaccio presents, of the two young princes violently enamoured of the same object, and still remaining in a state of amity. In Chaucer, the quarrel between the two friends, the foundation of all the future beautiful distress of the piece, commences at this moment, and causes a conversation full of mutual rage and resentment. This rapid transition, from a friendship cemented by every tie to the most implacable hostility, is on this occasion not only highly natural, but produces a sudden and unexpected change of circumstances, which enlivens the detail and is always interesting. Even afterwards, when Arcite is released from the prison by Pirithous, he embraces Palamon at parting; and in the fifth book of *La Teseide*, when Palamon goes armed to the grove in search of Arcite, whom he finds sleeping, they meet on terms of much civility and friendship, and in all the mechanical formality of the manners of romance. In Chaucer, this dialogue has a very different cast. Palamon, at seeing Arcite, feels a " colde swerde " glide throughout his heart: he starts from his ambuscade, and instantly salutes Arcite with the appellation of " false traitour ; " and although Boccaccio has merit in discriminating the characters of the two princes, by giving Palamon the impetuosity of Achilles, and Arcite the mildness of Hector, yet Arcite by Boccaccio is here injudiciously represented as too moderate and pacific. In Chaucer he returns the salute with the same degree of indignation, draws his sword, and defies Palamon to single combat. So languid is Boccaccio's plan of this amour, that Palamon does not begin to be jealous of Arcite till he is informed in the prison that Arcite lived as a favourite servant with Theseus in disguise, yet known to Emilia. When the lovers see Emilia from the window of their tower, she is supposed by Boccaccio to observe them, and not to be displeased at their signs of admiration. This circumstance is justly omitted by Chaucer, as quite unnecessary, and not tending either to promote the present business or to operate in any distant consequences. On the whole, Chaucer has eminently shewn his good sense and judgment in rejecting the superfluities and improving the general arrangement of the story. He frequently corrects or softens Boccaccio's false manners ; and it is with singular address he has often abridged the Italian poet's ostentatious and pedantic parade of ancient history and mythology.

Therefore it is to be remarked, that as Chaucer in some places has thrown in strokes of his own, so in others he has contracted the uninteresting and tedious prolixity of narrative, which he found in the Italian poet; and that he might avoid a servile imitation, and indulge himself as he pleased in an arbitrary departure from the original, it appears that he neglected the embarrassment of Boccaccio's stanza, and preferred the English heroic couplet, of which this poem affords the first conspicuous example extant in our language.

The situation and structure of the temple of Mars are thus described:

>   A foreste,[1]
> In which ther dwellede neyther man ne beste,
> With knotty knarry bareyn trees olde
> Of stubbes scharpe and hidous to byholde;
> In which ther ran a swymbul in a swough,
> As it were a storme schulde berst every bough:
> And downward on an hil under a bent,[2]
> Ther stood the tempul of Marz armypotent,
> Wrought al of burned[3] steel, of which thentre
> Was long and streyt, and gastly for to see.
> And therout came a rage of suche a prise,
> That it maad al the gates for to rise.
> The northen light in at the dore schon,
> For wyndow on the walle *ne* was ther noon,
> Thorugh the which men might no light discerne.
> The dores wer alle ademaunte eterne,
> I-clenched overthward and endelong
> With iren tough; and, for to make it strong,
> Every piler the tempul to susteene
> Was tonne greet of iren bright and schene.

The gloomy sanctuary of this tremendous fane, was adorned with these characteristical imageries.

> Ther saugh I furst the derk ymaginyng[4]
> Of felony, and al the compassyng;
> The cruel ire, as reed as eny gleede;
> The pikepurs, and eek the pale drede;
> The smyler with the knyf under his cloke;
> The schipne brennyng with the blake smoke;
> The tresoun of the murtheryng in the bed;
> The open werres, with woundes al bi-bled;
> Contek with bloody knyf,[5] and scharp manace.
> Al ful of chirkyng[6] was that sory place.
> The sleer of himself yet saugh I there,
> *His* herte-blood hath bathed al his here;
> The nayl y-dryve in the schode a-nyght;

---

[1] [Morris's *Chaucer*, ii. 61, ver. 1117.]

[2] [declivity].   [3] burnished.   [4] [Morris's *Chaucer*, ii. 62, ver. 1137.]

[5] This image is likewise entirely misrepresented by Dryden, and turned to a satire on the Church:

> "Contest with sharpen'd knives in *cloysters* drawn,
> And all with blood bespread the *holy lawn*."

[6] Any disagreeable noise, or hollow murmur. Properly, the jarring of a door upon the hinges. See also Chaucer's *Boeth.* p. [25, edit. Morris:] "Whan the felde *chirkynge* agrisethe of colde by the fellnesse of the wynde that hyşt aquilon." The original is, "Vento Campus inhorruit."

> The colde deth, with mouth gapyng upright.[1]
> Amyddes of the tempul set meschaunce,
> With sory comfort and evel contynaunce.
> *Yet* I saugh *woodnes* laughyng in *his* rage;
> The hunte ftrangled with wilde bores corage.
> *The caraigne in the busche, with throte i-korve:*
> *A thousand slayne, and not of qualme i-storve;*[2]
> *The tiraunt, with the pray bi force i-rafte;*
> *The toune destroied, there was no thing lafte.*
> *Yet saugh I brent the schippis hoppesteres;*[3]
> *The hunte*[4] *strangled with the wilde beeres.*
> The sowe freten the child right in the cradel;
> The cook i-skalded, for al his longe ladel.
> Nought beth forgeten the infortune of Mart;
> The carter over-ryden with his cart,
> Under the whel ful lowe he lay adoun.
> Ther wer also of Martz divisioun,
> The barbour, and the bowcher, and the smyth,
> That forgeth scharpe swerdes on his stith.
> And al above depeynted in a tour
> Saw I conquest sittyng in gret honour,
> With the scharpe swerd over his heed
> Hangynge by a sotil twyne threed.

This group is the effort of a strong imagination, unacquainted with selection and arrangement of images. It is rudely thrown on the canvas without order or art. In the Italian poets, who describe every thing, and who cannot, even in the most serious representations, easily suppress their natural predilection for burlesque and familiar imagery, nothing is more common than this mixture of sublime and comic ideas.[5] The form of Mars follows, touched with the impetuous dashes of a savage and spirited pencil:

> The statue[6] of Mars upon a carte stood,
> Armed, and lokede grym as he were wood;
> * * * * *

---

[1] This couplet refers to the suicide in the preceding one, who is supposed to kill himself by driving a nail into his head [in the night], and to be found dead and cold in his bed, with his "mouth gapyng upryght." This is properly the meaning of his "hair being bathed in blood." *Shode*, in the text, is literally *a bush of hair*. Dryden has finely paraphrased this passage.

[2] "slain—not destroyed by sickness or dying a natural death."

[3] A writer in *Notes and Queries* (1st S. ii. 31,) conjectures, that Chaucer may have misread the *bellatrici* of Statius *ballatrici*. Another writer in the same miscellany (2nd S. iv. 407) thinks that it should be *hoppesteres* quasi upholsteries= dock-yards. Now, a *hopyr* is the old word for the *trough*, in which the grain is placed to be ground, and there may have been a term, now lost, but known to Chaucer, founded upon *hopyr*, and having the sense of ship's stocks. This appears to be on the whole the most probable solution:

> "By God! right by the *hoper* wol I stande,
> Quod Johan, 'And se how that the corn gus inne.'"
> *Reeves Tale*, l. 4034, ed. Wright.]

[4] [The huntsman; from the Saxon *hunta*.—Tyrwhitt.]

[5] There are many other instances of this mixture. v. 319. "We strive as did the houndis for the bone." v. 403. "We fare he that dronk is as a mouse, &c." "Farewel physick! Go bere the corse to church;" "Some said he lokid grim and he wolde fight," &c. *infra*.

[6] [Morris's *Chaucer*, ii. 63, ver. 1183.] Statuary is not implied here. Thus he mentions the *statue* of Mars on a banner, *supr.* v. 117. I cannot forbear adding in

>   A wolf ther ſtood byforn him at his feet
>   With eyen reed, and of a man he eet;
>   With ſotyl pencel depeynted was this ſtorie,
>   In redoutyng[1] of Mars and of his glorie.

But the groundwork of this whole deſcription is in the *Thebais* of Statius. I will make no apology for tranſcribing the paſſage at large, that the reader may judge of the reſemblance. Mercury viſits the temple of Mars ſituated in the frozen and tempeſtuous regions of Thrace:—[2]

>   Hic ſteriles delubra notat Mavortia ſilvas,
>   Horreſcitque tuens: ubi mille furoribus illi
>   Cingitur adverſo domus immanſueta ſub Hæmo.
>   Ferrea compago laterum, ferro arcta teruntur
>   Limina, ferratis incumbunt tecta columnis.
>   Læditur adverſum Phœbi jubar, ipſaque ſedem
>   Lux timet, et dirus contriſtat ſidera fulgor.
>   Digna loco ſtatio? primis ſalit Impetus amens
>   E foribus, cæcumque Nefas, Iræque rubentes,
>   Exſangueſque Metus; occultiſque enſibus adſtant
>   Inſidiæ, geminumque tenens Diſcordia ferrum.
>   Innumeris ſtrepit aula Minis: triſtiſſima Virtus
>   Stat medio, lætuſque Furor, vultuque cruento
>   Mors armata ſedet: bellorum ſolus in aris
>   Sanguis, et incenſis qui raptus ab urbibus ignis.
>   Terrarum exuviæ circum, et faſtigia templi
>   Captæ inſignibant gentes, cœlataque ferro
>   Fragmina portarum, bellatriceſque carinæ,
>   Et vacui currus, protritaque curribus ora.[3]

---

this place theſe fine verſes of Mars arming himſelf in haſte, from our author's *Complaint of Mars and Venus*, v. 99:

>   "He throweth on him his helme of huge wyghte,
>   And girt him with his ſwerde; and in his honde
>   His myghty ſpere, as he was wont to fyghte,
>   He ſhaketh ſo, that almoſt it to-wonde;"

Here we ſee the force of deſcription without a profuſion of idle epithets. Theſe verſes are all ſinew: they have nothing but verbs and ſubſtantives.

[1] recording, [reverence, *T*.]

[2] Chaucer points out this very temple in the introductory lines, v. 1113:

>   "Like to the eſtres of the griſly place,
>   That hight the gret tempul of Mars in Trace,
>   In that colde and froſty regioun,
>   Ther as Mars hath his ſovereyn mancioun."

[3] Stat. *Theb.* vii. 40 [Edit. Paris, 1827, iii. 9-10]. And below we have Chaucer's *Doors of adamant eterne*, viz. v. 68.

>   "Clauſæque adamante perenni
>   Diſſiluere fores."

Statius alſo calls Mars, *Armipotens*, v. 78. A ſacrifice is copied from Statius, where, ſays Chaucer (v. 1435):

>   "And did hir thinges, as men may biholde
>   In Stace of Thebes."

I think Statius is copied in a ſimile, v. 1640. The introduction of this poem is alſo taken from the *Thebaid*, xii. 545, 481, 797. Compare Chaucer's lines, v. 870, ſeq. v. 917, ſeq. v. 996, ſeq. The funeral pyre of Arcite is alſo tranſlated from *Theb.* vi. 195, ſeq. See Ch. v. 2940, ſeq. I likewiſe take this opportunity of

Statius was a favourite writer with the poets of the middle ages. His bloated magnificence of description, gigantic images, and pompous diction, suited their taste, and were somewhat of a piece with the romances they so much admired. They neglected the gentler and genuine graces of Virgil, which they could not relish. His pictures were too correctly and chastely drawn to take their fancies: and truth of design, elegance of expression, and the arts of composition were not their objects.[1] In the meantime we must observe, that in Chaucer's *Temple of Mars* many personages are added: and that those which existed before in Statius have been retouched, enlarged, and rendered more distinct and picturesque by Boccaccio

---

observing, that Lucretius and Plato are imitated in this poem, together with many passages from Ovid and Virgil.

[1] In *Troilus and Cresside* he has translated the arguments of the twelve books of the *Thebais* of Statius. See B. v. p. 1479, *seq*.

But to be more particular as to these imitations, ii. 28, v. 40:—

"A companye of ladies, tweye and tweye," &c.

Thus Theseus, at his return in triumph from conquering Scythia, is accosted by the dames of Thebes, Stat. *Theb.* xii. 519:—

"Jamque domos patrias, Scythicæ post aspera gentis
Prælia, laurigero subeuntem Thesea curru
Lætifici plausus, &c. &c.
Paulum et ab insessis mœstæ Pelopeides aris
Promovere gradum, seriemque et dona triumphi
Mirantur, victique animo rediere mariti.
Atque ubi tardavit currus, et ab axe superbo
Explorat causas victor, poscitque benigna
Aure preces; orsa ante alias Capaneia conjux,
Belliger Ægide," &c.

Chaucer here copies Statius (*Theb.* v. 861-966). *Kn. T.* from [v. 70 to v. 151,] See also *ibid.* v. 70, *seq.* v. 930:

"Here in the Temple of the goddess Clemence," &c.

Statius mentions the temple of Clemency as the asylum where these ladies were assembled, *Theb.* xii. 481:

"Urbe fuit media, nulli concessa potentum
Ara deum, mitis posuit Clementia sedem," &c.

Ver. 2087.
"Ne what jewels men in the fyr caste," &c.

Literally from Statius, *Theb.* vi. 206:

"Ditantur flammæ, non unquam opulentior illa
Ante cinis; crepitant gemmæ," &c.

But the whole of Arcite's funeral is minutely copied from Statius. More than a hundred parallel lines on this subject might be produced from each poet. In Statius the account of the trees felled for the pyre, with the consternation of the Nymphs, takes up more than twenty-four lines, v. 84-116. In Chaucer about thirteen, v. 2060-2072. In Boccaccio, six stanzas, B. xi. Of the three poets, Statius is most reprehensible, the first author of this ill-placed and unnecessary description, and who did not live in a Gothic age. The statues of Mars and Venus I imagined had been copied from Fulgentius, Boccaccio's favourite mythographer. But Fulgentius says nothing of Mars: and of Venus, that she only stood in the sea on a couch, attended by the Graces. It is from Statius that Theseus became a hero of romance.

and Chaucer. Arcite's address to Mars, at entering the temple, has great dignity, and is not copied from Statius:

> O stronge god, that in the reynes colde[1]
> Of Trace honoured and lord art thou y-holde,
> And hast in every regne and every land
> Of armes al the bridel in thy hand,
> And hem fortunest as the luste devyse,
> Accept of me my pitous sacrifise.

The following portrait of Lycurgus, an imaginary king of Thrace, is highly charged, and very great in the Gothic style of painting:

> Ther maistow se comyng with Palomoun[2]
> Ligurge himself, the grete kyng of Trace;
> Blak was his berd, and manly was his face.
> The cercles of his eyen in his heed
> They gloweden bytwixe yolw and reed,
> And lik a griffoun loked he aboute,
> With kempe heres on his browes stowte;
> His lymes greet, his brawnes hard and stronge,
> His schuldres brood, his armes rounde and longe.
> And as the gyse was in his contré,
> Ful heye upon a chare of gold stood he,
> With foure white boles in a trays.
> In stede of cote armour in his harnays,
> With nales yolwe, and bright as eny gold,
> He had a bere[3] skyn, cole-blak for old.
> His lange heer y-kempt byhynd his bak,
> As eny raven fether it schon for blak.
> A wrethe of gold arm-gret, and huge of wighte,
> Upon his heed, set ful of stoones brighte,
> Of fyne rubeus and of fyn dyamauntz.
> Aboute his chare wente white alauntz,[4]
> Twenty and mo, as grete as eny stere,
> To hunt at the lyoun or at the bere,
> And folwed him, with mosel fast i-bounde,
> Colerd with golde, and torettz[5] fyled[*] rounde.

---

[1] [Morris's *Chaucer*, ii. 73, ver. 1515.] [2] [*Ibid.* ii. 66, ver. 1270.] [3] A bear's.

[4] Greyhounds. A favourite species of dogs in the middle ages. In the ancient pipe-rolls, payments are frequently made in greyhounds. *Rot. Pip. an.* 4, *Reg. Johann.* [A. D. 1203.] "Rog. Constabul. Cestrie debet D. Marcas, et x. palfridos et x. *laissas Leporariorum* pro habenda terra Vidonis de Loverell de quibus debet reddere per ann. c. m." Ten leashes of greyhounds, *Rot. Pip. an.* 9 *Reg. Johann.* [A. D. 1208.] "Suthant. Johan. Teingre debet c. m. et x. *leporarios magnos, pulchros*, et *bonos*, de redemtione sua." &c. *Rot. Pip. an.* 11, *Reg. Johan.* [A. D. 1210.] "Everveycsire. Rog. de Mallvell redd. comp. de I. palefrido velociter currente, et ii. *Laisiis leporariorum* pro habendis literis deprecatoriis ad Matildam de M." I could give a thousand other instances of the sort. ["Speght interprets *alaunz*, greyhounds; Tyrrwhitt, mastiffs. The latter was apparently misled by the fact that the wolf-dog, generally known by the name of the *Irish greyhound*, because used most recently in that country, is called by Buffon *le matin*."—*Bell*.]

In Hawes's *Pastime of Pleasure*, Fame is attended with two greyhounds, on whose golden collars Grace and Governaunce are inscribed in diamond letters. See next note.

[5] Rings; the fastening of dogs' collars. They are often mentioned in the inventory of furniture, in the royal palaces of Henry VIII. above cited. MSS. Harl. 1419. In the *Castle of Windsor*, article Collars, f. 409. "Two grey-

[*] Filed; highly polished.

> An hundred lordes had he in his route
> Armed ful wel, with hertes ftern and ftoute.

The figure of Emetrius, king of India, who comes to the aid of Arcite, is not inferior in the fame ftyle, with a mixture of grace:

> With Arcita, in ftories as men fynde,[1]
> The gret Emetreus, the kyng of Ynde,
> Uppon a fteede bay, trapped in fteel,
> Covered with cloth of gold dyapred wel,
> Cam rydyng lyk the god of armes Mars.
> His coote armour was of a cloth of Tars,[2]
> Cowched of perlys whyte, round and grete.
> His fadil was of brend gold newe *i*-bete;
> A mantelet upon his fchuldre hangyng
> Bret-ful of rubies reed, as fir fparclyng.
> His crifpe her lik rynges was i-ronne,
> And that was yalwe, and gliteryng as the fonne.
> His nofe was heigh, his eyen *bright* cytryne,
> His lippes rounde, his colour was fangwyn,
> A fewe freknes in his face y-fpreynd,
> Betwixe yolwe and fomdel blak y-meynd,
> And as a lyoun he his lokyng cafte.
> Of fyve and twenty yeer his age I cafte.
> His berd was wel bygonne for to fprynge;
> His voys was as a trumpe thunderynge.
> Upon his heed he wered *of* laurer grene
> A garlond freifch and lufty for to fene.
> Upon his hond he bar for his delyt
> An egle tame, as eny lylie whyt.
> An hundred lordes had he with him ther,
> Al armed fauf here hedes in here ger,
> * * * * *
> Aboute the kyng ther ran on every part
> Ful many a tame lyoun and lepart.

The banner of Mars difplayed by Thefeus, is fublimely conceived:

> The reede ftatue of Mars with fpere and targe[3]
> So fchyneth in his white baner large,
> That alle the feeldes gliteren up and doun.

This poem has many ftrokes of pathetic defcription, of which thefe fpecimens may be felected:

---

houndes collars of crimfun velvett and cloth of gold, lacking *torrettes*."--"Two other collars with the kinges armes, and at the ende portcullis and rofe."—"Item, a collar embrawdered with pomegranates and rofes with *turrets* of filver and gilt."—"A collar garnifhed with ftole-worke with one fhallop fhelle of filver and gilte, with *torrettes* and pendauntes of filver and guilte."—"A collar of white velvette, embrawdered with perles, the fwivels of filver."

[1] [Morris's *Chaucer*, ii. 67, ver. 1297.]
[2] Not of Tarfus in Cilicia. It is rather an abbreviation for Tartarin, or Tartarium. See [the] *Flower and Leaf*, [ibid. iv. 94, ver. 211:]

> "On every trumpe hanging a broad banere
> Of fine tartarium ful richely bete."

That it was a coftly ftuff appears from hence. "Et ad faciendum unum Jupoun de *Tartaryn* blu pouderat. cum garteriis blu paratis cum boucles et pendants de argento deaurato."—*Comp. J. Coke Provisoris Magn. Garderob. temp. Edw. III.* ut fupr. It often occurs in the wardrobe-accounts for furnifhing tournaments. Du Cange fays, that this was a fine cloth manufactured in Tartary.—*Glofs.* v. Tartarium. But Skinner in v. derives it from Tortona in the Milanefe. He cites Stat. 4, Hen. VIII. c. vi. [3] [Morris's *Chaucer*, ii, 31, ver. 117.]

> Uppon that other fyde Palomon,[1]
> Whan he wifte that Arcite was agoon,
> Such forwe maketh, that the grete tour
> Refowneth of his yollyng and clamour.
> The pure feteres of his fchynes grete
> Weren of his bitter falte teres wete.

Arcite is thus defcribed, after his return to Thebes, where he defpairs of feeing Emilia again:

> His fleep, his mete, his drynk is him byraft,[2]
> That lene he wexe, and drye as eny fchaft.
> His eyen holwe, grifly to biholde;
> His hewe falwe, and pale as affchen colde,
> And folitary he was, and ever alone,
> And dwellyng al the night, making his moone.
> And if he herde fong or inftrument,
> Then wolde he wepe, he mighte nought be ftent;
> So feble were his fpirites, and fo lowe.
> And chaunged fo, that no man couthe knowe
> His fpeche nother his vois, though men it herde.

Palamon is thus introduced in the proceffion of his rival Arcite's funeral:

> Tho cam this woful Theban Palomoun,[3]
> With flotery[4] berd, and ruggy afshy heeres,
> In clothis blak, y-dropped al with teeres,
> And, paffyng other, of wepyng Emelye,
> The rewfulleft of al the companye.

To which may be added the furprife of Palamon, concealed in the foreft, at hearing the difguifed Arcite, whom he fuppofes to be the fquire of Thefeus, difcover himfelf at the mention of the name of Emilia:

> Thurgh his herte[5]
> He felt a cold fwerd fodeynliche glyde:
> For ire he quook, he nolde no lenger abyde.
> And whan that he hath herd Arcites tale,
> As he were wood, with face deed and pale,
> He fterte him up out of the buffches thikke, &c.

A defcription of the morning muft not be omitted; which vies both in fentiment and expreffion with the moft finifhed modern poetical landfcape, and finely difplays our author's talent at delineating the beauties of nature:

> The bufy larke, meffager of *day*,[6]
> Salueth in hire fong the morwe gray;
> And fyry Phebus ryfeth up fo bright,
> That al the orient[7] laugheth of the light,[8]
> And with his ftremes dryeth in the greves
> The filver dropes, hongyng *on* the leeves.

---

[1] [Morris's *Chaucer*, ii. 40, ver. 417.]   [2] [*Ibid.* ii. 42, ver. 503.]
[3] [*Ibid.* ii. 89, ver. 2024.]
[4] fqualid. [*Flotery* feems literally to mean floating; as hair difhevelled (*rabuffata*) may be faid to float upon the air.—*Tyrwhitt.*]
[5] [Morris's *Chaucer*, ii. 49, ver. 716.]   [6] [*Ibid.* ii. 46, ver. 633.]
[7] For *Orient*, perhaps *Orifount*, or the *horifon*, is the true reading. So the edition of Chaucer in 1561. So alfo the barbarous Greek poem on this ftory, Ὁ Ουρανος ὁλος γελα. Dryden feems to have read, or to have made out of this miffpelling of Horifon, Orient.—The ear inftructs us to reject this emendation.
[8] See Dante, *Purgat.* c. 1. p. 234.

Nor must the figure of the blooming Emilia, the most beautiful object of this vernal picture, pass unnoticed:

> Emelie, that fairer was to seene[1]
> Than is the lilie on hire stalkes grene.
> And fresscher than the May with floures newe—
> For with the rose colour strof hire hewe.

In other parts of his works he has painted morning scenes *con amore*: and his imagination seems to have been peculiarly struck with the charms of a rural prospect at sun-rising.

We are surprised to find, in a poet of such antiquity, numbers so nervous and flowing: a circumstance which greatly contributed to render Dryden's paraphrase of this poem the most animated and harmonious piece of versification in the English language. I cannot leave the *Knight's Tale* without remarking, that the inventor of this poem appears to have possessed considerable talents for the artificial construction of a story. It exhibits unexpected and striking turns of fortune, and abounds in those incidents which are calculated to strike the fancy by opening resources to sublime description, or to interest the heart by pathetic situations. On this account, even without considering the poetical and exterior ornaments of the piece, we are hardly disgusted with the mixture of manners, the confusion of times, and the like violations of propriety, which this poem, in common with all others of its age, presents in almost every page. The action is supposed to have happened soon after the marriage of Theseus with Hippolita, and the death of Creon in the siege of Thebes: but we are soon transported into more recent periods. Sunday, the celebration of matins, judicial astrology, heraldry, tilts and tournaments, knights of England and targets of Prussia,[2] occur in the city of Athens under the reign of Theseus.

SECTION XIII.

CHAUCER'S *Romaunt of the Rose*[3] is translated from a French poem entitled *Le Roman de la Rose*. It was begun by William of Lorris, a student in jurisprudence, who died about the year 1260. Being left unfinished, it was completed by John of Meun, a native of a little town of that name, situated on the River Loire near Orleans, who

---

[1] [Morris's *Chaucer*, ii. 33, ver. 177.]

[2] The knights of the Teutonic order were settled in Prussia, before 1300. See also Ch. Prol. v. 53; where tournaments in Prussia are mentioned. Arcite quotes a fable from Æsop (v. 1179).

[3] [The one fifteenth century MS. of this poem that we possess (in the Hunterian Museum, at Glasgow) is a very faulty one. Mr. Bradshaw contends that it is not Chaucer's translation at all, but that of a fifteenth century poet, mainly because it contains so many false rhymes of the final *e*—false according to Chaucer's uniform

seems to have flourished about the year 1310.¹ This poem is esteemed by the French the most valuable piece of their old poetry. It is far beyond the rude efforts of all their preceding romancers: and they have nothing equal to it before the reign of Francis I., who died in the year 1547. But there is a considerable difference in the merit of the two authors. William of Lorris, who wrote not one quarter of the poem, is remarkable for his elegance and luxuriance of description, and is a beautiful painter of allegorical personages. John of Meun is a writer of another cast. He possesses but little of his predecessor's inventive and poetical vein; and in that respect was not properly qualified to finish a poem begun by William of Lorris. But he has strong satire and great liveliness.² He was one of the wits of the court of Charles le Bel.

The difficulties and dangers of a lover, in pursuing and obtaining the object of his desires, are the literal argument of this poem. This design is couched under the allegory of a Rose, which our lover after frequent obstacles gathers in a delicious garden. He traverses vast ditches, scales lofty walls, and forces the gates of adamantine and almost impregnable castles. These enchanted fortresses are all inhabited by various divinities, some of which assist, and some oppose, the lover's progress.³

Chaucer has luckily translated all that was written by William of Lorris:⁴ he gives only part of the continuation of John of Meun.⁵

---

practice in his genuine poems. For instance, the Romaunt rhymes the infinitives *ly-e*, *li-e*, with the adverbs *erly*, *tendirly*, l. 264, p. 2738; *maladie*, *jelousie*, with I, l. 1850, 3910, 4146, &c. &c. See *Temporary Preface to Six-Text Chaucer*, pp. 107-11. Prof. Child of Harvard also holds the *Romaunt* not to be Chaucer's.—F.]

¹ Fauchet, pp. 198-200. He also translated Boethius *De Consolatione*, [recently edited by Dr. Morris (1868, 8°) from Addit. MS. Br. Mus. 10,340, collated with MS. Univ. Lib. Cam. I. 3, 21,] and *Abelard's Letters*, and wrote *Answers of the Sibyls*, &c.

² The poem consists of 22734 verses. William of Lorris's part ends with v. 4149, viz:

"A peu que je ne m'en desespoir."

³ In the preface of the edition printed in the year 1538, all this allegory is turned to religion. The Rose is proved to be a state of grace, or divine wisdom, or eternal beatitude, or the Holy Virgin to which heretics cannot gain access. It is the white Rose of Jericho, *Quasi plantatio Rosæ in Jericho*, &c. &c. The chemists, in the mean time, made it a search for the philosopher's stone: and other professions, with laboured commentaries, explained it into their own respective sciences.

⁴ See Occleve (*Letter of Cupide*, written 1402. Urry's *Chaucer*, p. 536, v. 283), who calls John of Meun the author of the *Romaunt of the Rose*.

⁵ Chaucer's poem consists of 7699 verses: and ends with this verse of the original, viz. ver. 13105.

"Vous aurez absolution."

But Chaucer has made several omissions in John of Meun's part, before he comes to this period. He has translated all William of Lorris's part, as I have observed; and his translation of that part ends with ver. 4432, viz.

"Than shuldin I fallin in wanhope."

Chaucer's cotemporaries called his *Romaunt of the Rose* a translation. Lydgate says that Chaucer

"Notably did his businesse

How far he has improved on the French original, the reader shall judge. I will exhibit passages selected from both poems: respectively placing the French beside the English, for the convenience of comparison. The renovation of nature in the month of May is thus described.

That it was May, thus dremede me,[1]	Qu'on joli moys de May songeoye,
In tyme of love and jolité,	Ou temps amoreux plein de joye,
That al thing gynneth waxen gay,	Que toute chose si s'esgaye,
For ther is neither busk nor hay	Si qu'il n'y a buissons ne haye
In May, that it nyl shrouded bene,	Qui en May parer ne se vueille,
And it with newe leves wrene.	Et couvrir de nouvelle fueille :
These wodes eek recoveren grene,	Les boys recouvrent leur verdure,
That drie in wynter ben to sene ;	Qui sont secs tant qui l'hiver dure ;
And the erth wexith proude withalle,	La terre mesines s'en orgouille
For swote dewes that on it falle ;	Pour la rousée qui la mouille,
And the pore estat forgette,	En oublian la povreté
In which that wynter had it sette.	Où elle a tout l'hiver esté ;
And than by cometh the ground so proude,	Lors devient la terre si gobe,
That it wole have a newe shroude,	Qu'elle veult avoir neusve robe ;
And makith so squeynt his robe and faire,	Si sçet si cointe robe faire,
That it had hewes an hundred payre,	Que de couleurs y a cent paire,
Of gras and flouris, ynde and pers,	D'herbes, de fleures Indes et Perses :
And many hewes ful dyvers :	Et de maintes couleurs diverses,

"By grete avyse his wittes to dispose,
To translate the *Romans of the Rose*."

Prol. Boch. st. vi. It is manifest that Chaucer took no pains to disguise his translation. He literally follows the French, in saying, that a river was "lesse than Saine." *i. e.* the Seine at Paris, ver. 118. "No wight in all Paris," ver. 7157. A grove has more birds "than ben in all the relme of Fraunce," ver. 495. He calls a pine, "A tree in France men call a pine," ver. 1457. He says of roses, "so faire werin never in Rone," ver. 1674. "That for Paris ne for Pavie," ver. 1654. He has sometimes reference to French ideas, or words, not in the original. As "Men clepin hem Sereins in France," ver. 684. "From Jerusalem to Burgoine," ver. 554. "Grein de Paris," ver. 1369. In mentioning minstrells and jugglers, he says, that some of them "Songin songes of Loraine," ver. 776. He adds,

"For in Loraine there notis be
Full swetir than in this contre."

There is not a syllable of these songs and singers of Lorraine, in the French. By the way, I suspect that Chaucer translated this poem while he was at Paris. There are also many allusions to English affairs, which I suspected to be Chaucer's; but they are all in the French original. Such as, "Hornpipis of Cornevaile," v. 4250. These are called in the original, "Chalemeaux de Cornouaille," ver. 3991. [Cornouaille here mentioned was a part of the province of Bretagne in France. Mr. Warton must have consulted some French MS. respecting the singers of Lorraine, for the passage certainly occurs in some of the printed editions, and in several MSS. —*Douce.*] A knight is introduced, allied to king "Arthour of Bretaigne," ver. 1199. Who is called, "Bon roy Artus de Bretaigne," Orig. ver. 1187. Sir Gawin and Sir Kay, two of Arthur's knights, are characterised, ver. 2206, *seq.* See Orig. ver. 2124. Where the word Keulx is corrupt for Keie. But there is one passage, in which he mentions a Bachelere as fair as "The Lordis sonne of Windisore," ver. 1250. This is added by Chaucer, and intended as a compliment to some of his patrons. In the *Legend of Good Women*, Cupid says to Chaucer, ver. 329 :

"For in pleyne text, withouten hede of glose,
Thou hast *translated* the *Romaunce of the Rose*."

---

[1] [Morris's *Chaucer*, vi. 2, ver. 51.]

That is the robe I mene, iwis,	Eſt la robe que je deviſe
Through which the ground to preiſen is.	Parquoy la terre mieulx ſe priſe.
The briddes, that haven lefte her ſong,	Les oiſeaulx qui tant ſe ſont teuz
While thei han ſuffride cold ſo ſtrong	Pour l'hiver qu'ils ont tous ſentuz,
In wedres gryl and derk to fighte,	Et pour le froit et divers temps,
Ben in May for the ſonne brighte,	Sont en May, et par la printemps,
So glade, &c.	Si liez, &c.

In the deſcription of a grove, within the garden of Mirth, are many natural and picturesque circumſtances, which are not yet got into the ſtorehouſe of modern poetry:[1]

Theſe trees were ſette, that I devyſe,	Mais ſachiés que les arbres furent
One from another in aſſyſe	Si loing a loing comme eſtre durent
Five fadome or ſyxe, I trowe ſo,	L'ung fut de l'autre loing aſſis
But they were hye and great alſo:	De cinque toiſes voyre de ſix,
And for to kepe oute well the ſonne,	Mais moult furent fueilluz et haulx
The croppes were ſo thycke yronne,[2]	Pour gardir de l'eſte le chaulx
And every braunche in other knytte,	Et ſi eſpis par deſſus furent
And full of grene leves ſytte,	Que chaleurs percer ne lis peurent
That ſonne myghte there noon dyſcende,	Ne ne povoient bas deſcendre
Leſt the tender graſſes ſhende.	Ne faire mal a l'erbe tendre.
There myghte men does and roes yſe,	Au vergier eut dains & chevreleux,
And of ſquyrels ful gret plenté,	Et auſſi beaucoup d'eſcureux,
From bowe to bowe alwaye lepynge.	Qui par deſſus arbres failloyent;
Connies there were alſo playenge,[3]	Connins y avoit qui yſſoient
That comyn out of her clapers	Bien ſouvent hors de leurs tanieres,
Of ſondry coloures and maners,	En moult de diverſes manieres,[4]
And maden many a tourneynge	[Aloient entr'eus tornoiant
Upon the freſhe graſſe ſpryngynge.	Sor l'erbe freſche verdoiant.[5]]

Near this grove were ſhaded fountains without frogs, running into murmuring rivulets, bordered with the ſofteſt graſs enamelled with various flowers.[6]

In places ſawe I welles there,	Par lieux y eut cleres fontaines,
In whych there no frogges were,	Sans barbelotes & ſans raines,
And fayre in ſhadowe was every welle;[7]	Qui des arbres eſtoient umbrez,
But I ne can the nombre telle	Par moy ne vous ſeront nombrez,
Of ſtremys ſmale, that by devyſe	Et petit ruiſſeaulx, que Deduit
Myrthe hadde done come through condyſe,[8]	Avoit la trouvés par conduit;
	L'eaue alloit aval faiſant
Of whych the water in rennynge	Son melodieux et plaiſant.
Gan make a noyſe full lykynge.	Aux bortz des ruiſſeaulx et des rives
Aboute the brynkes of theſe welles,	Des fontaines cleres et vives
And by the ſtremes over al elles	Poignoit l'erbe dru et plaiſant
Sprange up the graſſe, as thycke yſet	Grant ſoulas et plaiſir faiſant.
And ſofte as any velvet,	Amy povoit avec ſa mye
On whych men myght hys lemman leye,	Soy deporter ne'en doubtez mye.—
As on a fetherbed to pleye,	* * * * *
* * * * *	
There ſprange the vyolet al newe,	Violette y fut moult belle
And freſhe pervynke[9] ryche of hewe,	Et auſſi parvenche nouvelle;

---

[1] [Morris's *Chaucer*, vi. 43, ver. 1391.]
[2] "the tops, or boughs, were ſo thickly twiſted together."
[3] Chaucer imitates this paſſage in the *Aſſemble of Foules*, v. 190, ſeq. Other paſſages of that poem are imitated from the *Roman de la Roſe*.
[4] ver. 1348.   [5] ed. Michel, p. 46.   [6] [Morris's *Chaucer*, vi. 43, ver. 1409.]
[7] A ſpecies of inſect often found in ſtagnant water.   [8] conduits.   [9] periwinkle.

And floures yelowe, white, and rede;	Fleurs y eut blanches et vermeilles,
Suche plenté grewe there never in mede.	Ou ne pourroit trouver pareilles,
Ful gaye was al the grounde, and queynt,	De toutes diverses couleurs,
And poudred, as men had it peynt,	De haulx pris et de grans valeurs,
With many a freshe and sondrye floure,	Si estoit soef flairans
That casten up ful good savoure.	Et reflagrans et odorans.[1]

But I hasten to display the peculiar powers of William de Lorris in delineating allegorical personages; none of which has suffered in Chaucer's translation. The poet supposes that the garden of Mirth, or rather Love, in which grew the Rose, the object of the lover's wishes and labours, was enclosed with embattled walls, richly painted with various figures, such as Hatred, Avarice, Envy, Sorrow, Old Age, and Hypocrify. Sorrow is thus represented:

Sorowe was peynted next Envie[2]	De les Envie etoit Tristesse
Upon that walle of masonrye.	Painte aussi et garnye d'angoisse.
But wel was seyn in hir colour	Et bien paroit à sa couleur
That she hadde lyved in langour;	Qu'elle avoit a cueur grant douleur:
Hir semede to have the jaunyce.	Et sembloit avoir la jaunice,
Nought half so pale was Avarice,	La n'y faisoit riens Avarice,
Nor no thyng lyk of lenesse;	Ne de paleur ne de maigresse;
For sorowe, thought, and gret distresse.	Car le travaile et la destresse, &c.
* * * * *	* * * * *
A sorowful thyng wel semede she.	Moult sembloit bien que fust dolente;
Nor she hadde no thyng slowe be	Car el n'avoit pas este lente
For to forcracchen al hir face,	D'esgratignier toute sa chiere;
And for to rent in many place	Sa robe ne luy estoit chiere
Hir clothis, and for-to tere hir swire,	En mains lieux l'avoit dessirée,
As she that was fulfilled of ire;	Comme celle qui moult fut yrée.
And al to-torn lay eek hir here	Ses cheveulx dérompus estoient,
Aboute hir shuldris, here and there,	Qu'autour de son col pendoient,
As she that hadde it al to-rent	Presque les avoit tous desroux
For angre and for maltalent.	De maltalent et de corroux.[3]

Nor are the images of Hatred and Avarice inferior:

Amyd saugh I a Hate stonde,[4]	Au milieu de mur je vy Hayne.
* * * *	* * * *
And she was no thyng wel arraied,	Si n'estoit pas bien atournée,
But lyk a wode womman afraied,	Ains sembloit estre forcenée,
Frounced foule was hir visage,	Rechignée estoit et froncé,
And grennyng for dispitous rage,	
Hir nose snorted up for tene.	Le vis et le nez rebourfé.
Ful hidous was she for to sene,	Moult hydeuse estoit et souilleè,
Ful foule and rusty was she this.	
Hir heed ywrithen was, y-wis,	Et fut sa teste entortilleè
Ful grymly with a greet towayle.	Tres ordement d'un touaille.[5]

The design of this work will not permit me to give the portrait of Idlenefs, the portrefs of the garden of Mirth, and of others, which form the group of dancers in the garden: but I cannot refift the pleafure of transcribing those of Beauty, Franchife, and Richeffe, three capital figures in this genial affembly:

---

[1] v. 1348. [Warton quotes a very late and poor French text, much modernized. —F.]
[2] [Morris's *Chaucer*, vi. 10, ver. 301.]
[3] ver. 300.
[4] [Ibid. vi. 5, ver. 147.]
[5] ver. 143.

The God of Love, jolyf and lyght,[1]	Le Dieu d'amours ſi s'eſtoit pris
Ladde on his honde a lady bright,	A une dame de hault pris,
Of high prys, and of grete degré.	Pres ſe tenoit de ſon coſté,
This lady called was Beauté,	Celle dame eut nom Beaulte.
And an arowe, of which I tolde.	Ainſi comme une des cinque fleſches
Ful wel thewed[2] was ſhe holde,	En elle aut toutes bonnes taiches :
Ne ſhe was derk ne broun, but bright,	Point ne fut obſcur, ne brun,
And clere as the mone-lyght.	Mais fut clere comme la lune.—
* * * * *	
Hir fleſh was tendre as dewe of flour,	Tendre eut la chair comme rouſée,
Hir chere was ſymple as byrde in bour ;	Simple fut comme une eſpouſée.
As whyte as lylye or roſe in rys,[3]	Et blanche comme fleur de lis,
Hir face gentyl and tretys.	Viſage eut bel doulx et alis,
Fetys[4] ſhe was, and ſmale to ſe,	Elle eſtoit greſle et alignée
No wyntred[5] browis hadde ſhe,	N'eſtoit fardié ne pignée,
Ne popped hir, for it nedede nought	Car elle n'avoit pas meſtier
To wyndre hir, or to peynte hir ought.	De ſoy farder et affaiĉtier.
Hir treſſes yelowe, and longe ſtraughten,	Les cheveulx eut blons et ſi longs
Unto hir helys doun they raughten.	Qu'ils batoient aux talons.[6]

Nothing can be more ſumptuous and ſuperb than the robe and other ornaments of Richeſſe, or Wealth. They are imagined with great ſtrength of fancy. But it ſhould be remembered, that this was the age of magnificence and ſhow ; when a profuſion of the moſt ſplendid and coſtly materials was laviſhed on dreſs, generally with little taſte and propriety, but often with much art and invention :

Richeſſe a robe of purpur on hadde,[7]	De pourpre fut le veſtement
Ne trowe not that I lye or madde ;	A Richeſſe, ſi noblement,
For in this world is noon hir lyche,	Qu'en tout le monde n'euſt plus bel,
Ne by a thouſand deelle ſo riche,	Mieulx fait, ne auſſi plus nouvel :
Ne noon ſo faire ; for it ful welle	Pourtraiĉtes y furent d'orfroys,
With orfrays leyd was everydeelle,	Hyſtoryes d'empereurs et roys.
And portraied in the ribanynges	Et encores y avoit-il
Of dukes ſtoryes, and of kynges.	Un ouvrage noble et ſobtil ;
And with a bend of gold taſſeled,	A noyaulx d'or au col fermoit,
And knoppis fyne of gold enameled.[8]	Et a bendes d'azur tenoit ;

---

[1] [Morris's *Chaucer*, vi. 31, ver. 1003.]
[2] Having good qualities. See *ſupr.* ver. 939, *ſeq.*
[3] [On the branch. Sax. hpıs, virgulta.]   [4] [well-made, neat.—*T.*]
[5] contracted.   [6] ver. 1004.   [7] [Morris's *Chaucer*, vi. 33, ver. 1071.]
[8] Enameling, and perhaps pictures in enamel, were common in the Middle Ages. From the Teſtament of Joh. de Foxle, knight, Dat. apud Bramſhill co. Southampt. Nov. 5, 1378. "Item lego domino abbati de Waltham unum annulum auri groſſi, cum uno ſaphiro infixa, et nominibus trium regum [of Cologne] ſculptis in eodem annulo. Item lego Margarite ſorori mee unam tabulam argenti deauratī et amelitam, minorem de duabus quas habeo, cum diverſis ymaginibus ſculptis in eadem.—Item lego Margerite uxori Johannis de Wilton unum monile auri, cum S. litera ſculpta et amelita in eodem." *Regiſtr. Wykeham Epiſc. Winton.* p. ii. fol. 24. See alſo Dugd. *Bar.* i. 234, a.

Enameled is from the French *email*, or enamel. This art flouriſhed moſt at Limoges in France. So early as the year 1197, we have "Duas tabulas æneas ſuperauratas de labore Limogiæ." Chart. ann. 1197, apud Ughelin.—*Ital. Sacr.* vii. 1274. It is called *Opus Lemnoviticum*, in Dugdale's *Mcn.* iii. 310, 313, 331. In Wilkins's *Concil.* i. 666, two cabinets for the hoſt are ordered, one of ſilver or of ivory, and the other *de opere Lemovicino*. *Synod. Wigorn.* A.D. 1240. And in many other places. I find it called *Limaiſe* in a metrical romance the name of which I have forgotten, where a tomb is deſcribed,

Aboute hir nekke of gentyl entayle
Was fhete the riche chevefaile,
In which ther was fulle gret plenté
Of ftones clere and bright to fee.
Rycheffe a girdelle hadde upon,
The bokele of it was of a ftoon,
Of vertu gret, and mochel of myght
For who fo bare the ftoon fo bright,
Of venym durft hym no thing doute,
While he the ftoon hadde hym aboute.

* * * * *

The mourdaunt, wrought in noble wife,
Was of a ftoon fulle precious,
That was fo fyne and vertuous,
That hole a man it koude make
Of palafie, and tothe ake.
And yit the ftoon hadde fuch a grace,
That he was fiker in every place
Alle thilke day not blynde to bene,
That faftyng myghte that ftoon feene.
The barres were of gold ful fyne,
Upon a tyffu of fatyne,
Fulle hevy, gret, and no thyng lyght,
In everiche was a befaunt wight.
Upon the treffes of Richeffe
Was fette a cercle for nobleffe
Of brend gold, that fulle lyghte fhoon;
So faire trowe I was never noon.
But fhe were kunnyng for the nonys,
That koude devyfe alle the ftonys
That in that cercle fhewen clere;
It is a wondir thing to here.
For no man koude preyfe or geffe
Of hem that valewe or richeffe.

Noblement eut le chief parè,
De riches pierres decorè,
Qui gettoient moult grant clartè;
Tout y eftoit bien affortè.
Puis eut une riche fainture,
Sainte par deffus fa vefture:
Le boucle d'une pierre fu,
Groffe, et de moult grant vertu:
Celluy qui fur foy la portoit,
De tous venins garde eftoit.—

* * * * *

D'une pierre fut le mordans

Qui gueriffoit du mal des dens.

Ceft pierre portoit bon eur,
Qui l'avoit pouvoit eftre affeur
De fa fantè et de fa vei,
Quant à jeun il l'avoit vei:
Les cloux furent d'or epurè,
Par deffus le tiffu dorè,
Qui eftoient grans et pefans;
En chafcun avoit deux befans.
Si eut avecques a Richeffe
Uns cadre d'or mis fur la treffe,
Si riche, fi plaifant, et fi bel,
Qu'onques on ne veit le pareil:
De pierres eftoit fort garny,
Precieufes et aplany,
Qui bien en vouldroit devifer,

On ne les pouvroit pas prifer:

"And yt was, the Romans fayes,
All with golde and limaife."

[Du Cange v. Limogia], obferves, that it was anciently a common ornament of fumptuous tombs. He cites a Teftament of the year 1327, "Je lais huit cent livres pour faire deux tombes hautes et levées de l'Euvre de Limoges." The original tomb of Walter de Merton, Bifhop of Rochefter, erected in his cathedral about the year 1276 [?], was made at Limoges. This appears from the accompts of his executors, viz. "Et computant xl l. v s. vi d. liberat. Magiftro Johanni Linnomcenfi, pro tumba dicti Epifcopi Roffenfis, fcil. pro Conftructione et carriagio de Lymoges ad Roffam. Et xl s. viii d. cuidam Executori apud Lymoges ad ordinandam et providendam Conftructionem dictæ Tumbæ. Et x s. viii d. cuidam garcioni eunti apud Lymoges quærenti dictam tumbam conftructam, et ducenti eam cum dicto Mag. Johanne ufque Roffam. Et xxii l. in maceoneria circa dictam tumbam defuncti. Et vii marcas, in ferramento ejufdem, et carriagio a Londin. ufque ad Roff. et aliis parandis ad dictam tumbam. Et xi s. cuidam vitriario pro vitris feneftrarum emptarum juxta tumbam dicti Epifcopi apud Roffam." Ant. Wood's *MS. Merton Papers*, Bibl. Bodl. Cod. Ballard, 46.

[1] I cannot give the precife meaning of *Barris*, nor of *Cloux* in the French. It feems to be part of a buckle. In the wardrobe-roll, quoted above, are mentioned, "One hundred garters *cum boucles*, barris, *et pendentibus de argento*." For which were delivered, "ccc barrs argenti." An. 21, Edw. III.—[*Clavus* in Latin, whence the Fr. *cloux* is derived, feems to have fignified not only an outward border, but alfo what we call a ftripe. Montfaucon, t. iii. P. i. ch. vi. A bar in heraldry is a narrow ftripe or fafcia.—*Tyrwhitt*.]

Rubyes there were, faphires, jagounces,[1]	Rubis y eut, faphirs, jagonces,
And emeraudes, more than two ounces.	Efmeraudes plus de cent onces:
But alle byfore ful fotilly	Mais devant eut, par grant maiftrife,
A fyn charboncle fette laugh I.	Un efcarboucle bien affife,
The ftoon fo clere was and fo bright,	Et le pierre fi clere eftoit,
That, alfo foone as it was nyght,	Que cil qui devant la mettoit,
Men myghte feen to go for nede	Si en povoit veoir au befoing
A myle or two, in lengthe and brede.	A foy conduire une lieue loing.
Sich lyght *tho* fprang oute of the ftone,	Telle clarté fi en yffoit
That Richeffe wondir brighte fhone	Que Richeffe en refplendiffoit
Bothe hir heed, and alle hir face,	Par tout le corps et par fa face,
And eke aboute hir al the place.	Auffi d'autour d'elle la place.[2]

The attributes of the portrait of Mirth are very expreffive:

Of berde unnethe hadde he no thyng,[3]	Et fi n'avoit barbe a menton,
For it was in the firfte fpryng.	Si non petit poil follaton;
Ful yonge he was, and mery of thought,	Il etoit jeune damoyfaulx;
And in famette,[4] with briddis wrought,	Son bauldrier fut portrait d'oifeaulx

---

[1] The gem called a jacinth. The knowledge of precious ftones was a grand article in the natural philofophy of this age; and the medical virtue of gems, alluded to above, was a doctrine much inculcated by the Arabian naturalifts. Chaucer refers to a treatife on gems, called the *Lapidary*, famous in that time. *Houfe of Fame*, L. iii. ver. 260 [edit. Morris].

> "And they were fet as thik of nouchis
> Fyne, of the fyneft ftones faire
> That men reden in the Lapidaire."

Montfaucon, in the royal library at Paris, recites, "Le Lapidaire, de la vertu des pierres."—*Catal. MSS.* p. 794. This I take to be the book here referred to by Chaucer. Henry of Huntingdon [has, among his minor productions (of which there is a copy in Royal MS. 13, c. 11), fome verfes on precious ftones. See Wright's *Biog. Brit. Literaria*, Anglo-Norman period, p. 169. This writer was living in 1154]. See Du Cange, *Gloff. Gr. Barb.* ii. *Ind. Auctor.* p. 37, col. 1. In the Cotton library is a Saxon Treatife on precious ftones. *Tiber.* A. 3, liii. fol. 98. The writing is [very] ancient. [The treatife referred to contains a meagre explanation of the twelve precious ftones mentioned in the Apocalypfe.] Pelloutier mentions a Latin poem of the eleventh century on precious ftones, written by Marbode, bifhop of Rennes [who died in the year 1123], and foon afterwards tranflated into French verfe. *Mem. Lang. Celt.* part i. vol. i. ch. xiii. p. 26. The tranflation begins:

> "Evax fut un mult riche reis
> Lu reigne tint d'Arabeis."

It was printed in [the folio edit. (1708) of the works of St. Hildebert,] col. 1638. This may be reckoned one of the oldeft pieces of French verfification. A MS. *De Speciebus Lapidum*, occurs twice in the Bodleian library, falfely attributed to one Adam Nidzarde, Cod. Digb. 28, f. 169. and Cod. Laud. C. 3, *Princ.* "Evax rex Arabum legitur fcripfiffe." But it is, I think, Marbode's book above mentioned. Evax is a fabulous Arabian king, faid to have written on this fubject. Of this Marbode or Marbodæus, fee Ol. Borrich. Diff. Acad. de Poet. p. 87, fect. 78, edit. Francof. 1683, 4to. His poem was publifhed, with notes, by Lampridius Alardus. The eaftern writers pretend that King Solomon, among a variety of phyfiological pieces, wrote a book on gems: one chapter of which treated of thofe precious ftones which refift or repel evil Genii. They fuppofe that Ariftotle ftole all his philofophy from Solomon's books. See Fabric. *Bibl. Gr.* xiii. 387, *feq.* and i. p. 71. Compare Herbelot, *Bibl. Oriental*, p. 962, b. Artic. *Ketab alahgiar feq.*

[2] ver. 1066. [3] [Morris's *Chaucer*, vi. 26, ver. 833.] [4] *famite;* fattin.

And with gold beten ful fetyſly,	Qui tout etoit è or batu,
His body was clad ful richely.	Tres richement eſtoit veſtu
Wrought was his robe in ſtraunge giſe,	D'un' robe moult deſgyſée,
And al to-ſlytered for queyntiſe	Qui fut en maint lieu inciſée,
In many a place, lowe and hie.	Et decouppeè par quointiſe.
And ſhode he was with grete maiſtrie,	Et fut chauſſé par mignotiſe
With ſhoon decoped,[1] and with laas,	D'un ſouliers decouppés à las,
By dru*e*ry,[2] and by ſolas.	Par joyeuſete et ſoulas,
His leef a roſyn chapelet	Et ſa neye luy fiſt chapeau
Hadde made, and on his heed it ſet.	De roſes gracieux et beau.[3]

Franchiſe is a no leſs attractive portrait, and ſketched with equal grace and delicacy:

And next hym daunced*e* dame Fraunchiſe,[4]	Apres tous ceulx eſtoit Franchiſe,
Arayed in fulle noble gyſe.	
She was not broune ne dunne of hewe,	Qui ne fut ne brune ne biſe;
But white as ſnowe falle newe.	Ains fut comme la neige blanche
Hir noſe was wrought at poynt devys,	Courtoiſe eſtoit, joyeuſe et franche,
For it was gentyl and tretys;	Le nez avoit long et tretis
With eyen gladde, and browes bente;	Yeulx vers rins, ſoureils ſaitis,
Hir here doun to hir helis wente.[5]	Les cheveulx eut tres-blons et longs,
And ſhe was ſymple as dowve of tree,	Simple feut comme les coulons.
Ful debonaire of herte was ſhe.	Le cueur eut doulx et debonnaire.[6]

The perſonage of Danger is of a bolder caſt, and may ſerve as a contraſt to ſome of the preceding. He is ſuppoſed ſuddenly to ſtart from an ambuſcade, and to prevent Bialcoil, or *Kind Reception*, from permitting the lover to gather the roſe of beauty:

With that ſterte outeanoon Daungere,[7]	A tant ſaillit villain Dangere,
Out of the place w*h*ere he was hidde.	De là ou il eſtoit mucè;
His malice in his chere was kidde;[8]	
Fulle grete he was and blak of hewe,	Grant fut, noir, et tout hericè,
Sturdy, and hidous, who-ſo hym knewe,	
Like ſharp urchouns[9] his here was growe,	
His eyes rede ſparkling as the fire glowe,	S'ot les yeulx rouges comme feux,
His noſe frounced fulle kirked ſtoode,	Le vis froncè, le nez hydeux
He come criande as he were woode.	Et s'eſcrie tout forcenez.[10]

Chaucer has enriched this figure. The circumſtance of Danger's hair ſtanding erect like the prickles on the urchin or hedge-hog is his own, and finely imagined.

Hitherto ſpecimens have been given from that part of this poem

---

[1] cut or marked with figures. From *decouper*, Fr. to *cut*. I ſuppoſe *Poulis windows* was a cant phraſe for a fine device or ornament. [Compare *infrâ*, p. 358, and Note 12.]

[2] [courtſhip, gallantry, T.]   [3] v. 832.

[4] [Morris's *Chaucer*, vi. 37, ver. 1211.]

[5] All the females of this poem have grey eyes and yellow hair. One of them is ſaid to have "Hir yen grey as is a faucoun," v. 546. Where the original word, tranſlated *grey*, is *vers*. v. 546. We have this colour again, Orig. v. 822. "Les yeulx eut *vers*." This too Chaucer tranſlates, "Hir yen greye," v. 862. The ſame word occurs in the French text before us, v. 1195. This compariſon was natural and beautiful, as drawn from a very familiar and favourite-object in the age of the poet. Perhaps Chaucer means "grey as a falcon's *eyes*."

[6] v. 1190.   [7] [Morris's *Chaucer*, vi. 96, 3130.]

[8] "was diſcovered by his behaviour, or countenance."

[9] *urchins*, hedge-hogs.   [10] v. 2959.

which was written by William de Lorris, its first inventor. Here Chaucer was in his own walk. One of the most striking pictures in the style of allegorical personification, which occurs in Chaucer's translation of the additional part, is much heightened by Chaucer, and indeed owes all its merit to the translator; whose genius was much better adapted to this species of painting than that of John of Meun, the continuator of the poem:

With hir Labour and Travaile[1]	Travaile et Douleur la herbergent,
Logged ben with Sorwe and Woo,	Mais il la lient et la chargent,
That never out of hir court goo.	
Peyne and Distresse, Syknesse, and Ire,	
And Malencoly, that angry fire,	
Ben of hir paleys[2] senatours.	
Gronyng and Grucchyng, hir herbejours,[3]	
The day and nyght, hir to turmente,	Et tant la batent et tormentent,
With cruelle Deth they hir presente.	Que mort prochaine luy presentent,
And tellen hir, erliche[4] and late,	Et talent de se repentir;
That Deth stondith armed at hir gate.	Tant luy font de fleaux sentir.
Thanne brynge they to her remembraunce	Adonc luy vient en remembraunce,
The foly dedis of hir infaunce,	En cest tardifve pesance,
Whiche causen hir to mourne in woo	Quant el se voit foible et chenue,[5]
That Youthe hath hir bigiled so.	Que malement l'a décéue Jouesce...

The fiction that Sickness, Melancholy, and other beings of the like sort were counsellors in the palace of Old Age, and employed in telling her day and night, that "Death stood armed at her gate," was far beyond the sentimental and satirical vein of John of Meun, and is conceived with great vigour of imagination.

Chaucer appears to have been early struck with this French poem.[6] [So were many other English poets. The author of the *Yle of Ladyes*, called generally *Chaucer's Dreme*,[7] supposes that the chamber in which he slept was richly painted with the story of the *Romaunt of the Rose*.[8] It is natural to imagine that such a poem must have been a favourite with Chaucer. No poet, before William of Lorris, either Italian or French, had delineated allegorical personages in so distinct and enlarged a style, and with such a fulness of characteristical attributes: nor had descriptive poetry selected such a variety of circumstances, and disclosed such an exuberance of embellishment, in forming agreeable representations of nature. On this account, we are surprised that Boileau should mention Villon as the first poet of France who drew form and order from the chaos of the old French romancers:

---

[1] [Morris's *Chaucer*, vi. 152, 4997.]   [2] palace.
[3] [providers of lodgings, harbingers.—T.]   [4] early.   [5] v. 4733.
[6] [See M. Sandras's *Etude sur Chaucer considéré comme Imitateur des Trouvères*, Paris, 1859, arguing that Chaucer owed nearly everything to Jean de Meun's and other French influence on him. See on the other side as to the greater influence of Italian on him.—Ebert's review of Sandras in the Chaucer Society's Essays, p. 5, and Prof. Ten Brink's *Studien*.—F.]
[7] [Mr. Bradshaw and Prof. Ten Brink contend that the poem called Chaucer's *Dreme* is decidedly not his.—F.]
[8] v. 322. Chaucer alludes to this poem in *The Marchaunt's Tale*, v. 1548.

> Villon fçeut le Premier, dans ces fiecles groffiers,
> Debroüiller l'art confus de nos vieux romanciers.[1]

But the poetry of William of Lorris was not the poetry of Boileau.

That this poem should not please Boileau, I can easily conceive. It is more surprising that it should have been censured as a contemptible performance by Petrarch, who lived in the age of fancy. Petrarch having desired his friend Guido di Gonzaga to send him some new piece, he sent him the *Roman de la Rose*. With the poem, instead of an encomium, he returned a severe criticism; in which he treats it as a cold, inartificial, and extravagant composition: as a proof how much France, who valued this poem as her chief work, was surpassed by Italy in eloquence and the arts of writing.[2] In this opinion we must attribute something to jealousy. But the truth is, Petrarch's genius was too cultivated to relish these wild excursions of imagination: his favourite classics, whom he revived, and studied with so much attention, ran in his head. Especially Ovid's *Art of Love*, a poem of another species, and evidently formed on another plan; but which Petrarch had been taught to venerate, as the model and criterion of a didactic poem on the passion of love reduced to a system. We may add that, although the poem before us was founded on the visionary doctrines and refinements concerning love invented by the Provençal poets, and consequently less unlikely to be favourably received by Petrarch, yet his ideas on that delicate subject were much more Platonic and metaphysical.

SECTION XIV.

CHAUCER'S poem of *Troilus and Cresseide* is said to be formed on an old history, written by Lollius, a native of Urbino in Italy.[3] Lydgate says that Chaucer in this poem

> made a translacion
> Of a boke which called is Trophe
> In Lumbarde tongue, &c.[4]

---

[1] *Art. Poet.* ch. i. He died about the year 1456.

[2] See Petrarch, *Carm.* l. i. ep. 30.

[3] Petrus Lambeccius enumerates Lollius Urbicus among the *Historici Latini profani* of the third century. Prodrom. p. 246. Hamb. 1659. See also Voss. *Historic. Latin.* ii. 2, p. 163, edit. Lugd. Bat. But this could not be Chaucer's Lollius. Chaucer places Lollius among the historians of Troy, in his *House of Fame*, iii. 380. It is extraordinary, that Du [Cange] in the *Index Auctorum*, used by him for his Latin glossary, should mention this Lollius Urbicus of the third century. Tom. vii. p. 407, edit. [1850.] As I apprehend, none of his works remain. A proof that Chaucer translated from some Italian original is, that in a manuscript which I have seen of this poem, I find, *Monesteo* for *Menestes*, *Rupheo* for *Ruphes*, *Phebuseo* for *Phebuses*, lib. iv. 50, *seq*. Where, by the way, Xantippe, a Trojan chief, was perhaps corruptly written for Xantippus, *i.e.* Xantippus. As Joseph. Iscan iv. 10. In Lydgate's *Troy*, *Zantiphus*, iii. 26. All corrupted from Antiphus, (Dict. Cret. p. 105). In the printed copies we have *Ascalapho* for Ascalaphus, lib. v. 319.

[4] Prol. Boch. ft. iii.

It is certain that Chaucer frequently refers to "*Myne auctor Lollius.*"[1] But he hints, at the same time, that Lollius wrote in Latin.[2] I have never seen this history either in the Italian or Latin language. I have before observed, that it is mentioned in Boccaccio's *Decameron*, and that a translation of it was made into Greek verse by some of the Greek fugitives in the fourteenth century. Du Fresnoy mentions it in Italian.[3] In the Royal Library at Paris it occurs often as an ancient French romance.[4] Much fabulous history concerning Troilus is related in Guido de Columna's *Destruction of Troy*.[5] Whatever were Chaucer's materials, he has on this subject constructed a poem of considerable merit, in which the vicissitudes of love are depicted in a strain of true poetry, with much pathos and simplicity of sentiment.[6] He calls it, "a litill tragedie."* Troilus is supposed to have seen Cresside in a temple,

---

[1] See lib. i. v. 395.   [2] Lib. ii. v. 10.
[3] [*L'Amore di Troilo e Griseida*, di Angelo Leonico, Ven. 1553, 8vo. Du Fresnoy, *Bibl. des Romans*, i. 217.—*Douce.*]
[4] "Cod. 7546. *Roman de Troilus.*"—"Cod. 7564. *Roman de Troilus et de Briseida ou Criseida.*"—Again, as an original work of Boccaccio. "Cod. 7757. *Philostrato dell' amorose fatiche de Troilo per Giovanni Boccaccio.*" † "Les suivans (adds Montfaucon ‡) contiennent les autres œuvres de Boccace."
[5] [See M. Joly's *Benoit de Ste.-More et le Roman de Troie*, 1870, and the very valuable Introduction by MM. Moland and D'Hericault, in *Nouvelles Françoises en prose du xive siecle*, 1858, where they have printed the prose French version of the *Filostrato*, entitled *Le Roman de Troilus*.]
[6] Chaucer however claims no merit of invention in this poem. He invokes Clio to favour him with rhymes only; and adds:
"To every lover I me excuse,
That of no sentement I this endyte,
But out of Latyn in my tonge it write."
L. ii. ver. 12. *seq.* But Sir Francis Kinaston who translated *Troilus and Cresseide* into

---

* L. ult. v. 1785.
† Boccaccio *Filostrato* was printed [at Venice before 1483 (see Brunet, i. 1013), and was reprinted at Bologna in 1498, and at Milan in 1499.] It is in the octave stanza. The editor of the *Canterbury Tales* [Tyrwhitt] informs me, that Boccaccio himself, in his *Decameron*, has made the same honourable mention of this poem as of the *Teseide:* although without acknowledging either for his own. In the Introduction to the Sixth Day, he says that "Dioneo insieme con Lauretta de *Troile et di Criseida* cominciarono cantare." Just as, afterwards, in the conclusion of the Seventh Day, he says that the same "Dioneo et Fiametta gran pezzi cantarono insieme d'Arcita et di Palamone." See *Canterb. T.* vol. iv. p. 85; iii. p. 311 [edit. Tyrwhitt.] Chaucer appears to have been as much indebted to Boccaccio in his *Troilus and Cresseide*, as in his *Knightes Tale*. At the same time we must observe, that there are several long passages, and even episodes, in *Troilus*, of which no traces appear in the *Filostrato*. Chaucer speaks of himself as a translator *out of Latin*, B. ii. 14. And he calls his author *Lollius*, B. i. 394-421, and B. v. 1652. The latter of these two passages is in the *Filostrato:* but the former, containing Petrarch's sonnet, is not. And when Chaucer says, he *translates from Latin*, we must remember that the *Italian* language was called *Latino volgare*. Shall we suppose, that Chaucer followed a more complete copy of the *Filostrato* than that we have at present, or one enlarged by some officious interpolater? The Parisian manuscript might perhaps clear these difficulties. In Bennet Library at Cambridge, there is a MS. of Chaucer's *Troilus*, elegantly written, with a frontispiece beautifully illuminated, LXI.
‡ Bibl. p. 793, col. 2. Compare Lengl. *Bibl. Rom.* ii. p. 253.

and, retiring to his chamber, is thus naturally described in the critical situation of a lover examining his own mind after the first impression of love.

> And when that he in chaumber was allon,[1]
> He down upon his beddes feet him sette,
> And first he gan to syke, and eft to grone,
> And thoughte ay on hire so, withouten lette,
> That as he satt and woke, his spirit mette
> That he hire saugh, and temple, and al the wyse
> Right of hire loke, and gan it new avise.

There is not so much nature in the sonnet to Love, which follows. It is translated from Petrarch; and had Chaucer followed his own genius, he would not have disgusted us with the affected gallantry and exaggerated compliments which it extends through five tedious stanzas. The doubts and delicacies of a young girl disclosing her heart to her lover are exquisitely touched in this comparison:

> And as the new abaysed nyghtyngale,[2]
> That stynteth first, when *she* bygynneth synge,
> When that she hereth any *herdes* tale,
> Or in the hegges any wight sterynge;
> And, after, syker doth hire vois oute rynge;
> Right so Criseyde, when hire drede stente,
> Opned hire herte, and told hym hire entente.

The following pathetic scene may be selected from many others. Troilus, seeing Cressïde in a swoon, imagines her to be dead. He unsheaths his sword with an intent to kill himself, and utters these exclamations:

> " And thow cité, in *which* I lyve in wo![3]
> And thow Priam, and bretheren alle isere!
> And thow *my* moder, farwel, for I go!
> And, Attropes, mak redy thow my beere!
> And thow Criseyde, O swete herte deere,
> Receyve now my spirit!" wolde he seye,
> With swerd at herte, al redy for to dye.
>
> But, as God wold, of swough she therwith brayde,
> And gan to sike, and " Troilus," she cryede;
> And he answerde, " Lady myn Criseyde,
> Lyve ye yit?" and lete his swerde down glide:
> " Ye, herte myn, that thanked be Cupide!"
> Quod she, and therwithal *she sore* sighte,
> And he bigan to glad hire as he myghte.

Latin rhymes, says that Chaucer in this poem "has taken the liberty of his own inventions." [The two first books of Kinaston's translation were printed in 1635; but a MS. of the whole work is in the possession of Mr. James Crossley, of Manchester.] In the mean time, Chaucer, by his own references, seems to have been studious of seldom departing from Lollius. In one place, he pays him a compliment, as an author whose excellences he could not reach. L. iii. v. 1330.

> " But sothe is, though I can not tellen all,
> As can mine author *of his excellence.*"

See also l. iii. 576, 1823.

[1] [Morris's *Chaucer*, iv. 122, lib. i. ver. 358.]
[2] [*Ibid.* iv. 275, lib. iii. ver. 1184.]   [3] [*Ibid.* iv. 349, lib. iv. ver. 1177.]

> Took hire in armes two, and kyſte hire ofte,
> And hire to glade, he dide al his entente,
> For which hire gooſte, that fliked ay o lofte,
> Into hire woful herte ayein it wente :
> But, at the laſte, as that hire eye glente
> Aſyde, anon ſhe gan his ſwerde aſpye,
> As it lay bare, and gan for feere crie,
>
> And aſked hym whi he it hadde out drawe ;
> And Troilus anon the cauſe hire tolde,
> And how hymſelf therwith he wolde han ſlawe ;
> For which Criſeyde upon hym gan byholde,
> And gan hym in *hire* armes faſte folde,
> And ſeyde, " O mercy God, lo, which a dede !
> Allas! how neigh we weren bothe dede !"

Pathetic deſcription is one of Chaucer's peculiar excellences.

In this poem are various imitations from Ovid, which are of too particular and minute a nature to be pointed out here, and belong to the province of a profeſſed and formal commentator on the piece. The Platonic notion in the third book about univerſal love, and the doctrine that this principle acts with equal and uniform influence both in the natural and moral world, are a tranſlation from Boethius.[1] In the *Knight's Tale* he mentions from the ſame favourite ſyſtem of philoſophy, the *Fair Chain of Love*. It is worth obſerving, that the reader is referred to Dares Phrygius, inſtead of Homer, for a diſplay of the achievements of Troilus :

> His worthy dedes, who-*ſo* left hem here,[2]
> Rede Dares ; he kan telle hem alle ifeere.

Our author, from his [ſomewhat unguarded imitation of Boccaccio] has been guilty of a very diverting and what may be called a double anachroniſm. He repreſents Creſſide, with two of her female companions, ſitting in a " pavid parlour," and reading the *Thebais* of Statius, which is called *The Geſt of the Siege of Thebes*, and *The Romance of Thebes*.[3] In another place, Caſſandra tranſlates the Arguments of the twelve books of the *Thebais*.[4] In the fourth book of this poem, Pandarus endeavours to comfort Troilus with arguments concerning the doctrine of predeſtination, taken from [Boethius

---

[1] *Conſolat. Philoſoph.* l. ii. Met. *ult.* iii. Met. 2. Spenſer is full of the ſame doctrine. See *Fairy Queen*, i. ix. 1, iv. x. 34, 35, &c. &c. I could point out many other imitations from Boethius in this poem.

[2] [Morris's *Chaucer*, v. 73, ver. 1784.]

[3] L. ii. v. 100. *Biſhop Amphiorax* is mentioned, ib. v. 104. Pandarus ſays, v. 106:

> " All this I know my ſelve,
> And all the aſſiege of Thebes, and all the care ;
> For herof ben ther makid *bokis twelve*."

In his *Boke of the Ducheſſe* (Works, v. 156, l. 47-51), Chaucer, to paſs the night away, rather than play at cheſs, calls for a *Romaunce* ; in which " were writtin fables of quenis livis and of kings, and many othir thingis ſmale." This proves to be Ovid, v. 52, *ſeq*. See *Man of L. T.* v. 54.

[4] L. v. v. 1490. I will add here, that Creſſide propoſes the trial of the Ordeal to Troilus, l. iii. v. 1048. Troilus, during the times of truce, amuſes himſelf with hawking, l. iii. v. 1785.

De Confolatione Philofophiæ—a book which Chaucer himfelf tranflated.¹]

This poem, although almoft as long as the Eneid, was intended to be fung to the harp, as well as read.

> And red wher fo thow be, or elles fonge.²

It is dedicated to the "morall" Gower, and to the "philofophical" Strode. Gower will occur as a poet hereafter. Strode was eminent for his fcholaftic knowledge, and tutor to Chaucer's fon Lewis at Merton college in Oxford.

Whether the *Houfe of Fame* is Chaucer's invention, or fuggefted by any French or Italian poet, I cannot determine. But I am apt to think it was originally a Provençal compofition,—among other proofs, from this paffage:

> And theroute come fo grete a noyfe,³
> That had hyt ftonde upon Oyfe,
> Men myght hyt han herd efely
> To Rome, Y trowe fikerly.

The Oyfe is a river in Picardy, which falls into the River Seine, not many leagues from Paris. An Englifhman would not have expreffed diftance by fuch an unfamiliar illuftration. Unlefs we reconcile the matter by fuppofing that Chaucer wrote this poem during his travels. There is another paffage where the ideas are thofe of a foreign romance. To the trumpeters of renown the poet adds,

> And alle that ufede clarioun,⁴
> In Cataloigne and Aragoun.

Cafteloigne is Catalonia in Spain.⁵ The martial muficians of Englifh tournaments, fo celebrated in ftory, were a more natural and obvious allufion for an Englifh poet.⁶

This poem contains great ftrokes of Gothic imagination, yet bordering often on the moft ideal and capricious extravagance. The poet, in a vifion, fees a temple of glafs:

> In whiche ther were moo ymages⁷
> Of golde, ftondynge in fondry ftages,
> And moo ryche tabernacles,

---

¹ [Book v. Profe 2-3, edit. Morris. See the extracts, *ibid*. vi-x.] Bradwardine, a learned archbifhop and theologift, and nearly Chaucer's contemporary, [treated this fubject] in his book, *De Caufa Dei*, edit. 1617. [Chaucer] touches on this controverfy (*Nonnes Preefts Tale*, v. 1349. See alfo *Troilus and Creffeide*, lib. iv-v, 961 *et feq*.)
² [Morris's *Chaucer*, v. 75, ver. 1811.]
³ [*Ibid*. v. 267, ver. 837. See *fupra*, p. 298, note 1.] ⁴ [*Ibid*. v. 247, ver. 157.]
⁵ See *Marchaunt's Tale*, ver. 1231. He mentions a rock higher than any in Spain, B. iii. ver. 27. But this I believe was an Englifh proverb.
⁶ He mentions a plate of gold, "As fine as *duckett* in *Venife*," B. iii. ver. 258. But he fays that the Galaxy is called *Watlyng-ftrete*, B. ii. ver. 431. He fwears by Thomas Becket, B. iii. ver. 41. In one place he is addreffed by the name of Geoffrey, B. ii. ver. 221; but in two others by that of Peter, B. ii. ver. 526, B. iii. ver. 909. Among the muficians he mentions "Pipirs of all the Duche tong," B. iii. ver. 144.
⁷ [Morris's *Chaucer*, v. 212, ver. 121.]

> And with perré¹ moo pynacles,
> And moo curiouſe portreytures,
> And queynt maner of figures
> Of golde werke, then I ſawgh ever.

On the walls of this temple were engraved ſtories from Virgil's *Eneid*² and Ovid's *Epiſtles*.³ Leaving this temple, he ſees an eagle with golden wings ſoaring near the ſun:

> That faſte be the ſonne, as hye⁴
> As kenne myght I with myn ye,
> Me thought I ſawgh an egle ſore,
> But that hit ſemede moche more⁵
> Then I had any egle ſeyne.⁶
>   *   *   *
> Hyt was of golde, and ſhone ſo bryght,
> *That never ſawgh men ſuch a ſyght.*

The eagle deſcends, ſeizes the poet in his talons, and mounting again, conveys him to the Houſe of Fame, which is ſituated, like that of Ovid, between earth and ſea. In their paſſage thither they fly above the ſtars, which our author leaves, with clouds, tempeſts, hail, and ſnow, far beneath him. This aerial journey is partly copied from Ovid's Phaeton in the chariot of the ſun. But the poet apologiſes for this extravagant fiction, and explains his meaning by alleging the authority of Boethius, who ſays that Contemplation may ſoar on the wings of Philoſophy above every element. He likewiſe recollects, in the midſt of his courſe, the deſcription of the heavens given by Marcianus Capella in his book *De Nuptiis Philologiæ et Mercurii*,⁷ and Alanus in his *Anticlaudian*.⁸ At his arrival in the confines of the Houſe of Fame, he is alarmed by confuſed murmurs iſſuing thence, like diſtant thunders or billows. This circumſtance is alſo borrowed from Ovid's temple.⁹ He is left by the eagle near the

---

¹ jewels.
² Where he mentions Virgil's hell, he likewiſe refers to Claudian *De Raptu Proſerpinæ* and Dante's *Inferno*, ver. 450. There is a tranſlation of a few lines from Dante, whom he calls "the wiſe poet of Florence," in the *Wife of Bath's Tale*, ver. 1125. The ſtory of Count Ugolino, a ſubject which Sir Joſhua Reynolds has lately painted in a capital ſtyle, is tranſlated from Dante, "the grete poete of Italie that hight Dante," in the *Monkes Tale*, ver. 877. A ſentence from Dante is cited in the *Legend of Good Women*, ver. 360. In the *Freeres Tale*, Dante is compared with Virgil, ver. 256.
³ It was not only in the fairy palaces of the poets and romance-writers of the middle-ages that Ovid's ſtories adorned the walls. In one of the courts of the palace of Noneſuch, all Ovid's *Metamorphoſes* were cut in ſtone under the windows. Hearne, Coll. MSS. 55, p. 64. But the *Epiſtles* ſeem to have been the favourite work, the ſubject of which coincided with the gallantry of the times.
⁴ [Morris's *Chaucer*, v. 224, ver. 497.]   ⁵ greater.
⁶ The eagle ſays to the poet, that this houſe ſtands
> "Right ſo as *thine owne boke* tellith."

B. ii. ver. 204. That is, Ovid's *Metamorphoſes*. See *Met*. l. xii. ver. 40, &c.
⁷ See the *Marchaunt's Tale*, v. 1248, and Lidg. *Stor. Theb*. fol. 357.
⁸ A famous book in the middle ages. There is an old French tranſlation of it. Bibl. Reg. Paris, MSS. Cod. 7632.
⁹ See *Met*. xii. 39, and Virg. *Æn*. iv. 173; Val. Flacc. ii. 117; Lucan. 1. 469.

house, which is built of materials bright as polished glass, and stands on a rock of ice of excessive height, and almost inaccessible. All the southern side of this rock was covered with engravings of the names of famous men, which were perpetually melting away by the heat of the sun. The northern side of the rock was alike covered with names, but being here shaded from the warmth of the sun, the characters remained unmelted and uneffaced. The structure of the house is thus imagined.

> me thought*e*, by seynte Gyle,[1]
> Alle was of stone of beryle,
> Bothe castel and the toure,
> And eke the halle, and every boure,
> Wythouten peces or joynynges.
> But many subtile compassinges,
> As rabewyures and pynacles,
> Ymageries and tabernacles,
> I say; and ful eke of wyndowes,
> As flakes falle in grete snowes.

In these lines, and in some others which occur hereafter, the poet perhaps alludes to the many new decorations in architecture which began to prevail about his time, and gave rise to the florid Gothic style. There are instances of this in other poems [ascribed to him.] In [the poem called *Chaucer's Dreme*,

> And of a sute were all the toures,[2]
> Subtily corven after floures,
> * * * *
> With many a small turret hie.

And in the description of the palace of Pleasant Regard, in the Assembly of Ladies:

> Fairir is none, though it were for a king,[3]
> Devisid wel and that in every thing;
> The towris hie, ful plesante shal ye finde,
> With fannis fresh, turning with everie winde.
> The chambris, and the parlirs of a sorte,
> With bay windows, goodlie as may be thought:
> As for daunsing or othir wise disporte,
> The galeries be al right wel ywrought.

In Chaucer's Life by William Thomas,[4] it is not mentioned that he was appointed clerk of the king's works in the palace of Westminster, in the royal manors of Shene, Kennington, Byfleet, and Clapton, and in the Mews at Charing.[5] Again in 1380, of the works of St. George's Chapel at Windsor, then ruinous.[6] But to return.

Within the niches formed in the pinnacles stood all round the castle,

---

[1] [Morris's *Chaucer*, v. 245, lib. iii. ver. 93.]   [2] [*Ibid.* v. 88, ver. 81.]
[3] Chaucer's Works, ed. Urry, p. 434, col. 2, lines 158-165.
[4] Chaucer's Life in Urry's edition. William Thomas digested this Life from collections by Dart. His brother, Dr. Timothy Thomas, wrote or compiled the Glossary and Preface to that edition. See Dart's *Westminst. Abbey*, i. 80. Timothy Thomas was of Christ Church, Oxford, and died in 1757.
[5] Claus. 8, Ric. II.
[6] Pat. 14, Ric. II. *apud* Tanner, *Bibl.* p. 166, note e.

> al maner of mynftralles,[1]
> And geftiours, that tellen tales
> Bothe of wepinge and of game.

That is, thofe who fang or recited adventures either tragic or comic, which excited either compaffion or laughter. They were accompanied by the moft renowned harpers, among which were Orpheus, Arion, Chiron, and the Briton Glafkerion.[2] Behind thefe were placed, " by many a thoufand time twelve," players on various inftruments of mufic. Among the trumpeters are named Joab, Virgil's Mifenus, and Theodamas.[3] About thefe pinnacles were alfo marfhalled the moft famous magicians, jugglers, witches, prophetefles, forcereffes, and profeffors of natural magic,[4] which ever exifted in ancient or modern times: fuch as Medea, Circe, Calliope, Hermes,[5] Limotheus, and Simon Magus.[6] At entering the hall he fees an infinite multitude of heralds, on the furcoats of whom were richly embroidered the armorial enfigns of the moft redoubted champions that ever tourneyed in Africa, Europe, or

---

[1] [Morris's *Chaucer*, v. 245, ver. 107.]

[2] Concerning this harper, fee Percy's Ballads.

[3] See alfo the *Marchaunt's Tale*, v. 1236, *feq.*

[4] See the *Frankelein's Tale*, where feveral feats are defcribed, as exhibited at a feaft, done by natural magic, a favourite fcience of the Arabians. Chaucer there calls it " An art which fotill tragetoris plaie," v. 2696. Of this more will be faid hereafter.

[5] None of the works of the firft Hermes Trifmegiftus now remain[s]. See Cornel. Agrip. *De Van. Scient.* cap. xlviii. The aftrological and other philofophical pieces under that name are fuppofititious. See Fabr. *Biblioth. Gr.* xii. 708. And *Chan. Yem. Tale*, v. 1455. Some of thefe pieces were publifhed under the fictitious names of Abel, Enoch, Abraham, Solomon, Saint Paul, and of many of the patriarchs and fathers. Cornel. Agripp. *De Van. Scient.* cap. xlv. who adds, that thefe *trifles* were followed by Alphonfus, king of Caftile, Robert Groffetefte, Bacon, and Apponus. He mentions Zabulus and Barnabas of Cyprus as famous writers in magic. See alfo Gower's *Confefs. Amant.* p. 134, b; 149, b; edit. 1554. In fpeaking of ancient authors who were known or celebrated in the middle ages, it may be remarked, that Macrobius was one. He is mentioned by Guill. de Lorris in the *Roman de la Rofe*, v. 9. "Ung aucteur qui ot nom *Macrobe.*" A line literally tranflated by Chaucer, " An author that hight *Macrobes*," v. 7. Chaucer quotes him in his *Dreme*, v. 284. In the *Nonnes Prieft's Tale*, v. 1238. In the *Affemblie of Foules*, v. 111, fee alfo *ibid.* v. 31. He wrote a comment on Tully's *Somnium Scipionis*, and in thefe paffages he is referred to on account of that piece. Petrarch, in a letter to Nicolas Sigeros, a learned Greek of Conftantinople, quotes Macrobius, as a Latin author of all others the moft familiar to Nicolas. It is to prove that Homer is the fountain of all invention. This is in 1354. *Famil. Let.* ix. 2. There is a manufcript of the firft and part of the fecond book of Macrobius, elegantly written, as it feems, in France, about the year 800. *MSS. Cotton. Vitell.* C. iii. fol. 138. M. Planudes, a Conftantinopolitan monk of the fourteenth century, is faid to have tranflated Macrobius into Greek. But fee Fabric. *Bibl. Gr.* x. 534. It is remarkable that in the above letter, Petrarch apologifes for calling Plato the Prince of Philofophers, after Cicero, Seneca, Apuleius, Plotinus, Saint Ambrofe, and Saint Auftin.

[6] Among thefe he mentions *Jugglers*, that is, in the prefent fenfe of the word, thofe who practifed legerdemain: a popular fcience in Chaucer's time. Thus in *Squ. T.* v. 239:

> " As jogelours pleyen at this feftes grete."

It was an appendage of the occult fciences ftudied and introduced into Europe by the Arabians.

Asia. The floor and roof of the hall were covered with thick plates of gold studded with the costliest gems. At the upper end, on a lofty shrine made of carbuncle, sat Fame. Her figure is like those in Virgil and Ovid. Above her, as if sustained on her shoulders, sat Alexander and Hercules. From the throne to the gates of the hall, ran a range of pillars with respective inscriptions. On the first pillar made of lead and iron,[1] stood Josephus, the Jewish historian, "That of the Jewis gestis told," with seven other writers on the same subject. On the second pillar, made of iron, and painted all over with the blood of tigers, stood Statius. On another higher than the rest stood Homer, Dares Phrygius, Livy,[2] Lollius, Guido di Columna, and Geoffrey of Monmouth, writers of the Trojan story. On a pillar of "tinnid iron clere," stood Virgil: and next him on a pillar of copper, appeared Ovid. The figure of Lucan was placed on a pillar of iron "wroght full sternly," accompanied by many Roman historians.[3] On a pillar of sulphur stood Claudian, so symbolised, because he wrote of Pluto and Proserpine:

> That bare up *than* the fame of helle;[4]
> Of Pluto, and of Proserpyne,
> That quene ys of the derke pyne.

The hall was filled with the writers of ancient tales and romances, whose subjects and names were too numerous to be recounted. In the mean time crowds from every nation and of every condition filled the hall, and each presented his claim to the queen. A messenger is dispatched to summon Eolus from his cave in Thrace; who is ordered to bring his two clarions called *Slander* and *Praise*, and his trumpeter Triton. The praises of each petitioner are then resounded, according to the partial or capricious appointment of Fame; and equal merits obtain very different success. There is much satire and humour in these requests and rewards, and in the disgraces and honours which are indiscriminately distributed by the queen, without discernment and by chance. The poet then enters the house or labyrinth of Rumour. It was built of sallow twigs, like a cage, and therefore admitted every sound. Its doors were also more numerous than leaves on the trees, and always stood open. These are romantic exaggerations of Ovid's inventions on the same subject. It was moreover sixty miles in length, and perpetually turning round. From this house, says the poet, issued tidings of

---

[1] In the composition of these pillars, Chaucer displays his chemical knowledge.

[2] Dares Phrygius and Livy are both cited in Chaucer's *Dreme*, v. 1070, 1084. Chaucer is fond of quoting Livy. He was also much admired by Petrarch, who, while at Paris, assisted in translating him into French. This circumstance might make Livy a favourite with Chaucer. See *Vie de Petrarque*, iii. p. 547.

[3] Was not this intended to characterise Lucan? Quintillian says of Lucan, "*Oratoribus* magis quam *poetis* annumerandus." *Instit. Orat.* L. x. c. 1.

[4] [Morris's *Chaucer*, v. 255, ver. 420.] Chaucer alludes to this poem of Claudian in the *Marchaunt's Tale*, where he calls Pluto, the king of "fayrie," ver. 1744.

every kind, like fountains and rivers from the sea. Its inhabitants, who were eternally employed in hearing or telling news, together with the rise of reports, and the formation of lies, are then humorously described: the company is chiefly composed of sailors, pilgrims, and pardoners. At length our author is awakened at seeing a venerable personage of great authority: and thus the Vision abruptly concludes.

Pope has imitated this piece with his usual elegance of diction and harmony of versification. But in the mean time, he has not only misrepresented the story, but marred the character of the poem. He has endeavoured to correct its extravagances by new refinements and additions of another cast: but he did not consider, that extravagances are essential to a poem of such a structure, and even constitute its beauties. An attempt to unite order and exactness of imagery with a subject formed on principles so professedly romantic and anomalous, is like giving Corinthian pillars to a Gothic palace. When I read Pope's elegant imitation of this piece, I think I am walking among the modern monuments unsuitably placed in Westminster Abbey.

SECTION XV.

NOTHING can be more ingeniously contrived than the occasion on which Chaucer's *Canterbury Tales* are supposed to be recited. A company of pilgrims, on their journey to visit the shrine of Thomas Becket at Canterbury, lodge at the Tabard Inn in Southwark. Although strangers to each other, they are assembled in one room at supper, as was then the custom; and agree, not only to travel together the next morning, but to relieve the fatigue of the journey by telling each a story.[1] Chaucer undoubtedly intended to imitate Boccaccio, whose *Decameron* was then the most popular of books, in writing a set of tales. But the circumstance invented by Boccaccio, as the cause which gave rise to his *Decameron*, or the relation of his hundred stories,[2] is by no means so happily conceived as that of Chaucer for a similar purpose. Boccaccio supposes, that when the plague began to abate at Florence, ten young persons of both sexes retired to a country house, two miles from the city, with a design of

---

[1] There is an inn at Burford in Oxfordshire, which accommodated pilgrims on their road to Saint Edward's shrine in the abbey of Gloucester. A long room, with a series of Gothic windows, still remains, which was their refectory. Leland mentions such another, *Itin*. ii. 70.

[2] It is remarkable that Boccaccio chose a Greek title, that is, Δεκαμερον, for his *Tales*. He has also given Greek names to the ladies and gentlemen who recite the tales. His *Eclogues* are full of Greek words. This was natural at the revival of the Greek language.

enjoying fresh air, and passing ten days agreeably. Their principal and established amusement, instead of playing at chess after dinner, was for each to tell a tale. One superiority which, among others, Chaucer's plan afforded above that of Boccaccio, was the opportunity of displaying a variety of striking and dramatic characters, which would not have easily met but on such an expedition;—a circumstance which also contributed to give a variety to the stories. And for a number of persons in their situation, so natural, so practicable, so pleasant, I add so rational, a mode of entertainment could not have been imagined.

The *Canterbury Tales* are unequal, and of various merit. Few perhaps, if any, of the stories are the invention of Chaucer. I have already spoken at large of the *Knight's Tale*, one of our author's noblest compositions.[1] That of the *Canterbury Tales*, which deserves the next place, as written in the higher strain of poetry, and the poem by which Milton describes and characterises Chaucer, is the *Squire's Tale*.[2] The imagination of this story consists in Arabian fiction engrafted on Gothic chivalry. Nor is this Arabian fiction purely the sport of arbitrary fancy: it is in great measure founded on Arabian learning. Cambuscan, a king of Tartary, celebrates his birth-day festival in the hall of his palace at Sarra with the most royal magnificence. In the midst of the solemnity, the guests are alarmed by a miraculous and unexpected spectacle: the minstrels cease on a sudden, and all the assembly is hushed in silence, surprise, and suspense.

> Whil that the kyng sit thus in his nobleye,[3]
> Herkyng his mynstrales her thinges pleye
> Byforn him atte boord deliciously,
> In atte halle dore al sodeynly
> Ther com a knight upon a steed of bras,
> And in his hond a brod myrour of glas;
> Upon his thomb he had of gold a ryng,
> And by his side a naked swerd hangyng:
> And up he rideth to the heyghe bord.
> In al the halle ne was ther spoke a word,
> For mervayl of this knight; him to byholde
> Ful besily they wayten yong and olde.

---

[1] The reader will excuse my irregularity in not considering it under the *Canterbury Tales*. I have here given the reason, which is my apology, in the text.

[2] [Le Chevalier de Chatelain finds the original of this tale in the old French romance of *Cléomadès*, in 19,000 lines, printed in 1866 by the Belgian Academy, written from Spanish and Moorish sources by Adam or Adénès Le Roy, King of the Minstrels of the Duke of Brabant, in the thirteenth century. The Chevalier printed a modern French verse sketch of the story of Cléomadès in 1858, and re-issued it in 1869 with a fresh preface, as a second edition. The French Romance has a wooden horse with springs in it, which is managed by " tournant les chevilles," (pegs, pins), and Chaucer's brass one is managed thus too : " Ye moote trille a pyn, stant in his ere." But here, and in the fact that the common people are, in both tales, astonished at the horses, ends the likeness of *Cléomadès* and the *Squire's Tale*.—F.]

[3] [Morris's Chaucer, ii. 357, ver. 69.] See a fine romantic story of a Comte de Macon who, while revelling in his hall with many knights, is suddenly alarmed by the entrance of a gigantic figure of a black man, mounted on a black steed. This

These presents were sent by the king of Arabia and India to Cambuscan in honour of his feast. The horse of brass, on the skilful movement and management of certain secret springs, transported his rider into the most distant region of the world in the space of twenty-four hours; for, as the rider chose, he could fly in the air with the swiftness of an eagle: and again, as occasion required, he could stand motionless in opposition to the strongest force, vanish on a sudden at command, and return at his master's call. The Mirror of Glass was endued with the power of shewing any future disasters which might happen to Cambuscan's kingdom, and discovered the most hidden machinations of treason. The Naked Sword could pierce armour deemed impenetrable,

> Were it as thikke as is a braunched ook.

And he who was wounded with it could never be healed, unless its possessor could be entreated to stroke the wound with its edge. The Ring was intended for Canace, Cambuscan's daughter, and while she bore it in her purse, or wore it on her thumb, enabled her to understand the language of every species of birds, and the virtues of every plant:

> And whan this knight thus had*de* his tale told,[1]
> He rit out of the halle, and doun he light.
> His steede, which that schon as sonne bright,
> Stant in the court as stille as eny stoon.
> This knight is to his chambre lad anoon,
> And is unarmed, and to mete i-sett.
> This presentz ben ful richely i-fett,
> This is to sayn, the swerd and the myrrour,
> And born anon unto the highe tour,
> With certein officers ordeynd therfore;
> And unto Canace the ryng is bore
> Solempnely, ther sche syt atte table.

I have mentioned, in another place, the favourite philosophical studies of the Arabians.[2] In this poem the nature of those studies is displayed, and their operations exemplified: and this consideration, added to the circumstances of Tartary being the scene of action, and Arabia the country from which these extraordinary presents are brought, induces me to believe this story to be [identical with one which was current at a very ancient date among] the Arabians. At least it is formed on their principles. Their sciences were tinctured with the warmth of their imaginations, and consisted in wonderful discoveries and mysterious inventions.

This idea of a horse of brass took its rise from their chemical knowledge and experiments in metals. The treatise of Jeber, a famous Arab chemist of the middle ages, called *Lapis Philosophorum*, contains many curious and useful processes concerning the nature of

---

terrible stranger, without receiving any obstruction from guards or gates, rides directly forward to the high table; and, with an imperious tone, orders the count to follow him, &c. Nic. Gillos, *Chron.* ann. 1120. See also *Obs. Fair Qu.* § v. p. 146.

[1] [Morris's *Chaucer*, ii. 360, ver. 160.]   [2] Diss. i. ii.

S. 15. *Ideas borrowed from the Arabian Philosophy.*

metals, their fusion, purification, and malleability, which still maintain a place in modern systems of that science.¹ The poets of romance, who deal in Arabian ideas, describe the Trojan horse as made of brass.² These sages pretended the power of giving life or speech to some of their compositions in metal. Bishop Grosseteste's speaking brazen head, sometimes attributed to [Roger] Bacon, has its foundation in Arabian philosophy.³ In the romance of *Valentine and Orson*, a brazen head fabricated by a necromancer in a magnificent chamber of the castle of Clerimond, declares to those two princes their royal parentage.⁴ We are told by William of Malmesbury that Pope Sylvester II. a profound mathematician who lived in the eleventh century, made a brazen head, which would speak when spoken to, and oracularly resolved many difficult questions.⁵ Albertus Magnus, who was also a profound adept in those sciences which were taught by the Arabian schools, is said to have framed a man of brass, which not only answered questions readily and truly, but was so loquacious, that Thomas Aquinas while a pupil of Albertus Magnus, and afterwards an Angelic doctor, knocked it in pieces as the disturber of his abstruse speculations. This was about the year 1240.⁶ Much in the same manner, the notion of our knight's horse being moved by means of a concealed engine corresponds with their pretences of producing preternatural effects, and their love of surprising by geometrical powers. Exactly in this notion, Rocail, a giant in some of the Arabian romances, is said to have built a palace, together with his own sepulchre, of most magnificent architecture and with singular artifice: in both of these he placed a great number of gigantic statues or images, figured of different metals by talismanic skill, which, in consequence of some occult machinery, performed actions of real life, and looked like living men.⁷ We must add that astronomy, which the Arabian philosophers studied with a singular enthusiasm, had no small share in the composition of this miraculous steed. For, says the poet,

---

¹ The Arabians call chemistry, as treating of minerals and metals, Simia; from Sim, a word signifying the veins of gold and silver in the mines. Herbelot, *Bibl. Orient.* p. 810, b. Hither, among many other things, we might refer Merlin's two dragons of gold finished with most exquisite workmanship, in Geoffrey of Monmouth, l. viii. c. 17. See also *ibid.* vii. c. 3, where Merlin prophesies that a brazen man on a brazen horse shall guard the gates of London.

² See Lydgate's *Troye Boke*, B. iv. c. 35. And Gower's *Conf. Amant.* B. i. f. 13, b. edit. 1554. " A horse of brasse thei lette do forge."

³ Gower, *Confess. Amant.* [ed. 1857, ii. 9.] L. iv. fol. lxiiii. a, edit. 1554.

" For of the grete clerk Grosteft
I rede how busy that he was
Upon the clergie an heved of bras
To forge and make it for to telle
Of suche thinges as befelle—"

⁴ Ch. xxviii. *seq.*

⁵ *De Gest. Reg. Angl.* lib. ii. cap. 10. Compare *Maj. Symbolor. Aureæ Mensæ*, lib. x. p. 453.

⁶ Delrio, *Disquis. Magic.* lib. i. cap. 4.

⁷ Herbelot, *Bibl. Orient.* v. *Rocail*, p. 717, a.

> He that it wrought cowthe *ful* many a gyn;[1]
> He waytede many a conftellacioun,
> Er he hadde do this operacioun.

Thus the buckler of the Arabian giant Ben Gian, as famous among the Orientals as that of Achilles among the Greeks, was fabricated by the powers of aftronomy;[2] and Pope Sylvefter's brazen head, juft mentioned, was prepared under the influence of certain conftellations.

Natural magic, improperly fo called, was likewife a favourite purfuit of the Arabians, by which they impofed falfe appearances on the fpectator. This was blended with their aftrology. Our author's *Frankelein's Tale* is entirely founded on the miracles of this art.

> For I am fiker that ther ben fciences,[3]
> By whiche men maken dyverfe apparences,
> Which as the fubtile tregetoures[4] pleyen.
> For ofte at feftes ha*v*e I herd feyen,
> That tregettoures, withinne an halle large,
> Han made in come water and a barge,
> And in the halle rowen up and doun.
> Som tyme hath femed *come* a grym leoun;
> Some tyme a caftel al of lym and fton.

Afterwards a magician in the fame poem fhews various fpecimens of his art in raifing fuch illufions: and by way of diverting King Aurelius before fupper, prefents before him parks and forefts filled with deer of vaft proportion, fome of which are killed with hounds and others with arrows. He then fhews the king a beautiful lady in a dance. At the clapping of the magician's hands all thefe deceptions difappear.[5] Thefe feats are faid to be performed by confultation of

---

[1] [Morris's Chaucer, ii. 358, ver. 120.] I do not precifely underftand the line immediately following.

" And knew ful many a feal and many a bond."

Seal may mean a talifinanic figil ufed in aftrology. Or the Hermetic feal ufed in chemiftry. Or, connected with *Bond*, may fignify contracts made with fpirits in chemical operations. But all thefe belong to the Arabian philofophy, and are alike to our purpofe. In the Arabian books now extant, are the alphabets out of which they formed Talifmans to draw down fpirits or angels. The Arabian word *Kimia* not only fignifies chemiftry, but a magical and fuperftitious fcience, by which they bound fpirits to their will and drew from them the information required. See Herbelot, *Dict. Orient.* p. 810, 1005. The curious and more inquifitive reader may confult Cornelius Agrippa, *De Vanit. Scient.* c. xliv.-vi.

[2] Many myfteries were concealed in the compofition of this fhield. It deftroyed all the charms and enchantments which either demons or giants could make by *goetic* or magic art. Herbelot, *ubi fupr.* v. *Gian.* p. 396, a.

[3] [Morris's *Chaucer*, iii. 14, ver. 411.]   [4] jugglers.

[5] But his moft capital performance is to remove an immenfe chain of rocks from the fea-fhore: this is done in fuch a manner, that for the fpace of one week "it femede that the rockes were aweye." *Ibid.* ver. 560. By the way, this tale appears to be a tranflation. He fays, "As thefe bokes me remembre." v. 507. And "From Gerounay to the mouth of Sayne." v. 486. The Garoune and Seine are rivers in France.

the ftars.[1] We frequently read in romances of illufive appearances framed by magicians,[2] which by the fame powers are made fuddenly to vanifh. To trace the matter home to its true fource, thefe fictions have their origin in a fcience which profeffedly made a confiderable part of the Arabian learning.[3] In the twelfth century the number of magical and aftrological Arabic books tranflated into Latin was prodigious.[4] Chaucer, in the fiction before us, fuppofes that fome of the guefts in Cambufcan's hall believed the Trojan horfe to be a temporary illufion, effected by the power of magic.[5]

> An apparence maad by fom magik,[6]
> As jogelours pleyen at this feftes grete.

In fpeaking of the metallurgy of the Arabians, I muft not omit the fublime imagination of Spenfer, or rather fome Britifh bard, who feigns that the magician Merlin intended to build a wall of brafs about Cairmardin (Carmarthen); but that being haftily called away by the Lady of the Lake, and flain by her perfidy, he has left his fiends ftill at work on this mighty ftructure round their brazen cauldrons, under a rock among the neighbouring woody cliffs of Dynevor, who dare not defift till their mafter returns. At this day, fays the poet, if you liften at a chink or cleft of the rock:

> Such ghaftly noyfe of yron chaines [7]
> And brafen Caudrons thou fhalt rombling heare,
> Which thoufand fprights with long enduring paines
> Doe toffe, that it will ftonn thy feeble braines;

---

[1] See *Frankel. Tale.* The Chriftians called this one of the diabolical arts of the Saracens or Arabians. And many of their own philofophers, who afterwards wrote on the fubject or performed experiments on its principles, were faid to deal with the devil. Witnefs our Bacon, &c. From Sir John Mandeville's *Travels* it appears, that thefe fciences were in high requeft in the court of the Cham of Tartary about the year 1340. He fays, that, at a great feftival, on one fide of the Emperor's table, he faw placed many philofophers fkilled in various fciences, fuch as aftronomy, necromancy, geometry, and pyromancy: that fome of thefe had before them aftrolabes of gold and precious ftones, others had horologes richly furnifhed with many other mathematical inftruments, &c. chap. lxxi. Sir John Mandeville began his travels into the Eaft, in 1322, and finifhed his book in 1364, chap. cix. See Johannes Sarifb. *Polycrat.* l. i. cap. xi. fol. 10, b.

[2] See what is faid of Spenfer's *Falfe Florimel, Obs. Spens.* § xi. p. 123.

[3] Herbelot mentions many oriental pieces, " Qui traittent de cette art pernicieux et defendu." *Dict. Orient.* v. Schr. Compare Agrippa, *ubi fupr.* cap. xlii. *feq.*

[4] " Irrepfit hac ætate etiam turba aftrologorum et magorum, ejus farinæ libris una cum aliis de Arabico in Latinum converfis." Conring. *Script Comment.* Sæc. xiii. cap. 3, p. 125. See alfo Herbelot, *Bibl. Orient.* v. *Ketab*, paffim.

[5] John of Salifbury fays, that magicians are thofe who, among other deceptions, " Rebus adimunt fpecies fuas." *Polycrat.* i. 10, fol. 10, b. Agrippa mentions one Pafetes a juggler, who " was wont to fhewe to ftrangers a very fumptuoufe banket, and when it pleafed him, to caufe it vanifhe awaye, al they which fate at the table being difapointed both of meate and drinke," &c. *Van. Scient.* cap. xlviii. p. 62, b. Engl. Tranfl. *ut. infr.* Du Halde mentions a Chinefe enchanter, who, when the Emperor was inconfolable for the lofs of his deceafed queen, caufed her image to appear before him. *Hift. Chin.* iii. § iv. See the deceptions of Hakem an Arabian juggler in Herbelot, in v. p. 412. See *fupr.* p. 229, 230.

[6] [Morris's *Chaucer*, ii. 361, ver. 210.]

[7] *Fairy Queen*, [lib. iii. c. 3, ft. 9-11, edit. Morris, p. 169.]

> And oftentimes great grones, and grievous ſtownds,
> When too huge toile and labour them conſtraines,
> And oftentimes loud ſtrokes and ringing ſowndes
> From under that deepe Rock moſt horribly rebowndes.
>
> The cauſe, ſome ſay, is this: A litle whyle
> Before that Merlin dyde, he did intend
> A BRASEN WALL in compas to compyle
> About Cairmardin, and did it commend
> Unto theſe Sprights to bring to perfeƈt end:
> During which worke the Lady of the Lake,
> Whom long he lov'd, for him in haſte did ſend;
> Who, thereby forſt his workemen to forſake,
> Them bownd till his retourne their labour not to ſlake.
>
> In the meane time, through that falſe Ladies traine,
> He was ſurpriſd, and buried under beare,
> Ne ever to his worke returnd againe;
> Nath'leſſe thoſe feends may not their work forbeare,
> So greatly his commandement they feare,
> But there doe toyle and traveile day and night,
> Untill that braſen wall they up doe reare—

This ſtory Spenſer borrowed from Giraldus Cambrenſis who, during his progreſs through Wales in the twelfth century, picked it up among other romantic traditions propagated by the Britiſh bards.[1] I have before pointed out the ſource from which the Britiſh bards received moſt of their extravagant fiƈtions.

Optics were likewiſe a branch of ſtudy which ſuited the natural genius of the Arabian philoſophers, and which they purſued with incredible delight. This ſcience was a part of the Ariſtotelic philoſophy which, as I have before obſerved, they refined and filled with a thouſand extravagances. Hence our ſtrange knight's *Mirror of Glaſs*, prepared on the moſt profound principles of art, and endued with preternatural qualities.

> And ſom of hem wondred on the mirrour,[2]
> That born was up into the maiſter tour,
> How men might in hit ſuche thinges ſe.
> Another anſwerd, and ſayd, it might*e* wel be
> Naturelly by compoſiciouns
> Of angels, and of heigh reflexiouns;
> And ſayde that in Rome was ſuch oon.
> They ſpeeke of Al*hazen* and Vitilyon,
> *And* Ariſtotle, that writen in her lyves
> Of queynte myrrours and proſpeƈtyves.

And again,

> This mirour eek, that I have in myn hond,[3]
> Hath ſuch a mighte, that men may in it ſee
> When ther ſchal falle eny adverſité
> Unto your regne," &c.

Alcen, or Alhazen, mentioned in theſe lines, an Arabic philoſopher, wrote ſeven books of perſpeƈtive, and flouriſhed about the

---

[1] See Girald. Cambrens. *Itin. Cambr.* i. c. 6; Holinſh. *Hiſt.* i. 129; and Camden's *Brit.* p. 734. Drayton has this fiƈtion, which he relates ſomewhat differently: *Polyolb.* lib. iv. p. 62, edit. 1613. Hence Bacon's wall of braſs about England.
[2] [Morris's *Chaucer*, ii. 361, ver. 217.]   [3] [*Ibid.* p. 359, ver. 124.]

eleventh century. Vitellio, formed on the same school, was likewise an eminent mathematician of the middle ages, and wrote ten books on *Perspective*. The Roman mirror here mentioned by Chaucer, as similar to this of the strange knight, is thus described by Gower:

> Whan Rome stood in noble plite,
> Virgile, which was tho parfite,
> A mirrour made of his clergie,[1]
> And sette it in the townes eye
> Of marbre on a piller without,
> That they by thritty mile about
> By day and eke also by night
> In that mirrour beholde might
> Her ennemies if any were.[2]

The Oriental writers relate that Giamschid, one of their kings, the Solomon of the Persians and their Alexander the Great, possessed among his inestimable treasures cups, globes, and mirrors, of metal, glass, and crystal, by means of which he and his people knew all natural as well as supernatural things. The title of an Arabian book, translated from the Persian, is, *The Mirrour which reflects the World*. There is this passage in an ancient Turkish poet: "When I am purified by the light of heaven my soul will become the mirror of the world, in which I shall discern all abstruse secrets." Monsieur Herbelot is of opinion, that the Orientals took these notions from the patriarch Joseph's cup of divination and Nestor's cup in Homer, on which all nature was symbolically represented.[3] Our great countryman Roger Bacon, in his *Opus Majus*, a work entirely formed on the Aristotelic and Arabian philosophy, describes a variety of Specula, and explains their construction and uses.[4] This is the most curious and extraordinary part of Bacon's book, which was written about the year 1270. Bacon's optic tube, with which he pretended to see future events, was famous in his age, and long afterwards, and chiefly contributed to give him the name of a magician.[5] This art, with others of the experimental kind, the philosophers of

---

[1] learning; philosophy. The same fiction is in Caxton's *Troye boke*. "Upon the pinnacle or top of the towre he made an ymage of copper and gave hym in his hande a looking-glasse, having such vertue, that if it happened that any shippes came to harme the citie suddenly, their army and their coming should appear in the said looking-glasse." B. ii. ch. xxii.

[2] *Confess. Amant.* l. v. [edit. 1857, ii. 195].

[3] Herbelot, *Dict. Oriental.* v. *Giam.* p. 392, col. 2. John of Salisbury mentions a species of diviners called Specularii, who predicted future events, and told various secrets, by consulting mirrors, and the surfaces of other polished reflecting substances. *Polycrat.* i. 12, p. 32, edit. 1595.

[4] Edit. Jebb, p. 253. Bacon, in one of his MSS. complains, that no person read lectures in Oxford *De Perspectivâ* before the year 1267. He adds that in the University of Paris, this science was quite unknown. *Epist. ad Opus Minus Clementi IV.* Et ibid. *Op. Min.* cap. ii. MSS. Bibl. Coll. Univ. Oxon. c. 20. In another he affirms that Julius Cæsar, before he invaded Britain, viewed our harbours and shores with a telescope from the Gallic coast. MSS. *Lib. De Perspectivis*. He accurately describes reading-glasses or spectacles, *Op. Maj.* p. 236. The Camera Obscura, I believe, is one of his discoveries.

[5] Wood, *Hist. Antiquit. Univ. Oxon.* i. 122.

those times were fond of adapting to the purposes of thaumaturgy; and there is much occult and chimerical speculation in the discoveries which Bacon affects to have made from optical experiments. He asserts (and I am obliged to cite the passage in his own mysterious expressions): "Omnia sciri per Perspectivam, quoniam omnes actiones rerum fiunt secundum specierum et virtutum multiplicationem ab agentibus hujus mundi in materias patientes," &c.[1] Spenser feigns, that the magician Merlin made a glassy globe, and presented it to King Ryence, which showed the approach of enemies, and discovered treasons.[2] This fiction, which exactly corresponds with Chaucer's Mirror, Spenser borrowed from some romance, perhaps of King Arthur, fraught with Oriental fancy. From the same sources came a like fiction of Camoens in the *Lusiad*,[3] where a globe is shown to Vasco de Gama, representing the universal fabric or system of the world, in which he sees future kingdoms and future events. The Spanish historians report an American tradition, but more probably invented by themselves, and built on the Saracen fables, in which they were so conversant. They pretend that some years before the Spaniards entered Mexico, the inhabitants caught a monstrous fowl, of unusual magnitude and shape, on the lake of Mexico. In the crown of the head of this wonderful bird, there was a mirror or plate of glass, in which the Mexicans saw their future invaders the Spaniards, and all the disasters which afterwards happened to their kingdom. These superstitions remained, even in the doctrines of philosophers, long after the darker ages. Cornelius Agrippa, a learned physician of Cologne about the year 1520, and author of a famous book on the Vanity of the Sciences, mentions a species of mirror which exhibited the form of persons absent, at command.[4] In one of these he is said to have shown to the poetical Earl of Surrey the image of his mistress, the beautiful Geraldine, sick and reposing on a couch.[5] Nearly allied to this was the infatuation of seeing things in a beryl, which was very popular in the reign of James I., and is alluded to by Shakespeare. [Aubrey, in his *Miscellanies*, describes the beryl, and a drawing of one accompanies the text. This still remains an article of practice and belief.]

The Arabians were also famous for other machineries of glass, in which their chemistry was more immediately concerned. The philosophers of their school invented a story of a magical steel-glass, placed by Ptolemy on the summit of a lofty pillar near the city of

---

[1] *Op. Min.* MSS. *ut supr.*   [2] *Fairy Queen*, iii. ii. 21.   [3] Cant. x.

[4] It is diverting in this book to observe the infancy of experimental philosophy, and their want of knowing how to use or apply the mechanical arts which they were even actually possessed of. Agrippa calls the inventor of magnifying glasses, "without doubte the beginner of all dishonestie." He mentions various sorts of diminishing, burning, reflecting, and multiplying glasses, with some others. At length this profound thinker closes the chapter with this sage reflection, "All these thinges are vaine and superfluous, and invented to no other end but for pompe and idle pleasure!" Chap. xxvi. p. 36. A translation by James Sandford [appeared in 1569].

[5] Drayton's *Heroical Epist.* p. 87, b. edit. 1598.

Alexandria, for burning ſhips at a diſtance. The Arabians called this pillar *Hemadeſlaeor*, or the Pillar of the Arabians.[1] I think it is mentioned by Sandys. Roger Bacon has left a tract on the formation of burning-glaſſes:[2] and he relates that the firſt burning-glaſs which he conſtructed coſt him ſixty pounds of Pariſian money.[3] Ptolemy, who ſeems to have been confounded with Ptolemy the Egyptian aſtrologer and geographer, was famous among the Eaſtern writers and their followers for his ſkill in operations of glaſs. Spenſer mentions a miraculous tower of glaſs built by Ptolemy, which concealed his miſtreſs the Egyptian Phao, while the inviſible inhabitant viewed all the world from every part of it.

> Great Ptolmœe it for his lemans ſake[4]
> Ybuilded all of glaſſe by Magicke powre,
> And alſo it impregnable did make.

But this magical fortreſs, although impregnable, was eaſily broken in pieces at one ſtroke by the builder, when his miſtreſs ceaſed to love. One of Boiardo's extravagances is a prodigious wall of glaſs built by ſome magician in Africa, which obviouſly betrays its foundation in Arabian fable and Arabian philoſophy.[5]

The Naked Sword, another of the gifts preſented by the ſtrange knight to Cambuſcan, endued with medical virtues, and ſo hard as to pierce the moſt ſolid armour, is likewiſe an Arabian idea. It was ſuggeſted by their ſkill in medicine, by which they affected to communicate healing qualities to various ſubſtances,[6] and by their knowledge of tempering iron and hardening all kinds of metal.[7] It

---

[1] The ſame fablers have adapted a ſimilar fiction to Hercules: that he erected pillars at Cape Finiſterre, on which he raiſed magical looking-glaſſes. In the *Seven Wiſe Maſters*, at the ſiege of Hur in Perſia, certain philoſophers terrified the enemy by a device of placing a habit (ſays an old Engliſh tranſlation) "of a giant-like proportion on a tower, and covering it with burning-glaſſes, looking-glaſſes of criſtall, and other glaſſes of ſeveral colours, wrought together in a marvellous order," &c. ch. xvii. p. 182, edit. 1674. The Conſtantinopolitan Greeks poſſeſſed theſe arts in common with the Arabians. See Moriſotus, ii. 3, who ſays that, in the year 751, they ſet fire to the Saracen fleet before Conſtantinople by means of burning-glaſſes.

[2] MSS. Bibl. Bodl. Digb. 183, and Arch. A. 149. But I think it was printed at Frankfort, 1614, 4to.

[3] Twenty pounds ſterling. *Compend. Stud. Theol.* c. i. p. 5, MS.

[4] *Fairy Queen*, iii. [c. 2, ſt. 20, edit. Morris].

[5] Hither we might alſo refer Chaucer's *Houſe of Fame*, which is built of glaſs, and Lydgate's *Temple of Glaſs*. It is ſaid in ſome romances written about the time of the Cruſades, that the city of Damaſcus was walled with glaſs. See Hall's *Satires*, &c. b. iv. s. 6, written [before] 1597:

> "Or of Damaſcus magicke wall of glaſſe,
> Or Solomon his ſweating piles of braſſe," &c.

[6] The notion, mentioned before, that every ſtone of Stone-henge was waſhed with juices of herbs in Africa, and tinctured with healing powers, is a piece of the ſame philoſophy.

[7] Montfaucon cites a Greek chemiſt of the dark ages, "Chriſtiani Labyrinthus Salomonis, de temperando ferro, conficiendo cryſtallo, et de aliis naturæ arcanis." *Palæogr. Gr.* p. 375.

is the classical spear of Peleus, perhaps originally fabricated in the same regions of fancy:

> And other folk have wondred on the swerd,[1]
> That wolde passe thorughout every thing;
> And fel in speche of Thelophus the kyng,
> And of Achilles for his queynte spere,
> For he couthe with hit bothe hele and dere,[2]
> Right in such wyse as men maye with the swerd,
> Of which right now ye have your-selven herd.
> They speken of sondry hardyng of metal,
> And speken of medicines therwithal,
> And how and whan it schulde harded be, &c.

The sword which Berni, in the *Orlando Innamorato*, gives to the hero Ruggiero is tempered by much the same sort of magic:

> Quel brando con tal tempra fabbricato,
> Che taglia incanto, ed ogni fatatura.[3]

So also his continuator Ariosto:

> Non vale incanto, ov'elle mette il taglio.[4]

And the notion that this weapon could resist all incantations is like the fiction above mentioned of the buckler of the Arabian giant Ben Gian, which baffled the force of charms and enchantments made by giants or demons.[5] Spenser has a sword endued with the same efficacy, the metal of which the magician Merlin mixed with the juice of meadow-wort, that it might be proof against enchantment; and afterwards, having forged the blade in the flames of Etna, he gave it hidden virtue by dipping it seven times in the bitter waters of Styx.[6] From the same origin is also the golden lance of Berni, which Galafron, King of Cathaia, father of the beautiful Angelica and the invincible champion Argalia, procured for his son by the help of a magician. This lance was of such irresistible power, that it unhorsed a knight the instant he was touched with its point.

> e una lancia d'oro
> Fatto con arte, e con sottil lavoro.
> E quella lancia di natura tale,
> Che resister non puossi alla sua spinta;
> Forza, o destrezza contra lei non vale,
> Convien che l'una, e l'altra resti vinta:
> Incanto, a cui non è nel Mondo eguale,
> L'ha di tanta possanza intorno cinta,
> Che nè il Conte di Brava, nè Rinaldo,
> Nè il Mondo al colpo suo starebbe saldo.[7]

Britomart in Spenser is armed with the same enchanted spear, which was made by Bladud, an ancient British king skilled in magic.[8]

---

[1] [Morris's *Chaucer*, ii. 362, ver. 228.]
[2] hurt; wound.   [3] *Orl. Innam.* ii. 17, st. 13.   [4] *Orl. Fur.* xii. 83.
[5] [In 1694 was printed the *History of Amadis of Greece, son of Lisuart of Greece, and the fair Onoloria of Trebisond*. This worthy is called the Knight of the Burning Sword.] See *Don Quixote*, B. iii. ch. iv.
[6] *Fairy Queen*, ii. viii. 20. See also Ariost. xix. 84.
[7] [Berni's] *Orl. Innam.* i. i. [43-4]. See also i. ii. st. 20, &c. And Ariosto, viii. 17, xviii. 118, xxiii. 15.
[8] *Fairy Queen*, iii. 3, 60, iv. 6, 6, iii. 1, 4.

Magic Rings.

The ring, a gift to the king's daughter Canace, which taught the language of birds, is also quite in the style of some others of the occult sciences of these inventive philosophers;[1] and it is the fashion of the Oriental fabulists to give language to brutes in general. But to understand the language of birds was peculiarly one of the boasted sciences of the Arabians, who pretend that many of their countrymen have been skilled in the knowledge of the language of birds ever since the time of King Solomon. Their writers relate that Balkis, the Queen of Sheba or Saba, had a bird called *Hudhud*, that is, a lapwing, which she dispatched to King Solomon on various occasions, and that this trusty bird was the messenger of their amours. We are told that Solomon having been secretly informed by this winged confidant that Balkis intended to honour him with a grand embassy, enclosed a spacious square with a wall of gold and silver bricks, in which he ranged his numerous troops and attendants in order to receive the ambassadors, who were astonished at the suddenness of these splendid and unexpected preparations.[2] Herbelot tells a curious story of an Arab feeding his camels in a solitary wilderness, who was accosted for a draught of water by Alhejaj, a famous Arabian commander, who had been separated from his retinue in hunting. While they were talking together, a bird flew over their heads, making at the same time an unusual sort of noise, which the camel-feeder hearing, looked steadfastly on Alhejaj, and demanded who he was. Alhejaj, not choosing to return him a direct answer, desired to know the reason of that question. "Because," replied the camel-feeder, "this bird assured me that a company of people is coming this way, and that you are the chief of them." While he was speaking, Alhejaj's attendants arrived.[3]

This wonderful ring also imparted to the wearer a knowledge of the qualities of plants, which formed an important part of the Arabian philosophy.[4]

> The vertu of this ryng, if ye wol heere,[5]
> Is this, that who-so luſt it for to were
> Upon hir thomb, or in hir purs to bere,
> Ther is no foul that fleeth under the heven,
> That ſche ne ſchal underſtonden his ſteven,[6]
> And know his menyng openly and pleyn,
> And anſwer him in his langage ayeyn;
> And every gras that groweth upon roote

---

[1] Rings are a frequent implement in romantic enchantment. Among a thousand instances, see *Orland. Innam.* i. 14, where the palace and gardens of Dragontina vanish at Angelica's ring of virtue.

[2] *Dict. Oriental.* v. Balkis, p. 182. Mahomet believed this foolish story, at least thought it fit for a popular book, and has therefore inserted it in the Alcoran. See Grey's note in *Hudibras*, part i. cant. i. v. 547.

[3] Herbel. *ubi supr.* v. *Hegiage Ebn Yusef Al Thakefi.* p. 442. This Arabian commander was of the eighth century. In the *Seven Wise Masters* one of the tales is founded on the language of birds, ch. xvi.

[4] See what is said of this in the *Dissertations*.

[5] [Morris's *Chaucer*, ii. 359, ver. 138.]   [6] [voice.]

Sche fchal eek know*e*, to whom it wol do boote,
Al be his woundes never fo deep and wyde.

Every reader of tafte and imagination muft regret that, inftead of our author's tedious detail of the quaint effects of Canace's ring, in which a falcon relates her amours, and talks familiarly of Troilus, Paris, and Jafon, the notable achievements we may fuppofe to have been performed by the affiftance of the horfe of brafs are either loft, or that this part of the ftory, by far the moft interefting, was never written. After the ftrange knight has explained to Cambufcan the management of this magical courfer, he vanifhes on a fudden, and we hear no more of him.

> And after fouper goth this noble kyng [1]
> To fee this hors of bras, with al his route
> Of lordes and of ladyes him aboute.
> Swich wondryng was ther on this hors of bras,[2]
> That fethe*n* this grete fiege of Troye was,
> Ther as men wondred on an hors alfo,
> Ne was ther fuch a wondryng as was tho.
> But fynally the kyng afked*e* the knight
> The vertu of this courfer, and the might,
> And prayd him tellen of his governaunce.
> The hors anoon gan for to trippe and daunce,
> Whan *that* the knight leyd hand upon his rayne,
> * * * * *
> Enformed when the kyng was of the knight,
> And hadd*e* conceyved in his wit aright
> The maner and the forme *of* al this thing,
> Ful glad and blith, this noble doughty kyng
> Repeyryng to his revel, as biforn,
> The bridel is unto the tour i-born,[3]
> And kept among his jewels leef and deere;
> The hors vanyfcht, I not in what manere.

---

[1] [Morris's *Chaucer*, ii. 364, ver. 294.]

[2] Cervantes mentions a horfe of wood which, like this of Chaucer, on turning a pin in his forehead, carried his rider through the air. [A fimilar fiction occurs in the *Arabian Nights' Entertainments*, and muft be in the recollection of every reader.] This horfe, Cervantes adds, was made by Merlin for Peter of Provence; with it that valorous knight carried off the fair Magalona. The reader fees the correfpondence with the fiction of Chaucer's horfe, and will refer it to the fame original. See *Don Quixote*, B. iii. ch. 8. We have the fame thing in *Valentine and Orfon*, ch. xxxi. [The romance alluded to by Cervantes is entitled "La Hiftoria de la linda Magalona hija del rey de Napoles y de Pierres de Provença," printed at Seville 1533, and is a tranflation from a much more ancient and very celebrated French romance under a fimilar title.—*Ritfon*. The French romance is confeffedly but a tranflation: "Ordonnée en ceftui languaige . . . et fut mis en ceftui languaige l'an mil ccccclvii." A Provençal romance on this fubject, doubtleffly the original, was written by Bernard de Treviez, a canon of Maguelone, before the clofe of the twelfth century. See Raynouard, *Poefies des Troubadours*, vol. ii. p. 317. On the authority of Gariel, *Idee de la ville de Montpelier*, Petrarch is ftated to have corrected and embellifhed this romance.—*Price*. Of this extremely popular book there were numerous editions in French and Spanifh, and there is one in German. See Brunet, laft edit. iv. 643-8.]

[3] The bridel of the enchanted horfe is carried into the tower, which was the treafury of Cambufcan's caftle, to be kept among the jewels. Thus when King Richard I. in a crufade, took Cyprus, among the treafures in the caftles are recited

By such inventions we are willing to be deceived. These are the triumphs of deception over truth:

> Magnanima menſogna, hor quando è al vero
> Si bello, che ſi poſſa à te preporre ?

The *Clerke of Oxenfordes Tale*, or the ſtory of Patient Griſelda, is the next of Chaucer's Tales in the ſerious ſtyle, which deſerves mention. The Clerk declares in his Prologue, that he learned this tale of Petrarch[1] at Padua. But it was the invention of Boccaccio, and is the laſt in his *Decameron*.[2] Petrarch, although moſt intimately connected with Boccaccio for near thirty years, never had ſeen the *Decameron*, till juſt before his death. It accidentally fell into his hands, while he reſided at Arqua, between Venice and Padua, in 1374. The tale of Griſelda ſtruck him more than any:—ſo much, that he got it by heart to relate it to his friends at Padua. Finding that it was the moſt popular of all Boccaccio's tales, for the benefit of thoſe who did not underſtand Italian, and to ſpread its circulation, he tranſlated it into Latin with ſome alterations. Petrarch relates this in a letter to Boccaccio: and adds that, on ſhowing the tranſlation to one of his Paduan friends, the latter, touched with the tenderneſs of the ſtory, burſt into ſuch frequent and violent fits of tears, that he could not read to the end. In the ſame letter he ſays that a Veroneſe, having heard of the Paduan's exquiſiteneſs of feeling on this occaſion, reſolved to try the experiment. He read the whole aloud from the beginning to the end, without the leaſt change of voice or countenance; but on returning the book to Petrarch confeſſed that it was an affecting ſtory: "I ſhould have wept," added he, "like the Paduan, had I thought the ſtory true. But the whole is a manifeſt fiction. There never was, nor ever will be, ſuch a wife as Griſelda."[3] Chaucer, as our Clerk's declaration in the Prologue ſeems to imply, received this tale from Petrarch, and not from Boccaccio: and I am inclined to think, that he did not take it from Petrarch's Latin tranſlation, but that he was one of thoſe friends to whom Petrarch uſed to relate it at Padua. This too ſeems ſufficiently pointed out in the words of the Prologue:

---

precious ſtones and golden cups, together with "*Sellis aureis* frenis *et calcaribus.*" Vineſauf, *Iter. Hieroſol.* cap. xli. p. 328. *Vet. Script. Angl.* tom. ii.

[1] [Morris's *Chaucer*, ii. 279. Mr. Thomas Wright ſtates in his ed. of the *Cant. Tales*, that Chaucer tranſlates his *Clerk's Tale* "cloſely from Petrarch's Latin Romance *De Obedientiâ et fide Uxoriâ Mythologia.*"—F.]

[2] Giorn. x. Nov. 10. Dryden, in the ſuperficial but lively Preface to his *Fables* ſays, "The Tale of Griſilde was the invention of Petrarch: by him ſent to Boccace, from whom it came to Chaucer."

It may be doubted whether Boccaccio invented the ſtory of Griſelda. For, as Tyrwhitt obſerves, it appears by a Letter of Petrarch to Boccaccio, pp. 540-7, edit. Baſil. 1581, *Opp. Petrarch*, ſent with his Latin tranſlation, in 1373, that Petrarch had heard the ſtory with pleaſure, many years before he ſaw the *Decameron*, vol. iv. p. 157.

[3] *Vie de Petrarque*, iii. 797.

I wil yow telle a tale, which that I[1]
Lerned at Padowe of a worthy clerk,
* * * * *
Fraunces Petrark, the laureat poete,
Highte this clerk, whos rethorique fwete
Enlumynd al Ytail of poetrie.

Chaucer's tale is also much longer, and more circumstantial, than Boccaccio's. Petrarch's Latin translation from Boccaccio [has been printed more than once].[2] It is in the royal library at Paris, in that of Magdalen College at Oxford, [among Laud's MSS. in the Bodleian],[3] and in Bennet College library.[4]

The story soon became so popular in France, that the comedians of Paris represented a mystery in French verse entitled *Le Mystere de Griselidis Marquis de Saluces*, in the year 1393.[5] [Before, or in the same year, the French prose version in *Le Ménagier de Paris* was composed, and there is an entirely different version in the Imperial Library.[6]] Lydgate, almost Chaucer's cotemporary, in his poem entitled the *Temple of Glass*,[7] among the celebrated lovers painted on the walls of the temple,[8] mentions Dido, Medea and Jason,

---

[1] [Morris's Chaucer, ii. 278, ver. 26]. Afterwards Petrarch is mentioned as dead. He died of an apoplexy, Jul. 18, 1374. See ver. 36.

[2] [See Brunet, last edit. iv. 569-71, for a tolerably copious account of the editions of this tract in Latin, French, and German. Also for the *Epistola in Waltherum*.] Among the royal MSS. in the British Museum, there is, "Fr. Petrarchæ super Historiam Walterii Marchionis et Griseldis uxoris ejus." 8. B. vi. 17.

[3] MS. 177, 10, fol. 76; 275, 14, fol. 163. Again, ibid. 458, 3, with the date 1476, I suppose, from the scribe.

[4] MSS. Laud, G. 80.

[5] [This piece was printed at Paris about 1550; it has been reprinted in facsimile from the (supposed unique) copy in the Bibl. Imperiale. See Brunet, iii. 1968-9 (last edit.) The earliest French] theatre is that of Saint Maur, and its commencement is placed in the year 1398. Afterwards Apostolo Zeno wrote a theatrical piece on this subject in Italy. I need not mention that it is to this day represented in England, on a stage of the lowest species, and of the highest antiquity: I mean at a puppet-show. The French have this story in their *Parement des dames*. See *Mem. Lit.* tom. ii. p. 743, 4to.

[6] [Catal. No. 7999, edit. Paulin Paris.]

[7] And in a Balade, translated by Lydgate from the Latin, "Grisildes humble patience" is recorded. Urr. Ch. p. 550, ver. 108.

[8] There is a more curious mixture in [Gower's] *Balade to king Henry IV.*, where Alexander, Hector, Julius Cæsar, Judas Maccabeus, David, Joshua, Charlemagne, Godfrey of Boulogne, and King Arthur, are [associated as the Nine Worthies]. Ver. 281, *seq*. But it is to be observed, that the French had a metrical romance called *Judas Macchabée*, begun by Gualtier de Belleperche, before 1240. It was finished a few years afterwards by Pierros du Reiz. Fauch. p. 197. See also Lydgate, [*apud*] Urr. Chauc. p. 550, ver. 89. Sainte Palaye has given us an extract of an old Provençal poem in which, among heroes of love and gallantry, are enumerated Paris, Sir Tristram, Ivaine the inventor of gloves and other articles of elegance in dress, Apollonius of Tyre, and King Arthur. *Mem. Chev.* (Extr. de Poes. Prov.) ii. p. 154. In a French romance, *Le livre de cuer d'amour espris*, written 1457, the author introduces the blazoning of the arms of several celebrated lovers: among which are King David, Nero, Mark Antony, Theseus, Hercules, Eneas, Sir Lancelot, Sir Tristram, Arthur duke of Brittany, Gaston de Foix, many French dukes, &c. *Mem. Lit.* viii. p. 592, edit. 4to. The Chevalier Bayard, who

Penelope, Alceſtis, Patient Griſelda, Bel Iſoulde and Sir Triſtram,[1] Pyramus and Thiſbe, Theſeus, Lucretia, Canace, Palamon and Emilia.[2]

The pathos of this poem, which is indeed exquiſite, chiefly conſiſts in invention of incidents and the contrivance of the ſtory, which cannot conveniently be developed in this place; and it will be impoſſible to give any idea of its eſſential excellence by exhibiting detached parts. The verſification is equal to the reſt of our author's poetry.

SECTION XVI.

THE *Tale of the Nonnes Prieſt* is perhaps a ſtory of Engliſh growth. The ſtory of the cock and the fox is evidently borrowed from a collection of Æſopean and other fables, written by Marie [de France[3]], whoſe *Lays* [have been publiſhed.] Beſide the abſolute reſemblance, it appears ſtill more probable that Chaucer copied from Marie, becauſe no ſuch fable is to be found either in the Greek *Æſop*, or in any of the Latin Æſopean compilations of the dark ages.[4] All the manuſcripts of Marie's fables in the Britiſh Muſeum prove, that ſhe tranſlated her work " *de l'Anglois en Roman.*" Probably her Engliſh original was Alfred's Anglo-Saxon verſion of Æſop moderniſed, and ſtill bearing his name. She profeſſes to follow the verſion of a king who, in the beſt of the Harleian copies, is called *Li reis Alured.*[5] She appears, from paſſages in her *Lais*, to have underſtood Engliſh.[6] I will give her Epilogue to the Fables:[7]

> Al finement de ceſt eſcrit
> Qu'en romanz ai treite e dit
> Me numerai pour remembraunce
> Marie ai nun ſui de France
> Pur cel eſtre que clerc pluſur
> Prendreient ſur eus mun labeur
> Ne voit que nul ſur li ſa die
> Eil feit que fol que ſei ublie
> Pur amur le cunte Wllame

---

died about the year 1524, is compared to Scipio, Hannibal, Theſeus, King David, Samſon, Judas Maccabeus, Orlando, Godfrey of Boulogne, and Monſieur de Paliſſe, marſhal of France. [*Les geſtes enſemble la vie du preulx cheualier Bayard*, &c., printed in 1525.]

[1] From *Mort d'Arthur.* They are mentioned in Chaucer's *Aſſemble of Fowles*, ver. 290. See alſo *Compl. Bl. Kn.* ver. 367.
[2] MSS. Bibl. Bodl. (Fairfax 16).
[3] [By M. Roquefort, 1820, 2 vols. 8vo. Dr. Mall is preparing a new edition of Marie's *Lais* for 1871, with a much improved text.]
[4] [See MSS. Harl. 978, f. 76.]   [5] [*Ibid.* 978, *ſupr. citat.*]
[6] See Chaucer's *Canterb. Tales*, vol. iv. p. 179 [edit. Tyrwhitt].
[7] MSS. James, viii. p. 23, Bibl. Bod.

> Le plus vaillant de nul realme
> M'entremis de cefte livre feire
> E des Engleis en romanz treire
> Efop apelum ceft livre
> Quil tranflata e fift efcrire
> Del Gru en Latin le turna
> Le Reiz Alurez que mut lama
> Le tranflata puis en Engleis
> E jeo lai rimee en Franceis
> Si cum jeo poi plus proprement
> Ore pri a dieu omnipotent, &c.

The figment of Dan Burnell's Afs is taken from a Latin poem entitled *Speculum Stultorum*,[1] written by Nigellus Wirecker [or Willhelmus Vigellus], monk and precentor of Canterbury cathedral and a profound theologift, who flourifhed about the year 1200.[2] The narrative of the two pilgrims is borrowed from Valerius Maximus.[3] It is alfo related by Cicero, a lefs known and a lefs favourite author.[4] There is much humour in the defcription of the prodigious confufion which happened in the farm-yard after the fox had conveyed away the cock:

> and after him thay ran*ne*,[5]
> And eek with ftaves many another man*ne*;
> Ran Colle our dogge, and Talbot, and Garlond,[6]
> And Malkyn, with a diftaf in hir hond;
> Ran cow and calf, and eek the verray hogges
> . . . . .
> The dokes criden as men wold hem quelle;[7]
> The gees for fere flowen over the trees;
> Out of the hyves cam the fwarm of bees.

Even Jack Straw's infurrection, a recent tranfaction, was not attended with fo much noife and difturbance:

> So hidous was the noyfe, a *benedicite!*[8]
> Certes *he* Jakke Straw, and his meyné,
> Ne maden fchoutes never half fo fchrille, &c.

The importance and affectation of fagacity with which Dame Partlett communicates her medical advice, and difplays her knowledge in phyfic, is a ridicule on the ftate of medicine and its profeffors.

In another ftrain, the cock is thus beautifully defcribed, and not without fome ftriking and picturefque allufions to the manners of the times:

---

[1] ver. 1427.
[2] [The name of the author is varioufly given, and in fome of the later impreffions the title of the work is: *Liber qui intitulatur Brunellus in fpeculo Stultorum*, &c. See Brunet, laft edit. v. 1215. The earlieft edition appears to be that *fine ullâ notâ*, folio (Cologne, between 1471 and 1478).] It is a common MS. Burnell is a nick-name for Balaam's afs in the *Chefter Whitfun Plays.* MSS. Harl. 2013.
[3] ver. 1100.   [4] See *Val. Max.* i. 7. And *Cic. de Divinat.* i. 27.
[5] [Morris's *Chaucer*, iii. 246, ver. 561.]   [6] names of dogs.   [7] kill.
[8] *Ibid.* This is a proof that the *Canterbury Tales* were not written till after the year 1381.

> a cok, hight Chaunteclere,[1]
> In al the lond of crowyng was noon his peere.
> His vois was merier than the mery orgon,[2]
> On maſſe dayes that in the chirche goon;
> Wel ſikerer[3] was his crowyng in his logge,[4]
> Than is a clok, or an abbay orologge.
>   *   *   *
> His comb was redder than the fyne coral,
> And batayld,[5] as it were a caſtel wal.
> His bile was blak, and as the geet it ſchon;
> Lik aſur were his legges, and his ton;[6]
> His nayles whitter than the lily flour,
> And lik the burniſcht gold was his colour.

In this poem the fox is compared to the three arch-traitors Judas Iſcariot, Virgil's Sinon, and Ganilion who betrayed the Chriſtian army under Charlemagne to the Saracens, and is mentioned by Archbiſhop Turpin.[7] Here alſo are cited, as writers of high note or authority, Cato, Phyſiologus or [Florinus] the elder, Boethius on muſic, the author of the legend of the life of Saint Kenelm, Joſephus, the hiſtorian of Sir Lancelot du Lak, Saint Auſtin, [Arch]biſhop Bradwardine, Geoffrey Vineſauf (who wrote a monody in Latin verſe on the death of King Richard I.), Eccleſiaſtes, Virgil and Macrobius.

Our author's *January and May*, or the *Merchant's Tale*, ſeems to be an old Lombard ſtory. But many paſſages in it are evidently taken from the *Polycraticon* of John of Saliſbury;[8] and by the way, about forty verſes belonging to this argument are tranſlated from the ſame chapter of the *Polycraticon*, in the *Wife of Bath's Prologue*.[9] In the mean time it is not improbable, that this tale might have originally been Oriental. A Perſian tale has been publiſhed which it extremely

---

[1] [Morris's *Chaucer*, iii. 230, ver. 29.]   [2] organ.   [3] [ſurer.—*Ritſon*.]
[4] pen; yard.   [5] embattelled.   [6] toes.
[7] ver. 407. See alſo *Monk. T.* ver. 399.
[8] "De moleſtiis et oneribus conjugiorum ſecundum Hieronymum et alios phi-loſophos. Et de pernicie libidinis. Et de mulieris Epheſinæ et ſimilium fide." L. iii. c. 11, fol. 193, b. edit. 1513.
[9] Mention is made in this Prologue of St. Jerom and Theophraſt, on that ſub-ject, ver. 671, 674. The author of the *Polycraticon* quotes Theophraſtus from Jerom, viz. "Fertur auctore *Hieronimo* aureolus *Theophraſti* libellus de non ducenda uxore," fol. 194, a. Chaucer likewiſe, on this occaſion, cites *Valerie*, ver. 671. This is not the favorite hiſtorian of the middle ages, Valerius Maximus. It is a book written under the aſſumed name of Valerius, entitled *Valerius ad Ruſinum de non ducenda uxore*. This piece is in the Bodleian library with a large gloſs. MSS. Digb. 166, ii. 147. [It is a common MS. and is one of the productions aſcribed to Walter Mapes. See Wright's edit. of Mapes, 1841. The author] perhaps adopted this name, becauſe one Valerius had written a treatiſe on the ſame ſubject, inſerted in St. Jerom's works. Some copies of this Prologue, inſtead of " Valerie and *Theophraſt*," read *Paraphraſt*. If that be the true reading, which I do not believe, Chaucer alludes to the gloſs above mentioned. *Helowis*, cited juſt after-wards, is the celebrated Eloiſa. Trottula is mentioned, ver. 677. Among the MSS. of Merton College in Oxford, is, "Trottula Mulier Salernitana de paſſionibus mulierum." There is alſo extant, "Trottula, ſeu potius Erotis medici muliebrium liber." Baſil. 1586, 4to. See alſo Montfauc. *Catal. MSS.* p. 385. And Fabric. *Bibl. Gr.* xiii. p. 439.

resembles;[1] and it has much of the allegory of an Eastern apologue.

The following description of the wedding-feast of January and May is conceived and expressed with a distinguished degree of poetical elegance:

> Thus ben thay weddid with folempnité;[2]
> And atte feft fittith he and fche
> With othir worthy folk upon the deys.[3]
> Al ful of joy and blis is that paleys,
> And ful of inftrumentz, and of vitaile,
> The mofte deintevous of al Ytaile.
> Biforn hem ftood fuch inftruments of foun,
> That Orpheus, ne of Thebes Amphioun,
> Ne maden never fuch a melodye.
> At every cours ther cam loud menftralcye,
> That never tromped[4] Joab for to heere,
> Ne he Theodomas yit half fo cleere
> At Thebes, whan the cite was in doute.[5]
> Bachus the wyn hem fchenchith[6] al aboute,
> And Venus laughith upon every wight,
> (For January was bycome hir knight,
> And wolde bothe affayen his corrage
> In liberté and eek in mariage)
> And with hir fuyrbrond in hir hond aboute
> Daunceth bifore the bryde and al the route.

---

[1] [Tales tranflated from the Perfian (by Alex. Dow), 1768,] ch. xv. p. 252.

The ludicrous adventure of the Pear Tree, in *January and May*, is taken from a collection of Fables in Latin elegiacs, written by one Adolphus in the year 1315. Leyfer. *Hift. Poet. Med. Ævi*, p. 2008. [They are printed entire in Wright's *Latin Stories*, &c. 1842, 174-91.] The fame fable is in Caxton's *Æfop*. [Adolphus took many of his ftories from Alfonfus.]

[2] [Morris's *Chaucer*, ii. 332, ver. 465.]

[3] I have explained this word, but will here add fome new illuftrations of it. Undoubtedly the high table in a public refectory, as appears from thefe words in Matthew Paris, "Priore prandente ad magnam menfam quam Dais vulgo appellamus." *Vit. Abbat. S. Albani*, p. 92. And again the fame writer fays, that a cup, with a foot or ftand, was not permitted in the hall of the monaftery, "Nifi tantum in majori menfa quam Dais appellamus." *Additam*. p. 148. There is an old French word, Dais, which fignifies a throne or canopy, ufually placed over the head of the principal perfon at a magnificent feaft. Hence it was transferred to the *table* at which he fat. In the ancient French *Roman de Garin:*

"Au plus haut dais fift roy Anfeis."

Either at the firft table, or, which is much the fame thing, under the higheft canopy.

[I apprehend that [dais] originally fignified the wooden floor: [*d'ais*] Fr. *de affibus*, Lat.] which was laid at the upper end of the hall, as we ftill fee it in college halls, &c. That part of the room therefore which was floored with planks, was called the *dais* (the reft being either the bare ground, or at beft paved with ftone); and being raifed above the level of the other parts, it was often called the *high dais*. As the principal table was always placed upon a dais, it began very foon, by a natural abufe of words, to be called itfelf *a dais;* and people were faid to fit at the *dais*, inftead of at the table upon the *dais*. Menage, whofe authority feems to have led later antiquaries to interpret *dais* a *canopy*, has evidently confounded *deis* with *ders*, [which] as he obferves, meant properly the hangings at the back of the company. But as the fame hangings were often drawn over, fo as to form a kind of canopy over their heads, the whole was called a *ders.—Tyrwhitt*.]

[4] "fuch as Joab never," &c. [5] danger. [6] fill, pour.

> And certeynly I dar right wel faye this,
> Imeneus, that god of weddyng is,
> Seigh never his lif fo mery a weddid man.
> Holde thy pees, thow poete Marcian,
> That writeft us that ilke weddyng merye
> Of hir Philologie and him Mercurie,
> And of the fonges that the Mufes fonge;
> To fmal is bothe thy penne and eek thy tonge
> For to defcrive of this mariage.
> Whan tender youthe hath weddid ftoupyng age.
>
> * * * * *
>
> Mayus, that fit with fo benigne a cheere,
> Hir to bihold it femede fayerye;[1]
> Queen Efther lokede never with fuch an ye
> On Affuere, fo meke a look hath fche;
> I may not yow devyfe al hir beauté;
> But thus moche of hir beauté telle I may,
> That fche was lyk the brighte morw of May,
> Fulfild of alle beauté and plefaunce.
>   This January is ravyfcht in a traunce,
> At every tyme he lokith in hir face,
> But in his hert he gan hir to manace.

Dryden and Pope have modernifed the two laft-mentioned poems. Dryden the tale of the *Nonnes Prieft*, and Pope that of *January and May*: intending perhaps to give patterns of the beft of Chaucer's Tales in the comic fpecies. But I am of opinion that the *Miller's Tale* has more true humour than either. Not that I mean to palliate the levity of the ftory, which was moft probably chofen by Chaucer in compliance with the prevailing manners of an unpolifhed age, and agreeably to ideas of feftivity not always the moft delicate and refined. Chaucer abounds in liberties of this kind, and this muft be his apology. So does Boccaccio, and perhaps much more, but from a different caufe. The licentioufnefs of Boccaccio's tales, which he compofed *per cacciar la malincolia delle femine*, to amufe the ladies, is to be vindicated, at leaft accounted for, on other principles: it was not fo much the confequence of popular incivility, as it was owing to a particular event of the writer's age. Juft before Boccaccio wrote, the plague at Florence had totally changed the cuftoms and manners of the people. Only a few of the women had furvived this fatal malady; and thefe, having loft their hufbands, parents, or friends, gradually grew regardlefs of thofe conftraints and cuftomary formalities which before of courfe influenced their behaviour. For want of female attendants, they were obliged often to take men only into their fervice: and this circumftance greatly contributed to deftroy their habits of delicacy, and gave an opening to various freedoms and indecencies unfuitable to the fex, and frequently productive of very ferious confequences. As to the monafteries, it is not furprifing that Boccaccio fhould have made them the fcenes of his moft libertine ftories. The plague had thrown open their gates. The monks and nuns wandered abroad, and partaking of the common

---

[1] A phantafy, enchantment.

liberties of life and the levities of the world, forgot the rigour of their institutions and the severity of their ecclesiastical characters. At the ceasing of the plague, when the religious were compelled to return to their cloisters, they could not forsake their attachment to these secular indulgences; they continued to practise the same free course of life, and would not submit to the disagreeable and unsocial injunctions of their respective orders. Cotemporary historians give a shocking representation of the unbounded debaucheries of the Florentines on this occasion: and ecclesiastical writers mention this period as the grand epoch of the relaxation of monastic discipline. Boccaccio did not escape the censure of the Church for these compositions. His conversion was a point much laboured; and in expiation of his follies he was almost persuaded to renounce poetry and the heathen authors, and to turn Carthusian. But, to say the truth, Boccaccio's life was almost as loose as his writings; till he was in great measure reclaimed by the powerful remonstrances of his master Petrarch, who talked much more to the purpose than his confessor. This Boccaccio himself acknowledges in the fifth of his eclogues, entitled *Philosotrophos*, which like those of Petrarch are enigmatical and obscure.

But to return to the *Miller's Tale*. The character of the Clerk of Oxford, who studied astrology, a science then in high repute, but, under the specious appearance of decorum and the mask of the serious philosopher, carried on intrigues, is painted with these lively circumstances:[1]

> This clerk was cleped heende Nicholas;[2]
> Of derne[3] love he cowde and of solas;
> And therwith he was sleigh and ful privé,
> And lik *to* a mayden meke for to se.
> A chambir had he in that hostillerye[4]
> Alone, withouten eny compaignye,
> Ful fetisly i-dight with herbes soote,
> And he himself as swete as is the roote
> Of lokorys, or eny cetewale.[5]
> His almagest,[6] and bookes gret and smale,
> His astrylabe,[7] longyng *to* his art,
> His augrym stoones,[8] leyen faire apart

---

[1] [Morris's *Chaucer*, ii. 99, ver. 13.]   [2] the gentle Nicholas.   [3] secret.

[4] Hospitium, one of the old hostels at Oxford, which were very numerous before the foundation of the colleges. This is one of the citizens' houses; a circumstance which gave rise to the story.

[5] the herb Valerian.

[6] A book of astronomy written by Ptolemy. It was in thirteen books. He wrote also four books of judicial astrology. He was an Egyptian astrologist, and flourished under Marcus Antoninus. He is mentioned in the *Sompnour's Tale*, v. 1025, and the *Wife of Bath's Prologue*, v. 324.

[7] astrylabe; an astrolabe.

[8] stones for computation. Augrym is Algorithm, the sum of the principal rules of common arithmetic. Chaucer was himself an adept in this sort of knowledge. The learned Selden is of opinion, that his Astrolabe was compiled from the Arabian astronomers and mathematicians. See his pref. to *Notes on Drayt. Polyolb*. p. 4, where the word Dulcarnon (*Troil. Cr.* ii. vol. iv. 933, 935,) is explained to be an

> On fchelves couched at his beddes heed,
> His preffe¹ i-covered with a faldyng reed.
> And al above ther lay a gay fawtrye,
> On which he made a-nightes melodye,
> So fwetely, that al the chambur rang;
> And *Angelus ad virginem* he fang.

In the defcription of the young wife of our philofopher's hoft, there is great elegance with a mixture of burlefque allufions. Not to mention the curiofity of a female portrait, drawn with fo much exactnefs at fuch a diftance of time.

> Fair was the yonge wyf, and therwithal²
> As eny wefil hir body gent and fmal.
> A feynt fche werede, barred al of filk;³
> A barm-cloth eek as whit as morne mylk
> Upon hir lendes, ful of many a gore.
> Whit was hir fmok, and browdid al byfore
> And eek byhynde on hir coler aboute,
> Of cole-blak filk, withinne and eek withoute.
> The tapes of hir white voluper
> Weren of the fame fute of hire coler;
> Hir filet brood of filk y-fet ful heye.
> And certeynly fche hadd a licorous eyghe;
> Ful fmal y-pulled weren hir browes two,
> And tho were bent, as blak as any flo.
> Sche was wel more blisful on to fee
> Than is the newe perjonette tree;
> And fofter than the wol is of a wethir.
> And by hir gurdil hyng a purs of lethir,
> Taffid⁴ with filk, and perled⁵ with latoun.⁶
> In al this world to feken up and doun

Arabic term for a root in calculation. His *Chanon Yeman's Tale* proves his intimate acquaintance with the Hermetic philofophy, then much in vogue. There is a ftatute of Henry V. againft the tranfmutation of metals in Stat. an. 4, Hen. V. cap. iv. [1416-17]. Chaucer, in the Aftrolabe, refers to two famous mathematicians and aftronomers of his time, John Some and Nicholas Lynne, both Carmelite friars of Oxford, and perhaps his friends, whom he calls " reverent clerkes." *Aftrolabe*, p. 440, col. i. Urr. They both wrote calendars which, like Chaucer's *Aftrolabe*, were conftructed for the meridian of Oxford. Chaucer mentions Alcabucius, an aftronomer, that is, Abdilazi Alchabitius, whofe [*Introductorium ad fcientiam judicialem aftronomiæ* was printed in 1473 and afterwards.] Compare Herbelot, *Bibl. Oriental.* p. 963, b. Ketab. *Alafthorlab.* p. 141, a. Nicholas Lynne above mentioned is faid to have made feveral voyages to the moft northerly parts of the world, charts of which he prefented to Edward III. Perhaps to Iceland, and the coafts of Norway, for aftronomical obfervations. Thefe charts are loft. Hakluyt apud Anderfon, *Hift. Com.* i. p. 191, *fub. ann.* 1360. (See Hakl. *Voy.* i. 121, *feq.* ed. 1598.)

¹ prefs.　　　　　　　　² [Morris's *Chaucer*, ii. 100, ver. 47.]

³ " A girdle [ftriped] with filk." The *Doctor of Phific* is " girt with a feint of filk with barris fmale." Prol. v. 138. See [Halliwell's *Arch. Dict.* in v.]

⁴ taffeled; fringed.

⁵ [I believe ornamented with latoun in the fhape of pearls.—*Tyrwhitt*. An expreffion ufed by Francis Thynne in his letter to Speght will explain this term : " and Orfrayes being compounded of the French *or* and *frays*, (or fryfe Englifh,) is that which to this daye (being now made all of one ftuffe or fubftance) is called frifed or perled cloth of gold."—*Price*.]

⁶ latoun, or chekelaton, is cloth of gold.

> There nys no man so wys, that couthe thenche
> So gay a popillot,[1] or such a wenche.
> For brighter was the *schynyng* of hir hewe,
> Than in the Tour the noble[2] i-forged newe.
> But of hir song, it was as lowde and yerne[3]
> As eny swalwe chiteryng on a berne.
> Therto sche cowde skippe, and make *a* game,
> As eny kyde or calf folwyng his dame.
> Hir mouth was sweete as bragat[4] is or meth,
> Or hoord of apples, layd in hay or heth.
> Wynsyng sche was, as is a joly colt;
> Long as a mast, and upright as a bolt.[5]
> A broch[6] sche bar upon hir loue coleer,
> As brod as is the bos of a bocleer.[7]
> Hir schos were laced on hir legges heyghe.

Nicholas, as we may suppose, was not proof against the charms of his blooming hostess. He has frequent opportunities of conversing with her; for her husband is the carpenter of Oseney Abbey near Oxford, and often absent in the woods belonging to the monastery.[8] His rival is Absalom, a parish-clerk, the gayest of his calling, who being amorously inclined, very naturally avails himself of a circumstance belonging to his profession: on holidays it was his business to carry the censer about the church, and he takes this opportunity of casting unlawful glances on the handsomest dames of the parish. His gallantry, agility, affectation of dress and personal elegance, skill in shaving and surgery, smattering in the law, taste for music, and many other accomplishments, are thus inimitably represented by Chaucer, who must have much relished so ridiculous a character:

> Now ther was of that chirche a parisch clerk,[9]
> The which that was i-cleped Absolon.
> Crulle was his heer, and as the gold it schon,
> And strowted as a fan right large and brood;
> Ful streyt and evene lay his joly schood.[10]
> His rode[11] was reed, his eyghen gray as goos,
> With Powles wyndowes corven in his schoos.[12]

---

[1] "so pretty a puppet." [This may either be considered as a diminutive from *poupée* a puppet, or as a corruption of *papillot*, a young butterfly.—*Tyrwhitt*.]
[2] a piece of money.
[3] [brisk, eager.—*Tyrwhitt*.]
[4] bragget. A drink made of honey, spices, &c.
[5] "straight as an arrow."
[6] a jewel. [It seems to have signified originally the tongue of a buckle or clasp, and from thence the buckle or clasp itself. It probably came by degrees to signify any kind of jewel.—*Tyrwhitt*.]
[7] buckler. [8] [See Morris's *Chaucer*, ii. 113, ver. 479.]
"I trow that he be went
For tymber, ther our abbot hath him sent:
For he is wont for timber for to go,
And dwellen at the Graunge a day or tuo."
[9] [Morris's *Chaucer*, vol. ii. p. 102, ver. 126.]   [10] hair.
[11] complexion.
[12] *Calcei fenestrati* occur in ancient Injunctions to the clergy. In Eton College statutes, given in 1446, the fellows are forbidden to wear *sotularia rostrata*, as also *caligæ*, white, red, or green, cap. xix. In a chantry, or chapel founded at Win-

> In his hoses reed he wente fetusly.
> I-clad he was ful smal and propurly,
> Al in a kirtel¹ of a fyn wachet,
> Schapen with goores in the newe get.
> And therupon he had a gay surplys,
> As whyt as is the blosme upon the rys.²
> A mery child he was, so God me save;
> Wel couthe he lete blood, and clippe and schave,
> And make a chartre of lond and acquitaunce.
> In twenty maners he coude skippe and daunce,
> After the scole of Oxenforde tho,
> And with his legges casten to and fro;
> And pleyen songes on a smal rubible;³
> Ther-to he sang som tyme a lowde quynyble.⁴

His manner of making love must not be omitted. He serenades her with his guittar:

> He waketh al the night and al the day,⁵
> To kembe his lokkes brode and made him gay.
> He woweth hire by mene and by brocage,⁶
> And swor he wolde ben hir owne page.
> He syngeth crowyng⁷ as a nightyngale;
> And sent hire pyment, meth, and spiced ale,
> And wafres pypyng hoot out of the gleede;⁸
> And for sche was of toune, he profrede meede.⁹

* * * * *

---

chester in the year 1318, within the cemetery of the Nuns of the Blessed Virgin, by Roger Inkpenne, the members, that is, a warden, chaplain and clerk, are ordered to go "in meris caligis, et sotularibus non rostratis, nisi forsitan *botis* uti voluerint." And it is added, "Vestes deferant non *fibulatas*, sed desuper clausas, vel *brevitate* non notandas." *Registr. Priorat. S. Swithini Winton.* MS. *supr. citat.* quatern. 6. Compare Wilkins's *Concil.* iii. 670, ii. 4.

¹ jacket.   ² [branch.]
³ A species of guitar. Lydgate, MSS. Bibl. Bodl. Fairf. 16. In a poem called *Reason and Sensuallite, compyled by Jhon Lydgate:*
> "Lutys, rubibis (l. ribibles), and geternes,
> More for estatys than tavernes."

⁴ treble.   ⁵ [Morris's *Chaucer*, ii. 104, ver. 187.]
⁶ by offering money: or a settlement.   ⁷ quavering.   ⁸ the [fire].
⁹ See *Rime of Sir Thopas*, ver. 3357. Mr. Walpole has mentioned some curious particulars concerning the liquors which anciently prevailed in England. *Anecd. Paint.* i. p. 11. I will add, that cider was very early a common liquor among our ancestors. In the year 129[4-]5, an. 23 Edw. I. the king orders the sheriff of Southampton [Hampshire] to provide with all speed four hundred quarters of wheat, to be collected in parts of his bailiwick nearest the sea, and to convey the same, being well winnowed, in good ships from Portsmouth to Winchelsea. Also to put on board the said ships, at the same time, two hundred tons of cider. The cost to be paid immediately from the king's wardrobe. This precept is in old French. *Registr. Joh. Pontissar. Episc. Winton.* fol. 172. It is remarkable that Wickliffe translates, Luc. i. 21, "He schal not drynche wyn & *cyser*" [edit. 1848]. This translation was made about A.D. 1380. At a visitation of St. Swithin's priory at Winchester, by the said bishop, it appears that the monks claimed to have, among other articles of luxury, on many festivals, "Vinum, tam album quam rubeum, claretum medonem, burgarastrum," &c. This was so early as the year 1285. *Registr. Priorat. S. Swith. Winton.* MS. *supr. citat.* quatern. 5. It appears also, that the *Hordarius* and *Camerarius* claimed every year of the prior ten *dolia vini*, or twenty pounds in money, A.D. 1337. *Ibid.* quatern. 5. A benefactor grants to the said convent on the day of his anniversary, "unam pipam vini pret. xx. s." for

Som tyme, to schewe his lightnes and maistrye,
He pleyeth Herodz on a scaffold hye.

Again:

Whan that the firste cok hath crowe, anoon [1]
Up ryst this jolyf lover Absolon,
And him arrayeth gay, at poynt devys.
But first he cheweth greyn [2] and lycoris,
To smellen swete, or he hadde kempt his heere.
Under his tunge a trewe love he beere,
For therby wende he to be gracious.
He rometh to the carpenteres hous.[3]

In the mean time the scholar, intent on accomplishing his intrigue, locks himself up in his chamber for the space of two days. The carpenter, alarmed at this long seclusion, and supposing that his guest might be sick or dead, tries to gain admittance, but in vain. He peeps through a crevice of the door, and at length discovers the scholar, who is conscious that he was seen, in an affected trance of abstracted meditation. On this our carpenter, reflecting on the danger of being wise, and exulting in the security of his own ignorance, exclaims:

A man woot litel what him schal betyde.[4]
This man is falle with his astronomye

---

their refection, A.D. 1286. *Ibid.* quatern. 10. Before the year 1200, "Vina et medones" are mentioned as not uncommon in the abbey of Evesham in Worcestershire. Dugdale, *Monast.* [edit. Stevens,] Append. p. 138. The use of mead, *medo*, seems to have been very ancient in England. See *Mon. Angl.* i. 26. Thorne, *Chron.* sub ann. 1114. Compare *Dissertat.* i. It is not my intention to enter into the controversy concerning the cultivation of vines, for making wine, in England. I shall only bring to light the following remarkable passage on that subject from an old English writer on gardening and farming : "We might have a reasonable good wine growyng in many places of this realme: as undoubtedly wee had immediately after the Conquest ; tyll partly by slouthfulnesse, not liking any thing long that is painefull, partly by civill discord long continuyng, it was left, and so with tyme lost, as appeareth by a number of places in this realme that keepe still the name of Vineyardes : and uppon many cliffes and hilles, are yet to be seene the rootes and olde remaynes of Vines. There is besides Nottingham, an auncient house called Chilwell, in which house remayneth yet, as an auncient monument, in a Great Wyndowe of Glasse, the whole Order of planting, pruynyng, [pruning,] stamping, and pressing of vines. Beside, there [at that place] is yet also growing an old vine, that yields a grape sufficient to make a right good wine, as was lately proved. There hath, moreover, good experience of late years been made, by two noble and honourable barons of this realme, the lorde Cobham and the lorde Wylliams of Tame, who had both growyng about their houses, as good wines as are in many parts of Fraunce," &c. [Heresbachius] *Foure bookes of Husbandry*, [translated by B. Googe,] 1578. *To the Reader.*

[1] [Morris's *Chaucer*, ii. 114, ver. 501.]

[2] Greyns, or grains, of Paris or Paradise occurs in the *Romaunt of the Rose*, ver. 1369. A rent of herring pies is an old payment from the city of Norwich to the king, seasoned among other spices with half an ounce of grains of Paradise. Blomf. *Norf.* ii. 264.

[3] It is to be remarked, that in this tale the carpenter swears, with great propriety, by the patroness saint of Oxford, saint Frideswide, [Morris's *Chaucer*, ii. 106, ver. 262]:

"This carpenter to blessen him bygan,
And seyde, Now help us, seynte Frideswyde."

[4] *Ibid.* ver. 264.

> In fom woodneffe, or in fom agonye.
> I thought ay wel how that it fchulde be.
> Men fchulde nought knowe [1] of Goddes pryvyté.
> Ye! bleffed be alwey a lewed man,[2]
> That nat but oonly his bileeve can.[3]
> So ferde another clerk with aftronomye;
> He walked in the feeldes for to prye
> Upon the fterres, what ther fchulde bifalle,
> Til he was in a marle pit i-falle.
> He faugh nat that. But yet, by feint Thomas!
> Me reweth fore for heende Nicholas;
> He fchal be ratyd of his ftudyyng.

But the fcholar has ample gratification for this ridicule. The carpenter is at length admitted; and the fcholar continuing the farce, gravely acquaints the former that he has been all this while making a moft important difcovery by means of aftrological calculations. He is foon perfuaded to believe the prediction: and in the fequel, which cannot be repeated here, this humorous contrivance crowns the fcholar's fchemes with fuccefs, and proves the caufe of the carpenter's difgrace. In this piece the reader obferves that the humour of the characters is made fubfervient to the plot.

I have before hinted, that Chaucer's obfcenity is in great meafure to be imputed to his age. We are apt to form romantic and exaggerated notions about the moral innocence of our ancestors. Ages of ignorance and fimplicity are thought to be ages of purity. The direct contrary, I believe, is the cafe. Rude periods have that groffnefs of manners which is not lefs friendly to virtue than luxury itfelf. In the middle ages, not only the moft flagrant violations of modefty were frequently practifed and permitted, but the moft infamous vices. Men are lefs afhamed as they are lefs polifhed. Great refinement multiplies criminal pleafures, but at the fame time prevents the actual commiffion of many enormities: at leaft it preferves public decency, and fuppreffes public licentioufnefs.

The *Reve's Tale*, or the *Miller of Trompington*, is much in the fame ftyle, but with lefs humour.[4] This ftory was enlarged by Chaucer from Boccaccio.[5] There is an old Englifh poem on the fame plan, entitled: *A ryght pleafaunt and merye Hiftorie of the Mylner of Abyngdon*,

---

[1] "pry into the fecrets of nature." [2] unlearned.
[3] Who knows only his Creed.
[4] See alfo *The Shipman's Tale*, which was originally taken from fome comic French trouvere. But Chaucer had it from Boccaccio. The ftory of Zenobia, in the *Monkes Tale*, is from Boccaccio's *Cas. Vir. Illuftr.* (fee *Lydg. Boch.* viii. 7). That of Count Ugolins in the fame tale, from Dante. That of Pedro of Spain, from Archbifhop Turpin, *ibid.* Of Julius Cæfar, from Lucan, Suetonius, and Valerius Maximus, *ibid.* The idea of this tale was fuggefted by Boccaccio's book on the fame fubject.
[5] *Decamer.* Giorn. ix. Nov. 6. But both Boccaccio and Chaucer probably borrowed from an old Conte or Fabliau by an anonymous French rhymer, *De Gombert, et de deux Clers.* See [Le Grand,] *Fabliaux et Contes*, Paris, 1756, tom. ii. p. 115—124. The *Shipman's Tale*, as I have hinted, originally came from fome fuch French Conteur, through the medium of Boccaccio.

with his wife and his fayre daughter, and of two poore schollers of Cambridge.[1] It begins with these lines:

> Fayre lordings, if you list to heere
> A mery jest your minds to cheere.

This piece is supposed by Wood [without much foundation, perhaps] to have been written by Andrew Borde.[2] It was at least evidently written after the time of Chaucer. It is the work of some tasteless imitator, who has sufficiently disguised his original, by retaining none of its spirit. I mention these circumstances, lest it should be thought that this frigid abridgment was the ground-work of Chaucer's poem on the same subject. In the class of humorous or satirical tales, the *Sompnour's Tale*, which exposes the tricks and extortions of the mendicant friars, has also distinguished merit. This piece has incidentally been mentioned above with the *Plowman's Tale* and Pierce Plowman.

Genuine humour, the concomitant of true taste, consists in discerning improprieties in books as well as characters. We therefore must remark under this class another tale of Chaucer, which till lately has been looked upon as a grave heroic narrative. I mean the *Rime of Sir Thopas*. Chaucer, at a period which almost realised the manners of romantic chivalry, discerned the leading absurdities of the old romances: and in this poem, which may be justly called a prelude to Don Quixote, has burlesqued them with exquisite ridicule. That this was the poet's aim, appears from many passages. But, to put the matter beyond a doubt, take the words of an ingenious critic. "We are to observe," says he, "that this was Chaucer's own Tale: and that, when in the progress of it, the good

---

[1] [Abingdon is situated on a mill-stream, seven miles from Cambridge. See *Remains of the Early Popular Poetry of England*, iii. 98, *et. seqq*. The scene of Chaucer's story is called *The Old Mill*. See Wright's *Anecdota Literaria*, 1844, where the fabliau, above referred to, will be found printed.]

Bibl. Bodl. Selden, C. 39, 4to. This book was given to that library, with many other petty black-letter histories, in prose and verse, of a similar cast, by Robert Burton, author of the *Anatomy of Melancholy*, who was a great collector of such pieces. One of his books, now in the Bodleian, is the *History of Tom Thumb* [1630, 8vo,] whom a learned antiquary [Tho. Hearne], while he laments that ancient history has been much disguised by romantic narratives, pronounces to have been no less important a personage than King [Edgar's] dwarf.

[2] See Wood's *Athen. Oxon.* v. *Borde*, and [*Reliq. Hearn.* 1857, 822.] I am of opinion that Solere Hall, in Cambridge, mentioned in this poem, was Aula Solarii,—the hall with the upper story, at that time a sufficient circumstance to distinguish and denominate one of the academical hospitia. Although Chaucer calls it, "a grete college," ver. 881. Thus in Oxford we had Chimney Hall, Aula cum Camino, an almost parallel proof of the simplicity of their ancient houses of learning. Twyne also mentions Solere Hall, at Oxford. Also Aula Salarii, which I doubt not is properly Solarii. Compare Wood, *Ath. Oxon.* ii. 11, col. i. 13, col. i. 12, col. ii. Caius will have it to be Clare Hall.—*Hist. Acad.* p. 57. Those who read Scholars Hall (of Edw. III.) may consult Wacht. *v.* Soller. In the mean time, for the reasons assigned, one of these two halls or colleges at Cambridge might at first have been commonly called Soler Hall. A hall near Brazenose College, Oxford, was called Glazen Hall, having glass windows, anciently not common. See Twyne, *Miscel. Quædam*, &c. ad calc. *Apol. Antiq. Acad. Oxon.* [1608].

sense of the host is made to break in upon him, and interrupt him, Chaucer approves his disgust, and changing his note, tells the simple instructive tale of *Meliboeus—a moral tale vertuous*, as he terms it; to show what sort of fictions were most expressive of real life, and most proper to be put into the hands of the people. It is further to be noted, that the *Boke* of *The Giant Olyphant and Chylde Thopas*, was not a fiction of his own, but a story of antique fame, and very celebrated in the days of chivalry; so that nothing could better suit the poet's design of discrediting the old romances, than the choice of this venerable legend for the vehicle of his ridicule upon them.[1]" But it is to be remembered, that Chaucer's design was intended to ridicule the frivolous descriptions and other tedious impertinences, so common in the volumes of chivalry with which his age was overwhelmed, not to degrade in general or expose a mode of fabling, whose sublime extravagances constitute the marvellous graces of his own Cambuscan; a composition which at the same time abundantly demonstrates, that the manners of romance are better calculated to answer the purposes of pure poetry, to captivate the imagination, and to produce surprise, than the fictions of classical antiquity.

SECTION XVII.

BUT Chaucer's vein of humour, although conspicuous in the *Canterbury Tales*, is chiefly displayed in the characters with which they are introduced. In these his knowledge of the world availed him in a peculiar degree, and enabled him to give such an accurate picture of ancient manners, as no contemporary nation has transmitted to posterity. It is here that we view the pursuits and employments, the customs and diversions of our ancestors, copied from the life, and represented with equal truth and spirit, by a judge of mankind whose penetration qualified him to discern their foibles or discriminating peculiarities, and by an artist, who understood that proper selection of circumstances and those predominant characteristics, which form a finished portrait.[2] We are surprised to find, in so gross and ignorant an age, such talents for satire and for observation

---

[1] [Warton seems to have been writing at random, when he described *Sir Thopas* as "a story of antique fame." It is, on the contrary, a broad burlesque of Chaucer's own invention, as the whole context appears clearly to show. Tyrwhitt gravely observes, as Price notes: "I can only say, that I have not been so fortunate as to meet with any traces of such a story of an earlier date than the Canterbury Tales,"—nor has any one else!]

[2] [Compare with Chaucer's sketches of 1380-90 with that of A.D. 1592, by Greene, in his *Quip for an Upstart Courtier*, copied and enlarged from Thynne's *Pride and Lowlines*, written before 1570. See *Temporary Preface to Six-Text Chaucer*, pp. 101-2.—F.]

on life; qualities which ufually exert themfelves at more civilifed periods, when the improved ftate of fociety, by fubtilifing our fpeculations, and eftablifhing uniform modes of behaviour, difpofes mankind to ftudy themfelves, and renders deviations of conduct and fingularities of character more immediately and neceffarily the objects of cenfure and ridicule. Thefe curious and valuable remains are fpecimens of Chaucer's native genius, unaffifted and unalloyed. The figures are all Britifh, and bear [comparatively faint marks] of Claffical, Italian, or French imitation. The characters of Theophraftus are not fo lively, particular, and appropriated. A few traits from this celebrated part of our author, yet too little tafted and underftood, may be fufficient to prove and illuftrate what is here advanced.

The character of the Priorefs is chiefly diftinguifhed by an excefs of delicacy and decorum, and an affectation of courtly accomplifhments. [French of Stratford-at-Bow appears, in our poet's time, to have been a fort of bye-word]:

> Ther was alfo a Nonne, a Priorefſe,[1]
> That of hire fmylyng was ful fymple and coy;
> Hire gretteft ooth nas but by feynt Loy;[2]
> * * *
> And Frenfch fche fpak ful faire and fetyfly,
> Aftur the fcole of Stratford atte Bowe,
> For Frenfch of Parys was to hire unknowe.
> At mete[3] wel i-taught was fche withalle;
> Sche leet no morfel from hire lippes falle,

---

[1] [Morris's *Chaucer*, ii. 5, ver. 118.]

[2] *Saint Loy*, i.e. [Sanctus Eligius. T. This faint is mentioned by Lyndfay in his *Monarche*.] The fame oath occurs in the *Frere's Tale*, v. 300.

[3] dinner. [The Priorefs's exact behaviour at table is copied from *Rom. Rofe*, 14178—14199.

"Et bien fe garde," &c.

To fpeak French is mentioned above among her accomplifhments. There is a letter in old French from Queen Philippa and her daughter Ifabel to the Prior of Saint Swithin's at Winchefter, to admit one Agnes Patfhull into an eleemofynary fifterhood belonging to his convent. The Prior is requefted to grant her, "Une Lyvere en votre Maifon dieu de Wyncefter et eftre un des foers," for her life. Written at *Windefor*, Apr. 25. The year muft have been about 1350. *Regiftr. Priorat. MS.* fupr. citat. quatern. xix. fol. 4. I do not fo much cite this inftance to prove that the Prior muft be fuppofed to underftand French, as to fhew that it was now the court language; and even on a matter of bufinefs there was at leaft a great propriety that the queen and princefs fhould write in this language, although to an ecclefiaftic of dignity. In the fame Regifter, there is a letter in old French from the Queen Dowager Ifabel to the Prior and Convent of Winchefter; to fhew, that it was at her requeft, that King Edward III. her fon had granted a church in Winchefter diocefe, to the monaftery of Leeds in Yorkfhire, for their better fupport, "a trouver fis chagnoignes chantans tous les jours en la chapele du Chaftel de Ledes, pour laime madame Alianore reyne d'Angleterre," &c. A.D. 1341, quatern. vi.

The Priorefs's *greateft* oath is by Saint Eloy. I will here throw together fome of the moft remarkable oaths in the Canterbury Tales. The Hoft fwears by *my father's foule*. Urr. p. 7, 783. Sir Thopas, by *ale and breade*, p. 146, 3377. Arcite, by *my pan*, i.e. *head*. p. 10, 1167. Thefeus, by *mightie Mars the red*, p. 14, 1749. Again, *as he was a trew knight*, p. 9, 961. The Carpenter's wife, by *faint Thomas of Kent*, p. 26, 183. The Smith, by *Chriftes foote*, p. 29, 674. The

> Ne wette hire fyngres in hire fauce deepe.
> Wel cowde fche carie a morfel, and wel keepe,
> That no drope *ne* fil uppon hire brefte.
> In curtefie was fett al hire lefte.[1]
> Hire overlippe wypude fche fo clene,
> That in hire cuppe *ther* was no ferthing fene
> Of grees, whan fche dronken hadde hire draught.
> Ful femely aftur hire mete fche raught.[2]
>
> * * * *
>
> And peyned hire to counterfete cheere
> Of court, and ben eftatlich of manere.

She has even the falfe pity and fentimentality of many modern ladies:

> Sche was fo charitable and fo pitous,[3]
> Sche wolde weepe if that fche fawe a mous
> Caught in a trappe, if it were deed or bledde.
> Of fmale houndes hadde fche, that fche fedde
> With roftud fleifsh, and mylk, and waftel breed.[4]
> But fore wepte fche if oon of hem were deed,
> Or if men fmot it with a yerde[5] fmerte:
> And al was confcience and tendre herte.

The *Wife of Bath* is more amiable for her plain and ufeful qualifications. She is a refpectable dame, and her chief pride confifts in being a confpicuous and fignificant character at church on a Sunday.

> Of cloth-makyng[6] fhe hadde fuch an haunt,[7]
> Sche paffed hem of Ypris and of Gaunt.
> In al the parifshe wyf ne was ther noon
> That to the offryng byforn hire fchulde goon,
> And if ther dide, certeyn fo wroth was fche,
> That fche was thanne out of alle charité.
> Hire keverchefs[8] weren ful fyne of grounde;
> I durfte fwere they weyghede ten pounde.

Cambridge Scholar, by *my father's kinn*, p. 31, 930. Again, by *my croune*, ib. 933. Again, for *godes benes*, or *benifon*, p. 32, 965. Again, by *feint Cuthberde*. ib. 1019. Sir Johan of Boundis, by *feint Martyne*, p. 37, 107. Gamelyn, by *goddis boke*, p. 38, 181. Gamelyn's brother, by *faint Richere*, ibid. 273. Again, by *Criftis ore*, ib. 279. A Franklen, by *faint Jame that in Galis is*, i.e. Saint James of Galicia, p. 40, 549, 1514. A Porter, by *Goddis berde*, ib. 581. Gamelyn, by *my hals*, or neck, p. 42, 773. The Mafter Outlaw, by the *gode rode*, p. 45, 1265. The Hoft, by the *precious corpus Madrian*, p. 160, 4. Again, by *faint Paulis bell*, p. 168, 893. The Man of Law, *Depardeux*, p. 49, 39. The Marchaunt, by *faint Thomas of Inde*, p. 66, 745. The Sompnour, by *goddis armis two*, p. 82, 833. The Hoft, by *cockis bonis*, p. 106, 2235. Again, by *naylis* and by *blode*, i.e. of Chrift, p. 130, 1802. Again, by *faint Damian*, p. 131, 1824. Again, by *faint Runion*, ib. 1834. Again, by *Corpus domini*, ib. 1838. The Riotter, by *Goddis digne bones*, p. 135, 2211. The Hoft, to the Monk, by *your father kin*, p. 160, 43. The Monk, by his *porthofe*, or breviary, p. 139, 2639. Again, by *God and faint Martin*, ib. 2656. The Hoft, by *armis blode and bonis*, p. 24, 17. [See *Popular Antiquities of Great Britain*, 1870, ii. 248-50.]

[1] pleafure, defire.
[2] [reached].
[3] [Morris's *Chaucer*, ii. 5, ver. 143.]
[4] bread of a finer fort.
[5] ftick.
[6] It is to be obferved, that fhe lived in the neighbourhood of Bath; a country famous for clothing [at that] day.
[7] [Morris's *Chaucer*, ii. 15, ver. 447.]
[8] head-drefs.

> That on a Sonday were upon hire heed.
> Hir hofen were of fyn fcarlett reed,
> Ful ftreyte y-teyed, and fchoos ful moyfte and newe
> Bold was hir face, and fair, and reed of hewe.
> Sche was a worthy womman al hire lyfe,
> Houfbondes atte chirche dore[1] hadde fche fyfe.

The *Franklin* is a country gentleman, whofe eftate confifted in free land, and was not fubject to feudal fervices or payments. He is ambitious of fhewing his riches by the plenty of his table: but his hofpitality, a virtue much more practicable among our anceftors than at prefent, often degenerates into luxurious excefs. His impatience, if his fauces were not fufficiently poignant, and every article of his dinner in due form and readinefs, is touched with the hand of Pope or Boileau. He had been a prefident at the feffions, knight of the fhire, a fheriff, and a coroner:[2]

> An houfehaldere, and that a gret, was he;[3]
> Seynt Julian he was in his countré,[4]
> His breed, his ale, was alway after oon;
> A bettre envyned[5] man was nowher noon.
> Withoute bake mete was never his hous,
> Of fleiffch and fiffch, and that fo plentyvous,
> It fnewed[6] in his hous of mete and drynke,
> Of alle deyntees that men cowde thynke.
> Aftur the fondry fefouns of the yeer,
> He chaunged hem at mete[7] and at foper.
> Ful many a fat partrich had he in mewe,
> And many a brem and many a luce[8] in ftewe.
> Woo was his cook, but if his fauce were
> Poynant and fcharp, and redy al his gere.
> His table dormant[9] in his halle alway
> Stood redy covered al the longe day.

The character of the *Doctor of Phific* preferves to us the ftate of medical knowledge and the courfe of medical erudition then in fafhion. He treats his patients according to rules of aftronomy: a fcience which the Arabians engrafted on medicine.

> For he was groundud in aftronomye.[10]
> He kepte his pacient wondurly wel
> In houres by his magik naturel.

---

[1] At the fouthern entrance of Norwich cathedral, a reprefentation of the Efpoufals, or facrament of marriage, is carved in ftone; for here the hands of the couple were joined by the prieft, and great part of the fervice performed. Here alfo the bride was endowed with what was called *Dos ad oftium ecclefiæ*. This ceremony is exhibited in a curious old picture engraved by Mr. Walpole, *Anecd. Paint.* i. 31, [reprefenting a *Spofalizio*, but fuppofed by him to reprefent the marriage of Henry VII. Refpecting thefe alleged hiftorical paintings, fee fome valuable remarks by Mr. John Gough Nichols in *Notes and Queries*, 3d S. x. 61, 131.] Compare Marten. *Rit. Eccl. Anecdot.* ii. p. 630. And Hearne's *Antiquit. Glaftonb.* Append. p. 310.

[2] An office anciently executed by gentlemen of the greateft refpect and property.

[3] [Morris's *Chaucer*, ii. 11, ver. 339.]

[4] See [*Popular Antiquities of Great Britain*, 1870, i. 303.]

[5] [ftored with wine.—*Tyrwhitt*.]   [6] fnowed.   [7] dinner.

[8] pike.   [9] never removed.

[10] [Morris's *Chaucer*, ii. 14, ver. 414.]

Petrarch leaves a legacy to his physician John de Dondi of Padua, who was likewise a great astronomer, in the year 1370.[1] It was a long time before the medical profession was purged from these superstitions. Hugo de Evesham, born in Worcestershire, one of the most famous physicians in Europe, about the year 1280, educated in both the universities of England, and at others in France and Italy, was eminently skilled in mathematics and astronomy.[2] Pierre d'Apono, a celebrated professor of medicine and astronomy at Padua, wrote commentaries on the problems of Aristotle, in the year 1310. Roger Bacon says, "astronomiæ pars melior medicina."[3] In the statutes of New-College at Oxford, given in 1387, medicine and astronomy are mentioned as one and the same science. Charles V. of France, who was governed entirely by astrologers, and who commanded all the Latin treatises which could be found relating to the stars to be translated into French, established a college in the university of Paris for the study of medicine and astrology.[4] There is a scarce and very curious book, entitled: "*Novæ medicinæ methodus curandi morbos ex mathematica scientia deprompta, nunc denuo revisa,* &c. Joanne Hasfurto Virdungo, medico et astrologo doctissimo, auctore. 1518."[5] Hence magic made a part of medicine. In the *Marchaunts Second Tale*, or *History of Beryn*, falsely ascribed to Chaucer, a surgical operation of changing eyes is partly performed by the assistance of the occult sciences:

> The whole science of all surgery,[6]
> Was unyd, or the chaunge was made of both eye,
> With many sotill enchantours, and eke nygrymauncers,
> That sent wer for the nonis, maistris, and scoleris.

Leland mentions one William Glatisaunt, an astrologer and physician, a fellow of Merton College in Oxford, who wrote a medical tract, which, says he, "nescio quid Magiæ spirabat."[7] I could add many other proofs.[8]

The books which our physician studied are then enumerated:

> Wel knew he the olde Esculapius,[9]
> And Deiscorides, and eeke Rufus;
> Old Ypocras, Haly, and Galien;
> Serapyon, Razis, and Avycen;
> Averrois, Damascen, and Constantyn;
> Bernard, and Gatisden, and Gilbertyn.

Rufus, a physician of Ephesus, wrote in Greek, about the time of Trajan. Some fragments of his works still remain.[10] Haly was a famous Arabian astronomer, and a commentator on Galen, in the eleventh century, which produced so many famous Arabian physi-

---

[1] See *Acad. Inscript.* xx. 443. [2] Pits, p. 370. Bale, iv. 50, xiii. 86.
[3] Bacon, *Op. Maj.* edit. Jebb, p. 158. See also pp. 240, 247.
[4] Montfaucon, *Bibl. MSS.* tom. ii. p. 791, b. [5] In quarto.
[6] v. 2989, Urr. Ch.
[7] Lel. apud Tann. *Bibl.* p. 262, and Lel. *Script. Brit.* p. 400.
[8] See Ames's *Hist. Print.* p. 147. [9] [Morris's *Chaucer*, ii. 14, ver. 429.]
[10] Conring. *Script. Com.* Sæc. i. cap. 4, pp. 66, 67. The Arabians have translations of him. Herbel. *Bibl. Orient.* p. 972, b; 977, b.

cians.¹ John Serapion, of the same age and country, wrote on the practice of physic.² Avicen, the most eminent physician of the Arabian school, flourished in the same century.³ Rhasis, an Asiatic physician, practised at Cordova in Spain, where he died in the tenth century.⁴ Averroes, as the Asiatic schools decayed by the indolence of the Caliphs, was one of those philosophers who adorned the Moorish schools erected in Africa and Spain. He was a professor in the university of Morocco. He wrote a commentary on all Aristotle's works, and died about the year 1160. He was styled the most peripatetic of all the Arabian writers. He was born at Cordova of an ancient Arabic family.⁵ John Damascene, secretary to one of the Caliphs, wrote in various sciences, before the Arabians had entered Europe, and had seen the Grecian philosophers.⁶ Constantinus Afer, a monk of Cassino in Italy, was one of the Saracen physicians who brought medicine into Europe, and formed the Salernitan school, chiefly by translating various Arabian and Grecian medical books into Latin.⁷ He was born at Carthage, and learned grammar, logic, geometry, arithmetic, astronomy, and natural philosophy, of the Chaldees, Arabians, Persians, Saracens, Egyptians, and Indians, in the schools of Bagdat. Being thus completely accomplished in these sciences, after thirty-nine years' study, he returned into Africa, where an attempt was formed against his life. Constantine, having fortunately discovered this design, privately took ship and came to Salerno in Italy, where he lurked some time in disguise. But he was recognized by the Caliph's brother then at Salerno, who recommended him as a scholar universally skilled in the learning of all nations, to the notice of Robert, Duke of Normandy. Robert entertained him with the highest marks of respect; and Constantine, by the advice of his patron, retired to the monastery of Cassino where, being kindly received by the abbot Desiderius, he translated in that learned society the books above mentioned, most of which he first imported into Europe. These versions are said to

---

[1] *Id. ibid.* Sæc. xi. cap. 5, p. 114. Haly, called Abbas, was likewise an eminent physician of this period. He was called *Simia Galeni. Id. ibid.*

[2] *Id. ibid.* pp. 113, 114.

[3] *Id. ibid.* See Pard. T. v. 2407. Urr. p. 136.

[4] Conring. *ut supr.* Sæc. x. cap. 4, p. 110. He wrote a large and famous work, called *Continens.* Rhasis and Almasor (f. Albumasar, a great Arabian astrologer) occur in the library of Peterborough Abbey, Matric. *Libr. Monast. Burgi S. Petri.* Gunton, *Peterb.* p. 187. See Hearne, *Ben. Abb. Præf.* lix.

[5] Conring. *ut supr.* Sæc. xii. cap. 2, p. 118.

[6] Voss. *Hist. Gr.* L. ii. c. 24.

[7] Petr. Diacon. *de Vir. illustr. Monast. Cassin.* cap. xxiii. See the *Dissertations.* He is again mentioned by our author in the *Marchaunt's Tale*, ver. 565.

> "And many a letuary had he ful fyn,
> Such as the cursed monk daun Constantin
> Hath writen in his book *de Coitu.*"

The title of this book is "De Coitu, quibus profit aut obsit, quibus medicaminibus et alimentis acuatur impediatur-ve." *Opera,* 1536.

be still extant. He flourished about the year 1086.[1] Bernard, or Bernardus Gordonius, appears to have been Chaucer's contemporary. He was a professor of medicine at Montpelier, and wrote many treatises in that faculty.[2] John Gatisden was a fellow of Merton College, where Chaucer was educated, about the year 1320.[3] Pits says that he was professor of physic in Oxford.[4] He was the most celebrated physician of his age in England; and his principal work is entitled *Rosa Medica*, divided into five books, and printed at Paris in 1492.[5] Gilbertine, I suppose, is Gilbertus Anglicus, who flourished in the thirteenth century, and wrote a popular compendium of the medical art.[6] About the same time, not many years before Chaucer wrote, the works of the most famous Arabian authors, and among the rest those of Avicen, Averroes, Serapion,

---

[1] See Leo Ostiensis, or P. Diac. Auctar. ad Leon. *Chron. Mon. Cassin.* lib. iii. c. 35, p. 445. *Rerum Italic. Script.* edit. Muratori, iv. In his book *de Incantationibus*, one of his inquiries is, " An invenerim in libris Græcorum hoc qualiter in Indorum libris est invenire," &c. *Op.* tom. i. *ut supr.*

[2] Petr. Lambec. *Prodrom.* Sæc. xiv. p. 274, edit. *ut supr.*

[3] It has been before observed, that at the introduction of philosophy into Europe by the Saracens, the clergy only studied and practised the medical art. This fashion prevailed a long while afterwards. The Prior and Convent of S. Swithin's at Winchester granted to Thomas of Shaftesbury, clerk, a corrody, consisting of two dishes daily from the prior's kitchen, bread, drink, robes, and a competent chamber in the monastery, for the term of his life. In consideration of all which concessions the said Thomas paid them fifty marcs; and moreover is obliged, "deservire nobis *in Arte medicinæ*. Dat. in dom. Capitul. Feb. 15. A.D. 1319." Registr. Priorat. S. Swithin. Winton. MS. *supra citat*. The most learned and accurate Fabricius has a separate article on Theologi Medici. *Bibl. Gr.* xii. 739, *seq.* See also Giannon. *Istor. Napol.* l. x. ch. xi. § 491. In the romance of *Sir Guy*, a monk heals the knight's wounds. Signat. G. iiii.:

"There was a *monke* beheld him well
That could of *leach crafte* some dell."

In Geoffrey of Monmouth, who wrote in 1128, Eopa, intending to poison Ambrosius, introduces himself as a physician. But in order to sustain this character with due propriety, he first shaves his head, and assumes the habit of a monk. Lib. viii. c. 14. John Arundel, afterwards bishop of Chichester, was chaplain and first physician to Henry VI. in 1458. Wharton, *Angl. Sacr.* i. 777. Faricius, abbot of Abingdon, about 1110, was eminent for his skill in medicine, and a great cure performed by him is recorded in the register of the abbey. Hearne's *Bened. Abb.* Præf. xlvii. King John, while sick at Newark, made use of William de Wodestoke, abbot of the neighbouring monastery of Croxton, as his physician. Bever, *Chron.* MSS. Harl. *apud* Hearne, Præf. *ut supr.* p. xlix. Many other instances may be added. The physicians of the university of Paris were not allowed to marry till the year 1452. *Menagian.* p. 333. In the same university anciently, at the admission to the degree of doctor in physic, they took an oath that they were not married. MSS. Br. Twyne, 8, p. 249. See Freind's *Hist. of Physick*, ii. 257.

[4] p. 414.

[5] Tanner, *Bibl.* p. 312. Leland styles this work "opus luculentum juxta ac eruditum." *Script. Brit.* p. 355.

[6] Conring. *ut supr.* Sæc. xiii. cap. 4, p. 127; and Leland, *Script. Brit.* p. 291, who says that Gilbert's *Practica et Compendium Medicinæ* was most carefully studied by many "ad quæstum properantes." He adds that it was common about this time for English students abroad to assume the surname *Anglicus*, as a plausible recommendation. [See Wright's *Biog. Brit. Liter.* 1846, A.-N. Period, 461-3.]

and Rhasis, above mentioned, were translated into Latin.¹ These were our physician's library. But having mentioned his books, Chaucer could not forbear to add a stroke of satire so naturally introduced:

His studie was but litel on the Bible.²

The following anecdotes and observations may serve to throw general light on the learning of the authors who compose this curious library. The Aristotelic or Arabian philosophy continued to be communicated from Spain and Africa to the rest of Europe chiefly by means of the Jews: particularly to France and Italy, which were overrun with Jews about the tenth and eleventh centuries. About these periods, not only the courts of the Mahometan princes, but even that of the pope himself, were filled with Jews. Here they principally gained an establishment by the profession of physic; an art then but imperfectly known and practised in most parts of Europe. Being well versed in the Arabic tongue, from their commerce with Africa and Egypt, they had studied the Arabic translations of Galen and Hippocrates; which had become still more familiar to the great numbers of their brethren who resided in Spain. From this source also the Jews learned philosophy; and Hebrew versions, made about this period from the Arabic, of Aristotle and the Greek physicians and mathematicians, are still extant in some libraries.³ Here was a beneficial effect of the dispersion and vagabond condition of the Jews: I mean the diffusion of knowledge. One of the most eminent of these learned Jews was Moses Maimonides, a physician, philosopher, astrologer, and theologist, educated at Cordova in Spain under Averroes. He died about the year 1208. Averroes, being accused of heretical opinions, was sentenced to live with the Jews in the street of the Jews at Cordova. Some of these learned Jews began to flourish in the Arabian schools in Spain, as early as the beginning of the ninth century. Many of the treatises of Averroes were translated by the Spanish Jews into Hebrew: and the Latin pieces of Averroes now extant were translated into Latin from these Hebrew versions. I have already mentioned the school or university of Cordova. Leo Africanus speaks of "Platea bibliothecariorum Cordovæ." This, from what follows, appears to be a street of booksellers. It was in the time of Averroes, and about the year 1220. One of our Jew philosophers, having fallen in love, turned poet, and his verses were publicly sold in this street.⁴ My author says that, renouncing the dignity of the Jewish doctor, he took to writing verses.⁵

---

¹ Conring. *ut supr.* Sæc. xiii. cap. 4, p. 126. About the same time the works of Galen and Hippocrates were first translated from Greek into Latin, but in a most barbarous style. *Id. ibid.* p. 127.
² [Morris's *Chaucer*, ii. 14, ver. 438.]
³ Euseb. Renaudot. apud Fabric. *Bibl. Gr.* xii. 254.
⁴ Leo African. *De Med. et Philosoph. Hebr.* c. xxviii. xxix.
⁵ *Id. ibid.* "Amore capitur, et dignitate doctorum posthabita coepit edere carmina." See also Simon. in Suppl. ad Leon. Mutinens. *De Ritib. Hebr.* p. 104.

The Sumner or Summoner, whose office it was to summon uncanonical offenders into the archdeacon's court, where they were very rigorously punished, is humorously drawn as counteracting his profession by his example: he is libidinous and voluptuous, and his rosy countenance belies his occupation. This is an indirect satire on the ecclesiastical proceedings of those times. His affectation of Latin terms, which he had picked up from the decrees and pleadings of the court, must have formed a character highly ridiculous:

> And whan that he wel dronken hadde the wyn,[1]
> Than wolde he speke no word but Latyn.
> A fewe termes hadde he, tuo or thre,
> That he hadde lerned out of som decree;
> No wondur is, he herde it al the day;
> And eek ye knowe wel, how that a jay
> Can clepe Watte,[2] as wel as can the pope.
> But who-so wolde in othur thing him grope,[3]
> Thanne hadde he spent al his philosophie,
> Ay, *Questio quid juris*, wolde he crye.

He is with great propriety made the friend and companion of the Pardoner, or dispenser of indulgences, who is just arrived from the pope, "brimful of pardons come from Rome al hote;" and who carries in his wallet, among other holy curiosities, the Virgin Mary's veil, and part of the sail of Saint Peter's ship.[4]

The Monk is represented as more attentive to horses and hounds than to the rigorous and obsolete ordinances of Saint Benedict. Such are his ideas of secular pomp and pleasure, that he is even qualified to be an abbot:[5]

> An out-rydere, that lovede venerye;[6]
> A manly man, to ben an abbot able.
> Ful many a deynté hors hadde he in stable:
>   *   *   *   *   *
> This ilke[7] monk leet forby hem pace,
> And helde aftur the newe world the space.
> He yaf nat of that text a pulled hen,[8]
> That seith, that hunters been noon holy men.

---

[1] [Morris's *Chaucer*, ii. 20, ver. 637.]
[2] So edit. 1561. See Johnson's *Dictionary*, in Magpie.
[3] examine.   [4] ver. 694, *seq.*
[5] There is great humour in the circumstances which qualify our monk to be an abbot. Some time in the thirteenth century, the prior and convent of Saint Swithin's at Winchester appear to have recommended one of their brethren to the convent of Hyde as a proper person to be preferred to the abbacy of that convent, then vacant. These are his merits. "Est enim confrater ille noster in glosanda sacra pagina bene callens, in scriptura [transcribing] peritus, in capitalibus literis appingendis bonus artifex, in regula S. Benedicti instructissimus, psallendi doctissimus," &c. *MS. Registr.* ut supr. p. 277. These were the ostensible qualities of the master of a capital monastery. But Chaucer, in the verses before us, seems to have told the real truth, and to have given the real character as it actually existed in life. I believe that our industrious *confrere*, with all his knowledge of glossing, writing, illuminating, chanting, and Benedict's rules, would in fact have been less likely to succeed to a vacant abbey, than one of the genial complexion and popular accomplishments here inimitably described.
[6] hunting. [Morris's *Chaucer*, ii. 6, ver. 166.]   [7] same.
[8] "He did not care a straw for the text," &c.

He is ambitious of appearing a conspicuous and stately figure on horseback. A circumstance represented with great elegance:

> And whan he rood, men might his bridel heere[1]
> Gyngle in a whistlyng wynd so cleere,
> And eek as lowde as doth the chapel belle.

The gallantry of his riding-dress and his genial aspect are painted in lively colours:

> I saugh his sleves purfiled[2] atte hond[3]
> With grys,[4] and that the fynest of a lond.
> And for to festne his hood undur his chyn
> He hadde of gold y-wrought a curious pyn:
> A love-knotte in the gretter ende ther was.
> His heed was ballid, and schon as eny glas,
> And eek his face as he hadde be anoynt.
> He was a lord ful fat and in good poynt;
> His eyen steep, and rollyng in his heed,
> That stemed as a forneys of a leed;
> His bootes souple, his hors in gret estat.
> Now certeinly he was a fair prelat;
> He was not pale as a for-pyned goost.
> A fat swan loved he best of eny roost.
> His palfray was as broun as eny berye.

The Frere, or friar, is equally fond of diversion and good living; but the poverty of his establishment obliges him to travel about the country, and to practise various artifices to provide money for his convent, under the sacred character of a confessor.

> A frere ther was, a wantoun and a merye,[5]
> A lymytour,[6] a ful solempne man.
> In alle the ordres foure[7] is noon that can
> So moche of daliaunce and fair langage.
> * * * *
> Ful sweetly herde he confessioun,
> And plesaunt was his absolucioun;
> * * * *
> His typet was ay farsud ful of knyfes
> And pynnes, for to yive faire wyfes.
> And certaynli he hadde a mery noote.
> Wel couthe he synge and pleye on a rote.[8]

---

[1] [Morris's *Chaucer*, ii. 6, ver. 169.]
[2] fringed.   [3] [Morris's *Chaucer*, ii. 7, ver. 193.]   [4] fur.
[5] [Morris's *Chaucer*, ii. 7, ver. 208.]
[6] A friar that had a particular grant for begging or hearing confessions within certain limits.
[7] of Mendicants.
[8] A rote is a musical instrument. Lydgate, MSS. Fairfax, Bibl. Bodl. 16.
> "For ther was Rotys of Almayne,
> And eke of Arragon and Spayne."

Again, in the same manuscript,
> "Harpys, fitheles, and eke rotys,
> Wel according to ther notys."

Where *fitheles* is *fiddles*, as in the *Prol. Cl. Oxenf.* v. 298. So in the *Roman d'Alexandre*, MSS. Bibl. Bodl. *ut supr.* fol. i. b, col. 2.
> "*Rote*, harpe, viole, et gigne, et siphonie."

I cannot help mentioning in this place, a pleasant mistake of Bishop Morgan, in

> Of yeddynges[1] he bar utturly the prys.[2]
>
> Ther was no man nowher fo vertuous.
> He was the befte begger in al his hous,[3]
>
> Somwhat he lipfede, for wantouneffe,
> To make his Engliffch fwete upon his tunge;
> And in his harpyng, whan that he hadde funge,
> His eyghen twynkeled in his heed aright,
> As don the fterres in the frofty night.

With thefe unhallowed and untrue fons of the church is contrafted the parfon or parifh-prieft: in defcribing whofe fanctity, fimplicity, fincerity, patience, induftry, courage, and confcientious impartiality, Chaucer fhews his good fenfe and good heart. Dryden imitated this character of the Good Parfon, and is faid to have applied it to Bifhop Ken. [The *Perfones Tale*, as Dr. Morris has pointed out, was partly borrowed by Chaucer, with large variations, from the French treatife, *La Somme de Vices et de Vertus*, by Frere Lorens, of which there are verfions in Englifh, both profe and metrical.][4]

The character of the Squire teaches us the education and requifite accomplifhments of young gentlemen in the gallant reign of Edward III. But it is to be remembered, that our fquire is the fon of a knight, who has performed feats of chivalry in every part of the world; which the poet thus enumerates with great dignity and fimplicity:

> At Alifandre he was whan it was wonne,[5]
> Ful ofte tyme he hadde the bord bygonne[6]
> Aboven alle naciouns in Pruce.
> In Lettowe[7] hadde reyced and in Ruce
> No criften man fo ofte of his degré.
> In Gernade atte fiege hadde he be

---

his tranflation of the New Teftament into Welfh, printed 1567. He tranflates the Vials of wrath, in the Revelation, by *Crythan*, i. e. *Crouds* or Fiddles, Rev. v. 8. The Greek is φιαλαι. Now it is probable that the bifhop tranflated only from the Englifh, where he found vials, which he took for viols.

[1] [The *Prompt. Parv.* makes yedding to be the fame as gefte which it explains thus: geeft or romaunce, geftio. So that of yeddinges may perhaps mean of ftorytelling.—*Tyrwhitt*.]

[2] [Morris's *Chaucer*, ii. 8, ver. 237.]
[3] convent.
[4] [*Ayenbite of Inwyt*, ed. 1866, Introd.]
[5] [Morris's *Chaucer*, ii. 3, ver. 51.]
[6] See this phrafe explained above, p. 354, note 3. I will here add a fimilar expreffion from Gower, *Conf. Amant.* lib. viii. [iii. 299, edit. 1857.]

> " Bad his marefhall of his halle
> To fetten him in fuch degre,
> That he upon him myghte fe.
> The king was fone fette and ferved,
> And he which had his prife deferved,
> After the kings owne worde,
> Was made begin a middel borde."

That is, " he was feated in the middle of the table, a place of diftinction and dignity." [See the Forewords to *The Babees Book*, E. E. T. Soc. 1868.--F.]

[7] Lithuania.

> Of Algesir,[1] and riden in Belmarie.[2]
> At Lieys[3] was he, and at Satalie,[4]
> Whan they were wonne; and in the Greete see
> At many a noble arive hadde he be.
> At mortal batailles hadde he ben fiftene,
> And foughten for oure feith at Tramassene[5]
> In lystes thries, and ay slayn his foo.
> This ilke worthi knight hadde ben also
> Somtyme with the lord of Palatye,[6]
> Ayeyn[7] another hethene in Turkye:
> And everemore he hadde a sovereyn prys.
> And though that he was worthy he was wys.

The poet in some of these lines implies, that after the Christians were driven out of Palestine, the English knights of his days joined the knights of Livonia and Prussia, and attacked the pagans of Lithuania and its adjacent territories. Lithuania was not converted to Christianity till towards the close of the fourteenth century. Prussian targets are mentioned, as we have before seen, in the *Knight's Tale*. Thomas, Duke of Gloucester, youngest son of King Edward III. and Henry Earl of Derby, afterwards Henry IV. travelled into Prussia: and in conjunction with the grand masters and knights of Prussia and Livonia, fought the infidels of Lithuania. The Earl of Derby was greatly instrumental in taking Vilna, the capital of that

---

[1] [Algesiras; a Spanish town on the opposite side of the bay of Gibraltar.—*Price*.]

[2] Speght supposes it to be that country in Barbary which is called Benamarin. It is mentioned again in the *Knight's Tale*, v. 1772.

> " Ne in Belmary ther is no fel lyoun,
> That hunted is," &c.

By which at least we may conjecture it to be some country in Africa. [Froissart reckons it among the kingdoms of Africa: Thunes, Bovgie, Maroch, Bellemarine, Tremessen. The battle of Benamarin is said by a late author of Viage de Espanna, p. 73, n. 1, to have been so called: "por haber quedallo en ella Albohacen, Rey de Marruccos del linage de Aben Marin." Perhaps therefore the dominions of that family in Africa might be called abusively Benamarin, and by a further corruption Belmarie.—*Tyrwhitt*.]

[3] Some suppose it to be Lavissa, a city on the continent, near Rhodes. Others, Lybissa, a city of Bithynia.

[4] A city in Anatolia, called Atalia. Many of these places are mentioned in the history of the Crusades. The gulf and castle of Satalia are mentioned by Benedictus Abbas, in the Crusade under the year 1191, " Et cum rex Franciæ recessisset ab Antiocheo, statim intravit gulfum Sathallæ.—Sathallæ Castellum est optimum, unde gulfus ille nomen accepit; et super gulfum illum sunt duo Castella et Villæ, et utrumque dicitur Satalia. Sed unum illorum est desertum, et dicitur Vetus Satalia quod piratæ destruxerunt, et alterum Nova Satalia dicitur, quod Manuel imperator Constantinopolis firmavit." *Vit. et Gest. Henr. et Ric. ii.* p. 680. Afterwards he mentions *Mare Græcum*, p. 683. That is, the Mediterranean from Sicily to Cyprus. I am inclined, in the second verse following, to read " Greke sea." [" Probably the part of the Mediterranean, which washes the shores of Palestine in opposition to the small inland Sea or Lake of Gennesaret and the Dead Sea."—*Bell*.] Leyis is the town of Layas in Armenia.

[5] " In the holy war at Thrasimene, a city in Barbary."

[6] Palathia, a city in Anatolia. See Froissart, iii. 40.

[7] against.

country, in 1390.[1] Here is a feeming compliment to fome of thefe expeditions. This invincible and accomplifhed champion afterwards tells the heroic tale of *Palamon and Arcite*. His fon the *Squire*, a youth of twenty years, is thus delineated:

> And he hadde ben fomtyme in chivachie,[2]
> In Flaundres, in Artoys, and in Picardie,
> And born him wel, as in fo litel fpace,
> In hope to ftonden in his lady grace.
> Embrowdid was he, as it were a mede
> Al ful of frefshe floures, white and reede.
> Syngynge he was, or flowtynge, al the day;
> He was as frefsh as is the moneth of May.
> Schort was his goune, with fleeves long and wyde.
> Wel cowde he fitte on hors, and *faire* ryde.
> He cowde fonges wel make and endite,
> Juftne and eek daunce, and wel purtray and write.

To this young man the poet, with great obfervance of decorum, gives the tale of Cambufcan, the next in knightly dignity to that of Palamon and Arcite. He is attended by a yeoman, whofe figure revives the ideas of the foreft laws:

> And he was clad in coote and hood of grene.[3]
> A fhef of pocok arwes bright and kene[4]
> Under his belte he bar ful thriftily.
> Wel cowde he dreffe his takel yomanly;
> His arwes drowpud nought with fetheres lowe.
> And in his hond he bar a mighty bowe.
> * * * * *
> Upon his arme he bar a gay bracer,[5]

---

[1] See Hakluyt's *Voyages*, i. 122, *feq.* edit. 1598. See alfo Hakluyt's account of the conqueft of Pruffia by the Dutch Knights Hofpitallers of Jerufalem, *ibid.* [The original documents relating to this expedition, and alfo to thefe knights' expedition to the Holy Land, are now in the Record Office in London, and ought certainly to be printed by fome learned Society.—F.]

[2] Chivalry, riding, exercifes of horfemanfhip, *Compl. Mar. Ven.* v. 144.

> "Ciclinius ryding in his chevaché
> Fro Venus."

[Morris's *Chaucer*, ii. 4, ver. 85.]

[3] *Ibid.* ver. 103.

[4] Comp. Gul. Waynflete, epifc. Winton. an. 1471, (*fupr. citat.*) Among the ftores of the bifhop's caftle of Farnham. "*Arcus cum chordis.* Et red. conp. de xxiv. arcubus cum xxiv. chordis de remanentia.—*Sagittæ magnæ.* Et de cxliv. fagittis magnis barbatis cum pennis pavonum." In a *Computus* of Bifhop Gerways, epifc. Winton. an. 1266, (*fupr. citat*) among the ftores of the bifhop's caftle of Taunton, one of the heads or ftyles is, *Caudæ pavonum*, which I fuppofe were ufed for feathering arrows. In the articles of Arma, which are part of the epifcopal ftores of the faid caftle, I find enumerated one thoufand four hundred and twenty-one great arrows for crofs-bows, remaining over and above three hundred and feventy-one delivered to the bifhop's vaffals *tempore guerre.* Under the fame title occur crofs-bows made of horn. Arrows with feathers of the peacock occur in Lydgate's *Siege of Troy*, B. iii. cap. 22, fign. O iii. edit. 1555.

> "Many good archers
> Of Boeme, which with their arrows kene,
> And with fethirs of pecocke frefhe and fhene," &c.

[5] armour for the arms.

> And by his fide a fwerd and a bokeler,
> * * * * *
> A Criftofre¹ on his breft of filver fchene.
> An horn he bar, the bawdrik was of grene.

The character of the Reeve (or Steward), an officer of much greater truft and authority during the feudal conftitution than at prefent, is happily pictured.² His attention to the care and cuftody of the manors, the produce of which was then kept in hand for furnifhing his lord's table, perpetually employs his time, preys upon his thoughts, and makes him lean and choleric. He is the terror of bailiffs and hinds: and is remarkable for his circumfpection, vigilance, and fubtlety. He is never in arrears, and no auditor is able to over-reach or detect him in his accounts: yet he makes more commodious purchafes for himfelf than for his mafter, without forfeiting the goodwill or bounty of the latter. Amidft thefe ftrokes of fatire, Chaucer's genius for defcriptive painting breaks forth in this fimple and beautiful defcription of the Reeve's rural habitation:

> His wonyng³ was ful fair upon an heth,⁴
> With grene trees i-fchadewed was his place.

In the Clerk of Oxford⁵ our author glances at the inattention paid to literature, and the unprofitablenefs of philofophy. He is emaciated with ftudy, clad in a thread-bare cloak, and rides a fteed lean as a rake:

> For he hadde nought geten him yit a benefice,⁶
> Ne was not worthy to haven an office.
> For him was lever⁷ have at his beddes heed
> Twenty bookes, clothed in blak and reed,
> Of Ariftotil, and of his philofophie,
> Then robus riche, or fithul,⁸ or fawtrie.
> But although he were a philofophre,
> Yet hadde he but litul gold in cofre.⁹

His unwearied attention to logic had tinctured his converfation with much pedantic formality, and taught him to fpeak on all fubjects in a precife and fententious ftyle.¹⁰ Yet his converfation was

---

¹ A faint who prefided over the weather. The patron of field fports.
² [See the Ballad of John de Reeve in the *Percy Folio Ballads and Romances*, ii. 550.]
³ dwelling.   ⁴ [Morris's *Chaucer*, ii. 19, ver. 606.]
⁵ [For the early Oxford Life and Studies, fee Mr. Anfty's *Munimenta Academica*, Rolls Series, 1868.]
⁶ [Morris's *Chaucer*, ii. 10, ver. 291.]   ⁷ rather.   ⁸ fiddle.
⁹ Or it may be explained, "Yet he could not find the philofopher's ftone."
¹⁰ [This opinion is founded on the following paffage:
> "Not oo word fpak he more than was neede;
> Al that he fpak it was of heye prudence,
> And fchort, and quyk, and ful of gret fentence."
> Morris's *Chaucer*, ii. 10, 304.

Mr. Tyrwhitt has given a happier and unqueftionably a correcter interpretation of thefe lines: "'In forme and reverence,' with propriety and modefty. In the next line, 'ful of high fentence' means only, I apprehend, full of high or excellent fenfe. Mr. Warton will excufe me for fuggefting thefe explanations of this paffage in lieu of thofe which he has given. The credit of good letters is concerned that

instructive: and he was no less willing to submit than to communicate his opinion to others:

> Sownynge in moral manere was his speche,[1]
> And gladly wolde he lerne, and gladly teche.

The perpetual importance of the Serjeant of Law, who by habit or by affectation has the faculty of appearing busy when he has nothing to do, is sketched with the spirit and concisenefs of Horace:

> Nowher so besy a man as he ther nas,[2]
> And yit he semede besier than he was.[3]

There is some humour in making our lawyer introduce the language of his pleadings into common conversation. He addresses the host:

> Host, quod he, *De par Dieux I assente*.[4]

The affectation of talking French was indeed general, but it is here appropriate and in character.

Among the rest, the character of the Host, or master of the Tabard inn where the pilgrims are assembled, is conspicuous. He has much good sense, and discovers great talent for managing and

---

Chaucer should not be supposed to have made a pedantic formality and a precise sententious style on all subjects the characteristics of a scholar."—*Tyrwhitt*.]

[1] [Morris's *Chaucer*, ii. 10, ver. 307.]   [2] [*Ibid*. ii. 11, ver. 321.]

[3] [*Ibid*. ii. 171, ver. 39.] He is said to have "oftin yben at the parvise," ver. 312. It is not my design to enter into the disputes concerning the meaning or etymology of parvis: from which parvisia, the name for the public schools in Oxford, is derived. But I will observe, that parvis is mentioned as a court or portico before the church of Notre Dame at Paris, in John de Meun's part of the *Roman de la Rose*, ver. 12529:

> " A Paris n'eust hommes ne femme
> Au parvis devant Nostre Dame."

The passage is thus translated by Chaucer, or the writer of the *Rom. R*. v. 7109:

> " Ther nas no wight in alle Parys
> Biforne oure lady at parvys."

The word is supposed to be contracted from Paradise. This perhaps signified an ambulatory. Many of our old religious houses had a place called Paradise. In the year 1300, children were taught to read and sing in the Parvis of St. Martin's church at Norwich. Blomf. *Norf*. ii. 748. Our Serjeant is afterwards said to have received many fees and robes, v. 319. The serjeants and all the officers of the superior courts of law, anciently received winter and summer robes, from the king's wardrobe. He is likewise said to cite cases and decisions, "that from the time of king William were full," v. 326. For this line see the very learned and ingenious Mr. Barrington's *Observations on the antient Statutes*. [This subject is better discussed (says Mr. Douce) in Staveley's *History of Churches*, p. 157. He thinks the term is from *parvis pueris*, i. e. the children who were taught in a certain part of the church so appropriated; as appears from the quotation above cited in the note from Blomefield. Herbert the press-historian adds, that Minster-church in the isle of Thanet and St. Dunstan's in the East, London, have portions of them assigned for schools; and no doubt but there are several others which have the same.—I can add from my own knowledge, that the chapel at Hughington in the county of Lincoln was appropriated to the purposes of a school, and that King Street chapel, Westminster, has a portion of its structure set apart for such purpose: for I received the greater share of my education in both those places.—*Park*.]

[4] [Morris's *Chaucer*, ii. 171, ver. 39.]

regulating a large company; and to him we are indebted for the happy proposal of obliging every pilgrim to tell a story during their journey to Canterbury. His interpositions between the tales are very useful and enlivening; and he is something like the chorus on the Grecian stage. He is of great service in encouraging each person to begin his part, in conducting the scheme with spirit, in making proper observations on the merit or tendency of the several stories, in settling disputes which must naturally arise in the course of such an entertainment, and in connecting all the narratives into one continued system. His love of good cheer, experience in marshalling guests, address, authoritative deportment, and facetious disposition, are thus expressively displayed by Chaucer:

> Greet cheere made oure oft us everichon,[1]
> And to the souper sette he us anon;
> And served us with vitaille atte beste.
> Strong was the wyn, and wel to drynke us lefte.[2]
> A semely man oure ooste was withalle
> For to han been a marchal in an halle;
> A large man was he with eyghen stepe,
> A fairere burgeys is ther noon in Chepe[3]
> Bold of his speche, and wys, and wel i-taught,
> And of manhede lakkede he right naught.
> Eke therto he was right a mery man.

Chaucer's scheme of the *Canterbury Tales* was evidently left unfinished. It was intended by our author, that every pilgrim should likewise tell a Tale on the return from Canterbury.[4] A poet, who lived soon after the *Canterbury Tales* made their appearance, seems to have designed a supplement to this deficiency, and with this view to have written a tale called the *Merchant's Second Tale*, or the *History of Beryn*.[5] It was first printed by Urry, who supposed it to be Chaucer's.[6] In the Prologue, which is of considerable length, there is some humour and contrivance: the author, happily enough, continues to characterize the pilgrims, by imagining what each

---

[1] [Morris's *Chaucer*, ii. 24, ver. 747.]
[2] we liked.   [3] Cheapside.
[4] Or rather, two on their way thither, and two on their return. Only Chaucer himself tells two tales. The poet says that there were twenty-nine pilgrims in company: but in the Characters he describes more. Among the Tales which remain, there are none of the Prioress's Chaplains, the Haberdasher, Carpenter, Webster, Dyer, Tapiser, and Host. The Canon's Yeoman has a Tale, but no Character. The *Plowman's Tale* is certainly supposititious. See *supr.* and *Obs. Spens.* ii. 217. It is omitted in the copy of the *Canterbury Tales*, MSS. Harl. 1758. These Tales were supposed to be spoken, not written. But we have in the Ploughman's, "For my writing me allow." And in other places, "For my writing if I have blame."—"Of my writing have me excus'd," &c. See a note at the beginning of the *Cant. Tales*, MSS. Laud, K. 50, Bibl. Bodl. written by John Barcham. But the discussion of these points properly belongs to an editor of Chaucer. [See Mr. Tyrwhitt's *Introductory Discourse to the Canterbury Tales.*—Price.]
[5] [Lydgate also wrote his *Sege of Thebes* as a supplementary Canterbury Tale. —F.]
[6] Urr. *Chauc.* p. 595.

did, and how each behaved, when they all arrived at Canterbury. After dinner was ordered at their inn, they all proceed to the cathedral. At entering the church one of the monks sprinkles them with holy water. The Knight with the better sort of the company goes in great order to the shrine of Thomas a Becket. The Miller and his companions run staring about the church: they pretend to blazon the arms painted in the glass windows, and enter into a dispute in heraldry: but the host of the Tabard reproves them for their improper behaviour and impertinent discourse, and directs them to the martyr's shrine. When all had finished their devotions, they return to the inn. In the way thither they purchase toys for which that city was famous, called *Canterbury brochis*, and here much facetiousness passes betwixt the Friar and the Sumner, in which the latter vows revenge on the former, for telling a tale so palpably levelled at his profession, and protests he will retaliate on their return by a more severe story. When dinner is ended, the host of the Tabard thanks all the company in form for their several tales. The party then separate till supper-time by agreement. The Knight goes to survey the walls and bulwarks of the city, and explains to his son the Squire the nature and strength of them. Mention is here made of great guns. The Wife of Bath is too weary to walk far; she proposes to the Prioress to divert themselves in the garden, which abounds with herbs proper for making salves. Others wander about the streets. The Pardoner has a low adventure, which ends much to his disgrace. The next morning they proceed on their return to Southwark: and our genial master of the Tabard, just as they leave Canterbury, by way of putting the company into good humour, begins a panegyric on the morning and the month of April, some lines of which I shall quote, as a specimen of our author's abilities in poetical description:[1]

> Lo! how the seson of the yere, and Averell[2] shouris,
> Doith[3] the bushis burgyn[4] out blossomes and flouris.
> Lo! the prymerosys of the yere, how fresh they bene to sene,
> And many othir flouris among the grassis grene.
> Lo! how they springe and sprede, and of divers hue,
> Beholdith and seith, both white, red, and blue.
> That lusty bin and comfortabyll for mannis sight,
> For I say for myself it makith my hert to light.

On casting lots, it falls to the Merchant to tell the first tale, which then follows. I cannot [of course] allow that this Prologue and Tale were written by Chaucer. Yet I believe them to be nearly coeval, [within, perhaps, fifty years of the poet's death.]

[APPENDIX TO SECTION IX.

In connection with the *Canterbury Tales*,[5] it will be well to say something of the MSS. of them, the classes of those MSS., the groups and order of the Tales, the stages of the journey, Chaucer's use of

---

[1] There is a good description of a magical palace, v. 1973—2076.
[2] April.   [3] make.   [4] shoot.
[5] [The following paragraphs on Chaucer are by Mr. Furnivall.]

the final *e*, and the genuineness of some of the poems attributed to him.

Of MSS. of the Tales we know at least forty-eight; and of these forty-two have been lately examined in order, 1. to choose the best six unprinted for the Chaucer Society to print, 2. to find out in what fragments and groups the Tales were left by Chaucer at his death, and 3. what great differences the MSS. show between themselves. Lord Ashburnham, who has three MSS. of the Tales, has declined to allow the examination of his MSS. for the purposes above stated, but the remaining forty-two MSS. show that they may be ranged under two types, if we classify by *readings*, namely that of the Harleian MS. 7334 (printed by Mr. Thomas Wright and Dr. Richard Morris) and that of the Ellesmere MS. (one of the type that Tyrwhitt printed). But if we classify by *structure*,—by the order of the fragments of the Tales, and the changes made in the text by the changes of that order,—which plan best exhibits the differences of the MSS., we must range our MSS. under three main types.

Text A. Gamelyn in (generally); Man of Law's end-link changed to serve as a Prologue to the Squire's Tale, which is misplaced, to follow the Man of Law, as the Merchant's Tale is, to follow the Squire. Consequently, the stanzas of the Clerk's end-link or envoy are misplaced, so as to break the join between it and the Merchant's Tale made by the lines

> And let hem care and wepe, and wyng and wayle.[1]
> Wepyng and wailyng, care and other sorwe.[2]

No Host-stanza between the Clerk's and Merchant's Tales; Squire's end-link (or Franklin's Prologue) used as the Merchant's Prologue. Generally, spurious Prologues to Shipman and Franklin. Second Nun and Canon's Yeoman kept up high in the order of tales. Modern instances in the Monk's Tale in their right places, after Zenobia.[3]

---

[1] End of Clerk, l. 9088, Wright.   [2] Line 1 of Merchant, l. 9089, Wright.

[3] The following are MSS. of the A type, though some vary from it in certain points:

Lansdowne, 851.
Lichfield Cathedral.
Harleian, 7333.
Harleian, 1758.
Sloane, 1685.
Royal, 17 D xv.
Royal, 18 C ii.
Camb. Univ. Ii 3. 26.
Sloane, 1686.
Petworth.
Camb. Univ. Mm. 2. 5.

Trin. Coll. Cambr. R. 3. 15.
Trin. Coll. Cambr. R. 3. 3.
Barlow, 20.
Laud, 739.
New Coll. Oxf.
Corpus Chr. Coll. Oxf. 198.
Hatton, 1.
Rawl. MS. Poet. 149.
Rawl. Misc. 1133.
(All the early printed editions.)

Other MSS. varying much in the order of Tales, or being incomplete, are

Harl., 1239.
Sion Coll.
Brit. Mus. Addit. 25, 718.
Hengwrt.
Rawl. MS. Poet. 141.
Laud, 600.

Arch. Seld., B 14, (the only MS. that rightly joins the Man of Law's and Shipman's Tales.)
Holkham.
Christ Church, Oxf. 152.

The three types of the Canterbury Tales.

Text B. Harleian, 7334. Gamelyn in; Man of Law's end-link left, but with nothing to join into it. Clerk and Merchant kept together (no Hoſt-ſtanza between). Second Nun and Canon's Yeoman kept up. Modern inſtances in Monk's Tale in their right places (that is, the 2 Peters, Barnabo, and Hugilin, come after Zenobia, and before Nero).

Text C, or Edited Texts.[1] Gamelyn cut out. Man of Law's end-link cut out. Hoſt-ſtanza inſerted between Clerk and Merchant. Second Nun and Canon's Yeoman placed late. Modern inſtances in Monk's Tale put at the end, thus breaking the join made by

> But for that *fortune* wil alway aſſayle, 16249.
>
> And cover hir brighte face with a *clowde*, 16252.[2]
>
> He ſpak, how *fortune* was clipped with a *clowde*, 16268.[3]

It is ſomewhat curious that not one of the MSS. yet examined exhibits the Tales in the order in which Chaucer himſelf muſt have arranged or meant to arrange them, as ſhown by the ſtate he left them in at his death. That order is the following, which falls in well with a three-and-a-half days' journey of the pilgrims to Canterbury, allowing about ſixteen miles a day,—enough for the women to ride along the bad miry roads of thoſe early times:

Groups.	Fragments.	Tales and Links.	Alluſions to Places, Times, Prior Tales, &c. (Wright's 2-col. ed.)	Diſtances and Stages.
A.	I	1 GENERAL PROLOGUE	In Southwerk at the Tabbard as I lay. (l. 20).	
		2 KNIGHT		
		3 Link		
		4 MILLER		
		5 Link	{ Lo heer is Deptford, and it is paſſed prime ; Lo Greenewich, ther many a ſchrewe is inne. (l. 3906-7).	
		6 REVE		
		7 Link		
		8 COOK		
		* * *	[? *End of the Firſt Day's Journey.*]	[? Dartford 15 miles.]
B.	II.	1 Prologue		
		2 MAN OF LAW	It was ten of the clokke, he gan conclude (l. 4434).	
		3 Link		
	III.	4 SHIPMAN		
		5 Link		
		6 PRIORESS		
		7 Link		
		8 SIR THOPAS		
		9 Link		
		10 MELIBE		
		11 Link		
		12 MONK	Lo, Rowcheſtre ſtant hee;-faſte by (l. 15412).	
		13 Link		
		14 NUN'S PRIEST		
		15 Link		
		* * *	[? *End of the Second Day's Journey.*]	[? Rocheſter 30 miles.]

---

[1] MSS. of the C type, *Edited Texts*, are :

Elleſmere.
Camb. Univ. Gg. 4. 27.
Camb. Univ. Dd. 4. 24.
Harl. 7335.
Addit. Brit. Mus. 5140, (or Aſkew, 2.)

Duke of Devonſhire.
Helmingham.
Bodley, 686.
Haiſtwell MS. (or Aſkew, 1.)

[2] End of Monkes Tale, ed. Wright, from Harl. 7334.

[3] 6th line of Prologue of Nonne Preſtes Tale.

Scheme of the Canterbury Tales.

Groups.	Frag-ments.	Tales and Links.	Allusions to Places, Times, Prior Tales, &c. (Wright's 2-col. ed.)	Distances and Stages.
C.	IV.†	1 DOCTOR 2 Link and Prologue 3 PARDONER		
D.	V.	1 Prologue 2 WIFE OF BATH 3 Link 4 FRIAR 5 Link 6 SOMPNOUR	Quod this Sompnour, "And I byschrewe me But if I telle tales tuo or thre Of freres, er I come to Sydingborne. l. 6427-9). My tale is don, we ben almoft at toune. (l. 7876). [? Halt in the Third Day's Journey for Dinner.]	[? Sittingbourne 40 miles.]

† This group may go on any morning. It is put here to make the Tales of the Third Day not lefs than thofe of the Second.

E.	VI.	1 Prologue 2 CLERK 3 Link 4 Link 5 MERCHANT 6 Link	For which heer, for the wyves love of Bathe (l. 9046). The wif of Bathe, if ye han underftonde, Of mariage, which ye han now in honde Declared hath ful wel in litel fpace (l. 9559-61) To tellen al; wherfor my tale is do (l. 10314). [? End of the Third Day's Journey.]	[? Ofpringe 46 miles.]
F.	VII.	1 Link (l. 10315) 2 SQUIRE 3 Link 4 FRANKLIN	I wol not tarien you, for it is pryme (l. 10387).	
G.	VIII.	1 SECOND NUN 2 Link & Prologue 3 CANON'S YEOMAN	Er we fully had riden fyve myle, (l. 12483) At Boughtoun under Blee us gan atake A man, that clothed was in clothes blake.. It femed he hadde priked myles thre (l. 12489) His yeman eek was ful of curtefye, And feid, "Sires, now in the morwe tyde (l. 12516) Out of your oftelry I faugh you ryde.... ..al this ground on which we ben ridynge Til that we comen to Caunterbury toun (l. 12552). [Paufe. Go up Blean Hill, and through the Foreft.]	
H.	IX.	1 Prologue 2 MANCIPLE	Wot ye not wher ther ftont a litel toun, Which that cleped is Bob-up-and-doun, Under the Ble, in Caunterbury way? (l. 16935)... Is ther no man, for prayer ne for hyre (l. 16938) That wol awake our felawe al byhynde? A theef mighte [him] ful lightly robbe and bynde... Awake thou cook, fit up, God gif the forwe! What eyleth the, to flepe by the morwe? Haft thou had fleen al night, or artow dronke? Or haftow with fom quen al night i-fwonke, So that thou maift not holden up thyn heed? (l. 16951).	
I.	X.	1 Link & Prologue 2 PARSON	By that the Maunciple [?] had his tale endid (l. 17295) The fonne fro the fouth line is defcendid So lowe, that it nas nought to my fight Degrees nyne and twentye as in hight [Four] on the clokke it was, as I geffe... As we were entryng at a townes end (l. 17306) Now lakketh us no moo tales than oon (l. 17310) I wol yow telle a mery tale in profe, (l. 17340) To knyt up al this feft, and make an ende; But hafteth yow, the fonne wol adoun (l. 17366). [End of the Fourth Day's Journey. Reach Canterbury]	[56 miles.]

For a juftification of the conclufions here given, I muft refer to my Temporary Preface to the Six-Text edition of *Chaucer's Canterbury Tales*, Part I. 1868; and to Part I. of the Six-Text itfelf for fpecimens of the changed Man of Law's and Squire's end-links, the fpurious Prologues, &c., as well as tables fhowing the order of the tales in thirty-fix MSS. and five old printed editions.

The language of Chaucer—efpecially his ufe of the final *e*—and by it the fettlement of what works attributed to him are genuine and what not, is a queftion of the higheft importance. The ufe of *e* final by Chaucer, in the excellent, though flightly provincial MS. of *Canterbury Tales*, Harl. MS. 7334, as printed by Mr. Thomas Wright, and by Gower in his *Confeſſio Amantis*, as reprefented by Dr. Pauli's edition, has been inveftigated with the greateft care by Prof. F. J. Child, of Harvard Univerfity, Maſſachuſetts. His refults have been incorporated by Mr. Alexander J. Ellis in his important work on *Early Englifh Pronunciation, with fpecial reference to Chaucer and Shakefpeare*, publifhed jointly by the Philological, Early Englifh Text, and Chaucer Societies. Dr. Richard Morris in his admirable *Selections from Chaucer*, has alfo ftated the main refults of Prof. Child's and his own inveftigations into the ufe of the final *e* by Chaucer; and as both the two laft-named works are fo eafily to be had, and fhould be in the poffeffion of every ftudent, a reference to them is all that is needed here.

Mr. H. Bradfhaw, Librarian of the Univerfity of Cambridge, the moft Chaucer-learned ftudent in England, ftated fome years back, that having put in one clafs the works undoubtedly Chaucer's,—thofe named as his by himfelf, or attributed to him by his cotemporaries, or good MSS.,—and having put into a fecond clafs the other works attributed to Chaucer on authorities other than thofe above fpecified, he found on tefting them by the *ye-y* rhyme teft, that all the works of the firft clafs ftood the teft and proved genuine, while all the works of the fecond clafs failed under the teft, and proved (in his opinion) fpurious. Having thus (as he fays) both external and internal evidence againft this fecond clafs, Mr. Bradfhaw rejects as Chaucer's works, the following poems contained in Dr. R. Morris's Aldine edition of the poet's Poetical Works, and *à fortiori*, all the fpurious matter introduced into *Chaucer's Works* by former editors:

Court of Love, iv. 1.
Boke of Cupide, or Cuckow and Nightingale, iv. 51.
Flower and Leaf, iv. 87.
Chaucer's Dream, v. 86.
Proverbs of Chaucer, vi. 303.
World fo wyde, *ib.*
Roundel, vi. 304.
Romaunt of the Rofe, vi. 1.
Compleynte of a Loveres Lyfe, or Black Knyght, vi. 235.
Goodly Ballade of Chaucer, vi. 275.
Praife of Women, vi. 278.
Leaulte vault Richeffe, vi. 302.
Virelai, vi. 305.
Chaucer's Prophecy, vi. 307.

Mr. Bradfhaw's refults have fince been confirmed by a wholly independent inveftigator, Prof. Bernhard Ten Brink of Marburg, in Caffel, whofe Chaucer *Studien*,[1] Part I. 1870, is at prefent the only book worthy of notice on the fubject. But Prof. Ten Brink does not agree with Mr. Bradfhaw in rejecting the *Romaunt of the Rofe* as Chaucer's, on the ground of its *ye-y* rhymes, &c. as he thinks that in this, the poet's earlieft work, he may have worked on lefs ftrict rules of rhyme than he did in his later works. I ftrengthened this fuppofition by fhewing that at leaft three of Chaucer's immediate predeceffors, Minot, William of Shoreham, and Robert of Brunne,

---

[1] Chaucer: *Studien zur Geſchichte ſeiner Entwicklung, und zur Chronologie ſeiner Schriften*, A Ruſſell, Münſter.

rhymed *ye* with *y*; and Mr. Joseph Payne has now shown[1] reasons for supposing that neither in Norman-French nor Early English was the final *e* generally a separate syllable; and that Chaucer is no exception to the rule. Mr. Payne's conclusion is, that on the ground of the *ye-y* rhyme, no work attributed to Chaucer can be declared spurious. *Adhuc sub judice lis est.*

Herr Ten Brink divides Chaucer's life into three periods, I. Up to the time of his Italian travels, 1372, when he was under French influence,[2] and produced the *Romaunt* in 1366, the *Boke of the Duchesse* in 1369; II. After his Italian travels to 1384, his works being [the *Compleynt upon Pite*], the *Life of St. Cecile*, 1373, the *Parlement of Foules*, [the *Compleynt of Mars*], and *Palamon and Arcite*, *Boece*, *Troylus*, [the *Former Age*,[3] *Lines to Adam Scrivener*], with the *House of Fame*, in 1384; III. Thence to the poet's death in 1400, comprising the *Legende of Good Women*, the *Astrolabe*, *Anelida and Arcite*, *Canterbury Tales*, *Complaynt of Venus*, with a few minor poems. Herr Ten Brink's *Studien* have been translated for, and will be published by, the Chaucer Society.

Early in Chaucer's third period I should put his *Gentilnesse* (the firste Fadir, &c.), *A B C*, and *Moder of God*. His touching ballad of *Truth* (Flee fro the preese) I suppose to have been written about the time of his losses in 1388; and perhaps the *A B C* and *Moder of God* may go with it. The short poems of Chaucer's old age are, the *Complaynt of Venus*, from the French of Sir Otes de Graunson, a knight of Savoy, who became liegeman to Richard II., *Lenvoy to Bukton*, *Balade to King Richard*, *Lenvoy to Scogan* (written after Michaelmas in a year of "deluge of pestilence," which Mr. Bradshaw thinks was 1393), *Compleint ageins Fortune*, and his *Compleynte to his Purse*, addressed to Henry IV. in Sept. 1399, for which Henry probably granted him forty marks yearly on Oct. 3, 1399. See further in the Trial-Forewords to my parallel-text edition of Chaucer's Minor Poems, Part I. Chaucer Soc. 1871.]

---

[1] [In the last section of his valuable paper on the Norman element in the written and spoken English of the 12th, 13th, and 14th centuries, *Phil. Soc. Trans.* 1868-9, pp. 428-448, but written in 1870.]
[2] [See M. Sandras's *Etudes sur Chaucer*, Paris, 1859.]
[3] [A beautiful verse translation of the fifth metre of the second book of Boethius, first found by Mr. Bradshaw in two MSS. in the Cambridge Univ. Libr., and printed in Dr. Morris's *Chaucer*, vi. 300, and at the end of his Chaucer's *Boethius*, p. 180 (E. E. T. Soc. 1868).

END OF VOLUME II.

www.ingramcontent.com/pod-product-compliance
Lightning Source LLC
Chambersburg PA
CBHW032027220426
43664CB00006B/396